The Papers of Walter Clark

WALTER CLARK AT SEVENTEEN

as lieutenant colonel in the 70th North Carolina Regiment. This was the first regiment of Junior Reserves, and Clark was elected lieutenant colonel July 3, 1864. He is said to have been the youngest officer of his rank in either army. From a daguerreotype in the possession of the Clark family.

The Papers of

WALTER CLARK

Edited by

AUBREY LEE BROOKS

and

HUGH TALMAGE LEFLER

Volume One 1857-1901

Chapel Hill

THE UNIVERSITY OF NORTH CAROLINA PRESS

TO THOSE WHO BELIEVE

THAT THE PUBLIC WELFARE IS THE SUPREME LAW

AND HAVE THE COURAGE TO FIGHT FOR IT

PREFACE

In the preparation of my previous volume, *Walter Clark: Fighting Judge,* I was confronted with a rich collection of manuscripts, newspapers, pamphlets, and books. In hand were more than four thousand Clark letters, and an even larger number written to Clark. These letters cover the period from his childhood days at Ventosa plantation to his death as Chief Justice of the Supreme Court of North Carolina, in Raleigh, at the age of seventy-eight. Some of his opinions while on the Supreme Court are still as live as an electric wire, and many of them have been written into law. Clark's addresses before various bar associations and other organizations, his speeches, and his newspaper and magazine articles would fill at least two large volumes.

Following the publication of the Clark biography, a few reviewers criticized and some friends complained because the book had not contained more documentary material. The general and wide interest shown in Clark's life, together with the very favorable reception of the book and the astonishment expressed that any man could have accomplished so much, has led to the publication of these volumes of *The Papers of Walter Clark.*

Neither his biography nor this publication would have been possible but for the help of John W. Clark, able and devoted son of the Chief Justice.

Wishing to make this work complete and of greater value to students, historians, and the reading public, I associated with me in the undertaking Hugh Talmage Lefler, Professor of History at the University of North Carolina. Together for hours and days we have read some ten thousand letters and hundreds of speeches and articles. In the process of selection, elimination, and editing, Professor Lefler's knowledge of North Carolina history and his discriminating judgment have been of invaluable service in making this publication reflect the life and labors of one of North Carolina's most distinguished sons, Chief Justice Walter Clark.

Aubrey Lee Brooks

Greensboro, North Carolina
April 30, 1947

INTRODUCTION

In the selection of the letters and addresses contained in these volumes we have had access to more than ten thousand letters, over four thousand of which were written by Walter Clark and the remainder to Clark. From the time he entered boarding school to his death, Clark kept most of the letters he received and, in later years, retained copies of most that he wrote. These letters, exchanged with political and intellectual leaders in North Carolina and the nation, throw a vivid, and frequently a new, light on significant political, social, and economic movements. All of this correspondence has been carefully examined and read, and from it we have selected for publication the most important and revealing items reflecting the life and labors of Walter Clark—the man, the soldier, the farmer, the lawyer, the jurist, the statesman, and the "prophet of the new order."

The greater portion of the Clark correspondence is in the hands of the Clark family, who have put it at our disposal and have been coöperative in every way. Special acknowledgment is due Mr. John W. Clark, son of Walter Clark, for his hearty coöperation in our efforts to make this publication a full and fair account of his father's private and public career.

There are more than one thousand letters in the Clark Papers in the State Department of Archives and History at Raleigh, and we acknowledge our indebtedness to Dr. C. C. Crittenden and his staff for their helpfulness. We are also under obligation to Dr. J. G. de R. Hamilton, head of the Southern Collection in the University of North Carolina Library, for permission to use the A. W. ("Gus") Graham Papers and the Marion Butler Papers, both of which contain many valuable Clark letters.

Some Clark letters are found in the Claude Kitchin Papers, the Lee S. Overman Papers, and the Matt Ransom Papers in the University of North Carolina Library. The Jesse Turner Papers and a few other collections in the Duke University Library also contain Clark correspondence, and for the use of them we wish to express our thanks to Miss Nannie May Tilley, head of the Manuscripts Division of that Library.

Walter Clark wrote many letters to the North Carolina newspapers, and the files of the Raleigh *Sentinel,* the Raleigh *News and Observer,* the Clinton *Caucasian,* and other papers have yielded a large number on matters of public interest.

The letters and other papers are here arranged by chapters and in chronological order. Beginning with Clark's youth, and with each chapter presenting, in point of time, a connected recital, the successive chapters in this and the following volume take the story up to the time of his death as Chief Justice of the Supreme Court of North Carolina. This combination of the topical and chronological methods will enable the reader to refer conveniently to *Walter Clark: Fighting Judge,* which gives added meaning and tone to the volumes of letters and addresses. Each chapter is preceded by an essay, or "headnote," which gives an overview of the matters mentioned in the letters, with particular emphasis on Clark's role. Many letters have been reproduced in full; others have been condensed by the omission of irrelevant and unimportant portions; and in some cases only a few pertinent sentences have been reprinted. Numerous footnotes have been used to identify persons, places, and things. Clark's most significant addresses are reprinted in special chapters following the letters, with footnote references to these addresses at the proper place in the earlier chapters.

When it is recalled that a great portion of Clark's correspondence, his judicial opinions, public addresses, and magazine articles were done by hand, the amount seems almost unbelievable. His working hours were long and incessant, but the manual labor involved and the time devoted to reading and research simply stagger the imagination. The following is a brief summary of his recorded efforts: approximately five thousand letters (some were lost or burned, since only about four thousand are extant); more than ninety magazine articles; over fifty addresses; approximately one hundred letters to newspapers; 3,325 opinions during the thirty-five years he served on the North Carolina Supreme Court. He wrote *The Code of Civil Procedure of North Carolina;* edited the *State Records of North Carolina,* 16 volumes; translated from the French of L. C. W. Constant, *Recollections of the Private Life of Napoleon;* collected and edited *Histories of the Several Regiments and Battalions from North Carolina in the Great War 1861-'65,* in 5 volumes, edited "Appeal and Error," 1300 pages, in *Encyclopedia of Law;* annotated 164 volumes of *North Carolina Reports, Cases Argued and Determined in the Supreme Court of*

North Carolina—and all the while successfully managed the 5,000-acre ancestral Ventosa plantation on the Roanoke River.

Walter Clark was without question one of the most controversial characters that North Carolina public life has produced. His views on economics, social welfare, and legislative and judicial reforms, and his interest in the welfare of the common man were a quarter of a century in advance of the thinking of any other Southern jurist or political leader. His published letters and addresses show that he foreshadowed much of the best contained in the New Deal.

In many respects, Clark was like Thomas Jefferson. He was born an aristocrat with a long and distinguished family connection. Endowed with an excellent mind, he cultivated it by diligent study and employed it incessantly at hard labor. His sympathy from the first was with the toiling masses, and he devoted his life to the cause of equal rights for all and special privileges for none. His watchword on the bench was: "The public welfare is the supreme law." Like Jefferson, his power was in his pen, not on the platform.

Walter Clark believed that the Constitution of the United States needed revision, and he thought that the country was being held back by an antiquated legal system. President Taft once said that he would not trust the United States Constitution overnight with Chief Justice Clark. But there were many people who believed that Clark was giving the proper application of the Constitution to the problems of his time, and today, in many cases, his "radical views" and his dissenting opinions have become the law of the land.

Aubrey Lee Brooks
Hugh Talmage Lefler

April 30, 1947

CONTENTS

ILLUSTRATIONS

I

Early Years and Education

1846–1861

WALTER McKENZIE CLARK WAS born at Prospect Hill plantation, North Carolina, on August 19, 1846, the oldest child of David Clark II and Anna Maria Thorne. Young Clark had a distinguished ancestry and was related by blood to many of the prominent families of North Carolina. Most of his boyhood was spent at Ventosa, a self-sustained and self-sufficient plantation, which was located in an arm of the Roanoke River and represented the best of ante-bellum plantation life.

The Clarks and most of their relatives were Episcopalians, but Anna, before her marriage, had become a Methodist, and ever afterwards was devoted to and active in the cause of Methodism. Walter seems to have been the idol of his mother, and this attachment grew with the passing years. To her, whether he was on the battlefield or on the bench, Walter was always her adored boy, and throughout life he manifested a never-failing affection and tenderness for her. Several hundred letters, preserved in the Clark Papers, reveal this mutual affection.

As a child Walter showed an early interest in reading, which his mother encouraged, especially along religious lines. A governess was employed to aid with the care and tutoring of the Clark children, but the mother directed their religious instruction, and by the time Walter had reached the age of six he had read the entire Bible.

When he was eight years old, he was sent to Vine Hill Academy, located near Clarksville on a tract of land which his grandfather had donated for the school and on which part of the present town of Scotland Neck is built. No records of this period of his life exist.

In the fall of 1857 Walter was enrolled at Ridgeway School in Warren County, under the supervision of Professor William K. Bass. Here he remained for about two years, and the letters and reports from Mr. Bass to his father indicate that he was a studious youth who always conducted himself "with entire propriety." The first letter from Mr. Bass to Clark's father reported that Walter was "very studious, and what is rather remarkable in a boy of his age, seems to be so from love of study," and then the Professor added, "If I had a school of such boys, most of the troublesome part of the business would be avoided." In a later report, Mr. Bass wrote that Walter was "in orthography very superior, in composition, besides writing a nice hand, he manifests considerable faculty in composing, as well as facility of expression for one of his age."

Several essays and compositions written while he was at Ridgeway have been preserved, and a few of them are reprinted in this volume.

Many letters were exchanged by mother and son during the Ridgeway period. The boy wrote about his studies—Greek, Latin, and others. He was "the only boy studying Greek"; he read Caesar and Ovid; he attended church services, usually the Methodist, but occasionally the Episcopal church in near-by Warrenton; he commented on the preachers; and he made many observations about the school, the people in the community, and political doings at Warrenton. All of his letters reveal a deep affection for the family and most of them ended with the request, "Kiss all the children for me."

Walter's mother wrote him about plantation routine, the state of the crops, the work of the slaves, the prices of crops and articles which were purchased, the operations of his father's boat, the *Kahukee,* and other things which she thought would be of interest to her son, and always she advised him to be a good boy, read his Bible daily, and brush his teeth.

In the spring of 1859 Walter was sent to Belmont Select School in Granville County, under the direction of Professor R. H. Graves. A report of his progress which has been preserved, along with an explanation of the method of grading, indicates that Walter made the highest possible mark in every subject except speaking. His minus in speaking ability is both significant and prophetic. He never became a great platform orator.

While at Belmont Clark developed an interest in biography and history. He read *Plutarch's Lives* and other biographical works, and he wrote an essay on "Napoleon Bonaparte." He also wrote an essay on "Hope," which, in the phrases of the boy, foreshadowed the philosophy of the man to be. "When in the hour of adversity," he wrote, "everything else is gone—friends, kindred, property, all—Hope, the charmer, excites him to throw everything into the scale, soul and heart and abide the result . . . and be a *man*. . . . give fair play to his enemies and leave no stone unturned that may further his cause; And in a good cause, such a man, with such resolutions never fails."

After a year at Belmont, Walter wished to enter C. C. Tew's Military Academy at Hillsboro, but Professor Graves advised Clark's father against such action, because he feared that "Walter's connection with a Military School will not add to his classical knowledge," and he thought it would be "a pity for the current of his intellectual aims to stagnate, or that there should be a chasm in his road to a finished education."

In spite of this advice, Walter Clark was enrolled at the Hillsboro Military Academy, August 1, 1860. This famous school was modeled after West Point, and its student body was made up mainly of boys from leading families in North Carolina, with a few from other Southern states.

While at Hillsboro Clark wrote many letters to his mother. He described the physical plant and conditions in the barracks; he commented on his roommate and friends; he expressed his opinion of all his teachers—Tew, Lightfoot, Hamilton, and Strudwick; he commented on various preachers in town; he told what he was reading and frequently asked that books be sent him. In one letter he gave a detailed account of the daily routine of a student in a military school.

His mother's letters for this period were numerous and interesting. In addition to describing conditions on the plantation, she answered many questions which her son asked relative to local and state politics. On the eve of secession, these letters contained many observations about the state of public opinion in northeastern North Carolina.

Before his first year at the Hillsboro Military Academy was completed, North Carolina, on May 20, 1861, adopted the ordinance of secession and became a member of the Confederate States of America. Governor Ellis, realizing the gravity of the situation, called for volunteer troops to assemble immediately at Camp Ellis, near Raleigh. He requested Colonel Tew to assign one of his cadets to act as drill master for the first contingent of raw recruits then assembling. Colonel Tew and his staff designated Walter Clark, only fourteen years old, for this important task. Clark was the youngest officer and the smallest boy in the barracks. His parents hesitated to let him enter the army, but the boy was "eager to be off to war," and so his parents consented.

WALTER CLARK'S FIRST COMPOSITION

Nov. 1857

The Dog

My Dog.—I have a large black and shaggy Newfoundland; his feet and breast are of a pure white, the tip of his nose is white also; Carlo is his name, he was so named because, I thought it was a pretty name; he is an intelligent dog, if while playing, I like to drop my hat, he would get it, and bring it to me without being told; he has been made to go nearly half a mile after a walking cane; he can open a gate; he can run very fast once, he ran a deer four or five hundred yards, and caught him; he has a very good disposition, he will allow children to ride on his back; he has a loud coarse bark; he is very watchful, especially at night; he makes himself useful in various ways, he is a good guard dog, he does not like strangers much, when his feet get dirty, he will go, and wash them before he goes in the house—The End

SCHOOL REPORT OF WALTER CLARK, 1857

*From William K. Bass * to Walter's Father*

Ridgeway N C
Dec 14th 1857

Your Son Walter, during his stay in my school, conducted himself with entire propriety. He is very studious, and what is rather remarkable in a boy of his age, seems to be so from the love of study.

I herewith enclose you a copy of a circular showing terms, the time of commencing &c. I should be pleased to have Walter return and several more like him. If I had a school of such boys, most of the troublesome part of the business would be avoided.

NORFLEET HAWKINS † TO WALTER CLARK

Belmont 8th Dec. 1857

I received your letter about a month ago and I have not had time to answer it before Prof Owen and Bob are here yet Gordon has gone to Chapel Hill Bullock is gone to Charlotte. Dick and Bullock were here about three weeks ago Dick is going to a navy school in Maryland instead of west point. Mr. Graves received a pamphlet for you but did not send it to you. We have 17 scholars only one new one from halifax named smith. Old baldy came very near sending Bob John B and John C off yesterday because they went off Friday night and did not get back until day break. Old baldy is heap stricter than he youster be. I do not expect to come back here next session. give my love to all when you write home all of the boys send their best respect to you. I staying in the room you were staying in with smith. I expect to be at the Raleigh fair.

* Superintendent of Ridgeway School, Warren County.
† Clark's cousin.

WALTER CLARK TO HIS MOTHER

Ridgeway
Wednesday April 22nd 1858

I hasten to respond to your kind and affectionate epistle of the 15th ultimo, which I received Saturday evening, too late for me to reply then.... The mail train ran off near Weldon the other day, no lives were lost, but considerable damage was done to the engine; it is reported that it was caused by somebody placing a sill across the track, purposely to throw it off I believe, the Company has a good many enemies down towards Weldon. I saw an annonymous letter, the other day, in a newspaper, which was rather severe against them (the Company) especially the President.... I like Greek as well as ever, but it is harder than it was at first, I have commenced reading it right well, I think considering the time I have been reading. I can't write you as long a letter as I would wish for I must study my lesson, or else I might miss it.... I am the only boy in school studying Greek. Kiss all the children for me....

WALTER CLARK TO HIS MOTHER

Ridgeway
May 11th 1858

...I like Algebra first rate, I wrote Pa in my last (which he doubtless received) that I had commenced studying it. The Examination is to come off Tuesday, the first day of June; it was to have been the twenty-eighth of May (as I wrote you before) but as that will be court week at Warrenton, Mr. Bass postponed it until the first of June. Dr. Hawkins,* Aunt Lucy,† Mr. and Mrs. Bass say you and Pa must come up to it, to hear us speak and bring all the children. Mr. Bass has given us our speeches already. Mine is "The Address of Governor Wise at the Inauguration of the Washington Statue in Richmond, February 22nd, 1858," Long enough Title don't you think so, the Speech itself resembles it, being very long also. I don't want to speak at all, I will need a new suit of clothes out and out for to speak in.... Kiss all the children for me; how is Sissie, is Duckie ‡ as great a tease as ever,

* Dr. William J. Hawkins, who married Alethea Clark.
† Mrs. Blake Baker Nicholson.
‡ Clark's sister, Anna Leila. She married the Reverend J. D. Arnold, a Methodist minister.

does Mittie * love her book like she used to. I know Eddie † is and always will be mischievous without asking anybody. It is nearly sixteen weeks since I saw you last, I don't believe I ever was away from you so long in my life before now. I was quite homesick at first, but by studying hard I have got quite used to it. I would like very much to see you before the Examination; now that they have changed the schedule, I could leave here at 12 o'clock Saturday & come back at 1 o'clock Monday. Give my love to all.

WALTER CLARK TO HIS MOTHER

Woodlawn
Ridgeway, Saturday, August 1st, 1858.

. . . I went to Warrenton Tuesday last to hear the famous renegade, Old-Line Whig, and Know-Nothing, (as he is facetiously styled by the Know-Nothings ‡ and Whigs up this way) deliver a first-rate speech (everybody, that I have heard speak of it, said they had never heard the like before; it was excellent, even the Know-Nothings hard as it was for them, confessed he delivered no second-rate speech). You know it was a first-rate oration if they confessed it (that is the Know-Nothings). O! I forgot to tell you his name (but you countless know who it is), Henry W. Miller is the gentleman I refer to. . . . I reckon you are tired of this trash, but I thought, while I was writing, that I had just as well write everything I could think of as not and that three cents could carry four pages of trash just as well as a quarter of page of facts, tho' I remember the proverb "A single fact is worth a ship load of arguments" but arguments and writing trash are different. I attended the Episcopal service in Warrenton last Sunday, I suppose you know it is the first time I ever attended any church whatsoever, except it was a Methodist church. . . .

P. S. . . . I have finished the second book in Caesar this week, the reason I finished it so soon is because as I had not Algebra, I got two lessons in Caesar every day, I finished it in 5½ days.

WALTER CLARK TO HIS MOTHER

Woodlawn Ridgeway, Thursday, August 12, 1858

. . . I read three chapters in my Bible regularly every day and five or ten every Sunday like you requested me to do; I go to

* Another sister, Louisa Mabbetta, who later married Frank Ballard.

† Edward Thorne Clark, brother of Walter Clark.

‡ A secret political party opposed to foreigners. Its official name was the American Party.

Sunday School and Church, also I clean my teeth every morning, and every thing else you requested me to do. I hope you are not sick much. Excuse writing. Love to all, especially to yourself Pa and all the children.

P. S. . . . I have most finished Caesar.

WALTER CLARK TO HIS MOTHER

Woodlawn Ridgeway, September 17th, 1858

. . . Inclosed you will please find two compositions, one of which (the shortest one) I wrote last session, the other I wrote this session, you will judge for yourself which is best, but I am rather inclined to think that the one I wrote last session is the best of the two, for as Mr. Bass said it was not quite long enough I stretched the last as long as I possibly could. You will see that there are a great many words in the letter which I had just as well (and better too I reckon) have left out. There are some mistakes too, for instance, I said azure purple for brilliant purple. You will please put them in my box of letters in my table drawer, and carry them down the country when you go.

Sept. 1858

Composition on Frogs

By Walter. M. Clark.

Eureka! Eureka!

Frogs are amphibious animals, of the Genus commonly denominated, by Naturalists, Rana (from the Latin Rana, a frog): They have a smooth skin, four legs, a thundering big head, (if I may use the redoubtable expression) and *no tail* (though their *Ancestors "The Tadpoles"* have one and no very short one at that either): Marshy places abound plentifully with them; They also grow to a very large size in fenny boggy swamps as in the lower part of this State, where my amiable neighbor over the left (Mr. Old) resides, he can tell you all about *big* Pasquotank, and the little bullfrogs: If I should judge from the deafening noise, they make at night-fall in the marshes, I should not think that "a thundering big head" was so very inappropriate after all: After a rain in Summer the fields seem alive with them, a person can scarcely hear another speak, though he is in ten feet of him; Pasquotank! Pas-quo-tank! Pas-quo-tank! here they go! from which any one would think that the; Elysium of all frogs of any note whatever, was situated on the banks of Pasquotank. I mus'nt (*as "My Friend" is unnecessarily obliged to do sometimes*) but I shall now close this imperfect Composition of mine

So good evening to you all

Yours Walter. M. Clark:

Onne tulit punctum.
Qui miscuit utile dulci, Walter. McKenzie. Clark.

Finis

see next page

Animals and their Countries
or
The Wind-up

O'er Afric's sand. the tawny lion stalks.
On Phasis' banks the graceful pheasant walks.
The lonely eagle builds on Kilda's shore.
Germania's forests feed the tusky boar.
From Alp to Alp the sprightly Ibex bounds.
With peaceful lowings Britannia's isle resounds.
The Lapland peasant o'er the frozen meer.
Is drawn in sledges by his swift reindeer.
The River-horse and scaly Crocodile.
Infest the reedy banks of fruitful Nile.
Dire Dipsas hiss o'er Mauritania's plain.
Seals and spouting Whales sport in the northern main.
And last but not least the humble Frog
His home he has beneath the moss-cov'ed log
But should I not say on the bank
Of the muddy, of the renowned Pasquotank
Where turtles and croakers in numbers untold
Raise up their heads, all besmeared, and look at Mr. Old.

Adieu
W. M. C.

The End

WALTER CLARK TO HIS MOTHER

Woodlawn Ridgeway, September 24th 1858

. . . I received the pants (sent by Buckston) you spoke of in your letter, yesterday, they were just in the nick of time for we have had very cold weather (considering the time of year) and I had nearly ruined my black pantaloons by wearing them every day. I have got the grey ones on now, they feel very comfortably, they both fit first rate and I dont think I hardly ever had any to fit better than the greys. I have finished the first book of Ovid, and I have a prospect of finishing the whole this session. I expect to finish my Greek grammar also this session, and probably my Algebra. I will be in Geometry soon I hope....

WALTER CLARK TO HIS MOTHER

Woodlawn. Ridgeway, Friday, October 2nd, 1858.

I received your very kind and affectionate epistle of the 28th ultimo yesterday, and I now hasten to respond at the first opportunity I could get. I wonder that you have not received my letter that I wrote last Thursday. I received your letter dated September 20th (which was Monday) Thursday the 23rd and as you wrote me to write soon about the clothes I wrote the self same day, (and I came very near missing my lesson by it too) and as the down mail came before I finished my letter I sent it to the depot the very next day and I had no idea but that you had received it and was wondering that you didn't write when yesterday one of the boys called out Clark! here is a letter for you! I was rejoiced that you hadn't neglected to answer my letter after all, I opened it! Lo behold! you hadn't received but one! One! O-N-E-! solitary letter, from me since I have left home the last time, while I know I have sent three besides this one, two of which I sent by the boys, and one I carried myself. There must be a great defect in the mail somewheres because I have been down to the depot two or three times and, I have made them take every letter out of the box; how could you think I could forget to write home, I never have and I never will forget to do that, don't accuse me wrongfully any more, if you don't receive a letter from me every week, rely upon it! it is miscarried. Aunt Frances says she will probably be at Littleton Friday the 8th with Cousin Mollie, Colin and myself. The clothes fit first rate, I wrote you all about them in my last. Tell Col.,* Colin † says he will pay him a visit soon. Send the carriage to Littleton Friday 8th, Aunt Frances, Cousin Mollie, Colin, Norfleet ‡ and myself will certainly be there then. I will

* Abbreviation for Colonel, nickname given to David, brother one year younger than Walter.

† Colin Hawkins, Clark's cousin.

‡ Norfleet Hawkins, another cousin.

commence Geometry next week, Mr. Bass says. All send love. Kiss all the children for me. Write soon. I thought the shortest composition was best myself, and I wrote you so in my last.

WALTER CLARK TO HIS MOTHER

November 29, 1858

How do you like the river? I used to like the River better than Airlie but I have got so now, that I like Airlie *best* in summer and Ventosa *best* in winter; A fire never looked cheerful to me at Airlie and Ventosa never looked cheerful *without* a fire; I shall always believe there are no two places else in the world beside like them and shall always believe (instead of 'There is no place like home') that 'There are no places like home'.

Again must I say give my love to all.

Kiss all the children for me and write soon.

Pa never has answered my last two letters neither has Duckie and Mittie answered my last to them.

Good bye.

Belmont
May 5th 1859

Composition on Religion

By W. A. M. Clark.

Religion! The link between heaven and earth, is the veneration of men for that Supreme being, who lives above the skies, and rules with an omnipotent yet fatherly hand.

Religion was and is still cherished under various forms by barbarous nations.

Before the True God was known, every nation worshipped idols, not even the chosen race of Israel excepted.

Religion whether true or false, when not tinctured with fanaticism, exerts an influence more or less favorable on the human race. In the Dark Ages when,

"When hope for a season bade the farewell
Closed her bright eye and curbed her high carreer"

When all vestiges had disappeared of its former civilization, when religion had retired to the sequestered closets of monks, when the utmost licentiousness prevailed, how deplorable! was this state of affairs, when compared with Persia under the teaching of the Magi; and to Arabia which rose under the doctrines of

Mahomet, to a pitch not only of power but also of moral refinement, unequalled by any other period before or since.

But Fanaticism, when combined with religion, is like a scythe cutting down all who oppose it, and turns green meadows into a parched desert;

When the relapse from the Dark Ages took place, Fanaticism was taken for a love of religion; and many found a cruel death by torture, by the racks of the Inquisition, and in various other ways, then,

"O! Sacred Truth! Thy triumph ceased awhile
And Hope thy sister ceased with thee to smile."

Everyone is familiar with the persecutions of our forefathers; how grateful we ought to be that in this country all are free from it.

WALTER CLARK TO HIS MOTHER

Belmont Thursday
July 8th 1859

. . . There is a show in Clarksville tomorrow, and as Mr. Graves has business there, and as the boys begged so hard, he concluded to let them go, they have succeeded in hiring a wagon, they will have to give about a quarter or half of a dollar apiece for it—I intended going to *"the Show"* until yesterday, when I found out that it was the same one that exhibited at Littleton, and which Pa didn't wish me to go to, so I'll be at Belmont tomorrow almost entirely alone, as all the boys are going except me (one of them speaks of staying but it is doubtful.) I'll be lonesome enough tomorrow, I guess, the boys have been making fun of me, because they say I'm too stingy to help pay for the wagon—Tell Col he must write to me, & be sure to write me how our chickens come on; has he any young chickens yet—Tell Mittie she has never answered my letter yet—Colin is here as I wrote Pa, but this place does not suit small boys, it takes all Mr Graves time to attend like he wishes to the larger classes, and has no time to devote to the smaller boys, and teach them as they ought to be, and in a school like this, where everyone has to scuffle for himself, it is no wonder that small boys come out second best occasionally, and moreover a boy of Colin's temperament is little fitted to encounter the temptations *here* presented, which though comparatively few, are nevertheless great—Have you forgotten to send me the Advocate; I haven't read a newspaper since I came here. . . . I'm in Virgil yet and I often think of a ditty I heard a year or two since 'Ovid is mighty terse, but Virgil is a deal sight worse' and I've found to my sorrow that for once poetry spoke the truth....

[P.S.]

I told Mr Graves about Cousin Al's coming here next session, he said he thought he was too young to come off from home so far and he thought it best for him to wait a session or two more and come when he gets older, he was not anxious to take Colin—Tell Aunt Tups * & Uncle William † to write to me—When you see or write to Aunt Mabb ‡ tell her she owes me a letter—I subscribed a dollar for erecting a Gymnasium here I suppose you and Pa did not object to that....

WALTER CLARK TO HIS MOTHER

Belmont
August 2 1859

...I wrote to you last Friday, when the boys went to Clarksville to the show; I wrote you, I expected a lonely time that day by myself, and I was not *Disappointed*—Bob Williams, Cousin Arch Williams' son, is here; Cousin Arch came up to bring him, he boards with Mr Graves, he is fourteen, and very little if any larger than I.... Mr Graves is building two new offices, and as he has plenty of room now, he wishes to have only two boys in a room, and as there are four in our room in the house, he contemplates moving two of them out—Cousin Eddie & one other—and as I am his classmate & Cousin and anxious to stay with a classmate, he has concluded to put me with him, in one of the new offices, the one nearest to the house, provided you do not object, I hope you will not for it is heap easier to get my lesson at night, with somebody to help me.... I do not expect as good a report this session as last for I've missed enough the first two weeks to throw me back considerably.... Mr Graves has at present sixteen boarders, and is expecting two or three more, he has 33 or 34 scholars in all—Give my love to all—Tell Uncle Blake § he must answer my letter....

* Temperance Davis Thorne, younger sister of Clark's mother. She married Samuel J. Clark and, after his death, married J. Buxton Williams.

† William Thorne.

‡ Mary Elizabeth Mabbette Thorne. She married Kemp Plummer Alston.

§ Blake Baker Nicholson, husband of Lucy Thorne, Clark's mother's sister.

[P.S.]
Dont forget to send me the Advocate.
Three of Mr Bass' old scholars are here (besides myself) but as it happened none of them went there at the same time.

WALTER CLARK TO HIS MOTHER

Belmont—Tuesday night
August 16th 1859

As Dick (Uncle Tom's carpenter) expects, leaving here tomorrow morning, to pass by Airle in the evening, I concluded to write tonight, (although it hurts my eyes to write at night) in hopes you would receive it sooner—I received today the largest *mail* I have ever received at one time, since I have been here, namely, two letters and a paper; it is the first paper I have received since I used to take the Sunday School Advocate, two or three years ago—Your letters one of the 10th and one of the 6th inst. were both received today, both were postmarked Littleton August 12th—I was glad you all had secured Mr Bruton's services, I heard Mr Cook express his opinion, before I left that probably he would take his place—How is Aunt Pattie's * baby, better I hope—We have had two or three rains lately up here—I am writing to Uncle Blake tonight and on that account, you must'nt expect as long a letter as otherwise—How has the election terminated, I havent heard, is Smith elected?—The death of his two daughters was heavy on Mr Biggs, poor man, how does he bear it—Cousin Eddie sends love and says he will write soon—Those 11 volumes will make quite a handsome edition to my library I see I am not quite forgotten by those at home—I suppose Aunt Eliza & Uncle Colin † are with you now—Give my love to all Write soon—Tell Pa and Col I am expecting a letter—Colin sends love—Goodbye

WALTER CLARK TO HIS MOTHER

Belmont Monday
Aug 29th 1859

. . . The commencement at Hampden College ‡ in Virginia commenced today, three boys left here Friday to enter there—Cousin Eddie asked me a week or two ago, where to send for

* Probably Mrs. William Thorne.
† Mr. and Mrs. Colin Clark, who lived at Scotland Neck.
‡ Hampden-Sidney, famous Presbyterian college in Virginia.

tracts, I told him I didn't know, but I supposed Mr Crowder's at Raleigh was the place, and sure enough he sent, and last Friday, he received a package of tracts, the price of the money he sent, and in addition to that about twenty others as a present. . . . Today is cold and chilly, I don't believe we've had but one or two hot days this month it has been cold! cold! cold! from beginning to end—We havent been in the New office yet, but expect to be next week, one reason I wish to be there is, because there, there will be only two in a room, and here in the house there has been four in a room, we can study so much with only two—Mr Graves has so arranged it that, when the new offices are finished there will be only two in a room, except the room in the house, which being the largest, will have three. . . . Mr Graves commenced a new rule lately, it is this, directly after day break a bell is rang at all our doors to get up, and about ten or fifteen minutes after that or just before sunrise another bell is rang at the Academy, when all the boarders seventeen in number have to march down and say a Dictionary lesson about a yard long—

WALTER CLARK TO HIS FATHER

Belmont Thursday
Sept 1st -59

. . . I haven't seen the full report of the Elections yet, but from what I can hear, four Whigs & four Democrats were elected, and I suppose Smith is among the former—I've read those chapters of Ezk, which you directed, I think they are very clear on the subject—Mr Grave's rule, about getting up at daybreak, is very hard upon us these cold mornings—We've had frost here three or four times, I have seen some myself once, and that morning there was a good deal, I reckon it will injure the tobacco planters a good deal—Mr G has had 37 scholars this session (three have gone to Hampden Sydney College) an increase of eight over last session, he had 29 then— . . .

WALTER CLARK TO HIS MOTHER

Belmont
Sept. 24, 1859

. . . Mr Graves says he intends to send our reports off tomorrow morning, says he would have sent our reports before now but always likes to think over and correct them—It is pretty near time for you all to move down,* is it not, When you do go, don't forget old Hallady, as I expect to have a good deal of fun this winter hunting—Mr Graves offices are all finished now, he has seven rooms in them and one in the house for boarders, the old has two lower rooms and one upstairs, the new offices have two rooms each, all down stairs; Mr Graves speaks of putting up another office in vacation just like the new offices that is with two rooms only. . . . This place does'nt suit Colin, although he seems to like it right well for in this school like all other schools of its character there are some pretty rapid chaps, if I were in Aunt Mabb's place I would'nt send Cousin Al,† until he was older, it is an excellent school for larger boys, but it is no place for small boys, and people will find it so when it's too late. . . .

COMPOSITION BY WALTER CLARK

Belmont
Nov 9th 1859

Napoleon Bonaparte ‡

"The Hero of hundred battles" has fought his last fight, and has sunk into his final resting place, and now the World looks back on him as the one, who once held it in suspense, and who at his will set up and dethroned kings, and of whom it may well be said, he never saw his equal.

He is without doubt the greatest general of ancient or modern times; and now that prejudices and hatred are buried in the tombs his merits and his actions are appreciated, and he rises superior to the petty animosities and jeleaousy of his time, of him it may be said 'he was a great man'

He has been accused of inordinate ambition, but with very little truth; He loved France, and it was his desire to lead her forth from the lethargy she had fallen into under the rule of the inergetic house of Bourbon to take her stand in the front rank of nations; he saw with one glance of his eagle eye that it needed the will of a Napoleon to do it and regardless alike of the envy and jeleaousy of his countrymen and of foreign intervention he attempted it and absorbed by that one desire he sacrificed everything at the shrine of his country. He made a false step when he

* Clark's family was still at Airlie, their summer home. In October they usually moved to the Ventosa plantation on the Roanoke River for the winter.

† Alfred Thorne Alston, son of Clark's aunt.

‡ Clark was always interested in Napoleon Bonaparte and later published some articles about him. In 1895, in collaboration with his wife, he published a translation of Constant's *Life of Napoleon*.

divorced Josephine but it was over-zealousness for the good of his country which made him do it, for he knew France so long accustomed to tyrranical sway could not rule alone he saw also she needed an energetic king he therefore took it himself and knowing that if he died without heirs France would be again involved in bloodshed and horror, he sacrificed his affections and divorced the partner of his life; But he made a false step when he took a wife from the faithless house of Hapsburg had he taken a princess of Russia no doubt his empire would have stood. He made a false step as I have said and his high position his numberous friends vanished like the morning dew, nations glorying in his fall banished him to the Island of Elba and his faithless wife refused to share his exile, but his energy of soul and love of France was unconquerable, and again we see him at the head of her victorious armies, but the whole of Europe combined was more than a match for France exhausted as she was and on the disastrous plains of Waterloo he ended his military career.

Great Britain afraid even of the conquered hero determined to banish him to the lone and rocky island of St Helena; here the great Napoleon longed to be once more free but England fearful of him had him guarded too well, and he perished in his exile. His last request shows beautifully the spirit and aim of his life 'he requested to be buried on the banks of the Seine amid the people he loved so well'.

It is said he died delirious ordering on his battalions in his country's cause. It was nearly twenty years before his dying request was granted and his remains were carried to France and were greeted with the greatest enthusiasm; the streets of Paris were crowded with the thronging populace And to this day fickle as the French are, his name is cherished with veneration and respect—The Cathedral of Rouen holds his bones, but the World itself his name, his actions, his deeds

TO WALTER CLARK FROM HIS MOTHER

Ventosa Jan 21st 1860

I must write you, if only a few lines, for I know you expect a letter & I do not like for you to be disappointed, in getting a letter *from home*—I deem it unnecessary to say how much we miss you & how *sad* I felt after you left, but went right to work, (which is a good antidote for sadness) & did quite a lot of work on my new sewing machine. I think of & pray much for you, *my dear boy,*

& commit you into the hands of that Great & Good Being, who careth for us, & never forsakes those who trust him, pray to him my child to lead you & guide you each day, yes, every hour & may he guide & protect you from the snares of the wicked & the wiles of the evil one, is the *oft repeated* prayer of your fond Mother— I hope you reached Mr Graves's safely—& now *enjoying your studies finely*—improve *well,* your time while young, you have advantages that so many would be thankful for (& I hope *you* are) —I am glad you were so fortunate as to meet up with your Cousin Eddie at Littleton, tell him, his being your classmate & companion makes him, feel much nearer to me, I love him, & appreciate his kindness to you very much. . . . Mr Fulford the colporterer came yesterday morning & Brother Hunt in the afternoon, the latter (together with your Pa) went out riding & hunting this morning brought home seven wild pigeons, the largest I ever saw, they have gone out again this afternoon—The two overseers came Tuesday night, your Pa seems very much pleased with them so far—Your Pa has finished his dam & now busy (or rather has me busy) making his flags, has the poles up—The Kahukee * & barges, did not get off until this morning Cousin Gavin lost that negro woman & was expecting to lose a boy, the last we heard from there, his other sick ones were better. . . .

TO WALTER CLARK FROM HIS MOTHER

Ventosa Jan 31st 1860

. . . Your Pa is more & more pleased with his overseers, says they are educated & have more than ordinary minds, can measure up a dam &c with great facility & (I suppose accuracy) which you know will be quite a relief to your Pa, he has heretofore had all such things to attend to himself, With good weather & no hindrance your Pa thinks he could finish draining this week, but he will have to stop, as he expects that man from Greensboro here tonight, to have his fruit trees set out, he has 1200 apple trees to put out, so I guess it will take him some time—Old Mr Young has been down to see us & went pigeon hunting with your Pa, dont think he killed any, but your Pa shot them by the dozen—Mr Jarrell has also been to see us, he seems highly delighted with his new home, in Craven County, says he can buy large trout there for a cent apiece, that large tract of land down there that your Pa

* A boat owned by David Clark in which he regularly sent the produce of Ventosa Plantation to Norfolk and Baltimore.

spoke of buying at $10,000 has been purchased by John E Washington & Deburnia Hooper at 16,000—I will send your books as soon as I am well—Hope you are studying hard & getting on finely with your studies, you must not think because you are tolerably far advanced, that you have time to lose, it is a mistaken notion & rather a dangerous one & one that I hope you will not imbibe—I hope you will ever remember the kind admonition I gave you on parting. . . .

TO WALTER CLARK FROM HIS MOTHER

Ventosa Feb 7th 1860

. . . I am glad you have so many of your relations & acquaintances to go to school with you this session, you must be kind & polite to them all & indeed to all of your schoolfellows & never forget to be *polite* & *respectful* to your teachers—How have you & Henry Webb made it? friendly I hope—I know very well who John Alston is, he is the son of an own Cousin of mine who is one of the finest ladies I ever saw—she was a particular favorite of your Grand-Ma's, so if he is not a good boy, he does'nt take after his Mother, I have heard that he was an excellent boy & if so I hope you may be good friends; but dont let your companions (or the wish to please them) interfere with your studies or your duties Dont neglect reading the Holy Word of God & praying for his blessing—Are you regular in cleaning your teeth, I shall expect to see them looking very nicely when you come home. . . .

R. H. GRAVES * TO DAVID CLARK †

Brownsville P.O.
Granville Co. N.C. 1860

Yours of the 19th inst. came to hand by our last mail. I enclose herewith a certificate for Walter.

I have not a catalogue shewing the prescribed course of studies at the Hillsboro' Military Institute, and therefore cannot speak with confidence as to what class he can join; but from what I have seen and heard should think that he could easily join any of the classes in Anct Languages, and the second or third in Maths.—the most prominent study of such schools. Indeed a cadet with

* Principal of Belmont Select School, Granville County.

† Walter Clark's father. David Clark had attended Round Hill Academy, Northampton, Mass. for four years. At that time it was headed by George Bancroft, who was Secretary of the Navy in 1845, Minister to Great Britain from 1846 to 1849, and author of the well-known *History of the United States.*

whom I conversed recently, whom I know to be a youth of good mind & who went to Hillsboro' with very decided advantages, has now been there, if I mistake not, two years without being as far advanced in Anct Languages and Maths as Walter is now.

I fear that Walter's connection with a Military School will not add to his classical knowledge and in short that the mental food will bear too small a proportion to the physical exercise for one of his character. It would be a pity for the current of his intellectual aims to stagnate, or that there should be a chasm in his road to a finished education.

With all deference to your judgment, permit me to suggest the enquiry, whether if your son is to plunge at once into the company of a large number of boys, and thereby be exposed to the temptations incident to college life, he ought not, along with this disadvantage, to have the accompanying advantages of collegiate training. Indeed, I think that Walter is much less apt to be led astray than most boys are at sixteen. And, again, if your objection to an early entrance upon college life is that he wd pass through the course before his mind is sufficiently matured to receive full & lasting benefit, may not that objection be removed by his taking a second course at the University of Va. or some such Institution after he has graduated at another college.

I must add that although I have consented to prepare boys for the Sophomore class, yet to prepare them for the Junior Class would require more time than we could spare in justice to lower classes which are always most numerous.

As to your next son, I should think it desirable that he should have the benefit of judicious educational training, and believeing as I do, in taking into consideration the natural disposition and temperaments of boys, and especially in the efficacy of encouragement, I should be pleased to take charge of him such pains as his case might require and of receiving from you such suggestions as your judgment aided by a knowledge of his character might dictate.

COMPOSITION BY WALTER CLARK

Belmont
March 1st 1860

Hope.

Hope sustains and buoys up the mind, and directs it to loftier and nobler aims, and without it man would yield to despair in circumstances, in which by hope he has been aroused from his lethargy, and come forth from the struggle stronger than ever.

In the hour of trial and need, ever-present and smiling hope comforts the dejected soul with bright prospects of success.

It has been said that 'Patience and Perseverance will accomplish all things' But what will Patience and Perseverance avail if the hope of success is wanting?

When in the hour of adversity everything else is gone—friends, kindred, property, all—yet in the language of the Poet 'Hope, the charmer, lingers still behind' and excites him to throw everything into the scale soul and heart and abide the result; it nerves him to throw off his dejectedness and be a *man,* to give fair play to his enemies and leave no stone unturned that may further his cause; And in a good cause such a man, with such resolutions never fails.

The renowned Robert Bruce, having been defeated in six successive battles, was tempted to yield to despair, but hope divine impelled him to try his fortune once more of the field of blood, and the seventh battle yielded to the *now* victorious arms of Bruce; and thus by hope was Caledonia saved, and an imperishable name for her bonneted Chieftain was won.

The mightly mind of Napoleon was restive in his banishment to Elba, and *hope* told him he could again be reinstated on the throne, and instead of sinking into supineness, he bent all his energies to the work, and the battle of Waterloo so fatal to his cause would have been added to his numerous victories, but for the untimely arrival of Blucher.

But for Hope the world long ago would have been an abyss of despair. Campbell says

"Eternal Hope! when yonder spheres sublime.
'Pealed their first notes to sound the march of time
'The joyous youth began—but not to fade—
'When all the sister planets have decayed
'When wrapt in fire the realms of ether glow
'And Heaven's last thunder shakes the world below
'Thou, undismayed shal't o'er the ruins smile.
'And light thy torch at Nature funeral pile"

TO WALTER CLARK FROM HIS FATHER

Littleton Feb 24th 1860

. . . You write that you are doing well that is if I am to Judge by the reports you & Col Tew send (I mean in your studies) but you do not say how you are getting along in the drill especially in the dogtrot Do they not give Marks & Reports on that as well as on studies, if so let me know how you stand as compared with others of your Class in time of Drill

I hope to be at the Fair but cannot be certain that I can come—I noticed your gun today it is in bad order—You left one barrell loaded—I intend to have it put in order tomorrow & put away—

TO WALTER CLARK FROM HIS MOTHER

Ventosa Apr 3rd 1860

. . . They still continue building up Clarksville laying off streets &c, your Uncle Colin gave a hundred dollars, for a small lot for the baptist church, they expect to commence a building it soon, they are also about to commence building the factory & many other buildings are now going on, Mr Hyman has got the town started & now he is going to move to Norfolk & leave it—They have issued the first No of the "Scotland Neck News" I will send you a copy of it, by this mail

There is nothing particularly interesting going on at home, just now, your Pa is very busy crushing guano, of which, he has just purchased a hundred tons & speaks of purchasing a hundred more, a good deal of his corn is planted, but it is so very dry, that he cant plant in his stiff lands until a rain—They have had some amusing scenes, getting the hogs out of the fields before planting, you remember Kit (the boy that waits on the overseers) he thought it such fine fun, kept begging the overseers to let him have a mule & help them, said the mule would'nt throw him, finally he started & after going sometime, he went to jump a ditch & the mule landed him the other side, flat of his back, your Pa & the overseer, happened to see him & when they came up, wanted to know what was the matter, Oh nothing sir, Kit said "only the mule & I went to jump the ditch & the mule stopped & I kept on" you may know, it amused your Pa, to see the boy's tact—We expect the Kahukee up the last of this week—I guess we will leave here in about four weeks, for Airlie & then I suppose it will be about four weeks before we see you study hard & the time will soon pass. . . .

TO WALTER CLARK FROM HIS MOTHER

Ventosa April 10th 1860

I suppose your Holiday is past & you are again much interested in your studies—Your Brother is taking quite a long Holiday has not returned home yet, we expect to send for him today—Your

Pa has just been up to the quarterly meeting at Farmwell, had some excellent sermons, from Brother Wyche Mangum & Kingsbury, says they are all good Preachers, I have never heard Kingsbury— . . . Well I suppose I must begin to answer your questions; as to the apple trees, part of them are planted at Drews, in between the old trees so that as the old orchard dies out, there will be a young one ready to bear, part of them all in front of Applewhite down to the bottom quite a large orchard, part of them in the well & hen lot & then the missing places in my orchard filled out, I dont think we have lost the first one, they all seem to be living & growing—I am afraid I will lose one of my magnolias— The carpenters are putting me up a lattice at the back porch, for my vines to run on, which is quite an improvement, makes the porch a pleasant place to sit in—We are expecting the Kahukee up every day, Capt Taylor hurried down, thinking he would get a cargo of the Merchant's goods, as return freight, but I am afraid he missed them, as the Loper came up a day or two since, guess she was ahead of him— . . . We have had a plenty of shad & now catching rock—I dont know about the pigeons at the Overseers house, they have some red birds squirrels & one thing & another taming, your Pa has eight very pretty wild pigeons in a large cage, I tell him I want them for pigeon pies but he wont consent to it, dont know what he intends doing with them. . . .

[P.S.]

Why dont you get a hat, what makes you wear that cap & freckle your face up so, it is a pity—You ought to have had a hat early in the Spring— . . . I have just returned from a delightful ride with your Pa, over to Beaver dam, saw the hands harrowing the corn to get the wire grass out, his corn is coming up very strong & pretty, it is a field he is trying the American Guano on & he is anxious to see the effects, as there is such a variety of opinion about that Guano, as a fertilizer—Your Pa thinks it will be the very thing—. . . The Scotland Neck news is to be neutral I believe in Politics—I sent you a copy did you get it? We have a second No, rather better than the first at any rate, it is printed on better paper I believe. . . .

TO WALTER CLARK FROM HIS MOTHER

Ventosa April 24th 1860

I received a letter from you last Tuesday, I suppose you have received my last, containing an account of your report, I sent you some newspapers, also, last week & week before—What do you think of the "Scotland Neck News", it serves to amuse us very much, sometimes (tho' there are some very good pieces in it) I think the Editor ought to keep a dictionary by him & a grammar occasionally, the last No had several female contributions, & was the most amusing of any, I have not sent it to you, but you can see it when you come home—there were some pieces in it, that I did'nt wish you to read, those I can cut out or let you know which they are—We have all been fishing twice, Brother Hunt was down last Friday, Saturday & Sunday, (came down to preach to the servants on Sunday & generally instructs them in catechism on Saturday) & as had'nt much else to do on Friday & Saturday & is very fond of fishing, he helped us to fix up the hooks & lines &c, & we all went fishing (from Ed up) but none of us had much luck but Mr. Hunt.... I sent yesterday & had you seven or eight very pretty poles cut—I always like to have anything done for you that I can, when you are studying well & being a good boy, it is a pleasure to me to gratify you—I want to get you the other No's of Abbott's Histories, let me know, if you have "Peter the Great" or what is the last volume you got—...We have no objection to your going to Chapel Hill to see your class join, but let me know if you will have time to come home first—...The Kahukee has been to South End, since I wrote you, & now taking in a load at Leggetts barn & expects to get off tomorrow evening, she gets more to do than she can accomplish—Your Pa has'nt sent off the first grain of his corn—Capt Taylor has discharged his particular friend Mike, said Mike got to being a bigger man than he was—I have nearly covered my sheet, so will have to say Goodbye—Be punctual to your duties & may the Lord bless you, is the prayer of your fond & Affet Mother.

WALTER CLARK TO HIS MOTHER

Hillsboro
Aug 2nd 1860

I arrived here last evening about 6 o'clock; Col Tew didn't come over from the town until very late, so I did'nt know what Class I would join until this morning—Col Tew put me in the fourth Class as Pa wished, though he remarked that I was'nt prepared and would undergo the risk of being turned back into the 5th—The studies have been changed some from last year's Catalogue, they don't study Trigonometry until the 3rd Class, and they have advanced French accordingly, the Class is reading the hardest French Authors fluently, so you see, I am well prepared on everything but French, but *sadly deficient* on that—I send Pa Col Tew's receipt. The amount was $105 instead of $106. I send Pa $50.00 over, I should send $5 more but the Col could not change it—I would rather stay in the 4th Class *if I can,* but Col Tew fears my standing (on account of French) wouldn't justify it; he wished me to join the 5th this morning telling me I could stand near 1st in that Class but that in the 4th Class no matter how good my other recitations I could stand no higher than last or next to last, I told him *I preferred the 4th*—I hated to leave you all *mighty bad* yesterday but I knew it was time for me to be doing something—Give my love to all—I couldn't be homesick here. they keep me too busy—Today is the Election, Write me who is elected in Halifax, . . .

COL. TEW * TO DAVID CLARK

Hillsborough, Aug 3rd 1860

Your son arrived duly on Aug. 1st was examined and assigned to the 4th class. Being almost entirely unprepared in French he will need an extra degree of attention to that apartment. In Algebra although he had not advanced as far as the class yet his knowledge of the subject is fair—certainly sufficient in general for the purpose of studying the higher mathematics. In Latin there was of course no difficulty.

Our 3rd class is far beyond his point, and I am very sure that there are not three young men anywhere in the State who could pass the examination in Mathematics requisite for admission into it. This class is already ahead of the Chapel Hill course.

I have no doubt of your son's entire success with us and trust his health and constitution may be benefited by his position here.

WALTER CLARK TO HIS MOTHER

Hillsborough, August 15th 1860

. . . I wish I had taken your advice and studied French in vacation but you remember you did'nt say anything about it, until a week before I thought I would leave (though it in fact was prolonged to a fortnight) yet I could have learned a good deal in that time.

* C. C. Tew, Superintendent of Hillsboro Military Academy, was a graduate of South Carolina Military Academy and later Colonel of the 2nd North Carolina Regiment.

As the marks are read out every Monday for the preceding week, I can very readily let you know what mine are at any time, My marks for last week were, Geometry 15: Latin 13¾: French 11¼: History 15: N.B. 15 a week or 60 a month is the highest on any one study, though, as I wrote Pa, in making out the *stands* at the end of the month 60 in Geometry is rated 3 times as great as 60 in History. There are 91 Cadets here at present. There have been in all upwards of a hundred.

Col Tew is a very good French teacher, having travelled all over France *on foot;* I recite Geometry & French to him.

Capt Lightfoot * is a *very good* Officer, and is thoroughly versed in Military-Tactics, though not so well in Latin, as I have seen him make some palpable mistakes; I recite Latin to him.

Lt Hamilton † is a very nice man, though as being the lowest in rank (Lieut is below Capt) he is made the butt for everyone to vent their spleen upon (as in Academies they do the Assistant and in College the Tutors) they do him bad I tell you. I recite History to him.

Dr Strudwick ‡ (the Attending Physician) is considered an Officer of the H.M.A. as he attends every day whether there is sickness or not, I know very little about him, I believe he is thought to be a very good Physician.

I have given you a general description of the Officers, as I thought you would like to know something of them, they are very inadequate (in numbers I mean), Col Tew intends getting some more by next session.

I think my teeth will improve now, I have commenced cleaning them three times a day; I don't think there is much danger of their being injured by *hot* food here.

I have got some demerits already, I was Orderly last week, therefore was responsible for all noises in my room &c, some of the Cadets took it into their head to kick up a frolic, they succeeded so well that they soon had Capt Lightfoot tumbling upstairs, whereupon they ran out and left me to enjoy the fun.

Tell Pa the "'Life & Times' of Judge Iredell" in cloth costs $5.00 in sheep $6.00. Is he willing for me to get it at that price; The one I allude to is by Griffith J. McRee who married Judge Iredell's grand-daughter, is he the one Pa spoke of.

* Charles E. Lightfoot, later Lieutenant Colonel of the 6th North Carolina Regiment and then Colonel of the 22nd Regiment.

† D. H. Hamilton, later Major in the 13th North Carolina Regiment.

‡ Dr. William Strudwick, later Surgeon in the Confederate Army.

WALTER CLARK TO HIS MOTHER

Hillsboro'
Aug 15th 1860

As everything up here is new to me, I might as well write you a long letter at once—There are three other Cadets in my room, two are from Alabama and one from South Carolina, they are not such room-mates as I could desire, but I reckon it is the best I can do this session, The Cadets here study *very* little, I wish there were only two in a room like it is at Graves'.... I haven't heard Mr Brent yet, though I have been here two Sundays, the first Sunday somehow or other after we got there, we found out there was no preaching; And last Sunday after I had attended Roll Call, I went to my room for something, and seeing my squad about to march, I hurried to get there before I would get reported, and as the steps were muddy I took a notion to roll *and* I *did* roll for sure enough, I rolled from the third Gallery down to the bottom of steps it is a wonder I wasn't seriously injured, but my position saved me I suppose, I took it *pig fashion* (*over and over*) though I was hurt, I could not keep from laughing at the figure I was cutting; By rubbing camphor on the bruised places I was well as ever next morning, though I think next time I would prefer rolling a shorter distance—It has been raining nearly every day since, I have been here and now, it has set in cold and we find a fire very comfortable, though not so comfortable making it up—

WALTER CLARK TO HIS MOTHER

Hillsborough, August 18th 1860

...I am glad to hear Pa's crop turned out so well, it is pity his horsepower did so badly and that too on the first trial—Pa, it seems, misunderstands me, I only meant that when you saw my name footing the Class roll you mustn't think by that I didn't study—The number of Cadets has risen since I came from 83 to 96, 4 came at once day before yesterday morning, Col Tew is beginning to see that his school is firmly established, and I am surprised at the difference in recitation even since I have been here, they are in barracks now where one don't know when an Officer will step in, there is a *difference* between that and boarding out—They haven't read out marks for this week yet (Monday is the day), but I have received 15 on Geometry & History again, I dont know what I've got on French & Latin, I could get 15 on Latin with all ease, but as I recite French & Latin near about the same time, I am so busy with the former that I generally overlook the latter, In fact I sometimes recite perfect lessons on it without having seen the lesson—Reports (Demerits) are published every Friday evening, and to my surprise I had none, and as I have had none before I am as yet without any report at all—We read by turns a chapter in the bible every night in my room—Tomorrow is my birthday, *I* dont *suppose* I will get a *cake* however, as don't even have *molasses* some Sundays—I like here a great deal better than at first, I think the drill here second to none, it is thorough, the Cadets are more studious than I supposed, as those who came to my room at first (who came to plague me) were necessarily the least studious, and I thought by the number they were most all the Cadets—Col Tew is hurrying up our squad, in order that we may be in ranks by the Raleigh Fair, will you be there, or will you go up to Greensboro' earlier, on you way to the latter place you will have to pass by here—

TO WALTER CLARK FROM HIS MOTHER

Airlie Aug 20th 1860

Yesterday was your birthday, did you think of it? it should have been a day of reflection & of firm resolutions with you to spend the next seven years of your life in establishing firm moral & religious principles & in obtaining an education, that will render you useful in the service of God & your fellowman from now until you are twenty one (if the Good Being should see fit to spare you) will be about the most important era of your life, & will require much watchfulness & prayer, your happiness for life & (probably for eternity) will in a great measure depend on the course you pursue for the next seven years I put up some fervent petitions in your behalf on yesterday thought of you a great deal, I know that you are exposed to many temptations & that many snares will be laid, to entrap you, but I do trust & pray that you may ever have strength to resist them all, always think of the anxiety & solicitude of the fond ones at home & I am sure it will enable you to take fresh courage in your duty & double your diligence in study, perfectly regardless of the wild & wicked—true courage is to do our duty, even in the presence of those, whom we think will ridicule, I would be perfectly indifferent to ridicule, when in the pursuit of right, & you will never regret it, when you grow older There is one thing I wish to admonish you on & that is the subject of prayer & reading your bible, never neglect getting on your knees, in humble submission, to your Maker, before you retire to rest, (never mind who is in the room) & read your bible every day, let others scoff if they will, but never, do you swerve from your duty to your God, remember, to him we owe our all, & on him are dependent for everything—You must try and set a good example for others & not be led off by wild & wicked boys—You know the promises in the bible to those who heed the instructions of their Parents—I am not satisfied with your room, wish you could get a room on one of the lower floors & have more studious roommates—I suppose I was mistaken about your roommates—Do destroy this letter—Always be certain to prepare your lessons well, I think you did very well in your report, but expected you would get higher on Latin than any thing else, as Col Tew seemed to think you were better prepared on that study, let me hear from every weekly report, the number of marks & particularly on deportment—I feel so anxious about you, was busy all last night (in my dreams) helping you to get your lessons—So dont follow the example of those boys, who dont study—Your Pa wants to know if they have got you in ranks yet & I want to know (& dare say he does) if you have heard Mr Brent preach yet? you must go regularly to the Methodist church, I am sorry you were so unfortunate as to take such a tumble, & particularly on Church day—I received your letter containing the notice about your clothes, last Friday, & your Pa answered it, that same evening & sent you ten dollars, to buy some, have you received it? let us know & if you cant get any ready made, we will have to send you some, when it is cool, wear one of your black cloth jackets every day, for they are getting too small for you anyway, in fact you can wear any that you have, every day & get you a nice suit, for church—I think they ought to be more particular in publishing their circulars, for if it had not have been specified that you would [need] clothes in a month, you would have carried aplenty with you, but I thought it useless for you to carry so many, just to throw them aside in a month—If you hav'nt money enough, let us know— . . .

WALTER CLARK TO HIS FATHER

Hillsborough, August 23rd 1860

. . . The books have been sent for, as soon as your letter was received telling me to get them, I sat right down and wrote for them, I am glad—I will now have something to read, as I haven't been able to get a book to read since I have been here; (it is true there are plenty of novels I could have borrowed but I thought they were worse than none), I understand Col Tew has ordered a Library but it wont be here until next session, he has also fitted up a Lecture room—We eat dinner in the new mess hall Monday, it is a good deal larger than the old one—Col Tew says my clothes will cost $20.00 (And my pocket money has fallen from 25 to 16 dollars since I have been here and *8 or 9* of that will go for books and freight) so I will lack $4.00 of having enough for my clothes, but I think, as the summer is far advanced, I can by bargaining with the tailor myself get fewer clothes for I dont need the entire forage, as Col Tew would be obliged to get if he got any—... As soon as I get to be better versed in French, I intend to devote my leisure moments to Summery's Surveying—Mr Hamilton is studying for the law, and I hear he will get his license before very long—Last week I got 15 on Geometry & History as before, 14 in Latin against 13¾ before and 12 in French against 11¼—Col Tew says he will send you a Catalogue next week when he sends you my monthly stand—I room with Fleming of S.C. and Young & Hatch of Alabama, the former studies very well, the latter *two* not much, though they don't disturb me at all, only by snoring a little when they think the Officers wont visit....

WALTER CLARK TO HIS MOTHER

H.M.A.
Aug 25th 1860

... I have just returned from town, where I spent the morning, I saw the tailor and got what clothes I wanted *ready made* for $8.50, so much for seeing the tailor *myself,* and not leaving it to Col Tew, I got two pr of pants and two jackets of forage that had been made for one of the Cadets, but had proven to be too small and the Col had to have him some more made—I intend to hear Mr Brent tomorrow if I can possibly do so, he inquired for me the other day—I like my room-mates very well, and as to my room I would not have a room on the 2nd Gallery if I could possibly help they are so noisy there—Tell Pa I won't be in ranks in three months yet, the shortest time possible is three months from time of entry, and even a twelve-month sometimes, I will not be in ranks at the time of fair, but I may be far enough advanced to go down in the company, and be detailed after I get there for some maneuvres, but if any of you go up, I will only see more of you—

I wrote Pa what my reports were for the two last weeks, those for the present week will be read out Monday—I sent a $10 bill to Pomeroy and he sent me "Life and Correspondence of Judge Iredell" neatly bound in *2 vol cloth*—and "Plutarch's Lives" in *4 vol calf* together with $1.25 over, you know I have a long time wished to get the latter books . . . I went to Church yesterday but didn't hear Mr Brent again, it seems I can't get to hear him at all; I went to every church in town yesterday; when we got to town upon calling the Roll, Col Tew ordered the Baptist squad to accompany the M. E. squad as he had heard there was no preaching at the Baptist Church, whereupon off we both marched to the M.E Church, when we got there we found the doors shut and no preaching whereupon here comes Capt Lightfoot and ordered us off to the Presbyterian Church, but when we got there we found the place crowded by reason of no preaching at the other churches, so as it was late we had to double-quick (hot work for such a day) about a mile to the P.E. Church, when we got there that too was crowded and the squad-marchers of both Divisions refusing to do anything at all, and being tired of standing in the hot sun, we resolved ourselves into a Committee of the whole, and *were taken with a leaving,* for the next thing we knew we were at the barracks, I dont like that kind of Church-*going* at all—We will discontinue History, my marks for last week as read out this morning were nearly as last one Viz Geometry & History each 15. French 12. Latin 15—The Officers of the Company will be appointed this week, All of them would be taken out of the 1st Class but as there is no such Class at present of course out of the highest at present which is the 3rd but as there are only 4 in it, most of them will necessarily be of the 4th (none however of 5th), and as I am probably not lower than 10th (10 is the number to be taken out of 4th as only 4 in other) I would have to be appointed a Corporal, if I was drilled but as I am not the one 11th in Class will take my place. . . .

WALTER CLARK TO HIS MOTHER

Hillsborough August 31, 1860

. . . Tell Col he ought to be here just to see the Cadets in the awkward squads tumble head over heels; sometimes when the Officers are not about, the squad marchers get a litle frisky and as we are bound to hold our heads up, they sometimes set us off at full pace and first thing we knew we are pell-mell in a ditch and when we get up our mouths, hands, eyes full of dirt, we hear him

Upper left, Walter Clark's maternal grandmother; *upper right,* his maternal grandfather, William Williams Thorne, who lived at Prospect Hill; *lower left,* his father, David Clark II; *lower right,* Anna Maria Thorne Clark, his mother.

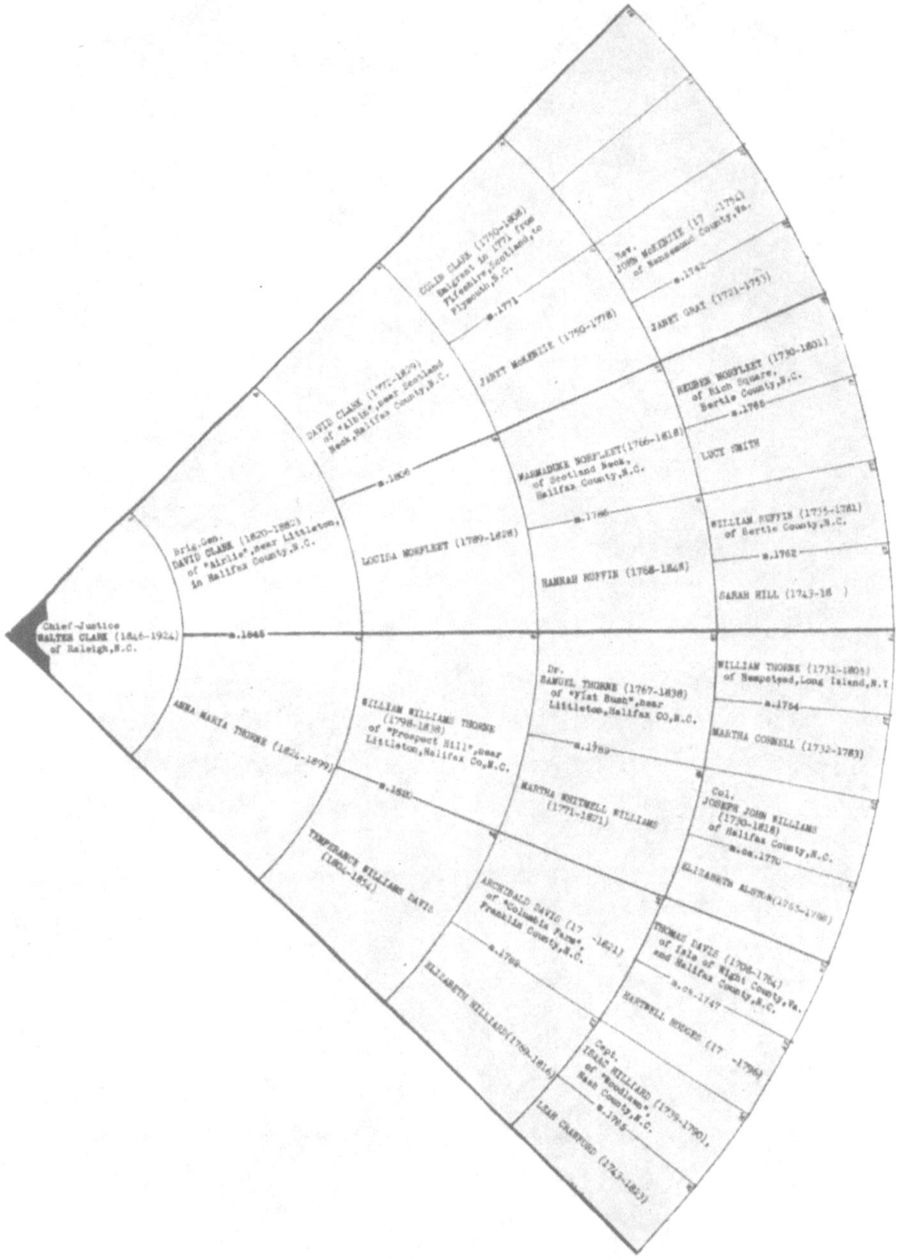

WALTER CLARK'S ANCESTRY

Prepared by W. A. Graham Clark, Chief of the Textile Division, U. S. Tariff Commission.

Report him! Report him again! But somehow or other such reports never find their way into the hands of an Officer for in that case the Cadet reported can write an *excuse,* and the squad marched would probably be suspended or dismissed; I don't mind it now, for I can generally tell when he intend[s] to do such, and look down and jump the ditch, and they dont dare to report me in such case for not holding head up in ranks for I can write an excuse stating reason why, in fact it is only alone for *fresh* and with the knowledge of the *rest* of the squad—Send me also some stamps as I am rather short of money to buy any. . . .

TO WALTER CLARK FROM HIS MOTHER

Airlie Aug 31st 1860

. . . Your Pa received a letter from you this week, informed us of the arrangements you had made, relative to your clothes, I think you did very well to engage them on such good terms, (that is, if they are good ones) we did not like to send you too much money at once, (as the mail is so frequently robbed) I will send you ten dollars more in this & guess you can make out with that, (for a while at least) unless you have more books to buy, if so, you can very readily let us know, for I much prefer your buying books to read, than having you to read novels, for they are in my opinion, one of the most pernicious things, of the present age—Whenever you need money, just write to your Pa what disposition you wish to make of it, & if proper, he will certainly send it to you—I am glad to see (from your number of marks in your last letter to your Pa) that you are improving in your French & Latin—Study hard & acquire industrious habits while young. . . . Your Pa was down the country last week, his corn crop had improved very much since the rains, but he thinks he will lose about a thousand bushels of wheat, from its sprouting this wet weather, did'nt get his thrashers in time, & when he did they did'nt work well at all, but all for the best perhaps, we have great cause to be thankful that it is no worse, for people many a time lose more than half of what they make & but for the rains, your Pa might have lost half of his corn crop—We have had & are still having precious revivals of religion through the country, have just had one at Shady Grove, at which there was 12 or 15 converts, . . . & one at Calvary & so on, I wish you could hear some of the good preaching, but the Lord is everywhere & as able to bless you at school as anywheres else. . . .

WALTER CLARK TO HIS MOTHER

Hillsborough, September 4th 1860

I received your affectionate letter of the 31st (Postmarked however Littleton *Sept 3rd*) this evening, I had been disappointed the last four or five days in not receiving your accustomed letter, and was getting uneasy about you all, when I received it this evening, I see from the Post-marks that the P. Master at Littleton is very negligent in sending *off* letters, and I am inclined to think he is *rather* so in sending you mine, for I recollect asking three successive days for a letter (you *know* when I went there so often) and finally *making* him look I found a letter that had been there a week or more—There was a fire in town last night, somebody's kitchen burnt down—I haven't heard of Mr Crowder's being here yet, I do not suppose he would pass without passing the barracks a visit, for I believe every body who comes to Hillsboro', comes out to see the Barracks—Will you please have the letters I received last session, and which by some unaccountable neglect I left at home, collected and tied up; I suppose they are in the trunk in the Lumber-room, I do not wish to lose them as I have all my previous letters tied up in Pa's safe on the river—Well! after all I heard Mr Brent last Sunday, he gave us a very good sermon indeed, I did not have a chance to speak to him however, Rev Mr Barringer preached there at night I could not go without permission from Col Tew who was absent, so I was disappointed in hearing him, he (Barringer) is P.E. of this District and a good preacher moreover—I am busy reading my books, though I have very little time for it....

WALTER CLARK TO HIS MOTHER

Hillsborough, September 8th 1860

...I am Orderly again this week, there are four in my room and of course I am Orderly once in every four weeks, I always dread for the time to come, it is always the time for *me* to get reports (demerits are called reports here, and merits are called marks) I have got I dont know how many this week—I will give you my routine while I am Orderly and see if you think I have much time for writing. Drum commences beating at 5.20 A.M. and continues beating 10 minutes until 5.30; in that time I have to get up, dress, wash my face, clean my teeth, fold up my bedstead and roll up my bed, be in ranks at the command "Front

Face" at exactly 5.30. answer to my name, then come back sweep out my room and put it to rights go after a bucket of water, then look over my Geometry about 5 minutes and go down at the striking of the steel at 15 minutes *to* 6 and recite until 7.15 carry my book to my room, by that time Drum beats for Breakfast hurry down, be in ranks at the Command "Face" answer to my name, We all then march into Mess-Hall, take seats at Command, stay there 20 minutes, each table rises at the Command (I am on the 5th table and have more time to eat as that rises last) form in order to march to Barracks (100 yrd off); It is then 8 o'clock I study my French Grammar until steel strikes at 9.00 (I have to get the Reader on the previous day) go down recite till 10. when steel strikes again, and I recite Latin till 11. then I go to my room, study my French Reader for next day till steel taps for Recreation at 12. Sweep out my room and go after a bucket of water, then I finish studying my Reader by 1. o'clock when I go down at beat of the Drum for. Dinner, be promptly in ranks, answer to my name, march into Mess-Hall, after marching back it is a quarter to 2. I take Recreation for a quarter of an hour, go to my room when steel taps for Study hours, then I study History until 4. when at taps of steel I go and recite until 5. then Drum beats for Drill, drill until 6 when Drum beats again for Supper, form, answer to name, march into Mess-Hall, after Supper bring water Sweep out my room, by that time Steel taps for Study hours; Light candle immediately, Get my Geometry & Latin by that time Drum beats at 9.30 when all unroll bed and bedstead and go to Roll-Call after that there is 20 minutes in which I read my Bible, say my prayers, clean my teeth, blow the Candle out at the tap of the Steel, jump in bed, sleep *soundly* until next morning when I am again awaken by the beating of the Drum....

WALTER CLARK TO HIS MOTHER

Hillsborough, September 8th evening 1860

I left off this morning after having given you *my routine* as Orderly, You will see from that what time I have for writing letters, I take only a quarter of an hour's recreation besides the Drill which is aplenty however, as it is the hardest sort of exercise to be running nearly an hour without hardly any intermission at Double-quick, it is a heap harder than running at pleasure, as the left foot of every individual has to touch the ground at *exactly* the same instant, and it is a great deal harder to do that than you suppose—A laughable circumstance took place the other day. Col Tew (he very rarely drills the Company himself, Lightfoot & Hamilton do it) had stepped out to correct some errors in the drilling, and running backwards before the Company as usual for an Officer in such case, he was so absorbed in noticing those Cadets who were drilling badly, that he carried them out of the Campus before he knew and the next thing he *did* know, he was rolling down a gulley four or five feet deep, they had to keep on as if nothing had happened, but those right behind the Col, stepping in the place where the Col had made the Clay sleek (it had just rained) slipped and about a dozen came pell-mell right on top of him and a muddy set they were, the rest kept on but you had better believe there was a pretty broad smile on their faces—I think I may possibly be in ranks, by the time of the Fair; You ought to be there to see the Company, I think it ought to be the *best* there, as I learned that at the last Fair, Col Tew had given them muskets but three days before, (this is an actual fact, for Col Tew himself said it) and they beat every Company in the State *then,* What ought they to do *now*—I received the University Magasin, which Pa sent me yesterday, do you think it is as ably conducted as before? . . .

WALTER CLARK TO HIS MOTHER

Hillsborough, September 13th 1860

. . . You must form a very erroneous idea of a Military school if you think that bustle and confusion are it's necessary accompaniments; the truth is that at a Military school everything is in the *strictest* order and regularity, precise to the second the *least* want of punctuality is punished with several demerits, even a laugh is reported and except at certain hours, there is no noise or bustle from one end of the Barracks to the other. . . .

I have had a good deal of fruit, though the watermelon and peach season is over now, there are plenty of chenquepens brought here every day, and sold at 10 cts a quart, I think that would be called rather cheap down with us—My marks for this week I am pretty sure of, (tho' they will not be read out until Monday) Viz Geometry 15. French 14. Latin 15. I am acquainted with these marks by one of Cadets happening to see them in the Recitation Book—I received the names and stamps you sent, I am very glad you sent them for I needed both very much at this time.

Has Pa returned from the River yet? What does he think of his crop at present? are there many deer on the plantation or have the Piney-woods people commenced killing them up yet? I wish so much Pa would post his lands, I am afraid if he don't I wont have a *chance* to *miss* another doe....

TO WALTER CLARK FROM HIS MOTHER

Monday Sept 15th 1860

...I hope by this time, you have become so expert in the drill, that they cant practice so many pranks on you, how many tumbles have you had at least one, *in the ditch,* I suppose, I think your report on your studies very good indeed thus far, so you must'nt give back, but let your motto be "onward, onward" both in your studies & deportment, remember the fond ones at home, whose happiness is so linked with yours—Dear Walter I am so much afraid, that amidst the noise & bustle of a Military school, you will neglect reading your bible & praying to the Great & Wise Creator of all things my dear child, it is a shallow foundation that any one stands on, where trust is not in the Lord—Obey the precepts of the bible & put your trust in God & he will be a lamp unto your feet to guide you in the paths of wisdom virtue & truth—Pray to God through Jesus Christ & he will hear & answer your prayers—I hope you will not tire of my writing to you on this subject, for it is of greater interest, than everything else, without the love of God in our hearts we can never be happy, Never let the foul stain of an oath, pollute your lips, always strictly observe the ten commandments....Did you get the University Magazine that your Pa sent? he wanted you to notice that letter it contained "From a Father to his Son."...

TO WALTER CLARK FROM HIS MOTHER

Airlie Sept 17th 1860

I have just received two letters from you, this morning, one dated the 8th & the other the 13th of Sept, it is quite provoking for the Post Masters to be so negligent, your letter of the 8th was written more than a week before I received it....Your Pa received your report while he was down the country, contents as follows, Geometry, 60 Latin 57, History 45, French 44, & two demerits, There was one thing I did not understand, it was made out, Cadet Walter Clark 5th class you certainly hav'nt been put back—The corn crop is very good on the river considering the dry weather, your Pa thinks the Guano was what saved him, says, but for that, his crop would have been unusually short, as there seems to be a general failure in the crops—Your corn here, I think is suffering from the present dry weather we hav'nt had a rain to wet the ground, in several weeks—I did not hear your Pa say any thing about the deer & turkeys on the river but he mentioned seeing some men hunting, on his plantation, with a knapsack full of squirrels that they had just killed, so I dont suppose you will find many squirrels, when you get home, they are very scarce in this neighborhood, your Pa cant find any to practice on, with his rifles—He has shot his rifles, but very little as he cannot procure lead for the balls, says he has tried at ten stores, & cannot get more than a pound.... Your Pa sent you three newspapers this morning, viz, the Observer, the Advocate, & the Intelligence, we could send them to you often, but dont suppose you have much time for newspaper reading, since it might cause you to neglect your studies I think you are getting on, bravo, in French but I would prefer your letters to me, written in plain English, as I am always so anxious to hear from you, would not have the patience to puzzle over one written in French—I think your time *fully* employed, when orderly, I guess you would'nt like to be so busy all the time, if practice will make perfect, think you ought to be a very good sweeper, by the time you get home.... You must not eat many chinquepins, if any, they are dangerous things to eat at this season, might give you an attack of Typhoid fever, for it seems to be very prevalent—Mind what I say be prudent in eating trash—

Have you heard Brother Brent preach again—I am glad you are punctual in reading your Bible & saying your prayers & also that you attend to your teeth—Your old Teacher Mr Bass has broken up his school near Petersburg & staying with his family at Capt Pearces—Mr Dick Smith's Son, was among the boys sent off from Chapel Hill, I have heard quite mortifying to his Father, I guess—I suppose you have heard of their sending off 9 more, since the 60, . . .

WALTER CLARK TO HIS MOTHER

Hillsborough, September 18th 1860.

. . . There were two errors in my report, the reason of which I couldn't explain to you unless I saw you, the report as it is filed in the Superintendant's Office, is Viz. Cadet Clark. Class 4th. Geometry *60.00,* French *44.25,* Latin *57.75,* History *60.00.* You will please make the corrections accordingly, and keep the report with all my others (I believe you have kept all my reports heretofore), I was the only Cadet in the Class that received 60.00 on History—You remember when I first came here, I knew scarcely anything about French, now my daily lesson consists in reading three pages in French, and turning (orally) a page of French into English and *two* pages of English into French (the hardest part of the lesson)—My marks for last week were Geometry 15, *French 15*, Latin *14.75*—Do try to get Pa to post his land, really if they kill up all the squirrels our fun is at an end, in the hunting line, and he had as well not bought his rifles, since he will have nothing to practice on; I write this because I love to hunt, and I do not know what I shall do with myself this winter, if there is no hunting to be done. . . . It seemed somewhat strange to me, but up here they call 10 cts a shilling, I always heard 16⅔ cts called a shilling before— . . .

WALTER CLARK TO HIS FATHER

Hillsborough, N. C.
Military Academy
September 26th 1860

. . . I did not know the River was high enough for the Kahukee to come up yet, do you reckon she will be as crowded with her loads this winter as last, last winter she had *more* than she could carry, how do you like her since she is lengthened. I don't suppose however it makes any material difference in her looks—Your cause-ways or crossing-places (I never could make the distinction) will be very useful and convenient this winter, at least I think you will find them so in passing about the plantation as well as in hauling, if they had been only constructed last winter, they would have saved you a good deal of useless riding, your team a good deal of severe hauling, and me *a good ducking*—I received the Observer yesterday (the first time I have received it) and from the receipt enclosed I saw that you had ordered it sent to me for a year until Sept-61, I am very much obliged to you for having it sent to me, it is undoubtedly the best paper of its class I have seen published—They do not give marks on Drilling but they *very often report* Cadets for Inattention or carelessness on Drill—The Building here is just completed, they are now engaged in tearing the scaffolding down, it is a beautiful building, I don't think the picture I sent Col does it justice— . . . This evening (a few minutes ago) one of the Squad-drillers had imprudently carried his Squad (which, by the way, was composed almost entirely of the smallest boys in Barracks) too far into the middle of the Campus, all of a sudden by an unexpected maneuvre the Company in full charge was thrown right upon them, The Driller took care of himself and as he was standing a little apart from his Squad he didn't have far to run to be beyond the flank of the Company, but the squad deserted by their Driller scared half to death were so frightened they didn't think to run aside and the little fellows took off like a flock of sheep. I don't think I ever saw such short legs travel so in my life, they ran like life depended on it, the Company soon righted about, but the little fellows never once looked around, they were sure the company was upon them and then they brought up, some of them were plunged head over heels in a brush-pile (at the end of the Campus) which obstructed their further progress. I don't know when I have laughed more, I wish you could have seen them....

TO WALTER CLARK FROM HIS MOTHER

Airlie Oct 24th 1860

...You all reached Hillsborough safely I suppose, (after your turnout) & I hope you are again at hard study, never halt, but continue to pursue with diligence your daily task, remember, we can never accomplish much in this life, without energy & perseverence—Watch well your deportment & never take the first step, in any bad or wicked habit, it is much easier to shun the first step, than the second Beware of bad company, the evil one uses every artifice to lure us from the path of duty, rectitude & honour, we have to be constantly on the lookout—*Watch* & *pray*—You are & have been the child of many prayers & I hope you will ever bear it in mind—I am not very well consequently dont feel much like writing a long letter—I have collected all of your letters that I could find, tied them in a package & put them over behind your books, in your bookcase but most of those that I have written you, I wish destroyed when you come home....

TO WALTER CLARK FROM HIS MOTHER

Airlie Oct 25th 1860

I wrote you yesterday, but having received your letter today, stating your number of marks & *demerits,* I feel so troubled at your getting so many demerits, (& that is so short a time) that I feel constrained to write & know what they were for—You know that I always look to your report on deportment, first thing & as you have always stood No 1. on that, at all the schools you have hitherto attended, I fear Hillsborough is doing you no good, for I am sure if it is to detract from your good behaviour, I shall wish you had never seen it & moreover if you wish to take a good stand in your studies, you ought to beware of demerits, for in your monthly reports every demerit, detracts from your grade as a scholar. I think you must have been in bad company, you know that I have always cautioned you about the choice of associates—Be certain to write me immediately on the reception of this I feel so anxious about you, such anxiety, as none but a Mother can feel—Never conceal your conduct to prevent demerits, but always let it be so correct, as not to deserve any—I think you are doing admirably in your studies & if you will only let your conduct accord, think I shall have great cause to be thankful. . . .

TO WALTER CLARK FROM HIS FATHER

Littleton
2 Nov 1860

I have just returned from Scotland Neck. I intended to go to the plantation but it rained (on Tuesday) so hard that I was stopped at Clarksville, where they were having a Military parade, with presentation of a flag by the Ladies to the L.N. Mounted Rifle—Present Rifle 46. Enfield Blues 60. Tarboro company about 70. The Halifax Ys did not come on account of the rain but a detachment of 15 came down in the afternoon. Flag presented by Ladies RH Smith spoke—Capt P Edmondson replied. Both good. & though it rained all day the troops paraded in the mud & water Had the weather been propitious there would have been a grand display for a country place, a large crowd of spectators as it was there were some five or six hundred present. . . . Bill has come back from New York He says that the Union ticket is gaining ground rapidly there. The Republicans have claimed one hundred thousand majority they now claim only thirty nine thousand but I hope the Union will carry the state if so all is safe. . . . I do not know that I care about your getting first distinction but should like for you to deserve it which you will do if you do your duty & take into consideration the disadvantage you started under—But if you do not think that you deserve it & should come to get it request Col Tew to let the right one Have it. . . .

TO WALTER CLARK FROM HIS MOTHER

Airlie Nov 7th 1860

. . . It is generally thought I believe, in this part of the world, that Lincoln is elected, & if so, we have much to fear, tho' I trust an overruling Providence will guide & protect us from evil—I dont think your Pa has seemed to apprehend much danger, tho' he thinks the South ought to be prepared, in case of an emergency—Your corn has been gathered & measured about 15 bbls, after what we used for corn puddings &c turned out better than I expected—I wish we could have you here, to help about setting out our fruit trees, when they come. . . .

[P.S.]
I have bought you another excellent book for your library, "Practical Truths"—Your Uncle William * was so taken with it that I loaned it to him, but put your name in it first—I wish you to read it as soon as you get home—

WALTER CLARK TO HIS MOTHER

H. M. A.
Sat. Feb 4th. 1861

. . . We came out here Wednesday, though we had no recitations until Friday, there being so many Recruits to whom *everything* had to be issued, that it was impossible to have recitations, it is said that Col Tew had 150 applicants this year, with how much truth I don't know! but it seems *very* probably there being here now 86 *Cadets & Recruits*, and 50 more *Cadets* being expected (as only 16 obtained honorable discharges) besides some 30 or 40 Recruits making an Aggregate of from 160 to 170; There is at Charlotte 95—Some of our Cadets have joined the army at Charleston (in vacation) still there are a good many South Carolina Cadets here yet—There are 3 Cadets here from Charleston and they state that Fort Sumpter will not be attacked before Friday night, the Batteries (of cotton bales) not being able to be finished before then, they say that the fort would have been taken long before now, but for the slowness (which the extreme secrecy of building the Batteries imposed upon them) with which the Batteries were erected, the South Carolinians being unwilling to the loss of life which any other manner of assault would ensure—Col

* William Thorne, who lived near Airlie.

Tew's Cannons have at last arrived, there are *two brass six-pounders* out before the Building now, and Col Tew has either *two* or *four rifled* Cannons at Newbern en route from Richmond Va; they are all furnished by the State; to my Class will belong the *Honor* of hauling them about, and scrubbing them up to keep them bright (won't it be an honor that we will not appreciate— It seems as if a body had been from home a month, I never hated anything so bad in all my life as I did my coming up here too soon, I felt as if I would rather be anywheres in the world than in Hillsboro, though a body don't have much time to think of home here except Saturdays and they *seem* as if they are going to take that little away from *us* for on Saturday we have Elocution (Speaking) and take Writing Lessons; Col Tew says this is the *hardest* year in the whole course; You may expect to see me about the bottom of the Class at the end of the year— . . .

I have had my overcoat made, I gave 6.50 for my dress pants (the usual price) and 13.50 for my overcoat (making $20 in all), I think the latter is *very* cheap, being made out of the finest Rock Island cloth the color of our uniform.

WALTER CLARK TO HIS FATHER

Hillsborough, Feb 19th 1861

. . . There are at present 101 Cadets (and recruits) here a pretty large number to open with—I think—I have my new overcoat. I had it made purposely too large so that it will fit me next Fall— Our new Registers will not be issued in a week or so, Col Tew sends one to every parent or guardian as soon as they are issued, he says he will send one as soon as *possible,* enclosed I send his Receipt—I dont have much time to write, but I *took* time tonight, to give you an idea of what I have to do I just give what I had to recite today: 9 to 10, Trigonometry. 10 to 11 Descriptive Geometry. 11 to 12 Latin. 12 to 1 P.M. Drill. 2½ to 3½ P.M. French. 3½ to 4½ Drawing. 4½ to 6 Drill and Saturday Elocution 6.45 A.M. to 8 A.M. I will do my best but to tell the truth I was not fully prepared last Fall when I joined the 4th Class and it hurts me now, however after a little we will have to drill only once a day and that will give us more time, If I find out that I will fall in July (I can tell in two or three week's how I will probably stand) what must I do? however you may rest assured of one thing that if *study* will carry me along I will rise; but *study* will carry you to a certain point and no farther; I will try to hope for the *best*—I will go to the Doctor Saturday and be vaccinated and send the scab from my arm as directed—Capt Pride Jones & Nash are Secession candidates for the Convention and Graham & Berry the Union—The Cadets are divided into two Companies A & B. I am in Company B, all the Cadet Officers have not been appointed yet, I will inform you when they are—The 3rd Class will have Artillery Drill this year; they have had us scouring the Cannon up already; Our Class is only large enough for managing 2 pieces as it takes *6* or *8* to manage a Gun and Our Class numbers 14 to which add 2 who are in the 2nd Class (who couldn't Drill last year on account of their numerical deficiency) gives us 8 to a Gun. . . .

TO WALTER CLARK FROM HIS MOTHER

Ventosa March 2nd 1861

. . . We have just heard the result of the election for Late Convention in this county—Mr Dick Smith & Dr Batchelor, your Pa did'nt vote at all; a good many were very anxious to nominate him & Cousin Tom Harriss, but he would'nt accept—You must let me know right away, how your vaccination took—I shall feel anxious until I hear—You have never written me, how you passed your time (& with what associates) until school commenced—Mrs Tom Hill from Hillsboro, has just been on a visit to Scotland Neck, but I did'nt see her, are you acquainted with her or not? How do you like drawing, you have always been so anxious to learn to draw, that I presume you are very fond of it. . . .

TO WALTER CLARK FROM HIS MOTHER

Ventosa
April 20th 1861

. . . I received your letter written to Mittie & me, hope you were not among the number engaged in hoisting the flag without permission—I think the Southern flag very pretty, but think the addition of a few more stars (which they will now have) will be quite an improvement—Your Pa & Cousin Gavin went up to Dawson's Xroads today as the election for Col comes off (I suppose you know that your Pa is the candidate that they think will be elected, he is also running for brigadier general, if he is elected to that office, will throw up Col, to someone else, his object is not to gain office for himself, but to defeat some who are not fit for it & get efficient men to take it—You wrote me the names of your roommates, but nothing of their character & disposition. . . . There is no news scarcely, but *secession, war* &c. presume you hear as much of that as I do, so I will not enter into any details—I suppose you attend the Methodist church every Sunday have you become acquainted with Brother Guthrie yet? Do you attend well to your teeth? & more than that, do you read your bible regularly & pray? dont neglect it, my dear boy, you will never regret doing it. . . .

II

"Little Clark," the Soldier

1861-1865

IN JULY, 1861, THE VOLUNTEER TROOPS AT Camp Ellis, numbering nearly one thousand men, were organized into the 22nd Regiment of North Carolina Troops under the command of Colonel James Johnston Pettigrew. "Little Clark," as he was called by many of the men, was chosen second lieutenant and drill master. Shortly after its organization this infantry regiment was ordered to join the Army of Virginia, and early in August it was encamped three miles northwest of Richmond. From this point Clark wrote his mother a long letter in which he described camp life, pointed out his own personal needs, told about the twenty-seven hundred "impudent" Yankee prisoners then being held in Richmond, and gave some interesting details about things he had observed in the Confederate capital.

After a few weeks, the 22nd Regiment was ordered to the Potomac to form part of the command of Brigadier General Theophilus H. Holmes. At first it was located at Brook's Station near Aquia Creek, a tributary of the Potomac. From this camp Clark wrote his mother, giving further details of army life and stating his frank opinion of Holmes, Pettigrew, and other officers. Soon thereafter the regiment marched to Evansport, a point on the Potomac River, the present Quantico Station, where batteries of heavy guns were to be established to blockade the river below Washington. Until March of the next year, the 22nd remained in support of the Evansport batteries.

Clark continued to act as drill master until November, 1861, when he was transferred to Camp Carolina near Raleigh to act in the same capacity for the recently formed 35th Regiment. The staff officers of the "harmless 35th," as Clark called it, were the Reverend James Sinclair of Robeson County, Colonel; Marshall D. Craton of Wayne County, Lieutenant Colonel, and Oliver Cromwell Petway of Edgecombe County, Major. It was not long until Clark had to "unfix here" and move to Camp Mangum, also near Raleigh. Here the 35th remained, perfecting its drill and discipline, until January 3, 1862, when, at the request of General R. C. Gatling, commanding the Department, it was sent to New Bern to take part in the defense of that strategic city against an anticipated Federal attack by General Ambrose E. Burnside.

About this time Clark resigned from the regiment and re-entered Tew's Military Academy. Consequently he did not participate in the New Bern campaign.

In the early summer of 1862, the 35th Regiment was reorganized by electing Matt W. Ransom colonel and Clark a first lieutenant. Colonel Ransom, a native of Northampton County, appointed Clark his adjutant on August 1. Shortly after, the regiment was ordered to join Lee's army then preparing for the Maryland campaign. Within the next two months Clark saw plenty of action. He joined Lee's army in time to witness the closing scenes of the Second Battle of Manassas; under Jackson he participated in the capture of Harper's Ferry; he was in the forefront of the Battle of Sharpsburg (Antietam), and he was actively engaged in the Battle of Fredericksburg.

Preparatory to Walter's joining the Army of Virginia, his father gave him a bodyguard and two horses. The bodyguard was a Negro boy named Neverson, only two years older than Walter, but intelligent and devoted to his young master. This devotion seems to have been mutual, for in Clark's letters home there are frequent references to Neverson which show genuine concern about his health and general well-being. Neverson remained with "Little Clark" throughout the war.

When Lee's army left Richmond to meet the Federal forces headed by General Pope at Second Manassas, Ransom's brigade was left behind to defend Richmond and Petersburg and to assist in the construction of fortifications around those key cities. On August 27 the brigade left Richmond en route to join Lee, then about to invade Maryland. They reached the Potomac on September 7 and waded through at Cheek's Ford; they marched as far as the Monocacy River, where they were ordered back to blow up the aqueduct over the canal; on September 11 they recrossed the Potomac at Point of Rocks, and, marching in the direction of the little town of Hillsboro, on the Harper's Ferry Road, reached and occupied Loudon Heights, September 14. From this point they shelled the enemy in Harper's Ferry until the Federal forces surrendered on the 15th. On the same day they marched twelve miles toward the Shenandoah and at 1 A.M. on September 16 started for Shepherdstown. At 1 A.M. the next day they crossed into Maryland, wading the Potomac for the third time in nine days. On September 17, Clark participated in the Battle of Sharpsburg, the bloodiest one-day battle of the war. On the next day the regiment retreated to the Potomac, crossing at Shepherdstown, and marched in the direction of Martinsburg, Virginia. From there they proceeded to the vicinity of Winchester, and remained there in bivouac until October 23, when they broke camp and marched through Culpeper Court House and Madison Court

House, and arrived near Fredericksburg on November 23, where they went into camp.

The Battle of Fredericksburg began about 4 A.M. on December 11, and Neverson rode with Adjutant Clark until the enemy opened fire at close range. Clark then dismounted and directed Neverson to take the horses to the rear so as to be out of danger—and for three days Clark saw neither Neverson nor the horses.

Following the Confederate victory at Fredericksburg, the 35th Regiment went with Lee into winter quarters near Richmond. Clark was troubled with a wounded hand which had been hit by a minie ball at Sharpsburg, and the severe winter was a tax on his strength. He wrote his mother asking for a pair of boots because he thought his "feet would freeze in these low shoes for they keep no more water out than if I had none." He finally received the boots.

His mother's letters at this period show great concern over her boy's health and she constantly urged him to resign and come home. Shortly before the Battle of Fredericksburg, orders had been issued to discharge all men in the regiment under eighteen and over forty years of age; but Clark, who was under eighteen, remained in the service, although some fifty men had dropped out.

The 35th Regiment, having become badly depleted from losses in battle and resignations, was ordered back to North Carolina for local service. On January 3, 1863, Ransom's brigade marched through Richmond and took the train at Petersburg for Kenansville, North Carolina. Soon after Clark reached camp, he had a letter from home informing him that his father had been commissioned a brigadier general in the North Carolina Militia, charged with the obstruction of the Roanoke River, and authorized to call as much of the militia of Bertie, Martin, and Washington counties as was necessary and to impress slaves, wagons, teams, and boats of every description into service. Walter was disturbed, and he wrote his mother to "Tell Pa by no means to enter the service. One day of such service as we saw sometimes in Virginia would be sure to kill him." The next day he wrote, "If anyone wishes to become used to the crosses and trials of this life, let him enter camp life."

These letters intensified his mother's concern over Walter's health and again she urged him to resign, but his father wrote and told him to use his own best judgment. Clark finally resigned in February and within a few weeks entered the University of

North Carolina, where he was graduated on June 3, 1864. Clark's letters reveal that he studied political economy and constitutional law under ex-Governor David L. Swain, then President of the University, and had other courses in law under Judge Battle. He said that he had "no idea of entering any profession except the army, but don't you think I am doing well enough to read Law."

On June 3, 1864, he wrote his mother: "I was graduated yesterday. Today I have been elected Major of the 5th Battalion Junior Reserves. Need I say that my first thought on the announcement of my election was yourself, & that I hastened to write. I had strong opposition. . . . I received, however, 16 votes out of 20. I have five (5) fine Companies, numbering nearly five hundred fine strapping Western lads. There is hardly a small man in my Battalion. My Battalion is composed of picked men and picked officers."

The demand for the organization of Junior Reserves in order to protect and defend the home fronts had been so insistent that the Confederate Congress on February 17, 1864, passed a law placing in the Reserves those between the ages of seventeen and eighteen, and forty-five and fifty. The Act also provided they were not to serve out of their respective states, but the North Carolina Junior Reserves saw action in South Carolina, Georgia, and Virginia.

The Sixth Battalion was organized at Camp Holmes, near Raleigh, and was ordered to Goldsboro on June 8. Ten days later it was ordered to Weldon and encamped at "Camp Ransom." On July 4, the First and Sixth Battalions were organized into a Regiment, the 70th North Carolina, with Charles W. Broadfoot as colonel and Clark as lieutenant colonel. Later in the month the headquarters of General Holmes were removed to Weldon, and soon thereafter he sent for the field officers of Clark's regiment and explained to them his earnest wish that his chief of staff, Lieutenant Colonel F. S. Armistead, might be made colonel of the First Regiment. Armistead was a West Pointer and brother of General Armistead, who was killed at Gettysburg. The field officers resigned, and at the new election Armistead was chosen colonel, Broadfoot, lieutenant colonel, and Clark, major—the rank which he held for the remainder of the war.

On October 16, the regiment went to Boykin's Depot, met a Federal raid from Blackwater River in Virginia, and returned to Weldon in a few days. Toward the end of the month the regiment was sent to Plymouth, to cover the approach to the eastern counties, from which large supplies were being drawn for the support of Lee's hard-pressed army. Early in November four companies were sent under Clark's command to Williamston. On one occasion Clark followed the enemy with part of the cavalry, three companies of infantry, and a section of artillery nearly to Jamesville, the remainder of the regiment being left to guard the road from Washington.

About the middle of February, 1865, the regiment moved to Kinston, and after it had been encamped there for about three weeks, news came that the enemy was advancing from New Bern in great force. At that time Sherman's army was marching up from South Carolina and on February 10 Clark's regiment retreated through Kinston, thence through Goldsboro, and on to Smithfield. On March 16 the Battle of Averasboro was fought and the next morning the regiment moved forward to meet Sherman. The night of the 18th they camped in the woods beyond the stream that runs through Bentonville.

On March 20 and 21, General Joseph E. Johnston, with about fifteen thousand men, faced General William T. Sherman with about seventy thousand in the last important battle of the war in North Carolina. The skirmish line of the brigade and the center was commanded by Major Walter Clark, and the Junior Reserves gave an excellent account of themselves. Years later General B. F. Hoke wrote about their gallant conduct: "At Bentonville they held a very important part of the battlefield in opposition to Sherman's old and tried soldiers, and repulsed every charge that was made upon them with very meagre and rapidly thrown up breastworks. Their conduct in camp, on the march, and on the battlefield was everything that could be expected of them."

The night of the 21st the Confederate Army recrossed the creek by the bridge near Bentonville. The Federals made repeated attempts to force the passage of the bridge, but failed. At noon the retreat was resumed and the troops camped near Smithfield.

On April 6, 1865, "the last great review held by any of the Confederate armies" was held, and "Governor Vance made one of his most inspiring speeches." On April 10 Johnston broke camp and the "final retreat began." Two days later his army reached Raleigh. The Junior Reserves marched on, and at Bush Hill, in Randolph County, on May 2, all that were left of them were paroled and they turned their faces sorrowfully homeward.

The next day Major Clark and Neverson began their weary horseback ride one hundred and fifty miles to Ventosa. On their way home they passed through Hillsboro and in sight of the military academy from which Clark had gone so ambitiously some years before. He knew that Colonel Tew had been killed at Sharpsburg, but he did not know until afterwards that every one of his instructors in the academy had gone to war and had been either wounded or captured.

When home was finally reached, there was no home—nothing but the land was there. Former slaves were wandering aimlessly about. The invading armies had burned to the ground the spacious Ventosa mansion, and its beautiful gardens had disappeared. All the happy memories of Walter's childhood lay waste before his eyes.

CLARK TO HIS MOTHER

Camp near Richmond
Monday Aug 10th /61

I am at present with the Regiment, which is stationed near Rocketts 3 miles Nor'west of Richmond, on a high bluff which commands a beautiful prospect of the surrounding country; I have seen even distinctly, with a large spyglass, in their encampments on the other side of the city 10 or 12 miles distant—The hills in the vicinity are dotted with tents; there are at present between 23 & 25,000 men lying encamped around Richmond and more arriving every day, Beauregard * has sent orders to send (until ordered by him) no more troops; It is said that he is attempting a crossing of the Potomac below Washington City about 10 or 12 miles, and that as soon as he crosses he will call for more troops, at any rate Col Pettigrew's † Regiment is expected to leave about the last of the week either for Manassas or the Mountains—The Yankee prisoners are confined in three or 4 large Tobacco Manufactories here,‡ the Officers are in a building to themselves; all the buildings are on Main street; There are 2700 of them in all, some are at work on vessels and *other things,* they are the most impudent things I ever saw, nobody hardly can pass without their making some remark across the street to each other; They have to shoot on an average a half a dozen or more every week for insubordination &c—I will want a sword & a piece of oilcloth (I wish now I had taken that piece of Aunt Pattie); *I will not need a*

* Confederate General Pierre Gustave Toutant Beauregard.

† James Johnston Pettigrew, Colonel of the 22nd Regiment, later Brigadier General, mortally wounded at Gettysburg, July 4, 1863.

‡ See W. B. Hesseltine, *Civil War Prisons,* for data on Richmond prisons.

servant, my Mess already has one and we would have no imaginable use for another; I am sorry Pa has had the trouble to hire one but the servant was hired you know when I was not here, however send the Sword & Oilcloth *by Express to me at Richmond. Va. Care of Col J. Johnston. Pettigrew. 22nd Regiment N.C. Vol.*— Col Stokes' * Regiment, the 1st N.C. State Troops, is quartered about a half a mile from here (it was at Warrenton you know), I saw Marks yesterday when I went down there—There is a large Steam Sugar Refinery here, I went all through it Saturday, it is 6 stories high and a perfect curiosity; Out of 20 hogheads of common sugar they get 5 barrels of dirt or filth, the dirt they get out of it is sold as Guano I believe—Winfield Scott † has *two children* buried not very far off from our encampment. "Breathes there a man with soul so dead. Who ne'er to himself hath said, This is my own, my native land"—Tell Pa I had to buy a pistol at last; One of Whitney's Navy Pistols, it has the same bore and is the same length of Colt's Navy Pistol but is stronger make and 5 oz lighter, and it outshoots as far as I have seen them shot together; I shot it the other day with not a *very great* elevation and it threw a little over 500 (five hundred) yards, It is a splendid thing to shoot squirrels with; Dr Hawkins drew on Rader Biggs & Co for the amount ($50) payable to the order of Mr Wilkinson, (the gentleman I bought it of), Mr Wilkinson has a whole trunk full he smuggled through from Louisville....

CLARK TO HIS MOTHER

Camp Bee ‡
Tuesday Aug 20th 1861

...It has rained ever since we have reached here and almost without intermission from the time we left Richmond up to the present moment. We asked an old negro when we got here how long it would rain, he said it generally rained *all August,* we then asked him how long was August in these parts he replied after a good deal of hesitation "just *three months adzactly*", since, I have come over to his opinion—I have me a better tent now if I hadn't got a better one I would have had to have almost waded out next morning—Col Tew's § Regiment was encamped about a mile

* Colonel Montfort Sidney Stokes of Wilkes County.
† United States General, Whig candidate for President in 1852.
‡ Apparently the camp at Brook's Station, near Richmond.
§ Colonel Charles C. Tew, graduate of West Point, head of Hillsboro Military Academy, Colonel of the Second North Carolina Regiment, killed at the Battle of Sharpsburg, September 17, 1862.

from here, it is so masked that a vessel might sail 50 or 75 yards of it and not perceive it; from the Batteries you can easily see the war steamers lying about 4 or 5 miles off (though it looks nearer); with a glass, you can see the men walking about on her—I have been a good deal perplexed about my pay, but I am in hopes now that it will be all right—Thursday. I have been sick with a sore throat and a headache attendant on it so that I have been compelled to wait till today to finish my letter; I am glad to be able to write that I am well—Give my love to all—Gen Holmes * from N.C. (*Pa's old acquaintance*) is Commander of this Department, he reviewed our Regiment today; He is not an Adonis in beauty by any means—The Battery down here at Aquia Creek (3 miles off) got to peppering Y. Doodle Esq again this morning, they get to pecking at each other every two or three days now—Direct my letters as I wrote you in my letter of Saturday Viz: To Accokeek. P.O. Stafford Co Va. Care of Col J. Johnston Pettigrew 22th Reg N.C.V—Tell Col next time you write to him, that he must write to me and send him an envelope directed as above—Excuse my writing as everybody is jostling me and talking all around me—It is uncertain when or for what place this Regiment will leave, a Regiment never knows when it is going to leave until the order is given Strike Tents nor where they are to stop until the command to pitch tents, This Regiment has moved 4 times since I have been with it and neither time did the Col have 5 minutes notice before hand—Give my love to all—*Write soon and write often*—I am well so dont be uneasy—If you want to know our position look on the Map for Stafford Co, you will see that about 10 or 12 miles North of Fredericksburg is a little creek whose name is not put down, that creek is Aquia Creek, at mouth of it are the Batteries and where the RR crosses it (the creek) is our camp—Good Bye— . . .

CLARK TO HIS MOTHER

Aquia Creek. Aug 28th 1861

. . . —Tell Frank to rub up my Sharp's Rifle as bright as a new pin. I am afraid it is getting rusty; with my Sharp's Rifle, Hallady gun, and my Navy Pistol in good order I think I will be well prepared for hunting this winter; my Pistol is a *Splendid* pistol, it carries a ball larger if anything than my rifle and one would be surprised to see the power of it. I should like for Pa to see it, I

* Lieutenant General Theophilus H. Holmes, commissioned October 10, 1862.

think it is just the weight for him and after a little practice he will go squirrel hunting with it altogether, he can shoot at a squirrel 6 times without loading and at 100 yds it is as good as a rifle and it is more convenient to carry—Tell Pa he must write to me—Did you tell Col to write to me—The *Prevailing* opinion in all the Regiments around from the highest to the lowest is that Peace will concluded by the 1st Nov notwithstanding that it is reported that we will cross over the Potomac into Maryland in week or 10 days, in fact, there *are* large wide flats building up these creeks in any quantity—Won't these continued rains injure Pa's crop on the River, I never saw such fine corn in all my life. (that is so much fine corn) as there is from Richmond to this place—Manassas is not more than 25 miles from here, we heard heavy firing in the direction of Fairfax C.H.* day before yesterday—Don't forget to tell Frank about my rifle, I saw a good many rifles in Richmond and there were none that for sporting I would give for mine—Camp writing will ruin anybody's handwriting so excuse this—...

RECOMMENDATION OF COLONEL J. J. PETTIGREW

Headquarters
22nd Reg. N.C.V.
Sept. 24th 1861.

This is to certify that Mr. Clark, Drill Master to this Regiment, has assiduously performed the duties of his position and in every way conducted himself with propriety. As this may be the last opportunity for some time of sending him home, I grant him a discharge from the present duty with orders to report to the Adj. General.

TO CLARK FROM J. A. C. BROWN †

Camp Holmes Near Evansport
Sept 30th 1861

I promised to write to you this week specially concerning your box. I have heard nothing of it. Some of our sick leave for Fredricksburg in the morning and I have instructed them to enquire after it at the Station & Fredricksburg and should I hear of it I will dispose of it according to directions—Well since you left

* Fairfax Court House.

† Native of Davidson County, Second Lieutenant and later Captain, Company L, 22nd Regiment of North Carolina Troops.

nothing strange or miraculous has come to pass—When you started will you believe it when I tell you how home-sick [I] was—I was attacked with a spasmodic fit of the blues. Why I was like a child—I am the worst fool in the known world about such things any grown man but myself would be ashamed to confess it—"Sic transit gloria mundi"—

"I feel like one Who treads alone
Some banquet hall deserted
Whose lights have fled
Whose garlands dead
And all but he departed"

I have been very unwell since you left and Lt Gray * on the sick list so I was pressed into service as the Capt. remains on the drunk list still. He is Oh! drunker than anything I ever knew to get. drunk tonight—Our Company was in line picket Friday and he powerful drunk down there and insisted very much that we should hold prayer meeting but could get no one to lead in prayer whereupon he gave a very pressing exhortation. it being dark some of the boys now and then would cry out Amen, and he would foam—My Uncle is coming out to see me in a few days when without some change is made—I am going to resign and go home with him—I dont mind a man's getting drunk once if he will get sober—that he may get drunk again, but to get drunk and never get sober is somewhat foreign to my schooling, and appears so very strange and unnatural to me—

We will move from this place nearer the river in a day or so. so said the Col—our Dress Parade this evening.

The sickness has abated none since you left us. one of our boys D.S. Nance † died last week. Lt. Nelson ‡ will die I guess—Harney § has been very sick but is improving—I ought to be on the sick list but I have to play Adjutant tomorrow—I am not able to tell you whether or not Dr Hall || has ever got sober—Col Long ¶ is sober or so drunk he cant go. which of the two is condition I am not able to say—and I cant say that I care—I think had I been the

* Claiborne Gray of Randolph County, Lieutenant of "Uwharrie Rifles."

† Died September 12, 1861, at Evansport.

‡ John N. Nelson, Sergeant and later Second Lieutenant of Company E, 22nd Regiment, died November, 1861.

§ E. C. Harney, Second Lieutenant, native of Randolph County, died Sept. 15, 1863, from wounds received at Gettysburg.

|| Dr. J. R. Hall of Davidson County, surgeon, resigned October 19, 1862.

¶ Lieutenant Colonel John O. Long, of Randolph County, taken prisoner May 31, 1862.

biggest drunkard in the civilized world would by this time become so thoroughly ashamed & disgusted that I would have just quit off without any moral suasion—

The fourth battery is to be finished tonight and Friday morning is the time set for the opening of the *ball*—They have been putting things through for a week—I hope they will do something this week—I will write to you when the fun is over I must stop as our light is about out—You must pardon me for being so hasty this time and be sure to write soon—

CLARK TO HIS MOTHER

Camp Carolina Near Raleigh
Nov 15th /61

... Our Camp is to be moved to 3 miles above Raleigh on the N.C. Central Railroad; It is now you know 3 miles below Raleigh on the Raleigh & Gaston RailRoad; they move it on account of the scarcity of wood at our present location; We will go into Winter Quarters there; The State has bought 500 acres for that purpose and 4 or 5 Regiments will have Winter Quarters there, one (Col Rob Vance's * the 29th) is already there and we will move over Monday.

Cols Sinclair † & Craton ‡ have not yet arrived so Maj Petway § has had all the trouble, of fixing out the Regiment and preparing to move, to himself; and by the way he is just 21 today.

I met 3 of my old school mates very unexpectedly the other evening when Vance's Regiment came down, they are all three Drill-masters, 2 of them were at Hillsboro and the other was one of Mr Graves' old scholars who subsequently went to Charlotte.

Major Petway went to Mr Graves only a session or two before I did.

Since Adj. Petway has been elected Major I have had to act as Adjutant of this Regiment, the regular Adjutant will be appointed as soon as Col Sinclair comes, I do not know whom he will be, though I think it is probable that one of the Lieutenants in the Regiment will be appointed.

If I was only 2 or 3 years older or 1st Class Drill-master I could

* Robert B. Vance of Buncombe County, Colonel of the 29th North Carolina Regiment, commissioned Brigadier General, March 16, 1863.

† The Reverend James Sinclair of Robeson County, Colonel of the 22nd North Carolina Regiment.

‡ Marshall D. Craton of Wayne County, Lieutenant Colonel of the 22nd.

§ Oliver Cromwell Petway of Edgecombe County, Major of the 22nd.

get the Adjutancy of the *Post* with all ease. I will buy the jacket if I can get one which I think is doubtful; if you could get the cloth it would not cost a quarter as much as if I bought one; I had to pay $7 for the making of my coat when you know I furnished everything and had to pay $8 for my pants (and now they are selling at $11) though they are very common indeed.

CLARK TO HIS MOTHER

Camp Carolina Near Raleigh, N.C.
Monday. Nov 18th. 1861

. . . Is there anything else you want me to buy in Raleigh? If so, let me know in time and I can get anything you want very readily.

I suppose Gen Martin * has never sent Pa his moulds yet, has he?

The Baptist Convention is at present in session in Raleigh; I have heard several of the Members preach out here at camp.

The State Convention meets today, I intend to go in tomorrow and see what kind of a monster this *legislatorial* bugbear is (for, to read the speeches delivered on the floor of the Legislature, it were a bugbear indeed, at which the stoutest Blackstone would quail) for aside from my desire to see this *Wise body,* I have not been in Raleigh for nearly three weeks although it is scarcely more than two miles off and I could go every day if I wished; I suppose Messrs. Smith & Batchelor will be up.

We move over to our new camp tomorrow; I hate to move as I am going away so soon, I will have to unfix here and by the time I fix up there I will have to leave; I would much prefer remaining here. . . .

They are at a loss whom to appoint as Adjutant of the Regiment or of the Post either; I have been told by those who have the appointing of both (without my ever having thought or said anything about it) that if I was only two or three years older they would appoint me and expressed their regret at their inability to appoint me as it was, as Gen Martin had ordered none to be appointed under a certain age; I feel confident however that if I was 1st Class Drillmaster I could get it with all ease, however all is for the best and if [I] had remained in camp in the Winter (as I should have done, had I been appointed Adjutant) I might have contracted some dangerous disease which would last me my lifetime.

* Adjutant General James G. Martin.

The nearer the time comes for me to come home the more I feel like coming and I regret now I did not write Col to meet me the 23rd instead of the 29th as he proposed; When I think of my hunting Burn's pleasant verses occur to my mind.

Now rustlin' winds and slaught'ring guns
Bring autumn's pleasant weather
The moorcock springs on whirring wings
Among the blooming heather.

By the way there is a volume of Burns in Pa's library, the duplicate of which I carried to Airlie.

Tell Frank to take my rifle mould and mold me some 90 or 100 Rifle balls by the time I come home.

CLARK TO HIS MOTHER

Camp Mangum Near Raleigh
Nov 26th 1861

... I have been acting Adjutant of this Regiment (with the exception of one or two days) ever since it was formed and I have been advised to apply for the permanent position of Adjutant of the Regiment by several of the Officers; Col Sinclair before his election pledged himself to appoint the person recommended by the majority of the Officers, I have at present the Recommendation of you may say the commissioned Officers of companies and a probability of my getting the *unanimous* recommendation of the Officers of the entire Regiment, though I don't think even then that it would be more than probable as Sinclair might have a favorite of his own to appoint and object to my age; To tell the truth I am not anxious for the position for the *disadvantages* nearly counterbalance the *advantages* of the Adjutancy, I had no mother no father to look up to for counsel and as it had [to] be decided then or never whether I should try for it so I had to rely on my own judgment for once; I weighed the matter carefully in my mind and as I knew that if I tried it was no means certain I should get it and even if I did I could resign and thereby have time to ask Pa's and your advice whereas if I refused it was all done with; besides I thought that in future life my being Adjutant at my age would be worth more to me than the knowledge I would probably gain in the next four or five months at school; I also felt that my country had a claim on my services as the other candidates for the Adjutancy were either totally incompetent or men of intemperate habits; As far as I am concerned I should certainly prefer the comforts of home to the liability to disease and all the numerous ills of a Winter Campaign or the chill & fevers and thousand & one ills produced by the indolence of Winter Quarters but I remembered that if I had been a poor boy I might be forced to make this my beginning and rise thereby to an *honorable* position in life, I know that this *incubus* of a *competency* has been the reason of many a man being worthless; I want my motto to be onward and upward, but I have left this matter with the Lord and whatsoever *He* does will be for my good "All's for the best"— is a true saying. It is uncertain whether I get the Adjutancy or not but one thing is certain I will be home as soon as I can, if I get the appointment I will be home to get my horse and boy & other things, if I do not get it I shall be home to stay for I have no idea of being a Drill master any longer; It is hardly *probable* I shall get the appointment. I may have erred in my judgment concerning this affair but I acted as I thought you and Pa would have wished me to have acted if I had had to have written you the circumstances.

We moved over to this our new encampment last Friday. I like it better than the other.

Direct your next to me thus: Lt W. McK Clark. 35th Regt Near Raleigh N.C. Care of Col Craton. (our Lieut. Col).

Being Adjutant has nearly ruined my handwriting however I wrote this in a hurry as my business takes up all my time.

TO CLARK FROM HIS FATHER

3 Dec 1861

By not coming with the Col you caused your Ma & myself no little uneasiness but as we recd your letter of the 27th next day with your reasons for not doing so She has become little though not entirely satisfied. As you say the writing was *very* bad. if not worse even than my writing. I think that I understand your motive for staying & think that in *justice* to you they should give you the Adjutancy even though they were certain that you would resign it immediately—that compliment you deserve. If you get it come Home & I will then say whether or not you may retain it or not. if any other person is appointed it is unnecessary to say come Home—You Have now served the State one four months & I want you to serve Me a short time in staying here while I am off on important business Say to the Lut General Col Martin that you can bring the Commission of the 35th Reg N.C. Militia down when you come. Your Ma wrote to you yesterday to Camp Carolina Write to me this week so that I may get the letter by Saturday

TO CLARK FROM J. M. HINES

Camp Mangum
Dec 6 1861

I have not handed in your letter of resignation as you directed thinking under the circumstances it would be best to get your furlough Signed; I presented your furlough to Col Craton this morning to get his Signature—He said with great pleasure would he sign it and expressed many regrets at your departure. Hopes you will soon return and yet be adjutant of the *harmless* 35. I will keep your furlough until I hear from you fearing it might be miscarried; should I send it in a letter if you cannot return within ten or fifteen days. If it is your request I will then hand in your resignation otherwise I will not. Write me soon I am your friend as ever

TO CLARK FROM C. C. TEW

Fredericksburg, Va. Dec. 9th 1861

Yours of the 2nd inst. is at hand and I reply without delay, sending to Col. Sinclair such a paper as I think you desire.

Should it add to your prospect of position or promotion I shall be much gratified. Many of your academic *confreres* are and have been doing very efficient service.

RECOMMENDATION OF COLONEL C. C. TEW

Fredericksburg, Va.
December 9th 1861

I take pleasure in stating on the part of Mr. W. McK.* Clark that he was for nearly a year a Cadet in the Hillsboro' Military Academy, having entered in July or Aug. 1860 a class somewhat advanced. While there he commended himself to my esteem by his uniform propriety of deportment, moral tone, and strict attention to military and other duties; he is a good soldier and you will find him entirely reliable. . . .

* McKenzie was Clark's middle name, but after the war he seldom used his middle name or initial.

TO CLARK FROM HIS MOTHER

Jan 9th 1862

Your Uncle Ed * has today received a letter from Genl Ransom † hastening his return to camp, & it has disconcerted my arrangements very much & forces me to write by candlelight, so I will have to be very brief—I fear you will be disappointed in not receiving all the articles you wrote for, but I have done the very best that I could under the circumstances I have sent you two large thick blankets, some soap to wash clothes with, a dozen candles, 2 cakes of soap for hands, a vial of *very nice* lip salve, some saleratus (instead of soda as I had no soda) I would not use much of either saleratus or soda, your Pa thinks it very unhealthy, saleratus is very much the same as soda, only a great deal stronger I have also sent you a first rate pr of gloves (think they will fit you exactly, your Pa says some gentleman in Petersburg offered him $9 a pr for some just like them) your beauregard & comfort for the neck, 3 prs of socks, (I had 8 pr. of your socks ready for you, but as you preferred cotton, I went to work & knit these since your Uncle Ed came)—The pants are some that you left at home & I had them fixed, thought they would answer for you to wear awhile, in case your Uncle Ed cannot get any in Petersburg for you, there was no chance for me to get you any, your Aunt Martha had to have some homespun for her boys & your Uncle Ed has a pr of Homespun, & I would gladly have had some for you, but had no means of getting it—Your Uncle Ed ordered a pr of boots for himself & a pr for *you* in Warrenton, he sent for them today, but I fear you will not get them, as Johnson is so slow & has so many orders to fill I also requested your Cousin Ed to order you a pr made in Chapel Hill, so perhaps you will get a pr after awhile—Toothbrushes are not to be had in this part of the world, I have been trying for sometime to get some for your Sisters I have asked your Uncle Ed to try & get you an overcoat & a pr of pants in Petersburg or Richmond as there are no such articles for sale about here—I send you a few cakes, ground peas, figs & a small piece of cheese & some butter for you and your Uncle Ed, if he can carry them all, wish he could carry you a box, but I think it very kind in him to carry what he does & he seems so willing to do it—He is very dear to me, I hate so much for him to leave & were it not that his return to camp will give you pleasure, I

* Captain Ed Thorne of Airlie, Mrs. Clark's brother.
† Matt W. Ransom, commissioned Brigadier General, June 13, 1863.

Walter Clark at Tew's Military Academy in Hillsboro when he was fourteen years old. From a daguerreotype in the possession of the Clark family.

TWENTY-SECOND REGIMENT.

1. Johnston J. Pettigrew, Colonel.
2. Thos. D. Jones, Captain, Co. A.
3. Graham Daves, 1st Lieut. and Adjt.
4. W. W. Dickson, 2d Lieut., Co. A.
5. Walter Clark, 2d Lieut. and Drill Master.

From *Histories of the Several Regiments and Battalions from North Carolina in the Great War 1861-'65,* edited by Walter Clark.—Volume II, facing page 161.

should regret it much more—Your Pa has been gone nearly all the time, so that he has seen very little of him Oh how I wish this horrible war would end—We all ought to pray unceasingly for *peace*—There is much apprehension now I believe that our State will be overrun by the Yankees—Your Pa has not moved his negroes yet—I hope he got his salt this week for his pork—... Your Uncle Ed had just vaccinated me & three of the children & one of the servants (from a scab your Pa got in Enfield) when we received the vaccine that you sent, but there are plenty more to be vaccinated, tho a great many of your Pa's servants were vaccinated when the small pox was in Scotland Neck, several years ago—It is night & I cant see so I must stop & write you again soon—My dear child dont neglect prayer & reading your bible read & pray often, it will be a great help to you—May the Good God guide & protect you & may I see you soon, is the earnest prayer of your Mother's heart—

I also send you some Apples that grew in my little trees at home....

I have sent you fifty dollars to buy your overcoat & pants & also another pr of gloves which you can give to one of the soldiers if you dont need them The pr for you is tied up with your beauregard & socks & comfort they will fit you better than this last pr—

CLARK TO HIS FATHER

H.M.A.* Jan. 16th 1862.

...It seems Jackson † is to be the Napoleon of this war; Some of his movements have been really similar to those of the "little Corporal" in his first Italian campaign. He resembles Bonaparte in his plan of beating the enemy in detail, in his rapidity of movement and of execution, in the attachment of his troops and above all in his good fortune which has never deserted him. He has put an entirely new face upon the appearance of this War.

What do you think of Beauregard's recent movements. They are very mysterious and the silence of the S.W.‡ press appears ominous. It seems certain that the enemy have complete possession of the Mississippi if not the Mississippi Valley.

Have you seen Gen Branch's § letter, about that piece in the papers containing an account of the battle of New Hanover Court

* Hillsboro Military Academy.
† General Thomas Jonathan ("Stonewall") Jackson.
‡ Apparently this refers to Southwest Press.
§ Brigadier General L. O'B. Branch of North Carolina.

House, which over the signature of *Hanover* (W. T. Nicholson *) seemed to call in question not only Gen B's abilities as a commander but also his personal courage? What do you think of Gen letter and what do you think of Hanover's letter and his recantation (so called)? I presume you have seen the pieces I allude to?

Judge Biggs was up here not long since. He has a son here. He reported all quiet down east. I expect the recent rains have caused your crop to be overrun with grass.

What is the general aspect of affairs on the River and in Scotland Neck? quite dull I presume.

It appears that the N.C. Troops covered themselves with glory at the late Richmond battle however tardy the Virginia papers may be in acknowledging it. I see the "gallant 5th" (Col McRae) † was again in the fight and acted with its usual bravery. The 22nd (formerly Col Pettigrew's) also covered itself with glory; It's Col Lightfoot ‡ was a Professor here you know; Its Lieut Col (Long) § who was taken prisoner after being wounded seriously and its Maj (Galloway) || who was also wounded were the Lieut Col and Maj when I was in the Regiment. Capt T.D. Jones ¶ (Co A 22nd Regt) who fell fighting so gallantly was a splendid Officer; I was well acquainted with him.

What do you think of the "Situation" now? Dont you think our chances are better now than ever?

...What do you think about the Gubernatorial contest? Do you think Vance will run? I expect he could be elected if he would run.

Spruill's Regiment has a good Col at last, Col Williams. Is Cousin Gail Adj yet. I presume Col Williams kept him as I believe he is very popular in the Regiment. Give my love to Ma and the children.

TO CLARK FROM BENNETT BAKER **

Hamilton N.C. Feby 25th 1862

You requested me by dispatch to have all the public stores in my shop to be transported to Palmyra immediately. I suppose the bulk in weight will be including the Ammunition &c will be be-

* A Kinsman of Clark, from Halifax County, Captain of Company E, 37th North Carolina Regiment.

† Duncan K. McRae of Cumberland County.

‡ Charles E. Lightfoot of Virginia.

§ John O. Long of Randolph County.

|| Thomas S. Galloway of Rockingham County.

¶ Thomas D. Jones of Caldwell County.

** Assistant Quartermaster.

tween eight and ten thousand lbs. and it is impossible to get team and send it so I will wait until the steamer goes up the river unless I get further orders. I understand today that Leventhorpe's * Regiment has been ordered back to this place and will be here Thursday evening. The Martin Militia was disbanded today. If Leventhorpe's Regiment does not come the Bacon will be needed here, but I shall obey your order and send it by the 1st boat.

TO CLARK FROM O. C. PETWAY †

Kinston N.C.
May 18th 1862

. . . Walter I was very glad indeed that you did not get the Adjutancy of this Regiment At first—not that I disliked to be with you, but because Sinclair turned out to be exactly what we always thought him to be—a cowardly scoundrel and you would have had to bear a portion of the disgrace, which he brought upon the Regiment by his cowardly acts; but as it is you suffered no disgrace and your chances for the Adjutancy of the Regiment is far better than they ever was before, and in case it is tendered you you will be more pleasantly situated. Col Ransom has not as yet appointed his Adjutant and he is somewhat upon a quandary who to appoint and upon consultation with Major Jones ‡ & myself your claims was urged pretty forcibly by us. He Rewiring your Father together with glorious description and good recommendation we gave you is somewhat prepossessed in your favor. I intended writing to you once before upon the subject I feared that you might be disappointed consequently I did not do it but now as everything seems to be in your favor—though not yet appointed I have seen fit to inform you of it, and rest assured that if any influence that I can exert in your behalf will secure you the position you shall have it: though not yet appointed, I confidently believe you will be; but do not really expect it, until you get the appointment. Your friends will do all they can for you. . . .

[P.S.]

What I have written to you concerning the Adjutancy Keep it strictly to yourself

The Regiment is getting along better than it ever did before.

* Brigadier General Collett Leventhorpe.
† Oliver Cromwell Petway, Major of 22nd North Carolina Regiment.
‡ Major John G. Jones of Person County.

Everything goes as smooth and regular as clockwork; We have five Rifle Companies three Enfield & two Miss Rifle Companies. Write immediately.

DAVID CLARK TO GENERAL J. G. MARTIN *

Scotland Neck
3 June 1862

I have just returned from Plymouth. On the way down the proper officers were directed to have a force ready to blockade & prepare infantry defences on the Bank & on the Road up the River at the crossings of streams. From four miles above Plymouth down to the mouth of the River the Bank is in Washington County. My instructions were to defend the River. But the Militia of that County were not made subject to my orders. Nevertheless supposing this might be an oversight, I place Col W. Littlejohn † in command of that section with written instructions. On my return I find in your order of the 31st that the Militia of that county are still left out—Therefore in that matter I may have done wrong—

A line of Couriers have been established from Plymouth to this point, to be paid for work actually done & no Dispatch sent unless actualy necessary—If an open dispatch is sent each officer on the line is to read it & know what duty he has to execute. The Road from Plymouth up is about one mile to half a mile from the River banks. Therefore without guns to defend the crossing at the creeks any position on the Bank can be burned. by the enemy landing below. If Plymouth is taken there is only a direct march of thirty-five miles to the town of Washington with a few old ships guns. many of which we bought at Norfolk unless I think that a stout defence may be made & the enemy at least delay long enough for an army to be formed behind me & this by a small force defending the bridges—At least if Gen Huger ‡ will give me a part of old guns which he will admit are worthless any where else We are willing to make the effort, if the guns are taken there will be only so much old iron lost & worthless to the enemy—The River can be easily blockaded in a few hours in such a manner that any advance by boats will be delayed for weeks but I am satisfied that this is unnecessary at this Moment, for up to Friday

* James G. Martin of Pasquotank County, Adjutant General of North Carolina; commissioned Brigadier General, May 15, 1862.

† William H. Littlejohn of New Hanover County.

‡ Major General Benjamin Huger, commanding the Department of Norfolk.

Night no enemy had appeared at Roanoke Island. & that place is now in a much better state of defence than I supposed for. They will either repel the enemy or delay him long enough to enable me to make all the necessary preparations (if the guns can be had) Having made arrangements as to what is to be done & who are to do it. I leave tomorrow to see what can be done with Gen Huger as to guns & ammunition If I can get some old carronains & by any means scrape up two or three light field pieces shall the attempt to defend Plymouth be made? The location of the batteries will prevent the enemy shelling & they must fight (with Boats) at two hundred yards (below the town) & at fifty yds. any place above Jamesville in passing the battery—There is a strong determination to defend their homes but the people say that they have want [of] a leader who is determined to make an effort—I believe most of the work can be done without pay—There are some Union men but most are demoralized through fear because nothing has been done to defend them in case of a failure at the Island—My plan of defence for the Town would be a battery at Stewards farm—Sawyers Mags plantation on the River below & opposite the battery—the field pieces & Mounted shot gun towards the Sound. Shall I make the defence?

In a call for the Militia shall I order a portion of them to be Mounted this will be necessary?

On my return I found Capt Meade * of the engineers making a reconnaisance of the River under order from General Gatlin † He promised to leave for me a sketch of his views as to best points of defence &c Mr. Thomas James will see you in a day or two as to procure lead & caps for some of the Regiments. My own regiment have enough on hand

Do not believe every lie you may hear about the people down here—they are much more frightened at Raleigh than we are.

TO CLARK FROM J. A. C. BROWN

Head Quarters 22nd Regt. N.C.T.
June 14th 1862

If I have answered your last I have forgotten it and as I have an unoccupied moment this morning I will devote it to your benefit. Well we have been into a fight as you know ere this. It was fierce indeed where our Regt was. We charged a musket battery through

* R. Kidder Meade.

† Richard C. Gatlin of Lenoir County.

a swamp and a thick wood & undergrowth. We were ordered to halt within twenty paces of the *Abs* & lie down the balls came thick as hail. Our Regt. acted very coolly and displayed unusual courage. We were fired into in front & rear. . . . We were ordered to fall back—I saw no man run and came very near being captured myself—Col. Lightfoot & Lt. Col. Long fell into the hands of the enemy. Our Regt. lost 147 killed, wounded & missing. Our company lost 10 among them some of our best boys. Bishop.* Bibb Russell.† Ab. Wellborn ‡—I did not receive a mark nor did Capt. Gray. nor Lt. Col. Gray—We elected our field officers yesterday—W. H. Comer of Hampton's Legion is Col. R.H. Gray of Co. S. Lt. Col—C.C. Cole § of Co E. Maj—I of course am now Capt. of our company a place I have always abhorred. My health is again declining & I fear I shall have to abandon the army—I have nothing to write & will stop & I hope you will write very soon—Lt. Charles is Adjt. though sick at present & I am now acting—but will be relieved shortly. I don't know who will be the permanent one—

TO CLARK FROM J. H. AVENT

Camp Mangum
June 18th 1862

. . . I have often thought of you since your departure from Camp, and never learned until a short time since that you were so near me.

I have had a hard time since I saw you. We have had about 10000 troops all the time, until the past 2 weeks. We have now only 3 Regt's and I assure you there is quite a change in the appearance of the Camp. I wish you could have been here when the great body of Troops were here. I had no assistance or, as good as none. Gage was in the same fix. By perserverence, and a display of more patience than I thought I possessed, I got through to the satisfaction I believe of all who came under my charge. Hanks is here with us yet, and is doing well, only he seems smitten with a little blue eyed "lassie" in the neighborhood with whom he seems rather intimate and familiar for "short acquaintance" I dont know what he is up to, but he generally visits of a night. Capt Gage is getting on very well, and since the last rush of

* W. D. Bishop of Randolph County.
† Probably J. B. Russell of Montgomery County.
‡ Absalom Welborne.
§ Columbus C. Cole of Guilford County.

Troops to the Camp, he has[nt] had time to play any old tricks—such as stealing like an assassin in the "stilly night", and confining one to his couch with a rope—sewing up pants &c.

Dr Little * is at the genl Hospital in Raleigh—saw him last night—He was very well. Dr. Leach † has raised a Company and gone off in the 53rd Regt—the one to which Maj. Iredell ‡ is Major.

Dr Hines § is Capt of Co K 45th Regt.—Col Junius Daniel,‖ and the last time I heard from him he was at Garysburg. I suppose he is still there.

I do not know how long I will remain at this place but think I will be able to get off soon in a better position than I now occupy. . . .

TO CLARK FROM J. A. C. BROWN

Camp 22[d] N.C.T.
June 19th 1862

I have but a moment to acknowledge the receipt of yours of the 14th Inst- and reply. I was laboring under the impression I had written to you since the battle. I know I have often thought & intended writing. I have had so much to look after that I have not a minute of my own—Our field officers were not elected until the 13th Inst. We regret the loss of Col. Lightfoot he would have been reelected without opposition had he not been a prisoner. We wanted a man to take command at once—Our officers are as follows—Col. James Connor—Maj of Hampton's Legion—A perfect gentleman and has been in eight fights since the war began—Lt. Col. RS Gray of Co. L. C.C. Cole of Co. E. So I am in command of the company—The other officers are sick and I am acting adjutant—You see I have my hands full—No Adjt has been appointed as yet. Col. Gray wants you and I beg at him like a child to have you appointed—Maj Cole wants his brother—I know not who they will select though I think the Col. intends taking him from the Lieuts. of the Regt. Col. W.D. Pender of the 6th N.C. is our Brig Gen—Ours is a N.C. Brig. entire composed of the 16th 22[d] 34th & 38th Regts. The Gen in taking command said the impression had

* Dr. William Little of Wake County, commissioned Assistant Surgeon in the Medical Corps, May 23, 1861.

† John Leach of Johnston County, Captain of Company C, 53rd Regiment.

‡ James Johnston Iredell of Wake County, killed at Spottsylvania Court House.

§ James M. Hines of Pitt County.

‖ Junius Daniel of Halifax County, commissioned Colonel, June 3, 1861, and Brigadier General, September 2, 1862; killed at Spottsylvania Court House, May, 1864.

gone forth that the 22[d] was the best that N.C. had sent out. I must say it did it credit on the 31st May. No set of men could have acted more gallantly under the circumstances. To my own knowledge many did not act so well. Col Connor in taking command said we had now a reputation we might well be proud of. He was near us in the fight. Pres. Davis. Gens Johnson. Gen. Lee. & Smith were present when we started in the fight & Davis spoke very complimentary of those under his immediate view—We made a charge on a musket battery. had to charge through a Swamp & Thick wood & undergrowth—We were halted in twenty paces of the battery & order to lay down. how any escaped is a wonder to me—I expected much of our Regt but was more than surprised at their noble conduct & coolness.... We were called out this morning and ordered in our rifle pits—I ran a narrow risk by foolishly standing on the rank in front while the men were loading. A shell passed within two or three feet of me—& fell just in our rear—When we made the charge on the 31st I had my hat in one hand & pistol in the other & when we lay down I was in front of the Co. I soon changed to my proper place when they commenced firing in rear—

...I am not anxious to get into another battle but if I do I want to have a fair showing....

CLARK TO HIS MOTHER

Hillsborough, June 28th 1862

Your affectionate letter containing such painful tidings * reached me late last night. I can not tell you how distressed I was. I have lost one who was as dear to me as a Brother could be and none but you can imagine how much I feel his loss. I feel like I was alone in the wide wide world. Both of my brothers have gone home to Rest while I alone of the three are left in this world of sin and sorrow. They are now both in Heaven and I solemnly ask myself the question "Will I meet them there? Ah! 'tis a solemn thought! I would freely give all my chances for Honor, Wealth, Position in this world, all in short, that I could ever hope or expect to be in this world for the simple assurance that my sins were pardoned. Pray for me, my Mother. Your prayers do me more good than anything else. I feel at times like I knew you were praying for me. I rarely ever express my inner feelings but really

* This refers to the death of David Clark who was two years younger than his brother, Walter Clark.

for the last two years I have had no peace of mind. I have determined time and again to be a Christian but somehow or other I always procrastinated. I have tried even, shall I confess it, to persuade myself to be an Infidel, but there was something in that so repugnant so terrible that I shuddered at the idea. I am convinced that there is no peace except in Jesus and I would give anything, yes everything to be an humble follower of the Cross. Such have been my feelings now for a long time but I can no longer keep from you the story of my soul's wrestling and I must ask your prayers to aid me to overcome my natural pride and wickedness and to humble myself at the foot of the Cross. I am not humble enough. I am too selfish. I fear I have lived too much for myself. You do not know how much I am distressed and what adds poignancy to my grief is I fear that I have not always treated the dear departed one with the gentleness and kindness I ought. I did not expect to hear of his loss so soon but the ways of Providence are inscrutable and I hope all is for the best. Give my love to all, and particularly to Aunt Sue, she is so kind I know she must have been a comfort in time of need. I should like very much for her to write to me. If you and Pa are willing I should like to come home about the middle of July on a furlough of two or three weeks. My mind needs relaxation.

I should have liked to have been at home but as you say his decline was so sudden. Give my love to Uncle Colin and Aunt Eliza.

Write soon.

Excuse my not writing more in the present state of my feeling. Be sure and write often.

TO CLARK FROM THOS. W. RICHARDSON *

Drury's Bluff
July 29 1862

I received your letter this day, and as the importance of the matter demands an immediate answer I hasten to do so. Col Petway has fallen, Col Ransom being wounded in the arm and side was forced to be carried from the field, and then Petway of course took command, ordering a portion of the regiment to advance, and charging with the whole, for the left wing was not in line exactly, and that was the portion ordered to advance, he

* First Lieutenant, Company D, 35th North Carolina Regiment, native of Chatham County.

fell when leading the Regt to the Charge. His leg was shattered by a cannon ball, or shell, and amputated. He died about three or four hours after being wounded it was a terible blow to the regiment. Capt Lassiter * shared a like fate—He was shot while gallantly leading his company to the charge. We lost 18 killed and 91 wounded, about ten of whom have died. The whole regiment fought very bravely. I shall start for Raleigh tomorrow where it would afford me much pleasure to meet you Capt Petty † sends his respects. All your old friends are well and would like very much to see you in the regiment again. We want an Adjt at present—our adjt resigned

TO CLARK FROM HIS FATHER

Littleton—20 Aug 62

I have just Red a message from Col Ransom to the effect that he wished you to become Adjt of his Regiment. If you have not taken that post under Col Gray & wish to accept Col Ransoms offer you may do so. I shall leave the matter with you. As all the offers of post have been made to you without solicitation from any one but have been rejected by me on account of your youth—& as you are now sixteen I do not see what grace the opposition can be continued You are therefore at liberty to accept it or not. If you accept let me know what money you will need. You should accept or reject without delay.

State the facts to Major Gordon ‡ & he will doubtless advise you what is best to be done

RECOMMENDATION OF MAJOR WM. M. GORDON

Hillsborough, August 20, 1862

Wm. W. McK. Clarke, the bearer, has been connected with the Hillsboro' Mily. Academy as Cadet for about two years. During the last six months he has performed the duties of Adjt. of the Post to my entire satisfaction. I have always found him prompt, energetic, & skilful in the discharge of all his duties; his departure for the army has caused me sincere regret.

I cheerfully endorse him & commend him to the favor of Colonels of Regiments as an invaluable assistant.

* Hardy J. Lassiter of Chatham County, Captain of Company D.
† Robert E. Petty of Chatham County.
‡ Major William M. Gordon, Superintendent of Hillsboro Military Academy.

CLARK TO HIS FATHER

Hillsborough, August 22nd 1862

I received your letter of the 21th inst this morning and now hasten to reply that my answer may go off by the first mail. As you left the matter to my choice I have carefully considered it in all its bearings pro and con with a mind unbiased as far as it could be by my inclinations. I have accepted and you can so signify to Col Ransom. I have made my preparations for departure and only wait your reply to leave. I expect an offer from Col Gray is now on the way but I will be as well satisfied in the 35th as there have been so many changes in Gray's Regiment that most of the Company Officers are strangers to me and I would go at the appointment of the *Col* (though it is true not *against* the wish of the Regiment) whereas in Ransom's Regiment I do not look upon the offer as coming from *Col Ransom* so much as from the *Regiment*. It would have been against all feelings of delicacy and proper regard for others to have rejected this position after the continued and expressed wish of the Regiment that I should be their Adjutant, and after their continued refusal to have any other. I have been preparing for this and have got so far ahead in my studies that I am now about where the regular course would be next November and therefore in case the war should end with a little study I can enter the 2nd Class next year thereby not losing any time whatever in my education by joining the army. I did not understand from your letter whether you wished me to come home or not. I will not carry my trunk and I will of course send it home if I do not come myself. All the clothes I will carry are at home together with my knapsack; the only outer clothing I will carry will be my gray suit at home and I will have my uniform made after I join the Regiment. I do not wish to carry any white shirts; Ma can make me three or four calico shirts or I can buy them in Petersburg. My uniform would cost me $90 or $100 dollars but from enquiry while in Richmond I learned that I can get beautiful cloth at the Government Bureau and have my uniform made for $35 at the most and I can get me a sword of Foreign make for $20. I would have to present my Commission however to procure the above as they are imported by the Government for the Army. My horse I rode at home last Winter will serve very well, she is blind in one eye but is quite spirited. Write soon and let me know how these arrangements suit you. I should like to hear by Sunday's mail so as to leave Monday. I have already made my arrangements with Maj Gordon and elsewhere. I have written to an Officer of the 22nd Regiment with my regrets at not joining that Regiment. I only await your reply. Write me the tenor of Col Ransom's message so I may know what he wants me to do. Invoking God's blessing I have devoted my feeble energies to the defence of all that is near and dear and I go into the struggle for Independence willing, if necessary, to offer up my life, on the altar of my country. May God smile on my future path through the dangers that may arise is the sincere prayer of your affectionate son. . . .

[P.S.]

I suppose of course Ma is willing for me to join now. I will be in the same brigade with Uncle Ed & Cousin David. Love to all.
P.S. I doubt now if I will hear [from] Col Gray in some time as he has been in a fight lately and may have been wounded.

TO CLARK FROM HIS MOTHER

Aug 22nd, 1862

. . . I received your letter, written Saturday after I had finished, the first of this written on Monday—I am glad to see you are better pleased & getting on so well in your class, you ought never to trust yourself to go to recitation, until you have studied over your lesson Your Cousin Billy N.* staid with us last night he expects to visit New York in a week or so & spend some time, for improvement & to see something of the world, I suppose, says he does'nt like to stay at home doing nothing—Capt Ed likes Chapel Hill very much, but keeps rather shy of the Soph's—I suppose you have heard of their sending off, about sixty students from the Hill, something about teazing the Fresh I believe—I had a long letter from your Aunt Eliza the other day, she is travelling up in the northern part of this state, & seemed highly pleased with her trip thus far, she was then at Asheville, & had been on an excursion to the Black (or Mitchell) Mountain & said she had a small Balsam tree for me that came from its top, she expected to visit the Warm & the Virginia Springs & several other places & then visit Airlie in route for home— . . .

* William Norfleet.

TO DAVID CLARK FROM MAJOR GORDON

Hillsboro, N.C.
Aug 26/62

I am in receipt of your letter in which you request me to give your son an unlimited furlough to join the army—

I am very sorry he has taken the notion to leave the school; he was making good progress & I was greatly pleased with his conduct & bearing—I hope it will not be long before his return to his duties—

TO CLARK FROM L. R. TINDAL *

Friendship S.C. Aug 27th, 1862

... I too, dear friends (Clark & Hill), regret the necessity very much, of leaving *you* all and the Institution—for truly there are some members of the Corps whom I have formed very strong attachments for, and even if there were no other reasons—you see the separation from friends would be sufficient to add to the troubles, of an already saddened heart; but when I reflect and look around in this wide world—unconsciously the feeling of the great importance that an education is to me here on earth arises to my mind & hence is more perplexed and irritated to know at this all important period, (of my improvement)—my school days & advantages of acquiring knowledge, in the proper sense, is broken into—at least until this Devilish War closes—and O God! forbid that the time shall be long when the tidings of peace shall be proclaimed from bound to bound. Yet when I look around, and know the condition of my country and that I am subject to its call—willingly do I reconcile myself to almost any sacrifice to do that which I feel to be a stern send to duty. You know it has been considered a rare thing during a man's life for him to even chance to serve his country; then, I think, it is an opportunity that we should all prize.

I regret so much my not being able to go on forthwith to Richmond, but so long as there is no battle and not much prospect of one *soon,* I can, in a degree, remain satisfied—away from the monotony of Camp life. I have been assured the place of Drill-Master, if I would not conclude to cast my lot with my bretheren in Richmond, but as you are aware of the trying time a fellow would have on drilling Conscript—I am constrained to decline this and accept the humble position of private in an Artillery

* Clark's roommate at Hillsboro Military Academy.

Company made up of *all* gentlemen, I may say, literally speaking.

As you know in every company there are a few characters always that, are not of the most select, but this company is, as near perfect composition as one generally gets to be.

The Officers are all *high toned honorable men*—either graduates of the S.C—College—Furman University, or Citadel,—and about ½ of the privates are particular school friends of the officers and equally as well educated. So you can imagine that the demoralizing effects that Camp life has on a person will be somewhat counterbalanced by so many congenial spirits working together as a unit.

I was quite surprised to know that Guion had certainly left on being exchanged, though I expect it was very gratifying to him. I received a letter from him the other day written at Lincolnton N.C. I wrote to old "No. 7A" soon after I arrived at home, but neither you nor Guion mentions its reception, hence must consider it as being lost. I also wrote to friend Roulhac. Has he received a letter from me?

I know you two, dear old fellows, must feel lonely in Old '14' if you haven't any one yet to fill the vacancies. Tell Maj. Hill I often think of him & the pleasant time spent together when all were absent, but he & myself—please give him my double breasted love with a kiss if it is not too sweet/rough business for two boys. I am very glad to know you have such a full school & so good a corps You didn't mention who were the Cadet Officers now, permanently. I am very anxious to know—and how do they get along generally—particularly reporting, Does Maj Gordon find much fault?

I am glad dear C— to learn that the 'Limoleon Society' was so full & prosperous, but do sincerely hope that all party spirit, and selfish feeling, existing in a degree between the Societies may die away finally & everyone work together for good. I have been disgusted at such principles being cultivated by different men several times; but then I suppose we may not notice such—the originators being only the *scum* you may say— . . .

CLARK TO HIS MOTHER

Camp near Martinsburg Va
Sept 26th 1862

I take advantage of this opportunity to again drop you a few lines. I had quite a journey to overtake my Regiment; I passed thousands of soldiers on the road every day (stragglers) and they had eaten up every thing so I had to do as I could. I marched on foot carrying our baggage (for it was impossible to get a conveyance) to Culpeper C H, thence I went to Warrenton thence on the road to Leesburg until I found that all troops were ordered to Winchester, I got back on the Winchester road at Salem, thence I went to Paris at the foot of the Blue Ridge, thence to Milwood beyond the Blue Ridge and across the Shenandoah River and thence to Winchester. I passed through a beautiful country, as we approached the Blue Ridge the dim indistinct line extending as far on each hand as the eye could see and then as the outline became more distinct the sight became treated to every variety of hue color and shape. The view from the top of the Ridge was sublime. I could not enjoy the scenery much however as I had a good deal of baggage to carry and Neverson * had his saddle to carry so we did not feel much like indulging in the Poetic. I staid in Winchester two days waiting for the Yankees to run out of Martinsburg; in the mean time I bought me a horse. I left Winchester as soon as Martinsburg was open and went there and thence I went to Williamsport (almost) when I found out my Regiment was not there; I came back to Martinsburg. I went thence to Harper's Ferry (or nearly there for I stopped over night at a place about six miles from the Ferry). Next morning about sunrise I was about three miles from Harper's Ferry where the Shepardstown road branches. There I found that our Brigade had left about 12 o'clock overnight (the night of the day of the Capture). After a ride of about 8 miles I overtook our Regiment on the banks of the Potomac waiting to cross and listening with intense though silent eagerness to quick and rapid cannonading over on the Maryland shore. The air was full of smoke, wounded men were passing along and every report indicated that a heavy battle was impending. I immediately reported 'for duty' and took my place at the head of my Regiment. I saw Uncle Ed who seemed really glad to see me and put Neverson under his charge with the wagons where he would be in no danger; I didnt see Neverson again until four days after the fight (the wagons being in a safe place of course).

I joined the Regiment about 12 o'clock M, we camped two miles over in Maryland that night about dusk and at midnight we marched out to the battle field. We took up our position on the extreme right but though the cannonading continued nearly

* Clark's Negro bodyguard.

all night no enemy appeared before us, at length however about 7 o'clock news came that the enemy was massing his troops against our left and we ordered there (four miles off) to be placed under Jackson under whom we fought all day. We made the best time we could and when we got in about two miles of our position (now the extreme *left*) the shells commenced dropping over our way. Our men were ordered to throw off their knapsacks and we pushed forward. Then commenced the long string of wounded coming from the Battle field, some carried on stretchers, some hobbling on with wounds in their legs arms feet head and of every imaginable shape. I can't describe a battle to you, no one can imagine anything like it unless he has been in one. We soon came near where we were ordered to take our place in line of battle. The Rattle of Musketry for the first time broke upon my ear. It is an indiscribable sound, it somewhat resembles dropping a hundred thousand leaden bullets on a loose tin roof. When we came in sight of the Field our troops were running out of the woods and forming every hundred yards and then breaking under the tremendous musketry and shelling the yankees poured in upon them. Our Brigade marched in between the two lines and relieved our broken and disheartened troops. We marched thus with our right flank exposed to the Yankees who attempted to take advantage of it. They got over the fence they were lying behind and started forward, immediately our brigade wheeled to the right thus placing the opposing lines about 80 y'ds apart and we gave the first fire. However in wheeling to the right we came through the woods and tho I was busy shouting and repeating commands and cheering the men up and though the shots were falling like hail I could not help occasionally noticing the poor Yankee wretches who were lying about in heaps with arms legs hands ears toes shot off mutilated in every form, for in the early part of the fight they held this identical piece of woods and after tremendous loss they had been driven from this woods which they had in turn driven our men from when our Brigade came up and took it. The execution was dreadful, files of Yankees dressed out in all their finery with occasionally a southern form in his ragged garments lying among them. Pistols, swords, etc. were scattered in confusion but there was no time to pause for one minute's loss would be our ruin and on us at that juncture rested the fate of the army north of the Potomac. I had to jump my horse over piles of the slain. The moment the first volley was fired by our men the entire Yankee line fell. Our men were then ordered to lie down. Col Ransom myself & the Lt Col of our Regiment had come into action on horseback though all the other Officers in the Brigade had left their horses in pursuance to orders. The Lt-Col, the enemy firing upon us, turned loose his horse and lost him for the firing made the horses unmanagable; I dismounted and squatted down at the foot of the rear rank men and held my horse and Col Ransom came up to me and asked me to hold his, so during the entire musketry Col Ransom and myself were the only two men not lying down in the Brigade. He being in command of the Brigade moved about a good deal of course and as I was determined not to let my horses go, I was up all time. I expected every moment to be hit or to see one of my horses fall over; they were rearing and necessarily attracting notice from the enemy. As I dismounted from my horse my hand was slightly grazed by a bullet which was no doubt aimed at me while on horse back. In about fifteen minutes however it slackened a little so I called a Drummer who took our horses and carried them to the wagons and we did not see them again in three days. It is useless to write more about the battle for I am tired as I have only given you the first 15 minutes of it and I am tired writing. I will write more soon so good bye....

TO CLARK FROM HIS MOTHER

October 1862

...I was sorry to hear of your suffering, hope it may prove, all for the best & I believe it will, if you will take it rightly & come home—If you cannot stand the climate, I would not risk it until too late in the season, for you might destroy your health & not be able to render any effectual service to your country at present or in future—Lay it all before the Good Being my dear child & ask his guidance & he will be sure to direct you aright—As for my part, when you left me to join the Army I gave you up into his hands entirely & scarcely felt as if you belonged to me at all (not that I am weaned from or love you less, for you are doubly dear to me since you embraced the cause of Christ)—I have given you to the Lord for his service & pray that you may live for his glory—He doeth all things well I believe that all things work together for good to those who love & trust him & that is what I endeavour to do—Study the scriptures I pray often—... You have great cause my child to thank the Good Being for kind preservation of you, amidst all the dangers through which you have just passed in your journey in the battle & then in sickness—I feel as if I could never praise & thank him enough—My heart swells with gratitude whenever I think of it—Oh who wouldn't love the Great & Good God. His infinite nearness & kindness to us, we cannot too highly appreciate—Many thanks to your Uncle Ed for his kindness—He is a great *personage* in my age & holds a deep place in my heart—I am glad that you can have his society—You must take care of your health & come home as soon as you can—I will send you a little blackberry wine (I hope you will not take anything stronger) & some rhubarb syrup by Mr. Pearson if he can take it—Wish so much that we could send your Uncle Ed & you a box—Your Pa leaves it to your Judgment about coming home, he has great confidence in you & thinks you will act right—He is not able to go for you, having been sick ever since he reached home & for several days was very sick. . . . Your Pa found Mr Moore busy making molasses (at the plantation) & expects to make some sugar. He had mended the mill & crushed a good deal of the cane, thinks he will make several barrels of molasses & two or three of sugar—We have not as yet made any preparation for moving on the river, but your Pa says if Gov Vance blocks or defends the river, as rumor says he intends doing, we will go down before long—He seems so anxious to go down Gov Vance (I heard) says the Yankees have got to leave the Eastern part of this State, if he has to lead our troops himself—I regretted so much to hear of Col Tew's death— . . .

[P.S.]

I have just written both you & your Uncle Ed (several days ago) a long letter, so it is useless for me to write more now. Hope you received the letters I suppose you do not need any clothes or you would have mentioned it—I would try & send you some but expect you home soon, so it would be useless do not put off coming until it gets so cold for you might have an attack of rheumatism How does Neverson like the service not so funny as he expected I presume

Miss Sallie & the children send much love—The servants make many enquiries after you & seem to look anxiously for a letter from Mass Walter Cook says Mass Walter promised to write often seemed to think you had not complied with it—

TO CLARK FROM HIS MOTHER

October 1862

. . . I do hope you will come home if not well, you had better come & stay awhile & recruit your health a little, even if you return afterwards—I had a letter from your Aunt Martha yesterday, saying when she last heard from your Cousin Will he was in Winchester (& that was two or three weeks ago) why is it? your Uncle Ed and you havent seen him?—Gil & Ed were at Culpepper C.H. both well, but said starvation stared them in the face—I sent you a small bottle of blackberry wine & some rhubarb syrup by Mr Pearson, wish I could have sent a large bottle of the wine to your Uncle Ed— . . .

CLARK TO HIS MOTHER

Camp near Winchester Va
Oct 13th 1862

I am now quite well. Uncle Ed * took me in his own tent and it is due to his care that I am now well; you really ought to write to him.

Uncle Ed very coolly informed me this morning that he had written to Pa to come on for me as I was unable to stand this climate. Of course Pa will have no idea of coming as I am accustomed to take care of myself and ought—certain—be able to do so under all circumstances but I write to prevent all uneasiness on your part. I am now well and Providence permitting I intend to stay with the army until I can tell whether there is any probability of our Brigade going farther south. If however the chances are that we will remain up in this country I expect to resign by the 1st of December as I do not think my health would permit of my staying in this country later than that. So give yourself no uneasiness, I will come soon enough but not before the 1st Dec in all probability. I am sorry Uncle Ed wrote anything about it though doubtless he intended it for my good (as he thought). I shall try to take care of myself *and if gets too cold I shall certainly come home* depend upon it. . . .

If you should wish you can telegraph to me at any time provided there was nothing contraband in your message.

I regretted very much to hear of Col Tew's death; The acceptance of his resignation in order to take charge of the Hillsboro

*Captain Ed Thorne, Walter Clark's uncle.

School with a high testimonial from the Secry'r of War was received only a few *hours* after his death. An old schoolmate of mine at Hillsboro and a Captain in a Regiment near us in the fight was killed. I hope to hear from you soon—

CLARK TO HIS FATHER

Camp near Winchester Va.
Oct 19th 1862

I write to advise you to have the children and all the negroes vaccinated. The "small pox" has made its appearance all over the army and the country generally and it is spreading (tho' somewhat slowly). We have two cases in this Brigade (in 24th Reg't) which was introduced by a man who left Petersburg three weeks ago. The Small pox is in nearly every Brigade (one or two cases only) in the Army and what is more it is in the Hospitals at Winchester and Staunton thro' which my letters pass and *by accident* (tho' not at all probable) a letter of mine might carry it home. The notice of this disease (*very properly*) is carefully suppressed but you know a person can catch the Small pox by the slightest contact and a great many of these sick soldiers on the cars have been hurried out of the very Hospitals in which these cases of small pox have appeared. There are only very few cases in the army and these with their mess mates are immediately quarantined so I hope there is no danger of its spreading. Most of the soldiers in the army are vaccinated and those who have not been are being vaccinated. Say *nothing of this* as it might prevent men at home from joining their Regiments where they are much needed or produce a panic in some way or other *but* as there are thousands of ways in which it can be taken without a person's dreaming of danger it would be best for you to go quietly to work and have the *children and negroes vaccinated* for if I judge not amiss it will *soon* appear among the people at home being carried by soldiers or in letters or by merely shaking hands with some one who has been in a half a mile of a Hospital. "An ounce of prevention is worth a pound of cure". I was today *vaccinated* and Uncle Ed was re-vaccinated in two different ways to make assurance doubly sure! You had better commence at once as Virus will be scarce and if Small pox gets hold in a country you know what a panic it produces. I do not wish to exaggerate the danger but I merely wish for you to know the danger. I was vaccinated with a good scab only four months old and by our Surgeon (who is actually the best doctor I ever saw—however it does not take a good doctor to vaccinate a person). I intend to have Neverson vaccinated as soon as possible. Be particular to say nothing of the above as it might produce a causeless and useless uneasiness in Ma, and Aunt Alice. I wrote to you yesterday. What have you done about my horse? if he has not started by the time this reaches you it will be best not to send him. Great love to all. Goodbye....

[P.S.]
All quiet along the lines to-day tho' there is not telling how long we will remain in status quo. It would be best to be somewhat particular about sending to Littleton just now.

CLARK TO HIS MOTHER

Camp near Upperville Va
Oct 28th 1862

...I have been sick a good deal and I have always had my hands full of business but altho' I received no letters from home whenever the time came for me to write home if I was able to sit up and write, no matter what I was doing I always made time to write *home*. My first letter to you after the Battle of Sharpsburg was written at 11 or 12 o'clock at night after a most fatiguing day's work. You do me a great injustice to think that I have one-tenth even of the time or opportunity to write that Uncle Ed has. Uncle Ed always has an opportunity to send off his letters being at Hd Qrs. he has scarcely anything to do and what little there is he has a clerk to perform it. he is with Gen'l Ransom's wagons which always go along and of course he always has his desk ink writing paper and tent whereas our wagons are very often separated from us three, four, five days or more at a time and I have nothing except what I have on my back or in my pocket. (Uncle Ed's wagons carry ammunition and of course must go wherever the regiment goes whereas it is often safest to leave our wagon train behind). Uncle Ed unless he has a mind to has not a bit more to do than at home I will now tell you a *little* of what I have to do and see if you do not think I would be excusable for not writing at all *especially* when I received no *answers* whatever, In the first place I rise before day to receive the reports of absentees at Reveille, by the time all the reports are received it is generally sunrise. I then issue the special orders of the day and as soon as the commander of the Regiment is up I have the numerous absentees from Reveille brought for punishment, by that time breakfast is ready and we sit down to a little raw bread and tough beef; Breakfast over I receive the Surgeon's Report of sick in the Regiment and order the Sergeants Call beaten and then up come the Sergeants with their Morning Reports half of which of course I have to rectify as it would be out of the order of things for them all to be right. Then I spend the next hour or more in consolidating the Sergeants Reports into a Voluminous Morning Report showing everything concerning the state of the Regiment in every particular. This Report is then sent to Commanding Officer of Regiment and then to Asst Adjt Gen'l of Brigade. Of course I have been interrupted in the mean time by five or six orders from Brigade Hdqrs and to issue as many to the Regiment. Then Guard Mounting. Then hurriedly write out orders to be published on Dress Parade and (at ten o'clock) have to hurriedly throw my sash around me and buckle my sword on to be in time to form my Regiment on the Parade Ground. Then comes all the tedious formality of Dress Parade. After Dress Parade, Drill or Inspection for hour or two and then a dinner of beef and bread. Before I have finished my dinner here comes an order for Brigade Drill or Review perhaps. Division Review (when we have to march four miles to the field and back again) by the time the Regiment is notified it is time to march out when I again have to put on sword and sash and form my Regiment. After two three hours or even more we return to camp thoroughly fatigued when here comes an order to send in immediately to Brigade Hd Q'rs a list of negroes in the Reg't. or an estimate of the number of guns wanted in the Reg't or any little frivolous order which has already been attended to three or four times but as there is generally a change of a gun or so or few rounds of cartridges in every two or three days I have to go to the trouble of seeing all the blockhead Orderly Sergeants in the Reg't and making out a new Report of the exact number of cartridges, bayonets, guns &c in the Regiment &c, then orders for Dress Parade; then Dress Parade, then a little supper then another list or Report to make out; Then receive Reports of absentees at Tattoo, then order culprits up for punishment and then—go to bed. Besides the above there are thousands of little things that can not be enumerated. I have to find time to wash my face &c, to read my bible, to clean my teeth twice a day, to send off to buy provisions, to have my clothes washed, then a dozen Officers will be up to see me on some special business &c &c &c &c—This is a day in camp not taking into account that perhaps it is raining, that the night before I slept out under a tree without covering, that I am bothered half to death with Quarter Master about forage for my horse, that I have to borrow pen ink & paper to make out orders &c. On a march it would fail me to tell *half* of what I have to do, galloping here and galloping there, arresting this man for going into an orchard another for something else, to put the Regiment in motion and halt it (about 10 or 12 times every hour) to see that rations are cooked that plenty of ammunition is in the cartridge boxes &c. I do not write to complain but merely to give you a *glimpse* of what I have to do if I do my duty (which I certainly try to do). If an Adjutant does his duty he has ten times as much to do as any other Officer in the Reg't (The Qr Master has as much but he has so many Assistants). I guess you are tired of this so I will take some other topic. Camp near Paris Va Oct 30th. I was interrupted just here by an order to report the number, names, health, company &c of the Shoemakers in the Reg't and just as I was half through an order came for Inspection and just as the Inspection was about half through an order came to march and pack up as we were to leave in five minutes (the Yankees having advanced) so we marched back, put the cooking utensils in the wagons and expected to leave right off. Well! we waited there until dark expecting a courier with orders every minute. At dark orders came to re-encamp (no attack being expected). We re-encamped and at ten o'clock quite tired I lay down to sleep expecting a good night's rest when at 12 what should come but orders to be ready to march *immediately,* the wagons were packed and started right off to start back to Paris as we were to follow in order to better protect the "Gap" (our object in coming down here). We waited and waited again until 12 o'clock (without supper or breakfast, as the cooking utensils were packed in the wagons) when all of a sudden we marched off and fell back to here (four miles and within a half a mile of the Gap). I had just got here and caused the Regt to stack arms when (an hour by sundown) an order came for the 35th to proceed . . . back to Upperville whence we had just come. When we got within two miles of Upperville Gen'l Ransom galloped up to superintend our movements and brought with him a Section of our Artillery as he had ascertained that the Yankee Cavalry had entered the town soon after we had left it. We advanced cautiously a half a mile farther, halted, posted our men behind a stone fence on both sides of the road, sent out advanced scouts and placed the Artillery so as to come quickly into Battery if necessary. Not one in twenty of our men have blankets and there we were ordered to lie on our arms in the cold without fires and without supper (having already gone without supper & breakfast—and with very little dinner). As soon however as the Reg'ts in camp had got their supper the 24th and a Reg't from Walker's Brigade came to relieve us and about midnight we got back and laying down by a fire I slept quite soundly until morning. Today I can't tell what I have been doing hardly; ever since Sunrise altho' the Reg't was under orders to march at a moment's notice I have been busy writing orders, giving & receiving orders, receiving Reports sending in Reports &c with barely time to eat dinner. About 20 minutes ago having a little leisure I started to finish this letter but have already been interrupted to write four orders. A movement of some kind is to take place tomorrow. Possibly a fight is on hand as Burnside is said to be 14 miles from here and our Brigade would like to meet him in pay for New Bern.

CLARK TO HIS MOTHER

Nov 3rd. 1862
Camp near Culpeper Court House

It seems I am doomed to write you a Diary of my proceedings. I last stopped writing near Paris Va., at the foot of the Blue Ridge & on the eastern side close to Ashby's Gap. Next morning we were awakened at 4 o'clock and went out on the Bi-Monthly Muster & Inspection and after that was over we started out on a march. After three days of *rough* marching last night found us here. I think we are on our way to Suffolk. The Army of No Va has been divided. The left wing under Jackson is left in the Valley while the right wing under Longstreet is either concentrated around here or is on the way here. Some of the Troops have already left on the train southward and we hope to go soon. You ought to have heard the cheering when the troops heard the whistle of the engine. They are in fine spirits at the idea of going nearer home. I neglected to state in the beginning of this letter where I was and how I got there. We left our Camp near Winchester on the 23rd of Oct and encamped the first night at Milwood, the next day we forded the Shenandoah, crossed the Blue Ridge at Ashby's Gap and encamped near Upperville where the first part of this letter was written. The Valley of Virginia in peace times is I presume the best country (agriculturally) in North America but now it is quite bare. Two Counties having in progress of this War supported two immense Yankee and the same number of Confederate armies. I will merely state that butter is $1 and 1.25 cts per pound. Common Apples 50 cts apiece. Honey $1.50 per pound. Chinese sugar cane molasses 4, 5, 8 & 10 dollars per gallon &c. Sugar & coffee is not be procured. We use wheat coffee and honey. Down here if anything is worse than the Valley. At Upperville everything was quite plentiful. I never saw such fine honey in my life. It has scarcely any comb and is raised in Patent beegums (invented by a resident of Upperville). They raise I think yearly 430 lbs of honey from one swarm. Just think of it! . . . I am in high glee at the prospect of coming 'down South' but I am afraid that we may be deceived about it yet. Write soon and often to me. Ransom's Brigade. Walker's Division.

CLARK TO HIS FATHER

Hd Q'rs 35th Regt N.C. Troops
near Madison CH. Va. Nov 9th/62

You will see from the heading of this that the cry of Ransom's 'foot cavalry' is on! still on! We had marched and countermarched until I thought, wearied of these muddy roads, we were about to 'change our base' and commence operations in the neighborhood of Suffolk and Blackwater but the Fortune of War has ordered otherwise. When we marched from Culpeper due South on the Rapidan road we were all certain that *our* General at least had adopted the "On to Richmond" policy and that after wading these mountain streams we would take a little trip 'down South' to dry off, but alas! for visions of sunshine and North Carolina yams, these roads have as many branches as the Roanoke has bends and just as we thought to catch sight of the Rapidan * a sudden turn took us across a stream cold as ice and set our faces in this direction i.e. on a countermarch towards Winchester, Upperville or some such place. Where your answer will reach me I know not but I do know that all a man can do in these roads is to follow his nose for his file leader will be *mighty* apt to carry him back to where he started from.

We left Upperville and Paris neighborhood on 31st Oct and reached Culpeper C H after a hard march on 2nd Nov . . . and on 4th we moved our camp down on Culpeper & Rapidan road, 6 miles from Culpeper, the same distance from Rapidan and within half a mile of the Battle field of Cedar Mountain (or Slaughter's

* River in eastern Virginia.

Mountain as the Yankees call it).* I walked over the Battle field and saw the Yankee graves in abundance, saw the woods cut up by the shells &c and all the sights which pertain to a hard fought field. It is evident that a good deal of the fighting took place in the open field. Jackson's right rested on Cedar Mountain (an excellent flank).

We left our camp yesterday at 3 o'clock and after fording a good many streams (as cold as ice) we arrived here to-day. The only forces in this immediate neighborhood is the 1st N.C. Cavalry; the rest of Longstreets Corps is at Culpeper C.H. I *think* that our Retreat here is for the purpose of letting Jackson get in their rear. Take a good map and you can see what I mean. We left Winchester 23rd of October and went down and protected Ashby's Gap (near Paris), in the mean time the rest of the 'Right wing' of the 'Army of No Va' took the lower route by the Front Royal Gap and when we reached Culpeper C H we found the whole of the Right wing there. Since we left Upperville & Paris our Cavalry advance guards have rapidly fallen back and the enemy have eagerly pursued and now our line may be seen stretching a line on the map from Madison C H to Culpeper C H while the 'left wing' under Jackson on the other side of the Mountain is as high up as White Post and Winchester. Does it not then seem that we have beguiled the enemy down here so that Jackson may cross over the Mountain and completely cut him off? Jackson can cross the Mountain at any of the Gaps between here and the Potomac. The 1st Cavalry have been in the fight nearly every day for the last week, yesterday they lost thirty or forty men (among them Capt. Houston).† I have heard Artillery every day for the past week and where there is so much skirmishing there is apt to be a fight soon. In Napoleon's language at Marengo 'We have retreated far enough today'. I think before the week is past that something 'decided' must take place. They say Burnside's is one of the foremost Corps, wouldn't this Brigade do their *best* to trap him? Tell Ma I shall do my best for Burnside ‡ as I know how she hates him.

Brig Gen'l Walker § (of Missouri) who has been commanding these two Brigades as Senior Brigadier set out yesterday for Richmond, having been made a Maj Gen'l and ordered to report to

* This battle, August 9, 1862, was the first encounter in the Second Bull Run Campaign and was a Confederate victory.

† William J. Houston of Duplin County, Captain of Company I, 9th Regiment Cavalry 1st.

‡ Federal General A. E. Burnside.

§ John G. Walker.

Gen'l Holmes * (in Arkansas). Col. Cooke † of the 27th N C has been made a Brigadier in Walker's place and Gen'l Ransom now of course commands these two Brigades as Senior Brigadier. Direct my letters hereafter to Ransom's Brigade, Ransom's Division, Longstreet's Corps. I am in Ransom's Regiment, Ransom's Brigade, Ransom's Division.

The principal object of my writing tonight is to ask what you wish me to do (or if you do not care) what you think best about me remaining in the army this Winter. When I entered the Army it was my expectation, nay, almost determination, to see the end of this struggle for Independence but I now fear that I shall be compelled to take an intermission as I am told that my constitution is totally unable to stand the rigors of this climate. It is now as cold here almost or fully as January, added to that our continued exposures, irregularity of life, half cooked fare, sometimes 20 hours without eating and then laying out with our only covering the canopy of heaven and our Reveille the distant booming of cannon announcing the fact that to night marches there is no end, may give you an idea of what a Soldier's life. (Yet after all I like the life and as long as the enemy treads our soil, if I am able I expect to be a 'soldier'). I ask you to say if you think I can stand it without serious injury; the Doctors say that I will have Pneumonia *certainly* but I feel no sickness and I am as hearty and as well as if I was at home and I am inclined to pay little attention to anybody's prediction about future illness for all *they* can do is like myself to *guess.* If I do not resign by 1st Dec I might as well make arrangements to stay on this Winter. If I resign I *expect* to go in again next Spring if nothing happens. The reason I write about resigning is because I know Ma is anxious for me to and if I do not, you know, and I were to be seriously sick—Do not ask Ma about this, for altho' she would advise as she thought best, yet I know her wishes *might* warp her judgment. Let me know *at once* if you will need me at home this Winter and if not if you think I would be doing my *country* justice to leave the army. In other words I want to know what is *right* and *best* for me to do taking into consideration *My duty to my country,* my respect for Ma's known wishes and my duty to myself as one who like others (if God permits) has a future to work out. Whatever you judge of the matter I will adhere to for I know you can instantly perceive and appreciate my dilemma. However I intend to remain with

* Theophilus H. Holmes of North Carolina.

† John R. Cooke, commissioned Brigadier General, November 1, 1862.

the Army until I am quite satisfied that the Campaign is substantially over (as far as fighting is concerned). I do not think Neverson can stand this climate as he has for some time back had a wretched cough which is not at all improved by wading these cold mountain streams, I am afraid it might settle on his lungs; he is and has been well ever since he left home (with a slight exception). . . .Neverson sends many howdys to Ed and all the servants; he waits on me *first rate,* he was a little green at first about camp &c but now I couldn't have a better (or honester) boy to wait on me. I (and I doubt not Uncle Ed) miss the warm fires at home I can assure you. . . .

[P.S.]

All I fear is that being sick this Winter might prevent my entering the army next Spring. It snowed all day last Friday (7th).

Before this reaches you the last Battle of the Campaign will (I hope) have been fought. I do not know whether we will have a chance or not.

Cousin David is well and *lively.* We started a gang of wild turkeys the other day at camp and Ransom's 'foot cavalry' caught *three directly.* Do you think the Yankees can get away from *us?* They will catch anything that starts from Yankees to squirrels & rabbits. . . .

It is useless for anyone to think of getting a furlough this Winter, for tho' I have not wanted or tried for one yet I have seen *hundreds* who have tried and failed.

I have been writing by firelight that you may get this as soon as possible. I hope you have made a good lot of sugar and molasses.

Whether I come home or not, I will need an overcoat if you can get one, for one cannot be procured up here.

CLARK TO HIS MOTHER

Camp near Madison CH. Va
Nov 11th 1862

. . . We moved our camp yesterday from two miles North of Town to this place, one mile 'South' on the Gordonsville Road. We now have a beautiful camp and the scenery here is unsurpassed, especially the appearance of the Mountains as the Sun first gilds them, some glittering in the early sunlight while the sides and hollows perfectly shaded afford a picturesque contrast while on the tops is seen the crusted snow (not yet melted) like crystal.

It is beautiful scenery wherever you go in this country and the deeds of man, evident in the desolation of farms, the torn fences, mined and deserted houses and the blackened & charred hearth-stones around which Peace and Plenty were wont to smile appear in awful colors to the beauty of Nature as beautiful now as before the Vandal hordes had entered this highly favored region and "Final Ruin fiercely drove his ploughshare oer Creation". It would make your heart sick to see the Desolation and Destruction in this which was once one of the finest countries the Sun e'er shone on. Literally 'facinnt desolationern et pacem vocant' They make a wilderness and call it Peace. I pray the Good Lord that they may never obtain a foot-hold in North Carolina and if the people of N Ca knew their habits upon obtaining possession of a country they would die to a man before their feet should pollute her fair name and 'sacred soil'. We are now encamped 18 (eighteen) miles from Gordonsville on Gordonsville & Madison CH road. I hear that Gov Vance has called out all the Militia between 35 & 50, I think Vance had better let the Militia stay home with their families and send for Ransom's Brigade and I will guarantee that we will drive every Yankee from the good old North State, A Brigade after having been up here is worth ten Brigades which have not left the State; you see they become emphatically 'soldiers' and learn to forget the way to dodge 'lamp posts'. The way we march if we were in Weldon—tonight—tomorrow would very quietly see us in Hamilton or beyond (and what is more not a man out of ranks) and next day would see us in Plymouth if every inch of ground had to be contested. It dont take us long to march any where's even if the roads are the worse in the world. I wish they would send us to Plymouth and Washington for about a fort-night. Our men have not had a tent since we left Richmond in August and as they lost most of their blankets at Sharpsburg they lay out at night by the fire and most of them in ragged clothes and without covering and strange to say there is barely *any* sickness whereas at Raleigh where they had good houses and at Newbern where they had tents with plank floors more than half were always sick! I have almost forgotten how coffee tastes, we have to use flour coffee that is just parch flour and make *coffee* of it—... Neverson would like to come home but don't want to leave me, he sends many howdys to Ed. I did not receive the Blackberry wine, what a pity! after you had been so kind as to think of it and send it. I am hearty but am anxious to see you all (as usual). Col Ransom has not yet returned but we are expecting him daily. I have no idea *where* we will be by the time you write again as we *keep moving*. . . .

[P.S.]
Tell all the servants howdy. Tell Frank if he had come with me he would have seen 'hard times' himself
I was in *strong* hopes that you could move down on the River this winter. If you were there I believe I should come home *at once.*

TO CLARK FROM HIS MOTHER

Airlie Nov 15th 1862

Your Pa returned from down the country last Tuesday, was down there in the stampede from the Yankees nearly all the families left Scotland Neck & your Pa took Mr. Pittman in the buggy with him & kept on to Martin (to Mr Tom Jone's) & came very near being cut off & taken prisoner. Your Uncle John & Aunt Eliza had just reached home Saturday, (to take up Winter quarters) & left Wednesday bag & baggage. Your Pa did not move any thing but some meat & molasses, his negroes he said might take the chances, except five (John Madison, William, Bryant, Donas & Ivan) whom he knew could'nt be trusted & he thought they corrupted the others, so had them taken & put in jail, with the intention of selling them—Mr. Dick Smith attempted to move his & 75 of them ran away, but have since returned, they did'nt want to move—Your Pa's ran away in the same way, but none returned only hid about under the houses & so on Report says 25 of Cousin Gavin's * have gone to the Yankees, & 8 of Ed Hall's & Jeremy Anthony's & Mr Urqhart's Just made a business of it, took wagons, carts, & whatever they wished & went in a body, the whole of them I understand except a few old ones they were more than a day crossing the river, & no one I suppose pretended to stop them I hav'nt heard that any of Cousin David's went off—Young Burgywn behaved very gallantly, it is said he saved the 17 Regt! they were down below Williamston when the Yankees attacked them with four times their number & Burgywn (who was Lieut Col of the Regt) repulsed & fought them five hours, holding them in check until he could be reinforced & says he could have whipped them (& I think he could judging from the way they acted at Hamilton, took fright & ran when no one was pursuing,

* Gavin Clark, first cousin of Daniel Clark and owner of a large plantation in Bertie County.

leaving wagons &c behind & their men straggling all through the woods, one Officer was picked up in the corner of the fence drunk & carried to Tarboro, we laugh & tell your Pa perhaps they heard Gen *Clark* was near & not knowing but he was some great Gen, with quite a force, may have caused the panic for our Army was retreating one way & they running the other, notwithstanding their Gen (Foster) told a lady, at whose house he staid all night that he had 12,000 men with him) if Radcliffe,* the Col whom it is said was drunk) had'nt have ordered a retreat—It seems we have the luck of drunken Officers in this State—Gen Martin had a sufficient force it is said & men who were anxious to fight but from some cause or other, he would'nt advance to tell the truth I guess he is timid—We had troops at Tarboro also (to stop their movement in that direction) & Vance was there (had gone down for the purpose of having the place put in a state of defence) your Pa thinks that we had about 6,000 troops & could have whipped the Yankees easily (for he does'nt think they had more than 4,000 the outside) if Martin had have let them fight, pretended he did'nt know where the Yanks were, to attack them & your Pa says he sent him word by Capt Thigpen (Capt of Artillery in the "Confederate Militia") who knew the country well & insisted on his moving up, & then he would'nt attack them—I suppose you think Ransom's brigade would beat this—We entrapped about 150 of Yankee cavalry, it seems we had a number of picked men in ambush, & Tucker's cavalry pretended to be retreating & thus drew the enemy on, to within range of our guns, when we fired & ruptured every saddle—I don't know that this is exactly correct, it may be a little exaggerated I guess you are glad that I did'nt move down, as I would have had to transfer back so soon—They are now fortifying the river below Hamilton, so perhaps I may be able to go down, before the Winter is over—Gov Vance has ordered out one fifth of the hands, in five counties to work on the fortifications, so I am in hopes they will have them complete—Half of Hamilton was destroyed by the enemy—Your Aunt Martha Clark has moved a good many of her things to Prospect Hill— . . . I am glad the Army is moving South, hope this letter will find you in Richmond & I would'nt care if you were still nearer home—Tell Neverson we can do very well without him at home, so hold on where he is & wait on you well & he will meet with a more welcome reception at home when he does come— . . .

* James D. Radcliffe of New Hanover County, Colonel in the 18th North Carolina Regiment.

TO CLARK FROM HIS MOTHER

Nov 20th 1862

. . . I am glad to see that you have some idea of coming home I can very well answer for your Pa, under the *circumstances,* I know he would advise you to *come home,* for he has been uneasy about you since the cold weather set in, in fact he tells me that he left it discretionary with you in the first instance, still he advised you not to go, he has no idea of bearing any of the blame, if any thing should happen to you—My advice is (and I dont think you have ever suffered from taking my advice) to come home *immediately,* without delay, & leave *old Burnside* to other Captors, & if you wish so much to assist in defending your country (a spirit I admire) to come to your own State—Gen Pettigrew now has command of the forces about Tarboro & perhaps you can get some position in his Army—At any rate I think there is a plenty for you to do nearer home—I must confess that I have felt less anxious about you, than I ever expected I could, but (as I wrote you before) when you left to join the Army, I gave you up into the hands of the Great & Good Being, & believed he would order all things right, if we would act our part right & I feel it to be one of my most pressing duties to advise you, according to the best dictates of my judgment, & pray that he may guide you to receiving it—I believe it is the Lord has led you to ask your Pa's advice relative to coming home—I dont think that either you or Neverson can stand that climate for it must be a great deal colder than this, as I now have some beautiful roses in bloom, gathered one of the prettiest "bouquets" I have seen in a long time, yesterday morning & sent it to Nina Harris—The weather today is comfortable without a fire, tho we had quite some cold weather about the time of the snow, which was very unusual for our climate in Nov—Your Pa left yesterday, was undecided whether he would go home, or go by Halifax & get those negroes he had in jail (I wrote you about them in my letter of the 15th a few days ago) & take them up to the salt works—If he went home I guess he will return tomorrow & I will get him to write you, right away, but if he went to the salt works, he will not be back in some time, so you needn't wait to hear from him, but come home before the weather gets colder. If you and Neverson both have a cough now, you may grow worse from exposure, until you cannot be cured, so you had better come & doctor yourselves in time—I will try to get Mr. Newsom to take your gloves & beauregard, to you, & would like for

him to carry you some socks (for you really ought to have them on) & you have a very nice comfort for the neck (a present from your Cousin Lou Bond) here, I wish you had that also—The boots shall be sent, if such an article can be had, or if your Pa has a decent pr I will send his—I saw a pr at Hunter's, much too large for you at $40. . . . I would get them if they fitted you, let them cost what they may—I will get your Pa to try and get you some, but fear I cannot get them in time to send by Mr. Newsom—
Dont Neverson need clothes? I wish you would let me know right away what you are going to do about coming home—I will make any exertion to get you an overcoat & send it if possible—General camp up from the river yesterday, Brother ——— wrote your Pa that all was getting on quietly & the negroes had been working & doing first rate, since the Yankees left—I hope they will never return to this State again. They committed great depredations while they were here, they took Gen Stubbs (house below us) prisoner & burnt his house, they also burnt the Waldo's house & many others at & near Hamilton—Some of the ladies determined to remain at home, but the Yankees commenced throwing shells & for fear of having their houses burnt over their heads, had to leave, one lady had to take up two sick children (with diptheria) & go into the woods or any where she could, & it was during that snow. Many of the people took their carpets & made tents of them & run their families & negroes into the woods—It was 18 of Cousin Gavin's negroes that ran off (instead of 25 as I wrote in my other letter) & 2 of Cousin David's—Jack Griffin who lives nearly opposite us on the river, shot himself. One of the Yankee Officers I understand, actually cried, at the ridiculous outrages committed on the people by the soldiers, & some of them said they were so anxious to stop fighting, that they didnt care which side whipped so the war would stop. They seem to be sick of fighting (or rather of marching through such a country, as the Roanoke region—I feel so much for the poor people down about Hamilton, some of them have been deprived of all their hogs, poultry &c. & cant tell how they are to live—Mrs Taylor, at whose house General Foster established his headquarters, said they took all of her poultry but did not take her meat, this is rather better than I expected of them—I wish Ransom's brigade could have been here, it would have been an easy task for them to have bagged the Yankees & taken their boats—I hear the "Raleigh Standard" puts it to Martin for his cowardice—I hope Pettigrew will act more gallantly, if another invasion of our State is attempted— . . .

CLARK TO HIS MOTHER

Camp near Fredericksburg Va.
Nov 26th 1862.

. . . It is not improbable that we may have a battle here at any time, a probability which will soon be solved into practicability or impracticability and as soon as I hear from Pa I will make up my mind to leave *at once* or make arrangements to take the winter through. I wouldn't *think* of resigning as long as there is a *prospect* even of a *fight*. It is mere folly for one to think of getting a furlough from *this* Army for any reason whatever this Winter. I would greatly prefer being at home this Winter as I really do not think I could stand this life and climate in a Winter campaign. Whatever arrangement I make I should make quickly. I hope by the time this month is out that I will have heard from Pa and as the affairs here will in all probability have taken an aspect by that time I may be able on the 1st Dec to offer my resignation or prepare for the Winter. If Pa should say it would be best for me to remain here I shall have to hurry up with preparations for Winter as it is quite late for that now. If I stay here I must send Neverson home for three or four more weeks here I am seriously convinced would permanently injure him. If I should stay I will need three good blankets, a pillow, a pr of good boots and overcoat and a great many other things which I will write for if I stay as it is impossible to get a furlough to go after them and equally impossible to procure them here where a man who can purchase a pr of boot formerly worth $4 at $40 or $50 is indeed lucky for it is *very* unusual that one can be purchased at all. It is now as cold here as Christmas time with you and feels even colder to us who live in the open air. I am anxious to come to a conclusion one way or the other as I think a person should always make up his mind at once (particularly in this case where a body must freeze a little if they delay long). . . .

I have been trying to persuade Uncle Ed to resign but I believe he intends to stay here. Being on Gen'l Ransom's * staff he will probably come home Christmas on a furlough as Gen'l's Staff Officers can get a furlough from the Gen'l on whose Staff they are, but other Officers have to get furloughs from Gen'l Lee who positively refuses to grant any furloughs whatever. I don't think Uncle

* Matt W. Ransom, Colonel of the 35th North Carolina Regiment, commissioned Brigadier General, June 15, 1863, and Major General in 1865.

Ed wants me to resign much and in fact I would hate to leave him.

We have a new way of shoeing our barefooted men (until we can procure shoes). As soon as the beeves are killed for Rations the hides are taken off and given to the Companies which have barefooted men and the Captains of those Companies then cause every barefooted man to make himself Moccasins (turning the hair side in). These moccasins protect the feet admirably and but for them our Reg't would have fifty or seventy stark-barefooted men.

We had a grand Brigade Inspection today and a wearisome thing it was standing in the cold six mortal hours.

Col Ransom is at home quite sick I understand. The Yanks I believe have given out the idea of shelling Fredericksburg.

TO CLARK FROM HIS MOTHER

Airlie. Jan. 12th 1863

...I had a short letter dated the 8th & your Pa a note (dated 10th) from you this morning, saying you were afflicted with boils, which makes me feel very anxious, I am so much afraid you were not vaccinated with good matter, you should be very careful to use matter from a person, whom you know is not diseased, for if they are diseased in any way, they will infect you—Do let me hear from you immediately—To be sure you hav'nt got the smallpox I think you had better resign & come home for it seems you cant get a furlough—Your Pa came up yesterday quite sick again—He has'nt got his salt yet & his hogs are consuming corn fast—He saw Mr Davis at the Depot today & he gave express orders for the salt to be brought up to Littleton tomorrow, so I am in hopes he will get it now & his wagons are here ready to take it down home right away—I could not hear whether Cousin David was going on today or not—If you cant get off & will let me know when you pass Enfield I will try & send Frank down with some eatables He says he must see you somehow or other if you come this way—Your Aunt Alice came to church & dined with me yesterday & came very near staying all night, that she might hear from Uncle Ed today as he promised to write as soon as he reached Petersburg, she will be much disappointed, not getting a letter today—Brother Brent preached for us yesterday & is spending today with us—Pa is Agent for the tract society. I have just handed him twenty dollars of your money that you so generously gave to the cause of Christ &

I pray God's blessing may go with it & that you may be blest as the donor—The tract society is certainly a good cause & we will always be blest in giving to the Lord, if we give with an eye single to the *glory of God*— . . .

[P.S.]
We are truly elated at our victory at Vicksburg—

TO CLARK FROM HIS MOTHER

Jan 22nd 1863

I had just written & sent you a letter (to Petersburg) yesterday, when your Pa came & told me your Regt had passed Enfield in route for Goldsboro so fearing that you may lose the nice box that I sent you last Saturday I write to inform you that it left Littleton under Mr. Heptenstall's charge (he belongs to Cousin David's old company) who said he was going directly to the Brigade—I directed it to the care of Donnans & Johnston Petersburg, expecting it would go by Express, but the Express refused to take it on account of its weight, so it was put under Mr H's charge & he said he would take it along with his baggage—It must have been in Weldon the same time you were—You had better make some inquiries about it, as some of the things would keep some time & might do you some good—I ventured to put a roasted turkey in, thinking you were near Petersburg & it would soon reach you, & the weather being very (*cold*) thought it would keep—I however had the precaution to put it in a separate petition so that if it spoilt, it would'nt spoil your cakes, cooked ham, biscuit &c—It may injure the butter (most of it) but dont think it could hurt the raw hams—I hope you did, or will get it—Let me know right away. . . . I do wish you could come home—Your Aunt Frances is at Dr Hawkins's—Horace Bennett (the one we teazed your Cousin Mollie about) was killed at Port Royal last year—Your Pa has killed 20,000 weight of pork & has'nt salt for the balance—We are all tolerably well, but your Pa—There has been a good deal of diptheria on the plantation but only one or two deaths. . . . Be certain to read your Bible & pray unceasingly to the Great & Good Being for his kind guidance & protection & dont forget to thank him for his kind preservation through so many dangers— . . .

Ed left to join Will's Regt last week—He wrote to the bootmakers in Chapel Hill about three weeks ago & he said he could make you a pr of boots but not just then I had a letter from Your Aunt Martha yesterday, giving me his address R H Lee Bootmaker Chapel Hill & saying she thought I had better write & hurry him up so I thought I would write to him today as you seemed to prefer his boots to Johnson's—Johnson sent me word he could make you a pr this week $40 if I would send the size. . . .

P S

Why did'nt you slip up from Weldon to see me? Tell Col Ransom he need'nt want ever to see me, unless he has the courage to brook a lady's scolding for I would be right apt to give him a *good scolding* for keeping you in the Army— . . . I think he might have obtained a furlough for you, as he took such a long one himself—Dont think he & I will ever be very good friends

TO CLARK FROM HIS MOTHER

Jan 29th 1863

. . . Your Pa's health is better—He has gone to Raleigh today on business—The last order for troops takes his Overseer again, he says he got a broken down man, one that had been discharged from the Army two or three times, thinking he could keep him, but it seems they are about to take *him*, & if they do your Pa says he will be obliged to have you at home, as they are now organizing the State troops into Regts, & he is liable to be called out himself—His Overseer went to Raleigh Tuesday to see if he could get off but I hav'nt yet heard whether he succeeded or not—Your Pa is greatly bothered. . . . I received the $400 you sent & took one hundred to use as you directed & intended putting the $300 out at Interest but your Pa said he needed it, so he has it, but I tell him he must pay you Interest, He says you ought to keep a part of your money to buy what you need—I wrote to Mr Lee, (the bootmaker in Chapel Hill) last week, (as he promised your Cousin Ed to make the boots) to send your boots by Express to Littleton. . . . I do not feel *very charitably towards Col Ransom*—We now have 8 Topographical Engineers staying up here at Bethel, taking a survey of the country around, but I am in hopes they will never be under the necessity of using the topography of this part of the country—(for Military purposes at any rate). . . . Your Pa wants to know if you have had Neverson vaccinated—Small pox seems to be spreading Dr Perry I understand has 16 cases of it . . . Do try my dear child to take care of your health & morals, & above all, dont forget the profession you have made—Take a firm stand for Christ & let your light shine, never bring reproach on the cause—It is a glorious cause & well worth all your energies to sustain it! Be a *whole* Christian, if you wish to be esteemed by God & your fellow man—I know you are exposed to many temptations, but (as I have written you before) "He that would be little in temptation let him be much in prayer" & as I have always told you, never take the *first step* in any bad habit—Prayer is the only weapon with which we can subdue our evil propensities, & keep our evidence bright—You know not half how gratifying it is to me, to think no foul oath ever polluted your lips (*unless* the Army has corrupted you & I trust it has'nt) & that you have contracted no wicked habit, that I can hear of & my sincere prayer to God is that you may come out of the Army as pure & uncontaminated as when you entered it—You cannot be too watchful my Son in guarding against the wickedness of a Camp life—If you are ever tempted to do wrong, think of *God* who has been so *kind* to you & then think of your *Mother* who loves you so dearly & how it would grieve her heart for you to yield to the wiles of the evil one—The Lord grant that his Grace may ever be sufficient for you—Be a *sincere Christian*—Christ is a very present help in every time of need—

CLARK TO HIS MOTHER

Hd Q'rs 35th Reg't—N.C. Troops
Jan 30th 1863.

. . . I am afraid these shoes I have will barely last me home. I have worn them ever since last August. *Any* boots from *anywhere* will do if I can get them. I tried all over Petersburg and couldn't get a p'r under 9's or 10's. It has been 6 or 7 weeks since I wrote home for boots and of course my shoes are pretty badly off as no one would have calculated that it would take a bootmaker 7 weeks to make a p'r of boots. Get Johnson's or anybody's that will have them quickest. I have thought my feet would freeze in these low shoes for they keep no more water out than if I had none. It is folly to think that persons in the Army can purchase at any time & anywheres what they need. If Uncle Ed starts back before I leave send the boots by him as my Resignation *may* not be accepted. . . .

CLARK TO HIS MOTHER

Camp near Kenansville N Carolina
Friday, February 6th in the evening. 1863

I received your letter of the 29th inst & had been wondering why you did not write. I think I have written nearly twenty times since I have been here. I can not imagine why you have not received them unless it is because they were *franked.* I can not buy or borrow a stamp in camp. There are none here. I borrowed a couple from Uncle Ed to put on one letter. . . .

Tell Pa by no means to enter service.* One day of such service as we saw some times in Virginia would be sure to kill him. For instance (as we did before Fredericksburg) to lie in an open *ditch* the rain pouring down without blankets or a mouthful to eat (and the enemy picking off every man who raised up to stretch his benumbed limbs) for two nights one day & the best part of another in succession, and then just the day before these two we lay flat on our stomachs on the wet ground in an open field and the livelong day the enemy firing at us from the housetops so that we had to wait till night to get a mouthful of raw bread to eat, and this again after the heat and excitement of the Battle the day before when of course our men ate nothing. Do you think he could stand that?

Neverson's vaccination took finely at Fredericksburg when mine failed to take. My vaccination at Petersburg took very finely (in two places).

CLARK TO HIS MOTHER

Hd Q'rs 35th Reg't–N.C. Troops.
February 7th 1863.

I received this morning the letter and pr of boots (!) you sent by Uncle Ed. I was truly glad to get the boots for my feet were nearly on the ground. I knew if they could be had that you would have them. I am only afraid you gave yourself too much trouble about them. If any one wishes to become *used* to the crosses & trials of this life let him enter camp life. There are millions of little petty crosses & trials in that kind of life which you can never imagine even.

I am quite bothered to-day. Someone came to my tent door last night & stole my oven & every thing I had to cook in, consequently

* David Clark, Walter's father, had just been commissioned a Brigadier General in the North Carolina militia, charged with "the obstruction of the Roanoke River."

to-day I am without any thing of the kind as I have sent miles out into the country trying to buy cooking utensils from some one but in vain....

I expect my Resignation this evening. Write soon. Give my love to all.

I am quite anxious to see you all, very anxious, but somehow I hate to leave the Reg't & my companions-in-arms. I will bring my horses home as Pa says so but I am afraid they will be expensive. Tho' I suppose I can sell them very easily. Uncle Ed got back this morning. He staid longer than the General (Ransom) expected. I hear that my box is at Weldon. If so could it not be sent to Littleton? That would be better than losing it altogether as something might not be ruined. Salt has gone up from $5 to $30 per bushel. I hope Pa bought his in time.... I know my boots *must* have bothered you. But for the pressing, urgent, imperative necessity for them I would not have written for them, but I thought Col. Ransom would hardly like to see his Adjt barefooted & besides it was pretty cool weather lately.

[P.S.]

I will try to beat this letter home! But don't let the probability of getting home soon deter you from writing as I may be here weeks yet. I would not be surprised to move a little farther South shortly. Towards Wilmington or Charleston.

Officers' expenses in the Army are very high. Some Officers' expenses are three times their salaries. I have kept an exact account of every thing I have bought.

Nothing of interest. It is said that the Yankees are moving troops to Carolina City as if they intended to move them away by sea.

TO CLARK FROM HIS FATHER

Littleton
9 Feb 1863

I have just recd your letter & also seen the one to your Ma. Bring both the horses through the country It would be best for you to come by Railroad. Neverson could bring the horses if Col Ransom would give him a pass to Scotland Neck. I expect to Leave in the Morning for Petersburg & am going nearly all the time. never in one place over two days together. on My return from the Burg it is probable the next move will be to the plantation unless French * or Green gets me in Hot water about the Negroes.

* General B. F. French.

There is & has been much sickness on the River & the Snow which was 11½ inches deep will hardly improve matters. The Fort on Rain Bend Bank is finished. The big guns upon the landing on the way across to it last Wednesday If the Garrison will fight as they should the River can be held against the Yankees For they can not & will not bring regular ships up it, but only some old Ferry Boats—As for English, French, Republicans & Democrats, I put no trust in any of them but have faith in hard fighting & the Almighty. All well & send love. Hoping to see you soon

TO CLARK FROM MAJOR W. M. GORDON *

Hillsborough, Feb 12 1863

Your favor of 28 inst. is to hand. I should have answered it ere this but have been waiting to ascertain the number of Cadets entering the 3rd Class. I am exceedingly sorry I cannot let you have the books mentioned in your note, but I have not enough for the Class already here—

We have a fine Corps, 94 being present with the prospect of a large increase—I wish you were here, the material of the corps being altogether different from what is was last year.

TO CLARK FROM C. H. HILL

Raleigh March 7th 1863.

. . . I am glad to learn that you passed through the fiery ordeal of Virginia & Maryland uninjured. The Soldier who passed through those bloody campaigns, should he survive the war, will be an object of interest, around whom the children of the next generation will gather & eagerly listen to his tales of Suffering & blood.

I should like to be a Surviving soldier of the noble army of the Potomac; an army, which, upon the battlefields of the first year, has written in letters of blood, the proudest page in the history of our young Confederacy. I have not been enjoying myself so much as you Suppose since we last met. I too have experienced some of the ineffable pleasures of camp life. About the first of last June, I volunteered in the 11th (Bethel) Regiment, & was out all the summer & two months of the Fall. We were stationed in & around Wilmington until the first of October, when we were ordered to Virginia & were sent over on the Blackwater, where I received my discharge. We received orders to go to Richmond, a

* Superintendent of Hillsboro Military Academy.

Short time before the battles there, but they were immediately countermanded & Col. Parker's Regt. was sent instead. The Swamps & sand-hills of New Hanover country will ever linger in my memory with unpleasant associations, for we were marched & countermarched through them until any place in the world was preferable to me.

And I did not belong to that class of gentry, who wear about four yards of gold lace twirled in the most fantastic manner upon their sleeves, but was very little above high private, being 1st Corporal. So you can imagine the delightful time I had. But I enjoyed more privileges than most men of my rank. The Surgeon of the Regt is a very particular friend of mine & I was permitted to tent with him. I consequently had better Society & a more pleasant time than I otherwise would have had—Walter Bullock is 1st Lieutenant in Mallett's Battalion, & is at the Camp of instruction near here. The Battalion was in the fight at Kinston, & Walter commanded his company. They suffered severely in killed & wounded & a great many were taken prisoners—Bullock behaved nobly & escaped unhurt—

TO CLARK FROM J. A. C. BROWN *

High Point N.C.
May 26th 1863

. . . I certainly could have had no other feelings than those of pleasure on hearing from an esteemed friend with such melancholy forebodings for such of late mostly possess me when I indulge my mind to run upon the war. The death of Col. Gray † surely I can not too deeply mourn—for in him I lost my best, kindest, truest friend—as a man he was frank, honorable—as an officer brave and decided, as a friend sincere & confiding. A peculiar sadness overcame me on account of Charlie Burgin's‡ death for he was my intimate associate among the company officers—And is it not strange what strong attachments spring up & shortly mature under circumstances adverse to nobler dispositions of our frail nature as camp life, and coincident barbarisms of war generally? I have often thought of a remark of Col. Gray made to me on this subject. "The army is *the* place to develop character"—If there be any condition in human life in which selfishness should

* Captain, Company L, 22nd North Carolina Regiment.

† Robert H. Gray of Cumberland County, died March 16, 1863.

‡ Charles H. Burgin of McDowell County, Captain, Company K, 22nd Regiment, wounded at Shepherdstown, died November 13, 1862.

with reason be endured certainly the army is the place to look for it, and correspondingly how pure & deep-seated must be that virtue that can take root, flourish & be evergreen amid the sterility of camp. I was forced to resign on account of my health though not until I was wounded again—I was wounded though not serious in the head, while making a charge at Shepherdstown Saturday after the battle at Sharpsburg—I was worn out & sick when we went into the fight, having marched almost day & night the week before beside having fought at Harper's Ferry & Sharpsburg—Three battles & no rest in seven days—A big week's work—We would not have been able to undergo such tire & fatigue, but for our nutricious & nourishing diet in the occasion—(green corn & dry crackers)—Charlie Burgin & I were wounded about the same time came off the field together & remained together until he started home he insisted that I come home with him—I at one time thought it very doubtful as to my ever being able to get home so did the Surgeons & express themselves—but I did & improved amazingly for a season but am at present on the decline. I greatly fear—I hope to be well once more though it is "hope against hope"—With the departure of my health my ambition (if I ever had any) was laid low—my prospects were blighted & decayed, like every spring flower visited by a frost—Physicians "with one accord" prescribed whiskey. I myself had an abiding faith in the efficiency of the blood of John Barleycorn—The good it at least had of causing me to forget my misfortune & that I was unhappy. As faith is strengthened by the exercise of faith so by indulgence I found the habit increasing. so I paused, deliberated, and chose death by natural disease than by the peril & disgrace of a drunkard's grave—I "taste not, touch not, handle not"....

I shall not overlook this mess for fear I would not send it—I am bored to death half my time—Oh: that I was able for Service. I had a hundred times rather be in the army than out—I have no respect for anyone who is keeping out—& consequently can have very little for myself

RECOMMENDATION FROM THE HONORABLE THOMAS BRAGG * TO J. A. SEDDON, SECRETARY OF WAR

Raleigh July 28th 1863.

Lt. Clark of this state informs me that he will apply for an appointment in the Regular Army—He will show you some testi-

* Governor of North Carolina, 1855-1859, native of Northampton County.

monials as to his service in the Provis. Army—Though formerly residing in the adjoining County owing to his youth I had not the pleasure of knowing him personally—His father, David Clark, of Scotland Neck, Halifax, Co. has been long known to me as one of the worthiest and most prominent citizen in his section of the State—A large planter upon the Roanoke, no man has more heartily devoted himself to the Cause of the South and I have no doubt that his son is all that is said of him by his Superior officers.

RECOMMENDATION FROM MAJOR J. M. RICHARDSON *

Ga. Mil. Inst.
Aug. 7th 1863.

Mr. W. McK. Clark was a cadet at the Hillsboro' Military Academy during my connection with said Academy in 1861, & a member of the 3rd class. When the Corps was disbanded on account of the war he entered the service, & has been, as I understand, adjutant of the 35th Regt. N.C.T. He is a deserving young man, of good character & ability, & I have no doubt that he would discharge the duties of a subaltern satisfactorily.

RECOMMENDATION FROM THE HONORABLE A. W. VENABLE † OF N.C.

Brownsville
Aug. 8, 1863

To the President of the Confederate States

Allow me to unite with the two Generals Ransom in presenting the name of Mr. W.M. Clark who desires a commission in the Regular Army he having determined to make arms his profession I am well acquainted with him and his is a most striking instance of the gallantry of our youth. On the first of August 1862 then not quite 15 years of age he left the Military Institute at Hillsborough with its highest honors was appointed drill master to Pettigrew's Regiment by the State of N. Carolina accompanied it to Aquia Creek and Evansport—was appointed Adjutant to the 35th Regt in the Maryland Campaign and highly complimented for his gallantry on the battlefront at Sharpsburg by his commanding generals. He was with his regiment at the battle of Shepherdton and the first battle of Fredericksburg 13 Dec 1862—He was in the

* One of Clark's former teachers at Hillsboro Military Academy. He was a Major in the 21st North Carolina Regiment, resigned in January, 1862, and became Professor of Mathematics at Georgia Military Academy, Marietta, Georgia.

† Representative in Confederate Congress, native of Granville County.

midst of the fight at Marys Hills. He continued with it until very recently he resigned because of the ill health of his father. He proposes to go to the University of N Carolina to finish his literary education. He is not quite seventeen years of age and having served with patriotic gallentry & capacity I should be much gratified at his success in his application He belongs to a most patriotic family and I think would make himself distinguished in the profession which he has chosen.

CLARK TO HIS FATHER

Chapel Hill, N.Ca.
Aug. 20th, 1863.

. . . I send by Willis my *"Political Economy"* which we have just completed (except one day's lesson for which I can borrow a book). It is an interesting work & it so nearly coincides with yours & Gov Swains opinion of Usury Laws that I send it. It's remarks on *Banks* & on *Paper Circulation* pages 224 and 288, on *Legal Rate of Interest* p. 324 & on *Protecting Duties on Tariff* p. 133 will I think please you. The Article on *Taxes* p. 388 is worth reading these times. At first sight the style appears rather simple & elementary but when we see the Author's full meaning that wears off. Gov Swain's * a splendid one to teach it he can give so many practical illustrations. Sometimes he gets to telling his Anecdotes & consumes nearly all the Recitation hour. Of course the Class laughs heartily at his jokes to encourage him to proceed till the hour is out before he knows it.

After "Political Economy" we take up *"Constitutional Law"* which we will also recite to Gov Swain.

I have commenced reading Law here under Judge Battle.† Next June (if I should continue here that long) if I pass well upon what I recite to him I will be entitled to a County Court License tho' I would not be entitled to *plead* until I am 21. I have no idea *whatever* of being a lawyer but as you wished me to have a complete education I thought that would benefit me some in after life at least as much as the Greek which I have bestowed so much time on & which I am studying to make up.

I have my hands *full* now. I have the *Full* Senior Course of Study, I have *Greek,* and I am reading Law. It takes up all my time. Judge Battle told me to-day that I was getting on *very* well,

* David L. Swain of Buncombe County, Governor of North Carolina, 1832-1835, and President of the University of North Carolina, 1835-1868.

† William H. Battle, Professor of Law.

Mr. Fetter to whom I am making up Greek told me I was doing remarkably well. I finished Herodotus having read in Six lessons all that it took the Fresh Class a Session to read as they had only two recitations a week in it. At that rate it will not take me long to make up the "two years Greek".

If there is a "Blackstone's Commentaries" in the neighborhood please send it to me by Willis as the one I am using is Judge Battle's....

I hope to be a full Student by the end of the Session which will entitle to me a Diploma next June just before the Supreme Court sits when I would get my license.

I have no idea of entering any profession except the Army but don't you think I am doing well enough to read Law as the only possible disadvantage that could arise would be that I might injure my eyes. Let me know what you think of it. I did not have time to write to you about it for as the ten (10) months requisite to read Law before procuring a License (the Annual Examination of candidates for Licenses takes place every June when the Supreme Court sits) was just commencing & if I had waited a week I would have had to have waited till June after next for a License & I wanted to get my license when I got my Diploma, besides I thought you wouldn't care just so I was improving my time.

TO CLARK FROM HIS MOTHER

Nov 3rd 1863

I received a short note from you last evening, saying you had'nt heard from home in nearly a fortnight. I cannot account for it—I wrote you a long letter on Friday 23rd Oct & your Pa wrote you on Friday 30th Oct & enclosed $100 bill—I fear your letters have been intercepted. Did any one know of your receiving money in your letters.... Your Pa wrote you immediately on the reception of your letter relative to the cloth & advised you to be sure & get as much of the cloth as you would for yourself & then a pr of pants for him, as it is much cheaper than we can get it down this way, in fact it is not to be had at any price—Any thing else you see that you want get it for goods are scarce in the country....

TO CLARK FROM HIS MOTHER

Airlie Nov 24th 1863

...I have some weaving now for you a coat & pr of pants & Your Aunt Martha gave me an overcoat that was your Uncle

William's, which I am having turned & made smaller for you, but if you are supplied they will answer very well for your Pa—I guess with what you have & what I can supply you with, you can make out—tho' if you see any very good for pants & can get it on good terms, you can get your Pa a pr of pants—We heard that calico was selling at $3.50 in Chapel Hill, if so, your Aunt Luce requests that you will get her 10 yds of light colored for her—She is willing to give as high as four dollars & so if you have the money to spare, & she can return it when you reach home. . . . Capt Taylor gave us a call the other day, just from Bermuda—he was third mate on board the Advance *—He sent us a box the other trip he made, & brought us a box up here &c this time, which was very acceptable—He inquired very particularly after you. . . .

TO CLARK FROM JAMES S. BATTLE

Tarboro. Dec 6th 1863

. . . I reached this place last night about 9 Oclock, after an exciting and unpleasant ride from Goldsboro. When I reached Goldsboro I heard that the Yankees were in eight miles of Tarboro and I did not know whether to come immediately on or wait until the excitement subsided, after thinking about it some time, I concluded to come on and see how everything was. But just before the Cars reached Goldsboro, the Commander of the Post received a Telegram stating that the mail train would not be able to take on any passengers as it was loaded with troops destined for Weldon, and when the cars arrived there was no place that I could get in, unless I went in the Baggage coach and I chose to come on rather than remain in Goldsboro another day. When I arrived here I found the home guard on duty and a regiment of soldiers stationed in town. The yankees were out on a raid but did not come quite as far as Greenville. I suppose they would have continued the raid as far as this place if they had not heard of the preparations that were being made for them. . . .

TO CLARK FROM C. J. AUSTIN

Tarboro Dec 15th 1863

Being alone in my room this evening & bored completly out with Tarboro I have come to the conclusion to while away a few moments in droping you a few lines thinking that you would be

* Noted blockade-runner. Before the war Taylor had captained the *Kahukee.*

much pleased to hear from an Old Friend and there is nothing that gives me more pleasure than writing to a friend except receiving a letter from one. Jimie & myself have been having a splendid time flying around the femail tribe. We visited Seven Young Ladies last evening and had a most pleasant time. The reason why I am so bored out today is that I am disapointed & cut out of a ride in the Buggy with a Lady this evening owing to my Horse being absent from home. The boy drove them off this morning in the country not knowing that I wished to drive and has not as yet returned. Do you not think that is enough to bore the "Devil" out? After anticipating Such a pleasant time this evening & then have it all broken up. Jimie just came by after me to go he has gone up & will no doubt have a delightful time. We both have lost our hearts I am sorry to say those young ladies are very nice they are from Virginia & expect to leave Thursday We will go with them I guess as far as Battlesboro & will no doubt have a Splendid time. After they leave it will be So boring here that I may leave and seek some place more pleasant....

TO CLARK FROM ANN S. HILLYARD

Chapel Hill 23 Decr 1863

Your very kind letter of the 20 Instant was received. I am very much obliged to you for your promptness in complying with my request. I will Take Twenty five Hundred pounds of Pork and One Bbl Lard. You can have the Pork Salted! It had better be put in Hogheads or Boxes. I will allow you whatever Pork Sells for with you. If you think it necessary Mr Urley will come down to Littleton when you send the Pork & Lard there Gov Swain has just come in and requested me to say to you to tell your Father to send him Twenty five Hundred pounds of Pork and send it with mine.

TO CLARK FROM C. W. BROADFOOT *

Camp Daniel Jan 12 64

...I think you are mistaken in regard to a Reg. being formed out of the Batts. now at Goldsboro I do not think that Genl Holmes will agree to it at present—

I would like very much to have one or two companies assigned to my Batt and then have yours & mine joined together—

* Charles W. Broadfoot, Major of First Junior Reserves.

Being the Sr Maj of course I would be entitled to the Lt Col'cy—

I shall write to Raleigh today to ascertain if the Batts now organized are to be thrown together in any way—

I hope you will keep me advised of any movements of this sort at Goldsboro.

I think it would be more pleasant for both of us if our Batts were together.

If a Reg were organized at Goldsboro the Col would rank *Armistead* and of course could not report to him—

I do not believe that any thing towards consolidation will be done at present— . . .

CLARK TO HIS FATHER

Chapel Hill
May 6th 1864.

If not elected Capt of the Orange Comp'y tomorrow expect me home, Monday evening or Tuesday morning. If I should be detained in Raleigh I should like for my name to be run for Captaincy of the Halifax Comp'y. At present there seems no *doubt* of my election here. Twenty four hours probably will decide the results of my first appearance for the suffrage of the people.

CLARK TO HIS MOTHER

Raleigh, N.C.
June 3rd, 1864.

I was graduated yesterday. To-day I have been elected Major of the 5th Battalion Junior Reserves. Need I say that my first thought on the announcement of my election was yourself & that I hasten to write. I had strong opposition. A Capt. of Cavalry and two or three Enrolling Officers were candidates against me. I received however 16 votes out of 20. I have five (5) fine Companies numbering nearly five hundred fine strapping Western lads. There is hardly a small man in my Battalion. My Battalion is composed of picked men and picked Officers. It was kept for a Government favorite tho' I disappointed them. By throwing in two additional Companies to beat me they had given me five Co's whereas the other four Batt's have only three each. There has been only 5 Battalions raised in this State so far. The 1st you know has been sent to Weldon. The other three are at Goldsboro to meet the raiders. I expect to be ordered off very shortly to one of the above named points with my command. If I pass by Littleton I will let you know.

Tell Pa please to have my bay (not the grey) filly brought up to Airlie.* I will let you know whether to send her to Goldsboro or Weldon. Neverson will have to get ready to be "off to the Wars again". I came off from home with only the shirt I had on and scarcely a cent of money as I expected to go by Weldon. I have no army shirts. If you have no materials I will get some here.

Gen'l Holmes † was much opposed to my election—I was too young. He doubtless thought 65 the right age to qualify a man for my position tho' it doesn't seem to fit *him* for Lt Genl by the way. Everything unfair and fraudulent was attempted to beat me. I gave the matter up entirely into the Lord's hands and asked that His will might be done. No one in camp except my few friends who were in the secret and the Officers who voted for me—they kept the matter entirely dark—thought five minutes before the election that I would get a single vote.

[P.S.]

I sent for Neverson. He will have to bring my blankets and oilcloth & his own ditto.

I will get home soon as possible. I have now to arm and equip my men & clothe them. I will be very busy until I leave here. Address for the present is Maj. W. McK. Clark, 5th Batt. Jun. Res., Raleigh, N.C.

RECOMMENDATION OF WM. T. DORTCH ‡ TO J. A. SEDDON, SECRETARY OF WAR

Goldsboro, N.C. June 16, 64

I most respectfully recommend W. McKenzie Clark, of North Carolina, for a position in the Regular Army, or on the staff of some General, if the former cannot be granted.

He had three years education at a Military School & at the commencement of the war, though under the military age, he entered the Army under Genl Pettigrew.

Was Adjt of the 35th Reg. N.C.T. & behaved very gallantly in several battles, receiving the commendation of Genl Robt Ransom & Mr W. Ransom. He afterward resigned to complete his

* Summer home of Clark family eight miles from Littleton, North Carolina.
† Theophilus H. Holmes.
‡ North Carolina Senator in Confederate Congress.

education & has recently graduated at the University of N.C. with distinction. He is a young man of high character & position in society, & now commands a Battalion of the reserve forces of the State with the rank of Major.

RECOMMENDATION FROM WILLIAM H. BATTLE

Raleigh June 20th 1864

My acquaintance with W. McKenzie Clark formed while he was a student in the Law Department of the University of North Carolina during the scholastic year of 1863-4 enables me to recommend him as a young gentleman of fine talents, studious habits and exemplary deportment—From my knowledge of him, thus obtained, I have no hesitation in expressing the opinion that he will perform with fidelity and ability the duties of any office to which he may be appointed, and which he would be willing to accept.

CLARK TO HIS MOTHER

Hd Q'rs 6th Batt Res Rorces
Camp Ransom near Weldon
June 21st 1864.

At last we are quite comfortably fixed. We are encamped about 1½ miles from Weldon in good log cabins—the Winter quarters of the 56th Reg't. We are well fixed and I am drilling my Battalion hard. Five Drills a day and the Officers recite on Tactics twice a day. My hands are pretty full. Last Saturday & Sunday I lay in the trenches around Weldon. I was given ½ mile of breastworks to defend. An attack was expected every minute Saturday and part of Sunday. If the enemy had penetrated my line all was gone for there were no troops to reinforce me. Major Reece's * Battalion was on my right and beyond that was four Companies of Hinton's † 68th N.C. We also had two Compy's of Artillery. On the Halifax side there was only the remaining Six Companies of Hinton. Lt Col Ed Yellowley ‡ was the Commanding Officer on our side of the River. He is a No. 1 Officer & a clever man. Genl Baker § took command of the Post Saturday but left for Goldsboro' on Sunday. Two thousand cavalry was the Force expected against us. My men were 'spoiling' for a fight....

* J. M. Reece, Commander of the Fourth Battalion of Reserves.
† Colonel James W. Hinton of Pasquotank County.
‡ Edward C. Yellowley of Pitt County.
§ Lawrence S. Baker of Gates County, commanding officer of the district.

I am in good quarters but can't answer for our fare. ⅛ pound of bacon is the ration Govt. issues per man and when I share that with Neverson you may be sure there is not much left. If you send anything down at 2 o'clock I will get the letter that night and go to town next morning. Send by Express or some one coming down. I have no plates &c. Have to cook in one Spider and eat with my hands. There is not a stove in Weldon. Send me a couple of tin plates, two knives & forks, and tin cup. Send me also a blacking brush. Hunter has some. I hope you have sent to Warrenton ere this for my Mess Chest. The way I am getting on is *decidedly* rich for a Commanding Officer. Fortunately I have had few visitors except men who come to get their sons discharged and as they eat with their sons *I* run no risks in asking them to dinner. If you have not my Mess Chest yet write immediately and I will try to have one made in Weldon but you will have to send me plates &c. I will also want another double blanket, or *two* double blankets and send home these two little blankets I have. They must be trundle bed blankets. Too short for any use.

TO CLARK FROM CAPTAIN W. S. LINEBERRY *

Gaston NC June 24th/ 64

Sir we got heer Safe last evening. we have got Splendid quarters good houses with Chimneys to them we are on the north side of the River. my men is very well contented. The water is very good. I feal very lonsom up heer by my Self I hope I will injoy it fore their is A very Pritey girle lives in the house joining my quarters & she is harde to beat on the Pianer....

I heer no account of Any Yankeys near heer I Dont think we are in any Danger of a Attact

TO CLARK FROM HIS SISTER

Airlie, June 28th 1864

I will write you a few lines as Ma wants [to know] whether you want your clothes sent in the mess chest or not, as it is nearly done. The clothes I speak of are the new suit Ma had made for you while you were at home. Pa received your letter last night. I am very glad you enjoyed your box. Ma says if you will save her jars, and send them back she can send you some more honey and

* Captain in the 70th Regiment, commanding Company C, Sixth Battalion, years later Superintendent of the Old Soldiers' Home in Raleigh.

butter. You wrote Sister that there were a great many cherries where you are, but Ma told me to tell you that if you eat too many they will certainly make you sick. We are all very well....

[P.S.]

Ma says she will write as soon as she can sit up. She also says you must not drink out of the tin cup she sent for if you do it will injure your teeth so much. The mug is for you to drink out.

TO CLARK FROM C. G. WRIGHT *

Camp Holmes †
July 1st 1864

Your favor of the 30th to hand this P.M. was pleased to find you well & in such good spirits. you have a fine lot of boys, and a good fight they will make.

I have just fixed up two recruits for you. the Reserves come in very slow. Our camp is very desolate, the Battalion has gone and most of our Officers. No doubt you have heard [about] the Raid on Camp Vance.‡ All were taking prisoners with the Exception of a few, particulars not learned. The Raiders composed chiefly of *Deserters & Tories....*

I will send the Boys soon as they come in (if any) to you. I trust you will be able to Keep up your number of men....

TO CLARK FROM HIS MOTHER

July 10th 1864

...I merely write a few lines to know how you are getting on & if you wish me to send you more eatables—I can send you some more honey as I have a very good supply, & some Irish potatoes, butter, &c Let me know what you would like to have most—I want to send you a bucket of lard also to cook with *since Neverson has come to be such a good biscuit maker*—I do hope you can pay us a short visit before long—I feel so anxious to see you.... I suppose I must send that suit of clothes to Gail by Will—I think it a very good plan, as they will not be of any service to you if you remain in the Army (& that you seem determined on) as they are so light, unless you would like such a suit to call on the ladies....

* Clement G. Wright of Cumberland County, Major in the 66th North Carolina Regiment, later Lieutenant Colonel.

† Near Weldon, North Carolina, named for General Theophilus H. Holmes.

‡ Two miles east of Goldsboro on the Wilmington and Weldon Railroad.

TO CLARK FROM J. A. C. BROWN

High Point N.C.
July 15th 1864

...Every thing is quite composed in this country and would appear uncommonly so to a soldier—Politics seems just now to have swallowed up all other subjects—Fighting has been going on so long that not much of it is noticed or talked of—Gen. Vance spoke at High Point last week. he killed off some of the Holdenites * & I am sorry to say they are as plenty as blackberries in this & the adjoining counties—I greatly apprehend the result in August. It does really seem people have gone crazy on the subject of peace—Holden has emboldened & given a chance for the disaffected to come out—What is to come of us I cant see—I intend to single out my man certain if the worst does come—I am not whipt nor *do I ever expect to be*—Again I must say I would like much to be with you though my health is very bad & the risk would be great—Still as the preachers say "No cross, no crown" & as the gambler—"no risk, no gain" The greater the sacrifice we willingly make the more noble & exalted our patriotism—I will say that I am at your bidding—I have learned that there is considerable sickness with you & some of the parents have expressed a desire that I would visit your Battalion at least—If you need my services in the medical department, you can cheerfully have them—I am not certain but I would prefer such a connection with your command to any other—The advantages to me personally would be more important.

TO CLARK FROM J. H. HOPE & CO.

Raleigh N C July 18th 64

I Recvd yours of date 15th In relation to a pair of Cavalry Boots the price is $275 instead of $175 If you want the boots at the price they were ordered at $275 you will please let me know. they are valuable and I can dispose of them

TO CLARK FROM HIS MOTHER

Airlie July 25th 1864

...I wrote you in my last to let me know, if there was anything that you wished me to send in the chest, but you said nothing

* William Woods Holden, candidate for governor against Vance in 1864, advocated "peace at any price." Vance was reëlected governor by an overwhelming vote, Holden carrying but two counties.

about it in your letter, so I only send some vegetables & a little butter—Your Pa has had your chest fixed very nicely & a screw put in the top to prevent injuring it by driving nails through the top—I wish we had a lock to put on it, but cant get one—You did'nt receive the shoes, (as I expected you would) the same day that my letter reached you—I have written you two or three times & Mittie wrote you, some time since, but as you hav'nt acknowledged the receipt of them, I suppose they never reached you—The money I guess your Pa will send by Neverson—I was not complaining (in my letter) of what you had spent (for I did'nt think you had spent any unnecessarily) but I was complaining of your not taking, what you needed with you, as it is inconvenient sending it to you, or rather more unsafe than inconvenient—Your Pa thinks it a perfect *outrage,* having that Virginian * elected Col, & seems much mortified that you should have submitted to it, thinks you should have had more independence.... Did your ink go safely in the box? How do you like the lamp I sent?! Let me know whenever you need anything—I will send you some more socks soon—I do wish you could come home to see us a little while—Was glad to hear that you had tents for your men & was better fixed—Did you enjoy the Apples & vegetables that I sent you—I only send some corn & potatoes this time as you dont seem to care for any other vegetable—You can roast your corn—Did you intend sending that paper of pens home, or was it an oversight? I send your bible, as I fear you have not been able to get one—Hope you will never neglect reading it—& following its precepts, for it is the only sure guide to happiness—As it seems I am to have so little of your company is this world, hope we may dwell together eternally in that blissful home above—My first & greatest ambition for my children is that they may be true & faithful Christians....

CLARK TO HIS MOTHER

Hd Q'rs 69th Regt N.C.T.
July 26th 1864.

Neverson came in last evening. Levi seemed sorry to see him. He and I were getting on very well. He makes a first rate boy. Mrs. Dr. Johnson got him to fix her loom while he was here. She seemed much pleased at it as she had never been able to set it to work before. I send home my cloth (4 yards) which cost $40. Make me a pr of pants and if you have the pattern the coat & vest also.

* T.S. Armistead, who was chosen Colonel of Clark's regiment.

I have bought 4 yards more from a Lieut at the price he gave for it ($40) which I will send home as soon as I get it. I send the lantern home as I do not need it here. Send me some postage stamps if you have them as there are none here. The shoes have never been rec'd. . . .

TO CLARK FROM HIS MOTHER

Airlie July 28th 1864

. . . I received your cloth & articles sent home. All came safe to hand—I write to know if you could go to Enfield some day & get the tailor to cut your clothes, if so I can send the cloth to him when your Pa goes down the country—I hav'nt your patterns, except those pants that were cut in Chapel Hill & I did'nt think they fitted near so well as those that were cut in Enfield. Let me know if you can go (right away) & I will then write you what day your Pa will go down & have the cloth there—I can have them made for you very nicely— . . . Your Pa said your boots would (those you bought) cost $175 So he sent you $65 more only, as he said he thought that was as much as you wanted, as you ought to draw $300 pay soon—Let us know exactly what you need—I hope your shoes are not lost. . . .

TO CLARK FROM HIS MOTHER

Aug. 1864

I had just written you by mail, to know what you wished me to send you & sent the letter before Neverson reached here. He reached here safely last evening & tells me you dont need any thing but some sugar & some socks, but I have taken care to send you other articles, thinking they will not go amiss—What you dont want, I guess you can readily dispose of to some of your men—Your Pa will insist on my sending some onions & your Cousin Will says you ought to learn to eat them, they are so healthy & a great improvement to beefsteak, when you have fresh beef—I send you a bucket of lard to cook with, & a jar of honey, vegetables, apples, cakes, &c. & one pr of new socks—Had some light bread, biscuit & crackers made for you to eat with your honey as Levi might not prove to be such a good biscuit maker as Neverson—I also send you some sugar and some tin plates that your Pa bought for you in Halifax & one more spoon—The lamp I send is one that your Pa had & he & your Cousin Will thinks the very thing for you (Will says he would give a good deal for one just like it) You can burn either oil, lard, or a short piece of candle in it—You can easily make another wick & put in, when this one burns out. (I will put in a ball of cotton for the purpose) & you can melt a little lard to replenish with every night—As Levi petitioned to go & wait on you, Your Pa and I have concluded that he will suit better than any one else that we can send, as he has been aboard the boat & has some experience in cooking & in travelling—I send you some slippery elm bark as a medicine—it is excellent to chew in cases of diarehea, or to allay thirst when you have had bad water to drink—You can give it to your men when they are sick—I have not sent much butter, I sent so much before, that you might share it with some of those who had been so liberal to you—I wish you had sent your socks for me to mend—I hope Neverson soon will be well enough to return—Dont eat too many cakes & apples, without eating solid food....

TO CLARK FROM DAVID L. SWAIN *

Chapel Hill, 2 Aug. 1864

I have just received your note of the 25.

The views expressed in my note of the 9th inst. were written *Current Claims* and were unavoidably hasty brief and superficial, and I am too busy at present to undertake to elaborate them. They present my opinions on all matters, as accurately as if my views were more fully and frankly set forth, and if you suppose my friends in your section of the country will attach any degree of importance to this, you may consider yourself at liberty to make such use of this as you may deem proper.

We are opening with nearly 100 students with no prospects of regular and steady increases. Our Professors with the exception of Prof Kimberly † (who is out on furlough) are at their posts. Prof Hepburn ‡ returned from Germany just in time to avoid the terrible conflict waged between Austria, Prussia, and Italy.

CLARK TO HIS MOTHER

Camp near Weldon
Aug 27th 1864

...I have been on an "Examining Board" for over a month. I guess you did not pay much attention to what I said in my letter

* President of the University of North Carolina.
† John Kimberly, Professor of Chemistry applied to Agriculture and the Arts.
‡ Andrew D. Hepburn, Professor of Metaphysics, Logic and Rhetoric.

about it for I was certainly explicit. We have examined between 50 and 60 officers. As Junior Officer of the Board I had all the records to keep and a great many cases took up two pages of foolscap. I am about through and you may be sure I feel relieved. I am now however ordered on a General Court Martial for the purpose of trying Deserters &c. I rec'd a letter from Cousin Ed a day or two since. He wants to get a position for me but can find no vacancy. My present position here is uncertain as you are aware....

CLARK TO HIS MOTHER

Camp 1st Regt Res. near Weldon
Sept 19th 1864.

We have been so busy fixing up in our Winter Quarters (three miles North of Weldon) that I have been unable to answer your letter rec'd a day or two since.

The firing Uncle William heard was really at Weldon. The 32-pounders on the fortifications having been loaded some time we took the occasion of Gen'l Baker's* visit to have them fired off, somewhat as a salute.

The coat I sent home I wanted Susan to turn. The cloth looks equally well on either side. In turning she might make the cuffs a trifle shorter than they are now.

I will take the first leisure to ride down to Halifax. It is 10 or 11 from our present Camp. Much love to all. Should you send me a box enclose Napoleon's Maxims, and one or two other little military books I have (not Tactics).

TO CLARK FROM HIS MOTHER

Sept 29th 1864

...As soon as I returned & Neverson told me how much you needed a boy—I concluded to send him any way, even if it made me a little backward with the Winter clothes—Your Pa intended sending down to the plantation for a boy, but I knew it would be some time before you got one at that rate & Levi seemed so anxious to go to you, that I sent him right off with particular injunction, for you to write me immediately on his arrival, but it seems that either you, or he, disregarded my injunctions, for I have not yet heard whether or not he reached camp—I had your coat made some time ago—Do you wish me to send it? And your

* Lawrence S. Baker, commanding officer of the district.

boots; shall I send them? If I were you I would not have the coat turned, only have the sleeves made shorter.... I think we had all better be praying for our country, these perilous times—There certainly seems a dark cloud overhanging the Southern Confederacy at this time & requires much prayer & faith to dispel it—Read your Bible & pray often my child & put your trust in God & all will work together for your good....

CLARK TO HIS MOTHER

Camp near Weldon, N.C.
October 15th, 1864.

Your *caution* in reference to the young ladies is *quite* amusing. You are just the reverse when I am at home for it is all I can do to be left to myself when young ladies make their appearance *there*. I should have thought that *caution* in that regard would have been unnecessary from one who was as well acquainted with my opinion of the 'feebler sex' as yourself. If I am but 18 as you hinted in your letter I am not a fool, And *most certainly* shall never entertain the most *distant* idea of tendering my "hand and fortune" when the one has yet to achieve the other. With the profession that I have chosen it is not probable that I shall own any land beyond my sabre's length. With a total disbelief in the *existence* of such passion as *Love*—at least as far as myself is concerned—I am not the one to exchange the hopes of the future—delusive they may be—for a few broad pieces of gold as *you* would insinuate. I thought that you had long ago penetrated the secret that I fain would keep from others—for "*Lowliness* is young Ambition's ladder"—that I have another aim in life than "to live as my sires have lived, and die as they have died". In my opinion "one crowded moment of glorious life is worth ten years of dull *existence*". It is my intention, and has been, should our young Confederacy go down in the billows which threaten to engulf it (which Heaven forbid) to collect a band of the brave around me and in a brighter clime and more unclouded skies seek *that* which Fortune denies me on my native shores. Maximilian of Mexico will not refuse a brave man's sword and I trust I know how to wear one. I live in the future as I live for it. These are my sentiments. Known to none, suspected by few. Think you that they are reconcilable with the pulsing sentimentalism of Love. The chords of my heart have been strung to a fiercer passion and echo not when struck by so unskilled a musician. I am as well aware Ma!

as you are of the snares used to entice young men into Matrimony. I am also pretty well versed in the duplicity of my own sex—you see I am fair, a blow at both sides of the question. But I fancy that an *early* and I might say *bitter* acquaintance with the World has learned me to beware of the one while I can laugh at the other. It has also learned me another thing—to keep my own counsel. *My real* opinion on any subject is known to few or none. And while there is nothing which I would keep from you yet as I suppose you were aware of my real sentiments on this subject my usual reserve in regard to my opinions prevented any allusions to it. I think that I have now expressed my sentiment pretty openly and in such a manner as to set the matter at rest for the next ten years, certainly until I am master of my own fortune or misfortune whichever it may be. As to the reason why "I wait on the girls from home and wont speak to them at home" your own letter is sufficient. I do not care to speak even to a lady where every one is ready to interpret a glance into a declaration of Love—and you see it was some of my innumerable *kinfolks* who tried to do it this time, Miss L—I believe it was.—Here, I am free. If any thing should occur to raise such a thought my *friends* are too polite to notice it and others dare not. As to M's pedigree it being a matter of indifference to me I know nothing. The only difference I have ever heard as yet between my "stock of folks" & M's is that my father's father brought money and respectability into our family while I believe he can only trace his as far back as his father. I call very frequently at Mr. M's. They are nice hospitable clever people. Not a night passes but some of the Officers from one of the Regts. are there. Aware of the awkwardness of manners which naturally results from unacquaintance with ladies' society and aware of the necessity of polishing my manners a little I took this opportunity of doing it when among a crowd of visitors my natural diffidence might pass unnoticed. As to my riding alone with Miss M my fair Cousin was mistaken—as kinfolks usually are. I never rode but once with Miss M and then it was in company with the sister of an old friend the young gallant and lamented Captain Durham. He was engaged to Miss M when killed and his sister was on a visit to her. I should of course have written about my visits there but for the fact that my letters generally reach more than one eye.

I made a mistake in writing for my boots. I found them in the carpet bag after I wrote. They are fixed very nicely.

The "Mercurial Ointment" you found in my pocket I had for

rubbing my spurs. A Capt. in the Regt. (formerly Capt. under Morgan) made me a present of a fine pr. of spurs. When the brass is well rubbed an application of Mercurial Ointment gives it an appearance of silver for two or three days. You have probably seen door knockers treated that way.

I rec'd the grapes you sent and jacket this morning. I enjoyed the grapes very much. The jacket and coat are both much improved. If I start to Richmond I will be at Littleton *Tuesday* morning. Wish I knew in which way Cousin Will intends going—By Littleton or Weldon. Tell Cousin Guil I could probably get him a Captaincy in the Junior Reserves if he wishes it. . . .

CLARK TO HIS MOTHER

Weldon
Oct. 20th, 1864.

. . . On Sunday evening we received marching orders as the enemy was reported crossing the Blackwater * with two Regts. and a Battery of Artillery. About 10 o'clock at night a telegram came from Gen'l Baker at Goldsboro ordering our Regt. to take the cars at once for Boykins.† We marched to Garyburg ‡ found the train ready and little before day the Regt. found itself at Boykins Depot. The next morning (Monday) dawned with a tremendous cannonade supposed to be the enemy shelling Nottoway Bridge 15 miles below on the R.R. Col. Armistead § immediately gave me a command of 125 picked men and three Officers (I believe the whole Regt. would have volunteered to go with me, they were anxious for a fight) pressed a train into service and away we started with a full head of steam for the scene of action. We had by this time received information from our *reliable* cavalry that the enemy with two Regts. and four pieces of Artillery were shelling the Nottoway Bridge. On getting to Newsom's Depot 5 miles from Boykins the cannonade increased so that the Conductor seemed unwilling to risk the safety of the Train. He was politely given to understand that Major Clark commanded the forces on board and that *that* train should go to Nottoway Bridge as ordered if I had to place a Sentinel over the Engineer and run the train down myself. Five miles farther on the firing ceased which seemed to intimate that the enemy had crossed. I

* River in eastern Virginia.
† Small town in eastern Virginia.
‡ Small town in northeastern North Carolina.
§ T. S. Armistead, Colonel of Clark's regiment.

then got on top the cars with one or two men so as to look out for bushwhackers. When in a mile of the Bridge we stopped the train (putting an Officer to watch the Engineer lest he might run off with the train and leave us 15 miles off from our nearest forces) and advanced carefully with a line of skirmishers to the Bridge. There we found about 20 of our Cavalry the worst scared set of men you ever saw. We then sent for the train and went down two or three miles farther to Murfree's * Depot (the end of the road). Found the Depot, P.O., and all the buildings laid in ashes. The enemy had also burnt at this place 15 bales of Cotton and carried off 125 head of Cattle penned there for Government. The ashes were still smouldering but the enemy had left a few hours before. Only fifty of the enemy had crossed the River (tho they had above mentioned force) and done this damage. Our cavalry numbering fully as many acted shamefully running without firing a shot. They plead their ammunition was out (shooting at Ducks). The enemy were fairly on their way to Suffolk when I got down. The firing we heard was probably due to the numerous water courses making the firing to seem nearer. There was of course nothing left for me to do except return which I did after reconnoitring to ascertain the force they had brought and see from the tracks if they had brought their artillery across. We reached Boykins again Monday night. The Regt. remained down there Tuesday and Wednesday and last night returned here after spending three days on Va. soil. They are very proud of their 'campaign' and I must say that the Regt. exhibited the very best spirit.

CLARK TO HIS MOTHER

Fort Branch
Near Hamilton
Nov 5th 1864.

I wrote you a few hurried lines as we passed through Hamilton last Monday. That day we marched 25 miles until in fact we got within ten miles of Plymouth when we met the fugitives from the town which had been evacuated two hours before. We took up position at Gardiner's Bridge that night expecting the enemy to advance. As he did not we fell back next day to this place. I am at present temporarily in command of Fort Branch at this place. My Garrison consists of 2 Companies of Heavy Artillery, 1 Company Light Artillery & 2 Companies Infantry (from my own Regiment).

* Present Murfreesboro, North Carolina.

The natural position of the fort is splendid. We have ten guns in position. I was placed in command by Genl Baker. I expect Col Pool * (of 10th Art.) with a portion of the Garrison at Washington to-day. If so I will rejoin my Regt which is about 3 miles distant as he will assume command of the Fort.

I need my Overcoat & gloves. If you will send them to the Plantation I can get them at any time as it is only 18 miles off. The 4 yds in one piece I sent home is for a Military Overcoat. The two yards nice cloth is for my uniform coat, as I have none. If the buckskin at home is tanned I will try to have me some gauntlets fixed up. . . . I intend to put in my application shortly for a furlough. All our furloughs now have to go up to Gen'l Lee as he is in command of the forces here.

TO MAJOR CLARK FROM COLONEL ARMISTEAD

Hd. Quarters Sub. District
Camp Baker Nov. 15th, 1864.

S O
Maj. Clark
1st Regt. Res. N.C.
No. 18 II

Maj. Clark will proceed with four (4) Companies of the 1st Regt Res N.C. to Williamsboro, and relieve the 50th Regt N.C.T. on picket duty near that place.

III

Lt. Col. Canhook † as soon as relieved will proceed with his Regt to Tarboro, N.C.

By order of
Col. F. S. Armistead
A. T. London
Adjt.

GENERAL ORDERS ISSUED BY MAJOR CLARK

Hd.Qrs. Biggs Farm.
Nov. 16th, 1864.

General Orders.
No.2.

Par.I. In assuming command at this outpost the Maj. Comdg relies upon the vigilance and devotion to duty of the Officers and

* Stephen D. Pool of Carteret County, Colonel of the 10th Artillery Regiment.
† John C. Vanhook of Person County, Lieutenant Colonel of the 5th North Carolina Regiment.

men under his command, to compensate for their paucity of number and to guard against surprise by the enemy. Discipline distinguishes the soldier from the recruit. Officers will be held to a most rigid account in the performance of their duties.

The attention of Officers and men is called to the following orders.

Par.II. No one will be allowed to pass the Picket lines going out, without written authority from these Hd.Qrs. This applies as well to Officers and men at the several Picket stations as to others. Officers are particularly enjoined to allow no straggling from their camp. Any one found more than a mile from his camp without written authority from his Comdg Officer approved at these Hd.Qrs. unless on duty will be severely punished.

Par.III. Commanding Officers will have at least three Roll Calls a day. Absentees will be punished. A Morning Report of each Company will be sent to these Hd.Qrs. every morning.

Par.IV. The Maj Comdg directs that every precaution be taken against surprise. At Fosters Mills there will be a Lieut of the guard every night. At the other posts select Sergts will supply the want of Lieuts. Comdg Officers are requested to visit their pickets at least once in 24 hours. Should they deem it advisable at any time to change the advance Picket stations they will report the fact at these Hd.Qrs.

By order of
W. McK. Clark.
Maj. Comdg.

W. H. Gregory
Lt. & Act. Ajt.

TO MAJOR CLARK FROM A. T. LONDON, ADJUTANT

Hd.Qrs. Sub. District
Camp Baker Nov. 18th, 1864.

Maj. W. McK. Clark
Comdg &c.
Williamsboro
Major

I am directed by the Col. Comdg. to say that, if the enemy makes any demonstration on Williamston, you will impress transportation for the removal of the torpedoes, as he has none to send you.

You have all the cavalry that is under his command. He expects to visit your post tomorrow.

I am Major
Very Resptly
Yr Obt Svt
A.T.London
Adjt.

CLARK TO HIS MOTHER

Hd Q'rs Williamston, N.C.
November 19th 1864.

I was sent down to this place four or five days since with four Co's of my Regt. to relieve the 50th. I am now in command of this Post. My command consists of 4 Co's Inf. (of my Regt), 2 Co's Cavalry and 2 pieces of Artillery.

My Cavalry Picket at Jamesville had a skirmish at Jamesville night before last, wounding one or two Yankees and capturing a Burnside Rifle. I went down with a reinforcement of Cavalry but the enemy were beyond pursuit. A Gunboat comes up by the Picket occasionally. I expected them to shell Williamston on yesterday but they did not. All the woman and children left the town. I had to press a wagon from Gen'l Stubbs * to move some torpedoes out of town which the inefficiency of our Naval Dep't permits to remain there when they ought to be in the River. Should the Gunboats stay up the River long enough next time to allow me to put my Artillery in position on the Bluff below Jamesville I intend to attack them on their return. I may be fortunate.

I sent up an application for 18 days leave of absence some 6 or 7 days since. As it has not returned I suppose it must have been App'd and forwarded to Gen'l Lee. If so I hope to be home shortly.

I am anxious to get a position on the Staff of some Gen'l in the Army of No. Va. I shall have a chance of promotion there. Whereas here old Gen'l Holmes would probably oppose my being promoted to Lt. Col. should a vacancy occur and besides I do not like to be under the Offr's I have over me. I do everything nearly that is done for the Regt. and get no thanks or credit for it. I am tired of the concern.

* Jesse R. Stubbs, Brigadier General of North Carolina Militia for the defense of Roanoke River.

RECOMMENDATION OF THOMAS BRAGG TO PRESIDENT DAVIS

Raleigh, Dec. 7th, 1864

This will be handed to you by Major Clark of the Pro. Army—He is the son of David Clark, an Extensive Roanoke planter of Halifax Co. and one of our best & most respected citizens—Young Clark was for three years a Cadet at the Hillsboro Military Academy in this State, and also graduated with much distinction at our University, read law and obtained license to practice—He entered the Army at the outset of the War & has seen much service—He was in Pettigrew's Regt. one of the best in the service, of which he was Adjutant, and has on several occasions, especially at Sharpsburg received the warmest commendations "for marked & distinguished gallantry"—A friend of his informs me that he desires to make the profession of army a permanent one and to be appointed a captain in the regular Army—I take pleasure in recommending him to your favorable considerations as a young man of decided merit, adding that his moral character & deportment have been uniformly good & that he is of the strictest sobriety and steadiness of behaviour.

RECOMMENDATION OF THE NORTH CAROLINA LEGISLATURE TO PRESIDENT DAVIS

Dec. 8, 1864

We respectfully recommend for appointment to the position of Captain in the regular Army of the Confederate States, Maj. W. McK. Clark of Halifax County, North Carolina: Maj Clark was for three years a cadet in the military academy at Hillsboro. Immediately on the secession of this State he entered the military service: He served in "61 in the Regiment. Commanded by the lamented Pettigrew to the entire satisfaction of that distinguished officer. The Maryland Campaign of "62 found him Adjutant of the Regiment commanded by Col (now Brig Genl) Matt. W. Ransom. On the field of Sharpsburg he elicited the warmest commendation of Genl Robt Ransom (then commanding his Brigade) for marked and distinguished gallantry. He at present holds the position of Major in the Provisional Army: Major Clark is a young man of fine talents and great moral worth and is a member of one of the most widely extended and influential families in the State: It [is] his desire to make arms his profession: The disruption of the old union alone prevented his completing his military

To

His Excellency President Davis

We respectfully recommend for appointment to the position of Captain in the regular army of the Confederate States, Maj Wm Mch. Clark of Halifax County, North Carolina. Maj Clark was for three years a cadet in the military academy at Hillsboro. Immediately on the secession of this State he entered the military service. He served in '61 in the Regiment Commanded by the lamented Pettigrew to the entire satisfaction of that distinguished officer. The Maryland Campaign of '62 found him Adjutant of the Regiment Commanded by Col (now Brig Genl) Matt. W. Ransom. On the field of Sharpsburg he elicited the warmest commendation of Genl Robt Ransom (then Commanding his Brigade) for marked and distinguished gallantry. He at present holds the position of Major in the Provisional Army. Major Clark is a young man of fine talents and great moral worth and as a member of one of the most widely extended and influential families in the State. It his desire to make arms his profession. The disruption of the old union alone prevented his completing his military education at the National Military Academy. He graduated at the University of North Carolina with the highest honors of the institution and was prepared for the practice of Law by Judge Battle of the Supreme Court.

Raleigh N.C.
December 8th 1864

Senate

M L Wiggins
W. Harris
Jesse H. Powell
W B Wright
A. F. Patterson
Saml. C. Bryson
Robt. P. Dick
M. L. McCorkle
C. S. Winstead
Wm Long
Wm. M. Greer
[illegible]
[illegible]
[illegible]
W. B. March
[illegible] Ellis
Wm T. Bagley
[illegible] Barrow

Giles Mebane S.S.
Thos B. Adams
E. A. Blount
R. W. Lassiter
John L. Bow[illegible]
W. D. Jones
Jonathan Horton
Thos J. [illegible]
George N. Lewis
H. Adams
Wm C. Smith
[illegible]
John Pool
R. S. Donnell
S.H.C.

Commons

H. Powell
Wm T. [illegible]
A. H. Davis
Thos J. [illegible]
M. Crawford
[illegible]
[illegible]
S. A. Powell
W. L. Brown
John R. Cowles
Paul F. Faison
[illegible]
W. P. Reinhardt
A. Costner
Saml L. Love
J. W. [illegible]
Allen W. Wooten
Zacheus Smith
J. H. K. Davis

Wm. H. Horton
G. H. [illegible]
C. S. Rogers
[illegible] West
C. Perkins
J. M. [illegible]
E. E. [illegible]
Danl. [illegible] Fowle
D. McLauren
S. D. Pool
B. F. [illegible]
E. J. Harrington
L. C. Benbury
[illegible]
J. M. [illegible]
J. C. [illegible]
[illegible] Horton
J. T. Henry
S. F. Phillips
J. H. [illegible]
J. H. Riddick
~~[illegible]~~
~~[illegible]~~

[illegible] committee
James Bond
Richd. H. Bond
Wm. F. [illegible]
[illegible] Patterson
D. McLaurin
S. S. Harrison
M. McGehee
W. A. Smith
J. S. A[illegible]
R. H. M[illegible]
[illegible] Cobb
L. A. Vann
[illegible]
G. [illegible]
Henry C. Gibbs

Ex. Dept. of N.C.
Raleigh Dec. 8th
I very cordially concur in this recommendation. Young Clark is esteemed a very promising & meritorious officer & I would be greatly pleased at his promotion.

Z B Vance

Governor & Legislature of N.C.
Dec 8th 1864

education at the National Military Academy: He graduated at the University of North Carolina with the highest honors of the institution and was prepared for the practice of Law by Judge Battle of the Supreme Court.

[Signatures of all members of the legislature follow as shown in the accompanying facsimile.]

Ex. Dep^{t}. of N. C.
Raleigh Dec. 8th

I very cordially concur in this recommendation. Young Clark is esteemed a very promising & meritorious officer & I would be greatly pleased at his promotion—

Z. B. Vance

RECOMMENDATION OF THE HONORABLE WM. A. GRAHAM *
TO PRESIDENT DAVIS

Dec 12th 1864
Richmond

I beg leave to add my recommendation to many testimonials of qualification of Walter McKinsey Clark for the appointment of Captain in the regular army—He is a native and citizen of North Carolina, and was educated at the University—has been in military service in the present war in which he has acquired considerable distinction—

TO CLARK FROM JONATHAN CHARLES

January 15—1865

Majer Clarke my dear sur I take this opportunity to inform yo that I recevd a letter from R I Wagner stating that my son L M Charles was left at the Camp near hamelton verry sick and no wone to tend to him but Wagner he rote to me by his reqest for me to Cum and se to him an bring him sum Clothing an sumthing to eat I fixet up as quick as I Cud it Cammest rainning an raind all nite an all next day I started the 11 am went to lexington thru the mud knee deep tha informed me that the bac rode briges was all swep a way so i Cud not go I regret verry much that he was not sent to Raleigh or greensbury hospittle whar he Cud a had medical attendance an sumthing fit for a sick person to eat an & bed to keep him warm if he is destitute of Clothing tel i Can Cum an bring him sum I want you to help him to get a

* North Carolina member of Confederate Senate and father-in-law of Clark.

furlo and send him home as quickly as he is able to Cum an if he is not able have him sent to Raleigh hospittle petagrue No 13 whare he was before Majer I want you to anser this letter as soon as you Can fale not

Martin you must take as good Care of yore self as possible an tri an git well and Cum home wonst more and rite as quick as you git this letter so I will no whare you are I must Close for the present

TO CLARK FROM HIS MOTHER

Jan 16th 1865

. . . We had quite a quiet time of it Christmas—Your Pa came up to spend Christmas with us, but heard Friday night that the Yanks were coming up the river, so he went down the next day & had his hogs driven up, & some corn hauled the next week—It was quite a relief to us all I assure you, when we heard they had been repulsed (the Yanks I mean) & then had two-fold gratification in hearing of their repulse at Wilmington also—I understand they are about to make a second attack on Wilmington & hope they will meet a similar fate— . . .

[P.S.]
Little Pat went to prayers for you two or three times, when she heard the Yankees were fighting where you were— . . . Your Uncle Plum lost 8 negroes at the salt works—The Yanks took them—

—Your Uncle Tom says the Yanks will whip us—*both,* dear, I think perfectly absurd.

TO CLARK FROM HIS AUNT MARTHA

Feb 4" / 65

I received a letter from your Mother requesting me to send you some rhubarb pills and some rhubarb syrup. Dr Hale has none of the syrup but he has promised to send you by mail today a box of pills. I have been waiting several days for an opportunity to send them by some person but as none offers I concluded to send them by mail thinking you might, if I waited longer, not have the *pleasure* of taking them before you recovered. I wished very much to send you something to eat but fear unless you send up that you will not get anything. It is not to far for Neverson to come and go in a day—why not send him when you get *hungry* for something different from your camp fare.

...I hope the rumours of recognition and peace may bring more important results than they have heretofore—We have a society for hunting soldiers sacks and if the men of your regiment are needy please write me immediately.

TO CLARK FROM HIS MOTHER

Feb 6th 1865

...I have a shirt ready for you & am waiting an opportunity to send it—If I do not hear from you, will send it to your Aunt Martha Clark's, day after tomorrow, when your Pa goes down—Also more shirts for Neverson—I only made one for you that I might know how you liked the fashion, before I make more—Always wear your flannel when it is cold—If you have not recovered from the disease you had, let me know immediately & I will send you some knit (woolen) shirts to wear next to your skin & I think they will be very beneficial—Your Pa came up last Wednesday—He does not seem in very good spirits about the war—I felt right much encouraged at one time about peace when I heard so many rumors of England & the United States going to war—But since our Commissioners * have gone to Washington, all seems veiled in mystery—I still pray & hope tho' for peace—Nothing new—...

TO CLARK FROM HIS MOTHER

Feb 9th 1865

I wrote you on the 6th that your Pa expected to go down the country Wednesday & that I would send you a shirt & so on, but the weather has been so bad, that he will not go until sometime next week—I hope the wagons will be up the last of this week however—I can then send you two shirts & the books you wrote for—Your letter of the 28th Jan reached me this morning & the one dated Feb 2nd (the one that I wrote you was misplaced or returned to the Office) came to hand Tuesday (day before yesterday)—I am glad that your health has improved—You must try & take care of it for your Mother's sake, if nothing else—The shirts I send are made of different material & the bosoms are little different, so you must let me know which you like best, as I have some more in hand for you—These have been much admired—Your Pa likes them very much—They are much like some that I saw Gail

* This apparently refers to the Hampton Roads Conference, February 3, 1865.

have—I have not yet pleated a piece of silk to make you a cravat—Mollie Hawkins promised to make a pretty one for you—Your Aunt Tups has been working hard on Col Armistead's gloves—I hope she will finish them in time to send with your things—I hope the Col will be promoted this time, if not, I believe it will all happen right—Do your whole duty & leave all wants to God—He [sees] all things & has promised that all things shall work together for good to those who love & trust him—You should pray for a believing, trusting, loving head my child & the Lord will never leave thee nor forsake thee—Be steadfast in Christ—unwavering in your faith in God & show your faith by obeying his commands—Never for a moment let the evil one get the advantage of you, to lead you into any violation of God's commands—The way of the transgressor is hard—We cannot any of us be *too watchful,* my child, so you must not think it attributable of any want of confedence, that I admonish you so often. I know the evil one is like a rearing lion, going about seeking whom he may devour, & I never want any of my children to get into his clutches—If we yield an inch to him, he will take an ell. So never make an acquaintance with his Majesty, through king alcohol, gambling, or any other vicious habit—You have had this long, free from all these bad habits & I trust & pray the Lord may give you strength, so to be to the end of your days (& may they be three score & ten) & then when you grow old, you can look back on your past life with peaceful tranquility—I imagine I see you smile as you read these lines, at Ma's useless anxiety (as you think) about you—But the bible you know, tells us, when we think we are strong, take heed lest ye fall & human nature is weak & you are surrounded by many temptations & ought to pray for much grace. . . . We have just heard of the return of our Commissioners, having effected nothing—No news in this part of the world. . . .

TO CLARK FROM HIS MOTHER

March 2nd 1865 Airlie

I am expecting Neverson today or tomorrow—However will write you a few lines by mail & enclose a private letter from Genl Lee to his Son, which breathes so much the sentiments of my own heart, that I wish you to read it attentively & treasure the advice, as if it came from your own parents, to you, for I certainly endorse the whole & hope you will profit by it—It never does any harm to read good advice & particularly when it emanates from such a noble speciman of humanity as Genl Lee—I hope to have your things all ready for Neverson—Have not yet received your boots, but Johnson said they would be done last week—If Neverson comes today, I will send Tony up for them tomorrow, as Neverson would have to rest his horse one day—I will send you some money if you need it—Let me know right away—Your Pa has'nt come yet—The wagons came up yesterday—All again quiet on the river—Young Mr. Slade from Lee's Army called here yesterday & he says the negroes in Va, a good many of them, are high up for going in the Army—I wouldn't be surprised (from paper accounts) if they put them in—I trust & pray we may have such a decisive victory over Sherman that we will not need the negroes, for I cant think they will be available in the Army— . . . I understand the Yanks are sending out recruits to get up negro soldiers, down the country & they are paid so much for everyone they carry in & those that wont fight they ship to Cuba & sell them—I see Singleton has gone to Richmond again—I dont understand it—I hope this will find you well & in good spirits—It is a Christian privilege to be happy at any place & under all circumstances—Try to keep a conscience void of offense to God & man & you will be happy—It is a great cross to be denied the pleasure of your company at home, but as long as I feel that you are at your post & doing your duty, I can be reconciled—It is certainly every man's duty to aid in the defence of his country now—The Lord grant us success—There are many prayers uplifted to Heaven, from the lips of poor feeble women in behalf of her bleeding country—It is her only weapon & may it have an effectual use in aiding our Husbands & Sons & Brothers to give us independence—Nature has denied us the right & strength to join in battle but our hearts & prayers are there ever—Put your trust in God my child, through the words of Christ—He is all powerful—The Yanks may outnumber us, but if we can secure God's favor, they will never prevail—All of you, in the Army who are professing christians should let your light shine & exert an influence for good—Try to win men over to the right way, influencing them to forsake evil—"He that turneth one sinner from the error of his ways, hideth a multitude of faults"—I am glad you are pleasantly situated—But from what I can learn there is a wicked state of society around Kinston & many snares to entrap a young man—Pray to God for grace to strengthen you in every time of need— . . .

CLARK TO HIS MOTHER

Camp 4 miles North of Smithfield.
Mar 27th 1865

Our Brigade was engaged in the battles of the 19th, 20th & 21st at Bentonville.* The Main fight was on Sunday (19)th when we attacked two Corps of Sherman's Army before the rest had come up and drove the Yanks two miles. On Monday they were reinforced and were the attacking party. They attempted to swing round our left (of which our Division formed the extreme left). They were well repulsed. On Tuesday they attempted to swing still farther round to the left and had got nearly thro' when Cheatham's † Corps which had just arrived on the field of battle met and drove them back taking some prisoners. Tuesday night we fell back beyond the creek. Wednesday we fell back to the Neuse & Thursday to our present Camp 7 miles north of Neuse on Louisburg Road. During the battles & the retreat I had no means to write and since then I have been too sick from the exposure—it was raining nearly all the time—I incurred during them. Since we have been in camp I have been confined to bed until to-day.

The Enemy at Bentonville were badly off for Provisions. His troops had positively nothing but parched corn. As to his animals that his Q.M. acounted were so fat when we captured some Artillery the horses were actually too poor to pull the pieces off. We captured about three hundred mules & horses all in same condition. Our teams are in better order than I ever saw them I think.

I commanded the Skirmish line of our Brigade on Monday. It was in a good wood for skirmishing with little or no undergrowth. We had a regular Indian fight of it behind trees. They charged my line twice but were both times driven back. That night the whole skirmish line kept up an almost continuous firing as they expected our Army to leave. That together with the scamps trying to creep up on us in the dark kept us up all night.

I suppose Neverson told you that my shirts suited me exactly. They are very pretty and have been much admired.

My Box came just in the nick of time and was I think the best you ever sent me. At least it seemed so while it lasted. I can't imagine where you got so many eggs. Not *one* of them was broken. I intended to have written you a long letter about the box shirts

* The last major engagement of the war in North Carolina.

† Major General Benjamin F. Cheatham of Tennessee.

&c but we have been moving so constantly and the wagons and generally been at the rear—besides no way to send letters—that I haven't had a chance....

Gen Hoke * complimented our Brigade *very highly*. Our loss 40 or 50....

TO CLARK FROM HIS FATHER

Littleton
30 March 1865

We have heard nothing of [you] since Neverson left & cannot know if he has returned to camp or not. I was ordered up to Raleigh last week & went up on Monday where I found they had no use for *me* & it seemed doubtful if they had for any of the others who were also ordered up there. Some of the Home Guard officers seem to think that organization a force & have come to my conclusion that the Militia alone should be organized & put on a war footing as Minute Men (Mounted) I think it would be well if the State could do this & set us to work, there is much work such a force could do & relieve Jonsons † troops, such as Depot Guards. To take up straglers, outer Guards to points not very important & upon a pinch to dismount & fight when there would probably be no men nearing—If not put to such work they should protect the farmers from the depredations of straglers for the amount of these rascals is causing immense damage to the cause. Men are actually afraid to leave home as they do not know at what time the plunderers might come & strip their families of everything, leaving them without anything to eat & nothing to look forward to as they take every horse & mule—People cannot send supplies for they cannot know into what hands the wagons & teams might fall even in a few miles of Home. If a stop is not put to these robbers whole Counties will go over to the Federals in sullen submission I think in such a time as this the State should resume her right over her people & put in the Militia every able bodied confederate exempt. RR Men &c so that all should assume service in cause.

I am just ready to plant corn & if it was not raining should plant today. All are well but your Ma & she is improving. Your Cousin Ed Nicholson was killed last Saturday at Petersburg. Robt Alston mortally wounded....

* Major General Robert F. Hoke of Lincoln County.
† General Joseph E. Johnston.

I expect to go to the plantation in a few days but as yet have here much of anything I shall find there. for I understand that the feds have an idea of trying to get the negroes to Volunteer. this will give them another fright or excuse to go to the Yankees instead of adding to an army [which] will strengthen them. If the Federals had the appointing of men & direction of affairs they could not have done more for our injury than we have ourselves. I do not know of a single measure that has not been wrong—that has not been persisted in when they saw it was usery or else attempted to patch up with something that was worse. Our officials have never turned back & tried to get in the right road When we begin to strip the speculators, beat drunken officers & place both in the ranks I then shall have a shadow of a hope & if such a course should be continued in I will feel sure of quiescence—without such action I can not see what good success would be to the people. Many a noble fellow is dying for the benefit of these *rascals*. . . .

CLARK TO HIS MOTHER

Camp near Smithfield
April 7th 1865

. . . It was rumored here a day or two since that the Yanks had Weldon. I am glad to see in yesterday's paper that it is not so. I would not be surprised however if they have it before the Month of April is out. Our situation—not on any leading roads—will protect us some but if they come expect to be pretty well pillaged—especially of valuables & gentlemen's clothing. It is useless to send things to any point for the place you send them to may be more exposed than home. If they take Weldon & come out any distance it will be for the purpose of going to Warrenton. Or they may cross the fords of the upper Roanoke and come to Warrenton by way of Ridgeway. I do not know when I can come home. If Halifax falls into the enemy's lines it will of course be some time. It is useless to talk at this stage of the War—Slavery is certainly abolished and the only use of the Institution now is to aid us in gaining our Independence—either as soldiers or by making a support for our brave defenders in the field. Since Gen Lee has evacuated Richmond it is impossible to say where our lines may be. All is yet unsettled.

I was much pained to hear of Cousin Ed's * death. It must be a

* Captain Edward Nicholson, cousin of Walter Clark. He and his brother were killed within a few days of each other just before the end of the war.

shock to his family. I was in hopes that it might turn out as it sometimes does that he was a prisoner & wounded but I saw last night a letter from an Officer in that Brigade to an Officer in ours in which he states that Capt Nicholson was struck by a piece of Shell mangling him terribly & causing immediate death. He spoke in the very highest terms of his courage, ability and fidelity as an Officer and stated that his loss was deplored by the entire Brigade. I had been thrown so much with Cousin Ed that his loss seemed nearer to me than almost any one else....

Don't leave home if the Yankees come. There is no place in the Confederacy that they will not enter before the War is over. I can't bear the idea of your being a Refugee. I have seen so much of the misfortunes of that unfortunate Class. They almost always express their regret in leaving home.

CLARK TO HIS MOTHER

Camp near Smithfield N.C.
April 10th 1865.

Your letter of 6th inst. was rec'd yesterday. I heard at the same time by a servant of one of our Officers just from Warrenton that Weldon had been evacuated, the bridge there and at Gaston burnt. That the enemy had been to Garysburg and at St Tammany's—on Roanoke 19 miles from Warrenton—and that hereafter the train would only run to Littleton. As I know not how long the privilege of communication with home may continue I hasten to write by this the first Mail in hopes that it may reach you.

I regret very much that I haven't Fanny with me instead of this horse of Uncle Blake's in order that I might save one more horse for Pa. As it is I have one of his horses here—the one Col Armistead has—. I wrote to Mittie on yesterday although it was Sunday as I then feared an interruption of communications. I wish I had a Cavalry Command so that if—as will be done—we should make raids upon the Yankee communications and detached garrisons I might have a chance to pass through old Halifax once more. Our Army I am glad to say is continually increasing. I do not think affairs can remain in this state of suspense much longer. Something decisive must be done shortly. It is beyond my ken to see any end to the War but while I am able for service I intend to stand by the cause while a banner floats to tell where Freedom and freedom's sons still support her cause. If the South is ever subjugated it is purely and simply the fault of the people. "It is in ourselves and not in our stars, dear Brutus, that we are underlings". In the numerous desertions from our Army and the consequent fall of Richmond & Petersburg we but behold the result of the senseless despondency of our people in /64. If the people are deserving of Freedom, if they are fit to be a Nation the struggle can not but close with the complete success to our Arms.

I was as you said opposed to the passage of the Negro Bill but when that Bill became a Law it was the duty of everyone who recognized the right of Congress to pass a Law, everyone who wished well to the cause and considered our Government a legal government to support the Law that had passed. It then became a mere matter of taste whether one would desire a Commission in these Troops. This I certainly do to being a private tho' I know that on *all* occasions these colored Troops will be placed in the fore front of the battle. The greatest objection to these troops is that they take from the cornfield those who would be more useful as producers than as soldiers. But when a Section of Country is given up to the enemy common sense would say that the negro men should be put into our Army. If left, they do not produce for our Army and but serve to swell the ranks opposed to us. The enemy already have several Camps of Instruction for the negroes in this State. They have formed of them Regts & Brigades that officered by Confederate Officers—men accustomed to govern negroes—should have aided to replant our Standard on the banks of the James. As to their efficiency and courage oppose them to the Yankee negro. Let Negro fight negro. This is an age of progressive ideas and mighty changes. The opinions of a lifetime must now vanish in a day. "The times change and we change with them." In one sense certainly.

Johnson's Army has on its Muster Rolls nearly 175,000 men fit for service. Of this 45,000 are Present. Quite a contrast. Lee's Army I suppose is much the same way.

The consolidation is daily going on [in] this Army. I understand that Gen'l Lee won a glorious Victory on Monday last. Have rec'd no account however.

I suppose that ere this you have concealed all that you think worth the while. Gentlemen's clothing and valuables are most apt to be taken by them. They always search in the garden for concealed thing. When in Fayetteville they fierced all over the garden of Col Broadfoot's mother for valuables but only succeeded in finding a large bowie knife which was concealed there. Not succeeding in finding any valuables in house or garden they gave up pursuit and behaved pretty well. Our Section of Country will not be subjected owing to its situation to the vicinity of any large Armies. The small raiding parties, if they dare trust themselves about in the country will be all that will trouble you and will not do much damage. You can hardly imagine how much the idea of your being in the lines troubles me. I hope Victory will soon enable us to free the State from this plague worse than that of locusts visited upon Egypt in days of old.

Give my love to all and kiss the children for me.

I hope this will be able to reach you. Again much love.

Be sure to write and let me know that you are well. Goodbye.

III

Farmer and Country Lawyer:

A Changed World

1865–1873

WALTER CLARK FACED A changed world when he returned to Ventosa in the spring of 1865. His father's health was ruined, his fortune gone, his home burned, and his hopes blasted. So Walter, the oldest son, accepted the responsibility of supporting a large family from the earnings of the run-down five-thousand-acre plantation. He proved equal to the task. He successfully rehabilitated the plantation and held the family together during this "tragic era."

Shortly before the close of the war, David Clark had given Walter a large plantation, known as Riverside, near New Bern, and he took over the management of this as well as that of Ventosa. Walter kept a diary for the years 1866-1872, which records in somewhat fragmentary fashion the strenuous and varied life of a plantation owner during the years of Reconstruction. On both estates he rebuilt destroyed houses and barns, bought livestock, collected a labor force, and established commercial connections with commission merchants in Norfolk and Baltimore. He kept an itemized account of all receipts and disbursements, now and then noting a cash loan from his uncles, Colin and Ed.

Young Clark refused to be overwhelmed by the numerous problems confronting Southerners of that day. While always interested in the history of the war and devoted to the cause of the Confederate soldiers, he realized that a new order was at hand and that the welfare of North Carolina and the South demanded a changed attitude on the part of the ruling classes. He thought that nothing was to be gained by weeping about the "Lost Cause" or the abolition of slavery.

In November, 1865, Clark began to publish letters in the newspapers, in which he criticized the baneful effects of slavery, urged the importation of free white labor, advocated the industrialization of the South, and pleaded with his fellow Southerners to forget the past and get to work. He insisted that the South must rid itself "of the dead body of slavery, and with it dispose of the perplexing problem of negro suffrage and negro equality forever." He maintained that North Carolina was "penniless, but not poor." All that was needed was competent labor to develop the immense resources of the state and the South, and he insisted that "the broad fertile fields, unexplored mines, unimproved water-power and dwarf cities of North Carolina are imperiously calling for the influx of population." He was particularly interested in the effort of North Carolina to procure immigrants from England, and the Clark Papers contain several interesting letters from the North Carolina Commissioner of Emigration, who had been sent to England for this purpose.

Clark thought that the South had nothing to gain by "styling as Yankee cuteness and cunning" the enterprise and energy in which he thought Southerners were signally lacking. He lamented the "cradle to the grave" dependence of the South upon the North, insisting that there was "but little of the comforts and conveniences, and few even of the necessaries of life for which we are not indebted to that same universal Yankee nation." He maintained that indolence was the besetting sin of the South and insisted that what his state and section needed was work, *work,* WORK. This he considered the "great panacea for all the ills that society is heir to. This will efface the ravages of war, suppress crime, organize and consolidate society, and cover our fields with harvest." He loved to refer to the Northwest as an illustration of what work would do for a region.

He hoped that the North Carolina General Assembly would place a heavy tax on all unimproved land and "either force the proprietors to make them productive of some good to the country at large, or part with them to those who will." This view foreshadowed the single tax theory of Henry George, and, needless to say, was not written into legislation.

Clark thought the South should, so far as consistent with honor, make every attempt to adjust her relations with the United States government. He maintained that politics had been a "fatal trade to us," and he thought the South needed "repose from political excitement." In several articles to the newspapers he sought to encourage the Southern people, imparting to them some of his concepts, ideals, and enthusiasm: "True, however, to the republican faith of our ancestors, we cannot but believe that the masses of the people mean well. They may be mistaken; they may be deceived; they may be misled by designing and unprincipled leaders but sooner or later the popular mind will discover the truth and the great popular heart will throb in unison to the true principles of liberty and right. For the present, however, the will of the predominating section, and with that the policy of the government, has been unmistakably settled. The only course, then, for the South is to develop her resources, encourage immigration, and bide her time."

In February, 1866, Clark became disturbed about the distressing situation at the University of North Carolina, and, in a letter to the press, made clear his views regarding the importance of education and the necessity of the state's supporting both the University and the public schools: "The cause of learning is the cause of civilization. Should North Carolina neglect her University she cannot be expected to provide for her common schools. The plea now abroad to excuse neglect of the one can as easily be urged for the abolition of the other." He believed that the University was the natural head of the state's school system.

In August, 1866, Clark decided to continue his study of law, since he was still too young to be admitted to the bar. He went to New York City to "see how the Yankees did it," and while there studied law and business. Then he studied for a short time at the Columbian Law School in Washington, D.C. In January, 1867, though not yet twenty-one, he was admitted to the practice of law in Halifax County and opened an office in Scotland Neck. Upon becoming of age he was licensed by the Supreme Court of North Carolina as a full-fledged lawyer, and his diary and letters disclose that he was soon employed as counsel in many cases. Within two years he transferred his law practice to Halifax and formed a partnership under the name of Clark & Mullen. His diary makes mention of arguing many cases before the Supreme Court, five in one session.

Fewer letters have been preserved for these years than for any other period of Clark's long and busy career. There is adequate material, however, to show that he was becoming well known as a planter and lawyer. In 1869, the University of North Carolina conferred upon him the degree of Master of Arts, and in 1870 he was chosen director of the Raleigh and Gaston Railroad. Two years later he was sent to Atlanta by Governor Tod R. Caldwell as a delegate to the convention of Southern representatives who were contemplating the construction of the Atlantic and Great Western Canal.

In the summer of 1871 Clark made an extended tour of the West, visiting practically all of the cities from Chicago, Indianapolis, and Detroit, to Omaha, St. Louis, Denver, Salt Lake City, and San Francisco. In a series of twenty-six lengthy articles, signed "Notes by the Way," printed in the *Roanoke News* (Weldon, N. C.), he gave excellent descriptions of the above cities and various other places visited, such as Mammoth Cave, Yellowstone, Yosemite, and Pike's Peak. He commented on agriculture, industry, education, churches, Indians, buffalo, Chinese in California, and many other things which attracted his attention. He was lavish in his praise of Western railroads and eloquent in his accounts of the phenomenal progress being made in various portions of the "Great West." He expressed the hope that his own South would awake from its lethargy and keep pace with the progress which he observed in the West.

Clark's criticism of the old order naturally aroused resentment in certain quarters. One of these letters gave offense to H. P. Pugh, who answered it with a letter to the *Norfolk Journal,* signed "Veritas." In this he reflected upon the author of the first-named article. Clark resented these aspersions and demanded an apology. When Pugh refused to apologize, Clark challenged him to a duel. The correspondence printed in this chapter throws light on this controversy and indicates the ultimate settlement without resort to arms.

DIARIES KEPT BY WALTER CLARK, 1866-1868 *

1866

Jan. 1—Left home this morning for my Newbern place.

Jan. 3—Walked over my plantation.

Jan. 4 & 5—Made purchases for plantation.

Feb. 8—About twelve o'clock started for Newbern plantation with 2 mules, 1 horse, 2 oxen, cow and calf. Six miles from Washington, N.C. on Saturday got on steamer "Bettie". After various adventures finally got a pilot and reached the plantation near Newbern at midnight Feb. 11—found things much upset.

Feb. 18—Discharged every hand I had.

Feb. 19—Got other hands.

March 20—The deed for my Newbern place dates from today.

March 25—Cousin Ed [Nicholson] killed a year ago today.

April 2—Cousin Will [Nicholson] was killed a year ago today.

May 2—One year ago today I started from the Army.

May 3—Letter from overseer on Plantation requires me to go down there at once.

May 7—One year ago today I reached home from the Army.

* The following extracts from Clark's diaries were prepared for publication by his daughter, Mrs. J. Ernest Ervin, formerly Susan Washington Clark.

May 15—Went to Plantation (Ventosa). At Enfield Dr. Joyner told me of my appointment as Col. and A.D.C. to Gov. Worth.*

May 22—In Raleigh called on Gov. Worth.

August 13—Left home for New York via Norfolk, Old Bay Line to Baltimore, Washington, Philadelphia and reached New York August 16 midnight. Entered Law Office of Messrs. Weeks and Foster, 58 Wall St. as Columbia Law College was not yet open.

August 19—My birthday. 20 years old.

August 20—Purchased Life Ticket in the Commercial College of Bryan, Stratton & Co.

Sept. 12—Called at Law Office and took my leave. Balance of my stay will devote myself to the Commercial College.

Sept. 20—Left New York on Steamer El Cid for Newbern at 1 P.M. Lay at Sandy Hook at anchor all night on account of stormy weather outside.

Sept. 23—Reached Hatteras at 10 A.M. and Newbern 7 P.M. Reached my farm next day. Put up machinery.

Oct. 10—This evening cut my hand in gin.

Oct. 16—Went to Newbern. Made arrangements about cotton. Had my finger dressed.

Oct. 22—Started for Airlie. At Goldsboro on sleeping car for first time.

Oct. 29—Went to Washington to enter Law School. Got room for $12 for month at 444 Eleventh Street.

Nov. 7—Entered Commercial College.

Dec. 5—Tonight was senior counsel for the plaintiff in the Moot Court. My first argument in a Law Case.

Dec. 12—Took my leave of the Law School.

Dec. 18—Got my diploma at Commercial College.

Dec. 20—Left by night boat for home. Christmas at home.

Dec. 27—Left by train for Newbern and plantation.

Dec. 31—Paid off hands. Hired four of them for another year. In review of the year I have much cause to be thankful. The Lord be praised for his manifold mercies.

* Jonathon Worth of Randolph County, Governor, 1865-1868.

1867

Jan. 7—Commenced work for year burning brush at Big Neck field.

Jan. 11—At home [Airlie].

Jan. 12—Went to Raleigh and on Monday the 14th got County Court License.

Jan. 14—Wouldn't let me stand for my Superior Court License.*

Jan. 16—Went back to Newbern and plantation.

Feb. 7—Took Cousin Sallie Nicholson to school at Hillsboro.

Feb. 18—At Halifax Court—Sworn in as Attorney at Law.

Feb. 26—Attended Warren Court.

April 17—Went to Littleton and sent off Ma's sewing machine to New York to be repaired.

April 24—Went to Newbern and plantation. Commenced planting cotton.

May-June—I am with the hands all day. Much trouble with hands.

July 9—Went to Newbern on way home to Airlie.

July 14—Started for Plantation on River (Ventosa).

Oct. 19—Sent 5 bales cotton to town—first shipment. Sick with chills.

Nov. 25—Cotton crop very short. Gloomy times with me. I trust to God.

Nov. 29—Finished reading Bible through 2nd time. 1st time was with Ma years ago. Oh happy days. Will I be happy like it again in this world?

Nov. 30—Commenced reading Bible through 3rd time.

Dec. 25—Spent Christmas at Newbern plantation.

Dec. 27—Received letter from Ma to come home.

Dec. 31—Rainy and blowing. The year has passed. It has not been a prosperous one but it might have been worse. I thank the Lord for His mercies and invoke His blessings for another year.

* Clark was not yet twenty-one.

1868

Jan. 1—May it be a prosperous year! Settling with my hands. Hired a new overseer.

Jan. 7—Mr. Armes takes charge for year [as overseer].

Jan. 9—Waiting for hands.

Jan. 14—In Raleigh. I get my Superior Court License. Snowing and sleeting.

Jan. 15—Great difficulty in getting hands.

Feb. 20—Left for Baltimore. Couldn't get hands so left for New York at 7 P.M.

Feb. 21—Arrived at N.Y. 6 A.M. Stopped at Tremont House. Snowing hard. Travelled about in city on business.

Feb. 26—Went to Randall's Island and got an apprentice. At 3 P.M. started home on steamer with 4 hands and 1 boy.

Feb. 27—Spent night at Fort Monroe.

Feb. 28—Reached home with my men.

March 2—Went to Halifax and then to Norfolk.

March 7—Went to Ventosa Plantation to settle with hands.

April 1—Started for Newbern Plantation.

April 8—Took train and went to Norfolk.

April 10—Went to Airlie.

April 16—Went to Ventosa Plantation.

April 20—Went to Halifax Superior Court.

April 21—Came back to Uncle Colin's as Court adjourns the 3 days of election.

April 22—Went down to Plantation & came near being drowned swimming my horse across swamp.

April 23—On plantation.

April 24—Went back to Court.

April 25—Went home.

April 27—Came down to Halifax with Pa to meet Negroes before Freedmen's Bureau.

May 3—Went to Plantation and stayed til May 18th.

May 16—Freshet rising.

May 17—Freshet very high.

May 18—Freshet falling—Swam my horse out—staid night at Uncle Colin's.

May 19—Got up to Court and arranged matters with Freedmen's Bureau.

May 26—Went up to Warren Court and staid all night with Aunt Mabb.

June 2—Went to Ventosa Plantation.

July 2—Went to Enfield on horseback to take train for Newbern. Got left by being in Whitaker's Office talking.

July 4—Staid with Chestnut all night. Next day he carried me down to farm in his buggy. Crop miserable. Cotton not even all chopped over.

July 6—Hire Taylor who comes down and takes charge. I discharge Armes.

July 16—Went up home.

July 24—Went to Plantation [Ventosa.] Raining—River rising.

July 28—Halifax Court. Couldn't get back to Plantation on account of freshet.

Aug. 3—Rode over plantation. Freshet did not do as much damage as I feared.

Sept. Trips to Petersburg and Norfolk on business.

Sept. 23—Go to Ventosa Plantation.

Oct. 6—Took steamer at Hill's Ferry and go down to Williamston Court.

Oct. 8—Back home at night & find boy with news of Uncle Colin's death. I go immediately.

Oct. 10—Burial took place at 3 P.M. W.R. Smith read the Burial Service.

Nov. 3—*Presidential Election.* Fix up 5th shovel on Sulky Plow—Go out to Election. Vote for the first time in my life.

Nov. 4—Very sick but I come up to Court.

Nov. 5—Leggett (my client in murder case) gets up to my room this morning. Have him bailed this evening.

Nov. 11—Leggett's trial (my first capital case) comes on. Submit the case without argument. W.A. Jenkins and myself for prisoner. Leggett cleared.

Nov. 17—Went to Spruill's and arranged Pa's matters with him. Went to see Mrs. Powell on business.

Nov. 28—Went to Palmyra Meeting for formation of new county.

Dec. 25—At home. Pleasant time. In evening all but myself and Cousin Temp go to the party at Mrs. Cooks.

CLARK TO HIS FATHER

Washington D.C.
Monday—Oct 23rd 1865.

I arrived here yesterday morning from Baltimore. I shall probably be here three or four days. After being at the expense of coming here it is best to go through with the matter. I saw Chandler in Norfolk. He said he had done *nothing* because he received a letter that you were to meet him in Washington. From what I can learn of your application for the return of your Boats is entertained the matter will be referred to Norfolk for investigation. This will simplify matters as you can prove the identity of the vessels there by witnesses on the spot. Chandler will arrive here this evening and I will go with him to see the Secr'y of War myself. Your application for Pardon I placed in the hands of the State Agent—Dr Powell—to whom I had a letter from Gov. Holden. He said that he would do all he could to *hasten* the matter. As it has to go through several Offices it will take two or three days for me to get it. It is necessary for me to have it to procure your Boats as their value alone would prove you to be in the $20,000 clause and it would be equivalent to proving a negative to attempt to prove to the Depts here that you were worth $20,000 and did *not* come within that clause.

Taylor was not in Norfolk—neither was Kader Biggs & Joe Biggs was sick. One bale of your Cotton had been sold at 25¢. I had the other two sold at 26¢. All the Merchants I spoke to thought that I had done the best that the market would justify. *Good* cotton was then at 53 *falling*. The three Bales averaged about 455 apiece and deducting the charges against you which I think somewhat large—174.00—the balance due you was $175.00 which I have with me.

In New Bern I saw Mr Lehman (lawyer) and got the order for the restoration of the land down there. His charges were quite moderate for his services—$15. They have three lines of Steamers running from New Bern to Norfolk. One line of Steamers and one of Sailing Vessels from New Bern to New York. The competition between the New and Old Line on James River is getting interesting. The day I passed through Norfolk the Old line reduced the fare (which I believe before opposition started was $6) from Richmond to Norfolk to 25 cts. The New Line not to be outdone came down *gratis* and sent a herald through the Streets with a general invitation for a *free* ride.

The Prices of *everything* remind one of Confederate times. Everything is at two or three prices....

LETTER TO THE "DAILY SENTINEL" (RALEIGH), NOVEMBER 30, 1865

WHITE LABOR IN NORTH CAROLINA

When the immortal Galileo forced by the bigotry of the age in which he lived to recant his heretical doctrine of the revolution of the world on its axis, was on his bended knees before the reverend father he suddenly paused in his recantation and sternly striking his bosom cried, *"But it does move though."* Yes, the world moves. The car of progress is moving on. The wilderness which but a few short years ago resounded with the cry of the panther and the war whoop of the savage now blossoms as the rose of the valley, and echoes with the loud hum of commerce. The basin of the Mississippi, and valley of the Lakes has become the seat of a mighty nation. Rolling on, the stream of civilization has leveled forests, and opened itself a way through the eternal barriers of the Rocky Mountains. On the golden sands of the Pacific the industry of the white man has found a home, in the trackless wilds of nature, he has created an empire. To any one who thinks at all the question must occur why is it that the cold bleak prairies of the North West should be overspread with cities and villages, and why is it that the still colder and the far off districts of Washington, Idaho and Montana should attract the stream of population, while our own sunny South with its streams, its valleys and its mountains with the finest lands and the loveliest climate of any country on the globe, should stand still in the march of improvement. The answer is found in the words of a distinguished man, "But for the incubus of African slavery," said he, "Virginia would today have been richer than New York." The force of circumstances has at length burst the chain that bound us. The cause that turned the fertilizing stream from our doors to that of our less favored neighbors and sent our youth, our talent and our enterprise to seek a field in the far West has ceased to exist. I am far from approving the means by which this has been accomplished, but the deed has been one of mercy in disguise. The South has awakened from her long lethargy. She has come out of the fiery ordeal of war penniless but not poor. For how can that nation be poor which has the soil upon which is grown two most important products—cotton and tobacco—for a supply of which the entire world looks almost to her alone. With thousands of miles of seacoast, with hundreds of harbors and navigable rivers, with millions of fertile acres, and with an untarnished record for the past and hope for the future how can such a country be poor?

The South during four years of a struggle unparalleled in history, has lost hundreds of thousands of her laborers, white and black, and when we take into consideration the decrease in the amount of work that will be performed by the negro under the new order of things, we may feel safe in saying, *the South is to-day minus one half of her labor*. Whence is this deficit to be supplied? She has millions upon millions of acres as virgin to the plough as when "the Indian warrior wooed his dusky maid" in the depths of her forests. Whence the labor by which they are to be cultivated? She has unrivalled water power, sites for harbors, cities and towns, the finest rivers of the continent and mines of inexhaustible store. Whence are these to be founded, and those to be made to subserve the grand purpose of the general welfare? No one expects that the negro will perform these grand purposes. No one anticipates that year after year, century after century the negro will remain here among us with a status undefined and a destiny unrecognisable. No, the white laborer *must* come here, sooner or later, he *must* come, and unless we are recreant to ourselves and country, he will come *now*.

The South has fought for independence. She has failed. When the South has put white laborers in her valleys, her mountains, her mines and her workshops, when her hillsides are dotted with homesteads, her water courses with manufactories, her valleys with cities and her harbors with shipping, I care not what flag shall float over her capitols, *the South will be independent*. When this is done, though her arms have failed, her independence will have been accomplished. Without this no matter what her arms might have achieved, she never, never could have been free, prosperous, happy or *independent*. Particularly do these remarks apply to North Carolina. Her immense resources are unknown, her mines unexplored, her lands uncultivated, and herself unappreciated. The white laborer is at your command. Wealth is in your lap. Bring him here, develop your resources, work your mines, till your lands and build your towns. The State is crying for capital! capital! Bring the labor here, put it to work, and a single year will bring a return of wealth that will set all the wheels of commerce a-going. The negro cannot live among us in the present state of things. *The proclamation of his freedom was the death knell of his race*. Like the red man of the forest, "he must read his destiny in the setting sun." Slavery is dead, let us rid us ourselves of the dead carcass. Let us bring white labor here and capital will follow. In Texas this year they have raised large cotton crops solely with whites. Next year we must do so in North Carolina. When our people appreciate their interest in this matter, and *act* upon it, then will our State take her stand where she was in 1790, and where she ought to be now—among the *first* on the roll of States. Our valleys will teem with population, our people be laden with wealth, our villages will become towns, and our towns will become cities, we will have weight at the ballot box and on the "field of bayonets", and will indeed become "A POWER IN THE STATE."

CAMILLUS.

Halifax County, N. C. Nov. 30th 1865.

LETTER TO "THE STANDARD," DECEMBER 2, 1865

THE INTRODUCTION OF WHITE LABOR

One hundred years ago Thomas Jefferson said: "It is written in the book of fate that the negro must be free, and it is also as certainly written there that the two races cannot live together in peace and equality." These were remarkable words. Five years ago, who among us would have believed his prediction in regard to the first? Who now disbelieves the second? The negro has fulfilled his mission. He must now pass from the stage. We must rid ourselves of the dead body of slavery, and with it dispose of the perplexing questions of negro suffrage and negro equality forever. Thus we must cut the gordian knot which cannot be untied.

The State has just emerged from a fiery ordeal. We are penniless, but not poor. We need but labor to develop our immense resources hitherto unappreciated because, to a great extent, they were unknown. Within our borders are almost everything to constitute a great State. We have fertile lands, navigable rivers, inexhaustible mines, and a brave and generous people. We need *labor* to develop these resources and improve the advantages which nature and nature's God has so lavishly bestowed upon us. To do this, however, the labor must be *certain*. The conduct of the newly emancipated freedman is a question yet to be solved by the future. The prosperity of a great State should not depend upon a contingency. North Carolina will not, cannot leave her future to the guardianship of the freed-negro.

The freedmen have almost universally, so far, exhibited antipathy to the cultivation of cotton. They solved the question in Texas by raising a fine crop this year, with German laborers. Even South-Carolina has entered the market and demands white labor to re-build her deserted cities, cultivate her fields, efface the ravages of war, and replace her household gods in her desolated homes. There is no State South, perhaps, that is more calculated by climate, by the simplicity of her customs and by her freedom from anything like an aristocracy, for the immediate introduction of white labor, than North-Carolina. Every one will admit that this labor must come *eventually*. The negro cannot remain here forever in his present anomalous condition. The future of the State cannot be made to depend upon the willingness to work of a race for whom hitherto, we have considered that now proscribed instrument, the lash, as peculiarly appropriate. The white laborer must come, but the interests of the State demand that he shall come now. I dread to consider the state of things, should we be left another year in the present uncertainty. The picture of abandoned farms, stagnated business, a dejected people and open lawlessness, is fearful to contemplate. Yet these must follow decreased production and uncertainty of labor. Gentlemen may go to Raleigh and legislate and legislate, but what does their collective wisdom amount to if the plough stands still in the furrow and the anvil rusts on its block? We are told that the State is suffering from want of *capital*. How, then do you propose to get it? Is it to be sent to us on demand? It was when Hercules bade the wagoner put his shoulder to the wheel, that his wagon came out of the mire. It is out of the *ground* that our capital must come. It is thence that our prosperity must spring. White labor is at our command. Experience has proven that it is cheaper and far more remunerative than forced labor.—The barriers that turned the fertilizing stream of population, energy and enterprise from our own doors to those of our less favored neighbors, are at length burst asunder. Fortune is at our doors. We must win her smile ere she takes her everlasting flight.

White labor to day can be procured at a cheaper rate than negro labor could be hired under the old system. It is more remunerative, is capable of being increased with the demand, and above all is *certain.* There is not a County in the State which would not be benefitted by the employment of several hundred white hands. Northampton County alone would to-day give sufficient employment to five thousand able bodied white laborers. I do not mean that she would have room for that number at some uncertain period in the unexplored future, for she has a territory that is capable at some time of supporting a population of which this number will be but a very small fraction, but I mean to say that at this moment the County mentioned could add five thousand able bodied whites to her producing force *profitably,* and with desirable results to herself and the State. Owing to the old system of buying up immense tracts to provide for the increase of negroes, there are few large farmers in North-Carolina that do not own five or six times the quantity of land capable of being worked by the force at their disposal. Thus immense tracts of the most fertile lands—for it is these mostly that have been bought up—have been rendered worthless to the owners and every one else. This course has been highly detrimental to the interests of our State, and has sent the working, industrial part of our population to seek a more congenial home in the new States. Our legislators now in session at the Capitol would do well to consider this matter, and by laying a heavy tax on all *unimproved* lands, either force the proprietors to make them productive of some good to the country at large, or part with them to those who will. The State has too long suffered herself to be drained of her wealth and population by this narrow-minded policy. Verily "he who maketh two blades of grass to grow where one grew before is a benefactor." *Let the Legislature see to it.*

The broad fertile valleys, unexplored mines, unimproved water power and dwarfed cities of North-Carolina are imperiously calling for the influx of population. The surrounding States are throwing open their portals and inviting white labor to their abandoned fields and workshops. Let not the "Old North State" be hindmost in the race of improvement, or like the fleece of Gideon be unbenefitted while all around us are moistened by the fertilizing shower.

OSSIAN.

LETTER TO THE "DAILY SENTINEL," DECEMBER 5, 1865

YANKEE CUTENESS AND SOUTHERN CANT

I am "native here and to the manor born"— Four long years through hardships, disease, danger and adversity I have endeavored to sustain the failing banner of a now fallen cause.— As I have witnessed their valor and ever admired their virtues, my countrymen may feel assured that it is not through anger or in malice, that I now advert to their failings. It has been too long customary with the Southern people to look with a certain degree of contempt upon everything in the manners, customs and opinions of those who live North of Mason's and Dixon's line which differs from their own. The North, and especially New England, has been so long the seat of all the *isms* and the abode whence the locust like clouds of humbugs, patent medicines and pseudo-philanthropism have arisen and overspread the land, that this feeling is natural, and to some extent justifiable. But it is much to be deprecated when we seek to excuse our own indolence by styling as Yankee cuteness and cunning the enterprise and energy in which we are so signally wanting and which has written in living light so many pages that record the progress of our country and the triumphs of our race. The "peculiar institution" has indeed been a curse to the country that gave it a domicile, and to the land that has witnessed its sudden extinction. Our daughters have grown up in frivolity and our sons without expectation of aught but pleasure. Our old men have lived in ease and the young have followed fast in the footsteps of indolence. Our magnificent country is unimproved, our factories unbuilt, our wants supplied from without, and the South, like the sun upon Gideon, has stood still in the onward race. The old have declaimed against Yankee enterprise as an abomination of Egypt, and the rising generation have lisped it in detestation.—Let them look around. From the inkstand from which I write and the pen with which I trace these lines, to the printing press on which they are promulgated, from the cradle in which we are rocked and the carved bedstead on which we repose, to the coffin that will receive us at our death, and the tombstone that shall commemorate our virtues to the succeeding generation, there is but little of the comforts or conveniences, and few even of the necessaries of life for which we are not indebted to that same universal Yankee nation. The very cotton that whitens our fields must pass through Yankee looms before it adorns our belles or clothes our laborers.

Nor does the spirit of cant stop there. Does one of our own citizens succeed in amassing a fortune by a laudable enterprise and a praiseworthy exhibition of energy, suspicion of unfair dealing and use of the tricks of the trade, is the reward of his deviation from the beaten paths of indolence and inactivity. Unaccustomed to labor themselves they either look with suspicion upon the reward of intelligent application, or excuse themselves to their own souls, that they are too honest to succeed in life! The Indians when they first saw the evidence of how much intelligence and enterprise may accomplish—the steamboat—unable to understand it and unwilling to concede the superiority of the white man, concluded that the evil spirit must be connected with it and give it the motive power. Surprised at the success which ever attends well directed *effort* our people must needs attribute unworthy motives or means to him who applies it. Let us away with this self excusing spirit of cant. We must foster enterprise. We must encourage energy and industry. Our people are *indolent.* This is our besetting sin, and possessing the country that we do it cries to Heaven against us.

When the greatest of orators was asked what was the first rule of oratory, he replied action! When asked what was the second he still answered *action!* and the third? ACTION! The story has its application and in our times. It is work, *work,* WORK that we need. This is the great panacea for all the ills that society is heir to. This will efface the ravages of war, suppress crime, organize and consolidate society, cover our fields with harvests and bring "smiling plenty" with her attendant train of household divinities to preside at our firesides. *Let our people go to work.* Work "in the living present" ere sorrow come and old age draw nigh. The climate is fine, and there is an abundance of good soil if properly improved. Heaven and earth seem to conspire to make us indeed a land of promise. Work we must and redeem this fine country from the hand of the slothful, and the sluggard, or a bolder and a hardier race must occupy our seats. Let us be true, true to our country and true to ourselves and leave not the regeneration of one of the finest countries on the globe to another people, and other times.

CAMILLUS

LETTER TO "DAILY PROGRESS" (RALEIGH), DECEMBER 12, 1865

BLACK LABOR VERSUS WHITE

Amid the weary changes of the passing year—a year which has witnessed the annihilation and disbanding of armies hitherto deemed invincible, the overthrow of a powerful government, and the sudden revolution in the opinions of eight millions of people, there is none more astonishing to our thinking men than to find themselves at entire variance with the sentiments of a life-time. While slavery existed the brain was cudgelled and reason was put to the rack to convince our people that the prosperity of the South depended upon its further maintenance. The subject was debated and re-debated. For more than forty years it divided the councils of the nation.—Like an apple of discord, for nearly half a century it was the subject of contention between opposing parties. "The irrepressible conflict" came. The question so long debated in the legislative halls was submitted to the stern arbitrament of war and argued on the field of battle. The issue of the conflict long seemed doubtful. The weight of a feather might have turned the opposing scales. The hidden leaf in the book of Fate has at length been turned, and there in unmistakable characters the doom of slavery has been written by the hand of Destiny.

Now that the fate of slavery has ceased to be questioned, and reason, which ever flees the arena of combat, has resumed her sway, it behooves us to look back over the course, and from amid the wrecks and fragments which strew the way to pluck the gem of truth. The peculiar institution has indeed been fatal to the best interests of the country. Like a black pall, it has hung over us and banished the sunlight of progress far from our borders. The North has built up with a rapidity truly astonishing. The Northwest, the *great* Northwest, with far fewer advantages of climate or soil than these States, has reached out her hand and received the reward of the wisdom of her policy an hundred-fold. Even the far off Pacific States have grown in population and strength, and in prosperity, beyond measure. But the South, the home of our childhood and the land of our birth, like the sun upon Gideon and the moon in the valley of Ajalon, has stood still in the march of progress.

Had the resolutions for the abolition of slavery introduced into the Virginia and Kentucky Legislatures in 1831-32 not been defeated by the menacing tide of fanaticism which even then desired to *force* an interference with our domestic affairs, our own interests would have long since led us to abolish an institution which, at variance with the spirit of our institutions and the genius of the age, has been fraught with the most baneful effects and finally been extinguished in the best blood of our citizens. The South has now to start anew. The labor of years has been destroyed in as many months. The industrial system has been completely prostrated, and until it is renovated we cannot hope for the stability of our remaining institutions or the security of our lives and property, much less the prosperity of the country. A blow aimed at the labor of a country is a stroke at its very vitals.—Render labor uncertain and you unhinge the very fabric of society and unsettle the edifice of good Government. Fill your villages, your towns and your workshops with a hard working, intelligent population, unembittered by distinction of race, and you place the prosperity of this State beyond the reach of envy or the votes of a Black Republican Congress.

In the Northwest, which is considered as the very type of progress, they are accustomed to regard every able bodied white man as $500 added to the wealth of the community. Annually between six and seven hundred thousand laborers are carried to the States bordering on the Lakes. The States composing the late Confederate States are now occupying the identical position that the Northwest held twenty, thirty and forty years back. We have advantages of soil and climate to which the Northwest is an utter stranger. We have an area capable of supporting untold millions, harbors in which ships of half the world should be able to find cargoes, and water power to put in motion wheels enough to fabricate all our cotton at our own doors. The four States of North Carolina, Tennessee, Kentucky and Virginia (including West Virginia) comprise an area as large as that of France, which supports more than forty millions of people. The State of North Carolina which at the first census in 1790 stood *third* in population, ranking in that regard above the State of New York, and by the eighth census taken in 1860, is only entitled to as many representatives as the city of New York alone sends by the same census.—We can see here in what respect slavery has benefitted us, and we can also see on what our hopes of the future prosperity of the State depends. If when we were able to make the negro work, the State retrograded with such frightful rapidity, what must be the result now that the colored race is diminished by one-third, and the remaining two-thirds are demoralized by sudden relief from the bondage of ages, and are intent upon keeping the jubilee of freedom by eating their bread in idleness. To say that the country can be prosperous in this state of things is folly. To rely upon it is madness.

In this posture of affairs it is evident that there is for the country but one course of relief. The fertilizing stream of population which has so long poured uninterrupted into the valleys of the Lakes, and has begun to roll down the slope of the Rocky Mountains, must be deflected into our own lovely and fertile valleys. The white laborer with the invincible perseverance of his race, must hew out for the noble old State the road to fortune through the adamantine walls that have so long surrounded her. With the influx of population, influx of capital will follow, and the ship of state which has been so long tossed upon the rough seas of adversity, with favoring gales, will gallantly sweep into the haven of *prosperity*.

L'ORIENT.

LETTER TO THE "DAILY SENTINEL," FEBRUARY 9, 1866

THE UNIVERSITY

"Whereas, in all well-regulated governments it is the indispensable duty of every Legislature to consult the happiness of a rising generation, and endeavor to fit them for an honorable discharge of the social duties of life, by paying the strictest attention to their education: And whereas, an University supported by permanent funds, and well endowed, would have the most direct tendency to answer the above purpose: Be it enacted, &c., &c."—*Act of General Assembly of North Carolina, 1789.*

It is the boast of the age, that it is a progressive one. Since the above act was penned, the discovery of steam, the invention of the telegraph, and of steam carriages by land and water, have revolutionized the world and electrified Science. Events have marched with gigantic strides. The Federal Union, to which North Carolina, after a decided rejection, but that very year gave her final assent, from a confederation of colonies, has grown to be the "first and foremost" power of the world. It has engaged in wars, but to emerge from each, as Anteus arose from his falls, stronger than before. Her three millions have become fifty, and where her twelve stars then shone on their field of blue, "the haughty astral banner" now floats to the breeze in every clime beneath the sun with nearly two score. Science too, has had her triumphs, and Learning no longer confined to cloisters, and the abodes of Philosophers, walks abroad like a beneficent deity, conferring her rewards on all who are willing to receive them.

It is here, in the full blaze of the glories of the 19th century, that we must pause, and as we look through the vista of more than three quarters of a century and read the above preamble to the act of the Legislature of 1789, and in the act itself a comparison will "unbidden rise" to our minds between the actions of the General Assembly in 1789 and of that convened in the year of our Lord, 1866. Then, as now, the State had but recently emerged from an exhausting war which had left the edifice of society unsettled. Then, as now, our people were penniless, yet more—they were *poor*. The debates concerning the adoption of the Federal Constitution were then at the acme of their intensity. The system of government was new and untried. The soldiery were demoralized by the long war, and its successful termination had rendered them difficult of control. Lawlessness was rife. Gloom was on the future. "Even the most ardent patriot" says one of the times "dared but hope for the future." Yet in that time and amid the bitter contentions then agitating the State, our General Assembly were not altogether unmindful of the "happiness of a rising generation" nor forgetful of the *"duty"* devolved upon them of fitting the youth of the State "for an honorable discharge of the social duties of life, by paying the strictest attention to their education."

It would appear strange indeed, should a Legislature which owes to the University the education, if I mistake not, of both the gentlemen who so ably preside over the discussions of its respective Houses, and who have but so recently elected two more of her sons to represent the State in the United States Senate. It would be strange, I say, that a General Assembly which numbers among its members so many who have participated in the benefits of the University, should, after the successful conduct of the Institution, which for seventy years has so fully vindicated the wisdom of its founders, refuse assistance, without which, we are told it cannot proceed. We are poor, it is true, but will the State be any richer when she allows an Institution, to which she owes so much that is bright in her past, to succumb for want of timely aid, and sends her youth to be educated at the Universities of more favored States? Will her record be any the brighter when she neglects an Institution which gave to the Union a President and to the State so many of her Chief Magistrates? Will she permit it to perish now, when during the eventful days of the past bloody struggle, its noble and devoted President struggled so gallantly, so heroically and so successfully to sustain it, while all the other abodes of learning were yielding to the necessities of the times and closing their doors.

The year 1789 should be noted in the history of North Carolina, for the passage of two acts, which perhaps more than any other, have reflected upon the future prosperity of the State. The ratification of the Constitution of the United States, and the act providing for the establishment of an University. The one was made to provide for the external relation, of the State, the other for her internal welfare. "Of two such lessons why forget the nobler one." The State was rendered subject to four years of terrible and devastating war, in an attempt to annul the one, and shall she be permitted to quietly render the other null and void by a refusal of requisite assistance in the hour of need? Will this desertion of her noblest work fail to bring a loss of honor and reputation, and a restriction of the blessings of education, which if not so terrible as the first, may prove more lasting and more detrimental to the real interests of the State. Should North Carolina neglect her University, she can not be expected to provide for her Common Schools. The plea now brought to excuse neglect of the one can as easily be urged for the abolition of the other.

It is earnestly to be hoped that no narrow minded policy will guide our course at the present juncture. If ever a far sighted liberal policy should be adopted it is now. Our system of government has been shaken to its very centre, and it is now before affairs become settled down into the old every day line of action, that we should mark out a new and liberal course. One more suited to this emphatically, practical and *progressive* age than that which has generally obtained in the late slaveholding States. Especially should our policy be more liberal, (when we become able,) in an educational point of view, for it is evidently upon the more general diffusion of intelligence among her citizens, that a State for the future must base the prosperity and happiness of her people. The cause of learning is the cause of civilization.

It is not my province, neither is it my wish, to criticise the acts of the present Legislature. Verily, *"they have their record,"* and will probably have their reward also. Still less do I desire to point out to that honorable Assembly, a course of action in the present emergency, but I believe that all true sons of the "Old North State" will unite with me in the hope, that she will rally to the aid of an institution to which she is indebted, for so much that has shed glory on her past and betokens hope of the future. There is something hovering under the shade of those venerable buildings and stealing along its now, almost silent corridors, something breathing through the tree tops and rustling over the lawn, that with an undefinable feeling of awe, calls to our minds the days when Polk, and Graham, and Manly and Pettigrew trod its halls, and recalls reminiscences of the sacred past, that we "would not willingly let die." Her sons have figured in every scene of American history. In the Presidential chair, in the Cabinet, on the Judicial Bench, as Governors, Statesmen, Prelates, Orators and Soldiers, the force of her influence, through her sons has been felt in every department of life. Should a broad and comprehensive policy mark our course, and should the noble old University, tried so severely by the "waves and weathers" of time, be enabled to emerge from the obscurity in which she now mourns the loss of her dead, and to prepare with new life and vigor to run with diligence the race set before her, there are thousand thousands, scattered from Maryland to Texas, whose hearts, in sympathetic unison, will bid her God Speed, but none more gladly or more proudly than each and every one of those, whose pride it is now, as it was in times past, to be deemed worthy even to be called

ONE OF HER SONS.

LETTER TO THE "DAILY SENTINEL," AUGUST 11, 1866

THE RADICALS AND THE FUTURE

Messrs. Editors:—General Sherman, in a speech to the young men of Yale College, has told them that the fighting was not done, and added that the future would present scenes of "woe, want and murder," to which those he had the honor to be engaged in would be mere *child's play*. These are remarkable words.—Coming as they do from the hero of the "March to the Sea," the modern Attila, who could boast that he had left a tract of desolation "forty miles wide and a thousand long," where the cry of the infant was stilled and the howl of the fox was hushed, they are significant. It were to be wished that he had been more definite.—The words, however, are doubtless as correct as they are remarkable. The destroyer of Columbia has the true instinct of blood. The situation of affairs at the North gives a solution of his meaning. Abolitionism and fanaticism have sown the wind and they well may reap the whirlwind. The recently proposed distribution of arms, the desperate propositions of the Radicals in their caucuses, the very speech of Sherman himself, betoken a diseased state of the body politic, and a state so far advanced in corruption, that the incision of the sword is the only remedy. In the march from Atlanta, Marius has learned the true art (*vide* his speeches) to conquer; now may he make the application nearer home....

In family quarrels of this kind among the victors, we, of the South, have no interest.—Verily we have no part in Israel and no lot in Judah. In any contest for power between copperhead and radical, Eastern and Western Yankeedom, it behooves us religiously to refrain. In such a struggle we have nothing to gain.—We have offered up, in a cause we deemed holy, the flower of our youth, the pride of our manhood, and the blackness of desolation marks where our habitations once stood. We have submitted in good faith to the powers that be, but in the struggle that Gen. Sherman foresees as to *what* shall constitute those powers, we have no further sacrifice to make. *Repose* is the first demand of an overwearied people. It is probably well that the South has resolved to be represented in the Philadelphia Convention. It behooves her, so far as consistent with honor, to make every attempt to readjust her relations with the general Government. But it is not well to be sanguine of the result. There will be unscrupulous Radicals in the Convention, in the garb of men of peace, and if the fund of corruption at the disposal of the dominant party will produce discord, then will discord divide its counsels. If the object or the result of the Convention is or will be to embroil the Southern people in the mazes of Northern politics, then it were to be wished, indeed, that the idea were never conceived. Yet it is proper and necessary to send our representatives, as indicative at least of our willingness, not of our confidence. Politics has been a fatal trade to us and ours.—We need repose from political excitement, increase of population, immigration of labor, influx of capital and development of our systems of general education and internal improvements. It is no time for contests for office.—The officers we have and "their adoption tried" it is well to return. To use a popular phrase, it is no time for "swapping horses." The time will come when the *State* may be able to recompense *all* her deserving men, but at present the *Territory* needs all her surplus activity diverted into a more profitable channel than that of political agitation.

The tone of the Radical leaders, the enunciations of their press, and the general aspects of matters of the Republic, recall forcibly to mind the earlier scenes of the French Revolution.—Had the French their Camille Desmoulins, their Heberts, their Couthons and St. Justs, these have their Beechers, Garrisons and Stowes without number. Had they a Chaumette, these have a Ben Wade, who can blaspheme without a blush. Had they a triumvirate of blood, these have the men who can clamor for the blood of a whole people and desire the population of the South "guarded in hell with a million of bayonets;" these had a Thad. Stevens,—Robespierre without his integrity,—and a Sumner,—a Danton without his talents. Had the French La Vendee attached to the old regime, these had the South as firmly attached to the old fashioned sentiments of liberty and personal rights of Washington, Jefferson and Madison. The wildest dreams of the wildest Jacobin have been surpassed by the legislative enactments of men who claim to sit in the seats, and possess the spirit, of Ames, Adams, Webster and Benton. If these modern imitators are without the abilities of the men who guided the fiery car of the French Revolution, they are also without their integrity. Bathed to the arms in blood, Robespierre and his companions would scorn to touch even a ring from the finger of their victim. What low political schemes, what record has been made of votes bought and sold, what tricks have been resorted to to enrich political adventurers, the Muse of History, which stands in silence in the Congressional hall, for the honor of America may well refuse the relation.

Affairs can not remain as they are. In mathematics, if a certain power be given, the resistance being known, we can calculate the results. Not so in history. The destinies of nations, as well as individuals, like the sword of Damocles, hang suspended by a single hair. We all know that Helen lost Troy, Lucretia expelled the Tarquins, and that even the cackling of the geese preserved the Capitol. Should not Providence, however, interpose, and should the Fall elections perpetuate, instead of defeating, Radical misrule, then the future is indeed to become a matter of mathematical calculation.—Accidents, events and contingencies, as has been said, may falsify the best drawn horoscope; but judging from probabilities—and in regard to all that concerns the future we can only reason as to the probable,—Gen. Sherman has drawn *his* inference, and so also will every true

FRIEND OF THE PEOPLE.

LETTER TO THE "DAILY SENTINEL," NOVEMBER 20, 1866

OUR WASHINGTON LETTER

WASHINGTON, D. C., NOV. 20, 1866. MESSRS. EDITORS: —One of those periodical simoons which sweep over nations, seems to have burst in its full fury upon the Northern section of this Union. France has had its Mississippi scheme, its revolution of '92; England its South Sea bubble; Germany its secret societies and Materialism, and the events of the passing year have shown, that the great North American Republic is not exempt from the national epidemics of the old world, which for a time overcome all principles and precedents, and leave right and wrong involved in inextricable confusion.

The recent elections have spoken to the world in a manner not to be misunderstood, and should the spirit of those elections and the principles they enunciate be taken as the settled policy of the people, we might well despair of republican institutions. True, however, to the Republican faith of our ancestors, we cannot but believe that the *mass* of the people mean well. They may be mistaken, they may be deceived, they may be misled by designing and unprincipled leaders; but sooner or later, the popular mind will discover the truth, and the great popular heart will throb in unison in the true principles of liberty and right. For the present, however, the will of the predominating section, and with that the policy of the Government, has been unmistakably settled. The only resource then for the South, is to develop her resources, encourage immigration and bide her time. Even should the Constitutional amendment be unlawfully adopted by excluding the vote of the "ten," by the next census, perhaps, it will cease to be injurious, and act *against* the States now most zealous in its adoption. The South owns more than one-half of the now settled territory; the climate is genial and the soil fertile. The wave of immigration will soon set in, and the little New England States just now so noisy, may find themselves shorn of those State rights which they are so willing now to ignore. They are treading on dangerous ground, for precedents in politics, as in law, are terrible things. It is *on dit* that an agreement with the Juarez government has been made by which the States of Sonora, Chihuahua and Lower California are to be turned over to the United States for annexation. It is said that the mission of Gen. Sherman is for the purpose of settling preliminaries and merely precedes an army of occupation. Certain it is, that unusual movements of troops have lately taken place in that direction. Should these rumors prove true, it indicates that the President has adopted a policy, perhaps the only one, which will restore his popularity in the Northern States. The Northern mind over-stimulated by the war and particularly its successful termination, is active, morbidly active, and must have something to feed upon. Any thing tending to the aggrandizement of the Republic is emphatically *popular*. Annexation of the Northern States of Mexico, while it would bring popularity to the administration, by turning public attention from issues on which it has already dwelt too long, would probably ensure the speedy admission of the excluded States. Viewed in this light, the measure would be a fine stroke of policy, but the ultimate effect of this vast increase of Territory, on the destinies of the Republic, is a question for the mature deliberation of the statesman and for time, which at last settles all questions from the minutest to the greatest.—The acquisition would indeed give us a shorter and more practicable route than any we now possess, to the Pacific. The shriek of the steam whistle which annihilates time and space may be allowed to compensate, in some degree, for the argument of those, if any, who may feel disposed to imitate the now annexationists of Polks administration.

The Capital has lately been enlivened by the presence of Parepa, the celebrated songstress, who is said to rival, if not surpass, Jenny Lind in her achievements.

Preparations are being made, at the Capitol, for the reception of the fortieth Congress, which is probably destined to be a memorable one in history, and whose first move on the board will be anxiously looked for by the whole American people.

C.

TO CLARK FROM HIS SISTER ANNA *

Airlie Jan. 1st 1868

A Happy New Year. Ma says her first prayer and her first stitch of work this morning was for you. She received your letter of the

* Later, wife of the Reverend J. D. Arnold, Methodist minister.

26th last night, says she has written to you twice since that was written, wrote to you to come home. I am very anxious to see you. Wish you could come I have been expecting you ever since Ma wrote. Pa says he is not able to send us to school this year, so I thought that if you would be willing I would recite to you when you came home, that is if you are going to stay any length of time.

I guess Martha, Mrs. Nichol & Sarah will stay if Pa is able to keep them. He says he can not hire any field hands except on shares. Old Sam is hired at Mr. Jack Johnson's. Uncle William is going to hire Tom. Don't know what Wynate is going to do.

Pa has not hired anyone yet, says he does not know what to do. Neverson has just been here and says his part of the crop will be one third of a bale of cotton, it will take all the corn he made to pay Cousin Sam Williams back what he borrowed last year. The people are giving negroes $72 and they find themselves. Cousin Tom Harriss has hired a white man and his family for their food and part of their clothes. Pa is going down the country tomorrow. What are you going to do this year. Pa is very low spirited he is troubled to know what to do.

Sister is going to teach the children and I am going to try to help Ma as much as I can. Study when I have an opportunity. I never thought of such hard times, nearly everyone is broke, Guess you are tired of hard times so I will close. I am thankful to say that we are all well. I think we have a great cause to be thankful instead of complaining so much. Don't think that we will ever starve. I heard that Uncle Blake was out of flour and lard, had been eating bread and meat for a week or so.

I believe that Ma has concluded not to keep Mrs. Nichols and Sarah. Pa is going to try to get another woman.

Sallie Hill says you must write to her. All join in love....

[P.S.]
Those who are working on shares, give them one third and they find themselves

TO CLARK FROM A. B. ANDREWS *

Henderson, July 31, 1869

No doubt you will be a little surprised to hear I am to be married September 1st to Miss Julia M. daughter of Col Wm.

* Superintendent of Raleigh and Gaston Railroad Company, later vice president and general manager of Southern Railway Company.

Johnston of Charlotte N.C. And I write this letter requesting that you will honour me with your presence on that occasion and act as one of my Groomsman. We will have a wedding on Wednesday night and leave Charlotte thursday evening. I will send you free Passes from Endfield to Charlotte & return. Hoping to receive a favourable answer from you.

TO CLARK FROM C. M. WESSON

October 6, 1869

I write this to ask your attendance in the capacity as a groomsman at my wedding on Nov the 10th—There will be quite a large reception at Mrs. R. H. Austin's after our marriage at the Church on the day or rather evening aforesaid—I am flattering myself upon my list of groomsmen—and hope you will honor me with your acceptance.... Halifax Ct. will be in session at that time and you can join us—with Robert Peebles *—thereby not losing much of the Session. The dress will be—black coat & pantaloons (such as you had at Morehead)—black vest buttoning low down—black *crevat* & white or pearl colored gloves—Let me hear definitely whether I can count upon you or not....

TO CLARK FROM THOMAS P. DEVEREUX †

Fresno County Cal
Oct 12th 1869

Yours of Sept 15 has been receid & I hasten to answer it. At this length of time I am unable to say positively what I did with the Jones mortgage; my impression was that I had given it to you along with the other papers, & this is still my recollection, but as you know nothing about [it] I may have sent it to Frank Jones you had better write him if you have not already done so, I will today write my father to look among some papers I left at home, to make sure that it is not there, but as I said above my recollection is that I handed it to you. Ask Frank Jones if there is not something said about it in your receipt to me which he has. As to the country out here I imagine that you know about all that I could tell in a letter, Your Eastern country has some advantages over this such as streams of running water timber etc but our advantages in other respects make up in a great measure for the

* Later Superior Court Judge.
† The Devereux family owned a plantation on the Roanoke River near Ventosa.

want of these. The climate is perfection, rather hot for some people, but all through the hot season the N W Trade winds prevail which so far do away with the heat that a man can labor here in the sun when the thermometer stands at 115 in the shade. Some of the land here is very fine but the great bulk of this valley is of a light sandy nature that produces from ten to twenty bushels per acre and the great advantage of farming such land is the quantity one man can cultivate—a good hand ought to plow & sow 300 acres if the rains set in by the 1st Nov which is about the average time. Society here is as yet in a rude state but the U.P.R.R.* brings us so much nearer to the refined & cultivated East that we will improve, people wont remain rough long after they become rich; and there is no doubt but that the wealth of the State is on the increase.

You must remember me to all my friends in your neighborhood I think of you all very often and still have the love for my native State strong within me Please make my respects to your father; With many thanks for your kind wishes and hopes for your complete success, I remain as ever your old schoolmate & friend

TO CLARK FROM THOMAS BRAGG †

Raleigh March 7th 1870

You will see from the papers that the case of Jones vs Hill has been decided in our favor, as I thought it would be after I had more fully examined it, and from the indications of the argument—I have just read the opinion, in which they say that after the purchase by Jones he had all the rights of Mortgager & Mortgagee and that he was entitled to *all* the settlements, but as he claimed only a reasonable rent treating Hill as his tenant he is now confined to that, and is entitled to it.

There is a suggestion that the mortgage debt was satisfied—they say the defendant may demand his answer to that effect & have an amount as to that matter, if he desires it—In that event, that Hymans Representative ought to be made a party, as he would be entitled to the rent if the mortgage debt had been paid—I hardly see the force of this reasoning—think it inconsistent rather, with the law that we were entitled to all the crop, but I suppose it is in the idea that we chose to treat and recognize Hill as our tenant—It would have been *hard* to have treated him otherwise.

* Union Pacific Railroad, completed that year.
† Governor of North Carolina, 1855-1859, native of Northampton County.

As in point of fact, I suppose, Jones debt is not all paid, we shall have no trouble on that score—

As the cotton is tied up by the Injunction, I think it would be best for you & Hill to argue that the cotton may be now sold by some safe third person and the funds held subject to the final decision of the case—

But I see no reason for further litigation, if our debt has not been paid, and therefore it seems to me that you & Hill could settle as to the amount of rent, let the cotton be sold and our claim and the costs of suit be paid out of the proceeds.

I congratulate you in the successful result of the suit, in which allow me to say, I was much aided by you, with authorities in its argument in the Supreme Court.

TO CLARK FROM AUNT MARTHA NICHOLSON

Glenview March 16th, 1870—

So you are "looking for my promised letter" are you? This I learn from a P.S. in a letter to your Uncle Tom rec'd a week ago, & He has been reminding me of it ever since. "Martha you ought to write to Walter, he says you promised to" dont think he intends to seal his letter till some scratches from my pen are enclosed with it; but must write very hurriedly tonight,—have just written two long letters, it is now half past Eleven o clock, quite time that I was asleep, besides I am getting so blind can scarcely see to write by Lamplight—I am so pleased to learn from a late letter, that you intend making us a visit soon, do come at your earliest convenience, & set your Uncle Tom right if possible. He is exceedingly low spirited. The one *idea* of a sale, haunts him by night & by day—

I beg him to dismiss all thoughts of it from his mind, & say every thing I can to cheer him, but it avails nothing, says his credit will be gone & he will go just as Dr Joyner did, now all this is very distressing to me, but I exert myself to be cheerful, knowing that it will never do, for both of us to get down. I believe though seriously, were a sale to take place, he would give up entirely, never make another effort; so you will do a deed of *Mercy,* dear Walter, to come & relieve his mind in some way, if you possibly can, all his hopes seem to be centered in you. I could see that your letter rec'd today, gave him a gleam of hope—His Physical disability too, unfit, him the more to bear these troubles—Let us know, when you will be here, in order that I may have my *Budget* of news ready for you, have lots of things to tell you on the Girls—know they wont like my reporting on them, but much I care for that,—More love letters &c, I cant begin to tell, will reserve till you come, dont know what I shall do with them, unless I turn their cases over to you, will you defend them or not? One of them recd yesterday the Express receipt for a Barrel of Oranges sent from N.Y. leave you to guess who it was sent by, & which one to, know you are Lawyer enough, to guess right—dont let them know that I told you—*We* had a nice time at Bet Wiggins Wedding. I say *we,* for would you believe that I turned out in that snow storm, to go to a Wedding, after being in Winter Quarters since the middle of Oct? it is even 80, Wonder will never cease. I have a heap to tell you about it when you come, have not time or space now—

I have not heard from your Ma in a long time, am anxious to make her a visit, but cannot think of leaving Husband, & of course he would think it impossible to go with me.

Excuse me for trespassing, fear you will not have time to read this scrawl—Cousin Blake is now in "Miss." * we will hear particularly from Gil, when he returns, he is expected home soon—

TO CLARK FROM THOMAS J. JARVIS †

Columbia N.C.
Sept. 7th 1870

Yours of the 18th Oct came to hand when I was prostrated upon a sick bed. I reply as soon as I am able. If you can show that Renfrow ‡ was not a citizen of the county twelve months before the election there can be no doubt about your defeating him. In this event the question would then be whether the House would seat you or send the election back to the people. I rather think the sentiment of the Democratic party is against the doctrine laid down by Wilkes the agitator in England years ago & recently revived by the radicals in Congress—The seating of minority candidates when the majority candidates are disqualified.

You will however do your county and yourself credit to keep the dirty Renfrow out whether you sit in or not.

* Mississippi, where Clark's relatives owned considerable land.

† Governor of North Carolina, 1879-1885.

‡ John H. Renfrow, Representative in General Assembly from Halifax County, 1868-1870.

TO CLARK FROM A. B. ANDREWS

Raleigh, N.C. Dec. 7th 1870

Yours of the 4th to hand—I am sorry that I cannot get the Annual Report of the S & R Road for you—But really I have never seen one—They never send them out and it is almost impossible to get one—But if I can will take pleasure in getting you one—Raleigh crowded

TO CLARK FROM THEOPHILUS PARSONS *

Cambridge—Feb 26/71

I hasten to acknowledge your kind note.

In the next edition of my contracts I shall endeavour to profit by your suggestions. It will not be published for a year or two.

In my work on Shipping and Admiralty & Insurance, I venture to state my doubts concerning the established doctrine, although it certainly is established by the decided weight of authority.

There is an effort now to extend the same rule to Telegraphs; that is, to hold that the amount is given & the bargain completed, when the Message of assent is given to the operator. But in my next edition, which will have a chapter on the Law of Telegraphic communication, I shall express my decided dissent from this,—unless upon further inquiry and consideration, my views change very much.

TO CLARK FROM JESSE J. YEATES †

Murfreesboro, N.C.
April 11, 1871

Your two letters were received by last nights mail. We are very glad to have your assistance in our enterprise. We will do the best we can, but a subscription obtained on an uncertainty as to where the road will be located will of necessity be less successful than if it were definitely known that we should get the benefits. I have just returned from Gates Court and have not yet had an opportunity of seeing our canvassers, but I hear they are doing well having the promise of between 7 & 8 thousand dollars. I am sure that we can get $15,000— with a good effort. I will endeavor to be at your meeting, but it will be too short a time for us to make much headway. There can be no doubt that it would be to the

* Massachusetts lawyer and author of a number of outstanding legal books.
† Lawyer and Democratic Representative in Congress, Dec. 6, 1875-March 3, 1879.

Charles Farrell

The law office built by Clark at Halifax when he was twenty-two. It is still in service as a law office.

interest of the company to run the road this way. It is the easiest thing in the world to prove it. Indeed it is a matter of astonishment to all with whom I have conversed on the subject that Margeritsville should have been selected as the eastern terminus. I hope you are progressing favourably in the work. It will be a great undertaking, but with energy we can succeed. The Edenton road has for the present suspended operations. When we commence let us push on until the engine shall drive its way in full speed from Tarboro to Boykins.

TO CLARK FROM C. M. HAWKINS *

Baltimore, Md.
April 12, 1871

Your favor of 5th inst. came to hand. I regret very much that you cannot go with me to Europe, and sincerely hope that you may yet so arrange your affairs as to be able to take the trip. I think it would be beneficial as well as pleasant to us both. If you find upon reconsidering the matter that you are compelled to visit California, let me know and I will try to go with you.

TO CLARK FROM J. H. WHEELER †

Elba near Washington City
29 April 1871

. . . In carrying out my purpose of bringing the History of my Native State down to the present time, I feel that I but discharge a final duty, and endeavour to do justice to a noble State which has more merit to be preserved, and upon which more obloquy has been cast than any State of our Union. I feel obliged for your kind sympathy, and shall receive any communication relative to the county of Halifax or any of her sons with gratitude. Since the publication of my reply to W Whitaker of Macon County (who took umbrage that his name had not been more fully noticed in my History;) and before, I have received many valuable contributions to the historic lore of N. C., and I have now a *reportoire* of *much* interest to me, and will be doubtless to my fellow citizens. My collection made in England is invaluable—and will present

* Hawkins, Williamson and Company were "Cotton Factors and General Commission Merchants."

† Member of General Assembly, 1827-1830; Superintendent of Branch Mint of the United States at Charlotte; Minister to Nicaragua; author of *Historical Sketches of North Carolina.*

the early history of N C in as bright and glowing colours which the endurance, fortitude and gallantry of her sons in later days has so nobly sustained. I am aware how dangerous to speak of events, the fires of which have yet not subsided. I shall have to tread on burning ploughshares. Yet in speaking of the illustrious dead I shall dwell as little as possible upon the characters of the living only to state their service—&c

FROM OCEAN TO OCEAN

(Selections from twenty-six articles appearing in the *Roanoke News* in the summer of 1871.)

We have now been four days in San Francisco. . . . The city, from one house in 1836, has grown to a population of 170,000 in 1871. It has perhaps the pleasantest climate of any city on the North American Continent. In San Francisco roses bloom in the open air the year round. . . . The hotels are the best imaginable. We have not seen the like anywhere else. . . . Nothing but gold and silver is current in the State. Ever since entering the boundaries of the State we have had to discard our paper money. The Banks and Brokers will readily buy your greenbacks, giving you the market price for them, but no one will take greenbacks in payment for anything. They are as little current as Confederate money would be. . . .

Now, indeed, our journey from Ocean to Ocean is complete. It is impossible to traverse the route we have, and see what we have seen, and to stand upon this plank dripping with the wet of the spray from the Pacific Ocean, without being deeply penetrated with the resources and power of the Republic. We may sit down in our little neighborhood at home and laugh at what we call Yankee bombast, but a trip across the Continent from New York to San Francisco, over a line 3,500 miles in length, will suffice to convince any man that he has no cause to be ashamed of being an American citizen. It is indeed a great nation. The sun never shone upon its like. . . .

We, of the South, undertook a large contract when we undertook to overthrow this Government—a larger one, as it turned out, than we could fill. The people of the South, certainly the people of North Carolina, did not desire this struggle. We were driven, AGITATED, into it by politicians, who, seeing they could no longer rule in Washington, like gamblers, risked all on the throw of the die. The politicians, the leaders, knew the odds we had to face. The masses of the people did not know and they do not today. Honor to the soldiery of the South, whose gallantry bore up a sinking cause on the points of their bayonets for two long years after that cause had been lost by the want of statesmanship at Richmond, honor to the heroism and devotion of our beautiful women, honor to the integrity and patriotism of our Southern masses, but may history pursue with an eternal infamy the impracticables who precipitated a struggle which they knew at the time to be hopeless, and protracted that struggle for months after it was evident that all hope of success by arms had passed. But you will say that these are dead or have lost their power. They have, indeed, lost their power for good, but not for evil. The same impracticable spirit animates them which caused one of their number to proclaim in Faneuil Hall, upon the very eve of the mighty convulsion, that he would yet "call the roll of his slaves from the foot of Bunker Hill Monument," and which made another declare in a public speech, here in the seventh year after Lee's surrender, that "he did not accept the situation—that he accepted nothing." These men are like the Bourbons. "They have learned nothing and they have forgotten nothing." They can see the sky red in the west at evening and say that it will be fair tomorrow, but they cannot read the signs of the times. Unfortunately, these men have imitators in every county in the South. And will you permit the writer, who, as a citizen of your State, feels a deep interest in her present and future welfare, to suggest that the defeat of the Convention at the late election was not due to the negro vote, but to the dislike of the people to these "men of reaction." With forty thousand white majority in the State, the defeat could not be due to the negro vote. The people doubtless desired a Convention. They were certainly tired of scalawag and carpetbag government. But these men too ill disguised the fact that they hoped in the movement a restoration of the old order of things (excepting, of course, slavery, which was dead beyond hope of reaction). The people were not ready for this. They did not desire reaction. And we think that a scrutiny of the ballot would show that there were two classes, whose power is every day becoming more felt in the State, that did not fully second the Convention move, *i.e.,* the poorer classes, who have never willingly followed the leadership of these men, and the young men who are naturally unwilling to entrust the control of their State again to the hands of men who for the past 50 years have curbed the destinies and fettered the progress, and so to speak, have, by their narrow selfish and exclusive policy kept her in bonds and swaddling clothes, while her sister States have been advancing on the high road to wealth and prosperity. If the true verdict was rendered it would probably be "Convention failed in North Carolina by 10,000 votes, not because the people were opposed to Convention, but because the reactionists were in favor of it."

Standing here, those sentiments naturally occur to us. They may give offence to some. It matters not. There has been too much proscription for opinion's sake in North Carolina. It is time that the truth was plainly spoken. It is time that dead issues were laid aside. It is time that men should cease to invoke the prejudices of days forever gone by. It is time that forgetting the past we should prepare to run with diligence the race before us. The writer loves North Carolina. Within her borders are all that is dear to him. Her prosperity is indeed the dearest wish of his heart, and, standing by this most distant shore of the Great Republic, he would fain waft across the mountains a wish that she may yet be

> "Great, prosperous and free,
> First pride of the land and first gem of the sea."

While in San Francisco . . . we were carried, also, into the haunts of the opium smokers, where hundreds of human beings—yet hardly human—lay on their little shelves, with hardly enough space to double themselves up in, and smoke themselves into a state of unconsciousness. We were told that some of these men had pursued this way of living for years. They are conscious for 3 or 4 hours in the morning, when they will go out and steal some petty article which will suffice to buy a little opium with and then they will coil themselves up and smoke until all consciousness leaves them. . . . The amount of degradation, of vice, of filth and poverty we saw in those few hours is beyond expression. It would however be as unfair to judge the Chinese by that standard as it would be to our white race by what one may see in a similar nocturnal visit to the "Five Points" at New York. It is noticeable that you never see a Chinaman drunk. There is a bitter hostility to the Chinese element throughout the State. But, strange to say, while everybody abuses the heathen Chinee, every one seems anxious to employ him. The real opposition seems to be based upon the fact that "John" works cheaper than the white laborer can, and that he hoards his money and will not spend it with the bar-keepers and shop-tenders. We are satisfied that they make excellent laborers. . . .

While on this railroad, we amused ourselves shooting at prairie dogs, elk and antelope. . . . On the train we saw S. S. Cox (Sunset Cox). He had been out to California making campaign speeches. Since leaving Congress, "Boss" Tweed has taken him up and we believe keeps him employed for Tammany. We reached Denver at 5 A.M. and left at 9 the same evening. Denver is the capital of Colorado, and is a flourishing, energetic, pretty town of 10,000 inhabitants. . . . Three railroads center at Denver. We noticed particularly the one which being built from here to Santa Fe, for it is "narrow gauge." . . . If a dozen or more narrow gauge branches could be built by the Wilmington and Weldon railroad, in your State, it would have a wonderful effect in developing Eastern North Carolina, and would doubtless pay the W. & W. R.R. handsomely in the bargain. The Northern roads have found the system of branch railways or feeders very profitable. . . . The portion of Colorado which lies east of the Rocky Mountains is a fine grazing country. We have met with nothing by which a fortune can be more rapidly, more surely and more easily made than by stock-raising in Colorado and Western Kansas. Cattle are bought very cheap in Northern Texas. They are driven up here on these prairies. Pasturage is fine, and free of expense. The snow never falls deep enough to interfere with the cattle. Those plagues of Egypt—tax gatherers and United States Internal Revenue men—never intrude, and there is no expense whatever except what is paid for the services of your herdsmen. . . . This range is a great favorite with the Buffaloes, who may be seen here by the thousands. The herds crossing the railroad track are oftentimes so dense, that the trains not infrequently have to stop to permit them to pass. Passengers on this road have evidently taken a pleasure in shooting these animals. We are certainly well within bounds when we say that we saw along the line of the road not less than one thousand buffaloes lying on the ground in varying stages of decomposition, bearing evidences apparently of having been shot in the last 5 or 6 weeks. Sometimes we would see 30 or 40 dead buffaloes in running a mile. If this wanton and wholesale slaughter is not stopped in some way, the buffalo will soon become an extinct genus. We must admit, however, that we could not resist the temptation, and fired away whenever we passed in range, though we can console ourselves, probably, with the reflection that we killed about as few of them as anybody. We saw some immense herds. At the eating stations, buffalo meat is a common dish. . . . Nearly the whole of western Kansas is entirely uninhabited. A member of the Kansas Legislature represents 8 or 10 counties up here. . . . The only known constituents he has, are the buffaloes, but from the condition we saw many of them in, along the line of the road, he seems to have the true modern legislator's regard for the interests of those who elect him. Many of the stations are merely military posts. The "Indian forts" at these posts are on the prairie dog order of architecture. They are adobe huts, built under ground, with a foot or 18 inches above the surface. The part that is visible is cresselated, or loop-holed for rifles, and roofed with rafters covered with earth and a thick growth of buffalo grass. They are the very best fort that could be devised for the Indian style of warfare. . . .

We have been in the "Mound City," as St. Louis is called, for two days. St. Louis is the third city in the Union. . . . The increase of railways built, leading directly to the city, last year alone, was 1,487 miles. . . . The city is as destitute as it can possibly be of fine Public Buildings, though it is true there are many handsome private residences. . . . There is but one good hotel in the whole place. The other hotels without exception, in appearance and otherwise, would not do justice to a country town. . . . There is most certainly, too, a lamentable want of public-spiritedness in St. Louis, for how else can we account for the almost entire absence of Parks and other places of public resort and recreation. . . . We have heretofore noted the tendency in Southern cities to neglect improvements of this kind. In every northern town and incipient town you will find provision for some place of innocent and healthy resort for the people. With the exception of Baltimore, we have never seen or read of a Southern city which paid any attention to matters of this kind. . . . Chicago, which has hardly a tithe of the local advantages of St. Louis, is far ahead in these two items of public spirit and public improvements. Consequently Chicago is building up and growing in a more rapid ratio. St. Louis is like the Southern country gentleman in this respect. We know but too well our advantage of position, of nature and climate, and we take too little trouble to turn them to advantage ourselves or to let the world know we have them. Meantime, those northern fellows are working like beavers. . . .

The Mississippi River furnishes an unbroken line of navigation from New Orleans to Fort Snelling, a distance of 2,131 miles.

It is across this river, in front of St. Louis, they are building the bridge which, when completed, will be the eighth wonder of the world. The plan of the bridge is original in many respects, and when completed, will probably be superior to any structure of any kind in the world. . . . This bridge will not only have the noblest arches in the world, but will be the first structure of its kind built of steel. The Engineer is Capt. Eads.

. . . . The Louisville and Nashville railroad do an immense business. They are virtually a monopoly, and such an influence have they over the Kentucky Legislature, that the latter has repeatedly refused to consult the real interests of the State by granting a charter for a competing Road across the State, from Cincinnati to Knoxville. . . . The L. & N. R.R. needs an opposition line. They crowded us all into dirty, filthy coaches that, from their appearance inside and out, had been in use for 20 years. The trains run to suit themselves, sometimes on schedule, sometimes out of schedule, and sometimes into one another. Everything about the road was in bad contrast to the railroads on the other side of the river. It may make money for the ring, but it is the worst managed road so far as the public is concerned, that we ever saw. . . . The appearance of the country, the soil and the growth of trees in this part of Kentucky, is very similar to that portion of Halifax County which lies between Gaston and Littleton. The population is sparse. The utter prostration of business, the depreciation of lands, the decay of plantations and buildings and the want of commercial confidence, the rural districts of Kentucky share in common with her sister States of the South. . . .

We are now nearing our journey's end. When we shall again have reached the borders of North Carolina we will have traversed 25 States and Territories, most of them twice, besides the Province of Ontario, in Canada, and will have travelled not less than 10,000 miles. We have seen larger and longer rivers than any in our State, broader Lakes, taller Mountains, higher Waterfalls, some more fertile lands, larger cities, better harbors and bigger ships in them, more banks and with more money than with us, we have traversed the Continent and stood upon the shores of the two great oceans, we have travelled through some of the finest country the sun ever shone on, but take it all in all—we say it candidly—we have seen no better country, no cleverer men, and certainly no handsomer ladies, than are to be found in good old North Carolina.

"Though wittlings may laugh at and scorners defame her,
Our hearts beat with gladness whenever we name her."

North Carolina is good enough for us. We think it ought to be good enough for anybody.

CORRESPONDENCE BETWEEN CLARK AND H. P. PUGH CONCERNING DUEL

Scotland Neck, November 18, 1871

SIR:—I beg leave to inform you that I wrote the letters in the *Roanoke News* over the signature of "Notes by the Way." I respectfully desire to know if you wrote the article signed "Veritas," which appeared in the *Norfolk Journal,* of the 14th inst., and if in that article you intended in any respect to reflect upon my character as a gentleman.

This note will be handed to you by my friend, Capt. W. H. Day.

Yours respectfully,

To H. P. Pugh, Hotel, N.C. WALTER CLARK

Hotel, Bertie Co., N.C. Nov. 18, 1871

WALTER CLARK, ESQ. Sir:—I received your note this morning desiring to know whether I was the author of the article over the signature of "Veritas." I am. Of your character I know nothing. I care to know nothing. If you take any exceptions you can do so.

Respectfully,

H. P. PUGH

This will be handed to you by my friend, W. E. Savage.

Scotland Neck, N.C.
November 19, 1871

SIR:—Your note of this date is received. I beg leave to request that you will meet me at your earliest convenience, at such point in Virginia or South Carolina as you may designate.

Very respectfully,

H.P. PUGH, ESQ., WALTER CLARK
Hotel, N.C.

Hotel, Bertie Co. November 19.

WALTER CLARK, ESQ.—Sir:—I will meet you at Fair Bluffs, South Carolina, on December 8th.

This will be handed to you by my friend, W. E. Savage, Esq.

Respectfully,
H. P. Pugh.

Scotland Neck, N.C. November 20, 1871

Sir—I have to acknowledge yours of yesterday, appointing Fair Bluffs, South Carolina, and December 8th, as time and place of meeting.

My friend, Capt. W. H. Day, will arrange the particulars of the meeting with any one you may select to act for you.

Respectfully,

H.P. PUGH, ESQ., Hotel, N.C. WALTER CLARK

Hotel, N.C., Nov. 22, 1871

Sir:—In reading your first note I misconstrued the tenor of it, as I was very much excited about other matters at the time, and did not give it due deliberation. I considered it altogether in a different light then from what I do now, after my friend, Col. W. E. Savage, and I have read it over and sifted the matter thoroughly between ourselves. The article in the *Norfolk Journal* was intended in no wise to reflect upon your private character. I only attacked it as I would any other public paper or correspondent of a public paper.

Respectfully,

TO COL. WALTER CLARK H. P. PUGH.

Scotland Neck, N.C. November 23, 1871

Sir:—Your note of the 22nd instant is received. I beg leave to say that your disclaimer of any intention to reflect upon my character as a gentleman, in the article signed "Veritas," comes late, but it is satisfactory.

I have the honor to be, very respectfully your obedient servant.

WALTER CLARK

TO H.P. PUGH.

IV

Raleigh Lawyer and Superior Court Judge

1873–1889

IN NOVEMBER, 1873, CLARK MOVED TO RALEIGH, where he was to reside for the remainder of his long and busy life. He soon had a good general law practice and, in addition, was director and general counsel for the Raleigh and Gaston and the Raleigh and Augusta railroads, and later of the Seaboard Air Line when these roads were merged.

Soon after he went to Raleigh, Clark induced Thomas M. Holt, later Governor of the state, to become associated with him in buying the Raleigh *News*, a daily paper which Clark managed and directed for a number of years. He made a considerable reputation with a series of well written and forcible essays, known as the "mudcut letters," criticizing the General Assembly for embarking the state on an expensive and wasteful undertaking in extending the Western North Carolina Railroad across the Blue Ridge Mountains. Large sums had been expended on this project, and the work had bogged down because of serious mud slides. Clark advocated the sale of the road to private interests, and his logical and merciless writings on the subject probably influenced the calling of a special session of the legislature in 1880, which sold the road to private interests.

On January 28, 1874, Clark was married to Susan Washington Graham, daughter of William A. Graham, former Governor, United States Senator, and Secretary of the Navy. The Clarks had a comfortable but inexpensive home, where they entertained many friends and reared their growing family. There were eight children—Susan Washington, David, William A. Graham, Anna M., who died in infancy, Walter, John Washington, Thorne McKenzie, and Eugenia Graham.

For the next decade Clark was very busy in many ways. In addition to his extensive law practice, he did considerable writing. In 1882, he published *Everybody's Book, Some Points in Law of Interest and Use to North Carolina Farmers, Merchants, and Business Men Generally*. He wrote and annotated *The Code of Civil Procedure of North Carolina,* commonly called *Clark's Code,* which was published in 1884 and passed through two later editions. At the request of the state, he also began the work of compiling and editing the *State Records of North Carolina,* which appeared in sixteen volumes (1886-1897). He also served as a member of the Democratic State Executive Committee until his appointment as Superior Court Judge in 1885. During this period he also found time to supervise the work at Ventosa plantation and to carry on considerable correspondence to encourage immigrants to settle in North Carolina.

When Clark moved to Raleigh he transferred his membership to the Methodist church and he became one of its most active laymen. He wrote a number of articles in the history of Methodism and, in 1880, delivered an address at Trinity College on the philosophy of religion. The next year he was chosen by the College of Bishops of the Southern Methodist Episcopal Church as a delegate to the Ecumenical Conference of Methodism at London. While in London he established credit at a bookshop with directions to furnish him with desired books and periodicals. In spite of his meager salary as a judge, Clark managed to build up one of the best libraries in Raleigh. He also had one of the first typewriters, if not the first, in the city. While Clark was abroad he travelled extensively on the continent studying social, economic, and political conditions, and wrote a series of letters for the papers about his experiences and observations.

Clark's first contact with Josephus Daniels began in 1885, as a result of an introductory letter from Henry Groves Connor. For a quarter of a century Clark and Daniels were friends, and Clark's opinions were publicized through Daniels' paper in Raleigh, *The News and Observer*. "This combination became awesome to the growing power of trusts, railroads, and political machines, while at the same time it gave a definite and able leadership to the advanced liberals in the state."

In April, 1885, Governor A. M. Scales appointed Clark to fill a vacancy on the Superior Court bench. In November, 1886, he was elected to this position, which he held until his appointment as a justice of the State Supreme Court in 1889. Some political leaders had urged his nomination for attorney-general, but he discouraged this movement and he withdrew his name voluntarily from the list of aspirants for the governorship in 1888, when the prospects for receiving the nomination were flattering.

The Superior Court judgeship paid only $2,250 a year, but Clark deliberately chose the bench for his life work. During his tenure of office, he established the rule that courts must open on time and that witnesses, jurors, and officers must be present in the courtroom when court opened. Promptness, efficiency, and justice ruled at all times in courts over which Judge Clark presided.

A. W. TOURGÉE * TO THE EDITOR OF "SOUTHERN HOME" †

(*Enclosed in a letter to Clark with a postscript by D. H. Hill*)

Greensboro N. C.
October 7th 1875

I see in your issue of the 27th ult., a reproduction of the charge, that I have, at some time, been an inmate of a penitentiary. I had supposed this slander to have been so utterly exploded, that even the bitterest of my enemies, would consider themselves thoroughly disgraced by its reiteration. I have no acquaintance with you personally and of course know nothing as to your information or intention in such publication. As an editor, I must suppose, that you have some knowledge of the contents of the public prints, and as this matter has been fully ventilated in them, and the most ample recantation given by several journals of the most unmistakable Democratic tone, I must conclude that your re-assertion of it is either from inadvertence to this fact, or a wilful design to perpetrate a slanderous and wilful lie.

If the former, then ordinary justice requires that you should make a retraction co-extensive with the circulation of the imputation. If this is not the case, in justice to a name which reaches back into the historic times of France without spot,—a family neither high nor low, but like their old keep on the Breton coast (La Tourgue,) rugged and true, as well as to myself and my children, I must take other means to rebuke the falsehood.

If you made the imputation in good faith from a belief in its verity, I desire to lay before you the most ample proof as to its utter and absurd falsity, to the end that you may make an explicit and candid denial of the same In that case I request that you will write me stating that fact and I will at once transmit to you the proofs alluded to.

If this is not done, or you are unwilling to take the course indicated, your silence will sufficiently inform me. If I do not hear from you within three days after receipt of this I shall conclude, either that you did not believe the statement you published or are unwilling to correct it when shown to be false and shall take other steps to vindicate myself from your aspersions.

* Albion Winegar Tourgée, noted carpet-bagger and native of Ohio, Superior Court Judge, 1868-1874, member of Conventions of 1868 and 1875, author of *A Fool's Errand by One of the Fools* and other novels.

† Daniel Harvey Hill, Lieutenant General in the Confederate States Armies, editor of "Southern Home" magazine. Hill's wife was a first cousin of Mrs. Walter Clark and sister of Mrs. Stonewall Jackson.

(D. H. Hill's Postscript)

I send you for your private edification, the letter of the "rugged & true" carpet-bagger, whose ancestors have their castle on the coast of Breton. I think that I made a mistake in touching his Penitentiary in Illinois instead of Ohio, but I corrected it afterwards & am all right with him now.

TO CLARK FROM A. M. SCALES *

Greensboro, Sept 5th, 1876

I am just on the eve of leaving home for my appointments in Stokes to be absent about a week & therefore write in haste I heard a discussion between Tourgee & Henderson at Wentworth in Rockingham County I think in 1870, in which discussion Henderson charged most explicitly that Tourgee was a penitentiary bird or in substance that, to which Tourgee after a denial replied that Henderson had stolen Daves mule this is my recollection at present & there are a no of others who will state the same. If the suit continues & yr pleas will admit of it it would be well to prove his general character in Greensboro;

TO CLARK FROM D. H. HILL

Charlotte N C
Sept 4, 1876

Tourgee threatened me with a libel suit. He wrote a very foolish letter claiming descent from Danish rovers, as I now recollect, and from an ancestral castle on some lofty crag. I replied to him my informers were Windy Billy, who had made the charge on the cars publicly and a gentleman of Greensboro, who said that a Yankee Soldier claimed to be a fellow convict with him, Tourgee. I did not give the gentleman's name, but he is W. A. Caldwell, now living somewhere in Tennessee. I think Mr C would be an important witness. Tourgee dropped the matter, I suppose. At least, I heard nothing more from him. If I can be of any service to you, command me. I would dislike, however, to be summoned as a witness.

* Alfred M. Scales of Rockingham County, Governor, 1885-1889.

Above: Susan Washington Graham, whom Walter Clark married in January, 1874. *Below:* Governor William A. Graham, Mrs. Clark's father; and Susannah Sarah Washington Graham, Mrs. Clark's mother.

Charles Farrell

Dike along the Roanoke River at Ventosa plantation. It is seven miles long, twelve feet high, and forty feet wide at the base. It was built about a hundred years ago by Slaves, who moved the dirt in wheelbarrows.

TO CLARK FROM D. H. HILL

Charlotte N C
Oct 30, 1876

I would not wish my name used in connection with the letter as I don't want to have any further trouble with the "nigger & true" scoundrel of Breton Castle, which is probably euphony for Ohio Penitentiary. My other use, in the way of ridicule that may be made of the letter with-out involving my name, would be admissible. Mr W. A. Caldwell of Greensboro told me that he heard a Yankee soldier say that he was a fellow convict of the nigger and true. Windy Billy charged him with being a convict in the cars on the N C R R. Joe Turner * made it fifty times. Why he is so tender of his reputation now surpasses my knowledge of carpet-bag nature. We think here that Dr Pritchard must know all about Holden's confessions & that he ought to speak out. It will injure him seriously, if he does not. Many charge him with too much friendship for Billy & say that he will not expose the fellow.

TO CLARK FROM WASHINGTON DUKE †

Durham, N.C. Dec. 13 1876

Please collect act of mine against D.J. Ezzill If possible & hurry up all the other claims you have of mine. How about the H Petersen claim at Houston Texas also the Gust Bischoff claim sent you some time ago?

TO CLARK FROM D. M. FURCHES ‡

Statesville, N.C.
Jan. 9, 1877

I have received your 'Index of Cases overruled.' &c, with the compliments of the author, for which I am obliged—And am satisfied it will be of practicle use to the profession.—

I have often thought that our Supreme Court neither did themselves, nor the profession Justice in failing to declare these opinions overruled, when they found it necessary to do so, & when their new opinions in effect do overrule their former opinions.

* Josiah Turner, Jr., editor of the Raleigh *Sentinel*.

† Manufacturer of Duke's Genuine Smoking Tobacco, founder of W. Duke Sons and Company, and father of James Buchanan Duke and Benjamin N. Duke.

‡ David M. Furches of Iredell County, Superior Court Judge, 1875-1879, Associate Justice of North Carolina Supreme Court, 1895-1901, Chief Justice, 1901-1903.

At anytime you might expect our courts to find it necessary to review and overrule their former opinions occasionally—Especially so for the last eight or ten years, under the new practice, and the many new questions growing out of the results of the war—For instance the case of Summers vs McCoy, is in effect overruled by the case of Sanders vs Jarman, and the case of State vs Bailey by the State vs Johnson—Yet it is not so stated, and the profession is left in doubt—I mention these two cases because they were mine, and occur to me now—& serve to illustrate what I have just said.

I have the very highest respect for our Supreme Court, their learning, and ability, but think they make a mistake in this.

TO CLARK FROM A. M. WADDELL *

Philada. Jan'y 11th 1877

Your favor of 28th of Dec. was forwarded from Washington to me at this place, and was received yesterday. In regard to the reduction of letter postage, I am, as you are kind enough to say, already tolerably well informed, but notwithstanding the great convenience it would be to the masses of the people, I fear that any attempt to reduce the rate of postage at this time, would meet with no success, for the reason amongst others, that the Post Office Department, requires now annually, its deficiency of appropriation, of about $8,000,000. So you see that retrenchment and reform, is sometimes a double-edged sword. I have frequently had my attention called to this subject during the past 12 months by some of the best informed persons in the country, but I can see no hope in the early future of any reduction of our rates upon letter postage....

TO CLARK FROM WASHINGTON DUKE

Jany 23rd 1877

I enclose claim against E.J. Moody Marion S.C. Please send it forward for collection at once & Oblige....

Have you heard anything from your atty in Houston Tex as regards the Petersen claim?

* Alfred Moore Waddell, Lieutenant Colonel of cavalry in Confederate army, Democratic Congressman, March 4, 1871-March 3, 1879.

TO CLARK FROM JAS. E. SHEPHERD *

Washington, N.C.
Jan. 25, 1877

I am glad to see it announced in the papers that you are preparing a digest for publication. I was about to commence one for my own use, but yours will save me the trouble. I suppose you will not tamely follow the headings or syllabuses, as Judge Battle has done. There is a mine of lore in the reports which Battle's Digest does not pretend to show and a Digest on the plan of Abbott's will be a great benefit to the profession. When do you think it will be ready?

TO CLARK FROM WASHINGTON DUKE

Durham. N.C.
June 21, 1877

Yours enclosing Flanigan's postal received. I enclose the postal together with a letter from Jas. E. Boyd to me, to whom I sent both of these claims last November. I have written him three or four times to send either claims or money, but have never succeeded in drawing a single word from him. I wish you would collect it from him right away. I have no doubt but that both claims have been collected by him & I merely sent them to you to ascertain whether he had done so or not.

TO CLARK FROM JOHN E. WOODARD

Wilson, N.C. June 23rd 1877

If it be entirely convenient, please favor me with two copies of the Memorial Oration delivered by Montford McGehee Esq. on the life and character of Hon. William A. Graham and oblige.

TO CLARK FROM WASHINGTON DUKE

Durham, July 16th 1877

Herewith I hand you a claim on G.W. Boroughs & Co Atlanta Ga which you will please forward to some good attorney and instruct him to make the claim safe. I drawed on him at the maturity of each Bill & the drafts was returned with the words (have remitted) on back of Dft which was not true I wrote to them &

* Native of Beaufort County, Superior Court Judge, 1883-1888, Associate Justice of North Carolina Supreme Court, 1889-1893, Chief Justice, 1893-1895.

they sent me their note at 60 Days & I returned at once to them & told them I could not accept & they returned it to me again & I sent it back to them & told them I would not accept Without they would get some reliable man to indorse for them & have heard nothing from them since. You must instruct your attorney not to belive their statements as regarding the Claim being for it certainly has not. I do not mind indulging them for a time if the claim can be secured in any way but if not secured I want the money made at once if possible. I have extended the time on several Claims which always resulted in giving them a chance to wind up their business & Break & never pay nothing. Your immediate attention will greatly oblige

TO CLARK FROM F. S. WILLIAMS *

Richmond 1877

A Strong effort is going to be made this Summer & fall to Settle up the line of the N.C. & R & D RR. with immigrants, from the North and East, and I want to get the names of parties having land &c for sale along these lines and a description of them. Can you refer to this in your local columns, as this increase of population will largely benefit your Section. All having land, can address me.

TO CLARK FROM DAVID SCHENCK †

Lincolnton, Aug 10 1877

I have the pleasure to acknowledge the receipt of your brief in Bunting vs Gales also the compilation of the Acts in regard to the Ral & Gas RR and Ral & Aug RR—The case of Bunting vs Gales was quite an interesting one but the Supreme Court has straddled the ditch so much, it is impossible to know on which side of it they are—Perry vs Campbell 63 N.C. & King vs Com[s] 65 NC seem to be irreconciliable—You have done much good to the profession by your digests of the Sup. Court decisions and we owe you gratitude.

In conversation with a number of lawyers the other day, it was suggested that we would ask you to give us two columns in the News called the "Lawyers and Legislators Column"—In this lawyers might express themselves on current opinions, on amendments to our statutes, suggest and publish new bills, recite

* President of the Richmond and Danville Railroad Company.

† Native of Lincoln County, Superior Court Judge, 1874-1881, author of *North Carolina, 1780-1781.*

interesting cases and points, diversify with anecdotes and incidents of the court room &c &c—They would make the News the pet of the profession—I would promise you a frequent article—What do you say to it? Lawyers have no medium of communication in the state and they feel the need of it—Did you see any suggestion to Gen Jones on making an Appendix to our next Reports of the Conflict of Jurisdiction cases? You are so competent and adapted to this work that I hope you will pardon me suggesting it—

TO CLARK FROM THOS. M. HOLT *

Haw River Aug. 11, 1877

Sometime since I *believe* when I was in Raleigh last, *One* gentleman spoke to me about consolidating the two Papers, to which I replied, if the other stockholders were willing to sell, I would sell mine. In a conversation afterwards, with Maj. Engelhard †, the same subject came up & was talked generally in which conversation, I told him that I felt great sympathy for Hale *especially,* his Father & my Father being old long & tried friends & that if Hale & Saunders ‡ would buy out the other stockholders, I would sell them mine on very good terms. As I took the stock money to establish a good Democratic paper, & to advance the interest of the party, than to make money. This I am sure is about all the conversation I ever had about the matter.

If you think they are *not able* to buy & *would* not pay what you thought it worth, that of course ends the matter. I am willing to sell them my stock, (& will do so at a much less figure than to any one else) *if they can buy the remainder,* but as I said before, my feelings still are, that I will not sell unless we make a clean sale of the whole thing. I expect to be in Raleigh Friday the 17th, when I would be glad to see you.

TO CLARK FROM B. N. DUKE §

Durham, N.C. Sept 24, 1877

I enclose my check no 452 for $25.00 amt due you on the Burroughs claim as collection fees. Our Mr. W. Duke would have

* Textile manufacturer of Alamance County, Governor of North Carolina, 1891-1893.

† Joseph A. Engelhard of New Hanover County, Secretary of State, 1876-1879.

‡ Peter M. Hale and Colonel William L. Saunders began the publication of the Raleigh *Observer*. Saunders was Secretary of State, 1879-1891, and editor of the *Colonial Records of North Carolina.*

§ Benjamin N. Duke, son of Washington Duke.

called on Mr Jefferies when in Atlanta—But did not know he was the attorney who had the matter in chge. Please acknowledge & oblige.

Can't you stir up some of our other delinquents & make them pay?

TO CLARK FROM W. N. H. SMITH *

Raleigh, N.C. Sept 25 1877

It is more convenient for me to communicate by note than to walk to your office, at the risk of finding you absent. I want to know if you have heard from your client in reference to the compromise of the suit against Hymans & Davy.

You remember I proposed to pay you 20 dollars, which will cover costs & I presume also excess of interest usually taken if any. Let me hear from you.

TO CLARK FROM C. H. BROGDEN †

Washington, D.C., Nov. 6, 1877

I duly received your letter calling my attention to the want of more mail facilities in Halifax Co., for which please accept my thanks.

It is my duty here to try to represent the wishes and interests of my constituents as far as I can, and I assure you that the new mail routes which you mention as necessary and desirable shall receive proper attention at the proper time.

TO CLARK FROM A. S. MERRIMON ‡

Washington, Nov. 9th 1877

I am in receipt of your letter of the 2nd inst. and have today made another effort to have mail routes placed on the [road] from *Halifax to Scotland Neck* as you suggest. The Deptmt. has no money that can be devoted to that purpose now, but I think—feel confident—that at an early day such routes will be granted.

* Chief Justice of the Supreme Court of North Carolina, 1878-1889.

† Curtis H. Brogden of Wayne County, Governor 1874-1877; Republican Representative in Congress, 1877-1879.

‡ Augustus S. Merrimon, United States Senator, 1875-1879; Associate Justice of North Carolina Supreme Court, 1885-1889; Chief Justice, 1889-1893.

TO CLARK FROM JOSEPH M. WILSON *

Washington, D.C.
Nov. 27, 1877

I thank you for the Memorial of Mr. Graham.† I remember him (as a public man) very well. I voted for him, and as an old line Whig, felt his defeat with that of Scott very keenly. He was one of the few Southern men, who identified themselves with the Secession movement, whose actions filled the hearts of Old line Whigs with grief. I read with profound interest of his efforts to prevent the great catastrophe, of his subsequent career in connection with the Confederacy. I knew very little hence the information given by the Orator was interesting to me. There is one thing that I have never yet been able to comprehend, and that is the claim of the soil upon a mans loyalty.—the *State* secedes, and hence the *Man* goes also—that is the old feudal idea that the man & the soil belonged together. With us the question of territory was subordinate. the *idea* of *government* was pre-eminent, but I find I am drifting into debateable grounds—and only refer to it because Mr G. was involved in that idea & followed it out. What the Orator says about the "North," leads me to believe that he dont testify to what he knows—though he doubtless does to what he believes. I suppose we are too near the events of the past 16 years to understand why God in his providence permitted such a war as our country was afflicted with. The question for *us* is to try & build up the "waste places," and to extend the area of good influences and good government, and thus advance the common interests of humanity. We all can do something for the good of our fellow man.

I often think of the pleasant visit I had to your city, and wish I could render the good and true men with whom I became acquainted, some aid in their efforts to develope the resources of the State.

TO CLARK FROM W. W. VASS ‡

Raleigh, N.C. Dec. 29, 1877

The Prest. has called a meeting of the Directors of this Co. and of the Ral Augusta and Sou RR Co. to meet at the Office of this Co. on Friday next, Janry 4, 1878, at 4 oclock, P.M.

* Secretary of the United States Department of Agriculture.

† William Alexander Graham, Clark's father-in-law, Governor, 1845-1849, and Whig candidate for vice president 1852.

‡ Secretary of Raleigh & Gaston Railroad Company.

TO CLARK FROM A. W. GRAHAM *

Hillsboro' N. C.
July 3rd 1878

Your letter and your postal card were received a few days ago, also your letter in regard to the Congressional nomination. I am much obliged for the statistics and information in regard to the Public Printing. It is a strong card for us to hold in this campaign, and I have already used it with good effect in one or two instances I am very much surprised that it was never published before and thus give the lie to the Turner advocates who say he never received any thing at the hands of the party. Turner † was in Raleigh last Friday for the purpose of raising money for his campaign & to start a paper, but I have not yet heard whether he was successful. He is intensely bitter now in attacks on Gov. Vance,‡ and tells the country people that Hampton § had the rogues in South Carolina punished and Vance let the great rascals in this State escape because some of his friends were concerned in the stealing. And strange to say a large number of our people are ignorant enough to believe him. It has occurred to me, though I have no proof of it that Merrimon's managers are encouraging him in his infernal rascality, for wherever you find a Turnerite you find a Merrimon man, and very frequently those who have heretofore been considered sound but who lean to M. have nothing to say against Turner. You must not mention this matter as it is, as yet, only an opinion of my own.

You have seen, I suppose, the result of the Prospect Hill convention. There was a strong under-current against Williamson in the Convention and our friends had some difficulty in quelling it, but we told them it would never do to go back on the recommendation of Caswell County. There is considerable dissatisfaction in Person & Orange with Wm's and I am fearful about his election; especially as Charles Winstead || of Person will be a candidate against us. Winstead is *very* popular in Person among the Democrats and will run as a no party man and will thus command a large vote from both sides, and Williamson being so unpopular in all three counties, Winstead stands a good chance

* Augustus W. Graham, lawyer, better known as Gus Graham. He was Clark's brother-in-law and closest friend.

† Josiah Turner, Jr., editor of the Raleigh *Sentinel*.

‡ Zebulon Baird Vance, Governor of North Carolina, 1862-65 and 1877-79.

§ General Wade Hampton, Governor of South Carolina, 1877-1879.

|| Member of General Assembly, 1860, 1864-1865, 1868, 1881.

to be elected. If he runs, of which I think there is no doubt now, it will be in Merrimons interest as he considers himself under obligations to M. for favors and assistance rendered him. *This is authentic but strictly confidential.*

Will you please examine the files of the Sentinel of 1874 and find what Turner had to say of Ruffin as an independent. I wish copious extracts made and as you will hardly have time to do it, if you will have some one to do the work I will pay for it. I think we will have the warmest campaign ever witnessed in Orange....

TO CLARK FROM A. W. GRAHAM

Hillsboro' N. C.
July 22nd 1878

Your postal and letter in regard to J. H. Moore * & the Public Printing were received last week. I am very much obliged to you for your promptness in the matter. Turner has the impudence to get up and deny that he ever received a dollar of the money. He says Moore & Ramsey his foremen made the contracts measured the printing and received the money and he never got one dollar of the profit. He can beat the devil in brass & lying. Do you suppose Moore would give me a statement in writing about it? I enclose a note to him which I would be obliged to you to hand to him and get an answer if possible and send to me at Durham care of M. A. Angier by tomorrow nights mail, as I think I can use it with good effect at Bladen Spring on Wednesday. He would have been defeated any way but Guthrie & Jenkins only render it more certain. Turner's friends charge that they were brought out by Democrats in Orange & Wake to defeat T. As Chairman of the Democratic Committee, being in a position where I would have been consulted by the party, I have given it the lie on every occasion. Guthrie & Jenkins cannot concentrate the Radical vote, not having the confidence of the party, but they will get a good portion of it. I suppose you have heard of the difficulty at Chapel Hill between John & Turner. He had said nothing about me until we reached Pattersons Mill and I of course said but little about him as we were candidates for different positions. But when we got there he thought being in his stronghold he could say what he pleased & criticised me pretty freely. I gave him as good as he sent & our friends say made a good many votes. At Durham he did the same thing and just laid himself open to attack & of course I did

* Author of *History of North Carolina from the Earliest Discoveries to the Present Time.*

not fail to wade in. Our friends say I drove a great many votes away from him. I went for him on his Swepson * correspondence & upon Lewis Jenkins affidavit & the Public Printing & of course he could not stand it. We speak at Mangum's Store today, his strongest place in the county and I expect he will crow loudly. But we have all the points on him so I do not fear anything. He & his son Tom are both going around the canvass heavily armed. . . .

TO CLARK FROM P. H. WINSTON †

Windsor 8 Oct 1878.

In this sequestered glen known as Bertie we cast our eyes (in mind) abroad now and then but we get no knowledge worth having.

I tax your busy moments with some few inquiries.

1 Who has charge of the Editorial Dept of the News? I wish to know the man who writes and does the including and excluding for the paper.

2 As to the Vance Merrimon wrestle I wish to know which will fling. I have the impression that the heterogeneous mixtry for Merrimon may be formidable. Indeed some say that he is as good as in. Write me and shed light on this head.

3 Tell me if you please what are the signs for the Raleigh lawyers Are they making money. Who get the cases and the money. Who eats the best breakfast among them.

Our crops are about average. Cotton I think is a shewing above the average. My crops are about 10 per cent above

The probability is that Jo Martin will crowd Yeates *very close*. Respass will not get 100 votes. Chamberlain not 10. What about Davis and his opponents.

I think you had better return to Halifax.

Do you like Raleigh? Is property rising or falling there.

I think you are a specie man. My doctrine is and as long as I am in debt will be that the currency should be watered. It is too strong. Those old Confederate times were good when a man could pay debt easy. Issue paper until gold goes to 200 and that would give us $100^{00} a bale for cotton to pay debts with.

Write me Clark and tell me especially about the senatorial contest. Who will get it.

* George W. Swepson, notorious figure of Reconstruction period in North Carolina.

† Bertie County lawyer and member of the General Assembly; father of Francis D., George T., and Robert W. Winston.

TO CLARK FROM P. H. WINSTON

Windsor 8 Feby 1879.

I got your esteemed letter and am always cheered by the magnetism of your writing. I have to thank you for sundry good suggestions in that and previous letters.

If I had been fairly whipped in the fight of June 1878 I would have taken it and subsided like a man. But it was not fairly done. They took underhold and the back lock, both together unfair in wrestling.

We are all very poor in Bertie. Dyspepsia, gout, obesity, and such like are all gone from here. The Anti fat medicine not needed in Bertie.

As Genl Leach in former years was wont to exclaim "What is the Country coming to"? . . .

Clark it looks to me like Raleigh is going to dry up some. As to Windsor it can live on Raccoons and roasting ears gathered from the adjacent corn fields. Raleigh is rather too far from Windsor for Raleigh's permanent prosperity.

Windsor has not shrunk any in one hundred years. Raleigh is remarkable for Injunctions Mandamus, Certioraris, Recordari's and supersnatchits. It is the only capital in the world where the State furnishes the lawyers with snuff and then pays them at the rate of 100^{oo} for each sneeze. I am going there Clark. I do not expect any snuff nor sneezing, but to hear it going on will be delightful. Every Key in the gamut will be sounded in the different sneezes, resembling in no little degree the frog harmony at Terrapin Point when the herrings come.

Our farmers are lively. Cotton is done. We are all singing

Old King Cole &c

We change it with

Begone dull care

TO CLARK FROM W. H. KITCHIN *

Washington May 16th/79

Yours received & noticed. I will try to have the service increased on the Route named. I tried to get the acts of the third session, but am told that they are not out yet—will send them when pub-

* William Hodges Kitchin of Halifax County, Democratic Representative in Congress, March 4, 1879-March 3, 1881, father of William Walton and Claude Kitchin.

lished—I am tired of politics & out of patience with this Congress & will say this City is the Sodom of America—There is no harmony in our party—we are as you may say at sea—No one with sufficient wisdom & backbone to lead—The South has yeilded that honor to the Northern democrats & they are as nervous as if walking on the brink of a burning Versuvius. We like wisdom & more oil in the spinal column of our party. Our so called leaders are worse on a retreat than Johnson with not half his strategy—The hard money wing of our side I fear will split us asunder—Every thing on the money side tends to consolidation & the curtailing of the rights of the people. And besides this, if we do not capture the Greenbackers * so called we are gone in 80—They hold the balance of power in the country—& in my opinion the only salvation of this country is the fusion or affiliation of these elements—If this should fail, I confess my hopes of the republic are clouded—Of course the Greenbackers are in the extreme, and off at a tangent, but we must advance none & draw them back so that we can get in the same ranks, or my fears may be realized, I hope not—Hill † has made a powerful speech—unanswerable, & Thurman ‡ shot his hundred-pounder to dry with telling effect, but its yet to be seen whether they will have the desired effect—We will hope for the best. . . .

TO CLARK FROM A. W. TOURGÉE

Raleigh, N. C.
May 26th 1879.

Knowing that you have examined my Digest of contest cases very carefully, I would like an expression of your opinion as to its merits, advantages &c

TO CLARK FROM A. W. TOURGÉE

Wentworth House
Denver, Colorado.

I had intended to have written both to you and the *News* long before this time; but at the same time, there was a sort of reserved promise in my mind that I would not write until I reached

* National political party.

† Benjamin Harvey Hill of Georgia, Democratic Representative in Congress, December 6, 1875-March 4, 1877; United States Senator, March 4, 1877-August 16, 1882.

‡ Allen Granberry Thurman of Ohio, United States Senator, March 4, 1869-March 3, 1881; member of Electoral Commission of 1876 and unsuccessful candidate for vice-president of the United States in 1888.

here, which I then expected to do some two months ago—However, I have loitered by the way, enjoying for the first time in many years, a month's immunity from labor and but a week ago, reached this place. I send enclosed for the *News,* my first impressions. They will have little interest for you but may amuse others.

I was much interested in your brief in regard to the Speaker's veto and must say that I think the court has covered itself with ineffaceable shame in its subserviency to a *clique*—not a party—and uselessly antagonizing and injuring the entire educational interests of the state. It opens the door to every species of fraud and chicanery and leaves the legislation of the state entirely under the control of the presiding officers or either of them.

It seems to me my friend, that the time of which we were speaking together a few months since, and wh— you have been writing for so long, has come. Those few months have been pregnant of great results. They have been pivotal in their character. Two things may be counted upon as settled—viz: The election of Grant as President and the disruption of the Democratic Party of the South. They are as certain as tomorrow's sunshine, *visi deas intersit.* The evidences of disintegration are too numerous to mention. Already they have lost control of Virginia. Georgia will follow next. Stephens and Crawford and Felton may have private grievances and personal aims, I do not doubt but they have; but they have correctly forecasted the future and taken stock in its revulsions. I do not doubt but the Grant *"boom"* and its inevitable success are largely the cause of this; but in any event it must have come sooner or later.

It seems to me that you will never have another such an opportunity offered you. You *could* not have a *better* one. In your place I would put myself avowedly at the head of the *News.* I would put up *Grant,* a *unified nation,* good schools and no speaker's veto. Just look at it square-headed my friend. It only needs a little tip to upset the predominant party in your state at the best. You *know,* as well as I, (though of course I will not ask nor expect you to acknowledge it) that N. C[a] was not *carried* by the Dems. in 1876 but was *counted* in by the aid of Tilden's money. The figures in regard to it are simply overwhelming. Think of Nash Co. giving *39 per-cent more votes than she had voters by the census of 1870!—As she did.* Of course you are *considered* as having been privy to some part of this. The men who managed it are perhaps uncertain just how much you know. Now, while they could well afford to pay no attention to the deductions of a Republican, a hint of such a thing from *you,* would disarm all assault. Then in addition to this such a movement would give you at once a national prominence. It would focalize you in the eyes of the nation —of the North as well as of the South. In short it is your chance. You have nothing to lose and everything to gain by it. You have the nerve if you do not wait too long in making up your mind. If you are to gain anything you must move at once and burn your bridges.

You must pardon me this. You know I am outspoken and I think you will credit me with some forecast in such matters. At all events let me hear from you. If you will not take good fortune when it is thrown in your way at least write and tell me so, in order that I may have the script to shake in your face, when we meet in that old age when all men lie about their past.

The People's Platform For The Extra Session *

1. Repeal immediately on assembling all appropriations for building the "Mudcut" R.R. The annual burden of that R.R. on the taxpayers is about $300.000 as follows

Interest paid by State on $850.000 Mortgage bonds	$59.500
Appropriations for iron, carts &c.	70.000
Expense feeding clothing & guarding 600 convicts	45.000
Sheriff's 5 per ct. comm. collecting above sums out of the people	8.725
	$183.225
Add value of labor of 600 able bodied convicts above expenses of clothing, feeding & guarding as per agreement between the R.R. & the Penitentiary Board	57.000
(if hired elsewhere this sum would come in to *reduce taxation*)	
Also add nett earnings of road from Salisbury to Asheville 150 miles—*say*	60.000
(This sum, if work is stopped at Asheville, instead of going into the Building the R.R. as now would reduce taxation by paying the annual interest)	
Annual cost to taxpayers	$300.225

* Manuscript in Clark's handwriting in the Clark papers, also reprinted in various newspapers.

As the total state tax raised by the tax list is $510.000 a repeal of this subsidy would relieve each taxpayer of about 3/5, considerably *over half,* of his State taxes. In view of the State Treasurer's Report of a deficiency of $240.000 in the State Treasury and an overwhelming public sentiment a repeal of the tax is *imperative.*

2. If the offer to buy the road on investigation turns out to be a fair price with sufficient guarantees, take it. Even if at a little under-price, if the guarantees are good, take the offer for the sake of getting the matter out of politics. But if the price is greatly inadequate or the guarantees are insufficient, let the State hold the 150 miles of R.R. from Salisbury to Asheville which has cost the taxpayers so much till we can sell at a fair price. The nett earnings would pay the $59.500 annual interest on the bonds. In the mean time, permit any parties who think the Paint Rock & Ducktown R.Rs are good investments for their money to build them free of charge to the taxpayers. The legislature has power to prevent discrimination in their tariffs against our own ports. *But sale or no sale repeal this $300.000 annual Railroad Subsidy.*

3. As an offset to the expenses of the Extra Session abolish the ornamental "Bureau of Agriculture" with its annual cost of $25.000 to the farmers, leaving only the Fertilizer Analysis Stations which is the only useful part of it.

4. Have the "School Bill" signed and give the children of the poor a chance.

The true solution of our troubles is to legislate for the interests of the whole State ("the greatest good for the greatest number") regardless of the clamor of the *politicians* of any one section, and relieve the taxpayers from all except *necessary* taxation regardless of the clamor of office-holders.

Many Voters

Cost of Mudcut R.R. To Date

State Bonds (recognized debt) issued before 1868	$4.400.000
Private subscriptions " "	1.000.000
4 years from May 1876 to May 1880 at $250.000	1.000.000
Cost of 150 miles from Salisbury to Asheville	$6.400.000

This is exclusive of the debt for which the road was sold in 1873 and exclusive of the $6.000.000 special tax bonds issued in 1868 of which it is claimed $600.000 of work was done on the Western Division.

All this expense has been incurred to get to Asheville. Now there is 47 miles to be built to Paint Rock and 140 to Ducktown and we have just gotten to the difficult part of the work. The Governor says, with the present subsidy it would take eight years to build to Paint Rock and twenty years to Ducktown and the President of the road in a recent speech admitted it would take $6.800.000 to build the two lines beyond Asheville. Considering how estimates of the cost of building of a R.R. when made before hand always fall under the mark it is fair to estimate that $15.000.000 (fifteen millions) and thirty years time are necessary to build the two R.R. beyond Asheville, and that too when the assessed value of the real estate of the eight small counties through which the two roads are to run is less than *one eighth* of the amount required to build the R.Rs through them. Whether we sell the completed Railroad from Salisbury to Asheville or not, *repeal the tax to build beyond Asheville.*

CLARK TO CHARLES A. COOK *

Raleigh, N. C.
24 Feb. 1880

Our "Tax-payers Boom" has become a tidal wave and an extra session has been called to repeal the R. R. tax. When the legislature meets repeal of the tax is certain. On the further proposition to sell or give away the 150 miles of road from Salisbury to Asheville as a bonus to parties to induce them to build the Paint Rock and Ducktown R. R. debate is likely to prove lively. Your judgment before proved so reliable and prophetic that I am bold enough to ask (if agreeable) your own judgment and public sentiment in your country on this question of the sale. Of the repeal of the taxation there is now no question *anywhere.*

TO CLARK FROM CHARLES A. COOK

It is almost the universal sentiment here that the road should be sold.

I am very scantily informed about the matter and therefore have no sufficient data upon which to base a decided opinion of *my own.*

The "tax payers boom" is heartily endorsed by the taxpayers of this section.

* Warrenton attorney, member of General Assembly, 1887, 1895-1897.

PATRICK HENRY WINSTON
"Winston of Bertie."

TO CLARK FROM HUGH F. MURRAY

Wilson, N. C.
February 26, 1880.

Yours received. My mind is not yet made up on the subject of the Western Railroad sale. When it is, I will let you hear from me. The Wilson Advance, edited by my law partner, will oppose the sale. Your paper has not favored the criminal circuits as I hoped it would.

My political "ticket" is Fowle * for Governor against the world!

TO CLARK FROM JOSEPH P. CALDWELL †

Statesville, N. C.
April 6, 1880

Yours of the 5th to hand. If nothing happens I will be in Raleigh to see you Friday morning (9th inst.) by the Raleigh and Augusta Air lines train and, as time as well as money is a consideration to as poor a man as myself, will expect to return by the Richmond and Danville train at 5 P.M. of the same day in order that I may be back as early as possible.

Hoping that this arrangement may suit you.

TO CLARK FROM G. E. MATTHEWS ‡

Ringwood, N. C.
June 19th, 1880

I think the chances first rate for you to get the nomination for Atty. General.§

All the Halifax delegates with whom I have conversed are for you and I wish you would make a fight for the nomination or at least endeavor to show through your friends why you should have the nomination.

I wish to come to Raleigh 15th, if I can leave my patients—and anything I can do to aid in securing the nomination for you I am willing to do.

Do you think it is now Fowle or Jarvis?

* Daniel G. Fowle of Wake County, member of General Assembly, 1862-1864, Governor, 1889-1891.

† Editor of the Statesville *Landmark*, 1880-1892, and of the Charlotte *Daily Observer*, 1892-1909.

‡ Halifax County physician and politician.

§ Clark asked that his name be withdrawn from consideration for this nomination.

Let me know at once whether or not you have consented to stand for the aforesaid nomination.

Spier Whitaker * told me yesterday he was for you for the position and I am sure your native county will go for you and you know "a prophet is not without honor" etc. . . .

C. B. DENSON † TO CLARK

Raleigh, N.C.
July 3, 1880

I have the honor to inform you of your appointment as a member of the Executive Committee of the North Carolina Agricultural Society for 1880, by Col. Thos. M. Holt, ‡ President.

TO CLARK FROM BRAXTON CRAVEN §

Trinity College
July 21, 1880.

The United States Government proposes to send twelve Cherokee Indian boys to Trinity College, to receive an English education.

1. The pay will be prompt and remunerative.

2. They are to be boarded in a house to themselves, and will not mingle with the other students.

So far as I can see, there is no objection, unless it should not be favorable to the public.

Please give me your opinion frankly and fully. Shall we receive them, would any of our patrons refuse to send their sons on that account? Would it in any way detract from our standing?

Would it aid our missionary work? Please answer at once.

TO CLARK FROM SAMUEL J. FALL ||

Wellingboro, England, Nov. 1880.

Yours duly received. I had almost started two or three other families as the three spoken of will live together (I hope it is a decent house) and work together. I reckoned them as one as I

* Halifax County lawyer; member of General Assembly, 1881; Superior Court Judge, 1889-1894.

† Secretary of the Society. Clark took an active interest in the State Fair and was a member of the Executive Committee from 1880 until the time of his death.

‡ Native of Alamance County and Governor of North Carolina, 1891-93.

§ Craven was president of Trinity College, then located at Trinity in Randolph County.

|| Commissioner of Emigration for the State of North Carolina in Great Britain.

know there is plenty of land. I expect now I shall have to let two young men who want to go with them, go. You can easily find a small place for them. I send 3 families to New Bern by the same ship, Dec. 11th.

I have another family on my hands, whom I scarce know what to do with, a Mr. Brimley,* wife, 3 grown sons, 2 grown daughters—have been farming on a large scale. 400 acres under plough, moved in best society, had a beautiful home, thoroughly well educated, the youngest son has just carried the prize and scholarship of the Royal Agricultural Society, for knowledge of scientific farming—a superior family. I have been arranging with them for 4 months past, fully expecting they would have ten or fifteen thousand dollars. They have sold off everything, given up the farm, and are now ready to start, and will come by the same ship. Their passage tickets will cost nearly $600 to Raleigh, and now I find that they will scarce have any left. What can be done? They certainly cannot buy a farm at present though they will have more money in a few years. Do you know a place they could rent on shares with a 5 or 6 roomed house on it? They are up in all kinds of sheep, cattle and corn farming, would make a splendid addition, would be good society in any community.

I have written to Mr. Chavasse of Henderson and to N.B. Broughton.† They will have through tickets to Raleigh but if between you, you can find a suitable place, at Littleton, Henderson or thereabouts, send a letter in enclosed envelope to meet them and they can stop and save the expense.

Personally I am exceedingly disappointed. I visited their place and have spent a deal of time over them and if they had the money, they would have been a credit to me.

It is all round the same, farmers cannot realize the value of anything just now. I came across a party last week in Lincolnshire who five years ago paid one hundred thousand dollars for a farm, they have put forty thousand into it in improvements, drainage, fences, the stock on it, and today they cannot sell it for the current debts incurred last year. Do the best you can for these. Let me know when you have any land vacant.

* The Brimley family migrated to North Carolina and Mr. C. S. Brimley was prominently connected with the State Museum for many years.

† President of Edwards, Broughton Printing Company and outstanding champion of education.

TO CLARK FROM SAMUEL J. FALL

(Enclosed in a letter from Walter Clark to his Father)

Wellingboro, Eng. Dec. 30, 1880

I will do the best I can to find you a customer for the Hotel. I know it, having stayed there 2 days.

I fear it is not the class of theirs an English Emigrant needs.

How much capital ought a man have to start it and run it with?

Let me know where you can find farms to rent on share. I have lots more getting ready to come.

Three more families leave London Jany 5th for Raleigh 2 for New Bern.

I have 2 Schoolmasters ready. would be glad to hear of an opening to start with.

No information you can give me, will come amiss, but will be gratefully received.

(Postscript by Clark)

Read & *return* me this. Do any of your neighbors want such renters?

How would you like one or two on the river on trial. You might reserve a two horse crop of good land for them & if you let me know at once they can be there *before* Mar 1—in plenty time for this year's crop. Love to all. Return me this letter.

[P.P.S.]
Many as you see are going to Newbern——Surely it is no sicklier & much better land on the River.

CLARK TO A. W. GRAHAM

Raleigh, N.C.
4 Jan 1881

. . . I am wholly opposed to *any* new counties anywhere & hope the Orange people will defeat Fuller's scheme.* Small counties are more expensive of course besides as our constitution gives each county a member there are already numerous counties voting hardly as much as one of your townships but with a member each. The result is that Orange, Wake & other large counties are not

* In January, 1881, a bill to create Durham County was introduced in the General Assembly, and to present the matter to the various committees of that body Thomas C. Fuller, a prominent Durham attorney, was employed.

proportionately represented & every new county tends to increase the disproportion....

CLARK TO A. W. GRAHAM

Raleigh, N.C.
15 Feb. 1881

There is now a splendid chance to kill the "Durham" bill.*

We had a meeting here, raised a little money & sent runners through the Wake "cut-off." † They have returned with a petition signed by a majority of voters in said cut-off *against* Durham. If Hillsboro will display a like activity I am sure you could in next two days send down at least a large petition from the Orange "cut-off" against it. That would kill the bill. Those people in the cut-off who are farther from Durham than they are now from Hillsboro would sign it, also that class who are constitutionally opposed to *anything* new, those who are opposed to being taxed to build a new jail & court house when they already have good ones, and also those who don't want Blackwell & Co ‡ to have a little county in which they will virtually appoint the members of the legislature & all the county officers. These classes combined would make a large petition from the "cut-off"—*there* is where you want them from.

If killed this time, you will never be troubled again for no members will ever come from Orange again to betray & divide her.

If your people will *promptly* send two men through the "cut-off" & send down signatures here we can kill the bill *easily*.

CLARK TO A. W. GRAHAM

Raleigh
22 Feb. 1881

... I think we will beat "Durham" again on Thursday but I shall not feel safe till it is done. Blackwell,§ Carr || & Morgan ¶ are hard at work trying to change votes.**

* The bill to create Durham County was introduced in the legislature by Caleb B. Green of Durham, then in Orange County.

† A small strip of land in Oak Grove and Cedar Forks townships which was to be cut off from Wake and added to the new county of Durham.

‡ Blackwell and Company had built the first tobacco warehouse in Durham and had become prominent in tobacco manufacturing.

§ William T. Blackwell and J. R. Blackwell were prominent tobacconists.

|| Julian S. Carr, prominent industrialist and partner of W. T. Blackwell.

¶ Samuel T. Morgan, who with Eugene Morehead, organized the Durham Fertilizer Company in 1888.

** The bill to create Durham County passed in 1881.

TO CLARK FROM SAMUEL J. FALL

Wellingboro, Eng. Feb. 28, 1881

I received your post card dated 12, Feb. yesterday, Sunday. and the one dated Jan. 17. this noon. so that it has been 6 weeks on the road. I have tried and shall try to send some one for the Hotel for I need the cash bad enough. They keep me so short that I don't know how to get along from week to week and must give up unless they alter. But it is very seldom I come across any one with cash enough to take it. I have several would like it but have not money enough, and I have several who have means but would not care for this Hotel.

I send a splendid wealthy family. 12 chill. out last week will arrive same time about as this with $1000. If you know a farm they could rent for a year, let them know (name Tysen).

In April I shall send 2 gentlemen, one a clergyman the other a retired Colonel, to Raleigh and the West. They want to look out a good home with good climate, good society, good educational facilities, (12 children each.) They want also good investment for capital having £12,000 or $60,000 each, moving in high class society. I will give them an introduction to you, and shall be glad if you can forward them to good society, make N.C. attractive. Let me know when I can send you any more tenant farmers.

Send me all the newspapers you can. any sort.

TO CLARK FROM H. N. MC TYEIRE *

Nashville, Tenn.
May 5, 1881

The College of Bishops desire you to act as one of the Delegates of our church to the Ecumenical Conference of Methodism, which is to meet in London, next September.

It gives me great pleasure to make this communication, and I earnestly hope you can so arrange as to serve the Meth. Episcopal South on that important occasion.

Don't let any ordinary business stand in the way, I beg you. Your church wants your services and your presence at the world-wide gathering of her sons.

* Methodist bishop.

TO CLARK FROM SAMUEL J. FALL

Wellingborough, England, Oct. 18th 1881

I take the liberty of asking your kindly interest in behalf of the bearer, Albert Galliene, Methodist Minister at Guernsey, who should feel deeply grateful for any counsel or courtesy you may extend, or influence you may secure for the son for whose temporal & spiritual welfare the father is most solicitous....

TO CLARK FROM A. W. GRAHAM

Hillsboro, N. C.
December 17, 1881

I have time for only a few words to congratulate you on your answer to Jarvis * fling at the "Mud Cut Boom". He was in no way justifiable in his attack on you and he will find that it will recoil upon him. Vance & the Railroads seem to have started him to writing and he does not know when to stop. They have put the party in a bad fix and do not seem to have the wisdom to extricate it. Unless the Legislature meets and patches up a truce between the various factions we are hopelessly gone at the next election....

CLARK TO A. W. GRAHAM

Raleigh, N.C.
20 June 1883

...That the "three" aldermen have committed a breach of party discipline is very clear. Whether there are reasons which make their course justifiable, or even commendable, is a question which they must fight out with their constituents. But that is not the question I was trying to ascertain public sentiment upon. To prevent the effect of a breach of party discipline a gross violation of *law* was resorted to in depriving 5 men of their rights without trial, without evidence & with a refusal to *hear* the parties. The matter will figure largely in next year's campaign. What I am trying to find out from you & others is to ascertain if there is any considerable feeling, or disposition, among democrats to endorse a violation of *law* and legal rights for the benefit of party organization. I want to find out the temper of the party upon it. If there is a feeling that *law* can be violated for *party,* we shall be beaten next year, for there is a conservative feeling in N.C. that will not

* Thomas J. Jarvis of Pitt County, Governor of North Carolina 1879-1885.

endorse illegality to favor either party. The feeling here is clearly expressed that the party is in no way responsible for the illegal act & should not make itself responsible by any seeming endorsement of it. The press generally seem of the same way of thinking—and that we should take on no more "load" to carry through the next campaign. But after all, it depends upon how the party generally view the illegality perpetrated here (in *the name* of party organization, but really for the benefit of one or two men). If the party is put in the attitude of endorsing a violation of law and individual rights, if done in the name of the party, it is very clear to me that the people who repudiated the radical party for doing that thing, will serve us the same way.

CLARK TO A. W. GRAHAM

22 Sept 1883

... Probabilities are for Merrimon *—there is a good chance for John.† If Judge Ruffin has written that letter I suggested, it is not improbable John will be appointed. I have done all I could in that direction. Public sentiment throughout the State would endorse his appointment. No better one could be made. If Merrimon is appointed, it will be an effort to allay dissatisfaction in the party—

CLARK TO A. W. GRAHAM

Raleigh
29 Sept. 1883

... As I foresaw, Merrimon is appointed.‡ If a strong letter from Judge Ruffin in favor of John had been there, it is by no means certain that he would have been appointed.

And just here—John would make a good Supreme Court Judge & his appointment would give general satisfaction. If he is willing to take the place his friends should quietly go to work *now*. Both Judges Smith § and Ashe || are over 71. It is really certain that one or both those places will be to fill before Jarvis' time is out. Their resignation (or death) may take place at any time. I make the suggestion because I know such a view of the matter is absent from no one, and when the vacancy occurs a *prepossession* will settle the matter.

* Justice Thomas Ruffin had resigned from the Supreme Court and Governor Jarvis appointed A. S. Merrimon to succeed him. In 1889, Merrimon became Chief Justice.

† John Graham of Hillsboro, Clark's brother-in-law.

‡ As Justice of the Supreme Court.

§ W. N. H. Smith, Chief Justice, 1879-1889.

|| Thomas S. Ashe, Associate Justice, 1879-1887.

TO CLARK FROM B. F. MOORE *

London, Oct. 1, 1883

I am in receipt of your card and letter since my arrival here in London, for which accept many thanks.

I came in an ace of returning home, but as you suggest, that I may never have another opportunity, I have quite reluctantly given my consent to go to Rome, Florence, Naples, &c. &c. I doubt if I will go to Constantinople or to the Nile as it takes a deal of money to travel with. I cannot get on with less than $10 per day on an average, sometimes less, sometimes more, and I live quite economical at that, much cheaper than the great majority of travellers. I have today spent including return telegram for $500 from home, $28, this was unavoidable, as I know that you & Alf † got around it, but I could not, so it goes. I have fished in the "Bonnie Doon", and saw the monument of Burns and the house in which he was born; thence to Dumfries and saw his tomb... and then thro' the English lakes, Windemere &c to Preston; thence via Birmingham to Warwick; the castle there also Kenilworth castle and Stoneleigh Abbey, thence to Stratford-on-Avon, and saw all there including... "the very spotted deer that Shakespeare stole his'n from". Saw oaks the like of which I never saw before, one 11 feet through at Stoneleigh Abbey. Thence to Oxford where I remained two days, going all about everywhere. In London I went to Windsor Castle and saw the galleries there, St. George's and the Albert Chapel, and have since then visited the galleries and museums by day and the theatres at night and to my surprise found that there was so much to see. If my money comes, I will leave here, Friday or Saturday direct to Florence... and then to Rome &c. Give my kindest regards to yr wife & sisters and to all inquiring friends....

TO CLARK FROM JAMES E. SHEPHERD ‡

Washington, N.C.
Oct. 29, 1883

...When is your code coming out? Please send me a copy as soon as you can. The profession is making inquiries about your digest. Do you think you will complete and publish it?

* Bartholomew F. Moore, native of Halifax County, Attorney General of North Carolina 1848-1851, and one of the state's most outstanding lawyers.

† Alf Haywood, prominent Raleigh lawyer and son-in-law of Governor Holt.

‡ Native of Beaufort County; Superior Court judge, 1882-1888; Associate Justice of Supreme Court, 1888-1893; Chief Justice, 1893-1902.

TO CLARK FROM JOHN M. ROBINSON *

Baltimore, Md.
December 6th, 1883

I am just in receipt of a letter from Maj. Winder † in reference to the personal damage cases. In this letter, Maj. Winder says that he deems it his duty as it is his pleasure, to let me know how well the Company has been served by you, and that he has never seen so much interest manifested by any of our attorneys as you have manifested in these cases. Under such a letter as this from Maj. Winder, I feel that I should thank you personally for what you have done.

TO CLARK FROM DANIEL A. LAMONT ‡

Albany, N.Y., June 20, 1884

Governor Cleveland has received your letter of the 13th inst., and directs me to convey to you his thanks for your congratulations and assurances.

CLARK TO A. W. GRAHAM

3 July 1884

. . . As to running for the Senate, it is a delicate matter for me to say, but as I believe in giving a frank answer, if I give any at all, I should say that if your wife's health & your business permits *you* should go to the Senate. You owe it to yourself. You have a bright future ahead. You have popularity. You would be helped by the prominence public service would give you.

John § already has all that can be made by going to the Senate. He has a good record, a fine reputation. He will not materially add to them by another term. He needs no additional prominence or reputation. What will *now* help him most in the contest two years hence for Congressional nomination is not more State reputation but a *personal acquaintance* with the local leaders and best men in the various counties & townships of this *Congressional District.* That he will not make on the floor of the Senate. I have seen & talked with men from Nash, Johnston, Franklin, Wake & Chatham, and "felt their pulse" so to speak. Not a man of them but knew *who* John Graham was, and *what* he was—all were satis-

* President of the Seaboard and Roanoke Railroad Company.
† Probably John C. Winder.
‡ Private Secretary to Cleveland.
§ John Graham of Hillsboro.

fied with his record and his capacity, what he had done & what he was capable of doing but—and here is the point, most of them objected "I don't know him, our people never saw him &c."

If John would go through the *District,* canvassing for Cox,* making acquaintances & friends, his record & the fact that his 3 counties are entitled to the nomination next time will give it to him. People told me yesterday that *no* Wake man could get it two years hence since Cox will then have had it six years & he thought John's chances the best. Bunn † will canvass the District as Elector & John should offset that—I give you my views—I do not mean to presume to dictate to, or advise John. He is the best judge of his own course, but I am replying to your enquiry & giving the reasons for my opinion. . . .

CLARK TO HIS MOTHER

Hillsboro, N. C.
24 July 1884

My telegram yesterday carried you the news of our affliction.‡ As you have been through the same trial you know what our feelings are.

The baby lived 24 hours after our arrival. I think she gave me one look of recognition but was too sick to put out her arms to come to me as was her habit. I sat by her bedside during the night and up to the hour she breathed her last. When I found she was really dying I brought Sudie in and put her on a bed by the cradle and put the baby in her arms. The day had past the hour of twelve and turned to the setting, and with the turning of the tide the bright little spirit floated out on the vast sea of Beyond. When our day was at its noon and brightest, her little eyes opened on a brighter and an endless day. Timid and shrinking from new faces, as you know she did, the shining one who came for her must have been attractive beyond loveliness, for she left us without shrinking, not a convulsion, not a throb, told of her going and she went so sweetly that it was hard to tell exactly when the little heart had ceased to beat and the pulse to flicker.

Partly from her name, partly from her bright, merry, good,

* William Ruffin Cox, Brigadier General in Confederate Army; Democratic Representative in Congress, March 4, 1881-March 3, 1887; Secretary of United States Senate, 1893-1900, first cousin of General David Clark.

† Benjamin Hickman Bunn, Democratic Representative in Congress, March 4, 1889-March 3, 1895.

‡ Due to serious illness, Mrs. Walter Clark did not arrive in Hillsboro, where her children were visiting their grandmother, until the day before the fifteen-month-old Anna died.

loving disposition, and possibly from an instinctive feeling that we were to lose her, she has always been my special pet and companion. For months, I have looked forward to seeing her at noon and night. She learned my steps and always met me as I came to dinner or at night, always with her little smile and accompanied me to the door or gate to bid a reluctant goodbye as I passed back to my daily toil.

Today at 6 P.M. we will bury her little body in the Presbyterian grave yard here by the side of her grandfather and aside her mother's kindred, but I shall leave her there with profound and sincere conviction and trust that I shall meet her again. It may be soon, it can not be very long, for no matter how the span of man's days are lengthened they are quickly past like a dream in the night or a tale that is told; till then, dearest brightest best little baby good bye. May Christ receive her, God accept her.

Sudie sends much love to you and all and says tell you not to regret that you did not come with us, that she had much rather that you should remember the baby as she was, than as the deepened lines of pain and suffering now work themselves on that face once so bright and merry.

Sudie bears up under the blow as well as in her prostrate condition and with her warm, ardent, temperament, I could expect, for which I am thankful.

What our future plans now are for the summer I can not tell. I fear that the cold you took will make you ill and shall be uneasy till I hear that it is better.

Time will, I trust, with us as with all others bring healing to the wound which now so severly grieves us; but while it may allay the pain of parting, no length of time will dim the recollection of the bright little being that brought us so many days of happiness, who loved everybody and whom every body loved. Love to all and a more than double portion to yourself

TO CLARK FROM THOMAS M. HOLT *

Haw River, N.C.
Nov. 15th, 1884

If you can secure for me the members from Halifax, and any others, from your eastern friends, I would be greatly obliged.

* Manufacturer and agriculturist of Alamance County; Lieutenant Governor of North Carolina, 1889-1891; Governor, 1891-1893, following death of Governor Daniel G. Fowle.

From what I can learn, Busbee * will be my strongest competitor. I think there will be several dark horses hitched out to be brought in, in case neither of us can get a majority. Will be thankful for anything you can do for me.

TO CLARK FROM HENRY GROVES CONNOR †

Wilson, North Carolina
March 21st, 1885

Your very kind letter reached me yesterday and I assure you that I heartily thank you for your congratulation. I trust that it was your modesty that prevented you from giving me the opportunity to present mine to you. Your appointment I have always regarded as certain. I think that we are extremely fortunate in receiving the appointment with so little opposition & I think with so much popular approval. I shall devote all of the energy and talent wherewith I am possessed to the discharge of the duties of the position & trust that my friends, who have been so kind, will not have cause to regret my promotion. Please give my kind regards to Haywood, his kindness to me together with his many admirable qualities attached me to him. I regard myself as particularly fortunate in the friendships formed while in the Senate.

TO CLARK FROM GEORGE T. WINSTON ‡

Chapel Hill, N.C.
March 23, 1885

I fear you will deem me presumtuous, but relying upon your friendship for my father and his regard for you and yours, I venture to ask a great favor of you. It is that you address letters to Senators Vance and Ransom requesting that my brother Pat be let alone in possession of the Idaho office—I see by the Charlotte Observer that a "Mr. Williams of Iredell" is after the place.

My brother Pat is really a good Democrat today—He has been mad with Jarvis and others; hence his recent display.

This office is remote from North Carolina and is no part of

* Fabius H. Busbee, Raleigh attorney and counsel for the Southern Railway Company.

† Superior Court Judge for many years; Associate Justice of Supreme Court, 1902-1909; appointed Federal Judge by President Taft in 1909 and served until his death, November 23, 1924.

‡ President of the University of North Carolina, 1891-1896.

North Carolina political perquisites. My brother's long, valuable and disinterested services for the party ought to entitle him to be let alone in this petty office.

TO CLARK FROM FRANCIS D. WINSTON *

Windsor, N.C. Mch 24, 1885

You will please enter my name among the members of the State Bar Association.

I read with pleasure the announcement that you are likely to be appointed Judge of your district.

Your friendship for my father has been and will ever be greatly appreciated by the members of his family and we rejoice at any success you may attain—especially so when the position is one in accord with your desires and ability—as the Judgeship is.

CLARK TO A. W. GRAHAM

6 April 1885

I am glad to know that your course in the Legislature is so thoroughly endorsed by your constituency. I knew that it would be so. When a man does what he knows is right & legislates for the *intelligence* of a constituency he always wins a permanent and abiding popularity because it is a popularity based upon respect for his character and sound judgment. . . .

CLARK TO A. W. GRAHAM

Raleigh, N.C.
8 April 1885

. . . A committee of 8 or 10 lawyers headed by Fowle † & Fuller ‡ went up to see the Governor & some plain words passed.

They told him that I had never *desired* the place, that it was a matter of pecuniary importance to *them* as to the kind of man who should be the resident judge of the district, that they had selected a man with an unparalleled unanimity, that he (the Governor) had passed him over for Mr Battle, that they had acquiesced in that (tho' they did not desire Battle) for they recognised it as a fit appointment, but when it was intimated that there was a prospect

* Bertie County lawyer; member of General Assembly; Superior Court Judge, 1901-1903.

† Daniel G. Fowle, Governor, 1889-1891.

‡ Probably Thomas Fuller, Raleigh lawyer.

of saddling Bachelor on them whom nobody wanted, and everybody did not want, it was time to express themselves. The Governor got a little warm too. They told the Governor that if he was opposed to their *first* choice, they could furnish some other men—not Batchelor.

My own impression is that the proper course for me to take is to say nothing—and if it *is* tendered to decline. If John came I wished to consult him & take his judgment on that. The bar wanted him to come for a different reason.

I understand that a delegation from Wayne & Johnston bars will both be here to-morrow—Harnett is too far off. The bar is stirred up not of course because *I* am not appointed but because their unanimous recommendation is disregarded & especially at the prospect of Batchelor being put over us. I do not know what the Governor will do & I am sincere in saying I don't care, I write you fully that you may show it to John. I am glad that he has been saved the trouble of coming, tho' I believe he would have cheerfully done so if at home.

TO CLARK FROM A. W. GRAHAM

Hillsboro, North Carolina
April 9, 1885

Scale * seems to be having sort of a "monkey & parrot" time. As you have had nothing to do with the appointment and have not been active in the matter, if Scales shall be forced by the demands of the bar and the public to appoint you, I think you ought not to decline. I have no doubt it would gratify him to have you do so, but it would be a disappointment to the profession and your friends. The Judge does not have to come in contact with the Gov. nor be under any sort of obligations to him. Certainly neither you nor your friends would be beholden to him in any way.

The appointment lasts only two years and then the people will take charge of the matter.

Scales has certainly made no friends by his course so far. It is unfortunate for him that he has lived out of the State so much, he does not know the needs or the wishes of the people.

Do not decline the appointment if tendered. It will not be the Governor's but the people's appointment.

* Alfred Moore Scales of Rockingham County, Governor, 1885-1889.

TO CLARK FROM H. G. CONNOR

Wilson, N.C.
April 18, 1885

As you well know the announcement of your appointment gave me real, genuine pleasure and my congratulation is hearty and sincere. No man ever had the endorsement of the profession more unanimously than yourself and what is better no man was ever more entitled to it. Now let us go to work and show what the young men can do on the bench—I will probably see you in a few days.

TO CLARK FROM THOMAS M. HOLT

Haw River, N.C.
April 25, 1885

Absence, has prevented me from sooner offering my congratulations upon your appointment.* You were my first choice and I *earnestly* hoped all the time that the Governor would have wisdom enough to appoint you. I feel that one more honest & impartial Judge has been added to the list, one who knows the law, and knowing it, will administer it, without fear, or favor. I am glad to see the papers endorsing your appointment. I enclose what friend Yates † of the Charlotte Democrat says. I wish you success in this and all other things.

TO CLARK FROM H. G. CONNOR

Snow Hill, N. C.
October 10, 1885

Accept my hearty congratulations upon the fine work which you are doing. I feel that, I shall appear to great disadvantage in following you, but congratulate myself upon the example set for me....

I write to call to your attention, and ask your good offices in the way of kind words, etc. for my young friend Josephus Daniels ‡ who began his career as a Metropolitan Editor. I have known, intimately, "Joe" from his boyhood and can say for him that in all of the qualities of character, disposition &c which constitute

* As Superior Court Judge.

† Editor.

‡ This letter "laid the foundation for one of the most important friendships in Clark's life." Daniels became owner and editor of the *News and Observer* in 1894.

and makes up a first class, high toned, honorable and entirely reliable young man he *Excels.* I know of none superior and not many Equals. He has enjoyed that priceless blessing, better than wealth or station, the affectionate careful training of the most pious and devotedly Christian mother, and right nobly has he profited thereby. As a young man he needs kind words, expressions of confidence and esteem from men like yourself. I can assure you that they will never be abused, and you will find him worthy of all the encouragement which you can give him.

I am here for two weeks and will go to Vance. I hope to meet you and talk over matters before beginning work in your Dist.

TO CLARK FROM C. N. ARMFIELD *

January 8th, 1886

I am instructed by Governor Scales to enquire of you, if you desire to sell your calegraph † and if so what amount would you take for it? The Governor would also like to know your opinion of its merits as a writing machine.

TO CLARK FROM W. W. HOLDEN ‡

Raleigh, N. C.
Jan. 11, 1886

Allow me to express my high gratification at your action as Judge in relation to the crime of gambling. The sentence pronounced is moderate and just.§ For months and months that foul gambling house has glared on the main street of our City, inviting young and old men to bankruptcy, desperation, and ruin, and I have wondered if there was no law to extinguish that baleful light. Thank God, you have done that work! It is not what we have done for ourselves, but what we have done for others, that will give us most joy when we come to die; and this will be one of the joys of the inflexible Judge who has shielded the innocent and unwary in danger and in temptation. Accept, Sir, my hearty

* Private Secretary to Governor A. M. Scales.

† Typewriter, said to have been the first one in Raleigh.

‡ Appointed Governor of North Carolina by President Andrew Johnson in May, 1865; elected Governor in 1868, impeached and removed from office in 1871.

§ A man by the name of Miller was indicted for operating a saloon and gaming house, which was located next to the Yarborough House in Raleigh. Miller plead guilty to one count in the indictment and Clark imposed a sentence of "Two thousand dollars fine and thirty days in prison." Editorials, telegrams, and letters praised him for his action.

thanks, and the thanks and commendation of every thoughtful parent and of all good citizens, for what you have done. The Solicitor and the Jury have also acted worthily and nobly.

TO CLARK FROM S. T. NICHOLSON *

Washington, N. C.
January 27th, 1886

Your course in the "Miller Case" † is meeting with great applause in this section, as I suppose it is doing in every part of the State. It is noble & just and you will be rewarded. If persevered in it will do more to extinguish the flames of Sin in our land than any course adopted for ages. It has created quite an enthusiasm with the good people, of our country & everybody of any consequence is ready to rally to your Support & to "heap blessings upon you".

I feel highly pleased & gratified at your honorable conscientious & fearless move in this matter, & your giving such entire general satisfaction. It shall be fully attended to in our County Paper. God will surely bless you in your effort to do right. . . .

TO CLARK FROM T. M. ARGO ‡

Raleigh, N.C.
February 26, 1886

Judge Connor requested that some of us would write to ask if you left your key to your private office in Raleigh, or through inadvertence carried it with you. He is very desirous to have access to it that he may consult your excellent library in regard to the many questions arising in the cases now trying before him. Please let him know as he seems eager to get at the law of every matter.

I trust you are well, and not fatigued by your arduous labors.

CLARK TO A. W. GRAHAM

Durham, N.C.
12 Mar 1886

I learn that you have wooden benches for the Jury in Orange. In every county I have been in I have gotten the Chm of Comrs

* Physician and surgeon, cousin of Clark.
† See footnote in previous letter for facts in this case.
‡ Raleigh attorney.

to put in Revolving Arm Chairs. Those for this county are already ordered. They were put in Wake & Granville as you know—also in Guilford & Alamance. I don't want Orange to be behind. As I hold only one term—and only one week in Orange, I would be glad if you see the Chm or the Sheriff and have them ordered *now* as to be in place when I get there.

They can write to Sheriff Wheeler at Greensboro to telegraph for a dozen chairs just like those put in Guilford—or write to Clerk Sup Ct at Raleigh to telegraph for a dozen like those put in there. I mention this as they may not know exactly *what kind* to get or *where,* and we want them right away. By making a *start* this way, you may follow it up hereafter improving yr Court Room.

You can say to Mr Hall that it will cost the county nothing for I will save more than that by pushing the business of the court—and if he is afraid of the responsibility, tell him that I will take it when I come by making an order that they are necessary for the Court. He can order the chairs now & I will make the order (if he wishes it) then to cover it—...

CLARK TO A. W. GRAHAM

Raleigh, N.C.
7 Aug. 1886

I am sincerely gratified at Jno's nomination. I was satisfied that if Durham would *stand* he would get it. Two years ago he would have gotten it easily if his friends had stood. I know what work you must have had. I wished I could be here to help you.

I see Connor is taking a whack at Miller. The Supreme Ct says in the first Miller case (there are 3 of them in the 94th) 94 Reports page 903. that it is not appealable. Phillips did the right thing in sending him to jail tho' it would have been better to have done so promptly. Remember me kindly to Connor.

I am sorry for Winston's defeat....

CLARK TO A. W. GRAHAM

Raleigh, N.C.
24 Sept 1886

You have noticed the radical ticket for judges. They have no idea of electing their ticket but Miller and his crowd will try to have me cut so as to run some behind the other judges. I shall have quietly to get at some points votes of Republicans to run me up for losses. This of course between us. Are there any points in the Fifth District where by proper management I can quietly have this done.

Now as to a more serious matter. I have been here a week off duty and have investigated the ground carefully. This Cong. District is in *serious danger.* The Knights of Labor * are quiet but their votes will be felt. They are being assiduously worked. Then too there is great danger of apathy and indifference among our voters. I do not know how to talk to John about this matter. But I feel interested in it and can write to you. I shall be here till Tuesday morning.

There is great danger in this district & *no mistake.* The danger is all the greater because it is underground. If I were John I would get all the speakers I could into the district & make it a live campaign to bring out the vote. With the vote *brought out in* full we would be safe. John knows his own business & I will not presume to advise him, but knowing that there is danger I would be hardly doing right not to give warning that you may advise with him of it if you think best.

CLARK TO A. W. GRAHAM

Raleigh, N.C.
20 Nov 1886

I see that Jarvis † is trying to get up a boom for Governor in 1888— He has been Gov. 6 years and now has a 4 yrs place at $12.000 a year. It is *enough* for his services and talents. It is time we younger men had a showing. It is very probable my own name will be before the Convention with a strong backing. I would be glad if you would think over the matter, consult with friends and after a while at your leisure give me your advice and judgment. When you see Bob Winston ‡ you might get his views as to Granville. I don't want to be announced as a candidate nor to let it get into the papers this early but I have been solicited to run and desire the advice of a few friends like yourself, in whose judgment I have confidence, before I decide. If it were *announced* this early that my name would be used I would be the mark of attack by the friends of other gentlemen. I would also be glad to know John's § views when you have leisure to talk it over with him.

* National labor organization which was begun in 1869.
† Thomas J. Jarvis, Governor, 1879-1885; Minister to Brazil under Cleveland.
‡ Robert W. Winston, prominent attorney; Superior Court Judge, 1890-1895.
§ John Graham of Hillsboro.

PENCILLED NOTE FROM PRISONERS IN THE WAKE COUNTY JAIL TO CLARK

1887

We do as prisoners of Wake County Jail do appeal to you to please have the windows raised as we suffer almost to death with the heat it is twice as hot down here as it is up there but the windows is down and painted so the heat is intensely hot please oblige us as to have them raised.

CLARK TO A. W. GRAHAM

1 Sept 1887

. . . I thought there was some change in Will Fuller * tho' I could not account for it. Though not *committed* until recently I understood he was with us— Before he goes too far how would it do to have it suggested to him (& Winston) that by the custom of rotating the man must come from the East this time & besides Greensboro can't have the place *8* years. As their object is not Gilmer, but a vacancy their *best chance* is to support Gilmer † for one of the new Supreme Ct. Judges. Our friends could help them on that and they could be on good terms with the power who would *appoint* Gilmer's successor.

Armfield ‡ will not practically be in the race. I am just from his county. He is as a political speaker not only *nil* but a "wet blanket", though he is a good jury advocate. Then too he is *no* organiser and the fight between his faction & Robbins § is as bitter as between Stedman || & Waddell.¶ It is too soon to "bring out" any man but the quiet securing of leaders of public sentiment and of men in each county and township is none too soon. It is in that way Ransom succeeds—making tho' very little show on the surface. I think Iredell & Rowan will both be with us.

I write you freely at the risk of tiring you. *Our friends* are organising throughout the State & I believe (without some accident) we *shall win.* I supported Winston's father for Judge & his brother ** for Prof. at Chapel Hill and I was in hopes he could

* Durham attorney.

† John H. Gilmer of Greensboro, member of General Assembly, 1893.

‡ Probably Robert F. Armfield of Iredell County, Superior Court Judge, 1888-1895.

§ William M. Robbins of Iredell County, Conservative Representative in Congress, December 1, 1873-March 3, 1879.

|| Charles M. Stedman of Greensboro, Lieutenant Governor, 1885-1889; Democratic Representative in Congress, April 4, 1911—.

¶ A. M. Waddell of Wilmington.

** George T. Winston, later President of the University.

help us in this fight. Strudwick * is a man of talent & can be of great help to us if he will take hold.

TO CLARK FROM BRAXTON CRAVEN

Trinity College, N.C.
Sept. 19, 1887

. . . I shall yet bring stronger influences to bear on the Governor. He dare not refuse this appointment † we ask. He has received other letters and the whole subject is beginning to attract attention. I receive letters on the general subject almost daily, some of them from persons in the ring; some of them have been disappointed and are sore on the University question. They threaten me privately as well as publicly. I like that. I am for a University strongly and firmly, but not for a mere High School. Let them act fair, manly and right, that is what I want. I am amazed at the News; it was thought to be the organ of that ring. No step has ever added so much popularity to it in this direction. . . . I see no escape. Right or wrong, I attribute this move to you.

If the Gov does not give you the Judgeship, we should come out with facts he cannot stand.

TO CLARK FROM JOHN F. CROWELL

Trinity College, N.C. [n.d.]

I have the pleasure of officially informing you of your election to the position of Trustee of Trinity College. Your nomination by the trustees was unanimously confirmed by the conference. You are therefore considered as an active participant in the deliberations of that body, upon your acceptance of the office. Believing that you will gladly share the efforts now being made to promote the progress of the development of the college I gladly welcome you.

TO CLARK FROM E. J. HALE ‡

U. S. Consulate
Montevideo
November 25, 1887

. . . As you have been abroad you can appreciate my feelings when I arrived here and knew no one and was unable to speak the

* Probably R. C. Strudwick, member of General Assembly, 1883.

† As Associate Justice of Supreme Court.

‡ Edward Joseph Hale, editor of the *Fayetteville Observer;* American Consul at Manchester, England, 1885-1889; Minister to Costa Rica, 1913-1921.

language—though as you, I believe speak both French and German, you were not troubled with this inconvenience of inability to talk. I am catching on to much of the language and hope in six or eight months more to speak and write it quite correctly. Montevideo I find quite a nice city. The girls here are nearly as pretty as those in N. C. and they dress very much like the French girls. The men are sharp active business men and know quite well all the tricks of trade. The government is a disgrace. The "spoils" is the only thing on which the party lines are drawn and it has been reduced to that point unless each side gets a share not so much of spoils but of *stealage,* there is a revolution. The chief duty and privilege of a government official is to steal and rob. His term of office and popularity is not measured by his patriotic deeds as an official but by the distribution of the stealage to his henchmen. How different from good old N. C.! I watch the papers quite closely for information and news but see very little that has any definite bearing upon the Gubernatorial question. The latest that I have is from the "N. & O.", and it is to the effect that Gen. Jarvis will doubtless be in the race. The Senatorial bee has struck his hat and not the Gubernatorial, I should think. I have written to my Duplin friends but the political winds shift there so often that Duplin is rather an unknown quantity until the Convention comes. The long term of court that you held there made many friends for you and the railroad to Kenansville idea at the time quite took the heart of the Kenansville men, and Clark for Governor was quite the talk. Gen. Steadman is making a fight for Duplin so I am informed but he has some active personal opposition and among the opposition is Sheriff Kenan who at the present time I think comes nearer running the County politics than any man in the County. Thanking you again for your kindness in remembering me and trusting that on my return to N. C., I may be able to shake hands with Gov. Clark.

TO CLARK FROM WALTER A. MONTGOMERY *

Warrenton, N.C.
January 20th, 1888

. . . I understand the peculiar difficulties in the way of your making any canvass to secure the nomination for Governor, and I know you appreciate thoroughly that you will have to rely almost entirely upon your friends to manage your interests.

* Associate Justice of North Carolina Supreme Court, 1895-1905.

My judgement is worth something as to how the people among whom I live would act under stated conditions, *provided* their passions were not excited by demagogues, and provided further their wishes could be fully and fairly expressed. I think Warren County, in the State Convention, will support you, if the delegates shall represent the best orders of our people, and their preference. Two elements among the people, however, are to be considered in the election of delegates, viz; the "fast set," and the political farmers: the first, may organize and move against you because of the position you have taken, on the bench, in favor of public morals, and the latter, for the purpose of helping the claims of some farmer candidate. A. H. Davis (Baldy) can distract the organization of the "fast set," and Mr. H. B. Hunter can help you with the farmers. Probably Mr. Ed. Thorne can be of service to you with these two gentlemen. My individual influence is for you, and will be, unless Charles M. Cook * should aspire, in which event, I would from peculiar considerations support him.

I do not however, now, see this in the way.

CLARK TO A. W. GRAHAM

Yadkinville, N.C.
21 Feb. 1888

I return Manly's letter. I think he expresses the situation east of W & W. clearly & rightly. See his last 2 lines. S—— † has no great strength west. His *main* reliance is Kope Elias ‡—he has no strength in the centre & Piedmont to speak of.

The only men in Raleigh against me are Faison, Snow, the Busbees, A. Jones & Ryan—I know of no others. S—— is trying to make the most of that. Carr § is his club-mate & he is working on him. Can you get Carr to work. Is he reliable?

I know of no change in Andrews. When you see him, suppose you talk with him frankly—write me what he says. S—— is *always jubilant but never nominated.* Dr. W.A. Lash Walnut Cove is an old schoolmate & W.W. King, Danbury an old army friend. When you have leisure write them....

When you get down to Raleigh, ask Bob Gray, Stamps & A.D. (Buck) Jones as to Raleigh sentiment. Snow diligently tells it Carr is not sincerely for us. Quietly let Carr know this.

* Secretary of State, 1895-1896; Superior Court Judge, 1903—.
† Charles M. Stedman of Greensboro.
‡ Active lawyer and politician in western North Carolina.
§ Julian S. Carr, Durham industrialist.

CLARK TO A. W. GRAHAM

Raleigh
3 Mar/ 88

...I can not *find* the dissatisfaction here with bar or people. Only 4 members of bar against us out of 50. Snow told Jo. Daniels to-day he was for Stedman but he would not make any fight on me in Wake. When you come down next week consult with *Pace, Whitaker, Peele* & others who are with us and when [you] go back straighten up Carr and put him to work.

The "Fowle" boom is gotten up to divide Wake. Fowle takes it in dead earnest but has not consented to run yet. Our friends are saying nothing to irritate & I hope by good management to conciliate him & get him off—

We can't afford to *say* Andrews & Winder are for us. Still their weight will be felt for us in Convention. It has been reported to A. that you said "Andrews is for Clark but isn't helping any." I know it isn't so but it probably is a misrepresentation by Carr. It is a difficult matter not to get misquoted in politics.

Pace tells me L.L. Polk * (who is running Alexander) says Syd would be satisfied with Lt. Gov. Suppose you talk with Pace & see if thro' Polk the arrangement can be made. I don't think we can do better....

TO CLARK FROM W. H. MOORE

Washington, N. C.
March 8, 1888

I received the "Quarterly Statement" you were kind enough to send me, for which please accept my thanks. I would like to know more of the Societies Publications. All Christians, and especially all Ministers, must feel a deep interest in anything that tends to throw light on Biblical history.

I wish also to say that I have talked freely with leading citizens throughout my District, regarding your candidacy for Governor of the State in the approaching canvass, and I know that they would give you a hearty support. No one has been mentioned *the people* here would support with more enthusiasm than yourself.

In my judgment much depends (more than ever before) on the moral character of the candidate the Democratic party shall nominate for the office.

* Leonidas Lafayette Polk, founder of the *Progressive Farmer,* national president of the Farmers' Alliance, and first Commissioner of Agriculture, 1877-1880.

The Prohibition sentiment is strong, and constantly growing in this Section. They will have a County Ticket in this County, as well as in others, and, if an immoral man is put up, the Democratic party will lose many votes they have been receiving.

Your record as Judge of the Superior Courts would make you acceptable to the Prohibition element, so far at least as to draw many of these to your support, and they will not vote for any other Democrat who has yet been named.

I have talked freely with gentlemen (Democrats) in Washington, Tyrell, Hyde, and Beaufort, Counties, and they will give you a stronger support than any candidate yet named can get.

Personally, I desire your election not only from friendship, but patriotism, and, if I can contribute anything to consummate it, you have only to command, and shall find me at your service.

O. A. WIGGINS TO DR. W. R. WOOD

Wilmington, N.C.
April 10th, 1888

Being a native of Halifax Co. and personal friend of Judge Clark from early boyhood days, I of course took interest in his probable nomination by the State Convention for Governor and am consequently much disappointed on reading his letter of withdrawal. Cannot some means be brought to bear on him which will cause him to reconsider and allow his name to come before the Convention. His most formidable opponent (who it seems is from this place) is by no means a favorite among the business people even of his own place, as evidence he has tried for the last ten years to get to Congress but has never been able to receive the nomination from his District Convention. If not able to control his own District can it be supposed that he is able to control or bring out the full Democratic vote of the entire State? My own opinion is, it would jeopardize the Democratic cause to nominate him. While people of his own city are loath to take an active part against him they can at least see the danger. It is the interest of white people and the Democratic party (for which I have labored for twenty years without being a politician) that induces me to write this letter and I beg that you will regard it as a personal one and not for the public. When Judge Clark's name was first mentioned for the Governorship I think it met the hearty approbation of at least one half the business people of this place. The time has come when the people should cease to be the cracker to the whip of political aspirants, but instead bring forward the best men who will serve the whole people justly, regardless of consequences. Excuse the liberty I have taken, but the occasion is great, and I think the cause justifies the action.

CLARK TO A. W. GRAHAM

Winston, N.C.
15 Apl 1888

. . . I replied to *Carr*—that I had withdrawn in favor of no candidate—from fear of none & by an understanding with none *but* to save the party from another Cooke-Bunn or Jarvis-Fowle fight.

I replied to Dr Wood I must stand *honestly* & *squarely* by my letter of withdrawal & to allow no letters written to papers. That if at Convention there should be a dead-lock (which is a mere chance) and a third man is necessary my friends could use my name then if they see fit. But I do not propose to withdraw & keep on actively running.

TO CLARK FROM H. G. CONNOR

Wilson, N. C.
April 25, 1888

I thank you for your very kind thoughtfulness in writing me. The loss of my house is not only a very great temporary inconvenience but a financial loss which with my small salary and large family it will take me many years to overcome. For the first time in several years, I am without insurance. It has required all my fortitude to rally from the blow which came upon me so suddenly. I hope, however, that with the assistance of kind friends and good health to live to see another home arise from the ashes of my old so that when you reach this District and County I may be able to entertain you. I note your suggestion about the pleasant place to have my family—but I can not think the Sovereign ever contemplated that the Judges should indulge themselves and families out of their salaries. I have found the 8th a very pleasant Dist. and was glad to hear many pleasant things said of you. The bars have been unusually kind to me. While I like the bench and would be glad to make it my life work I feel that duty to my family will force me from it. . . .

TO CLARK FROM W. R. JERNIGAN *

Osaka, Japan
July 31, 1888

You are very good to think of me and write me such a kind letter. I appreciate it and send you my sincere thanks.

I have read your speech with the greatest pleasure. It is like every thing else you write and say—ornate and purely eloquent. When I first heard that you were going on the bench I knew that you would impress the people of N. C. just as you have. Your bearing and fine judicial reputation have not surprised me, but let your distant friend assure you that it has given him the most sincere gratification.

You would enjoy a visit to Japan. Can't you come over and spend some time with us? We have comfortable quarters and will try to make you comfortable. There are a great many laughable scenes in Japanese Character "Sunset" Cox should never have written his book, "How to Laugh" until he had visited Japan.

The Japanese are an interesting people too. They have much in their civilization that is admirable but there is no country like our own. Its greatness and superiority is more marked when viewed and contrasted from a distance. I do not mean, that we should leave our own country in order to love it better, but when standing on foreign soil, we have a more accurate conception of its beautiful and free system of government....

* United States Consul at Osaka and Hiogo, Japan.

V

Honeymoon in Public Life

1889–1896

ON NOVEMBER 14, 1889, GOVERNOR FOWLE appointed Walter Clark Associate Justice of the Supreme Court of North Carolina. In November of the following year, he was elected to fill the unexpired term, and in 1894 he was elected for the full eight-year term.

When Clark took his seat on the Supreme Court he was just forty-three, the youngest member of the bench of five judges, in perfect health and a glutton for work. During the thirty-five years that he was to remain on the bench, he wrote 3,235 opinions, of which 182 were concurring and 371 dissenting.

The writing of nearly one hundred opinions a year—probably a record—did not occupy all of Clark's time. His restless spirit and inexhaustible energy drove him to labor in other fields and to wage war for overdue reforms in government and society. Many outside demands were made upon him. He delivered many addresses and he served as a member of the Board of Trustees of Davenport College and also of Trinity College. He was on the committee of the latter board which brought about the removal of the college from Randolph county to Durham.

During these years, Clark published a score of articles, largely relating to law, government, history, and agriculture, in such outstanding magazines as *The Green Bag, The Arena, Harper's,* and the *American Law Review*. The editor of the last-named publication wrote: "We will welcome anything from your pen." George T. Winston, then president of the University of North Carolina, wrote him: "I do not see how you find time for such researches. Surely we all owe you a debt of deep gratitude." In 1892, Clark published an article on "The Supreme Court of North Carolina," an address on "William R. Davie," an obituary of Judge A. S. Merrimon, and a noteworthy essay on "The Telegraph and the Telephone Property Parts of the Post Office System." In 1894, he published "The Election of Postmasters by the People," "The Election of Senators and the President by Popular Vote, and the Veto," "The True Remedy for Lynch Law," and "Inventions Needed at the South." In 1895, he published "The Telegraph in England," "The Telegraph and Telephone," "Should the Government Control the Telegraph?" and, in collaboration with his wife, a translation of the three volume *Life of Napoleon* by Constant.

The next year, Clark visited Mexico and published four articles in *The Arena* relating to that country. He was an ardent free silver man and printed an article on "Free Coinage Indispensable, but Not a Panacea." He likewise published an article on "The Vice-President: What to Do with Him."

By 1894 Clark had made an enviable place for himself on the Court and his dissenting opinions were already attracting much attention. In 1893, James S. Manning wrote him that his dissenting opinion in *Vanstory* v. *Thornton* was "the clearest exposition of Homestead I have ever read." His decisions as well as his articles were attracting national notice. But his term of office was ending that year, and the Democratic party was facing a critical political situation, occasioned by the "Farmer's Revolt" and the formation of the Populist party.

The state conventions of all three parties met in Raleigh in the spring of 1894. The Democrats, as a matter of course, renominated Clark. To the surprise of many people, probably of Clark himself, the Populists and Republicans both endorsed his nomination. A few conservative Democrats advised him not to accept their endorsement, whereupon Clark publicly announced that the action of these two conventions had been taken without his knowledge. Even Simmons advised his acceptance, and J. P. Caldwell, editor of the powerful Charlotte *Observer,* wrote him that "no one can question your democracy."

Clark subscribed to many of the reforms and demands contained in the Ocala Platform of the Populist party and he carried on an extensive correspondence with Marion Butler, outstanding Populist leader in North Carolina. One suspects that some conservative Democrats never forgave Clark for his "Populist leanings" during these eventful years.

When the Democrats met in Raleigh in 1896 to nominate a candidate for governor, they faced a discouraging situation. It appeared almost certain that the "fusion" of Republicans and Populists would sweep the state and some of the delegates thought it would be wise to try to wean back the Populists by the nomination of a man who was relatively sympathetic with Populist views. James H. Pou, Chairman of the Democratic State Executive Committee, thought that Clark was the only Democrat who could be elected governor and urged him to head the ticket. Colonel R. T. Bennett put Clark's name before the convention as a man "who can certainly be elected governor." Then a delegation went to visit Clark to see if he would accept the nomination. Addressing the group, he assured them of his willingness to serve the state, but said that he felt it his duty to serve out the term on the bench to which he had been unanimously elected two years before. He also emphasized the fact that he was a poor man and could not bear the expense of the campaign. The Democrats then nominated Cyrus B. Watson, a friend of Clark, to wage a losing battle against Daniel L. Russell, Republican, and William A. Guthrie, Populist. In view of the fact that Russell polled only 8,521 more votes than Watson, and that Guthrie polled some 31,000 votes, many people believed that Clark could have been elected, maintaining that he would have received many of the Guthrie votes.

Many North Carolinians thought that Bryan's nomination for president in 1896 made Clark's nomination for vice-president a logical one but feared putting a Southerner and an ex-Confederate soldier on the national ticket. In spite of this fear, the Democratic National Convention, meeting in Chicago, gave Clark 50 votes for the vice-presidential nomination on the first ballot, and he continued to receive the 22 North Carolina votes until the fifth ballot, when Arthur Sewall of Maine was nominated. Bryan's views on many matters were similar to those of Clark, and in the years to follow the Great Commoner wrote Clark many letters expressing admiration for his devotion to the cause of the common people and for his relentless fight against monopolies, trusts, and combines.

TO CLARK FROM FRANK MC NEILL

Rockingham Feby 20 '89

I was pleased to receive your favor of 11th inst. I will always remember with greatest pleasure our circuit together. The good effects of your administration of the criminal law is very noticable here yet. You doubtless remember Beasly— Since that time there has been no complaint of gambling at Laurinburgh. The conviction & punishment of Pool virtually stopped the sale of Liquor at Cameron, and the Walters case in Columbus will do good there for years and years. I think your plan of issuing instanter copies and trying offenders at first term unless they have legal excuse for continuance is by far the best. When offenders know that speedy, prompt punishment awaits them they will be deterred. I succeeded in getting Judge Connor to adopt this rule and he saw and told me that it was by far the best way to enforce the criminal law. Since that time the Judges have been disposed to hold that the Defts were entitled to continuance if they desired as matter of right & without excuse at the first term.

I am obliged to you for securing passage of law simplyfying

indictments for perjury. The law in reference to indictments for Murder has saved me good deal of unnecessary labor.

TO CLARK FROM B. R. LACY *

Raleigh, N. C.
November 16, 1889

I am not writing to congratulate you on your appointment, as I think the boot is on the other foot, and the State should be congratulated on your accepting it, and Governor Fowle, on making the best appointment that could possibly have been made. My object is to thank you for your picture. I appreciate and value it very highly, and would have acknowledged it sooner but I hoped to see you and thank you personally.

TO CLARK FROM S. F. TELFAIR †

Raleigh, Nov. 16th 1889

I am instructed by the Governor to enclose your Commission as Associate Justice of the Supreme Court of North Carolina, vice Hon. A.S. Merrimon, resigned, and request that you will please send your resignation as Judge of Superior Court. The Governor will notify you when your Commission will take effect, as he hopes to make arrangement for it to take effect at once. I shall not accept your resignation as Superior Court Judge until Arrangement for holding your Court in Madison County next week has been made. If there is any difficulty about filling your place, he will request you to hold your Court next week, before you qualify on the Supreme Court bench....

TO CLARK FROM R. B. GLENN ‡

Winston-Salem, N. C.
Nov. 26, 1889.

Yesterday I did not see you before Court met, & left before it adjourned, so did not have a chance to shake your hand & congratulate you upon the high honor conferred upon you. I did not know that you aspired to this place and am told the appointment was not sought by you, but I feel assured that you will fill the high office with dignity and credit to yourself and as you did as

* Benjamin R. Lacy, Commissioner of Labor and Printing, 1893-1897; State Treasurer, 1901-1929.

† Private Secretary of Governor Daniel G. Fowle.

‡ Prominent attorney, Governor of North Carolina, 1905-1909.

Superior Court Judge, you will likewise as Supreme Judge, win the esteem and respect of all the people and especially of the bar. I wish you great success in your new role, and predict for you a brilliant future.

TO CLARK FROM MRS. "STONEWALL" JACKSON

Charlotte, N. C.
March 22, 1890

I trust I am not taking too great a liberty in appealing to you upon a matter of much importance to me and mine, that it must be my apology for so doing.

My Father regarded you as the most conscientious and fearless Christian jurist in the State, and I feel sure that I can rely safely upon any advice and assistance you could give me.

My trials, of late years, have been peculiarly heavy, as in addition to the loss of my only child, her husband has taken her children from me, and he is totally incapable of rearing them himself. However, he has a father and maiden sister, who will support and take good care of them, and for that reason, I made no effort to keep the children by law. Every one who knows Mr. Christian's profligate habits, encourage me to hope that the return of the children to me is only a question of time, but God only knows how this will be, and I must submit to His will, whatever that may be.

What I wish to do now is to secure what little property I have to the children, beyond all possibility of Mr. C's ever getting a cent of it into his hands. When he married my daughter, I settled one half of all I had upon her and she unfortunately made *him* her trustee. In less than a year, the bulk of all she had was gone, and now but a very small part remains. After her death, he was magnanimous enough to transfer this remnant to me, in trust for the children. Now, in making my will, I must put all my property in trust for them, and I know of no one whom I could select as trustee so suitable and competent as *yourself*. I know I could not place it in safer hands, and you will not only do me a life long favor by accepting this trust, but will be rendering a great benefit to the grand-children of General Jackson, for whose sake alone, these children ought to be sacredly cared for, and given the best advantages. My estate is in good shape & I owe no debts, so that I do not think it would be troublesome to manage. The property consists of one house and lot here, one in Lexington, Va., 1 small tract of land in Ark., a few unimportant lots in St. Paul, Minn., and a few also in San Diego, California. In each of these places I have reliable agents. Col. Brown could act in conjunction with you here, and John Graham could settle Robert's debt to me with you, in case it is not done during my lifetime. You may ask why I do not appoint Col. Brown or one of my Brother's as my trustee. The Col. is too old a man and my brothers do not desire to undertake it, and in my opinion none of them are as capable or suitable as Judge Walter Clark!, whose discharge of *Christian duty* points him out as the man above all others, to whom I would commit this trust, with the assurance that it would, under God's blessing, be faithfully kept and well executed.

Please remember me affectionaly to my aunt Susan and to Sudie and with kindest and best wishes for you and yours.

CLARK TO MRS. "STONEWALL" JACKSON

Raleigh, N. C.
24 March 1890

I appreciate the high compliment implied in your request and thank you for your kind expressions.

In reply I can only say that there is no southern man, more especially none who, like myself, had the honor of serving under Gen. Jackson, who would not deem it a privilege to render any service, however slight, to yourself or his grandchildren. I sincerely trust however that you may be spared till long after your grandchildren become of age and live to be your own trustee.

Our household were pained to learn some days since that your grandchildren were not to remain with you as we know it would be a grief to you. We will be glad to hear that they have been returned to you, as doubtless will be the case, for it seems so much more suitable and appropriate for you to have them.

I trust you will need no assurance, Mrs. Jackson, that in this, or in any other matter, in which you may think I can be of service to you—I am certainly at your command.

TO CLARK FROM J. M. SPAINHOUR *

Lenoir, N. C.
June 10, 1890

The North Carolina Conference at its last session elected you a Trustee of Davenport Female College, located at this place, and

* Lenoir dentist and Secretary of the Board of Trustees of Davenport College.

it becomes my duty and pleasure to request you to attend a meeting of the Board of Trustees during Commencement week, on Tuesday June 17th, at 3 P.M. . . .

CHARLES W. TILLETT * TO JOSEPH G. BROWN †

Charlotte, N. C.
24 July 1890

In reply to your favor I will say that there is not the slightest movement on foot in this section to defeat Judge Clark. Every body is for him so far as I can hear.

Yes, you are right, I am his friend and ready to do anything I can for him. I think I can assure you there is no danger.

TO CLARK FROM GEORGE W. GRAHAM ‡

Charlotte, N. C.
July 24th, 1890

There is not the least opposition to you or Merrimon § in this section of the state. No one is even spoken of as a substitute for either of you. And you will find that you will be endorsed by nine tenths of the County conventions that send delegates to Raleigh. If any counties go against you they will be in the Winston-Womack || district. Your reputation as a Supreme Court judge would save you even if your friends were not at work. So there is no cause for anxiety on your part. Vance,¶ however, had better be at work. For unless the meeting of the Alliance ** at Greensboro this week does something to check it he is going to be strongly opposed. Right here at home the farmers are opposed to him and the same feeling exists elsewhere as you will see in the "Progressive Farmer". Syd †† [Alexander] did not have any trouble because we got every thing ready in May and quietly waited for the Conventions of the different counties to meet and give an acct. of the alliance work done therein. Our County Convention meets tomorrow and like all the others in the district will

* Charlotte lawyer.
† Raleigh banker.
‡ Eye, ear, and throat specialist.
§ Judge Augustus S. Merrimon.
|| Thomas B. Womack of Chatham County, member of General Assembly, 1883-1885; Superior Court Judge, 1889-1890.
¶ Zebulon B. Vance, former Governor and then United States Senator.
** Farmers' Alliance.
†† Sydenham B. Alexander of Charlotte, member of General Assembly, 1879, 1883-1887.

endorse Syd for Congress but is divided between the four candidates for judges.

Our convention for state officers meets sometime in August.

TO CLARK FROM F. S. SPRUILL *

Louisburg, N. C.
July 26, 1890

My object in writing is to assure you of my aid and influence in securing you the nomination to succeed yourself.

I note with grave apprehension the tendency of the people to rebuke Fowle † through his appointees. My opinion is that your great personal popularity will prevent anything of the sort in your case.

Anything that I can do, please command me to it without hesitation. You may feel assured at the same time that I will carefully keep inviolate any confidence of the kind bestowed. I know how indecorous it is considered of Judges to electioneer. Still I think they have a right in justice and propriety to direct their own canvass in a quiet way. MacRae ‡ is doing it. Who do you wish me to see or write?

TO CLARK FROM JOHN F. CROWELL §

Trinity College, (P. O.) N. C.
October 2, 1890

At the annual conference of N. C. held in Greensboro, December 18, '89, yourself, Mr. Mauney and myself were appointed as Committee to carry out the voluntary resolution.

"Whereas, Trinity College by legislative enactment is located in Randolph Co., And whereas by the action of this conference, it is now to be removed to Raleigh, N. C., therefore resolved that a committee of three be appointed to secure such legislation as may be necessary for such a removal."

I will be in Raleigh on the 16th, of this month, and hope that you may find time to do what work may be necessary to comply with the terms of the resolutions. Mr. Mauney cannot be present;

* Lawyer, member of General Assembly, 1893, and division counsel of the Atlantic Coast Line Railroad.

† Daniel G. Fowle, Governor 1889-1891.

‡ James C. MacRae of Cumberland County, Superior Court Judge, 1882-1890; Associate Justice of Supreme Court of North Carolina, 1893-1895.

§ President of Trinity College, then located in Randolph County.

at least he does not expect to. I will, however, let him know of our meeting.

TO CLARK FROM A. H. MERRITT *

Pittsborough, N.C.
April 28, 1891

If the Trustees should elect you President of the University, would you accept the position?

I have great confidence in your integrity, learning and executive ability, and I am not the only one of the Trustees who think that you are the man we are in search of.

TO CLARK FROM ALFRED MOORE WADDELL

November 20th, 1891

. . . I fear my letter made a wrong impression on you. I come, as you probably know, from Federalist stock, and my early education was decidedly colored with ideas of the party. I expect you and I think very much alike in regard to the nature of our government as originally established and as gradually developed, and finally fixed by the last 30 years of its history.

I don't know what Kingsbury † wrote to you, but I know he claims to be a strict Jeffersonian Democrat, and it has been my fortune to "sail into" him upon several occasions in the past because of his apparent unconsciousness of the effect of current events on the relations of the States to the Union. Daniel Webster, as I was taught to believe, had the true conception of these relations, but events have carried us away beyond his position, and (as I have said in some of my speeches) this is not the same government we once lived under.

You are right in desiring to utilize all the beneficent powers of the govt. for the public good, and when it can be done without straining the Const. old fogyism ought not to be allowed to stand in the way.

My rather cynical tone in the letter I wrote to you was not addressed to *your* ideas, but to the wearisome and untimely objections of those who are eternally opposing every advance in American civilization with the ghost of theories—that murdered if you choose—are certainly dead.

As I said, I am not a centralizer, but I believe this is a nation,

* Chatham County Superintendent of Public Instruction.

† Theodore B. Kingsbury, Methodist minister and editor of the Wilmington *Messenger*.

and not a confederation merely, and I will support the exercise of all just powers conferred upon it by the Const. whenever I think they are to be used for the good of the people.

I repeat that I consider your argument for the postal telegraph etc. excellent and that I believe the system will be adopted before many years in accordance with public sentiment, but there are dangers in it I fear, which may lead to trouble. However, I may be all wrong.

Excuse me, but I didn't want you to misunderstand me.

TO CLARK FROM SEYMOUR D. THOMPSON *

St. Louis, Mo.
Jan. 28, 1891

Your favor of Jan. 17th, has been sent to me by the publisher of the *American Law Review* in their customary way, with the expectation that I shall answer it.

The rewards of legal journalism are very small. The *American Law Review* has never been able to pay more than $2.00 per printed page for contribution, and, then only after the date of publication. They get a great many more contributions than they can possibly use. They do not get enough from men occupying high positions, like yourself, whose opinions will be valued because of their station. I think that an article from your pen, upon some subject of general present interest, would be appreciated by the readers of the *Review*.

I sympathize with a judge who attempts to live respectably upon the salaries paid by some of the states. I get the largest judicial salary which is paid to any judge in Missouri, which is $5500 a year, and I find myself unable to support my family and educate my children properly upon that. If I did not have other sources of income, I could not get along at all. May I make the suggestion that you might increase your personal revenue by writing a book,—unless your judicial duties are too severe to allow you to shoulder so much extra labor.

TO CLARK FROM JOHN F. CROWELL

Rochester, N.Y.
January 28, 1891

It seems to me that it might be sufficient to have an act incorporating the 62½ acres of land known as Trinity College grounds

* Associate editor of *American Law Review,* St. Louis, Mo.

near the city of Durham to be governed according to Charter and by laws to be made subject to the approval of the Board of Trinity College.

The board can decide for itself who shall be electors and who not.

I have failed to get the Boundaries but will have them sent by mail from home by my brother.

If you will make a draft of Charter, I think it will be all right.

I will be in Raleigh on the 5th of Feb. and if it is not through by that time I will do what I can to effect its passage.

TO CLARK FROM DAVID DUDLEY FIELD *

New York
January 21, 1892.

I have to thank you for a copy of your annotated Code of Civil Procedure, which you were good enough to send me. It is a monument to your labor and skill. New York has adopted three of the five codes prepared by her commissioners. Our code of Civil Procedure you took as a pattern for your own. Our Penal Code and Code of Criminal Procedure, which have been in practice some years, I will send you, if you wish. Perhaps you have them already in your library. The Civil Code and Code of Evidence I send you. They have passed both Houses more than once, but failed for want of the Governor's signature, having been generally passed in the last days of the Session.

The pamphlet, which I send you, being a reprint of an article I wrote for the American Law Review, will acquaint you with the progress of codification in this country. It would be a great pleasure to see all the codes prepared for New York adopted in North-Carolina. You seem to be the very man to take the lead as law-reformer in your State. Command me if I can help you. Please let me hear from you again on the subject, and oblige

TO CLARK FROM JOHN WANNAMAKER †

Washington, D.C. March 8th, 1892

I am extremely obliged to you for your kindness in sending me a clipping in regard to Henry Clay's views on the telegraph.

* New York attorney, chief counsel for "Boss" Tweed; also counsel for Tilden before the Electoral Commission in 1877; early champion of law reform and codification of international law; author of a number of legal books.

† Famous "merchant prince" and Postmaster-general under Harrison.

TO CLARK FROM C. A. CILLEY *

Hickory, N.C. Mar 12, 1892

I am now, and for two weeks have been, studying your "Code"— The further I go the more I admire the labor, patience & genius for bookmaking displayed.

It is a positive necessity, it seems to me, to every lawyer, and exhausts the subject. I find cases there which none of our Digests contain. It is as interesting to me as a novel, for I am all the time hitting upon some new thing.

I could not forbear stopping in my reading just now, on purpose to say this, & having said it, I will go to reading again.

TO CLARK FROM ROBERT P. DICK †

Greensboro, N. C., Mar 22d 1892

Yours of the 17th has been received, and I was pleased to learn that you had agreed to furnish "The Greenbag"—a sketch of the Judges of our Supreme Court,—for I know that the work will be well done.

I am now engaged in preparing an address for the Y.M.C.A. of Reidsville to be delivered in a short time. In two weeks my courts will commence, and I will be much engaged on the circuit I will not have time to prepare a condensed sketch of my associates on the bench.

I have had occasion to deliver funeral addresses on the life and character of Justices Pearson,‡ Ruffin § and Settle || I regret that I have no extra copies to send you. I think that Col Kenan can furnish them. I have a bound volume that I could send you if you so desire

I think the decisions of Judge Pearson on *habeas corpus* cases—during Civil War and Reconstruction,—are as interesting and important as any he ever delivered.

Hon Kemp P Battle wrote a sketch of my life in No 4 of University Magazine 1889. I have no extra copy. I can send you photograph.

* City attorney and counsellor for First National Bank.

† Associate Justice of North Carolina Supreme Court, 1868-1876; Judge of the United States District Court for Western North Carolina.

‡ Richmond M. Pearson of Yadkin County, Associate Justice, 1848-1858; Chief Justice, 1858-1878.

§ Thomas Ruffin of Orange County, Chief Justice, 1833-1852.

|| Thomas Settle of Rockingham County, Associate Justice, 1868-1876.

Mr Justice Boyden * was very remarkable for his knowledge of all questions of Practice that came before the court. All the judges of the court recognized his great usefulness and *authority* upon such questions. He was also a very good man and of the highest integrity

Mr Justice Rodman † was the most learned judge that I ever met with. He had great familiarity with the English Reports, and most all other law books. He was a constant reader and wrote opinions with much facility

Mr. Justice Reade ‡ is a man of real genius. He was the finest advocate before a jury that I ever knew. I regarded him as a model Judge. He was pure and upright and was always conscientious in the discharge of duty. He did his best in the administration of justice and "his best" was of a very high order.

I wish I had time to write more fully of my Brethren of the Bench. We were truly Brethren—as no unkind word ever passed—and we were cordial in conference and in our Social intercourse

My memories of those days are all pleasant—and are often recalled

TO CLARK FORM WILLIAM B. RODMAN §

Washington, N. C.
April 28, 1892

My son showed me your favor of 19th March last. I have been a long time without making a reply to it. I intended to comply with your request which I certainly appreciate the kindness of: but my health is such that I hate work of any sort, as much as I used to enjoy it. I am downright lazy, and half blind. I have proposed a sketch of the labors of my life however, which I enclose with this. I fear it is too long to suit your purpose, or rather that of the Periodical that you refer to. If so—strike out freely all that will not suit his views. The hardest work I ever did was in preparing the legislation which as one of the Committee to certify our laws, I reported to the Legislature in 1868-1869—including the Code of Criminal Procedure which they failed even to notice. I do think these Acts of Assembly will endure on our Statute Books and in every code hereafter, for many years, and it will

* Nathaniel Boyden of Rowan County, Associate Justice, 1871-1873.

† William B. Rodman of Beaufort County, Associate Justice, 1868-1878.

‡ Edwin G. Reade of Person County, Associate Justice, 1868-1878.

§ Native of Beaufort County and prominent member of the 1868 Convention, which drafted the so-called "Canby Constitution"; Associate Justice of the Supreme Court of North Carolina, 1868-1878.

never be known that I am entitled to any credit for them, unless I put up my claim to it now.

P. S. As to my opinions while on the bench, like all others Coke's-Eldon's-Ruffin's-Gaston's they will necessarily become obsolete,—as the buildings of each generation of men, are covered up by the accretions which the next builds over them. Where are the palaces of the Caesars in Rome? buried many feet under the surface, only occasionally dug up by antiquarians. I do not know that this thought has ever occurred to you, but it will do so, as you get old and it is the less sad—the older one grows.

TO CLARK FROM JAMES DINWIDDIE *

Raleigh, N.C. May 9, 1892

We should be pleased to have you present our medals for us at the approaching commencement (May 30th), and I write this evening to request that you grant our young ladies that honor.

I assure you that I shall also appreciate very highly the honor of having you do so.

TO CLARK FROM WILLIAM R. COX †

July 8th 1892

I have just read an imperfect synopsis of your speech at the Battle Ground of Guilford C.H. subject Gen Wm R Davie. I write to congratulate you upon your success & to request that should your speech be published in pamphlet form—& you should see that it shall be—you will send me a copy for preservation among my valuable documents.

TO CLARK FROM R. W. BROWN ‡

Halifax, N. C.
July 11, 1892

The Board of Commissioners desire to return their thanks and also the thanks of the people of Halifax County for your offer to present to the County the portrait of Gen. W. R. Davie and to assure you that the gift will be appreciated and preserved by our people.

* Principal of Peace Institute.
† Democratic Representative in Congress, December 5, 1881-March 3, 1887.
‡ Register of Deeds and Chairman of the Board of County Commissioners.

TO CLARK FROM A. C. AVERY *

Raleigh, N.C.
July 14th 1892

I have just returned from a trip to Asheville and find your letter awaiting my return for reply. I approve of the idea of postponing session till Tuesday of each week and sitting four hours instead of three till the end of the week or till the docket for the district is finished.

I have not caught up with the news yet; but the outlook politically is not entirely satisfactory to me.

CLARK TO DAVID SCHENCK †

[n.d.]

I appreciate your courtesy in sending me a pass over the R & D system. As I have refused all passes since occupying this position I take the privilege of returning this. I know you will not think me churlish or intending the slightest disrespect to one I esteem so highly as yourself. Nor do I mean to intimate that any judicial officer is guilty of impropriety in accepting these compliments which have the sanction of years and many of the best and finest judges. But I simply defer to what in the greatest of modern times is given as a motive for public conduct "a decent regard for the opinions of mankind" and a still higher authority which is equally familiar to you. I Corinthians, 8 Chap. 13 V.

TO CLARK FROM A. M. WADDELL

Wilmington, N. C.
August 15th 1892.

I have your letter, enclosing the article on Gen[l] James Hogun ‡ and inquiring in regard to Gen[l] Nash.§

I had read the article, with great interest, upon its first appearance in print, and am very glad somebody has at last tried to rescue the name of that brave soldier and patriot from oblivion. I never could find out anything about him, and have always been disgusted at the ungrateful and criminal disregard of common

* Alphonso C. Avery of Burke County, Superior Court Judge, 1879-1888; Associate Justice of North Carolina Supreme Court, 1889-1897.
† Superior Court Judge, 1874-1871; native of Lincoln County.
‡ Brigadier General in the American Revolution.
§ Francis Nash of North Carolina, Brigadier General in the American Revolution.

decency exhibited by our people in regard to preserving the record of the achievements of their forefathers. For more than thirty years I have never lost an opportunity of reminding them of it, and I shall continue to do so as long as I live.

As to Gen Nash I am sorry to say that while there may be a letter somewhere in the possession of some one of the Waddell family I do not know of it. I remember seeing in my boyhood a letter from him to his wife giving an account of a dinner he had attended the day before at Gen Washington's tent—but what became of it I dont know— My uncle John Waddell wore Gen Nash's sword (and sash I believe) during the Mexican War in which he was a Major. After his death in Louisiana the relics disappeared, as I am informed— There never was a picture of Gen Nash that I ever heard of, and I am quite sure that such papers as existed in regard to him were destroyed by fire when Judge Alfred Moore's house was burned—as I know all the valuable plate, library &c were then destroyed. Judge Moore, as you know, was Gen N's brother-in-law, the latter having married his sister—Gen N's will is recorded in Brunswick and I have a copy of it.

I hope you will write the sketches of our Genl Officers in the Revolution. We sadly need all the literature of that sort we can get.

TO CLARK FROM GEORGE T. WINSTON

Chapel Hill, N. C., Sep. 7 1892

Please be assured of my grateful appreciation of your kind letter with the article on Gen. Hogun, the extracts from Moultries Memoirs * and the notices of Judge Toomer.† I shall hope to have *them all* printed in the first number of the University Magazine and to have the facsimile of Gen. Hogun's signature. I do not see how you find time for such researches. Surely we all owe you a deep debt of gratitude. Your address on Davie we shall be glad to print also in the Magazine, with the portrait, probably next month (No. 2). Please send me a printed copy of the address. The Magazine No. 2. will be issued the same month as University Day, and the publication of the article in that number will be especially appropriate. Please let me know the cost of the engraving, so that we may pay our share.

* William Moultrie, American Revolutionary leader from South Carolina.

† John D. Toomer of Cumberland County, Superior Court Judge, 1818-1819, and 1837-1840; Associate Justice of North Carolina Supreme Court, 1829.

TO CLARK FROM DAVID SCHENCK

Greensboro', N. C.,
October 7th, 1892.

. . . I thank you for your congratulations on my speech at Lincolnton. "Being native there and to the manner born", I only followed all the other speakers, who made very find arguments. Mine was only by way of exhortation on the application of the subject illustrated with a little humor and anecdote, but I feel confident that great good was done by the four speeches at old Lincolnton this week. I spoke there because there are a number of men in that County who were going or had gone to the Third Party,* who were very anxious to hear my views upon the subject, and they came out and listened to me with great patience. There is an anomaly that I found at Lincolnton and that is that the Negroes in large numbers are voting the Democratic ticket, and they are open and outspoken about it and are not afraid to avow it. This is a strange change since I left. The magnificent victory in Georgia will be worth ten thousand votes to us in North Carolina in my opinion.

TO CLARK FROM JAMES H. POU †

Smithfield, N. C., Nov 11th 1892

Mr. Busbee ‡ writes me today that he will probably not be an applicant for the U. S. Dist Attyship; and that being the case I have decided to apply for it.

If you can give me your assistance in the matter I will very greatly appreciate it.

TO CLARK FROM S. D. THOMPSON §

St. Louis, Nov. 12th 1892.

I have read with the greatest interest and pleasure the whole of your address upon the life and character of Judge Davie. I am glad that you have done this much to rescue from oblivion the name of this great man. I am ashamed to say that I do not recall

* Populist or People's Party, organized in 1892.

† Prominent attorney of Johnston County and later of Raleigh; member of General Assembly, 1885-1889; at one time chairman of Democratic State Executive Committee.

‡ Fabius H. Busbee, Raleigh lawyer and division counsel of the Southern Railroad Company.

§ Associate Editor of the *American Law Review.*

ever having heard of him before reading your address. Near the close of your address, page 30, there is a quotation relating to the tomb of Napoleon at St. Helena. This is a stanza which I learned when a boy, but I have partly forgotten; and yet it runs in my mind that the quotation (except the last two lines) is different from the way in which you give it. Can you tell me who the author of that poem is and where it can be found?

I ought to add that I have read with equal interest the first instalment of your sketch of the Supreme Court of North Carolina and its judges in the *Green Bag*.* It is very far above the generality of sketches of that kind published in that journal. The *American Law Review* would welcome anything from your pen, though the rewards of legal journalism are disgracefully small....

TO CLARK FROM JAMES H. POU

Smithfield, N. C., Nov 19th 1892

Upon consideration I have decided not to apply for the position of District Attorney. Mr Aycock † tells me he will apply. He has done more for the party than I and I am not willing to be in his way. I may be an applicant for some other position under the national government, and I would like to have a letter of general endorsement from you.

I will also be a candidate for President *Protem* of the Senate and I would highly appreciate any good word you might speak for me in that behalf

TO CLARK FROM DAVID SCHENCK

Greensboro', N. C.,
December 14th, 1892.

...I have reflected upon the matter which you suggested to me at Raleigh and I am very highly pleased with your suggestion and very much interested in having it carried out. I have a reference to the Acts of the Legislature under which Colonel Saunders ‡ published his Colonial Records, but I have not yet examined them closely. Won't you do me the kindness to draw up the Bill just as you want it and send it to me confidentially. I find that there will be a number of Bills before the next Legislature asking

* Legal magazine.

† Charles B. Aycock of Wayne County, Governor, 1901-1905.

‡ Colonel William L. Saunders of Wake County, Secretary of State, 1879-1891; editor of the *Colonial Records of North Carolina*.

aid to perpetuate the Historical events of North Carolina. Professor E. A. Alderman * will be on hand asking some aid to his Historical Society.† He was around to see me the other day and we had a long conference. I mentioned to him the great importance of publishing the Records of our Revolutionary History and told him confidentially that you would undertake the work if the Legislature would give you proper recognition and assistance, and that I was much interested in it. He suggested that you should print it as a part of the documents of the Historical Society of North Carolina and deposit it with that Society, meaning the Society which was organized at Morehead last summer.

I merely give you this information in order that you may keep apace with the current events.

I will apply th[r]ough our Senator Mr. King ‡ for an increase of the appropriation to the Guilford Battle Ground of from $200.00 to $500.00. I hope to get it. We must have some aid or we cannot keep up the ground decently and in order....

I notice that you are working yourself more than you can bear. I could see traces of weariness on your face. Your spirit is stronger than your body, and as your friend I want to warn you not to break yourself down in your early life. Don't follow my example in that respect. The State needs your services in the future and I know of no man now who can be a successor to Colonel Saunders except yourself, but you must not undertake to do too much at once. "Make haste slowly."

TO CLARK FROM A. M. WADDELL

Wilmington, N. C.
Dec[r] 30th 1892.

Knowing from experience, the lack of appreciation among North Carolinians of efforts to perpetuate the memory of our great men, or elevate in any way the State pride of our people—to say nothing of gratuitous labors to excite a taste for literature of any kind—and apprehending that you have probably had a similar experience I want to say to you that I take the "Green Bag," and have read your articles on our Supreme Court with very great pleasure and interest.

* Edwin A. Alderman, President of the University of North Carolina, 1893-1900; later President of the University of Virginia.

† Historical Society of North Carolina.

‡ J. L. King, State Senator from Guilford County, 1885, 1891-1893.

There is and has always been a pitiful and disgraceful ignorance and indifference among the people of this State in regard to the history of the State, and an apparent aversion to asserting the least claim to the *respect* of the world, much less to its admiration. It is for this reason that the State has no higher place in the sisterhood, for that she is regarded as about the "sorriest" of the original thirteen there can be no doubt, and the people of the State have only themselves to blame for it.

There is no encouragement to a man to engage in anything intellectual in N° Carolina, but, thank God, the pleasures arising from culture do not depend on the value placed on it by others. Still, when a man renders a service to his State by rescuing from oblivion (which would otherwise engulf them) the names and deeds of her worthy sons, he would at least like to receive credit for a noble purpose.

If our people possessed the characteristics of almost any other American citizens how different a place the State would occupy in public estimation:—

But I've got off on one of my hobbies, and by your pardon, I merely intended to let you know that there is one man in N. C. who appreciates your work in these, and the other biographical articles which you have written, and to say that I hope you will continue your labors.

TO CLARK FROM FABIUS H. BUSBEE

Raleigh, N.C.
January 14, 1893

Please write me the letter "To the President" recommending Charles * for the post office as you kindly offered to do. Send it to me and I will keep it until after inauguration.

TO CLARK FROM DAVID SCHENCK

Greensboro, N. C.
January 14th, 1893.

. . . I feel great interest in your bill.† It is a matter I have had in view for years—the publication of these old manuscripts, but did not know how to get at it.

* Brother of Fabius H. Busbee.

† For the organization of the Guilford Battle Ground Company. The bill was passed and Schenck became president of the company.

These sections of The Code were called to my attention by Professor Alderman and I believe that he would accept this Act as a substitute for his North Carolina Historical Society. That is, if the main purposes be embraced in this Act, to wit: Allowing the Trustees to appoint you to edit certain papers and there may be others that his Society would desire to publish.

I want to give everything that I have got on North Carolina History to the State where it will be kept, and I think I shall do it before I die and not put it off to be done by my executor. If I knew exactly when that event would come I would try to anticipate it, but during my life I have frequent reference to my papers and like to enjoy them.

This Legislature is a liberal one and we must not lose the opportunity to do all we can for the State during its session. I would suggest to you to have your bill introduced at once, and could you not have some friend to move the appointment of a Committee on Historical Matters that all papers, resolutions and bills relating to the History of North Carolina might be referred?

TO CLARK FROM DAVID SCHENCK

Greensboro, N. C.
January 17th, 1893

The bill for the Battle Ground Company will be introduced on the 21st and I will be down perhaps about a week from now.

I send you a copy of your bill for fear you did not keep a copy yourself and I think you had better have "Bill Day" * to introduce it for you or somebody else whom you think is better suited for the purpose. Professor Alderman will introduce his bill also to incorporate "The William L. Saunders Historical Society of North Carolina".

He will ask for the use of the old State Library Room in the Capitol and for a thousand dollars to begin with. I think he will get the room but doubt whether he will get the thousand dollars, but if a man don't ask he will never receive. Maybe they will give him five hundred dollars. I drew the bill for him. It provides in one section for the collection and distribution of pamphlets and it also has a section in it that provides for the publication of anything that the Trustees of the State Library may request them to publish—same section of the Code referred to in your bill.

* Captain William H. Day, State Senator from Halifax County.

TO CLARK FROM MARTIN H. HOLT *

Raleigh, N. C.
January 27th, 1893

Your letter and bill enclosed to hand and duly considered. I am in hearty sympathy with the idea, and am willing to do all I can to secure the passage of the Resolution. It ought to pass; it will pass. It is a burning shame on our state that the niches in our Capitol stand empty, monuments to our lack of patriotism. I shall be glad to confer with you at such a time and place as you suggest to consider the matter further before introducing. I have consulted quite a number of the leading gentlemen here, and all are agreed as to the wisdom of the Resolution.

TO CLARK FROM JACOB BATTLE †

Raleigh, N. C.
February 20, 1893

The letter sent by you this morning I handed to Mr. Holt. I went over in the House this morning and got up our Motto Bill.‡

If you have the time I can fix up a provision to be inserted in the Machinery Act in regard to tax on corporations with a unit showing how the new law proposed will operate in comparison with the old law, I will be very much obliged. . . .

TO CLARK FROM ERNEST HAYWOOD §

Raleigh, N. C.
March 25th, 1893

Can you give me a history of the picture called "The First Trial by Jury" or at least tell me what particular incident (if any) it really represents? I think you have one of these pictures and there is one in the Clerks' office. I have one and am anxious to know what it really represents.

* Founder of Oak Ridge Institute and Representative in General Assembly from Guilford County.

† Superior Court Judge, 1893-1895; native of Nash County.

‡ Clark had suggested to Battle that the State's motto should be "Esse Quam Videri," which means "to be rather then to seem," and the General Assembly of 1893 (chapter 145) adopted the words "Esse Quam Videri" as the State's motto and directed that these words with the date, "20 May, 1775" should be placed with our Coat of Arms upon the Great Seal of the State. See article by Walter Clark, "Our State Motto and Its Origin," in *The North Carolina Booklet,* Vol. IX, No. 3, reprinted in Volume II of *The Clark Papers.*

§ Raleigh attorney.

I write to you simply because you are considered an authority on such subjects.

TO CLARK FROM HORACE W. FULLER *

Boston, Mass
April 8th, 1893

Your favor of April 6th is at hand with enclosures for which accept my thanks. Contributions to the "facetiae" column are particularly acceptable and if the judges in our other states would manifest the same interest in the "Green Bag" that you kindly show, I should be able to keep that column filled with a great deal of interesting matter.

CLARK TO JESSE TURNER †

Raleigh, 1 May 1893

Your esteemed favor to hand & address on Gen. Davie sent you as requested. I appreciate the compliment of the request.

The epitaph was by *Gov* Gaston of S.C. who was somewhat earlier in date than our *Judge* Gaston of N.C.

I had the pleasure a while back of reading a very interesting letter written by you to Judge Aiken of Danville, Va., a grandson of Judge Murphey,‡ in reference to your early recollections of Justice in Orange. I feel a peculiar interest in that county, as my wife is from Hillsboro being the daughter of Gov *Wm* A. Graham whom you probably knew.

[P.S.]

If you feel an interest in N.C. history you may find something to amuse a leisure hour in an *illustrated* series of sketches of all the Judges of the N.C. Supreme Court contributed by one to the "Greenbag" Magazine in *Oct. Nov. & Dec.* No's 1892. I particularly refer to Murphey and Ruffin whom you knew so well.

CLARK TO JESSE TURNER

Raleigh 3 May 1893

I trust the "Davie" pamphlet reached you safely.

A gentleman of Greensboro says Judge Murphey used to go to his father's house very often and he says "Murphey was a small

* Editor of *The Green Bag*, legal magazine.
† Native of North Carolina, lawyer and judge at Van Buren, Arkansas.
‡ Archibald D. Murphey, educational leader and Superior Court Judge, 1818-1820.

man, extremely handsome, and an eloquent and persuasive speaker and one of the most delightful companions in the world, but that he was very licentious and would not pay his debts and would borrow all the money he could from his friends and get them to go his security. It was one of his sureties who had a large amount of money to pay for him who had him imprisoned in the jail at Greensboro for debt. He was also an infidel."

I would appreciate it if you will let me know how this agrees with your own recollection & knowledge of Murphey.

I will be glad to be favored with any information as to him or other leading men of that day—as to their appearance, manner, characteristics, with incidents or anecdotes which you may be willing to give. I will highly esteem the favor.

I note you say your father was at the battle of Guilford C.H. Did he ever give you an account of that fight? I presume you have seen Judge Schenck's book * vindicating the conduct of the N.C. troops on that field.

TO CLARK FROM DAVID SCHENCK †

May 16th, 1893.
Greensboro, N. C.

Accept my thanks for your letter of May 15th 1893. I did not know that Theo. H. Hill ‡ was yet alive. If I remember correctly he is a man of my age or older. I remember to have seen him when I was in the Convention of '62, if I am correct in his identity. If you would be kind enough to suggest the matter to him perhaps he would be patriotic enough to write us a poem without charge. If he will agree to it I will send him all the data necessary in type, so that he will have no difficulty in getting the ideas. I think it would add very much to his reputation if he would write a poem for this occasion; it would be handed down among our archives. I do not want a long poem—8 or 10 stanzas would do, or maybe a dozen if he prefers. I do not know Mr. John H. Boner,§ though I fear it is arguing "myself unknown."

I am extremely gratified that the Governor and Council have requested you to complete Colonel Saunders work from 1775 to 1781. Couldn't we stretch it a little so as to include 1781? I think

* *North Carolina, 1780-81.*
† Schenck was President of the Guilford Battle Ground Company.
‡ North Carolina poet, best known for "The Star Above the Manger."
§ North Carolina poet.

if I were you I would collect everything that bears upon the battle of Guilford Court House. To simply give the correspondence and documents leading up to the war and omitting this battle, which was the cap stone, would leave the work very incomplete. By all means in the world do all you can in that direction and I promise you all the help in my power. I have been trying for some time to go to Washington or Richmond, but have not been physically able to do so. At times I feel very uneasy about you. I know that you are doing exactly what I did—overtaxing your mental strength —and if you work during your vacation, work slowly,—"Make haste slowly".

I have all the communications made to the University Magazine, bearing upon the history of 1780—'81, collected in one Volume, and I have all the biographies of distinguished men of that day, which were published in the Magazine, collected in another Volume. These I will place at your command. The Volumes are indexed, which will facilitate your examination of them. Any book that I have will be at your service of course.

I did not know that you were looking in the direction of West Point when I asked you to sign Alderman's recommendation. It was very magnanimous of you to give way to him. I know of no one who will enjoy it more or fill the duties better than Professor Alderman. He will make his mark in North Carolina before he dies and I feel that you and I will not be forgotten as long as his tongue and pen shall live and he has many years ahead of him yet, I hope.

TO CLARK FROM JESSE TURNER *

Van Buren, Ark.
May 19, 1893

Your letter of the 1st and 3rd inst. recd., but the *Davie pamphlet* has not yet come to hand. . . . My reply to what is said by the gentleman of Greensboro about Judge Murphey I have to remark that I was born and grew up to manhood within five miles of his home. I saw and heard him often at the bar, at his home and elsewhere, and think I know him fairly well, and I never heard it charged or intimated that he was "licentious," or that he was a man "who would not pay his debts," and that "he would borrow all the money he could from his friends, and get them to be his security," and that he was an "infidel."

* Turner studied law under Judge Murphey.

These charges I am thoroughly convinced have grossly misrepresented Murphey's character. The *living Murphey* was usually regarded as a *Model of decorum* and *propriety* in every walk of life. In conversation and conduct he was courteous and defferential, and never indulging under any circumstances in profanity, vulgarity or indecency. These were foreign to the innate purity of the man, and the most fastidious lady would have no occasion to have found fault with his *earnest* and most *heated* utterances at the Bar or elsewhere. Murphey during a great part of his life carried on various branches of business, He was a successful lawyer, he was also a farmer, merchant, and miller. Unlike most lawyers, he preferred a country life to a town life. He had settled down in the midst of a most comfortable and prosperous rural plantation with whom he was always a great favorite. In these various branches of business which he followed for nearly 20 years his dealings and business transactions with his friends and neighbors have been extensive and varied. In conducting a variety of pursuits such as he was engaged in it must necessarily have often happened that his relation to neighbors and friends and persons with whom he had dealings was sometimes that of *creditor* and *often that* of *debtor.* Now I wonder how he got along with his business if he would not pay his debts? Perhaps the Greensboro gentleman can explain. It seems to me that the mere statement of these facts is a refutation of this unjust charge. If it had been said that these came [at] a time in the busy and active life of this great and good man when he could not pay all his debts it would have been true then such has been the fate of many good men and since Murphey's day, but then it can be truly said in Murphey's case that [he] did all the highest type of an honest and honorable man could do to pay his debts. He surrendered all of his large estates and property both real and personal for the benefit of his creditors and it was all sold under the hammer of the Sheriff of Orange County. This sale took place in February or March 1821. I was then a boy about 15 years of age and was present at the sale, and remember its incidents as of yesterday. His large estates were held in his own name, and no debts were secured by *Mortgages, Deeds of Trust* or any kind of *lien* whatever. It seemed that most of Murphey's debts had been made on his *individual* responsibility and only in exceptional cases that personal security was required. Murphey in the days of his prosperity had made no provision for his family or kinfolks in anticipation of reverses of fortune. No *concealment* or *covering up fraudulent conveyances* or settlements of property to wrong or injure creditors. But all his property thus surrendered was *unincumbered.* Hundreds of people were present at the sale. *Murphey* was there and his *creditors* were there, either in person or by representatives. All was *fair* and *open,* and Murphey's large amount of property failed to satisfy all his creditors and left a considerable amount of indebtedness still unpaid. Years after Murphey's property had all been swept away some of his creditors whose debt had not been satisfied had writs of *Ca. Sa* issued against him and his person was seized and kept within "prison Bounds", both at *Hillsboro* and *Greensboro* for a time. And thus was illustrated in the person of Judge Murphey, *broken down by misfortune* and suffering from disease that cruel relict of a barbarous age *imprisonment* for debt, A law which I am pleased to know has been long since stricken from the Statute book of my native State.

I have never had the shadow of a doubt, that if Murphey had lived and his health preserved he would have paid every dollar of his *unsatisfied indebtedness. But a hard fortune, Oh, how hard it was,* all said otherwise.

CLARK TO JESSE TURNER

Raleigh 22 May 1893

... I am much gratified at your complete vindication of Judge Murphey whose fame is so dear to all North Carolinians.

You could doubtless get a copy of Judge David Schenck's book of him, or his publishers at Greensboro, N.C. ...

WALTER CLARK TO FRIENDS

Raleigh, 24 May, 1893

At the instance of the Governor and Trustees of the Public Library, I have undertaken to carry on Col. Saunders' Colonial Records from 1776 where he left off work down to 1781 as authorized by the Act of General Assembly. There is no compensation whatever attached to the labor except the consciousness of endeavoring to aid in the vindication of our past and our heroic dead. Knowing your feelings and services in that respect I beg that you will aid me with your advice, suggestions and information as to what should be published and the best means of procuring materials.

I shall much appreciate any aid you may be able and willing to give me.

TO CLARK FROM KEMP P. BATTLE *

Chapel Hill, N. C.
May 30, 1893

I will assuredly afford you all the aid I can in your laudable enterprise.

I have waited before writing you in order to consult Dr. Winston † in regard to your having copies of the MS owned by the University.

He will recommend the Trustees to allow you to have these copies but does not see his way clear to allowing them to be taken from Chapel Hill. Could you not employ one of our students to do the work? We have a considerable number of valuable originals. It is the rule in all Libraries to have the copying done in these limits. I suppose of course the Trustees of the State Library will allow you the expenses of copying.

If you consent to this I will superintend the execution. Please state whether you will require type-writing.

TO CLARK FROM JAMES S. MANNING ‡

Durham, N. C. June 3rd, 1893

I have just read your opinion in Vanstory v. Thornton, and it is, in my judgment, the clearest exposition of the Homestead I have ever read. I regret exceedingly that the views you express are not the views of the entire Court and the law of this state. It seems to me to set aright the whole matter, after many years of confusion and conflict, and to make the matter clear, plain, and simple. How unfortunate it is that this impartial matter, after 25 years of decisions, should not finally be determined!

From my knowledge of the views of the members of the professions, your opinion is sustained, and it must be a matter of daily regret, that it is not the law of the land.

* Professor of History and former President of the University of North Carolina, 1876-1891.

† George Tayloe Winston, President of the University of North Carolina, 1891-1896.

‡ Lawyer, member of General Assembly, 1907-1909; Associate Justice of North Carolina Supreme Court, 1909-1917; Attorney General of North Carolina, 1917-1925.

TO CLARK FROM JAMES C. MACRAE *

Fayetteville, N. C.
June 6, 1893

Yours of yesterday recd. I will go to the Court House and examine the old records and write you as to what is worth perpetuating. I fear they are in fearful condition.

Cumberland, as you know, was part of Bladen and was not formed until 1754 and the records which show the earliest settlement of the Cape Fear section are in Bladen; but I note that you are concerned only with those from 1876. I hope I will be able to find some thing of interest.

I have read Manning's letter in reference to your dissenting opinion in Vanstory v. Thornton. I wish our predecessors had taken your view of it in the beginning.

TO CLARK FROM ROBERT D. GRAHAM †

Washington, D. C.
June 8, 1893

...I have talked over the matter with both Col. D. R. Goodloe,‡ and Woodbury Wheeler. From the first I learned that an old MS taken from the War D. records and secreted when the British captured this place in 1814, was kept by a Mr. Bird until 1883, 69 years, and then restored, probably to the State Department and that Mr. G. had made out a copy of it and sent to Col. Saunders. It is a list of army officers in the Revolutionary War, from N. C. If not found, another copy can be made.

Mr. Wheeler wrote today for the return of the MS copy made by his father, John H. Wheeler in the London Rolls Office. It is now loaned to a party on Am. Encyc. in N. Y. When it is recd., I will see what it has in it that has not been given in "Wheeler's Reminiscence of N. C."

Have you in Raleigh "Graham's Colonial History". There is one copy here at the Columbian University Library. It has a little on N. C.

Now as to the Pension Office, the labor and expense of getting to and selecting the *N. C. papers* from the mass there is so great

* Superior Court Judge, 1882-1890; Associate Justice Supreme Court, 1893-1895; native of Cumberland County.

† Lawyer.

‡ Daniel Reaves Goodloe, native of North Carolina; prominent anti-slavery writer; later editor of the *National Era;* author of a number of books.

that I almost despair of your getting anyone to go through them. Outside of the declarations filed by the veterans of the Revolutionary War, there appear to be nothing there beyond the names of the commanders of North Carolina Regiments of the Continental Line—a copy furnished to the Pension Office by the State of North Carolina. So I suppose you still have the original at Raleigh. When I resigned from the Civil Service Commission, I spent over three weeks in going through the declaration filed in the B. P. by the revolutionary soldiers. I did not get much of general interest, though the declaration of Gen. Wm. Lenoir is an exception and I sent a copy to Col. Walter Lenoir in the West. I will try and go through my hasty, penciled notes made at the time and write you further. Will also go to the Congressional Library again.

I understand Col. Saunders to say he had the material for May 1775. He said he would send that section to me for review before publishing, and I supposed he had forgotten this and gone to print without it.

TO CLARK FROM W. E. DANIEL *

Weldon, N.C.
June 9 1893

At the last Commencement at Wake Forest College a Committee of the Trustees consisting of Mr. Holding, Mr. Gulley and the writer was appointed to provide for the Establishment of a Law Department at Wake Forest College, to select the teacher and to make the necessary arrangements for opening the same in September.

Before we left the Commencement, it was agreed that you were the man to take charge of it, and Mr. Holding has written me that they had already spoken to you. An engagement prevented my attendance or I would have seen you in person. We meet again Thursday evening, but I want to write to you and express my earnest desire that you may accept the position. There are several reasons which I can give—The time has come for the establishment of a Law Department at Wake Forest College and our people are going to do it, and it will merit their patronage. Its success will be assured and quick if a lawyer and a judge of your recognized fitness, learning, ability and character shall have charge of it.

In late years, a large number of young men who leave Wake

* Lawyer.

Forest College are studying law; everyone will take the course there, if there is a course—If you take the chair, others will be attracted; and the place, the cheapness of living, and the good influence which is thrown around every young man, will be great inducements.

I believe that after the first year, the remuneration would be sufficient for your work, and in a few years, your reputation as a teacher and in the standing of the boys who would go from your classes would make it ample.

I have always been your friend and an admirer and I think such an opportunity as this at your time of life and in your present position comes to few men. In after years, who could measure your influence throughout North Carolina with a man in each community who had learned the law under your teaching?

I hope to see you when I come to Raleigh and discuss this matter with you further, let me express the wish that you may consider favorably this matter and that your consideration may lead to your acceptance.

TO CLARK FROM GEORGE T. WINSTON

Chapel Hill, N. C.
June 15, 1893

Dr. Battle and I have decided to lend you what material you wish to use, although it is not according to our rule. You will protect it, I am sure, you will use it for the State, And you, in fact; secured much of it for us. Dr. B[attle] reports that it is not catalogued. I think your best plan to come here and *see* it and select what you choose, unless indeed you can wait for Prof. Alderman till Sept. or can secure Dr. S. B. Weeks's * aid *now*. He is here.

By the way, Weeks is the very man to travel over N. C. and *collect material*. He would do it most admirably.

I am so ignorant of the value of this material that I cannot offer my services. Shall I see Weeks, or will you write him?

TO CLARK FROM STEPHEN B. WEEKS

Durham, N. C.
19th July, 1893

I found your postal awaiting me on my return from a little bit of a vacation. President Winston told me last week that he would

* Stephen B. Weeks, author of many historical books and articles on North Carolina.

be glad to go to Raleigh and go before the committee on the library in the matter of the historical agency if it would be of any service. I write you this so that you may ask him to come down and go with you before the committee if it will add weight to your own arguments. I am very anxious to do the work. I become more and more interested in it the more I think of it and hope that it can be finally arranged as we desire. I think that I am on the track of one or two new finds that promise to be rich in Revolutionary matters but I cannot tell as yet what is in them.

TO CLARK FROM B. F. STEVENS *

London
19 July 1893

I am favoured with your letter of the 3rd inst. and I take pleasure in congratulating the North Carolina authorities upon their success in having secured your good services in supervising and editing their Colonial Records.

I hardly know how to answer your enquiries shortly and lucidly. By "supervising and editing" I presume the intention is to print the Colonial Records. I do not know how complete your files of Records are. In New Hampshire their Records are nearly complete and they were printed from their own material in hand. I subsequently read these New Hampshire volumes with the Official Records that are now preserved in the Public Record Office of England and I was able to note many differences of more or less importance and fill up many deficiencies in the Proceedings of the Council and of the Assembly and also of Governors Speeches and Official Correspondence. The Acts in the Public Record Office include those that were disallowed and also the private Acts, some of which were never printed. The English Minutes of Council among almost innumerable subjects include the reasons for disallowing particular Acts &c &c.

In New York it was thought best to obtain transcripts of every document relating to that Colony. In New Jersey they have been doing very much the same thing. South Carolina is now employing a gentleman to make up their records.

My Notes upon the manuscripts in the Public Record Office

* Famous bibliographer and purchasing agent in England for many American libraries. Stevens made facsimiles of 2,107 important historical manuscripts in many European archives for the years 1773-1783, which were printed in twenty-five volumes.

relating to America are so copious that I could make a preliminary Report upon the North Carolina documents without very much labor but before your settling down to the expenditure of any large amount of money or to carrying out any comprehensive scheme it will be desirable to know what documents you already possess and with what thoroughness you want to collate, compare, and transcribe such documents as will go toward completing your series. To this end I venture to suggest that a personal interview and cursory examination of the papers would not only be much more satisfactory to you but I think, in the long run, it would be more economical.

I could assist you in quickly surveying the material in England and with these facts clearly in your mind you could report the details so clearly and so fully to your Board that they could make such a plan, more or less comprehensive, as they might like to carry out, and they could proceed from beginning to end upon absolutely definite lines.

If you want to employ my services in carrying out your plans when they are formulated, I am at your disposal; but whether you employ me or not I shall willingly do what I can to assist you in deciding upon your line of procedure and to this end I respectfully repeat the suggestion that it will be economical for you to come to London to see the enormous mass of manuscripts relating to North Carolina, and its immediate surroundings, that are preserved in the Public Record Office and in numerous other Archives.

I shall have pleasure in sending you Catalogues of Americana but I venture to suggest that it will be both more economical and much more expeditious if you will prepare, or cause to be prepared, as full a bibliography of North Carolina books as can be readily made, and then having ticked off those which you already possess, your agents in America and on the Continent can search for the remaining items in many Collections where no Sales Catalogues are being issued. Perhaps Mr. Poole of the Newberry Library of Chicago, or Mr. Winsor of the Harvard Library, or Mr. Spofford, the Librarian of Congress, may have so classified their Americana that they can give you the North Carolina block very readily in case you yourself or your own State Librarian shall not have already prepared a better bibliography. The Catalogue of the British Museum and of certain other well known Libraries may perhaps readily supply some items.

The Periodical Publications for which you ask will be sent to you.

Wishing you the best possible success in your great undertaking.

TO CLARK FROM W. NOEL SAINSBURY *

Boulogne, Mer, le
10 Aout, 1893

. . . I have also to acknowledge and thank you for Draft for £20–& soon after my return to England I hope to send you some transcripts which I have noted as valuable additions to the N. C. records already sent–In going thro' the So. Car. records there are many quite as interesting and pertinent to North as to South Carolina but it was quite impossible without great sacrifice of time and very great expense for me to examine that large series & as a matter of fact I did not then think the game would be worth the candle but I am noting them all now while proceeding with the So. Car. records for that Governt. I note your remarks about Carthagena & St. Augustine & you may be sure they shall have my best attention in my resuming work at the office. . . .

TO CLARK FROM W. NOEL SAINSBURY

Roll House
Chancery Lane,
London, W. C.
14 Oct. 1893

I have recd your letter of the 28th Sept. last which acknowledges receipt of the parcel of copies I sent you by Book post–I have now the pleasure to forward you a *second* parcel of copies by Book post which I hope you will find interesting–I expect to find other papers relating to *North* Carolina in the *South* Carolina correspondence–I will shortly look into the papers of Carthagena & Louisburg Expeditions & see if I can find anything of interest to your State–I am very hard pressed at the moment completing another Vol. of my Colonial Calendar of State Papers which I trust will be published before the end of the year or at all events printed.

I will see if the Journals of Council or Assembly of N. C. contain anything of the Expeditions.

* Head of the British Public Records Office.

TO CLARK FROM STEPHEN B. WEEKS *

Baltimore, Maryland.
October 21st, 1893.

I am anxious to find out the years in which Joseph Martin represented Sullivan county, now in Tennessee, in the legislature of North Carolina. He was there most of the time between 1780 and 1790 but I have no way here and know of no way by which I can arrive at the exact years. Can you help me out of the hole? Wheeler prints the representatives of all the counties in North Carolina after the division but leaves out those which went with Tennessee as much as to say they were never a part of the old State.

I hope you are meeting with success in the work of the colonial records. I think that my own interest grows instead of decreasing from distance. I am on the track of the Blount papers and have written concerning them. They may not be of much service for the period you are now on but will certainly come into play from 1784, if we are so successful as to get that far. Unless there is some radical change in my own program from which I now contemplate it is very probable that I shall offer you my services for the work we have talked so much about late next spring for the summer at the mere matter of expenses. You can keep this in mind and we will await developments for you and for me.

CLARK TO ROBERT O. LEINSTER

Raleigh, N.C., 25 April 1894

Yours to hand. I have delayed replying till I could hear definitely from the RR's to whom I applied for reduced rates. I have now heard and they refuse any reduction. It could hardly be expected otherwise as all our R.R's are now owned in New York by Yankees, and they can hardly feel about this matter as we do. Our present calculation is to get to Washington on May 23, and go out on 10:30 A.M. train next day to Sharpsburg with the Federal Commissioners—one of whom Gen. H. Heth served in our Army. There is a R.R. station now in 3 miles of Sharpsburg. This 3 miles we will go by Stage.

Your section sent a splendid set of soldiers to the war and I am very glad you are to represent them. Our members are thinning out every day. We have to make this trip at our own expense but

* Weeks received his Ph.D. degree in History at Johns Hopkins.

I feel we owe it to the memory of our gallant dead to do so. If we do not, other states will claim the honor of taking & holding positions which North Carolina held on the day of battle....

TO CLARK FROM JULIAN S. CARR *

Durham, N. C.
June 4th 1894

There is considerable talk here and hereabouts regarding your election to the Presidency of Trinity College. You don't know how glad such talk makes me. Of all men in my knowledge I would rather Judge Walter Clark was President of Trinity College, and I write to know if there is any possibility of you being persuaded to consider the acceptance of the position. To be frank with you I am for you first, last and all the time, if you will allow your name presented to the Board, and I would like to have the distinguished honor of presenting your name to the Board. At your convenience I trust you will drop me a line touching this matter.

TO CLARK FROM JOHN F. CROWELL †

Durham, N.C.
June 8 1894.

No name mentioned in connection with the Presidency of Trinity College receives half so much approval as your own. I wish to know whether you are in any sense a possibility, that is, whether you would accept if elected on any terms or conditions. If so, I want to know so that I may have the assurance of the college's being in the safest possible hands. I would like exceedingly to put your name in nomination next Tuesday.

CLARK TO THE EDITOR OF THE "CHARLOTTE OBSERVER"

Raleigh, N.C. July 28, 1894

I notice in your issue of yesterday, that a correspondent refers to me as a "doubting Thomas" and states that I am uncertain as to which nomination I will take—the "democratic" or the "so-called fusion." In justice to myself I wish to say that your correspondent has been misinformed. At no time have I been uncertain in my views as to any matter of public importance. As a judge

* Prominent Durham industrialist.
† President of Trinity College.

I thought propriety required that I should take no active part in political discussions, nor did I feel called upon to rush into print whenever a newspaper correspondent attributed to me views I never entertained. It is proper however to say once for all that I am not and have not been at any time a candidate for any nomination other than the democratic nomination for the office I now hold. My democracy has not been questioned by those who know me. There is no foundation whatever for any assertion or surmise connecting my name with any party other than the one to which I have given my means and my time from the first ballot I cast.

CLARK TO R. L. LEATHERWOOD

Raleigh, N.C.
August 2, 1894

I am gratified to notice your endorsement by renomination. Your services entitle you to this honor, and I had no doubt that you would receive it if you desired it.

The Populists here gave me a genuine surprise yesterday by endorsing me as a Democrat as my own successor. On hearing it, I immediately consulted our party leaders, and the card you will notice in today's paper was drafted by their advice. I hope my friends will not allow my position to be misunderstood. Placing a Judge on both tickets is very common at the North, and indeed is the rule in some States, but in this State has only been done, I believe in 1868, when both parties placed Pearson, Reade, and perhaps others on their tickets. Hence I was very much taken aback at first what to do.

LETTER TO "THE SOUTHERN CULTIVATOR AND DIXIE FARMER," NOVEMBER, 1894

INVENTIONS NEEDED AT THE SOUTH

By Judge Walter Clark

The common field pea, whether the cow pea, clay pea, the Unknown pea, or other variety, is the clover of the South. It will grow when clover will not. It will furnish more forage than clover and will improve land more rapidly. It can be sown, when desired, in a crop of corn, and thus improve land without losing a year's use of it for cultivation. At the North the pea is coming into wider use in lieu of clover for forage and as a land improver.

This will furnish a growing market for our peas, as they will not mature seeds there. The great drawback in the raising of peas for seed is the great cost of harvesting and beating them out. At the North where beans are largely raised they have satisfactory bean harvesters and threshers. Southern inventive genius has always been equal to the demands upon it. If some one will invent a satisfactory pea harvester and a good pea thresher, he will not only make a fortune for himself, but he will bring back fertility to the South. It will increase ten fold the growing of field peas, besides making a new crop for us to ship to the North. These inventions will stimulate the growing of field peas, just as the invention of the cotton gin stimulated the increased crop of cotton.

Then, too, a good peanut thresher is badly needed for the peanut crop. Picking off by hand is slow and expensive, and none of the peanut threshers invented so far are satisfactory. They break and shatter too many peanuts.

The price of cotton does not bid fair to go up. The new area added every year in Texas will continually overbalance the world's increased consumption. Then there is the steadily increasing production in India, Egypt and Brazil. In Mexico the cotton plant lives eight years and produces two crops a year. Production there has heretofore been small, owing to the lack of railroads and reliable labor. This is being remedied. To compete with a country which can produce sixteen crops of cotton from one planting is like using a muzzle loader against a sixteen shooter. Besides, all countries south of us, irrespective of fertility, and no matter how rich we shall make our lands, have the advantage of us in the length of the season. We can not overcome the disadvantage of our short seasons for cotton. In North Carolina it is doomed, sooner or later, to disappear as a market crop. We can substitute many things. Grass is very profitable if the land is made rich enough because it takes so little labor. Two weeks out of the fifty-two—one week in June to mow and one week later to bale up, is enough—while cotton or tobacco require the year round. The field pea offers the advantage of abundant forage, a steady improver of our lands, a good fattener for cattle and hogs, and a crop to ship North. The drawback in the great expense of harvesting and preparing for market should be overcome. The South will reward with wealth and honor the man who will furnish the harvester and thresher that will enable us to increase ten fold this crop.

TO CLARK FROM STEPHEN B. WEEKS

Washington, D. C.
January 1, 1895

The Laws of North Carolina were duly received. They will be used and returned in a short time. Please accept my thanks and the thanks of others in the Bureau for your kindness in this matter.

I went to Philadelphia week before last to look into the Archdale Papers which are there in private hands for information on his life for my Quaker book. I found some things of interest to me and quite a number of interest and service to the colonial history of North Carolina and which will serve as a supplement to the published first volume. I have secured the permission to have these copied for you. I enclose a memorandum of papers that I think should be copied. Some of them relate directly to N. C.; some refer to Carolina only and it is difficult to say whether they mean South or North Carolina or both. In such cases I think it best to err on the side of inclusiveness and suggest that they be copied. The copying will cost 30 cents an hour. Of course, my own trouble and expense is not to be counted in this connection as that has been paid in another way. If you desire to have these copied please return the memorandum with them so marked and I will forward it at once.

TO CLARK FROM HORACE W. FULLER *

Boston, Mass.
January 4, 1895

Yours of the 1st at hand. I beg to differ with you in regard to your modest estimate of the services you have rendered me and shall most gladly continue sending you "The Green Bag" so long as you are willing to read it. If it will ease your conscience in the matter, occasional contributions of "Anecdotes" will more than repay any imagined indebtedness.

Thank you for you kind offer to write up some desired subjects for me, and I shall ere long avail myself of it. . . .

CLARK TO MRS. REBECCA A. TURNER †

Raleigh, 25 Jan. 1895

I thank you very much for your kindness in sending the notices of the death of your distinguished husband and especially for your

* Editor of *The Green Bag, A Monthly Magazine for Lawyers.*

† Widow of Jesse Turner, lawyer and judge at Van Buren, Arkansas.

letter. Such men never die. Their example and their influence live on in ever widening circles, passed on by one generation to the next, for all ages that are to come.

North Carolina is proud of the honors and the fame that her son won for himself in Arkansas. Two States deplore his loss. But he has gone to his reward like a ripe sheaf in full maturity. He lived beyond the Psalmist's alloted span of life. Life's duty nobly done, his life work crowned he laid aside the cares and troubles which infest this pitiful life of ours. The star of his life went not down behind the darkened west but it set like the morning star which melts in the brightness of the coming day.

I am glad that you and your son will prepare a Memorial Volume. I should be glad of a copy not only for myself, but one to place in our State Library that our young men may have ever accessible the life record of one of North Carolina's noble sons whose fame will ever be dear to her....

TO CLARK FROM FRANK E. EMERY

Jan. 26, 1895
Raleigh, N. C.

Since you have taken so much interest in the development of the farming interests and have written several letters to leading papers in the state on these topics, I wish first to express my own thanks for those articles and the encouragement which they have given to farmers not alone but others who have those interests at heart.

To your interest in the pea thresher and the cheapening of processes we owe a trial soon to come off at Goldsboro, N. C. one of the successful machines.

A trial is set for Feb. 4th at Mr. T. B. Parker's Goldsboro, N. C. of The "Success" Pea Thresher manufactured at Dalton, Ga. by J. H. Gardner. We hope to get both the machine and the man to the Farmer's Institute at the A. & M. college about Feb. 14th or 15th, date not yet absolutely fixed.

May we count on you about a ten minute speech on any agricultural topic you may select at some one of the three sessions? A varied and interesting program is expected....

TO CLARK FROM ENOCH W. SIKES *

John Hopkins University
Baltimore, Md.
February 1, 1895

In the Economic Conference of the University, the *Status of Southern Industries* is to be discussed in a few weeks. *Cotton and its Manufacture* is the feature assigned me. I wish to discuss it especially from the standpoint of a border state of the cotton belt.

An article written by yourself sometime ago contained figures and conclusions that I think will be serviceable to me and instructive to the conference.

Will you kindly give me the figures or reference, on any source from which helpful information may be secured? I take this liberty from your very kind offers of assistance made me when I saw you at Wake Forest.

TO CLARK FROM S. F. TELFAIR †

Raleigh, N.C.
March 22, 1895

I am instructed by the Governor to state that you have his permission to continue Major Daves ‡ at the work and also engage Dr. S. B. Weeks to do the indexing, but would be glad if you would get the consent of another member of the Library Board.

TO CLARK FROM ROBERT W. WINSTON

Durham, N. C.
April 9th, 1895

Please permit me to thank you for your kind favor of the 5th instant. Our Court has been continuously in session ever since I heard from you, both night and day, and I have been unable to see the parties and make the changes you suggested. I trust that the matter is now in good shape. It seems to have met public expectation in all particulars, and I think the State ought to be heartily congratulated in having upon the Bench one who is so alive to the best interests of the country and so thoroughly competent to discharge the duties of his high office.

* Sikes obtained his Ph.D. degree at Johns Hopkins. He was Professor at Wake Forest and later President of Clemson College.

† Private Secretary to Governor Elias Carr.

‡ Graham Daves, author of a large number of articles about the Civil War.

TO CLARK FROM CHARLES A. SUMNER *

San Francisco, Dec. 12, 1895

In response to your request, I have the honor to send you at once several printer copies of the Bill † I introduced and pressed, & which I still think the best offered up to date (others offering substantially the same measure)....

CLARK TO MARION BUTLER

Raleigh, Dec. 18, 1895

I enclose you copy of Mr. Sumner's bill, which is an excellent one. I do not put it into "Type-writer" as you may wish to make changes. I also enclose you Mr. Sumner's letter. I hope you will have success in this matter. It will place the masses under lasting obligations to you.

TO CLARK FROM W. P. WILLIAMSON ‡

Mobile, Alabama
February 6th, 1896

Some friend has sent me a copy of the New Berne Journal containing your letter on the silver question written from the City of Mexico.

While I stand with my party for the principle of a protective tariff and for sound money (gold standard), I must confess that the condition of affairs you found in Mexico surprised me.

Your letter will be sneered by the creditor class as an argument *ad captandum vulgus,* but to the debtor class it will appeal with the irresistible force of a mountain torrent....

TO CLARK FROM B. O. FLOWER §

Boston, Mass.
February 17, 1896

... I think that two comparatively brief articles in the May and June numbers will be preferable to a long and yet condensed paper in the May number, especially as the nation is becoming

* San Francisco lawyer and congressman-at-large from California, 1883-1885; author of *A Governmental Postal Telegraph* and many other books. Sumner was the "earliest political advocate of a government telegraph."

† The bill provided for the creation of a "government telegraph."

‡ Official of Mobile and Ohio Railroad Company.

§ Benjamin O. Flower, editor of *The Arena: A Twentieth Century Review of Opinion.*

tremendously aroused at the present time on the monetary question. The arrogance of plutocracy and the subserviency to the dictates of the Bank of England are becoming more and more manifest all the time. . . .

Your papers are admirable, being well written, thoughtful, and delightful in every respect.

I send you today an advance copy of the March Arena, containing pictures which I think will please you. Later I shall send you several copies.

I do not know of any person whom I could get to draw the map you suggest; that is, one that would be satisfactory and accurate, but will try and give the subject further attention when I have time. You must remember, however, my dear friend, that with the treasurership of our Company, the strain of the constant and unremitting opposition of plutocracy, which is becoming more and more alarmed at the strength of the Arena, my editorial duties, and my very large correspondence, . . . I have not been able to do much additional work that I wished to accomplish.

TO CLARK FROM THOMAS J. JARVIS

Greenville, N. C.
Feb. 20, 1896

I am sorely disappointed in not being in Raleigh this week. I am interested in the case of Hooker vs. Latham and others and I fully intended to go there to argue that case and while there I have to talk with you about many things. . . .

I appreciate your position on the bench preventing your taking an active part in politics yet it cannot prohibit your taking an interest in the welfare of your state and does not make it improper for you to discuss with a friend the best way of securing that welfare. Thus understanding your position I desired to have a long confidential talk with you about North Carolina politics and the best way to save the state from the curse of Republican rule. I am glad to see you are so emphatic and strong on the silver question. It is right. The single gold standard will make in this country, as in Europe, an aristocracy of wealth. The equal use of both gold and silver will best promote the interest of the *people* and should, in my humble judgment, be the fixed policy of this country. Some way should be devised to bring the silver men together, but I fear nothing but two or three good thrashings will do it. . . .

TO CLARK FROM B. O. FLOWER

Boston, Mass.
March 9, 1896.

I hope you will write to The World, as I suggested in my letter a few days since. The World published my letter on Saturday, excepting the part which referred to your visit to Mexico and the prosperity of that country; and all of my criticism in regard to the query they put to Senator Tillman *—"Does Senator Tillman imagine that the farmers are more prosperous in the silver countries, Mexico, Germany, France, etc., than they are in the United States?" they cut entirely out of the letter, but published all the rest. Now, I think if you were to write them a letter they would publish it, as I understand that the attack made by their correspondent, Creeland, on Senator Tillman after the delivery of his speech created such angry comment in the South, that The World sent for Senator Tillman to come up and study Wall Street and present his views, untrammelled, in The World. This, of course, is not for publication, but it shows that The World is aware of the sentiments of the South, and it does not want to tread too heavily upon an enormous portion of its clientele.

TO CLARK FROM MARION BUTLER †

Washington, D.C.
April 14, 1896

Your esteemed favor of Feb. 11th received. Allow me to thank you for your very kind words. I will try to have the speech published as widely as possible. Please ask the Progressive Farmer to publish it. After they have published it, I will publish it in the Caucasian.‡ I will send a copy of the speech and the bill to the parties you name.

Answering a question in one of your former letters I will say that I feel sure that the telegraph monopoly has offered franks to every member of the Senate and the House, and I fear that most of the Congressmen have accepted them. I had not been in my seat as Senator more than a day before a telegraph frank was offered me. It is needless to say that I did not accept it. I will not be able to

* Benjamin Ryan ("Pitchfork Ben") Tillman, United States Senator from South Carolina, 1895-1919.

† United States Senator from North Carolina, December 2, 1895-March 4, 1901; native of Sampson County and a Populist.

‡ Butler's paper, published in Clinton.

do much with the bill in Congress this session, but I intend to press it from the beginning of next session until I get a report and then I will make it lively for the monopoly on the floor of the Senate.

I had your articles and Prof. Parton's articles printed as a Senate Document. I send you one.

TO CLARK FROM J. W. GRAINGER *

Kinston, N. C.
April 21, 1896

...Yesterday morning before your letter came, I had written and mailed to Ed Chambers Smith a long letter in regard to the situation, etc. In that letter, I wrote him that you could poll ten thousand votes more for Governor than any man in North Carolina. That is my honest candid opinion and I do not say so because you are my preference of any man in the State, but I say it because I fully believe every word of it. Your clearly defined position on the Silver question and the further fact of all the parties having voted for you, it is much easier for them to do so again, to say nothing of your other qualifications. Yes, I am fully of the opinion that we should make a fair, open, honest, proposition to the Populist and Conservatives—some satisfactory arrangements with them at an early day as possible. It is the height of folly for the Democratic party to hope to do anything else. It will take close united action upon the part of both to win. The Republicans are going to make a desperate united effort and I think will effect fusion in some counties. The local offices are going to be the trouble. If the Chairman of the Democratic Executive committee was in sympathy with us we might hold another meeting and get matters in shape, but I do not think he is with us.

...I am frank to say I am open to any plan for success that the good white people shall hold the State, and I shall give you my opinion freely after carefully considering all the surroundings. The question is: Will the laced-jacket Democrats vote for Maj. Guthrie? † I do not believe they will. If he is nominated for Gov. I rather believe the Gold Democrats will run a ticket and I fear they would poll a good many that would otherwise vote with us. These matters must and should be considered. I think the decidely better plan would be for you to run for Gov. and then let

* Prominent businessman and former member of the General Assembly.
† Populist candidate for Governor in 1896.

Maj. Guthrie be nominated for Lt. Gov. and then you would have the credit of saving the state and no man could head you off for anything your friends might see proper to name. As to the division of the other officers, I think the plan laid down in the News and Observer would be accepted. I know, holding the position you now occupy, would hamper you very greatly and just how it could be managed, I am not prepared to even suggest. But one thing I am sure of and that is you can poll more votes and my humble opinion is you are the only man in N. C. that can be elected Governor.

I think there would be a few extreme gold Democrats would not vote for you or any other Silver man, but I think they would be comparatively few. When a man does a thing once, it is much easier for him to do so again. I refer to Populist voting. I had a long talk with Dr. Cy. Thompson * and I rather believe he will fall in with Butler and his friends. If Chambers Smith could get a good number of Silver men, Democrats only and Silver Democrats including the Silver Executive Committee to have a conference in Raleigh, he would find a good number of our very best leaders and map out some formulated plans, it might be well. I am not sure but it might have a good effect in educating our party up to accepting and offering terms, etc.

... One thing you may be absolutely sure of; anything I can do for you I am with you until the end. I have not found a Democrat or Populist but what will vote for you and it looks to me if any satisfactory deal can be made with our Populist friends, you ought to be our standard bearer. However, I will agree to News and Observer plan, but I am candid to say I fear Maj. Guthrie's success. I do not think he could carry any Republicans to speak of and I fear it would be a Horace Greely waterloo. Lots of Democrats would not vote for him (Greely) notwithstanding Governor Vance whooped him up all he could. I may be mistaken. These are my private views to you.

CIRCULAR LETTER SIGNED BY B. R. LACY †

Raleigh, N. C.
May 10, 1896.

At the Chicago Convention the friends of silver will doubtless nominate a Western man for President and a Southern man for

* Cyrus Thompson, M.D., native of Onslow County; member of the North Carolina General Assembly, 1883-1885; Secretary of State, 1897-1901.

† Commissioner of Labor and Printing, 1899-1901; State Treasurer, 1901-1929.

Vice President. The Northeastern States will give us no electoral votes, and there is no need in wasting a nomination upon them.

The necessity of carrying North Carolina and the belief that Judge Walter Clark can solidify the silver vote in the State and hold its eleven electoral votes makes it strongly probable that with a strong backing from this State, fortified with a resolution of instruction from our State Convention, the honor of the Vice Presidency may come to North Carolina.

I would be glad to have your views as to the advisability of introducing such resolution and what support, in your judgment, it would receive from your section. To be effective in procuring this honor for North Carolina the resolution should be adopted as nearly unanimously as possible by our State Convention and be backed at Chicago by an earnest delegation in his favor. It is for the lack of these that North Carolina has had so little recognition in the past. The opportunity now offers to honor our State by the selection of one of its citizens for this high office if there is an earnest support given by our people.

J. W. B. NEAL TO B. R. LACY

Scotland Neck, N. C.
May 19th, 1896

. . . I am afraid that eastern money and Cleveland brains are going to capture that same Chicago Convention and I don't know if that would not be the best thing that could happen for our State, for then the silver people would surely get together and save North Carolina from the thieves & scalawags who are trying to get her by the throat.

I read the editorial in the News & Observer and endorse every word contained in it, & would be very very glad to see Judge Clark nominated for Vice-Prest & will do my utmost to further his interest. Walter Clark knows Halifax Co. as well as I do, and he also knows that one has to work in many ways to accomplish his end. I am unable to say at this writing what can be done, but of this you may rest assured that I shall do my level best for his interest, & if I fail to carry my point it will not be because I have not tried. One Col. Carr will also do his level best to help the Judge to an endorsement, if for no other reason than that he wishes to get him out of his Gubernatorial road. . . .

TO CLARK FROM J. HARVEY HENDERSON

Charlotte, N. C.
May 19, 1896

I have not had the pleasure of being personally acquainted with you, although have long known of you as a soldier, statesman, and jurist, and am pleased to see you hold on to the old school democracy of our fathers and such as our glorious old Zeb Vance preached. Our State has been without a leader for sometime, and our staunch old democrats both in the city and county have their eyes on you as the man to lead them to victory again, and to establish our state once more on a foundation of true democracy. I will admit we have a few gold-bugs in the city, but 9/10 of the people of Mecklenburg are for the restoration of Silver, and it is my honest opinion that North Carolina can be carried by a good majority by you as their leader for Governor.

TO CLARK FROM A. W. GRAHAM

Washington, N. C.
May 25, 1896

Just before leaving home, I receive a letter from Mr. B. R. Lacy informing me that an effort would be made to have you nominated for Vice-President at Chicago, and asking my assistance and cooperation in the movement.

Of course, I will gladly do anything that will further your interest, or that you desire, after careful consideration.

I do not believe the time will come until after you and I are gone, that a Southern man can be elected to a place when an accident could place him at the head of the government. The feeling in the large cities of the North has very much softened against us, on account of their trade relations and associations with us. But in the rural districts and small towns, the bitterness toward the South, though latent, is as intense as ever and only needs such a thing as the nomination of a Southern man to bring it out.

Would the use of your name for this position tend to injure your chances for the Senate? . . .

A. W. GRAHAM TO B. R. LACY

Washington, N. C.
May 25, 1896

...I wish I could have a short personal interview with you so as to express fully my views upon the proposition contained in your letter. You know my relations to Judge Clark and my fondness for him and that I am willing to do anything to further his interests. But I cannot believe it possible to elect any Southern man to a position where he might have an opportunity to become the president of this country. We hear a great deal about "bridging over the bloody chasm", "burying the past", "the dead issue of the war", etc. That feeling does prevail to a great extent in the great trade centers of the North where the people come in direct contact with Southern men. But in the rural districts and the small towns and villages the feeling towards the South is as intensely hostile as in the days of 1861 and it needs but the nomination of a Southern man, with the possibility of his becoming chief executive to arouse all of that latent feeling. The Course of the G. A. R. and the present congress on the subject of pensions is but a slight exhibition of the slumbering hate. Not until you and I are dead, and all others who had only personal knowledge of the war, though we were too young to participate, do I believe it will be possible to elect a Southern man to the presidency of this Country.

I have an idea that there is a position of great honor and usefulness that we can secure for Judge Clark and I would be glad to confer with you about it when we meet.

But if Judge Clark desired us to proceed with this matter you can rely upon me to aid you in any way in my power.

W. W. KITCHIN * TO B. R. LACY

Roxboro, N. C.
May 26, 1896

Yours of yesterday relative to the candidacy of Judge Walter Clark for Vice-President received. No one has a higher opinion of him than myself or will be gladder to see him obtain any honor he desires.

Every effort must be put forth for silver for the crisis in the

* William Walton Kitchin of Person County, Democratic Representative in Congress, March 15, 1897-March 3, 1909; Governor, 1909-1913.

financial battle is at hand. Nothing will give the silver sentiment in this section a greater impetus than his nomination. I think this section will favor the resolution though I can tell nothing of the advisability of introducing it, not knowing how other sections will receive it.

Personally, I would hate to see him off the bench.

GEORGE GRAHAM VEST * TO JOSEPHUS DANIELS

Washington, D. C.
June 1, 1896

. . . I have heard Judge Clark spoken of as a gentleman of the highest character and of great ability. His claims to the nomination for Vice-President at Chicago will certainly receive from me earnest and respectful consideration.

In this connection, by way of suggestion and not of bargain, I would be glad if the delegates from North Carolina to the Chicago Convention would help us to nominate Richard P. Bland † for President. It is not necessary for me to write anything in regard to his claims upon our party. He has for twenty years been the foremost figure in the struggle for bimetallism, and if any man living can be safely trusted upon that question, he is the man. His calm, level-headed intellect, and unquestioned integrity and courage, will give us a good President, and one from the people.

TO CLARK FROM R. A. DOUGHTON ‡

Sparta, N. C.
June 6, 1896

I regret that we did not have time to discuss the political situation more fully at Chapel Hill. On my return home, I was informed that Mr. Carr's § friends are telling the people that if *he* is nominated, the Populists will nominate no one and will give *him* their support. This is being freely circulated. It seems to me that in this crisis in the history of our party, great care should be exercised and no one should act selfishly. While some counties

* United States Senator from Missouri, 1879-1903.

† Representative in Congress from Missouri, March 4, 1873-March 3, 1895, and March 4, 1897-June 15, 1899; co-author of Bland-Allison Silver Purchase Act of 1878.

‡ Rufus A. Doughton of Alleghany County; lawyer; member of General Assembly for many terms; Lieutenant Governor of North Carolina, 1893-1897.

§ Julian S. Carr, Durham industrialist.

MARION BUTLER

United States Senator from North Carolina.

have instructed for me it has been wholly without any effort on my part. I am in no sense a candidate. It will be more congenial to me to push my law practice and remain away from actual participation in politics. But I feel a great interest in this contest and would be glad to see the defeat of Russell. A great many of us think that you are the strongest man in the party at this time. I am convinced that you are several thousand votes stronger than Mr. Carr. Let me hear from you fully and give me your opinion of the situation. I assure you that you can write me in the fullest confidence.

TO CLARK FROM CHARLES M. STEDMAN *

Atlanta, Ga.
June 11th, 1896

I send you a short note, from my new home, to say that I am greatly gratified to see from the columns of the Fayetteville Observer, edited by my special life long friend Capt. E. J. Hale, that your name will probably be presented by the N. C. delegation to Chicago, for the nomination for the Vice-Presidency—I am rejoiced to feel and know that the great rebellion of the *people* against the tyranny and insolence of gold is bringing to the front men like yourself who has had the prescience to know the right and the firmness to defend it, even in the face of misrepresentation and injustice. I may possibly be of some service with influential people here in forwarding the wishes of the democrats of my native state, to which my heart ever turns with remembrance and love.

TO CLARK FROM DAVID SCHENCK

Greensboro, N. C.
June 13, 1896

Nothing has so distressed me as your refusal to run for Governor. This beats us and delivers us to the negro. We want no candidate going around again with a "wet nurse" nor a poetical character whose only hope is mushroom charities and pretended wealth. Russell † will run such men off the stump. I am sincerely pained....

* Greensboro attorney; Democratic Representative in Congress, April 4, 1911-Sept. 23, 1930.

† Daniel L. Russell of Brunswick County, Republican Governor, 1897-1901.

TO CLARK FROM W. G. LEWIS

Statesville, N. C.
June 30, 1896

Many of us, your friends in this section of N. C. regretted that you could not see your way to accept the nomination for Gov. which the people had practically tendered to you. We, however, indulge the hope that at Chicago you will be put on the ticket with a western man and that by consultation then, the silver forces can be united in which event we can carry the country.

I talked with Mr. Klutz * and Mr. Turner † from this District and I feel that every thing will be done by them to secure your nomination for the V. P. and I feel that you will secure it.

The getting together of the silver men is all we need to make success certain and I hope when they all come together that such action of one party will be taken so as to secure the endorsement of the two conventions that will meet at St. Louis....

TO CLARK FROM IREDELL MEARES ‡

Wilmington, N. C.
July 1, 1896

...In a discussion as to your views on the subject of the telephone and railroad recently, I said that you were in favor of the control by the Government of the telephone and telegraph, but not of the railroads. A friend insisted that he had read a published article by you in which you advocated both. Is he not mistaken? My recollection of your several articles, all of which I think I have read, is as stated above. I think you have likewise stated your position to be this in several personal conversations....

I regret that you should not have seen your way clear to have accepted the nomination for Governor. I believe that it would have attracted to us many votes that we may not now get. However, I feel that we have a most creditable ticket and will enter into the canvass with a feeling that all will be right.

One of the great difficulties which seem to me now to confront any advocate of reform measure, who is actuated by high motives and is conservative, that the mouthing demagogue, like some of

* Probably Theodore F. Klutzz of Rowan County, Democratic Representative in Congress, Dec. 4, 1899-March 3, 1905.

† W. D. Turner of Statesville, member of the General Assembly, 1887-1891; Lieutenant Governor, 1901-1905.

‡ Prominent lawyer and Progressive candidate for governor in 1912.

those we have in this State, pushes himself in the advance guard, and, forgetting that he is advocating a principle, gives utterance to socialistic sentiments, which affords the opposition occasion to cry down a good measure, like that which you are advocating as to the telegraph and telephone, simply because it is advocated by extreme Populists who care less about the principle than their elevation to office.

TO CLARK FROM C. SELDON SMART *

Boston
July 1, 1896.

. . . Either our Editor, Mr. B. O. Flower, or myself, will go to Chicago, leaving tomorrow or tonight. Mr. Flower's health is not good and if he is not able to go and it happens that I cannot, we will send a representative. However, I expect either Mr. Flower or I will go. Our object will be to do all we can to unify the Silver vote, and I beg to assure you, as far as I am personally concerned, and I think I can speak the same for The Arena, the ticket that has been named with you on it will be entirely satisfactory to us. I had thought of you as an altogether good nominee for the *first* position on the ticket but indications now strongly point to Teller † and with Teller and Clark and a unified Silver People's Party vote, this ticket will win in my opinion.

TO CLARK FROM G. W. HINSHAW ‡

Winston, N. C.
June 22, 1896

Since I saw you, I have been in several counties,—Yadkin, Surry, Guilford, and Randolph—and found that you can carry more votes than any man in the state. Owing to the recent political changes, I am clearly of the opinion that the strongest state ticket we can possibly make is you for Governor and Hon. R. A. Doughton for Lieut. Gov., National ticket Boies § for President and Teller || for Vice-President. The Populists and Republicans voted

* Business manager of Arena Publishing Company.
† Henry Moore Teller of Colorado; United States Senator, December 4, 1876-April 17, 1882; Secretary of the Interior in President Arthur's cabinet, April 6, 1882-March 4, 1885; United States Senator, March 4, 1885-March 3, 1909.
‡ Prominent wholesale merchant.
§ Horace Boies, Democratic governor of Iowa, 1890-1894.
|| United States Senator from Colorado.

for you the last election and the Populist, so far as I can learn, are for you now. They are in this section, The man who redeems the state is entitled to be elected Senator and if we can elect you Governor, we can make you Senator. I expect to be in Raleigh Wednesday morning. Bryan would like very much to have the vote of this state. I know him very well personally.

W. O. TEMPLE TO JAMES M. WOODS

Rapid City, South Dakota.
July 3rd, 1896.

Since your departure for Chicago, I have learned that the North Carolina delegation will place Judge Walter Clark of that State in nomination at Chicago for the vice-presidency. I write to ask that you will secure for Judge Clark the unanimous support of our delegation, if possible, or as much of it as you can. I would esteem as a great personal favor to me anything you may do in this direction. Judge Clark needs no introduction, and no endorsement from me. His reputation is a national one. Judge Clark is a man of the finest mold, and alike in private and public life he has always enjoyed the implicit confidence of the people in his State. He is not only a profound lawyer, a ripe scholar, but he is also a deep student of political events, and I doubt if the name of any man will be presented to the Chicago convention who is his superior in capacity for statesmanship and grasp of the great political and economic questions of the day.

TO CLARK FROM R. A. DOUGHTON

Sparta, N.C.
July 3, 1896

Allow me to thank you for yours of the 29th ult. and also your article on the Telegraph and Telephone.* I have read the article with great pleasure.

You were kind enough to refer to my candidacy for Congress in this District.

I am greatly obliged to my friends throughout the District for the interest taken in my behalf. But I am a practical man and want to be *elected* when I become a candidate. You are situated where you can gather the political sentiment of the State, and I

* This article is reprinted below, page 432.

want you to give me your opinion on the outlook. Will the Republicans and Populists get together on a State ticket?

It is my opinion that we ought to get local fusion with the Populists in the Counties where it can be done on honorable terms.

You have no friend in N. C. who would rejoice more than myself if you should be nominated for Vice-President at Chicago.

G. S. FERGUSON * TO THE NORTH CAROLINA DELEGATION TO THE DEMOCRATIC CONVENTION

Waynesville, N. C.
July 4th, 1896

I would not venture at this distance to suggest a plan of campaign for you. I have every confidence in your tact as well as earnest work in the accomplishment of the mission on which you are sent. I know you will do all in human power to secure the financial plank of the platform to be such as meets the wants of your constituency.

You will permit me to urge that you do all in your power for the honor of our State deserving as She is, of fame in peace, as she merited it in war.

In asking for the second place on the National ticket, She asks for no more than she deserves from her history and status on the present issues of the day. In the selection of Walter Clark as her favorite son, she named one who if his career had ended with 1865, the State might well have been proud of him.

He has been a patriotic student of history, an accurate reader of current events, and master of the philosophy of American politics, a conservative, determined and out spoken as well as able advocate of Silver. The Honor of the State would be safe in his hands, as it is now rightly committed to your care.

The people at home will read your influence by the vote he polls, and each will be rewarded by the work he does. For the financial policy of the party the whole country looks alike to all the Silver delegates and in my opinion North Carolina looks to each of her delegates to do his utmost for the man she has mentioned as her favorite, and will no more pardon carelessness or inactivity in his interest than in the securement of the principles held sacred and dear by her people.

* Garland S. Ferguson of Haywood County, Superior Court Judge.

TO CLARK FROM S. B. ALEXANDER *

Charlotte, N. C.
July 4th, 1896

I have read Senate Document No. 205 † with much interest. As it is right that the Government should use the Telegraph and Telephone in the mail service, it ought to be good policy to make it an issue in this campaign, and we ought to gain considerable advantage from it. The Populists will fight us for promising a new election law and will, in my opinion, fuse with the Republicans on state issues on account of said election law and this might aid in capturing many in spite of there leaders. The abuse that many Democratic papers and persons have heaped on the Populist have got them so wrought up that even if the St. Louis Populist convention endorsed the Chicago nominee, I think they will put out a state ticket and have county, and in some districts, Congressional fusion, to preserve their election law, six per-cent, and county government, Unless the Democratic state nominees will give it a cordial we may not be able to make as much out of it as we should. I hope you may receive support enough to bring it before the people in this campaign.

CLARK TO JOSEPHUS DANIELS

Raleigh, N. C.
July 7, 1896

Congratulation on your election to represent our State on the National Committee. It is an honor which your abilities and services richly merited and it is a position in which you can be of great service to us in N. C.

By the time, this reaches you I presume the V. P. matter will be over. However it terminates, will you and Mr. Lacy kindly say to the N. C. delegation that you are commissioned by me to express to them, singly and collectively, my deep appreciation for their support and earnest effort.

I think Bryan is the choice of this State for Pres. and I hope when this reaches you he will have been selected. Could you get Dr. Mott ‡ to render us any assistance or did his crowd and their wishes have any weight.?

* Sydenham B. Alexander, Democratic Representative in Congress, Dec. 7, 1891-March 3, 1895.

† Reprint of Clark's *Arena* article on Telegraph and Telephone.

‡ J. J. Mott of Statesville, leader in Republican party.

TO CLARK FROM CHARLES F. WARREN *

Washington, N. C.
July 16, 1896

I am satisfied that you or some other Southern man could have been nominated for Vice President but for the opposition of Southern men. Mr. Bryan stated in the conference, when Mr. Blackburn and others were opposing the nomination of a Southern man,† that he did not share any such feelings. I am satisfied that the Republicans could have made no capital out of the nomination of a Southern man. There is not another President for the Republicans in the bloody shirts. The west and the South are the sections making this fight, and a Southern man ought to have gone on the ticket. Just as long as Southern men do not assert the claims of their section, just so long will Northern and Western party friends ignore us. It is now 31 years since Appomattox. When Chicago erects a monument to Confederate dead it ought to reach the end of the animosities growing out of the war. I think the nomination of Mr. Sewall ‡ was unfortunate for many reasons. I found at Chicago a number of delegates who had read your article on Mexico, and were much impressed by them. I would suggest, with the consent of the publishers of the Arena that they be published as a campaign document. This could be arranged through Joe Daniels, who is upon the National Committee. It would help the cause, and besides I think it would help you and my only regret is that we could not secure your nomination at Chicago.

TO CLARK FROM CHARLES W. TILLETT

Charlotte, N. C.
November 16th, 1896.

I made a request of the Supreme Court in yesterday's issue of the Charlotte Observer to the effect that they make a rule requiring the briefs of lawyers to be bound, indexed and placed in the Supreme Court library. I know that you are ever ready to further any plan that will be of practical help in administering justice, and I write this personal letter to you, and ask that you take the matter in hand, and have the rule passed. So far as having the

* Attorney and at one time State Senator from Beaufort County.
† Clark received 50 votes for the vice-presidential nomination.
‡ Arthur Sewall of Maine was nominated for vice-president on the fifth ballot.

books of uniform size is concerned, it will be very easy for you to say in the rule that the books shall be of the size of our Supreme Court reports, and any printer can have access to one of the volumes of our reports, when he comes to print the brief.

It is now about time for you to give us another article on the "Progress of the Law", as I have not forgotten the promise you made in your former communication, and I shall be very glad to receive another one, as soon you find time to write it.

TO CLARK FROM CHARLES S. DAVIS *

Asheville, North Carolina
November 26, 1896

Smith D. Atkins of Freeport, Illinois, a son-in-law of Gov. D. S. Swain informs me that Hon. Richard H. Battle and you were the executors of Mrs. Swain's will and that to you gentlemen was left the possession and final disposition of all Gov. Swain's historical collections and manuscripts. Will you kindly inform me whether, among Gov. Swain's papers, you found anything pertaining to the Society of the Cincinnati. If so, and you will kindly loan me any such papers, for a definite period not exceeding one month, I will, with your possession, be glad to make copies of them. I can assure you they will be well cared for and promptly returned to you without any expense to you.

TO CLARK FROM P. H. WINSTON

Spokane, Washington
Dec. 11th, 1896

I am greatly obliged for your letter.

My father was very fond of you and I have always entertained for you the highest regard, admiration and respect.

I sincerely trust you will be elected U. S. Senator. I read all you write for the *Arena* to my family. My heart is with the old places and old people. At night when alone I live for hours in the past, at Bertie, at Chapel Hill, at the refugee home in Franklin County. During these hours you are often present. When you came to the University you were the handsomest and brightest young gentleman I ever saw—I hope yet to see you & all the the North Carolina friends who are so near and dear to me. George's removal to Texas was a great blow to me. I cannot bear to think of returning to N. C. and not see him.

* Secretary of the North Carolina Society of the Cincinnati.

I want to see you and talk over the past; the present; the future. Did you get the copy of the book I sent you of which I am the author.

TO CLARK FROM MARION BUTLER

Washington, D.C.
Dec 26-96

Yours inclosing amendments to R.R. Com. law with clippings recvd—I had it but to fight for 2½ & 2 cents for 1st and 2nd class fares respectively, but I am very much impressed with your arguments for making fight now for 2 & 1½ rates. I think all the other provisions in the bill you send good & should be passed—What do you think of the inclosed bill? The greatest burden [on] our people are the interstate rates which our State Commissioners can not reach—The present high rates on truck to the Northern markets are especially burdensome to the people in the extreme part of the State. I don't know of any better way moving in this matter than to give to the State Commissioners the power to prosecute such cases before the elected State Commission. I know how slow & almost useless & powerless this latter body is, but still something may be done—Give me your opinion as to the provisions of the bill inclosed—I will make it a part of the bill which you send—

TO CLARK FROM CHARLES M. STEDMAN

Atlanta, Ga.
Dec. 28th, 1896

I send you this note to say that you must not blame me for my long delay in forwarding to you the history of of 44 N. C. Regiment. I could have sent you my personal reminiscence in a very few days after receiving your request to write the history of the Regiment. I have found it most difficult to obtain necessary information after strenuous efforts. I shall be able to send you what I have written within sixty days.

I often, in fact all the time almost, am thinking of the Dear Old State where I was born, reared and spent the best days of my life. Am I very frequently thinking of you, Judge, and regret the Democratic party in N. C. do not follow the pathway to which you pointed them. I trust the coming years may bring to you increased honors and that you may long live to be of service to a people whom I shall ever love.

TO CLARK FROM MARION BUTLER

Washington, D. C.
Dec 31 1896

Yours of the 28th rec'd—I thought of the very provisions which you added when drawing the bill, but I left it discretionary with the Commissioners to prosecute these cases before the Interstate Com. for two reasons, 1st I feared the expence that the Commission might incur on behalf of the State if every complaint against Inter State rates had to be prosecuted without discretion, 2nd If the commissioners desire to do their duty by the people they will prosecute every meritorious case, and if they act against the people, the quicker that fact is exposed the better—If the State Commission is given the power & left with discretion, the truckers & other Instate shippers will soon see who is to blame—

The item of expence to the State is however the important consideration, if all complaints are to be prosecuted &ct—Please consider this & give me your opinion—If these objections are not serious, then I prefer the law to be as you indicate—Your suggestion about having the Legislature to pass a resolution favoring a Postal Telegraph is good & I will try to manage it—Do you not think the Legislature should pass an act to prevent the removal of certain cases to the Federal Courts? I want to talk to you about this & also the Lease of the N.C.R.R. when I go to Raleigh—

VI

Dissenter and Reformer

1897–1901

UNTIL 1896 WHEN HE WAS TENDERED the nomination for governor and endorsed for vice-president of the United States, Clark's career, in both law and politics, was an uninterrupted honeymoon of success. But now this adulation ceased, and for the next six years he became the central figure in a series of conflicts that shook the state from center to circumference.

The first conflict resulted from his denunciation of the recently organized American Tobacco Company and its practices; the second, from his exposure of the evils resulting from the consolidation of the Southern Railway Company, the Seaboard Air Line, and the Atlantic Coast Line into three powerful systems which he alleged were violating the law and dominating state and local politics. By 1896 Clark had come to believe that the control of the national government had passed from the people to the railroads, trusts, and banks, and he was convinced that the masses were being oppressed by a vicious combination of evil forces that were operating under cover and through various aliases. He insisted that the state and nation were dominated by "railroad judges, congressmen, and legislators," and that the railroads, "like Pharaoh, were not willing to reduce the people's burden." He said the real issue was MEN OR MONEY.

In numerous dissenting opinions, in a score of public addresses and articles, and in letters to newspapers and to private individuals, Clark condemned the ruthless practices of railroads, especially the Southern, which he considered the chief political agency of the "money power" in North Carolina. He maintained that the railroads were guilty of flagrant violations of the law, that they were illegally extorting two million dollars from the people of the state each year by excessive passenger rates, and that an "army of 100,000 free pass toters" was being created annually—a "cheap mode of controlling politicians." He said that "monopolies were in the saddle" in North Carolina and that A. B. Andrews' manipulation of the Democratic party, plus Matt W. Ransom's re-election to the United States Senate, had aided the spread of Populism in the state. He felt that the North Carolina Railroad Commission was not doing its legal duty and urged that this body be made elective. He thought the legislature was derelict in its duties and that it was suffering from "lobbyitis and legislative leprosy." He insisted that the Federal courts were "packed with railroad appointees," and he saw no way to prevent control by the "money power" until the federal judiciary was made elective. He was afraid that his party was becoming a "compromise party" under the influence of wealthy interests. Clark knew that the "fight between railroads and the people as to the mastery is no child's play but real war," and he was ready and eager to take up the gage of battle.

Between 1897 and 1902, Clark waged incessant warfare for many governmental and social reforms. He published more than twenty magazine articles, advocating among other things, postal savings banks, one-cent letter postage, election of postmasters, popular election of senators, and a revision of the Constitution of the United States. He was one of the earliest and most zealous proponents of an income tax and, in 1898, said that "aggregate wealth of the country proposes to neither fight nor pay." He was eager to fight and was probably the only Supreme Court judge to offer his services in the Spanish-American war. His application was rejected and he continued to "wage war" on the home front for numerous reforms which he felt had to come. Bryan wrote him that "reforms come slowly and usually one at a time." Clark tended to agree with this idea, but he continued to fight for many governmental and social changes.

Clark's greatest year of publication was 1897. In that year he published: "The Right of the Public to Regulate the Charges of Common Carriers and of all Others Discharging Public, or Quasi-Public Duties," "Maladministration of the Post-Office Department," "The Rights of the Public over Quasi-Public Services," "The Progress of the Law," "The Election of United States Senators by the People," "Twelve Reasons Why the Telephone Should be Restored to the Post Office," "Open Letter to the Railroad Commission of North Carolina," "Jamestown Settled 81 Years Before John Smith," "The Political Teachings of the Gospel," "The Physical Napoleon," "The Right to Regulate Railroad Fares and Freight Rates," "Revision of the Constitution of the United States—Election of Judges, Senators and Postmasters by the People," and one of his finest articles, "Where Shall the Governing Power Reside?"

CLARK TO MARION BUTLER

Raleigh, N.C.
30 Jany 1897

At request of Hon. C. A. Sumner,* M.C. from California I have this day sent him a letter of introduction to you. I want you to know him. He is the earliest practical advocate of a Govt Telegraph & the most persistent and earnest.

I congratulate you upon the passage through the State Senate yesterday of your brother's† Resolutions, including ownership of Pacific R.Rs, Telegraph & Postal Savings Banks. I am glad the Democrats all voted for it. I trust you will manage to have it pushed through our lower House. If these Resolutions can be placed on our Statute book it will work a signal advance from corporation rule. Would it not be well for you to mail some copies of Sen. Doc. 205 to some members of the House of Representatives here?

The corporations have had a tremendous weight in N.C. politics & legislation. They conceived so low an opinion of this legislature after Pritchard's‡ election that they turned its control over to Andrews private secry as being beneath a "boss's" care, but the passage of your brother's resolution through the Senate & House's (inquiring into fancy R.R. salaries) through the House will scare the "bosses" back into the saddle.

CLARK TO MARION BUTLER

Raleigh, N.C.
11 Feb. 1897

. . . Both your brother and mine, have been disappointments—especially mine—in the vim & capacity to push the rate reduction and anti-Free Pass bills. My position on the court and the jealousy & criticism of a judge taking part in politics, prevents my getting round among the members. Unless *you* are here there is no one who has the ability & influence to save these bills to prohibit free passes or to reduce railroad, telegraph & telephone charges. Unless you come & prevent it, the monopolies are in the saddle.

As the validity of the act annulling the lease (if it should pass) might come before the court, I have not expressed and can not

* Charles Allen Sumner, Democratic Representative in Congress from California, March 4, 1883-March 3, 1885.

† George E. Butler, State Senator from Sampson County.

‡ Jeter C. Pritchard, Republican United States Senator from North Carolina, Jan. 24, 1895-March 4, 1903.

express, any opinion, or exert any influence as to it—as you will see at once.

Your brother & mine, by putting their heads together could do good work for themselves and the State—*if they only would.*

CLARK TO MARION BUTLER

Raleigh, N.C.
20 Feb. 1897

. . . The "Reduction of Rates" bill failed in Senate 24 to 23 and in House 55 to 54 (tho' it is now claimed the vote stood 55 to 55). The anti-Free Pass bill passed Senate 23 to 21 on 2nd reading but was then postponed till Feb 27. Both these measures would have passed both Houses but that J.W. Wilson & S. Otho Wilson * went before Committees & said it would be a reflection on them & to save that reflection the people of N.C. must pay several hundred thousand dollars more than they ought for next two years—

Your splendid work in getting R.R. Commission passed in 1891 has been more than nullified by Andrews' † getting J.W. Wilson made Chairman. He uses the position as vantage ground against removing the extortions the Commission was created to prevent. He has for 6 years run the Commission as a Bureau of Andrews' office.

We can never do any thing till—

1—We get through an anti-Free Pass bill. Cant you help now to get the pending one through.

2—Till we make the R.R. Commers *elective by the people.* It ought to be done by this legislature.

CLARK TO MARION BUTLER

Raleigh, N.C.
22 Feb. 1897

As you are already aware the bills to reduce R.R., telegraph & telephone rates failed in Senate & House each by *one* vote. The anti-Free Pass bill passed second reading in Senate & is postponed & made special order for next Saturday—27th. *With a little more help* the latter could be passed yet, and the "reduction of rates" bills could be re-introduced & passed, but we do not know where to look for help—

* Members of the North Carolina Railroad Commission.

† Alexander B. Andrews, Vice President and General Manager of Southern Railroad Company.

Has your Committee reported on your "Postal Telegraph" bill? I believe the best way to help on the measure is to have 50 centres of agitation & education—instead of one—by pushing bills in *every* State & Territory to restrict Telegraph rates within a State to 10 cents & annual rental of telephones to $12 and $18. The discussion will show the people (which they do not know) that these great monopolies are subject to their control. In this connection I write *specially* to call your attention to the fact that Gov. Pingree * is making a legislative fight for *2 cents R.R.* fares in Michigan and that if you (or some friend of yours in Congress who knows him well) will send him a copy of S.D. 205 and write him a letter asking him to *add* a clause for 10¢ telegrams & 12 Phones it may help on the cause here. as well as every where else.

CLARK TO A. W. GRAHAM

Raleigh, N.C.
10 March 1897

Gov. Russell has answered the Injunction by removing all the State Directors & Proxy. He had to do it to prevent their filing an answer giving away the case. The Charter empowers him to do this.

He wants to appoint a strong Board of Directors, irrespective of party. Remembering you wanted to be a Director years ago & believing your name & services in the Board will be of great value to the State at this juncture—a call you have never refused—he tenders you the appointment of Director. He will naturally expect you either to vote for his choice of Prest. & Secry or not vote at all. They are Dr Norment & Cam. Pearson, I think Judge Avery † will also be on the Board with you. Under the circumstances I hope you will accept.

CLARK TO MARION BUTLER

Raleigh, N.C.
12 Mar. 1897

The R.Rs with their Federal bench packed with R.R. appointees think they are in the saddle. The people in fact have the power through their right to fix rates.

* Hazen S. Pingree, Governor of Michigan, 1897-1901.

† Alphonso C. Avery of Burke County, Superior Court Judge, 1879-1888; Associate Justice of North Carolina Supreme Court, 1889-1897.

Otho Wilson *ought* to be on the people's side. Beddingfield * being about to return to the people is getting more patriotic. These two are a majority of R.R. Commission. Let them cut down "Southern's" rates (now yielding 20% nett profits) to say, 2%—and *all* passenger rates on Standard lines to 2 cents and 1½ cents. If this is promptly done, J.W. Wilson & Abbott † will not *dare* to entirely revoke & raise rates after April 1—and even if they do, the R.Rs & people will have learned the valuable object lesson as to *who* has the whip hand. Can't you write S. Otho. This fight between R.Rs & the people as to the mastery is no child's play but real war. I dont hesitate to call on you & leave it to your judgment.

CLARK TO A. W. GRAHAM

Raleigh, N.C.
15 Mar 1897

The Populists & Reps are now so wide apart that they will *never* act together again *unless* we let the Dem. party make the mistake out of deference to Carr,‡ Overman § &c—of being the "compromise party"—The secession from us to the Populists will then be terrific. To prevent that, any Democrats Russell shall put on the Board ought to accept. I am as far as you from wishing to reflect as Carr, Overman & Co—they were simply *overreached* by Andrews. But we can't afford to commit the party to Pierpont Morgan & Co because his overseer was sweet enough to delude our Gov. into a bad trade. Indeed but for Andrews' manipulation of our party & his repeated re-elections of Ransome we never would have had the Populist party.

I am glad you accepted for the above reason so that the fight against R.R. domination shall not seem to exclude democrats from being on the people's side.

There is but one danger in your accepting—Russell is bull headed. He might want to file an answer charging Carr & Co with fraud &c. If so, let *him* file that answer. If he should insist on Directors doing so, I presume you would quietly resign, without publicity. I didn't think it possible tho' he will do that. He will prefer the credit if charging fraud himself.—if it is done—in his

* E. C. Beddingfield, member of Railroad Commission; later a member of Corporation Commission.

† Member of the North Carolina Railroad Commission.

‡ Julian S. Carr, Durham industrialist.

§ Lee S. Overman of Salisbury, United States Senator, November 9, 1903-December 12, 1930.

own answer & besides as Avery is counsel he will not draw an answer for Board charging fraud on Carr, Alexander, Overman &c. I merely suggest possibilities.

We have been too tender footed on the R.R. matter, Andrews is simply another Swepson & has debauched more young men than you have any idea of. They can be kept straight if the leaders were only outspoken—

CLARK TO MARION BUTLER

Raleigh, N.C.
3 April 1897

I enclose you an article which you may not have seen as N.C. papers seem afraid to print it. I do not know whether the "Caucasian" * will copy it or not.

The people have *felt* for long that "conditions" are not right but it takes time & experience to locate the disease & ascertain the remedy. Of one thing I have become convinced—the people can *secure* no victory, if indeed they can win it until the U.S. Judiciary are made elective and for a term of years. With a life tenure and appointments made by the corporations, they can construe away Acts of Congress as fast as we can enact them—vide "Income Tax." The movement must be begun some time. It can not win at first but the agitation will be educational. If you are disposed to introduce the bill to amend the Constitution to make judges elective & will make a speech on if I will draw it and send it to you.

CLARK TO MARION BUTLER

Raleigh, N.C.
1 May 1897

You have small time to read other men's speeches but I send you to-day copy of my Richmond speech † that you may read *that part of it* upon the election of U.S. Judges & Senators by the people & the Transportation question.

I notice the P.M. Genl. has app[d] *6* delegates to "Universal Postal Union." I have studied that question for years & have taken much interest in it. I should be glad to be appd—as I suppose the number is optional & that the Govt. only pays personal expenses. I think I could be of some service. If it were an *office* I could not accept, and you would not wish to ask for it—but if it

* Butler's newspaper, published at Clinton.
† This speech is reprinted below, pp. 442ff.

is a mere honorary appointment with expenses I should be glad to get this if you have any friends through whom you could get it done.

I am preparing an article on Reduction of R.R. rates. I presume the Inter State Commission have a table of passenger fares all over the country. If printed, please have it sent me. If not printed, can you call on them for information & send to me. I would not trouble you but you see that I am writing in the public interest & without compensation of course.

CLARK TO MARION BUTLER

Raleigh, N.C.
10 June 1897

Some time since I wrote an article on "Mal-administration of the Post Office" which has been widely copied. It was largely based, as you must have seen, on data furnished by speeches of yourself & others in the Senate. As to one statement I have had doubts i.e. that the Govt. uses "*500* postal cars." It seems to me that the number must be much larger. You can turn to your speech of Feb last in the Congl. Record & you know the sources of your information. Will you please inform me if you are sure that *500* is the correct No.

I have noticed with pleasure your efforts for Postal Savings Banks. Will you have sent me a copy of the "Reports received by State Dept from U.S. Consuls as to telegraphs, telephones & Postal Savings Banks" in other countries, which were ordered printed upon your motion—also copy of "Annual Report of Librarian of Congress" & oblige.

CLARK TO THE RAILROAD COMMISSION OF NORTH CAROLINA

Raleigh *News and Observer,*
July 13, 1897

In compliance with your request, I respectfully submit some of the reasons which occur to me why you should accede to the public demand, already granted in some States, for a substantial reduction of passenger and freight rates. At no time in the last six years have numerous, able and skillful counsel been lacking to represent to you the opposition to any concession to the public wishes. I wish, therefore, that your invitation to present the people's side of the question had been extended to some one far abler than I to express the justice of that demand, and with power to persuade you to grant it.

The right of the public, either through a legislative act or by means of a commission, to REGULATE AND FIX THE RATES of all common carriers, and especially of railroads, has always been recognized as law. Repeated decisions of the United States Supreme Court have of late years re-affirmed this law, and so conclusively and clearly, as to be beyond chance of recall.

The somersault of a judge of that court, which reversed the precedents of 100 years, in order that an income tax of $60,000,000 might be transferred from the rich syndicates, corporations and millionaires, to the backs of the toiling producers sent a thrill of indignation through the country, whose last vibration has not yet been felt. But a decision which should attempt to change the immemorial law and put in the hands of the railroad corporations the unrestricted power to fix the tolls we should pay on the internal commerce of the country, would place the value of every man's land, of every man's cotton, or other produce, at the mercy of these corporations.

To turn over the fixing of the tariff upon our foreign commerce, absolutely and without disguise, to the syndicates and trusts who grow rich upon it is not a circumstance to the effect upon the public welfare, and the public mind, which would follow the turning over this tariff on our internal commerce (which is many hundred times greater than that which comes from foreign countries through our custom houses), to be fixed, at their will, by those who are to receive the profits of their own action. If the millers were to combine to fix the tolls of their mills, without regulation by the public, it would place the bread of the people at their mercy. But that combination is absolutely nothing to the power (if they possessed it) of corporations to levy at will their own rate of toll upon every pound of freight, and every passenger that is moved by steam in this land.

The very act of assembly to which you owe your existence expressly confers upon you the power to fix rates for passengers and freights, and for telegraph and telephone messages. Unless your Commission is a nullity you have the power, and you were CREATED TO EXERCISE IT. The public demand for a reduction of railroad charges must have been strong indeed, which in spite of the well-known influence of those corporations and their long experience in defeating legislation could force through the act which created your commission. It was not established to compliment three gentlemen with office, nor to add to our taxation and expense of some $12,000, annually, but the Commission was created because the public was overwhelmingly convinced far back—certainly prior to 1891—that the railroad charges were excessive, and oppressive, and that relief could not be had from the voluntary reduction of them by those receiving railroad incomes, but must be ordered by the people, in right of their sovereign power to fix the rates of common carriers.

The only restriction upon your power to fix rates ever suggested by any court, is that the rates should not be too low to afford a reasonable interest upon the actual value of the property. This valuation you have placed at $26,000,000, upon all the railroads in this State. The railroads have contended that even this is too high.

There being about 3,450 miles of railroad in this State, this is an average of about $7,800 per mile. If this sum in cash would replace, as is probable, the railroads of the State, then it is a sufficiently high valuation. You have said, after careful investigation, I presume, that it is the actual valuation of the railroads, including their franchise. Acts 1895, chapter 119, section 45.

The question then is what is A REASONABLE INTEREST upon the investment of $26,000,000. Upon so large an investment as that three per cent. is a good interest, for government bonds at that figure are at par. Or take the North Carolina value of money; our State four per cent. bonds are at par, and even Raleigh five per cent. bonds lately sold at $9 above par. Even in small loans to individuals bearing six per cent. not more than four per cent. net, after paying taxes, is received by those living in towns. The Supreme Court of the United States in the late case of Livingston vs. Sanford, 164 U.S., 578, say that rates high enough to earn four per cent. will not be disturbed by the courts, and in Dow vs. Beidelman, 125 U.S., 680, the same court says that rates high enough to earn 1½ per cent. are sufficient when the present holders have bought the railroad, or its stock, below par, as is the case with all the large railroad systems in this State.

You have fixed the railroad valuation at $26,000,000, but the bonds and stocks of the railroads in this State amount to $94,000,000. It is clear, therefore, that rates high enough to pay interest or dividends upon the latter sum are grossly in excess of what is just to the public. Freight and travel are thus being taxed to pay dividends and interest on nearly $70,000,000 of fictitious capital.

There are THREE DIFFERENT METHODS, each of which will demonstrate that the present rates are grossly excessive.

1. Take the three great railroad systems of the State, which embrace nearly four-fifths of the total valuation. Your report for 1896 shows as follows:

	Valuation	Net Earnings	Miles
Atlantic Coast Line	$6,852,000	$963,000	685
Southern R.R. System	8,104,000	1,345,000	1,004
Seaboard R.R. System	5,265,000	667,000	618
	$20,221,000	$2,975,000	2,307

That is to say, property invested of $20,000,000 (but costing present owners far less), is allowed rates high enough to earn nearly $3,000,000, net or fifteen per cent. interest annually out of the people of North Carolina. Your report says the property is worth $20,000,000, including franchise. Your report says the net earnings are nearly $3,000,000, and even in this we are at the mercy of the corporations. There has not yet been a cross examination or inspection of their books. We do not know whether in pro rating they have allowed the North Carolina portion of their roads as much as an impartial calculation might prove to be just. We do not know how much the net earnings would swell if only moderate salaries were allowed, and improper charges disallowed, and the Supreme Court of the United States say in Wellman vs. Railroad, 143 U.S., and they say it again in Reagan vs. Trust Co., 154 U.S., at page 412, that no rates will be held too low until the salaries are shown to be not excessive, or that improper charges have not been made, and that the rates fixed by the public authority cannot be supervised till these matters are shown up. In the absence of any examinations by your board of the original books, it is proper to say this in support of a suggestion that an auditing of the books might show that the net earnings upon calculation by impartial accountants are probably FAR MORE THAN FIFTEEN PER CENT.

The railroad returns as made to you are *ex parte,* and among very many things requiring explanation is this: In 1891, the gross receipts were returned by the railroads at $8,551,000, and net earnings as $3,120,000. In 1896 the gross earnings had increased nearly $1,200,000, but in some unaccountable way there is an increase of operating expenses of over $1,050,000, or in other words, the more business these corporations do the larger the percentage of expenses, which is contrary to experience. Besides, we know that improvements cheapening the cost of operation have been constantly made in the railroad world, and that the wages of the men, the rank and file, have been rather decreased than diminished. The Inter-State Commerce Commission report a sharp reduction as to the pay of the men, and an increase only in the salaries allowed by the higher officials to themselves, but it would take a great deal of this to account for the addition of $1,050,000 to operating expenses in North Carolina in five years out of an increased business of less than $1,200,000.

The North Carolina Railroad, 223 miles long, reported its *pro rata* contribution to salaries of "general officers" in 1891, $21,500 the same item in 1894 was $24,089 (more than the total salaries paid by this great State to the Governor and all the heads of the Executive Departments combined), while in 1896, after public criticism, this same item has shrunk without explanation to $5,875. This and many other matters which seem unaccountable, may, it is true, be explained. THEY NEED IT.

As I have said, the value of "the investment" of these three chief lines in North Carolina is reported by you as being $20,000,000. At four per cent. net the rates should be high enough to allow them $800,000 net earnings, but the actual net earnings reported upon the showing of these three companies for 1896 is $2,975,000, i.e., they carried off to their non-resident owners the sum of $2,175,000 in excess of the fair and legitimate rate of four per cent. of the investment. The excess extorted out of us alone is, therefore, far more than double the entire sum we pay to support our State government and the public schools, and this illegal excess goes to New York and London bankers.

It must be remembered that this proposed four per cent. net is above charges for railroad wrecks, betterments, repairs, law expenses, taxes, high salaries, and every possible charge which the corporations have seen fit to crowd into their expenses, for the sum total of the money received by these three lines for their operations in North Carolina in 1896 is admitted to be $8,476,000.

Thus the sum in excess of a reasonable allowance of four per cent. on the investment which these three systems have carried out of North Carolina since the day your Commission was established to reduce rates—the excess above legal rates in these six years—has been NEAR THIRTEEN MILLION DOLLARS, exclusive of interest. This sum under the decisions of the highest court in this land could justly and properly have been kept here, and its presence today would make this State blossom like a rose. Talk about frightening capital from coming into the State by "knowing our rights, and daring to maintain them." What we need is to keep a just part of our own capital in the State, and not to permit it to be carried off, to be used by Wall Street and London bankers to wreck other corporations elsewhere; to bid them in at under price and thus repeat the process over and over again.

It may be adroitly urged that you cannot reduce through rates. True enough, but you can protect your own people by reducing fares and freights between any two points in this State, so that the gross receipts of all kinds, through and local, shall not net more than four per cent. on the value of the money invested. Peik vs. Chicago, 94 U.S., 164.

2. But there is another proof that RATES ARE TOO HIGH. The value of money began increasing with the demonetization of silver and went on decreasing, as evidenced by the fall in prices of everything else, till 1891. At that time your Commission was established to reduce railroad rates. It is impossible to understand the tenor of the debates for and against the measure in that and in previous Legislatures, nor the intense struggle by the railroad lobby and the railroad newspapers against it upon any other basis. Indeed the power to do that is the very kernel of the act creating the Commission.

Whatever change your Commission felt able to make did not amount to any "cut," but was a "raise" for comparing the Railroad Commission report of 1892 with that of 1891, it appears that while gross earnings had increased $80,000, the net earnings had increased $83,000—a greater profit than before. Had rates merely remained the same, an increase of $80,000 in gross earnings would have shown $30,000, not $83,000 increase in net earnings. If the public demand, as evidenced by the establishment of your Commission, could have been complied with, there would have been a substantial cut in 1891. For a stronger reason there should be a greater one now. Since the repeal of the purchasing clause of the Sherman Act the value of the money in which we pay our freights and fares has gone on increasing, but railroad charges HAVE REMAINED THE SAME.

Cotton, which for six years ending in 1891, had averaged eleven cents, in the six years since has averaged barely seven; a fall of over 33 1/3 per cent. The railroad rates ought in fairness to be 33 per cent. less than the figure to which they ought to have been cut in 1891.

We know that the great railroads contributed great sums in the last campaign to maintain the gold standard. We are now paying these sums back by high rates, and thus paying them to increase the load resting upon us. A commission established by our people ought, it is respectfully submitted, to have that mercy upon us which we cannot expect from the non-resident owners of these corporations who know no more about us and care as little, as the English landlords do for their Irish tenants, or their Hindoo subjects.

One of these great systems saw the justice of the public demand and the wisdom from a business standpoint, of recognizing the enhanced value of money by reducing rates. Its owners made a very handsome cut, with great profit to themselves and to the gratification of their patrons. WHY THOSE REDUCED RATES were stopped, and the public and the line deprived of an arrangement so highly satisfactory to both, and by what methods it was done, is known by your commission already.

3. There is still another demonstration that rates are too high as to passenger rates. The rate now, as in 1891, is still 3¼ cents per mile, and it is higher than that on some of our roads, yet the railroads report the average received per passenger mile two and one-fifth cents. Clearly, therefore, there is a vast number of people who ride either absolutely free or at less than the general public pay. The Railroad Commission act contemplates that there shall be no discrimination, and could there be worse discrimination than to pile up 3¼ cents on the general public so that they shall pay enough not only for their own riding, but for reduced rates and free rates to others.

There are occasionally excursions, and the immense crowds which go upon them show the demand for lower rates. If a reasonable permanent rate of two cents per mile were given all the time it would save the public great inconvenience from over-crowding, and the railroads from the pressure for cars on these semi-occasional fits of concession. There would be a steady stream of travel which would be equally, and probably more, remunerative to the railroads (as has been the experience elsewhere), and it would be far more satisfactory to the people, who, after all, are the only support of the railroads.

Then the system of granting 1,000 mile tickets at two cents, or 2½ cents to men who have $40 or $50 to spare, and exacting 3¼ cents from those who need the reduction still more is only less OBJECTIONABLE THAN FREE PASSES.

I commend to your consideration the following extract from the report of the Railroad Commissioner of Michigan: "To sell 1,000 mile tickets at a less rate per mile than that for a less number of miles is a gross discrimination between passengers entitled to the same treatment. It violates the principles of justice the same as if 100 car loads of freight could be carried at a less rate per car than ten car loads between the same points." The doctrine of "equal right to all, and special privileges to none," is especially applicable to the rights of the public over a common carrier. No man should be charged higher for the same accommodation because he is poorer.

I do not advocate a two cents per mile rate on all railroads, but wherever one man travels at two cents another should not be charged more for the same grade of accommodation. The rate should be graded, as in many States. Those whose gross receipts exceed $4,000 per mile should not charge more than two cents per mile. Those whose gross receipts are over $3,000, but less than $4,000, should charge not over 2½ cents per mile, and all others not over three cents. The same or similar reduction and grading should be made in freight rates, the object being to allow a fair, just percentage of net profits on the actual value of the "plant."

There are 180,000 miles of railroad in the United States. They have been built with great difference in cost and through sections differing vastly in the amount of travel and freight. Ingenious tables could be made, which by skill in grouping, would make almost any given rate the average. There are roads charging LESS THAN ONE CENT PER MILE, and a few charging as high as the highest allowed in this State. The German government recently sent a commission to this country to investigate our system. With German patience and plodding thoroughness as to detail, they reported that upon a fair average two cents per mile was the average American rate. Lord Bryce, in an article written in the railroad interest in the North American Review for March, 1897, also says that the average American rate is two (2) cents per mile. As far as I can judge, it is about the figure, and considering the enhanced value of money, it would require a larger quantity of cotton, corn, or labor to buy a passage for 100 miles now at two cents per mile, than would a few years back have brought a passage for 100 miles at 3¼ cents per mile.

I hope your Commission will see proper to grant the public this concession, which is so eminently just. I am confident that the railroads would make more money as well as more friends by themselves voluntarily conceding this reduction. These agitations for two (2) cents fares, wherever they have been begun have never ceased till the demand has been granted. The demand is so just and reasonable in itself that it could not be otherwise.

I have preferred the above methods, which demonstrate clearly from your own reports that the rates here are too high, to entering into a comparison with rates elsewhere, which are so various and so numerous that contention could easily be raised on this collateral question by railroad advocates, anxious to divert attention from the real issue. That inter-State rates to North Carolina are higher than either to Virginia or South Carolina, was clearly shown by two late conventions of manufacturers at Greensboro and Charlotte, and it is not to be supposed that these corporations in their local rates have been more considerate of a people who have been so forebearing and patient under corporation imposition as those of this State have so long been. But my own investigation has been thorough, and has satisfied me that the railroad rates in this State, everything considered are the highest on the continent.

I learn that the answer filed by the Seaboard Air Line, when it was contending (against an injunction brought by a rival line) for the privilege of reducing their rates, set out this fact. But, however, it may be as to the answer, I am confident as to the fact that our rates are the highest. Wherever the rates elsewhere approximate ours it will be found that they are in those States where the railroads have almost without disguise taken possession of the government.

It is true that some States have more people than this, but they have more railroads, too. Only twelve States have as many people per mile of railroad as North Carolina.

The reduction of transportation charges IS NO SMALL MATTER to the public. The railroad freights for twelve months in the United States amount to eight hundred millions of dollars. It is the most burdensome tax we pay, and is equal to four times what this year's cotton crop will sell for, estimating it at ten millions of bales at five cents per pound. Adding the receipts from passengers, carrying mails, and other sources the people of this country annually pay the railroads five times the total receipts from the entire cotton crop of the country. Each family in the U.S. pays on an average $60 a year for freight alone. As the government statistician, Commissioner Wright, estimates the average income of each head of a family at $500 per annum, each family works one and a half months per year to pay the freight. There is no escaping this tax. It is added into the cost of every yard of cloth, every pair of shoes, every pound of sugar, coffee or flour that is bought, and is deducted from the price of every pound of cotton, or bushel of wheat, or corn, or other product sold. A reduction of this internal tariff will give the greatest relief. If all freight could be carried as cheaply as wheat is carried from Duluth to Buffalo this burden would be cut down to one-tenth of what it is now, from $800,000,000 to $80,000,000, a saving to the wealth producers of $720,000,000 per year. You can not do that, but you can justly reduce freights and fares in North Carolina to four per cent. net on what you yourselves say is the true value of the railroad property, and this would lift from the backs of our people, at a stroke of the pen, $2,300,000 per annum, which is now illegally and unjustly extorted out of them, for the use of the London and New York bankers who have bought up our railroads at a song.

The taxes paid by the railroads here are admitted by that one of the officials of the lines in this State who is perhaps best acquainted with the subject to be the lowest paid by railroads in any of the States. The property tax paid by them here is not supplemented by any tax on gross earnings, or stocks, as is usual elsewhere.

I know that there is always the threat that we will drive capital from the State. That was threatened if the six per cent. interest law was passed, but today North Carolina's 4's are at par, and Raleigh's five per cent.'s are $9 above par. What we need is to keep our own capital in the State, and with $13,000,000 saved every six years, as above shown, could be done, we can build railroads and get us a good school system upon our own money. Foreign capital will come here, not because we are humbly respectful and submissive to the owners of it, but because four per cent. net above taxes and all other charges is more than can be had by investing in United States three per cents.

In conversation recently with a director of one of these lines, though a North Carolinian himself, he said: "The truth is, this is getting to be an old country. Our laborers must come down to European wages and our farmers must live cheaper and be content with European small profits. They cannot help themselves." That is the way in which the banker-owners of our railroads, and all within their influence look—with perfect complacency, too—upon the situation. But if it is true that our farmers must surely and steadily be TURNED INTO PEASANTRY and tenant holders, and our laborers into semi-serfs, the net reduction should be all round—top as well as bottom—and the capitalists who have $20,000,000 invested in our three systems should take two per cent. net profits—for two per cent. per year is the bank rate in London and Paris.

But I take it the railroad owners would now be perfectly satisfied with the four per cent. net which the Vanderbilt roads in New York pay. They would not grumble at that. What they strenuously object to is getting four per cent. only on their investment. They would be satisfied with four per cent. on the $26,000,000, but they want you to go on and allow them four per cent. on something which you and they both say does not exist, i.e., their property in these roads above $26,000,000. There is the sore point.

They want dividends on that $26,000,000, which they say is even more than they have invested here, and which your Commission says is every cent they have here, and then they wish to tax the people fares and freight high enough to pay four per cent. on, on, on up to $94,000,000, i.e., on $70,000,000, for which they have not paid a cent nor struck a lick of work, but which is evidenced simply by so many pieces of paper on which they have stamped their decree that the people of North Carolina are mortgaged to pay them interest, and it is their decree also that unborn generations of North Carolinians must come into the world to pay them interest thereon. One generation does not satisfy their greed, but their long fingers must reach down into the pockets of those who are to come after us. We neither gave nor authorized that mortgage and we will not be bound by it. THERE IS A REASON, personal to yourselves, permit me to say, with the greatest respect, why you ought to grant a reduction. In the last Legislature bills to reduce fares and freights were defeated by only one majority in each house, and two of your commission went before the committees against the bills. It is reasonable to suppose on that narrow margin that but for your opposition those bills would have passed. It was understood that you opposed them because you thought that it would be a reflection on you for the Legislature itself to make the reduction which you had the power to make. It is certain that members who voted against these bills have attempted to justify their course to their constituents at home by the allegation that they expected fully that you would yourselves make the reduction.

If $26,000,000 will replace the property that is the value of the plant, and an enormous addition for the valuation of the franchise can only be made on the basis that the excessive rates and profits make the property worth that much more than it could be built for. I think the valuation should be placed at whatever the plant is really and truly worth, and that fares and freights should be reduced, taking the previous years' figures as a basis, so that four per cent. on that valuation, above taxes and all expenses of every kind will be the net earnings.

To swell the valuation by an estimate of $28,000,000 as one of your number has proposed, for the value of the franchise is simply an admission of grossly excessive rates of fares and freights. It would merely put into the treasury a tax which cannot exceed two-thirds of one per cent. on that sum, while letting the corporations put their fares and freights high enough to earn six, ten or fifteen per cent. on this $28,000,000 of "wind." If the treasury prefers it as a method of taxation, the rates might be fixed to yield six per cent. net on $26,000,000 (above property tax and all other expenses) and then a tax could be laid by the Legislature on the gross earnings sufficient to reduce the net earnings to four per cent. THIS IS RESORTED TO IN SOME STATES. This method would give much of the desired reduction of freights and fares and at the same time add considerably to the tax receipts. In Massachusetts the railroads pay $3,680,000 taxes in addition to the property tax. This is about nine per cent. on their gross earnings from passengers. In Illinois the Central Railroad pays the State seven per cent. on gross earnings. In many other States a similar tax is levied. In Indiana the railroads pay $2,250,000 tax, and even in Pennsylvania, whose government openly belongs to them, they pay $3,500,000. In New York the railroads, in one way or another pay over $8,000,000 taxes annually. Wisconsin, which has about our population, collects over $1,200,000 from railroads. In Minnesota the tax on railroad gross earnings is $1,000,000. and the railroads in the little State of New Jersey pay over a million dollars in taxes. In North Carolina all the railroads combined pay the State a little over $100,000 on their $26,000,000 of property, and not one cent on their nearly $10,000,000 of annual gross earnings, or on their $3,285,000 of net earnings. The three great railroads of the State earn fifteen per cent. usury on their investment and pay the State back less than $100,000 in taxes.

But should your Honorable Commission think it wise to increase the valuation for taxation by some millions for valuation of the franchise, as has been suggested, I earnestly ask you IN JUSTICE TO THE PUBLIC, not to overlook the fact that in fixing rates they should not be high enough to give the railroads four or six per cent. net, on the franchise valuation. They are only entitled to four or six per cent. (as you may grant) on the value of the plant, i.e., on their investment. If that is $26,000,000, then the net earnings should be calculated to be earned on that. The franchise valuation is simply the "wind," the "water" added by reason of the excessive profits and this "wind" having cost them nothing to allow them a net earning on that would be the very matter against which our people have most earnestly protested.

Our people have no hostility to railroads. The charge is an old device of their officials whenever justice is demanded in regard to them. There is hostility against the methods of some of their managers and against the free pass system, which in many instances is a thin veil for corruption; and against the enormous sums in excess of reasonable net earnings which are being exacted by the present high rates and sent out of the State never to return, to the permanent impoverishment of this Commonwealth. It is these abuses, not the proper uses, of railroads, which are repugnant to us.

You are North Carolinians entrusted with a great and sacred responsibility. YOU HAVE IT IN YOUR POWER to render long delayed justice to a long suffering people. You can lighten the load which a blind and exacting avarice has bound on their shoulders and makes heavier and heavier with the passing years; for money is still enhancing in value and hence the rates for freight and passengers are increasing in effect, though not in nominal amount, each year, and almost each month.

I pray you grant the people that justice and that relief in the confident hope of which your commission was created. In your wisdom you have thought proper to defer it till now. Six years is a long time for a whole people to suffer. The facts and figures I have laid before you are taken from your own reports. They tell a sad tale of insatiable avarice on the one hand and of patient endurance on the other.

I thank you for the compliment of asking me to present the cause of the people in this matter. Nothing is nearer to my heart than their welfare. Nothing will be a higher honor than to be able to secure at your hands some alleviation of the burden so unsparingly laid upon them. I would that I possessed eloquence so that I might present their cause with the force its justice and its importance demands.

As plainly and as clearly as I could, in my humble way, I have called this matter to your attention. In the name of 300,000 voters in North Carolina, I say that you harken to their cause. However arrogant, however domineering, however omnipotent in our government the railroad kings seem to be, the real sovereigns, are the patient burden-bearers, the voters of the State.

They have been very patient, they have been patient a long time, but they may be patient no longer. Two and a quarter millions of dollars of illegal exactions each year is too heavy a burden to carry much longer, and our history tells us that when these toil-worn and sun-burned men of North Carolina have been moved by tyrannical exactions and justice too long delayed, they know how to assert their sovereignty.

Into your hands I now commit their prayer for relief.

CLARK TO MARION BUTLER

Raleigh, N.C.
23 July 1897

The agitation for Postal Telegraphy has not been as "seed sown on barren ground." It is bearing fruit. The Times-Democrat of New Orleans, the News & Ob. here & numerous other democratic, and republican papers too, are now supporting it.

The Times-Democrat has written me for data. Kindly mail *Page M. Baker, Editor Times-Democrat New Orleans,* La. (marked personal) a copy of Sen. Doc. 205 of last year. Please send *at once.* It contains you know the Postal Telegraph articles.

The suggestion for *State* action was defeated by our legislature last winter, as you know, by one majority but our R.R. Commr has now fixed the rate at "15 cents for 10 words" between any two points in N.C. If this is followed by other States it will force U.S. Telegraphy.

The strongest feature to be urged is a government telephone at every country P.O. This will for the first time—*53 years* after its introduction—place this great invention in the reach of the masses and will double the receipts of over 60.000 country Post Masters. These are *two strong clubs* to use against the Monopoly.

By invitation, I am to address the Bar Association of Tennessee at Nashville, Tenn July 30. In it, I shall open the fight for *elec-*

tion of U.S. Judges by the people. The appointive system for U.S. judges is the "ace up the sleeve" by which the corporations trump away every move for popular emancipation. The speech will be nearly 4.000 words but if you should wish the Caucasian to print it (few papers, if any, will *dare* to do it) notify them—and myself—and I will furnish them copy.

I have not had full opportunity to get up such article as I wish on Postal Savings Banks—though I am heartily in favor of that measure—but will have it ready long before Congress meets again....

My speech at Nashville for election of U.S. judges by the people will be the first gun fired in a campaign which must be won before anything can be won in behalf of the people.

TO CLARK FROM EDWIN A. ALDERMAN *

Chapel Hill
Sept. 1, 1897

As I understand it the papers referred to in your letter to Dr. Battle were given to the University and I could not consent to part with them without minute inquiry into the circumstances of their coming into our custody. If you will kindly send them I will make this inquiry and let you know.

I congratulate you on your great service to the State and your fruitful and unflagging zeal.

TO CLARK FROM OTTO PATZER †

Madison, Wis.
Nov. 17th, 1897

After full investigation, our Committee has come to the conclusion that government acquisition of the telegraph in this country should include the telephone. We are led to this conclusion by our study of conditions in England and Europe, and especially by the competition here existing between telegraph and telephone in spite of the contract and strong bond between them. We understand your writings on the subject to include both but we do not wish to quote you in our work without consulting you. Could we

* President of the University of North Carolina, 1896-1900.

† Professor, University of Wisconsin and Chairman of the Committee of Investigation of the Telegraph.

quote you to the effect that public good would best be furnished by government acquisition of both telegraph and telephone, and that the acquisition of telegraph alone without the telephone would not be a wise step?

You have already given us much aid in our investigation and we beg leave to thank you for your recent favor.

CLARK TO MARION BUTLER

Raleigh, N.C.
11 Dec. 1897

I hope you will take advantage of the tide that is setting in for Postal Savings Banks to *press* your Bill for Postal Telegraphs & Telephone. All the latter measure needs is to be brought into active agitation. The Western Union has always defeated it by the chloroform process.

What has become of your Constitutional Amendment to elect Senators by the people—and to make the Federal Judiciary elective? It was Senator Tillman * who wrote me he would introduce the latter measure but I hope that will not deter you from proceeding with your bill, if he has done nothing.

I received a telegram from N.Y. World yesterday saying that they had seen an article of mine in *Dec* "New Time" (which you have probably seen) and asking for a column for their editorial page to-morrow (Sunday). I sent it on & I suppose you will see it in the Sunday "World"—

TO CLARK FROM SAMUEL FOX MORDECAI †

Raleigh, N. C.
Dec. 21st 1897

Thank you very much for "Proceedings Bar Associations of Tenn." I read your speech with much interest and profit. It is a bright and able presentation of those views of the constitution entertained by you in common with very many other patriotic citizens. It was doubly interesting to me because it presented in a readable form—a very rare thing to my notion valuable historical events connected with the constitution. Accept my congratulations.

* "Pitchfork Ben" Tillman of South Carolina, United States Senator, 1895-1918.

† Lawyer and for many years Dean of the Law School at Trinity College and Duke University.

CLARK TO MARION BUTLER

Raleigh, N.C.
21 Dec. 1897

We have an exceedingly heavy docket. As soon as the holidays come I will draw & send you the Cons[l] Amendment to elect *judges* by the people.

I see the Amendment to elect *Senators* by the people is unanimously recommended by the House Committee. Can't you introduce it in the Senate, push it along to a report & when the same bill comes over from the House, substitute that bill for yours—thus head off delays.

If you can bring forward *one cent* letter postage, it will give you an opportunity to impress on the public mind again your telling figures about the renting of Postal cars.

[P.S.]
If I were in the Senate, instead of the colleague * you have, possibly I might help you some in pushing these and other much needed reforms.

TO CLARK FROM ALEXANDER BUCHANAN †

Adelaide, Australia
Dec. 10, 1897

I have brought this matter under the attention of the Right Hon. The Chief Justice who considers that the North Carolina Reports will be useful in the Supreme Court Library, and approves the suggestion that, in the absence of current reports, such Volumes of the South Australian Law Reports as are available or obtainable should be forwarded in exchange as requested.

TO CLARK FROM REV. J. D. HUFHAM ‡

Henderson, N. C.
1898

Since the publication of the last number of the Baptist Historical Papers, I have been asked many times whether the horrible sentence pronounced by Chief Justice Howard on the Regulator, Capt. Benj. Merrill, at Hillsboro 1771, was unusual; or whether it was according to an established formula provided in such cases.

* Jeter C. Pritchard, United States Senator, December 2, 1895-March 4, 1903.
† Master of the Supreme Court of Australia.
‡ Prominent Baptist clergyman and at one time editor of the *Biblical Recorder*.

I am unable to tell and no lawyer whom I have consulted has given me any definite or satisfactory information.

Knowing you to be expert in all questions of law and history, I venture to ask you. You will recall the sentence, that Merrill was to be taken to the place whence he came and thence to the place of execution; to be hanged by the neck; to be cut down while yet alive; his bowels taken out before his eyes while yet alive, etc.

Was this formula provided by the old English law or was it devised by Howard? Merrill and the other five Regulators were tried, I think, under the Johnston law which was passed by the legislature in session at New Bern.

Just a little information in reference to this matter will be a great kindness to me.

TO CLARK FROM L. H. HARDY *

Roxboro, N. C.
January 5, 1898

I have read with much pleasure your article entitled, "If Christ Should Come", and I desire to recommend it for I believe you must have written that article by the grace of God.

The principles you set forth are the very principles which are and have been advocated by every true Primitive Baptist Minister since I have known anything of their teachings.

I am very glad that the good Lord of heaven, who rules in the armies of heaven and among the inhabitants of the earth has so wrought in your heart as to enable you to rise up in opposition to the leading sentiments of the worldly-great and write for the public those words of truth.

CLARK TO MARION BUTLER

Norfolk, Va.
12 Jan. 1898

The Hanna † election has so sharply called the attention of the country to the evils of the present mode of electing Senators that the present would be a good time to *press* the bill for election of Senators by the people.

Senator Tillman wrote me he favored (& would introduce) an amendment providing for election of U.S. judges. If you can get

* Primitive Baptist minister.

† Marcus Alonzo Hanna, chairman of the Republican national committee in 1896 and United States Senator from Ohio, March 5, 1897 until his death, January 15, 1904.

him to speak on your bill when you do, it will add to the publicity which it needs.

I learn that Board of Visitors to West Point are purposely selected from different political parties & from different parts of the country—

TO CLARK FROM EDWIN A. ALDERMAN

Chapel Hill
January 18, 1898

I thank you warmly for your generous gift of the valuable booklet containing so many of your recent address and articles....

I have given the number of those indicated for the Professors and the Library....

However, I shall try to think out a scheme and assure you that the young men will appreciate the gift and its motive. I always read what you write with interest and pleasure and with some amazement at your industry and fecundity.

TO CLARK FROM FRANK R. WRIGHT *

New York, N. Y.
January 20th, 1898

Mr. Graham Daves has suggested that we write you in regard to illustrative material pertaining to the Revolution, and we understand that you are at present compiling the state records. Can you inform us of the whereabouts of any interesting relics, documents, maps, etc., relating to the affairs of the South at that period?

TO CLARK FROM JAMES S. SENER †

Fredericksburg, Va.
Jan. 25, 1898

This Commission organized at the instance of the City of Fredericksburg and the Counties of Spottsylvania, Stafford, and Orange, for the purpose of marking and preserving the great Battlefields of Fredericksburg, Chancellorsville, The Wilderness, and Spottsylvania C. H., is about to become incorporated under the laws of Virginia by the Legislature now in session. There is no job or syndicate in it. The charter follows closely on the lines of that granted to the Chickamauga incorporation. Soldiers on both sides of the lines are lending their names and influence to

* Official of Charles Scribner's Sons.
† Vice-chairman of the National Battlefields Park Commission.

the work. We expect no contribution of money and the charter expressly declares that no one is to have personal gain or benefit from it. Under these circumstances we should be glad to include your name as one of the incorporators from the State of North Carolina. As we are anxious to have the bill passed as soon as possible, please let us hear from you at your earliest convenience....

[P.S.]
It is the purpose of the Association when organized to apply to Congress to take up and take charge of the matter as was done in the case of Chickamauga.

CLARK TO MARION BUTLER

Raleigh, N.C.
3 Feb. 1898

I note in a late speech of Rep. Maguire * of Cal. that he says he was on platform committee at Chicago & the plank against life tenure of office was against *all* life tenures, including judges, and not against merit system nor in favor of "spoils." I saw N & O here & succeeded in getting it to *copy & endorse.*

I have written him to-day & asked him to introduce a Const. Amendment for an elective judiciary. Can you not in some way get this done? The measure is indispensable. Without it, the life judiciary, with irreviewable power to hold acts of Congress & the President *unconstitutional* will "hold the fort" for the Money Power *no matter by what majority* the people carry the country. We have no chance (without the amendment) except the slow process of the garrison (put there by the Money power) dying out.

I see that Chief Justice Faircloth † has been put on the Board of Visitors to West Point. I suppose another North Carolinian will hardly be put on.

CLARK TO MARION BUTLER

Neal Station ‡ 4 Feb 1898

Permit me to suggest to you—if you have not already thought of it—that if Hawaii is admitted to have ready & promptly introduce a bill for a *Govt.* cable, as part of P.O.—There *will* be a cable

* James G. Maguire, Democratic Representative in Congress, March 4, 1893-March 3, 1899.

† William T. Faircloth of Wayne County, Chief Justice of North Carolina Supreme Court, 1895-1901.

‡ In Halifax County, near Ventosa Plantation.

of course and if you do not have this ready, there will be a Western Union bill, *asking a subsidy* of course for their private line. It will be a good opening to introduce Govt. Telegraphy.

I write from here where I am at my farm for a day or two. I should think Mr Maguire would support this—

TO CLARK FROM KEMP P. BATTLE

Chapel Hill, N. C.
Feb. 11, 1898

. . . I think the change to written examinations is an admirable one and your suggested increase of requirements wise. Lawyers are in large measure teachers of the people and ought to know something.

CLARK TO MARION BUTLER

Raleigh, N.C.
12 Feb. 1898

. . . Your plan of election by the people is the best. No more popular plank could be put in a National platform.

There is no need to pension present judges. It was not done when any State changed from life to elective judges. The pension idea would kill it.

I have thought over what you said as to Hawaii. If the *world would stand still* and our population did not increase we do not need it. But with our steady increase in population, and of our commerce in the Pacific, it will be a great mistake to reject it and let Great Britain take it. A few years hence our commerce in the Pacific will be 50 fold what it is now—or more, if China awakes to new life as Japan has done, and then Hawaii will be *indispensable to us.* If annexed, I hope you will introduce a bill to organise it as the "Territory of Honolulu" or the "Territory of the Pacific" or something to get rid of the awkward and malodorous "Hawaii"—

CLARK TO MARION BUTLER

Raleigh, N.C.
28 Feb. 1898

The R.Rs endeavored to defeat reduction of rates. Now it is done, they fear to arouse public indignation by Injunctions & resultant investigation of their high salaries and doctored returns.

The Southern has very *adroitly* proposed to Governor: If he will

1. Restore the "cut" of passenger rates (which they estimate at $300.000 in the State) and will contract to pardon the countless penalties incurred for violation of law as to free passes and freight discriminations & will let judgment be taken in their favor on the 99 year-lease investigation, *then* the Southern will

2. Lease Atlantic R.R. at $30.000 per year and pay all expenses of lease investigation, including *liberal* fees to *State's Counsel!* Hence these last are open mouthed running Commrs down to *rescind!* I saw a letter one of them this P.M. had cajoled the Gov., introducing to Pearson & Caldwell * demanding a restoration of rates to 3 cents till legislature met—well knowing of course that if this is done the people losing all confidence will let the Southern elect a legislature to repeal the R.R. Commission act—and put us back *10 years.*

The Gov. threatens not to employ counsel for State if R.R-s get out injunction &c &c. There ought to be manhood enough in the Bar to punish volunteers as in the Kirk legal troubles. But if not, Commrs ought to have manhood enough to let Gov. take responsibility of *not* employing counsel.

Every pressure, & every influence, from every quarter is being brought to bear upon Pearson & Caldwell to rescind. I write hastily for *you* should write them both (in duplicate here & at their homes) *at once* to stand firm. It is the last chance for the people.

In truth the "cut" will be less than $200.000. As the R.Rs in N.C. yearly extort two millions *nett in excess* of what the law would allow, this is 1/10 only of what a Commission *might* do & even this $200.000 could be made good in 3 different ways— 1—By making the army of over 100.000 free pass toters in N.C. pay their way as the law requires— 2—By cutting down Spencer's $50.000 salary & other exorbitant salaries. 3. By natural increase in travel, from lower rates.

Write Pearson & Caldwell, & telegraph them you have written. It is the crisis. Hold firm now, or lose *all* the gain we have made in 10 years for the people.

CLARK TO MARION BUTLER

Raleigh, N.C.
2 April 1898

You have seen J.H. Pearson's resolution which was adopted, to require 1.000 mile & 2.000 tickets to be made transferable, i.e.

* Members of the North Carolina Railroad Commission.

valid in hands of *holder*. If Caldwell does not again "flop" this puts the R.R's in a hole. They already sell those tickets at 2½ & 2¢ per mile and therefore can't appeal or enjoin. Their excuse for these tickets has been that the interest on $25, (for 1.000 miles) and $40 (on 2.000 miles) made the difference. But this rule will make them put in more than $25's & $40's than before—while on the other hand in practice it will probably throw open 2¢ and 2½¢ rates to the public that Caldwell's late "flop" in rescinding the reduction will amount to little good for them. If this is adhered to it will *force* the general reduction.

The R.R's while always professing willingness to do away with free passes always defeated every bill towards that end. It is their cheap mode of controlling the politicians & officeholders of the state by making the masses pay for *all* the R.R. travelling. Then too as a R.R. man said "they can buy a man with a free pass to whom they can not offer money." The "Southern" is the political agency of the Money Power. To take away its free passes is to cut off its right hand.

Have you noticed the R.R. action as to free passes? For 7 years, since Comm. Act was passed in 1891, they have issued an average 100.000 illegal passes annually in N.C. Each of these violations is liable to a "penalty of not less than $1.000 nor more than $5.000." After thus making 700.000 violations of the law, they were indicted in 2 cases last Oct. They put off trial from term to term till Mar 31—6 mo's delay. Then they plead *ignorance* of the law—they who have all the high priced lawyers hired! Then they plead that they had violated the law so long & so uniformly! as if that was not an aggravation. Then they pleaded that it was "persecution," enforcing the law in 2 cases! out of 700.000 violations—Then they were let off with the minimum fine allowed $1.000 each & $2.000 thus goes into the school fund of Wake. Then though the case regularly should come up to this term of the Supreme Court, they are allowed 60 days delay by the Solicitor so as to put the cases off another 6 mo's. Nor is this all—so determined are they not to lose the chance of controlling through these illegal favors—One road announces that it will issue all its free passes "good over Va. & N.C. lines so as not to be under State laws." The answer to this should be made. 1. The inter State Commerce law forbids free passes as well as State Law & has been so construed by the Inter-State Commission 8 times when Judge Cooley was at its head—the most eminent Constitutional lawyer in the country. 2. The State law forbids *free carriage* between points in the State, not the issuing free passes, and when a person is so carried illegally it makes no difference that the person the R.R. carries has an order in his pocket which would authorise the conductor to carry him free into Va.

Another R.R. is pretending to take up its editorial free passes with a view to make the editor howl on its side, for it will take care to take up the passes of those only who do not.

There is no chance to carry this State for Bryan two years hence unless the hold of the Money Power is broken. That hold is the political machine called the "Southern" which controls editors, lawyers and every influence it can exert. Its cheapest (to itself) but most effective weapon is the free pass system. Hence the importance of attacking it. Already these corporations are moving to nomination by *each* party of railroad judges, congressmen & legislators—this done they will let the sham battle go on knowing however it may end theirs is the spoil.

I write hastily. If the ideas strike you put them in your own words and use—as you *can* use them—

CLARK TO MARION BUTLER

Raleigh, N.C.
14 April 1898

If war comes, taxes must be increased. When it is sought to lay them on coffee, sugar, tobacco & beer, I hope that there will be a determined effort in the Senate to add an *income* tax, in several different phases, so as to emphasise *by debate* that the aggregate wealth of the country proposes to *neither fight nor pay*. This can't be done in the House, but a few determined men in the Senate can make the issue so sharp the country will respond next Nov. The Money Power will try to bulldose & dragoon their measure through on the ground that *any division* will be *unpatriotic!*

Again when bonds, certificates of indebtedness, or notes are issued I hope they will be *legal tenders,* not payable in coin, but worded like the greenbacks "which saved the life of the nation" and whose unconstitutionality has been approved by the supreme court.

The "necessity" of these taxes & money issues is the people's opportunity.

I am glad that you propose to nominate two R.R. Commr's at your State Convention. The Republicans set a precedent for this in nominating Pritchard for Senator. I hope (as your Convention meets first) you will *emphasise* the demand for reduction of railroad rates. The people are solid on it. A leading democrat (who is opposed to such resolution) told me this week very sadly that the Democratic State Convention *must* pass a resolution demanding such reduction or we would be hopelessly beaten.

You will note that the "Southern" files an exception to the last reduction which it says will amount to $12.000 through its reports show that its increase of *nett earnings* last year over the year before was $100.000 and its total increase of nett earnings in one year was $622.000—nearly 2/3 of a million—yet like Pharaoh it will not reduce the people's burdens even the finger nail of $12.000. Its real fight is to deny the public right to control Pierpont Morgan. The *real issue* is shall his combination of London & N.Y, bankers who own our railroads *continue* to control N.C., select its governors, judges & legislatures or shall we control *them.*

TO CLARK FROM WILLIAM H. S. BURGWYN

Charlotte, N. C.
April 27, 1898

Though I thanked you at the time for your kind act in going to see Gov. Russell in my behalf; as I think over it, the manner in which it was done and the generous terms in which you spoke of me coupled with the statement that it was the first request for appointment to office that you had made of the Governor, that I feel that I must write a few lines just again to express my thanks. You have always been ready and willing to oblige me, and you may rest assured, I shall be happy at any opportunity of being service to you.

CLARK TO MARION BUTLER

Raleigh, N.C.
28 April 1898

I have a son at Cornell University N.Y.—David Clark—who is to graduate in June. In common with many of his classmates he has applied for appointment as Engineer in the Navy under the late act. Many of his class-mates have received orders to report for examination & as he stands towards the head he thinks he has been overlooked from not "having a friend at court." Could you, without much trouble call his case to attention of Navy Dep't, I should be obliged.

He will be 21 next mo. has had 4 yrs at A&M College, as student

& then 2 more as Instructor & now a year at Cornell and is, I presume fairly well equipped as an Engineer, as he has always taken honors in his classes & is recommended by Faculty at Cornell. Is of perfectly steady habits.

Mr. Bryan's letter to Mr Daniels in favor of Co-operation has had a *fine* effect. The Pierpont Morgan officials are much alarmed I learn, fearing that the Dem. State Conv. may pass resolutions denouncing "99 years lease" & demanding "lower fares & freights and no free passes." This will be prevented by them, if possible.

CLARK TO A. W. GRAHAM

Raleigh, N.C.
26 May 1898

Do you know of a good saddle horse at Oxford which can be bought from $75 to $100. David is Adjutant & wishes to buy one but they have formed a "combine" here & put the price up to $125 to $150.

If you know of one, please telegraph me—at my expense.

Andrews was supreme in the convention. Of 52 men of different committees 49 were lawyers, of these 23 were So. R.R. lawyers & many others were R.R. lawyers.

CLARK TO MARION BUTLER

Raleigh, N.C.
30 May 1898

Will you please present the within to the President with such endorsement as you think proper to give it.

The position I wish is General of Brigade, and if possible with N.C. troops. If appointed, I want a command that will *go to Cuba.* My record is that I was a cadet at a Military School when the Civil War broke out & entered the Confederate service in the spring of 1861 at the age of 14, and served most of the four years and surrendered under Jos. E. Johnston in May 1865. At 17 years of age I had risen to be Lieut Colonel.

Since the War I was 4½ years on the Superior bench & for the last 9 years on the Supreme Bench on which my term will expire Jan. 1. 1903.

I have small expectation that the President will appoint me or any other Silver man. But I would like to have my tender of services with my record laid before him. You can also give the facts to the Associated press, if you like. I am probably the only Supreme Court judge who has offered his services.

The Silver men would have carried the late Democratic Convention easily for Co-operation—in my judgment—if they had had *pluck.* Andrews' Attys were so blatant that they over-awed and ran over those who should have stood by Mr Bryan. Andrews, I learn, has scolded his attys well & soundly for letting the Convention condemn free passes & demand lower R.R. rates—in the platform.

CLARK TO A. W. GRAHAM

Raleigh, N.C.
1 June 1898

. . . You will see in this morning's News & Ob. my Opinion in Greenlee's case which the Char. Ob. calls *communistic* & which has set the R.R. *fices* barking. Read it. Six years ago we held that a R.R. was liable for negligence if a *passenger* was injured for lack of self couplers. This opinion says that the 10.000 R.R. *employees* in N.C. are entitled to the equal protection of the law, that the defendant has issued $76.557 of bonds & stock per mile for the public to pay interest on and out of that sum should be able to protect their employees by putting in car couplers which cost $18. per car. And this *they* call communistic! Are there any papers whom you can get to present this view to the public? They cut off all information from the people wherever they can.

[P.S.]
I send you "Prog. Farmer" on our Convention. It is well sometimes to see "how others view us."

CLARK TO MARION BUTLER

Raleigh, N.C.
6 June 1898

Was the recommendation for Brig. Gen laid before the President! if so, what is the prospect.

I believe most, if not all, our delegation in the House would sign the recommendation, if Capt Lloyd has time to present it for their signatures. Mr Linney * was in the C.S. Army & is friendly. I see that Loge Harris reports that Spier Whitaker will be appt.

* Romulus Z. Linney of Alexander County, Republican Representative in Congress, December 2, 1895-March 4, 1901.

Brig Gen. As he has recently had an attack of paralysis and was only a Lieut in C.S. service, if this is true, the "Southern" must be backing him—as he has been applying to A.B.A.* for help.

Some one, will be appointed from N.C. If it is not already settled, I would be glad to go—I believe I am the only Supreme Court judge in the Union who has tendered his services.

CLARK TO MARION BUTLER

Raleigh, N.C.
24 June 1898

I presume the annexation of Hawaii is a certainty—and that of Cuba and Porto Rico is almost equally so.

As an advocate of Postal Telegraph, would it not be well to get in a bill to lay a Postal cable to Hawaii (as soon as annexed) before some monopoly asks a bill *with a subsidy*—which (as in the case of Pacific R.Rs) will amount to U.S. furnishing the funds & *giving* the line to the promoters. If the P.O. works a line from San Francisco to Hawaii, why not between any other two P.O's in U.S!

Public sentiment in this State is strongly in favor of annexation of Hawaii, and ever since Jefferson's day the South has been desirous of annexing Cuba. I write you about Postal cable as in the midst of other cases you may possibly not have thought of it.

TO CLARK FROM CHARLES D. MC IVER †

Greensboro, N. C.
June 25, 1898

Upon my return from Asheville, I find your letter of June 23, for which I beg you to accept my grateful acknowledgment. It is gratifying to me that you should take the trouble to write and make this or any other suggestion in regard to the work of the State Normal and Industrial College. I had thought of Spanish as a possibility. I do not care for it to displace German, but if I can make arrangements to do so, I shall put it on the same footing with French and German. I am now in correspondence with a young woman with a view of employing her to teach French and Spanish.

* A. B. Andrews, Vice President and General Manager of the Southern Railroad Company.

† President of the State Normal and Industrial College, now the Woman's College of the University of North Carolina.

CLARK TO A. W. GRAHAM

Raleigh, N.C.
12 Sept 1898

I am glad to see the compliment paid you by the unanimous endorsement of Granville. I hope you will sacrifice your inclinations & take the nomination of the District. You will be *badly needed* here & you can never serve your State better. The R.R.'s are *packing the nominations* & are trying to elect a *Railroad legislature* with a view to repealing the R.R. Commission act & the anti-pass law and assuming untrammelled sovereignty of public affairs. They are systematically at work all over the State. Your presence in the next legislature will be a great service to N.C.

CLARK TO A. W. GRAHAM

Raleigh, N.C.
20 Sept. 1898

. . . The R.R.'s in confidence—have so taken possession of our party & contemplate such *Revolutionary Measures* that for the sake of the State & Party you ought to come to the legislature if you can—Mr. Bryan's renomination and election may possibly turn on the action of N.C. You ought to come—if you have to make some sacrifices—if not *too* great.

TO CLARK FROM EDWIN A. ALDERMAN

Chapel Hill
October 1, 1898

I was in Raleigh during the examination of the candidates for license and wished to see you, but I have had too much experience with looking over examination papers to interrupt a man in that process. I wish you to know that I rejoice without measure over the action of the Board in the matter of written examinations. I know of nothing that will do more in elevating and dignifying the legal profession in North Carolina. It pleases me to know that fifteen out of sixteen of our men who had done the work here have passed it.

I wanted to call at your house and have a long conversation with you about a number of matters of public interest, but I was told that you were up to your ears in work the whole time, hence postponed it until my next visit.

TO CLARK FROM HERIOT CLARKSON *

Charlotte, N. C.
November 30, 1898

Capt. Alexander † has referred me to your letter of the 25th concerning the Mass. Law in regard to "Land Registration"—now in use in Australia and Chicago; would you be so kind as to write on for a copy of the act for me to look over.

Could you tell me where I could get some act establishing a Reformatory for young Criminals? This is a matter of great importance and about as important as Church Building, though it may be expensive.

TO CLARK FROM J. A. BALDWIN ‡

Charlotte, N. C.
Dec. 28, 1898

I desire to thank you most cordially for your kind words in reference to my article on "Mill Life". I appreciate what you say all the more because I know you have given much thought to this and kindred subjects.

We have sent copies to all Legislators and most of all the preachers of the state.

Mr. D. A. Tompkins,§ one of the most progressive mill men of the South, has formulated a bill which Mr. Heriot Clarkson will offer. It provides for an eleven hour law, a prohibition of children under twelve years working in mills during public school terms, and some provisions to prevent so much moving. It is not all that I would like, but I think under the circumstances it is the best that can be done. Many mill owners will be opposed to any legislation at all.

As a pastor these things so got hold of me that I could not conscientiously keep quiet any longer.

You can do a very great deal in helping to secure this legislation, and I am glad to know it is your desire to do so. I would have been surprised and disappointed had it been otherwise.

A better system of schools is very much needed for all our people. We need more day school and S. S. Libraries. I am working with a most excellent and cheap Sunday School library, and it is my intention to put it in as many schools as possible.

* Later Associate Justice of North Carolina Supreme Court.
† Probably refers to S. B. Alexander of Charlotte.
‡ Charlotte minister.
§ Daniel A. Tompkins, prominent industrialist.

CLARK TO A. W. GRAHAM

Raleigh, N.C.
14 June 1899

Yours to hand. As you surmised David * did not consult me, and naturally—from local associations, and Sudie & Mrs. Primrose being schoolmates, pledged himself to Primrose.

The whole trouble was caused by Geo Winston coming out so late. When he was announced, I told David that while I had nothing against Primrose Winston was the best man to build up the College &c. I urged him, if he could not vote for W. *at least* to throw off in Lacy, or Whitsett, but he said he was honorably bound to go for Primrose, and that when he left him he wanted to go to Winston. I think he would have done that at last meeting but for an attempt (he thought by W's friends) to get Alumni meetings to *instruct* him to vote for W— which he resented. He told me that when he left here, W. would be elected next meeting.† Bailey & his crowd are at the bottom of the fight on W— and David & all A & M boys are down on Bailey. I write David about the matter by this mail, emphasising this view from admissions in Bailey's card yesterday. David is a boy of his own will, besides I feel more delicacy in persuading him, than I would others, lest it might seem authority instead of persuasion, and I wish him to discharge his duty, in the post as he sees it, free from any thing more than his knowledge of my views & judgment which he knows are for Winston.

The Winstons have always been friends of mine, but I have been of theirs. I think I seconded Dr W's election as Latin Prof (tho a man may easily overestimate his own efforts) and I have done all I could for each & every member of the family on all other occasions when in my power. But I will not count such mutual support—it is enough to say I have *always* been for them and this occasion is no exception. Just now I think Dr Winston could probably do more for the College than any man I know of and his coming would be endless vexation to Bailey and his crowd.

You have been working too hard. Let us go down July 4 to Morehead to State Bar Association. I wish to talk over some matters with you any way & we can there renew our acquaintance with brother lawyers. . . .

* David Clark, son of Walter Clark, now editor of the *Southern Textile Bulletin*.

† George T. Winston was elected President of the North Carolina Agricultural and Mechanical College by a majority of one vote, the deciding vote being cast by David Clark. Walter Clark was a member of the Watauga Club, which had much to do with the founding of the College.

[P.S.]
You can let W— see this letter if you think best.
I am anxious for you to go to Morehead, if you can. They are laying *some plans* to be hatched out there.
Destroy this note.

TO CLARK FROM E. J. HALE *

Fayetteville, N. C.
July 4th, 1899.

...I am much perplexed as to how we shall be able to get a Bryan and free silver delegation to Chicago next year—I mean, of course, a genuine one.

If we could have had a vote on the negro suffrage amendment this year, we would then have been easily able to control the Democratic party in 1900, because we could have drawn the line sharply against the gold boys in that year's primaries. If, however, the same primaries which select delegates to the State Convention and the same State Convention are to be entrusted with the widely dissimilar tasks of selecting a State ticket to conduct the State campaign for white supremacy and of choosing delegates to represent the Bryan and pro-silver sentiment of the State at Chicago, we shall, without the shadow of a doubt, be confronted, in the State committee meeting that issue to call for the State Convention, with the proposition that the carrying of the amendment is the supreme issue and that consequently we must open our primaries to the same constituency which gave us the victory last year—that is, to all *white* men, including Republicans, (10,000 to 15,000), goldboys (10,000), etc. Last year, after we had set the pace by rejecting the Populist offer of co-operation, our County Conventions were filled with goldboys and other McKinleyites. These anti-Democratic elements, happened to be white and therefore came within the terms of the call, while the other whites, Populists and extreme silver Democrats, abstained from our Conventions through disgust and resentment.

The same composition of our Conventions next year will mean a solid delegation to the National Convention of silver-plated goldboys. At the same time, such a state of affairs would so complete the alienation of the Populists that McKinley would carry the State in a canter—even if Bryan were our nominee.

* Editor and proprietor of the *Fayetteville Observer*.

That the carrying of the State for McKinley in 1900 was the governing factor in all last year's performances—from the rejection of co-operation to the superhuman efforts to justify that rejection by seeking and securing the aid of the McKinley Railroads in carrying the State election and by the employment of open fraud and intimidation, aided and abetted as the latter were by the Washington Post and many other Republican and goldboy papers—I have never entertained a moment's doubt. Tillman, when here last fall, declared that the chief obstacle to co-operation had been the ambition of the senatorial aspirants for Butler's place in 1901. No doubt that played a part.

When it was supposed that the vote on negro disfranchisement might be taken this year, so that a purged and therefore free electorate could tackle the Bryan versus McKinley issue in 1900, the machine (including), I was sorry to see, the News and Observer as well as Olds and the rest decried my urgent demand (issued immediately after the election) that the mandate of the white victory be recognized by the disfranchisement of the negro. They described it—some by headlines, some by direct affirmation as a Republican and a Populist demand. In the midst of this, when I was standing practically alone, Jarvis discovered that the Constitution prevented an election on the question of amending it in an off-year. Instantly, the machine faced about; and they have since out-Heroded me as an advocate of negro disfranchisement. My interence is that they perceived the opportunity which this soul-tearing issue presented for degrading—or at least for complicating—the Bryan issue in 1900.

Now, unless the present Bryan wave becomes so pronounced that a renewal of the old-time requirement may be secured at the hands of the State committee—viz: that only those be admitted to the primaries who agree to support the National as well as the State tickets—we will have no showing at all in the State Convention.

After the election returns of 1896 revealed the continued existence of the usual majority of 20,000 *whenever* the Democrats of Vance's time chose to unite, there arose again an opportunity to recover the Populists by holding out a hand to them. The committee's resolution to that effect (introduced by Winston) was supplemented by an amendment to the plan of organization (by H. L. Stevens) inviting all whites into our primaries. This proved to be our undoing; for at once, and as if in obedience to a common direction, nearly all the papers in the State (including the

News & Observer) commenced to assail Butler and the Populists. And they did so in such vile terms that all chance of enticing them out of their organization into our primaries was destroyed. As soon as this was accomplished, the machine employed that originally well meant invitation to cover the introduction of Republicans and other goldboys into our Conventions. Instead, therefore, of a co-operation of Bryanites, we have a fusion of Republicans, Clevelandites and Democrats, all training under the banner of Democracy. The point is, how can we reverse this state of affairs so as to be prepared for the inevitable bolt of the Republicans and Clevelandites when Democratic issues are at stake.

I am so cut off from the opportunity of observing political movements which those at the capital enjoy, that I can at best work out but an imperfect conception of the situation by the intense study which I devote to the country press. I would be very glad indeed if you could enlighten me as to the drift, as seen from your commanding position.

CLARK TO A. W. GRAHAM

Raleigh, N.C.
10 July 1899

. . . A large turn out down at Morehead *—175 lawyers, including nearly every R.R. lawyer in the State. My presence had its deterrent effect—I was not expected. You probably saw Price's † speech & mine, in yesterday's *Post*—if not, some friend probably has the paper.

Price went down the day before I did, and on the cars, told some gentlemen "The Supreme Court must be reformed and it can best be done through the Bar Association. *"Our people"* will not invest their money down here unless the Court is more satisfactory to them, they can not *risk* their properties, especially we must get rid of that man Clark." He probably had a drink but he expressed the real animus of that crowd, who hope to do through the Bar Ass[n] what they fear a Convention of the People would not do. Say little about this except where you know your man. I will see Gov. about Directorship. He readily appointed you two years ago at my instance, but I think he is now absolutely in Andrews' keeping. They say so here.

It would be well to have Benehan ‡ refresh his memory.

* Annual meeting of the State Bar Association.
† Charles Price.
‡ Benehan Cameron.

TO CLARK FROM CHARLES D. MC IVER

Greensboro, N. C.
August 4, 1899

...I am organizing an Alumnae association with branches in every county, which I hope will accomplish the purpose which you suggest.

If a woman cannot be a "Notary Public", as was decided in Governor Carr's administration, I doubt whether she can hold office in a Board of Trustees. However, I shall hope to talk to you about this matter when I have an opportunity to see you again.

It seems that Dr. Winston * is taking hold of matters, and is fulfilling the expectations of his friends and some of his enemies. I think that those who are responsible for his coming back to the state have done the state a service.

By the way, would you consider a proposition to take charge of the Law School at the University?

I was discussing the possibility of your going there to one or two of the members of the Board of Trustees, and one of them in particular expressed his anxiety to have the place offered to you, if you could afford to accept it....

P. S. Bailey seems to take it pretty hard.

TO CLARK FROM O. B. EATON †

Winston, N. C.
Aug. 17, 1899

I am one of the "Forgotten Men" whom you represented before the Convention of Railroad Commissioners at Denver Col.,‡ and wish to thank you for the very able manner in which you presented our cause. I, like millions of others, feel gratified to you for championing the side of the man who "pays the freight". I trust that the influence for right and for justice that you are setting in motion will stir the people so that their great government will see what the awakening portendeth and right the wrong of the "Forgotten Man".

I have not forgotten the noble stand you made some months

* George T. Winston, President of the University of North Carolina.
† Mayor of Winston.
‡ This refers to address of Clark to the National Convention of Railroad Commissioners at Denver, Colorado, August 10, 1899. Reprinted below, pp. 470 ff.

ago in the interest of Education and Methodism in N. C. and I hope it will bring a rich reward.

TO CLARK FROM CLYDE R. HOEY *

Chapel Hill, N. C.
Sept. 4, 1899

What the extraordinary remedies in a civil action are in N. C. is a mooted question with the law class and some of us have agreed upon a "coment reference" and you are requested to give us what you regard as the extraordinary remedies as contradistinguished from the provisional remedies enumerated in the code.

I have been spending the summer here at the law school. The course is quite comprehensive and the examinations are particularly rigid, but I have passed all examinations in both classes so far, and the course is now nearing the end. If there is any branch of the law upon which one should be *especially* well prepared preparatory to standing the Supreme Court examination this month, I should appreciate the suggestion....

TO CLARK FROM ALFRED MOORE WADDELL

Wilmington, N. C.
Sept. 12, 1899

Since writing to you (at the Mayor's office where I was very busy) I had an interview with Maj. Duffy † of the *Star* about the subject of our correspondence, and he, after reminding me that he had written several articles in favor of Primaries, &c &c, said he would soon take up the subject as referred to in the article of the *Patron & Gleaner*. I am sorry to say that Kingsbury ‡ is offended (as I am informed) because of the undue credit given to me for the Nov. Revolution when really *he* was the man who brought about the revolution! His "bosses" of the *Messenger* have never said one kind word of the present City gov't, and are owned by the W. & W. R. R. Co. (or by Walters) § and I wouldn't speak to them about anything political.

Kingsbury, in today's issue, sneers at the "self-sacrificing" candidate for U. S. Senator, numbering me among them and says my

* Native of Shelby; Governor of North Carolina, 1937-1941; now United States Senator.

† Editor of the Wilmington *Star*.

‡ Theodore B. Kingsbury, editor of the Wilmington *Messenger*.

§ Harry Walters, president of the Wilmington and Weldon Railroad.

name is mentioned for both Senator and Govr. but that he supposes I would "hardly run for both offices".

You need expect nothing from the *Messenger* until after others have settled matters.

I believe we can lick out "the machine" if we organize and stand up to the rack.

Kingsbury seems to favor Carr * for Senator, but he is not allowed to write all he would like to say. The paper is a temporizer with a collar on.

I am determined to fight "the machine" with all my power.

Of course you know that June Davis, Rountree,† and the gold bugs here, are against you for anything, as they are against me. The two named above voted for Frank Stedman for Mayor against me! They are W.&W. R. R. attorneys and will of course support Simmons for Senator, if the Atlantic Coast Line requires it.

TO CLARK FROM W. S. PEARSON ‡

Morganton, N. C.
Sept. 14th, 1899

. . . To be wholly frank with you we can not elect the Senator unless we get control of the party machinery at the Spring Convention and no stone should be left unturned to accomplish that by careful selection of county delegations.

If we win nationally, as there is a chance to do with restored harmony, the Committee becomes of first importance to the office seeking class, who will have great weight with the Legislature.

If we lose, the gold bug element will feel that their policy has the future with it and will give free reign to the corporations, in which event the Committee, held by us, would be the sole "break" left.

Selfishness enters so largely into all plans looking to the accomplishment of the platform pledges that one becomes disheartened with his co-workers. I was about to give names but I forbear.

I have the very highest regard not only for your patriotism, (since Vance's death I know no other man, who is even charged with having much of that virtue) but for your judgment as to the probable movements of the parties here and hence with diffidence submit views not wholly in accord with yours, and differing only in the ways and means tending to a common purpose. With the

* Julian S. Carr of Durham.
† George Rountree of New Hanover County; later Superior Court Judge.
‡ Editor of the Morganton *Herald*.

notion of dividing the forces I said what I did of Carr and frankly asked him the question if he intended being a candidate, receiving an evasive reply, though I am on close terms with him.

The feeling is quite strong among Western lawyers against the Simmons-Aycock, Connor-Allen * Combination pronouncing it hoggish and I see the Tarboro Southerner would have Gen. Cox † in the race—at least I infer as much. Frank Osborne ‡ and Mike Justice § have a combination on private account, which is the only movement I know of in the West that has any even the least adhesiveness.

I hear within the past few hours of Theo. Davidson's || ambition for Governor and that it is being quietly but well worked in the extreme West. If Aycock is nominated for Governor I regard it as a death blow to Simmons' hope for the Senate and S. is unquestionably the choice of the Railroads. Unless you yourself will agree to oppose him he will in my opinion have a walk over in the event of a Western Man being nominated for Governor. The fact is we have no man in the West fit for Governor so far as my acquaintance extends and whether Aycock is or not I am not prepared to say. He made a most favorably impression here in 1898 upon both Populists and Democrats, Corporation attorney as he is, and owns to being.

I have an ambition to be on the State ticket myself and am promised the 8th Dist solid by its leading men. Frankly I care nothing for the Auditorship the only place not pre-empted, but its associations with an Executive that would do right gives it some weight in a council of State and therein I might be of some use to N. C. and my children.

TO CLARK FROM EDWARD A. MOSELEY ¶

Washington, D. C.
September 16, 1899

... I am obliged for your favor and the accompanying copy of your address at Denver. I have since received several papers containing a copy of the address.

* William R. Allen of Wayne County, Superior Court Judge, 1894-1895, 1903-1910; Associate Justice of North Carolina Supreme Court, 1911—.

† William R. Cox of Wake County, Representative in Congress, 1881-1887.

‡ State senator from Mecklenburg County, Attorney General, 1893-1897.

§ Michael Justice of Rutherford County, Superior Court Judge.

|| Theodore F. Davidson of Buncombe County, member of General Assembly, 1879-1881, 1903; Attorney General, 1885-1893.

¶ Secretary of the Interstate Commerce Commission.

It is with no spirit of criticism, but on the contrary with the greatest diffidence and only at your earnest request that I venture to point out what I am sure you have already noted in your introduction to the discussion of passenger rates, and that is the comparison which you institute with freight rates.

It is unfair as a statement, not more to the roads than yourself and is the only jar I could detect in your splendid paper, which was a credit to you and a treat to the Convention, and I renew my congratulations, for it reads well in type, which all papers do not. But passenger transportation in speed, appointments, regularity, train service, terminal expenses and accomodations is so far removed from freight carriage as to make a reference to the weight of the average passenger as an element in the value of service in the nature of an absurdity.

In freight hauling the dead weight of car may be less than pound for pound, while the passenger train with baggage, dining, and sleeping car may be thousands for each passenger carried. My suggestion goes no further than the omission of the weight, which to my mind weaken your very clear and able argument.

It might be suggested that the criticism on reduced rates accorded Ministers of religion, may be regarded from some quarters as inexpedient. In all trade relations with those whose livelihood depends on the free will offering of those religiously inclined, a concession from the commercial price is universally conceded. But reference to this, dear Judge, is only a question of policy and whether you should eliminate this from your speech is purely one of which you are the best judge. . . .

TO CLARK FROM R. A. SANKEY *

Wichita, Kansas.
September 30th, 1899.

I write to thank you for the copy of your address delivered at Denver at the meeting of the Railroad Commissioners.

I have read the address with a great deal of interest and pleasure. It seems to me it strikes the key note of the situation. The difficulties, however, in the way of a satisfactory adjustment of freight rates under existing conditions seem to me insurmountable. There is so much capital involved and which is so easy of concentration, that it can always bring pressure enough to bear

* Member of law firm of Sankey and Campbell.

upon the legislators to prevent legislation. This is especially true in the Federal legislation.

The people who support the railroads and pay the excessive tolls levied are so widely scattered, their interests so disunited and they are so easily led off by partisan cries that at present it seems impossible to unite them, or to make any determined and successful resistance to the constant aggressions of organized capital. I am, however, very glad to have such men as yourself present the matter so ably and forcibly to the public.

TO CLARK FROM JOHN E. WOODARD *

Wilson, N. C.
Nov. 22nd. 1899

Permit me to say to you that I have been highly edified and instructed by a careful perusal of your masterly dissenting opinion in Abbott vs. Beddingfield. It is as refreshing, as it is rare, to find, in these corrupt days, a Judge with the courage, as well as the ability, to declare from principle, and the reason of the thing, unterrified by the "antiquated precedents", persistently flaunted in his face, the rights of the sovereign people, as declared by their Representatives. Your premises are well supported by the authorities cited, and your conclusions seem to me to be absolutely unanswerable. If, as is reported, Judge Ruffin said, after delivery of the dissenting opinion, in Spruill vs. Leary, 13 Ire., he was unworthy longer to sit as Chief Justice, while Pearson was a member of the same court, the same degree of candor would leave no room for doubt, as to who, by reason of his learning, ability, and courage, was preeminently entitled to preside over our present Court.

TO CLARK FROM FRANK S. SPRUILL †

Louisburg, N. C.
November 23, 1899

Letters of congratulation are not very much in my line, but I must indulge my wish to congratulate you on your dissenting opinion in Abbot v. Beddingfield. Outside and beyond the scholarly training and attainments discovered in the opinion, there is a breadth and sweep to it that are delightful exceptions to a great deal of our modern judicial literature. So far as the

* Lawyer and former member of the General Assembly.
† Lawyer.

argument is concerned, I apprehend that there is no division of sentiment amoung the lawyers of the State as to where the weight of it lay. It isn't for having the best side I am congratulating you; it is for your masterly presentation of that side. This dissenting opinion must, in time, and will, become the law of N. C.

TO CLARK FROM LOCKE CRAIG *

Asheville, N.C.
November 23rd 1899

As a citizen of North Carolina I wish to thank you for your dissenting opinion in Abbott v. Beddingfield. It is a powerful stand for democratic representative government and must have a telling influence on this eventful period of our history. In my humble judgment it is the finest opinion that has emanated from the bench of North Carolina.

TO CLARK FROM CHARLES B. AYCOCK †

Goldsboro, N. C.
December 4, 1899

I am in receipt of your favor of the 28th ult. I have written Mr. Small,‡ congressman from the 1st District to procure for me, if possible the work which I desire. I am indebted to you for your kindness in this matter.

I am afraid from talk among the brethren of the Bar that your dissenting opinion in the Railroad corporation case will be taken to be an attack upon the right of the Court to declare any act of the Legislature unconstitutional. Our Court has gone so far and seems so ready to declare any and all acts unconstitutional that a dissent in a particular case is likely to be drawn pretty strongly, but it would be a dangerous doctrine to engraft into our law that the Court cannot declare any act unconstitutional. The people may always be trusted in the long run but there comes times of passion to us all and even the wisest men need the restraint of constitution. This feeling is so strong that I am apprehensive that your dissenting opinion may cause fear in the State and redound to your injury and to the injury of that which we both love. I

* Member of the General Assembly, 1899-1901; Governor of North Carolina, 1913-1917.

† Governor, 1901-1905.

‡ Representative in Congress, Dec. 4, 1899-1921.

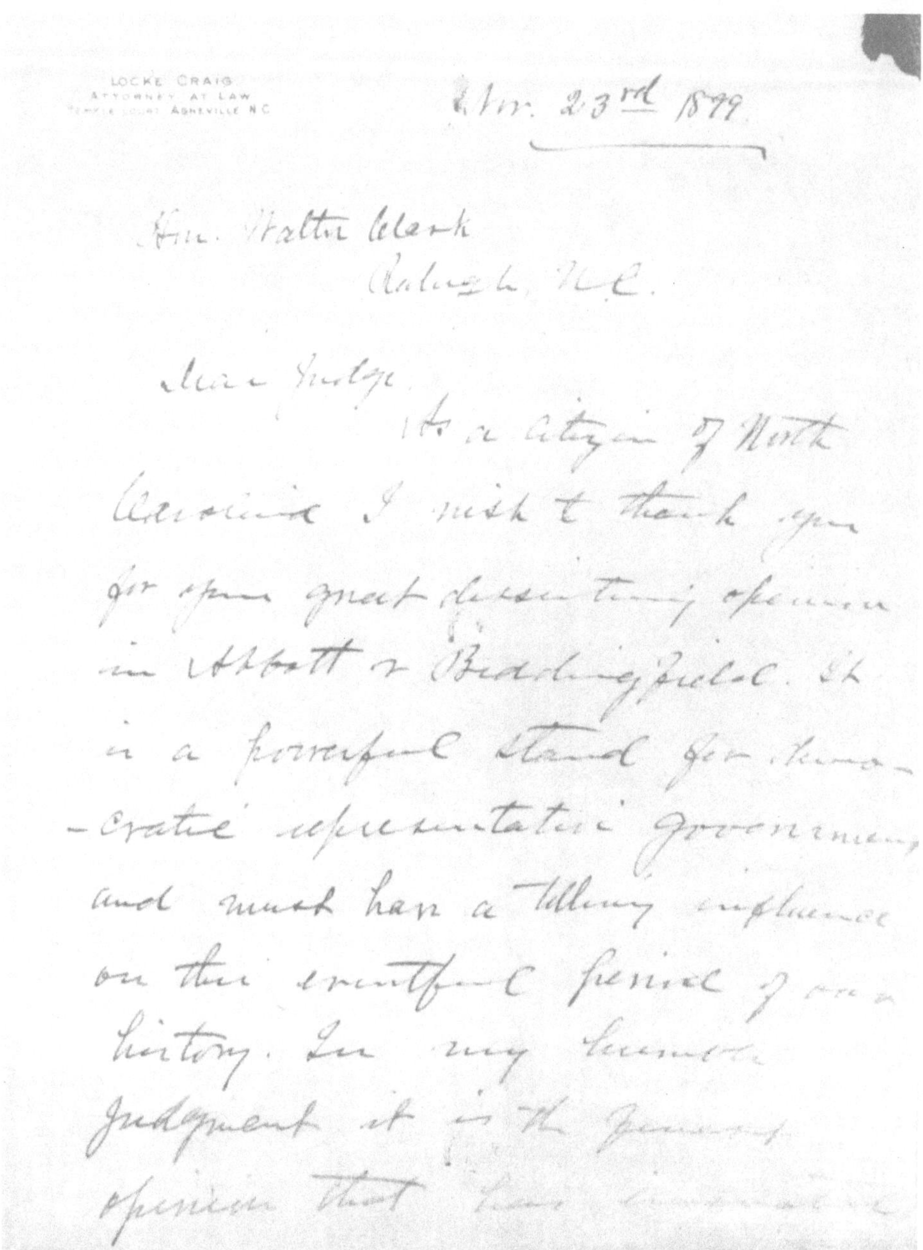

LOCKE CRAIG
ATTORNEY AT LAW
TEMPLE COURT ASHEVILLE N.C.

Nov. 23rd 1899

Hon. Walter Clark
Raleigh, N.C.

Dear Judge,

As a citizen of North Carolina I wish to thank you for your great dissenting opinion in Abbott v Beddingfield. It is a powerful stand for democratic representative government, and must have a telling influence on this eventful period of our history. In my humble judgment it is the greatest opinion that has [illegible]

One of the many letters received by Judge Clark congratulating him on his dissenting opinion in the case of *Abbott* vs. *Beddingfield,* a reversal of the decision in the celebrated case of *Hoke* vs. *Henderson*. Locke Craig was later Governor of North Carolina.

From the bench of North Carolina.
With kindest regards,

Sincerely

[illegible]

hope you will pardon me for making this suggestion and that you will believe that I have no further purpose in making it than the good of our commonwealth.

CLARK TO MARION BUTLER

Raleigh, N.C.
13 Dec. 1899

I am glad to see you have again introduced your Bill for Postal Savings Bank & purchase of Postal cars. The progress of measures for the interest of the people is slow in these days when combinations of capital control, but eventually the fetters that now bind us will be broken, and your attitude in these matters will be remembered to your lasting honor. I hope you will press to a vote this session your bills for election of Senators by the People and for a Postal Telegraph. The Govt. cables to Philipines & Hawaii, & possibly to Porto Rico, will open the way for Postal Telegraphy.

I regret that our court held to the antiquated & untenable doctrine that *public office is a private contract*—a doctrine in which they stand alone against the civilized world. If they had had any consideration to parity advantages (with which some have inconsiderately charged them) a shrewd consideration would have shown them that for a temporary benefit, future opportunity was sacrificed—for as the political opponents of a majority of the court are in power, the late decisions give them the legal right to fill every office for 8 years, or longer, or for life and as long the *duties* of those offices remain in any shape or mode to be discharged, the change of political supremacy at the ballot box can not change the *administrative* officials. I think the court was simply "chained to the past" by an ultra-conservative, natural in the two oldest members of the court, whom the other two followed.

CLARK TO MARION BUTLER

Raleigh, N.C.
18 Dec. 1899

. . . If you will read the decisions referred to "Wood v. Bellamy" is *no authority* for the "Day" case, nor for "Abbott v. Beddingfield." Wood v. Bellamy was a mild form of Hoke v. Henderson, in fact did not go as far, for it merely held that the new act merely changing titles of officers would not oust them, it was merely "same old horse under a new blanket." In fact the legislative act itself declared it was only an amendment. In Day's case the legislature declared an abolition, & prescribed new officers with new duties. The court for *the first time* in its history declared if duties survived, in any shape, the office survived—which is equivalent to saying no necessary office can be abolished, & hence the incumbent must stay as long as his original term was limited. "Abbott v. Beddingfield" went still further and held the old incumbent was entitled to discharge the additional duties and received additional pay of new office altho no legislation gave them to him.

The cases really in point are not Wood v. Bellamy but "Ewart v. Jones 116 N.C. 570" by Faircloth C.J. which held that a change in Criminal Court which was less than the change made in Day's case put Jones out & Ewart in—and Ward v. Elizabeth City 121 N.C. which held that a new charter adding a few acres of land authorised outting Ward, City Atty, out & new incumbent in. The court has *gone back* on these two direct precedents—and have gone miles beyond what was dreamed of in Hoke v. Henderson—which itself (as you well say) is bad law.

Some day when you sit down to read the late decisions, *as a lawyer,* you will be astonished & surprised.

Nor would my dissent in Abbott's case justify Simonton's judgment as to taxing power of Commission, as I should in my recent opinion (speaking for the court) that the Southern R.R. was liable for issuing a free pass, *equally* whether the majority, or the dissenting opinion in Abbott v. Beddingfield was the law.

These late decisions can not stand. If they could, then popular govt. is at an end, for the Corporations have only to secure 3 judges of this Court to be "the State." They are worse in principle, than the "Income Tax Cases."

TO CLARK FROM F. L. RILEY *

University, Miss.
December 23, 1899

Please let me know the amount of money your State has expended for collecting, preserving, and publishing the facts pertaining to her history. I am preparing a Memorial to be presented by the Historical Society of Mississippi to the Legislature of our State in which we shall ask for an appropriation for the historical

* Professor of History at the University of Mississippi and Secretary of the Mississippi Historical Society.

work that needs to be done in our midst. I desire to cite the worthy example of your State as one that has provided for the perpetuation of her history.

Please give me as accurately as possible: (1) The amount that has been expended by North Carolina in the last year (2) The total amount that has been expended on her history from the first appropriation to the present time.

TO CLARK FROM WILLIAM JENNINGS BRYAN *

Austin, Texas, Dec.30,1899

Your favor of July 19th has just come to light from my accumulated mail as I was too busy during the summer to look at my letters and since the election I have been resting.

Am obliged to you for the report of the situation there, and fully agree with you as to the election of U.S. Judges by the people, and advocated it in several lectures that I delivered prior to the last National Convention. We had so much in the last platform, that I have been kept busy defending what we had without adding anything new.

Reforms are secured one at a time. I believe that the election of Senators is ripe now. I note what you say in regard to the Philippine question. Ever since the subject has been before the public I have done what I could to call attention to the dangerous principle involved. I do not believe that the people would be willing to admit the Philippine Islands with the idea of allowing their people to become full fledged citizens. The McEnery Resolution † expressly negatived that. The only other alternative is for us to govern them as subjects. We cannot do this without placing ourselves upon European ground and denying that the people are the source of government. Our plutocratic class already despise the plain people. What shall be our fate if the plain people themselves surrender the doctrine of self-government?

Upon what ground except that of brute force can we then rest our arguments? In my judgment Hoar ‡ did not state it too strongly when he said that it would be the beginning of the end of the republic.

* Democratic candidate for President of the United States, 1896, 1900, 1908.

† A resolution, introduced by Senator Samuel Douglas McEnery of Louisiana, declaring that the provisions of the Treaty of Paris of 1898 need not necessarily determine the future policy of the United States regarding the Philippine Islands.

‡ Rockwood Hoar, United States Senator from Massachusetts, 1877-1904.

I believe that the party must hold all the ground that it took in '96 and then go forward to meet the new questions.

TO CLARK FROM THOMAS R. ROULHAC *

Sheffield, Ala.
January 12th, 1900

... I have had the purpose of writing you ever since I received the copy of your address to the railroad commissioners, and thanking you for it. I have always been the most conservative of men, in respect to changes in the policies of our government, and especially in regard to those, which would involve it in undertakings, which we have been accustomed to consider as properly belonging to private enterprise. I see many good reasons for adhering to that principle; but I must admit, that your address made a profound impression on my mind, if it did not entirely convert me. I see a huge and threatening danger-cloud in front of this country, in the strength and extent of corporate power; and there could be less injustice, and less wrong, or bad policy, it may be, in the government's regaining functions, which are derived from the sovereign power, than there would be in its entering upon business which sprung from no such source, or depriving, or in competing with, individuals in undertakings not begotten or protected by chartered powers. Still, I fear that our form of government does not admit of such a civil service, as would keep railroad and telegraph operations out of the baneful influence of partisan politics; and if it does not, what a fulcrum and lever of unrepublican institutions and administration such an enhanced patronage would confer. I would prefer to confine the Federal Government to three things: maintaining our relations with other countries, including its defense of course; furnishing money of the highest value and a public credit of the highest order; and a judicial authority, to settle controversies between the different states and the citizens of different states. Byond this, I am, in all respect, a home ruler. Yet we have been reckless, in bestowing corporate powers; and, I fear, we will be driven to exert some power and compulsion to regain, and certainly to restrain, much of what we have is heedlessly parted with. If so, the highways and postal intercommunication more nearly belong, in strictness, to governmental functions, and a better operation and administration would more greatly contribute to the interests of the public.

* Lawyer, former schoolmate of Clark at Hillsboro Military Academy.

TO CLARK FROM E. J. HALE

Fayetteville, N. C.
Jan. 18, 1900

... I agree with you entirely that it is our bounden duty to be charitable. The circumstances force me to say that I so behaved towards Mr. Daniels in 1893. Without the slightest provocation, when I was defending Vance from the assaults of Caldwell,* Ransom,† (via Harris), Olds,‡ &c., he made an outrageous attack on me in his paper. I received a letter from Raleigh informing me of the circumstances of his fathers death, and saying that I could demolish him by publishing them in my reply. Instantly, I dropped all controversy with him and turned my attention to Simmons & the others.

Of course, I have not alluded to his misfortune as coming from you, or, indeed, from any one, or at all. I have frequently heard it, especially in Raleigh when he was opposing the carrying out of the Cumberland Democratic pledges to the liquor men.

As to his suffering from his political course, we all suffer from that, and, I think, I do & have far more than he. But I cannot be blind to the fact that we all in North Carolina seem to be in an inextricable bag because of his course at and before the State Convention in '98. When he was standing in with Caldwell against co-operation as urged by National headquarters, Jones was forced to make me his agent here, (I did not seek it.) Daniels was re-instated upon the understanding that he would advocate the party policy. The caucus of the regular Democrats, at the State convention, of which caucus he was a member, adopted my resolution declaring adhesion to the national Democracy. When the getting of the resolution before the convention by the "first intention", failed, Daniels sent to me, asked for my resolution and assured me that he would introduce it as a minority report of the platform committee. That threw me off. The result is that the old Ransom machine is re-instated in power more secure than ever.

I think, under the circumstances, that I have exercised great forbearance toward him; for, notwithstanding what I have suffered at his hands, I have, over and over, put myself out with Furman (who is, personally, very friendly, and often makes overtures to me in his paper) in order to avoid giving aid & comfort

* J. P. Caldwell, Editor of the *Charlotte Observer*.
† United States Senator Matt W. Ransom.
‡ Colonel Fred A. Olds of Raleigh.

to Daniels enemies. But we shall never get straight in this State as long as our organ at the capital pursues it half-hearted course. As I told Daniels at Washington in '98, if he would only fight straight I would make it my business to work up all the support I could for him. And I am always ready to co-operate with him, if he will let me; but there seems to be always some *impasse*.

TO CLARK FROM THOMAS M. PITTMAN*

Henderson, N. C.
March 7, 1900

I used to think you a little too advanced on public questions. I am not sure whether you are growing more conservative or I more radical, but your address before the R. R. Commissioners struck me exactly in the right place. Nearly all the prominent movements of the present day seem to me subversive of Democracy. Your argument in behalf of the people is powerful and just. I shall preserve it permanently.

TO CLARK FROM RISDEN T. BENNETT †

Wadesboro, N. C.
March 16, 1900

Tell me the name of the case where you have criticised the custom on the part of clerks of the Superior Courts in appointing themselves commissioners to sell land ordered by such clerks to be sold in cases pending before them.

In McLean vs. Patterson 84, N. C. and in a case in 102 the practice was upheld....

CLARK TO MARION BUTLER

Raleigh, N.C.
20 Mar 1900

The Republican National platform 4 years ago demanded & promised 1 cent letter postage. They have taken no steps to redeem that pledge. With reform as to postal cars and in railroad rates to Government, it is possible. *One cent* letter postage is of no consequence to the idle rich but it is to all business men and to the masses.

* Lawyer.
† Wadesboro attorney and former Superior Court Judge.

Why not make that amendment, and speak to it, in giving point to your advocacy of above reforms?

CLARK TO A. W. GRAHAM

Raleigh, N.C.
30 April 1900

I hope you can get the same amendment to the libel law, as has been made to recovery for "personal injuries resulting in death." There is the same reason for it and if you can get to a jury your share in the recovery will probably pay for your trouble in getting the amendment passed—which (will) not be great unless Duke learns of your purpose to get it passed. Kilgo's "article" in "Trinity Archive" * for March is being distributed in pamphlet form & doubtless any friend in Durham could get you a copy—or you could get some friend in Oxford to write to Kilgo for a copy.

Webster † has raked him editorially since I wrote you. No other paper, however, has done so, so far as I know.

You certainly ought to come to State Senate this fall.‡ The RRs are trying to pack this legislature, *especially the Senate* and if you are here you can prevent much deviltry—especially the intended emasculation of the R.R. Commission Act and the repeal of the law forbidding free passes. This latter law, though imperfectly enforced, alone, "smashed the slate" at the last convention.

Joe Daniels recently said to a friend that he could easily get Aycock nominated for Vice President but for his fight for White Supremacy. He was asked why he did not get me nominated. He said Possibly I might be—but my *Confederate* record was in the way.... But you can tell when you get to Kansas City whether it is worth while to bring the matter forward. Daniels himself told me that Mr. Bryan said, while here, that it would be very agreeable to him [if] I were put on the ticket.

TO CLARK FROM CHARLES F. WARREN §

Washington, N. C.
May 2 1900

... I know you have given much thought to the subject of legal education and the standard of admission and I would be glad to

* Literary magazine of Trinity College.

† John R. Webster of Reidsville, Editor of *Webster's Weekly*.

‡ Graham was a member of the General Assembly, 1901-1905, and again in 1909 and 1913.

§ Lawyer and former member of the General Assembly.

have your views, generally and especially as applied to present conditions in the State. Let me hear from you by Saturdays mail if possible.

The written examination was a step and a long one, but only a step toward the desired end.

It seems to me also that the Association might well take some action upon the subject of legal ethics in the beginning of its career.

Every bar is cursed with some Shyster. I know codes and rules of ethics are largely empty sentences unless there is a vigorous sentiment in the association behind them.

I would like to hear from you upon that topic also.

It seems to me that there must have been something radically wrong in conditions in this State before the adoption of the written rule when classes numbering fifty-five could pass as a whole.

In the four terms preceeding the written rule 195 passed and 23 were rejected. In the four terms since the rule has been in effect 122 have passed and 90 failed. That is of course better. Any observant man can see that it has been made too easy to enter the bar, easier than in any other profession in this State, and as a result the bar has suffered and in many instances caught what the other professions would have refused.

. . . What is the number of lawyers in the State in active practice? With over 300 admissions in the last four years, the number is far beyond what I had thought. . . .

TO CLARK FROM ROBERT M. DOUGLAS *

Greensboro, N. C.
July 31, 1900

Judge Cobb of Georgia has written to me asking the name and whereabouts of the case in which we sustained the validity of compulsary vaccination ordinances. I cannot remember the name, nor can I find the case in any of the numbers of the Southeastern that I have here.

I wish you would tell Mr. Bradley where to find it, and ask him to send me the Southeastern containing the case.

If he cannot find it in my room, ask him to send me the court Copy and I will return it. Excuse my troubling you, but you remember everything.

* Associate Justice of the North Carolina Supreme Court, 1897-1905.

TO CLARK FROM J. BRYAN GRIMES *

Grimesland, N. C.
September 26, 1900

There will be a meeting of the N. C. Tobacco Growers in Raleigh Oct. 24th.

Knowing your sympathies are with the people in every movement looking to the betterment of their condition. I have the honor to invite you to address this association along such lines as seem to you most pertinent to our interests.

I hope you can do us this favor as your counsel will be valuable.

TO CLARK FROM CHARLES B. AYCOCK †

Goldsboro, N.C.
October 22, 1900

I am in receipt of your kind favor of the 20th. I shall carefully re-read the White case and particularly your dissenting opinion in the 126th. It has been my intention to devote the most of my Inaugural Address to the subject of education and the change in the election law. My idea is that we have promised, and must fulfill it, to educate the children in the State and certainly we have reached the time when our duty demands that we shall have an election law so fair that the opposition party will admit its fairness. With the elimination of the negro we ought to have a greater freedom of opinion in the State and that opinion ought to be given adequate and exact expression at the polls. I will thank you for any further suggestions which you may wish to make me concerning my Inaugural Address. I believe it is not expected that I should send a message to the Legislature as this is done by the outgoing Governor. As to the Chief Justiceship there are many friends of yours who are likewise friends of Judge Shepherd and they are going to find themselves much embarrassed by the situation. I am impressed by the strong way in which you state the precedents which have heretofore been followed. This view of the matter had not presented itself to me before. I will talk with you about this matter when I come to Raleigh. Please do me the kindness to make as many and full suggestions of what I shall say to the Legislature as you can with your many duties.

* President of the North Carolina Tobacco Grower's Association; Secretary of State, 1901-1923.

† Governor, 1901-1905.

AYCOCK & DANIELS,
ATTORNEYS AND COUNSELLORS AT LAW
EAST WALNUT STREET,
GOLDSBORO, N. C.

Oct. 22, 1900.

Hon. Walter Clark,

Raleigh, N. C.

My dear Judge:-

I am in receipt of your kind favor of the 20th. I shall carefully re-read the White case and particularly your dissenting opinion in the 125th. It has been my intention to devote the most of my Inaugural Address to the subject of education and the change in the election law. My idea is that we have promised, and must fulfil it, to educate the children in the State and certainly we have reached the time when our duty demands that we shall have an election law so fair that the opposition party will admit its fairness. With the elimination of the negro we ought to have a greater freedom of opinion in the State and that opinion ought to be given adequate and exact expression at the polls. I will thank you for any further suggestions which you may wish to make to me concerning my Inaugural Address. I believe it is not expected that I should send a message to the Legislature as this is done by the outgoing Governor. As to the Chief Justiceship there are many friends of yours who are likewise friends of Judge Shepard and they are going to find themselves much embarrased by the situation. I am impressed by the strong way in which you state the precedents which have heretofore been followed. This view of the matter had not presented itself to me before. I will talk with you about this matter when I come to Raleigh. Please do me the kindness to make as many and full suggestions of what I shall say to the Legislature as you cam with your many duties.

With best wishes, I am,

Very truly yours,

C. B. Aycock.

Facsimile of a letter in which Governor-elect Aycock asks Judge Clark's advice in the preparation of his inaugural address.

VII

The Clark-Kilgo Controversy

1897-1898

THERE IS NO OTHER ENGAGEMENT IN Clark's long career which so completely reveals his convictions and courage and so thoroughly shows his determination to fight the evil influences of corporate wealth than his famous controversy with John C. Kilgo, President of Trinity College.

In 1889 Clark had been appointed to the Board of Trustees of Trinity and he had been on the committee which brought about the transfer of that institution to Durham. In June, 1894, Dr. Crowell, the retiring president, wrote Clark asking for permission to submit his name for consideration for the presidency of the college. Clark expressed appreciation of the compliment but declined to permit his name to be used. John C. Kilgo, of South Carolina, was elected president, and Clark gave his enthusiastic approval. At the inaugural exercises he declared Kilgo an equal to any former president of Trinity College.

It was not long, however, until Clark became skeptical of Kilgo's political views and educational policies. He thought Kilgo was "making himself an apostle of money and the detractor of all who dared to disagree with him." Many North Carolina newspapers took a similar view. The Kinston *Free Press* said, "It would be better for North Carolina, for Christianity, and for Trinity College, in the long run, if a different sort of man was at the head of the leadership of the leading Methodist school in North Carolina, even though the school was less prosperous from a worldly point of view," and the Raleigh *News and Observer* reported Kilgo as saying: "I am bigger than North Carolina."

Clark had denounced trusts time and again, while Kilgo had said, "Trusts and monopolies are not the awful curse of society that we are led to believe by demagogs. Great wealth can and does make happiness." Utterances of this kind were too much for Clark. Yet Dr. Paul Garber, in his *John Carlisle Kilgo,* says that "Clark challenged the right of Kilgo as president of Trinity College to express views on issues if they were contrary to the public opinion of the state. He could not accept the idea that any educational institution should present opinions that were contrary to those commonly accepted." Garber seems to infer that Kilgo was a liberal, Clark a conservative or reactionary. This is somewhat amazing, since Clark was probably the most outspoken man in North Carolina or the South in advocating economic and social reforms, many of which were so radical for that day that he was denounced by some people as a socialist and even a communist.

The famous Clark-Kilgo controversy began in June, 1897, when Kilgo recommended that the Board of Trustees change the policy of electing faculty members for one year and elect them for a term of four years or longer. This proposal was referred to a committee of which Clark was chairman and it received an adverse report.

Shortly after this meeting, Kilgo wrote Clark that he had heard Clark had said that this proposal was "really an effort on my own part to secure the presidency of Trinity College for a longer term." Further correspondence between Clark and Kilgo and between Clark and James H. Southgate, President of the Board of Trustees, ensued. Some of this correspondence has been reprinted by Garber and also by A. L. Brooks, in his *Walter Clark, Fighting Judge*. The editors have attempted to go beyond either of these books and reprint all of the Clark-Kilgo-Southgate letters, as well as a number of the hundreds of letters in the Clark Papers pertaining to this controversy.

The Clark-Kilgo controversy became a kind of free-for-all, and many prominent North Carolinians engaged in it—openly or under cover. On July 16, 1897, J. W. Bailey wrote Kilgo that Clark "carries a knife under his shirt for you.... If he shows his hand I will drive him back; else he isn't the demagog he is said by some to be." Josephus Daniels defended Clark and denounced the "tobacco trust." In his recently published *Editor in Politics,* he says: "At that time Bailey and Kilgo were singing a duet of adoration of trusts when not opposing decent appropriations to the University and other state educational institutions."

The story of Clark's resignation from the Board of Trustees, the exoneration of Kilgo by the Board, the newspaper accounts of the controversy, and the story of the Kilgo-Gattis trials may be found in the biographies by Garber and Brooks mentioned above—but from very different points of view.

Clark realized that he was waging a hard battle, and he wrote a friend that he "had rather fight a dog with a spade than an unprincipled preacher-demagog." In his last letter to Southgate, he really "opened up" on Kilgo, the Dukes, the tobacco trust, and corporate wealth in general. He declared that "Kilgo is the only man who can get big donations from the cigarette trust, that he is the only man who can 'milk the cow' . . . and that I ought to have said nothing to irritate the feelings of this artist in milking, whose touch is so soothing and irresistible and whose services are so indispensable."

Following his "defeat" and Kilgo's "vindication," Clark received hundreds of letters, many from clergymen, endorsing his position. One very prominent minister wrote that "a jury of preachers is the last tribunal on earth from which to expect even-handed justice," while another declared that the Methodist church was becoming a laughing stock and he hoped that God would "have mercy upon us." A distinguished historian wrote, "They cannot at this late date undertake to put Inquisition methods into force." A prominent lawyer declared, "If I had a dozen boys to educate and a barrel of money for each boy I would not send them to Trinity while he [Kilgo] is at its head." Another writer said, "The cowhide well laid on is the punishment for him, and I hope he will have it before he leaves the State." A former professor at Trinity College wrote, "Every one of us is asked to give up his convictions, and fall down and worship Kilgoism." And, of course, the classic remark of the whole controversy was the one made by Clark's friend, Cyrus B. Watson, in his closing argument to the jury in the Kilgo-Gattis trial: "Over the gateway to the entrance of Trinity College there is this inscription, 'Eruditio et Religio!' It should be now changed so as to read, 'Eruditio et Religio et Sugario et Cigarro et Cherooto et Cigaretto et Kilgo.' "

TO CLARK FROM JOHN C. KILGO *

Trinity College
June 1897

I have recently heard that since the meeting of the Board of Trustees you remarked that my motion to elect professors for a four years' term, was really an effort on my own part to secure the presidency of Trinity College for a longer term. I am not disposed to believe this rumor, yet I think it but just to you, as well as to myself, to inform you of the rumor. If it is true, I would be very glad to know upon what basis you made the statement. I trust you are all well.

CLARK TO KILGO

Raleigh, N.C.
July 1, 1897

Yours to hand. Whoever made the report to you has evidently misconceived what I said. I did not say what you state. But I have no objection to saying what I did say, if you will give me the name of your informant.

* President of Trinity College, 1894-1910; Methodist Bishop, 1910-1922.

TO CLARK FROM KILGO

Durham, N.C.
[n.d.]

Yours of recent date has been received.

Prof. R. L. Flowers,* of Trinity College, informed me of the statement which I called to your attention. I will be very glad to get this matter corrected, as it is of importance to me personally.

CLARK TO KILGO

Raleigh, N.C.
July 2, 1897

Yours to hand. Does Prof. Flowers say that I had such conversation with him? I have no recollection of any talk with him on any subject. If so, let him state time and place, so I can recall what was said.

I have not the slightest objection to stating what I said about any matter that you feel any interest in, but I wish to know the party who states the conversation, that I may recall exactly and fully what I did say to him. I feel sure that I had no talk with Prof. Flowers that could bear that construction, and he can certainly refresh my recollection by stating time and place, if I did.

TO CLARK FROM KILGO

Durham, N.C.
[n.d.]

Prof. Flowers did not tell me that he had had any conversation with you on the matter involved. He simply stated that he had heard that you had made the statement to which I referred in my first letter. Rev. N.M. Jurney,† who had heard of your making the statement told me on yesterday that he understood that you made it to Mr. J.G. Brown.‡ I have not seen Mr Brown, nor have I communicated with him concerning the matter. However, the only matter which concerns me is, whether you impugn my motive in making the suggestion to the Board of Trustees to elect Faculty for a longer term. All this is very painful to me, and I would be glad to have it cleared up.

* Professor of Mathematics and President of Duke University since 1940.
† Methodist minister and member of the Board of Trustees of Trinity College.
‡ Raleigh banker and member of Board of Trustees; later chairman.

CLARK TO KILGO

Raleigh, N.C.
July 7, 1897

I write you directly in reply to your first letter that the party, whoever he was, had misconceived what I said, but if you desire to know what I said I should state it, if you would say who alleged he had the conversation with me.

It now turns out that Prof. Flowers told you that he heard that Rev. Mr. Jurney heard that some one else said that I had told Mr. Jos. G. Brown something like it. This is too much like "the three black crows." Mr. Brown and I are fellow-trustees. As such I had a conversation with him. I did not understand that it was usual for such conversations to be repeated. In that conversation I did not use the language you state. But if you are curious to know what passed in a private conversation between two members of your Board, let Mr. Brown state, if he wishes, what it was. If it differs from my recollection in any way, I will point it out, and then you will be in possession of a private conversation and my personal views as fully as it will be possible for you to get information.

When I wrote you in my first letter that what I said was misconceived, and when you discovered further that whatever was said was not publicly, but in a private conversation between two Trustees, whose privilege it is to discuss the management of the College in fullest freedom and confidence, I should have thought that you would have seen the propriety of letting the matter stand. But if you wish to investigate private conferences between Trustees, and Mr. Brown wishes to repeat to you, I shall give you frankly and fully what I said.

[P.S.]
You are at liberty to send a copy of this to Mr. Brown if you wish to pursue the matter.

TO CLARK FROM KILGO

Durham, N.C.
[n.d.]

Your last letter has been received. I confess a great degree of surprise at what you have to say in this letter as well as in your former letters. I do not think I am guilty of any impropriety in corresponding with you concerning this matter. I am quite capable of distinguishing between the business of the Trustees and an impeachment of my personal character. It is not the function of any Trustee, under any circumstance, to malign my character by impugning my motives. This is the question which has been at issue and is still the question. I do not feel that I am called upon to work for any man or men who set so little value upon my personal integrity as to charge me with sinister motives. From all that I have been able to learn, I regret to say that the original report has been confirmed.

Let me assure you again that I am not concerned with any discussion you may have had, or may yet have, concerning the business management of Trinity College; but at the same time I assure you that I will not submit to any Trustee assuming guardianship over my personal character. I do not so understand their duties. I regret this whole matter, and hoped in the beginning that it might be easily adjusted, but you have not seemed to be disposed to be generous in your treatment of it. No doubt you remember the time and place of your conversation. I leave you to settle that. At my earliest opportunity I will lay the matter before the Trustees for their decision.

CLARK TO KILGO

July 14, 1897
Raleigh

Yours to hand. Its tone impliedly asserts that it is a very grave misdemeanor not to entertain for you the same good opinion which you hold of yourself.

In conversation with another Trustee I told him of your growing unpopularity, and I expressed my thankfulness that the Trustees had defeated your recommendation which would have made you irremovable for four years. Your recommendation that the Faculty should be elected for four years, was unheard of and unnecessary. You made no exception of yourself from its provisions, and as men are presumed to intend the consequences of their own acts, I inferred that your motive was to do exactly what your recommendation would have done (if we had adopted it), i.e., given you, as well as the professors, protection from removal for four years.

The growing opposition to you, which has become intense with many, in the tobacco section especially; your reported speeches attacking the honesty of the silver men (who constitute nine-tenths of the white men of North Carolina); the attacks you have made on the State University; the quarrels you have managed to get up and keep up with Dr. Kingsbury,* Rev. Mr. Page,† Mr. Webster ‡ and others, have created antagonism which must shorten your stay, unless you are protected by a four years' term or some influence not based on public esteem. I am sorry that your energies are so little occupied that you are even now seeking to add a controversy with myself to your amusement.

The attempts of Northern multi-millionaires to capture by gifts and endowments the control of the education of the children of the people, has created a sensitiveness on that subject in the public mind. The charges in the public prints, however, intimating that the consideration of the gift by members of the Tobacco Trust to Trinity was that the youth were to be proselyted and taught political heresy foreign to the faith of their fathers, would have had small effect with so just a people as ours, if, by your parade of your gold standard views (which must have an untoward effect on the minds of the young men in your care), and your reiterated and ostentatious assertions of your superiority to public opinion had not given color to their charge. If your perseverance in that line of conduct shall deepen in the public mind suspicion into conviction (however unjust it may be in fact), wealthy syndicates may give you money, but the public will not send you boys.

In 1868 the State University had behind it the State Treasury and the then dominant political party, but it failed, because the public opinion of those who furnish college students was against it. You may think, however, you can carry it over an adverse public sentiment. You will know better after you have tried it.

I regret to write you this. Your administration promised success, and you ought to have won it with less ability than your friends credit you with possessing.

I do not understand your threat to lay my views before the Trustees, but as you somehow seem to think that the Board has jurisdiction of the offense, my views are herein plainly expressed, that there may be no controversy as to what they are.

TO CLARK FROM V. BALLARD §

Raleigh *News and Observer*
June 15, 1898

At the annual meeting of the Trustees of Trinity College, held June 6, 1898, the correspondence between Dr. John C. Kilgo and

* Theodore B. Kingsbury, Editor of the *Wilmington Messenger*.

† Methodist minister.

‡ John R. Webster of Reidsville, publisher of *Webster's Weekly*.

§ Ballard had resigned as treasurer of Trinity College in June, 1897. At the time this letter was written he was Secretary of the Board of Trustees.

yourself was referred to a committee who made a report on the same, and I was instructed to send you a copy, which please find enclosed.

CLARK TO BALLARD

Raleigh *News and Observer*
June 17, 1898

Yours to hand yesterday.

It contained the first notice I had of the appointment of the committee or of any investigation by it.

Will you please inform me at whose instance the committee was raised, and as it had 'ample evidence' for its conclusions will you inform me what witnesses went before it, what documentary evidence was permitted, if any, and if any argument was made before it except on Dr. Kilgo's side. You will please state whether the report of the committee was adopted by the Board. If it was, kindly give me the names of those voting on it and if there was no roll call, please give me the names of those actually present as far as you can recall them.

The re-election of Dr. Kilgo is evidence that the majority of the Trustees (certainly a majority at least of those present) were of opinion that he is a fit person to carry on the college, as the chief agent or servant of the Board. I belong to the minority on that question, but I am not aware of any provision of law that authorizes the majority, or any portion of them to censure me for my divergence of views on that subject or request me to resign. As the committee must have thought they had such authority, will you please cite me the provision under which they acted.

I am sorry to put you to so much trouble, but it is so unusual among North Carolinians to pass in judgment upon any man and condemn him in his absence, without notice and without opportunity to be heard, that I would be glad of any information you can give me from your records or from your own knowledge as to this very remarkable transaction.

P.S.—If there is any of the above information which you cannot give, by sending a copy of this letter to each of the committee possibly they can furnish it.

TO CLARK FROM V. BALLARD

Durham, N.C.
June, 1898

I beg to acknowledge receipt of your favor of the 17th and duly note contents.

In my first letter to you I failed to inform you that the report of the committee was adopted, and now inform you it was.

The Executive Committee will meet one day next week. I will then submit your letter to them, and write you further.

TO CLARK FROM V. BALLARD

Durham, N.C.
June 1898

At a meeting of the Executive Committee of Trinity College, held yesterday, I submitted to them your letter.

It was the opinion of the committee that your letter required no further answer, you having already had copy of the report of the committee appointed by the Board of Trustees.

CLARK TO JAMES H. SOUTHGATE *

Raleigh, N.C.
June 25, 1898.

I am in receipt of Mr. Ballard's letter in which he informs me that your Executive Committee declines to permit him to give me the information I requested.

As a Trustee I have a legal right to any information contained in the minutes and I should have thought as a measure of courtesy and of just dealing to one who had been afforded no chance of being heard, that you would have given me the fullest information as to all proceedings affecting myself even that not reduced to writing,

If any portion of the Board of Trustees had stated to me in a Christian spirit that it was unpleasant to have a difference between Dr. Kilgo and myself and that it would smooth matters if I would resign, I would cheerfully and promptly have done so. I had no intention of such a wish from any one. On the contrary, at Dr. Kilgo's instigation a committee is appointed, I am given no notice, no chance to put in evidence, nor present an argument, I am tried, found guilty and requested to resign. When I even then

* President of the Board of Trustees of Trinity College.

ask for the names of the witnesses and the nature of the evidence, and the names of the trustees who voted against me so that I may see what weight is to be given to their wishes and if there was a majority present, I am abruptly told I am entitled to know nothing but the verdict. Then in addition to that, this morning information is given to the public, through the Charlotte *Observer,* that I have been asked to resign.

The motive which actuates such proceedings is too plain to need comment. A verdict obtained by a jury appointed at the instance of the prosecution without any evidence or argument except from that side, and no opportunity to me to give any, and with refusal subsequently of all information as to the proceedings, will command no respect from any impartial or intelligent man. I shall give no weight to it and shall decline to accede to any request based upon it.

I think I know the 135,000 Methodist people in North Carolina, with whom I was raised and among whom I have lived all my life, well enough to say that they will give no weight to proceedings conducted in such a manner. They will at once divine who "ran" the proceedings and the motive was not the good of the college nor the vindication of justice, but to gratify the wounded vanity of Dr. Kilgo, and vengeance on the man who had ruffled it. As there were expressions in my letter not gratifying to those who make their millions by illegal trusts (at the expense of the toiling masses) there were doubtless some who felt it was necessary to propitiate them by condemning, unheard, the man who had been bold enough to let it be seen he did not fear "injustice, though wrapped in gold."

I would have resigned as I have said, if requested in a proper spirit for the good of the college. But if a trial had been instituted on and opportunity given, I could, and would, have laid before the committee, evidence that would have satisfied an impartial body of men that I was justified in every word of my letter of the 14th of July, 1897.

For eleven months I heard not a whisper about that letter and then on the 15th of June, 1898, I am suddenly informed I have been tried, found guilty and asked to resign for having written it. In his letter of July 13th, Dr. Kilgo stated that he would lay my conversation with Mr. Brown before the trustees, but I was aware they had no more jurisdiction to pass upon it than to try a law suit between Dr. Kilgo and myself, and I did not dream, no one would have dreamed, that if the Board assumed jurisdiction any committee would try the matter without giving me notice and opportunity to produce evidence—but that was the last thing Dr. Kilgo intended I should have a chance to do.

This proceeding, Mr. Southgate, was not instituted for the benefit of the college. It was palpably done to soothe Dr. Kilgo's vanity and to placate the Trust that more money might be obtained from it.

None know better than yourself that the Trustees had no jurisdiction of the matter. I was not elected by them. I was their peer. If the Board are judges I was one of the judges and not subject to them. At the meeting of the Board a year ago a resolution to endorse the Common School System of the State was introduced. You spoke against it. You said that it was contrary to primary right to tax one man to educate the children of another; that "if a man would admit he was a pauper you would contribute as charity to help educate his children, and you would contribute to educate orphans who were paupers, but you protested against being taxed for the common schools; that it was socialism, and you would not pander to such sentiments." I think I quote your exact language. You said more, of course, and eloquently and strongly. To the credit of the Board, the resolution was adopted over you, but such language coming from the President of the Board of Trustees of Trinity College is more calculated to damage the College than my views of Dr. Kilgo, expressed to him in a private letter. If the Trustees have jurisdiction of the views of its members, why did they not try those utterances and repudiate them by requesting you to resign?

Recently Dr. Kilgo, in an affluence of syophancy, led a procession to the house of Mr. Duke, and in a public speech extolled him as the greatest man the State had ever produced, and as superior to all the sacrifices of blood and treasure the State had ever made; that in comparison with his gifts of money, the primacy at Mecklenburg, the thousands who had offered up their lives at Moore's Creek, at King's Mountain, and all these years down to Cardenas, were as dust in the balance. In substance he said: "My Lord Duke, Give Us Money and Your Name Shall Be Exalted Above All Names." This deification of wealth—no matter how obtained—is not Christian education. This is not the language, these are not the thoughts, which a college president should teach his pupils. How much personal gratuity had so grateful a man received? Why did the Board not try him? You have jurisdiction of him. He is your elected servant to manage under your supervision this great institution, which the Methodist Church in North Carolina has placed in your hands.

Dr. Kilgo's reputation in South Carolina was that of a wire-puller, of the ward politician type. His performances in this State have justified his reputation. Length of years has not reformed him. He was a short time in Tennessee. One of the most distinguished members of our church in that State (not a layman) said to me: "We know the fellow well. He is a scrub—a scrub politician." If your committee wanted information, I could have given it to them. Dr. Kilgo did not intend they should have it. He got up the prosecution. He put in the evidence. He gets the report to suit him; my respectful request for information as to how it was all done, is denied; and then it is promptly advertised to the public that I had been requested to resign. Trinity College has put forward its claim for patronage that it creates Christian character. Is this a specimen of it?

Do you expect Trinity to succeed when, as is now well known, no man can remain as a Trustee who is not acceptable to this creative public respect when the language and conduct of its President would make it an annex to Duke's cigarette factory—an asset of the trust through which boys may be educated in due respect for the superiority of great wealth, when acquired through a trust over the sacrifice of life by thousands (who had nothing else to offer) at the call of their country.

I do not believe that any considerable portion of the board voted for the resolution, and that few of those, if any, outside the Duke-Kilgo syndicate, knew the violation of the elementary principles of justice by which it had been obtained.

To the honest, fair minded, intelligent people of North Carolina, and especially to the people of the honored church of which I have been a member for over thirty years, I am willing to submit this matter, and I will accept their verdict—not yours.

STATEMENT IN THE "CHARLOTTE OBSERVER," JUNE 25, 1898

JUDGE CLARK'S RESIGNATION AS A TRUSTEE ASKED FOR

It is learned in Charlotte that a controversy by letter has recently been in progress between Judge Walter Clark, of the Supreme Court, and Dr. J. C. Kilgo, D.D., President of Trinity College, and that at a meeting of the Trustees of the institution last week, Dr. Kilgo laid the correspondence before the Board, asked for an investigation of the charges brought by Judge Clark, and stated that if they were sustained his resignation would be forthcoming. The investigation was made, the result being that Dr. Kilgo was sustained, and that the resignation of Judge Clark as a member of the Board of Trustees was requested.

TO CLARK FROM JAMES H. SOUTHGATE

Durham, N.C.,
June 28, 1898

Responding to your favor of the 25th inst., you will recall being present at the June, 1897, meeting of the Trustees when the President's report was referred to a sub-committee consisting of yourself, Judge Montgomery and Dr. Swindell. The first recommendation in this report was "That the law which requires the election of the Faculty every year be changed so as to elect them not oftener than every four years, if indeed any time should be fixed other than the faithful discharge of duty. This should not refer to the election of a new member of the Faculty. He should always be put on probation 'till he proves his fitness for a permanent election." One of the Trustees moved that the President of the College be included in the recommendation, but the motion was withdrawn at the request of Dr. Kilgo. Your committee reported non-concurrence on this item of the report, "Judge Clark explaining to the Board that its adoption was liable to lead to legal entanglements." Dr. Kilgo promptly arose, explained his motive in making the recommendation, which was to avoid having the members of the Faculty in suspense as to their election from year to year, and gracefully consented to a withdrawal of the suggestion because of the light you threw on it from a legal standpoint of observation. In all other particulars the report was concurred in and adopted as a whole and ordered spread upon the minutes. In the organization of the College, its literature, in the method of approach to and disposition of this matter, there appears to be no real way to confound Dr. Kilgo, the President, with the Faculty, or to misconstrue the benign effort of one on behalf of the other.

You will further recall that later in this June, 1897, meeting, along towards adjournment, a resolution was adopted by a rising vote, you voting, cordially approving and endorsing the efforts of the Faculty, especially of Dr. Kilgo, the President of Trinity

College, in behalf of higher Christian education with a pledge to encourage and aid them more actively and unitedly in the future than in the past. This meeting of the Trustees was harmonious, pleasant, in which all, including yourself, appeared to take an active, intelligent interest.

Within three weeks of adjournment reports reached the President of the College which were calculated to damage him personally and, if true, the institution which he so ably represents, the nature of which is set forth in the correspondence which follows and with which you are conversant.

From this correspondence opportunity abundant was given to deny or retract, and failing to secure either, the inference was clear that you meant what you said and said what you meant, whereupon the President of the College notified you in his last letter that at his earliest opportunity he would lay the matter before the Trustees for their action. In your letter of July 14th you acknowledge this notice, enlarge and emphasize the criticism, and plainly express your views that there may be no controversy as to what they are. You were present in the meeting of the Board when the order was passed that its regular meetings shall be held during commencement week at the call of the President; and the Secretary of the Board informs me that he sent you, in common with all the other members of the Board, a notice of the June, 1898, meeting, so that with your acknowledgment of the notice given by Dr. Kilgo, that this personal matter would be brought before the Trustees, and the filing of your views in full—that there might be no misunderstanding as to what they were, with the further notice that the Board would meet Monday, June, 6, 1898, the Trustees cannot be blamed for your absence or the absence of additions of amendments to the written bill of complaints against Dr. Kilgo.

The Trustees met June 6th, 1898, according to call, and the following were noted present:

Rev. A.P. Plyler, Rev. G.A. Oglesby, Rev. J.R. Brooks, D.D., Rev. W.C. Norman, Mr. V. Ballard, Hon. W.J. Montgomery, Mr. R.A. Mayer, Mr. A.H. Stokes, Rev. P.L. Groom, D.D., Mr. J.H. Southgate, Mr. E.J. Parrish, Rev. S.B. Turrentine, Mr. B.N. Duke, Mr. W.H. Branson, Mr. P.H. Hanes, Rev. T.N. Ivey, Rev. N.M. Jurney, Rev. F.A. Bishop, Mr. W.R. Odell, Dr. W.S. Creasy, Mr. J.G. Brown, Col. G.W. Flowers, Prof. O.W. Carr, Rev. W.C. Wilson, Rev. J.B. Hurley.

Two Trustees had died during the year, one had removed to

another Conference, one was infirm and could not come, another was out of the State; so that of a possible thirty-one, there were twenty-five present.

When opportunity presented, Dr. Kilgo rose to a question of personal privilege, the right enjoyed by every member of a deliberative body, stated his grievance, read the correspondence between himself and you, and on motion the said correspondence was referred to a committee of five worthy men—men who perhaps rank second to none in North Carolina—according to you in honor, respect and fraternal devotion, namely: Revs. G.A. Oglesby, F.A. Bishop, W.C. Wilson, S.B. Turrentine, and Col. G.W. Flowers, which reference resulted not in a trial of yourself, as you seem to think, but the investigation of statement that you had made concerning another, and if any one was on trial it was Dr. Kilgo. Neither of you appeared before the committee, which, after a careful consideration of the correspondence, herein referred to, brought in a report to the Board of reaffirmation and a hearty endorsement of Dr. Kilgo and his administration, with the pledge of continued support; a deprecation and condemnation of the uncharitable and unfair spirit manifested by you in your correspondence with and charges against him; a positive affirmation, in the light of ample evidence, that your charges against him as including himself to be elected as President of Trinity College for four years, which was to secure for himself "protection from removal for four years," were not only unsupported, but actually contradicted by facts, and the expression of opinion that you ought to resign as a Trustee of the College.

These conclusions, in the form of resolutions, sent you by the Secretary, Mr. V. Ballard, were read, discussed and carried, there being only one dissenting vote. Three of the Trustees are known to have been absent when this committee's report was adopted. One was sick, two others left the afternoon before and arrived too late to take part in the proceedings the following morning.

Your request for data, made of the Executive Committee through the Secretary Mr. Ballard, could not then be granted for the reason that so far as you were concerned the case was considered closed until something else appeared. Your every complaint against Dr. Kilgo has been investigated with the result as announced to you and to that you were referred.

Concerning the publicity given to the subject through the Charlotte Observer, and in which you find justification for publishing your letter in the papers, the following telegram was submitted:

Durham, N.C. June 27, 1898

Mr. J.P. Caldwell, Editor Charlotte Observer, Charlotte, N.C.:

Item in Saturday's issue of Observer concerning Trinity College and Judge Clark was not authorized by our Board. Will you kindly inform me by wire at whose instance or on whose information the item was based.

J.H. Southgate,
President, Trustees, Trinity College.

J. P. CALDWELL * TO JAMES H. SOUTHGATE

Charlotte, N.C.
June 27, 1898

See to-day's *Observer*. It is enough for me to say that item "Clark's resignation asked" was furnished without procurement or even knowledge of anybody connected with Trinity.

JAMES H. SOUTHGATE TO CLARK

Durham, N.C.

Respecting the question of jurisdiction:

First. You will admit the right of a deliberative body to investigate charges against its members.

Second. You will admit the right of our Board to deal with Dr. Kilgo, an employee of the Board.

Third. By reference to section three of the College charter you will find that no person can be elected a Trustee by the Conference till he has first been recommended by a majority of the Trustees at a regular meeting; and that the Trustees shall have power to remove any member of this body who may remove beyond the boundary of the State or who may refuse or neglect to discharge the duties of a Trustee.

If a failure to respond to that part of your letter which refers to the political opinions or the professional or business calling of any one or more members of the Board should cause you to think there is an unpardonable weakness and infirmity and a species of tyranny manifest in the life of this beloved institution, let it go at that. The record fails to show where any one connected with it

* Editor of the Charlotte *Observer*.

has suffered or been discounted for opinion's sake in matters of public policy. This record speaks for itself no less than the meritorious work the institution is doing, and this, after all, is and should be the standard by which it will be measured. So judged, it is not to succeed; it is pronounced a success. Already the pride of North Carolina Methodism, its phenomenal growth has attracted the admiring gaze of the church at large. It courts not honor nor popularity save as these may come through right thinking and right acting.

With assurances, if such be necessary, that such an institution may be depended upon to defend the character of the man who bears its standard before the people from the mountains to the sea against unjust and unwarranted attacks by whomsoever made.

CLARK TO JAMES H. SOUTHGATE

Raleigh, N.C.
June 30, 1898.

The day of miracles has returned: "The dumb are made to speak." Information abruptly denied to me has been (in part) conceded to an outraged public opinion, but with so little clearness that the miracle was hardly worth working.

Your theory of defence, that it was Dr. Kilgo and not myself who was on trial, does credit to your ingenuity, and would be convenient if correct. The verdict and judgment show who it was intended to be tried and condemned. Read your resolutions:

"We, the committee, to whom was referred the matter of correspondence between Dr. John C. Kilgo and Judge Walter Clark, respectfully submit the following:

"*Resolved* 2. That we deprecate and CONDEMN the uncharitable and unfair spirit manifested by Judge Clark in his correspondence with and charges against Dr. Kilgo.

"*Resolved* 4. That it is the sense of the Board of Trustees that Judge Walter Clark ought to resign as Trustee of Trinity College."

If I was not on trial, then without a trial you deprecate and "condemn" me, one of your associates, and find that I have been guilty of being "unfair" and "uncharitable." If you did not find me guilty, upon what was it that you based your other resolution that I "ought to resign?" I would like to be informed. If only Dr. Kilgo was on trial, the resolutions expressing your satisfaction with him would have ended the matter. But when you go further and condemn me you either did so by trial without notice (as I complained) or without any trial, as you now assert, which is making the matter worse.

I notice you deny none of the material points of my complaint.

(1) Though the telephone in the building in which your committee sat is immediately connected with the telephone in the court-room in Raleigh, where I was, and three trains a day went from Raleigh to Durham, no summons, nor even a whisper ever came to me, in that or any other way, during your session of three or four days, that I was being investigated and condemned. It will not do to say that because I knew the Board would be in session I was "constructively" fixed with notice that Dr. Kilgo's threat to lay the matter before the Board would be followed by my trial and condemnation. As well say that because every citizen of the county knows when court will meet, that when one man says to another "I will lay the matter before the grand jury," that the latter can be sentenced by the Jury, without notice and without chance to offer evidence or argument.

(2) You give no excuse why, on my application, after judgment, you refused me even the limited information you now give the public.

(3) You have shown no jurisdiction in your Board to sit in judgment on me. And if your only object was to endorse Dr. Kilgo, did he want a "whitewashing" only, for it is nothing more when no one is given a chance to be heard in opposition.

(4) If your Board is empowered to sit in judgment on the views of its members, you do not answer why it did not try your views on matters of public importance as well as my private views as to Dr. Kilgo.

(5) You say nothing as to the laudatory declarations of Dr. Kilgo that the possessor of wealth, who gives money to the college which pays his salary, is the greatest possible object of respect. These degrading views are not proper to be taught college students in North Carolina without rebuke and I know the Board by its silence would not be taken as endorsing them.

These things you do not answer.

As to the new matter, that after Dr. Kilgo introduced the recommendation for a four years' term, that in reply to my objection he stated verbally that it did not embrace himself, I solemnly aver that I never heard it. "The written word abides," and proves the fact I asserted. The recommendation in his report, is broad enough to embrace the President, and if he did not wish to include himself, why did he not exclude himself. If he made that verbal exclusion of himself why did he make no reference to it in all his correspondence with me and leave it unasserted till now?

In my first letter to him I stated that the conversation was misconceived for my remark was not as to his motive, but upon the fact that it would have given him a four years' term, and that we were wise to vote his suggestion down. To Mr. Brown's query, I had said, I "didn't think he intended to leave himself out." In a desire to avoid a squabble with him I wrote him it was a private conversation and that he did not have it reported to him exactly right. It is his own folly that he misunderstood my repugnance to controversy as awe for his importance.

In reference to the advertisement of the matter by the Charlotte Observer, the information did not go from me, it must have gone from some one cognizant of the action of the Committee; Who was it? I recall to your attention a statement in that publication which throws a flood of light on the "true inwardness of this matter." Says the Charlotte Observer article: "Dr. Kilgo laid the correspondence before the Board, asked for an investigation of the charges brought by Judge Clark and stated that if they were sustained his resignation would be forthcoming. The investigation was made, the result being that Dr. Kilgo was sustained and that the resignation of Judge Clark was requested." Now look, without prejudice, at the letter of July 14, 1897, which is the only letter which can be construed to make any charges. What are they? Read it again, I pray you. 1. That Dr. Kilgo seemed to think it an offence for me not to have as high opinion of him as he had of himself. 2. I admitted I had said that "owing to Dr. Kilgo's growing unpopularity it was cause of thankfulness that the Trustees had defeated his recommendation which would have made him irremovable for four years (as any lawyer looking upon the report will say would have been its legal effect) and that I inferred that he intended just what his recommendation would have accomplished, if it had passed. 3. That his quarrels with Dr. Kingsbury, Rev. Mr. Page and others and his reported speeches assailing the honesty of silver men would shorten his stay unless he was protected by a four year's term or some influence other than public esteem, and that if he progressed further along that line, wealthy syndicates might give him money; but the public would not send him boys. Read the letter over and that is all you can find in it. Yet that is the letter whose charges the committee find on "ample evidence" were not sustained, under Dr. Kilgo's threat to resign if they did otherwise, and for writing which (at Dr. Kilgo's insistence) I am convicted of high treason and requested to resign.

There are many most excellent men on the board. They did not scrutinize this matter. Your letter shows you did not. Dr. Kilgo had satisfied the Board that he is the only man who can get big donations from the cigarette trust, that he is the only man who can "milk the cow" and when the awful threat was made that if he was not "sustained" they would lose their milker, he was "sustained" and I doubt if one in ten of the Trustees ever noticed the other part of the resolutions "condemning" me or that it occurred to them that they were committing the injustice of passing in judgment on an absent man, without a hearing or an opportunity to be heard. It is true there is wide complaint among the public that the cow makes her milk by eating up the collard patch of other people and that it is against the law for her to run at large (for both State and National law declares trusts illegal) but then the milk is good and you have kept your milker. It was unjust to condemn me without a hearing, but then barbarian that I am, I ought to have said nothing to irritate the feelings of this artist in milking, whose touch is so soothing and irresistible and whose services are so indispensable.

In the days of the glorious old Dr. Braxton Craven the college did not find an employee of that kind necessary or desirable. It stood broad-based on popular support, and though it was remote in the forests of Randolph, his number of students ran up to a higher figure than we can now boast, with all our magnificent "plant" and endowment. He turned out sturdy, self-respecting, young graduates who have been an honor, a blessing and an ornament to our Church and State. Such sentiments as we now hear did not then echo from the President's chair. I would that we could look upon his like again.

TO CLARK FROM THE REVEREND J. D. HUFHAM *

1898
Henderson, N. C.
Friday A.M.

. . . The calm courage and lofty courtesy with which you met a jury which you knew to be hostile and whose verdict you knew to be already made up fills me with fresh admiration for your character.

* Prominent Baptist clergyman and at one time editor of the *Biblical Recorder*.

I also thank you for requesting that the ordinary conditions, which prevail in court trials, whether ecclesiastical or secular—a jury unbiased and uncommitted—be observed. It is a good service to the cause of truth and righteousness, to call attention afresh to this fundamental and self-evident principle.

And I should have been amazed at the decision of the Trustees if I had not learned long ago that a jury of preachers is the last tribunal on earth from which to expect even-handed justice. The preacher by education, by office, and by habit is a one-sided man, incapable of weighing evidence or of investigation in matters of every day life. His teachings are accepted without question and he is the spiritual law of his congregation; in some respects the temporal law as well. His studies are also in abstract questions of ethics or theology. A few years of such life as that place a man at the farthest possible remove from the judicial frame of mind and from the view point of men who are engaged in the struggle to labors of our work-a-day world. And so our fathers were wise in disbarring the preachers from all part in the making and execution of the law. The darkest chapters of human history are those which tell of the framing or execution of law at the instance or by the dictation of the clergy.

I am not surprised, therefore, at the decision of your Trustees. From the nature of the case, they were incapable, as other preachers would have been, of seeing their position as others see it. Nor could they see how sad a blow they were striking at what they call "Christian Education" and how mightily they were helping "State Aid". But pardon me for saying so much. It is an old man's fault.

I count it a special mercy that we were born in the same century and that you were brought into the circuit of my life.

TO CLARK FROM HOWARD ALSTON

Littleton, N. C.
June 27, 1898

Allow me to say that your case Vs. Dr. Kilgo is absolutely safe in the hands of the jury—"The fair minded, intelligent people of N. C." Such conduct on the part of the Board of Trustees of Trinity College will be tolerated no more by the honest people of this state than were those "star chamber performances" abolished in the time of Charles 1st. You are right in saying that Trinity College may have all the money possible, but if the people are against it, she will get no boys—She will have "a pocket full of rocks and nothing to chunk at"—You know my father is a Methodist and though an Alumnus of the University, and a loyal one, he would like to lend a helping hand to the College of his denomination. He is one of the thousand who is becoming more against Trinity because of its being in the hands of such fellows as Kilgo—A sycophant—...

TO CLARK FROM STEPHEN B. WEEKS *

Washington, D. C.
July 3, 1898

I have the pleasure of informing you that I have completed the indexing of the first 13 volumes of the North Carolina Colonial and State Records and that I am now well under way on volume 14. I shall be glad to know when I may expect to have volume 15 and subsequent volumes in hand. If any or all of 15 is printed it is not necessary that it be bound for my use, but I can use the unbound pages. I should prefer however the bound volume. I shall be ready for it about the middle of August by the latest. Of course, it is not necessary that I have the future volumes at that time. I still have a great deal of work to do in the matter of alphabetizing the cards already made. This will take me two or three months. If other volumes do not appear this summer I can very well put my time on alphabetizing, but should prefer to go on with the indexing itself as this would hasten somewhat the completion of the whole work.

I have read with amusement the account of your recent fracas with the distinguished president and trustees of Trinity College. I see that the latter have forgotten none of the tricks which they knew so well how to play in 1893 when they had six or seven professors as a unit against the president and preferred to believe what the president said rather than take the words of all the faculty who, on the general line of complaint, were practically unanimous. I congratulate you on your manly letter to Southgate. Perhaps it would be well for them to learn that they cannot at this late date undertake to put Inquisition methods into force! Perhaps your letter will make them a little wiser, that is, if they are capable of being taught.

* Professor of History and Political Science at Trinity College, 1891-1895; author of many books relating to North Carolina history.

TO CLARK FROM O. H. BLOCKER

Old Fort, McDowell Co., N. C.
July 4, 1898

Mr. C. A. Webb of the Asheville bar spent the day with me yesterday and asked me if I had yet written you a letter of congratulation in re of Kilgo and his "Dukedom" and expressive of regret that Trinity College was being bought up by the gold standard "benefactors". I answered him that I had not because as you were all ways right you need not be everlastingly told of so patent a fact—but seeing in the press an effort to fix public opinion to the idea that the majority of Methodists were "with Dr. Kilgo", I write to say that I am not in that "majority" if it exists and which could not exist in reason.

Many occasions have served the people of North Carolina to thank God for our Judge Clark.

TO CLARK FROM THOMAS L. LEA

Hamer, N. C.
July 7, 1898

Allow me to congratulate you how well you handled Kilgo and the rubbing you gave the trusts. He made a speech at District Conference two years ago near me and a good many members left the church. I am a Baptist, but I could not stand it, so I was among the number that left.

I see from Websters Weekly that John E. White says the Baptists are with Kilgo. I would like to inform the gentleman that the Baptists are not but are with Clark. I wish some plan could be devised to run that trust out of N. C. for its ruining the tobacco section. They are stealing with one hand and donating with the other to benevolent purposes. I am truly glad and proud to know we have one man in the State that is not afraid to tackle them.

With best wishes for you and yours and hoping to see you elected to the U.S. Senate.

TO CLARK FROM CHARLES D. MC IVER *

Greensboro, N. C.
August 23, 1898

I write to say that after thinking the matter over, I concluded that it was not wise to write to Rev. Mr. Page. I think if you will get what he said at the Maxton Conference as reported in the

* President of the State Normal and Industrial College, 1892-1906.

Charlotte Observer a year ago last July, it might be put in as documentary evidence. Prof C. L. Raper, who lives in High Point, told Prof. Claxton that on one occasion he knew of a certain subject to be proposed for a debate among the students of Trinity College, and that the faculty prohibited them from debating the subject. I do not know what the subject was, but it either touched the labor question or trusts or some such modern topic. I have told Col. John R. Webster about this and I think he would cheerfully go to High Point to see Prof. Raper. . . .

TO CLARK FROM W. A. BLAIR *

Winston, N. C.
Aug. 26, 1898

Your favor of the 24th has reached me. I have not heard a word from Bandy or Claxton either, though I wrote the day I wrote you. Claxton, I see from the paper, is away in the institute work, which accounts for his silence. Bandy's conversation was along the line of Kilgo's record as a politician and a "swell head". He seemed to think there was nothing to him but brass and trickery. He had a number of incidents which came under his personal knowledge and a number of things he had heard to corraborate his statements. Of course, I do not remember the circumstances nor the names as I did not know at that time that I should want to refer to them again.

Claxton's talk is along the same line, and it was filled with quotations absurd and ridiculous from sermons and addresses. Claxton is a Methodist too, but was exceedingly sarcastic in his remarks. One story about God whittling sticks for Dr. Kilgo, was very striking and bitter. This was taken from a sermon which he had heard sometime before. I hope that it will be possible for me to see Bandy before Saturday night, but I am not sure, of course, as I have not heard from him. I see from the papers that K. is in South Carolina getting up affidavits, etc. I have heard many people express their belief that you were right in this matter, and I sincerely regret that I cannot get hold of the data which you ought to have and which I believe to be my duty to give you. As you say, it seems that the Doctor has been working one way and another to shut off the free speech and honest conviction of these people. Bandy surprises me very much as he was so strong in his statements.

* William A. Blair, member of State Board of Charities for many years and prominent banker in Winston-Salem.

CLARK TO A. W. GRAHAM

Raleigh, N.C.
27 Aug. 1898

Am sorry we could not meet & talk over matters. The *facts* are dead against Kilgo, if I only had compulsory process for witnesses, but Kilgo's machine & Duke's money has frightened off *all* they could.

To give you an instance. Gattis * & his son travelled extensively in S.C. They told me and others about K's being a notorious wire-puller &c. I had an interview with Carr † and told him the jury was packed & would decline to answer their request to furnish evidence in a case they had already once decided—but if he wanted the fight made I would do so if he would make Gattis & son testify. He agreed to it & to pay Boone's ‡ fees & expenses *if I would keep his name out of it*—so don't mention it. Some one got hold of Carr & intimidated him & next thing I heard he was insisting to Bryant § (Boone's partner) that Gattis must not testify. He would now testify but for Carr's opposition who is on his note in bank. Boone went to S.C., got up valuable information making him a necessary witness, but with Carr's defection he slacked off and now has gone to Chase City to recruit! Whether he will be back to trial, or whether this is to *flank out* at Carr's suggestion I can't tell. I *need him* badly for a witness. Is there any way to find out? or to insure his return? If you have any business that way, I will gladly pay your expenses there to casually see him & let me know if he will return—and if doubtful (which I do not want intimated to him) procure his return.

I had rather fight a dog with a spade than an unprincipled preacher-demagog. He has every advantage.

CLARK TO A. W. GRAHAM

Raleigh, N.C.
29 Aug. 1898

Many thanks for your kindness. Let me know the expense you were at that I may refund it—though I know your *time* you could ill spare. . . .

The jury is packed, the witnesses are bulldosed. I can only do

* Thomas Jefferson Gattis, superannuated Methodist minister who was operating a book store in Durham. For further details about Gattis see Brooks, *Walter Clark, Fighting Judge*, pp. 114-121 and Garber, *John Carlisle Kilgo*, pp. 224-227.

† Julian S. Carr, Durham industrialist.

‡ Durham attorney.

§ Victor Bryant, R. B. Boone's law partner.

the best I can trusting the public will grasp the "true inwardness" of the situation.

I am still doubtful of Boone being on hand.

TO CLARK FROM MAXEY L. JOHN *

Laurinburg, N. C.
Sept. 2, 1898

I have just finished reading the conclusion of the News-Observer's report on the so-called trial by the trustees of Trinity... and I must say that the very proceedings of that body show that Kilgo had the board "cooked",—par boiled, fried, stewed, and on the half shell too—and proves beyond a shadow of a doubt that your very just charge of wire pulling is even more than true. While your learning, talents, and attainments put you above criticism of the ordinary public, I wish to tell you that I have made it a point to ascertain what is the judgment of the citizens of this town as expressed on the street, and find that one and all accord to you full vindication and believe that you have conclusively proved every charge—without the admirable help given by Kilgo himself.

Every JOHN I know is a Methodist, and so am I. I would be proud to see Trinity move out on right lines; but she cannot do it with J. C. Kilgo at the head of it. While here summer before last he talked scandalously; and, now that it occurs to me, I am sorry I did not write you before, that he belittled the office of Presiding Elder of the Methodist church in the most contemptible manner and with the most disgusting tones. This in private, I being present. In an address he used the most glaring sophistry and indirectly said to his audience that he would not sign, were the real sentiments written down and handed him for signature. I was proud to hear that he told the Methodist pastor that he felt handicapped here more than at any place he had ever spoken. This is on account of the intelligent sentiment here on the matter of sectarian schools.

TO CLARK FROM D. W. BULLOCK †

Wilmington, N.C.
Sept. 2, 1898

I have read with very great sorrow of what has been going on at Trinity. So kindly as I feel toward you, in my humble opinion

* Lawyer.
† Wilmington physician.

the simple fact that you or any other man should be treated unfairly is a matter of minor importance to a primary principle of Justice, Compared with the weighty and all important question involved in the Unfortunate Trinity Affair. The attempt to humiliate you is not the real object aimed at. As wise a councillor as I know you to be, your withdrawal from the government of Trinity College is a very small portion of the damage that will be done to Christian progress and exalted manhood. We judge 'tis not the fact that you entertain an unfavorable opinion of Dr. Kilgo that has brought you into condemnation, but the fact that you should publicly entertain an opinion at all in the presence of that august assembly. Ten cent magazines, two penny newspapers, circuses, free or cheap excursions and our free schools have educated the people to that extent that they demand democratic principles in church as well as state, and that some people will no longer down at the command of their ——. I hope that you will continue to stand up for the churches best welfare in future as in the past. Now we have our churches arrayed as a laughing stock for every intelligent man out of it, if these and many other grievances do not call aloud for help from our best men the signs of the times count for nothing. I with many others in the state wish that you will write fully and let the public know the inwardness of the whole matter, believing that the only way to remedy the growing evil of Ministerial intolerance of lay opinion. . . .

I am not yet disposed to believe the N.C. Methodist Ministry bad and we must confess that in the past many of them were not fools, which puts me at a loss to account for the present state of affairs.

In my effort to do so I find myself wandering off in the domain of superstition and fanaticism. Can these brethren be under the influence of some heretofore unknown evil power that has temporarily bereft them of all sense of reason, justice and expediency or has Dr[.] Kilgo succumbed to the magic influence of hypnotism? Surely these men are under some strange and uncontrollable influence. Otherwise what power is it that makes men fall down and blindly, wildly, insanely worship at the feet of a fellow mortal—and in so doing seek the best interest of an institution for whom they and their ancestors have labored for generations, forgetting every principle of highminded Justice and exalted magnanimity. In their wild delerium of adoration unable to see that they are not only rendering themselves and the cause they espouse the laughing stock of every sober uninfatuated man woman child and dog in the state Jeopardizing not alone their own aspirations for sincerity, but the very future welfare of those whom they claim to be leading to the views of the blessed. God have mercy upon us....

TO CLARK FROM T. J. GATTIS

Durham, N. C.
Sept. 3, 1898

I am sorry you had to leave in the night and I failed to see you any more. Jno. C. Kilgo, the Dukes and Co. and the Trustees, unless I am greatly mistaken are bandying my name around considerably, and insinuating falsehood, etc.

I send you copy of THE HERALD this morning. You will see on third page marked article. I think I have spotted the one who gave the information. Not positive, however, but you will know who to deal with.

I decided, after long, serious prayerful consideration, to serve the church and Society as best I could in the matter, and I leave the results in the hands of Him whom I trust, and my friends, and the friends of justice and truth....

I am fifty-nine years old, have been a minister of the M. E. Church, South and member of the North Carolina Conference about thirty-eight years, have answered to my name during all this time, and presiding elder has been able to say during all these years that there is nothing against T. J. Gattis. I think I have been regarded as conservative during all these years. But enough of this, may God give you success in the work you are attempting to do for North Carolina Methodism and for Humanity.

TO CLARK FROM CHARLES D. MC IVER

Greensboro, N. C.
September 3, 1898

I write especially to congratulate you upon the able manner in which you conducted yourself and your case at Durham. I look forward with interest to reading your speech in tomorrow's News and Observer.

I thank you for your letter or September 1. I am surprised at the testimony of Rev. Mr. Grissom,* because I do not see that it has anything to do with the main question. I do not remember to

* W. L. Grissom, Methodist minister and author of *History of Methodism in North Carolina.*

have said that you were prepared. I did express to Dr. Crawford * my sympathy for you, though I do not remember to have told Dr. Crawford that I had done so at Durham. I did say to him that I was surprised to see you at Durham, and that in my opinion, the Board was surprised, but that you usually did the thing which people were not looking for.

ARTICLE IN "THE NEWS & OBSERVER," SEPTEMBER 4, 1898

At the late Clark-Kilgo trial the board refused to let Judge Clark speak unless he would promise not to print his speech, (which he had with him reduced to writing). He would not accept the terms. The speech he desired to deliver is as follows:

JUDGE CLARK'S SPEECH

Gentlemen of the Board of Trustees:

If this were an oratorical contest I would say what I have to say without manuscript. But as I might have the fate of Dr. Kilgo, at the coronation of Mr. Duke, and the notes of my speech taken down by another might differ from my recollection, I have reduced my argument to writing that I may read it. Especially is this prudence when Dr. Kilgo's unsworn stenographer alone is allowed in this room, and my request to have a stenographer present at my own expense has been refused at Dr. Kilgo's instance. I regret that it may be more tedious to you, but it will prevent all controversy as to what I shall say.

At the meeting in July, 1897, Dr. Kilgo made a report in which he recommended as follows: (I quote from Mr. Southgate's letter), "That the law which requires the election of the faculty every year, be so changed as to elect them not oftener than every four years." I opposed the proposition. It was referred to a committee of which I was a member, and which reported against it and it did not pass. The Trinity Catalog of 1894-5, which I hold in my hand has the word, "Faculty" in large letters, and the first line under it is:

JOHN C. KILGO, A.M. President and Professor of Philosophy.

In the present Catalog, it is headed: FACULTY AND OFFICERS
And the first name under that is:

JOHN C. KILGO, A.M., D.D. President and Professor of
Avera School of Biblical Literature

* L. W. Crawford, Editor of the *North Carolina Christian Advocate.*

So it is clear, beyond cavil, that if his recommendation had been adopted, Dr. Kilgo would have had a four years' term instead of one year. It is alleged that he disclaimed at the time, including himself. The place to have done that was in the recommendation itself, or by amending it. If he made such oral disclaimer, it must have been when I was out on the committee, or when my attention was otherwise occupied. I did not hear it. Some weeks later, having visited the Tobacco section and heard large numbers of Methodists express themselves adversely to Dr. Kilgo, on my return I mentioned this to Mr. Jos. G. Brown, a fellow trustee, with whom I had transacted my banking business for over twenty-five years, and said to him that it was well that we had defeated the resolution for a four years' term. This getting to Dr. Kilgo's ears, he seemed very much offended. Whether it was because he wished to pose as being so altruistic that he was only looking after the rest of the Faculty and was absolutely indifferent to his own interest, or whether he would have it understood that he was absolute master here, and nothing could shake him out, I do not know.

To his letter I replied, endeavoring to avoid a difficulty. I thought when I showed him it was a private conversation he would desist. In truth, I did not wish to tell him what I had said about his unpopularity. He persisted, and when he finally threatened to lay the matter before the board, I gave him, in my letter, July 14th, 1897, the conversation and the reasons in plain Anglo-Saxon. When that

"Chunk of old red sand-stone
Struck him in the abdomen,"

there were no subsequent proceedings. The correspondence suddenly stopped. When the board met in June, 1898, I did not care to come here to vote for his re-election, and not knowing any proceedings affecting me were in progress, I staid at home where I had some business needing me.

When I received the short note informing me that in my absence, a committee had sat on me, condemning me and asking me to resign, and the board had adopted their report, I was deeply pained that men who had been my associates for years, and whom I had deemed my friends, could have taken such steps, especially without any notice to me or opportunity to be heard. There was a telephone in the building in Raleigh, where I sat, connecting with one in this building, where you were sitting, and four trains a day each way between the two places, and your board was in session two days or more. Yet not a whisper of these proceedings came to my ears. I respectfully asked for information. Your secretary put me off several days. Possibly Mr. Duke was absent. Then I received a curt note, in effect that I knew the verdict and the sentence, and that was enough for me to know. Still I said not a word to any one. The punishment for questioning Dr. Kilgo's supremacy here was not enough. It must be published to the world. In the Charlotte Observer, June 25, appeared the following:

JUDGE CLARK'S RESIGNATION
AS TRUSTEE ASKED FOR.

"It is learned in Charlotte that a controversy by letter has recently been in progress between Judge Walter Clark of the Supreme Court, and Dr. J. C. Kilgo, D.D., President of Trinity College and that at a meeting of the trustees of this institution last week, Dr. Kilgo laid the correspondence before the Board, asked for an investigation and stated that if they were sustained his resignation would be forthcoming. The investigation was made, the result being that Dr. Kilgo was sustained, and that the resignation of Judge Clark as a member of the Board was requested."

This was the first time that the matter was put in the papers. It did not come from me. I did not know then of Dr. Kilgo's threat to resign if you did not find his way. This going into print came necessarily from some one who was on the Board. A telegram from the Charlotte Observer has been printed to the effect that it did not receive the news from any one connected with the college, which is true, so far as the paper is concerned. But a part of the process was disclosed at the meeting here on July 18th, when Rev. N. M. Jurney stated that Major Jas. W. Wilson told him a preacher had told him (Wilson) and he was going to have it published in the Charlotte Observer. Mr. Jurney said Major Wilson did not have it exactly correct, and he gave it to him straight. So we have an authentic statement of the threat, and the resultant proceedings, for Mr. Jurney is not only a member of the Board who voted for the resolution, but he is travelling agent in the employ of the college, and so a member of "the administration" that was endorsed. Who the preacher was who first told

Major Wilson, and who had not told it exactly straight, according to Mr. Jurney, I do not know, but he must necessarily have been a member of this board, or have gotten it from one who was.

When it was published that any one has been requested by his associates to resign, no matter from what kind of a board, it is a stigma (and this publication was so intended) and calls for explanation. To the reporter who called on me for an interview, I gave the correspondence, including my letter to Mr. Southgate, in which I said that if I had been asked in a proper manner for my resignation, it would have been cheerfully given, but that it was unheard of to try me in my absence without notice; without opportunity to be heard or submit evidence, and to condemn me and publish that, and that my resignation had been asked for. I said further that the Board had no jurisdiction to try its members for their individual views, and if it had, why had the Board not tried and condemned him (Southgate) for his speech condemning public schools, which was calculated to be far more injurious to the college than my unpublished views as to Dr. Kilgo, for whose views the Board is responsible, being the employe, for his excessively laudatory speech to Mr. Duke, of the Cigarette Trust, which was a deification of wealth. I spoke of his reputation as a wire-puller in South Carolina, and that he had not reformed in North Carolina, and mentioned that a clergyman in Tennessee had said he was a scrub politician. Mr. Southgate replied, saying among other things, I had not been in trial, only Dr. Kilgo, to which I replied that if I was not on trial, then the condemnation and sentence passed upon me was still less justifiable.

Dr. Kilgo then came out in an interview. I could have answered him very conclusively, but believing that the interest of the church and college could not be served by a continuance of the controversy, at a sacrifice of my impulse and to my own injury possibly, I was silent. The other side having had the first article in the paper, and the last, the opening and the conclusion as it were, it would seem that the "incident was closed."

But since I would not further reply, Dr. Kilgo had the ingenuity to re-open the fight and selected his own ground. He asked for an investigation of himself by this Board which had just endorsed him under threat of losing his valuable services if they did not, (for Mr. Jurney said the article containing that statement had been corrected by him for Major Wilson) and summoned me as a witness. I received the following letter:

Durham, N.C. July 7, 1898.

Judge Walter Clark, Raleigh, N.C.

In your recent letters to me given to the public through the press, there are accusations against the President of Trinity College, which require investigation by the Board of Trustees. As Dr. Kilgo is an employe of the Board this investigation which will be confined to him, is not in order, but is necessary for the protection of the Trustees in their purpose to employ no man in any capacity, whose character is not worthy of the fullest confidence.

Among others your attention is called to your statements that Dr. Kilgo wished to evade the evidence you had against him; the speech which you quote him as making on Mr. Duke's porch and other references as to this speech; his reputation in South Carolina; his residency and reputation in Tennessee and his record in North Carolina.

The Board will meet Monday, the 18th inst, in the Benefactor's Parlor of the Duke Building at 5 o'clock P.M.

It is earnestly desired that you present to the Board at the mentioned time and place in person or in writing all the evidence you have which will go to establishing these accusations.

Very truly yours,

J. H. SOUTHGATE
President Board of Trustees Trinity College.

In obedience to that request I attended here on the 18th. What then happened and how I was received are fresh to your memory. Rev. Dr. Oglesby, (pastor of Mr. Duke's church and chairman of the committee which had condemned me unheard) was appointed prosecutor and I was required to give the names of my witnesses to him and time was given both sides till Aug. 30, to get up the evidence.

This brings us to the evidence submitted here on this occasion. This resume has been necessary to its better consideration. Before I enter upon it, I wish to call attention to two points in Dr. Kilgo's interview which I refrained from answering—in the vain hope thereby to end this controversy. He said therein that on a rising vote at June session, 1897, I endorsed him. It is true that at that time I was willing to re-elect him for one year, but I knew enough to be opposed to risking him for four years. When shortly thereafter I found my views confirmed and told Mr. Brown we had done wisely to defeat the four year term, this racket began. Till then there had never been the slightest friction between Dr. Kilgo and myself.

In the same interview, he said on a rising vote to thank Dr. Duke and accept his gift I was present and did not protest. Note the difference. On the rising vote to endorse Dr. Kilgo, he says I voted (as I said above) but on a rising vote to thank Mr. Duke he merely says I did not protest. He is correct that there was a difference. The fact is when the rising vote was taken to thank Duke I (and I believe one other) did not rise. I thought that protest enough, if protest were necessary. While I did not vote to thank Mr. Duke I wish to call your attention to the fact that nowhere in this controversy have I raised the debatable question (whatever my opinions may be) whether the college ought to receive money made by a cigarette trust, which is a business not only condemned by the church, but which like all other trusts is illegal. What I have condemned was the laudation which endorses the method of making the money. Whether eating meat that had been set before idols was unlawful the great apostle left an open question but he certainly condemned the worship of the idol.

Nor have I said aught against the Methodist church or college. I know Dr. Kilgo's friends would like to give it that turn but he is neither the Methodist church nor is he Trinity College. To criticise him is not to attack either. Without my knowledge or desire the Conference elected me a Trustee of the college and I have endeavored to serve the best interests of both. If I shall satisfy you that Dr. Kilgo is not a proper person to manage this institution it will be no pleasure to me. I shall feel that I have discharged a painful duty.

I will now proceed to review the evidence brought out on this investigation.

In no court of justice could matters be properly investigated unless there was process to compel the attendance of witnesses. You have no compulsory process for witnesses and that has been the only chance of escape for the defendant. Of course those not Methodists can not be made to obey your subpoena but when I accepted your request to get up the evidence, I understood that Methodists, especially ministers, would obey it. But many of the most material witnesses, among them ministers who would readily have proven the charges in a few minutes, by testifying to what they had repeatedly stated, have refused to testify and you admit you are powerless to compel them. Some refuse because it is unpleasant and they do not wish to mingle in the affair. Others frankly say they fear they will be injured by the influence of the agents of the Duke Cigarette Company, and of Dr. Kilgo. Others still, who had promised to testify after their names were furnished to the defendant were touched by some magnetic influence that changed their minds. With this absence of power to compel witnesses the prosecution is called to prove a case. We have done so we think, but it is nothing to the case we would have in reference to the charge that Dr. Kilgo was a wire puller in South Carolina, the following evidence has been offered you:

B. C. Beckwith, a graduate of this college, a Methodist, a gentleman of the highest character, a lawyer of fine ability was sent by you to South Carolina to get up evidence. He testified here that he was absolutely indifferent and told Dr. Kilgo who went with him that he would report the fact as he found it. He went through South Carolina from one end to the other, stopping at several important points. He said he conversed with fifty to seventy-five gentlemen of standing in the Methodist church including four out of six delegates to the General Conference, and with note book in hand he told you could tell what each one had said, that witnesses would talk freely, but that few were willing to have depositions taken. He told you that while Dr. Kilgo has some strong partisans there that his character is that of a wire-puller and ecclesiastical politician, that it is generally believed that he, John O. Wilson and Dr. Kirkland formed a combination at the Memphis General Conference to secure certain offices, Dr. Kilgo's share to be the presidency of Columbia Female College. He took two depositions, Rev. T. C. Ligon and J. K. Jennings, which supported this view, but after that those who expressed those views would no longer go into deposition. As soon as Dr. Kilgo got a statement from Bishop Duncan favorable to him, the preachers possibly out of respect to him, ceased giving depositions, but they continued to give Mr. Beckwith statements which he took down. On cross-examination Dr. Kilgo drew out of Mr. Beckwith the conversation he had with three men who were favorable to Dr. Kilgo, but when Mr. Beckwith asked in justice to himself to give his conversations with others, and I asked it, Dr. Kilgo strenuously objected. The door was closed that you might not have the truth. My charge was that his reputation in South Carolina was that of a wire-puller and this could only be shown by statements of people who knew it. Reputation is what people say of a man. It is necessarily hearsay. Yet Dr. Kilgo had further examination of Mr. Beckwith as to his reputation ruled out because it was hearsay.

R. B. Boone, a lawyer of this place, a gentleman of well-known character, the son of a Methodist minister and a Methodist himself testified to you that he formerly lived in South Carolina, has two uncles who are Methodist ministers in South Carolina and on a recent visit to Spartanburg, S.C., he inquired particularly as to Dr. Kilgo's reputation in that State and found it was that of a wire-puller and politician, who had made combinations to run the Conference and had split it up badly. He offered to give the names of parties with whom he had talked, who he said were gentlemen of high social and church standing, but again Dr. Kilgo objected. Evidently he wanted an "investigation that does not investigate."

Rev. T. J. Gattis, a minister of the North Carolina Conference, whose character has never been impeached, told you he had travelled in South Carolina two and a half years and in that time he had attended every District conference in that State, 26 in number, and knew personally every Methodist minister in it and most of the leading laymen. He said that Dr. Kilgo's general character in South Carolina was that of a wire-pulling politician, that he had badly split the church there by his "combine" with John O. Wilson and Dr. Kirkland and the church was much relieved when he left, but that Dr. Kilgo still had his friends and partisans there.

At your last meeting Dr. Kilgo had this same Rev. John O. Wilson here and asked leave of you for him to sit at the table as his counsel. Afterwards he took his deposition. In it, Mr. Wilson has to admit that he had heard that Dr. Kilgo had been charged as being a wire-puller, but said it was not true. Of course, he thinks that, for if Dr. Kilgo is a wire-puller, the evidence is that Mr. Wilson was his associate. He also took the deposition here of Mr. Chreitsburg who formerly lived in South Carolina and who it seems now has made friends with Dr. Kilgo, though there are depositions here showing it was not "ever thus." Dr. Kilgo told us at our last meeting that he could bring the whole South Carolina Conference here. In truth, besides the two just mentioned, which were taken here in July, in his late tour through the State of South Carolina he got ten depositions. There are largely over a million people in South Carolina. He formerly lived there, still has his partisans there and he brings you from his tour ten certificates of character. Some of those say they have heard these charges, but disbelieved them, he also found some who said they had not heard them. Two of the ten were Senator McLaurin and his former class-mate Gov. Ellerbee. These gave him a good character, but there was no one present to cross-examine them when Dr. Kilgo took their statements and who would expect two public men to volunteer, without cross-examination, a modification of a certificate of good character. Possibly these men may have thought wire pulling a necessity and not a reflection upon or abatement of good character. Then he relied greatly on Bishop Duncan's statement that he had no knowledge of his being a wire-puller. As the Bishop is his known friend the Bishop is the last man to whom such reports would be carried. The Bishop has been placed, out of his turn, in charge of South Carolina Conference this year and when it was known he had given this certificate, the preachers stopped giving depositions which would clash with it. They, however, talked freely and Mr. Beckwith stood here, note book in hand, to tell you what the leading preachers and laymen in South Carolina said about Dr. Kilgo's character as a wire-puller. But Dr. Kilgo shut this off, except as to three men who had spoken favorably to Beckwith as to him.

In his speech Dr. Kilgo bitterly denounced Rev. Mr. Gattis for testifying against him when he had been kind to him. Mr. Gattis told you he came very unwillingly and only in obedience to your summons, and his kind relations to Dr. Kilgo heretofore did not require him to testify falsely. You heard Dr. Kilgo's thinly veiled, if veiled at all, threats of vengeance. As surely as Dr. Kilgo is the wire-puller and politician this evidence abundantly proves him to be you will see his efforts to have Mr. Gattis removed from his position at the next annual conference—not because Mr. Gattis is not faithful and competent and has been so deemed all these years—but he has testified against Dr. Kilgo, he has revolted against his "machine." The ward politician and "boss" must punish him. Watch my prediction.

Mr. Beckwith was sent by you to South Carolina to learn what Dr. Kilgo's character was. Dr. Kilgo thinks that Mr. Beckwith took his mission too seriously. He contends that Mr. Beckwith should have formed his opinion of Dr. Kilgo's reputation in South Carolina from the ten who gave depositions in his favor—who were of course specially selected by Dr. Kilgo—and not from the fifty or seventy-five others whom Mr. Beckwith selected at random among Methodist preachers and laymen, and who talked freely with him. It is common sense that from the latter a more accurate opinion can be formed of the truth as to Dr. Kilgo's reputation. I have lived in Raleigh twenty-five years. There are men there whose general character I do not know. A man does not know Dr. Kilgo's reputation simply because he lives in South Carolina. If I wish to know a man's general character in Raleigh would I confine myself to a few selected names he gives me, or would I go generally to people of his associates, his church, his trade, his lodge? This latter course Mr. Beckwith took. He is intelligent, he is impartial, he was selected and sent there by this board, and he tells you "Dr. Kilgo's general character in South Carolina is that of a wire-puller and ecclesiastical politician."

After Mr. Beckwith and Dr. Kilgo who were travelling together in South Carolina separated, the latter took the statements of Senator McLaurin and Gov. Ellerbee in Mr. Beckwith's absence (he being given notice just as he was leaving on the train) and those depositions were admitted. Mr. Beckwith procured the following affidavits from two laymen of high standing in the church, one of them assistant secretary to the annual conference in the absence of Dr. Kilgo and they have been rejected. As we justly complain of the rejection of valuable evidence which would have aided you to a just conclusion, I read them:

State of South Carolina
Sumter County.

Personally appeared John M. Knight who, being duly sworn, deposes and says:

That he is editor and proprietor of the Sumter Herald, a newspaper published at Sumter in said State, and resides in the city of Sumter. That he is a member of the Methodist E. Church, South, and has attended as a delegate from his church several sessions of his District and Annual Conferences. That he is now a member of the Board of Colportage of the South Carolina Conference.

Deponent further says that he has long known Dr. J. C. Kilgo, formerly of S. C. Conference, now president of Trinity College, and that his relations with Dr. Kilgo have always been pleasant. That at the 1893 S. C. Conference held in Sumter deponent first heard of the said Dr. Kilgo as a politician; and knows that he made himself very offensive to former friends, at the 1893 and other conferences by manipulation and wire-pulling and is sure that the church in South Carolina suffered much injury from the coterie of wire-pullers composed of Dr. Kilgo and others, who directed their efforts in controlling appointments—to the hurt of the church and injustice to meritorious ministers. . . .

HIS RECORD IN NORTH CAROLINA

Your invitation to me to prove that is broad. It is impossible to cover the whole ground. You know that from the time Dr. Kilgo set foot in this State till now there has been a continued turmoil. The effect can be better seen than the incidents described. You know that notwithstanding this magnificent plant and the "largest endowment" in the State (as Dr. Kilgo advertises) Trinity had last session fewer students by a good deal than Dr. Craven ran your attendance up to in Randolph. We have hardly half as many as Wake Forest under the quiet, peaceable management of Dr. Taylor. We have not as many as Davidson College, which represents a denomination of 30,000 members, while we have a membership of about 135,000 to draw from and at Chapel Hill there are more Methodist students than of any other denomination and the number of Methodist students there has steadily increased ever since Dr. Kilgo started in here. There were 115 Methodist boys at the University 1896-97. There must be a reason for this. Methodists are as loyal to their church and institutions as any people and certainly as loyal when with half of our membership they gave Craven 171 students. Yet last year (excluding young ladies who were not admitted in Dr. Craven's time) there was here 141, counting every one who attended any day during the year. And that reason must rest, where the praise would be claimed, if there was a large attendance, i.e., with the administration of your President. I said in my letter, I thought he had proven himself unfit, and this result is strong evidence of it. Then there are the difficulties he has had especially with that much-loved minister of the gospel, Rev. Jesse H. Page, and with that genial gentleman and Methodist, who has friends wherever he is known, T. B. Kingsbury, L.L.D., and many other difficulties might be recalled by you. Then I offered you evidence of his sermon in which he said that "the average woman can be led anywhere by a diamond ring." It was excluded from this investigation, but it has not been excluded from the knowledge of the people of North Carolina. Can the pure and noble women of our church be expected to send their sons to a college whose President says that the average woman has her yielding point—in a diamond ring. Did he speak this upon his own experience or upon hearsay? I cannot trust myself to speak my sentiments upon this declaration as to my fair countrywomen, who are as pure and as chaste as any that adorn God's footstool. I am not here to denounce but to suppress my indignation as best I may. Here is the affidavit:

Roxboro, N.C., July 26, '98

We hereby certify that we were present at a lecture delivered by Rev. John C. Kilgo in Roxboro and heard him use the following language, "The average woman can be lead anywhere with a diamond ring." The ladies present were severe in their condemnation of the statement and the low estimate placed by the speaker on the fidelity and constancy of our women.

The above language of Dr. Kilgo was published in the next issue of the Person County Courier and has never been denied so far as we know.

IDA LANSDELL.

Many other ladies have concurred in this statement. . . .

Then I also offered you, as further proof of his record (when you asked for) the personal evidence of Hon. John R. Webster, ex-Speaker of the House of Representatives, Methodist, a graduate of this college well and favorably known all over North Carolina, that he had heard Dr. Kilgo lecture in Madison last year and he said that the primary department of our graded schools are "baby ranches into which parents, careless of their children, pitched them and if he was looking for vice and immorality he would not go into the so-called dark corners but into the graded schools."

He testified in person, but the evidence was voted out on objection from Dr. Kilgo, on the ground that it did not tend to prove Dr. Kilgo's "record in North Carolina," or his "unfitness," and you refused to let it go on your minutes that the evidence had been offered. Furthermore though Mr. Webster had come here under your subpoena to testify, after his evidence was rejected, on Dr. Kilgo's motion he was ignominiously expelled from this room because he was "a newspaper editor." . . .

I offered the affidavits of as highly respected men as are to be found in the county of Caswell that Dr. Kilgo proposed to cure the free silver men by the application of 16 lashes to each back and a large portion of the audience rose and went out. The people of North Carolina are in the habit of thinking for themselves and when the President of this college proposes to punish them with the lash for opinion's sake it is a part of his "record in North Carolina" that will do the college no good. Your prosecutor excluded this also. Here is the affidavit I offered:

JOHN CARLISLE KILGO

From a painting by Wiltschek.
Courtesy of the Duke University News Service.

North Carolina,
Caswell County.

C. G. Lea being duly sworn says that he was present at a lecture at New Hope church in Caswell County, when Dr. J. C. Kilgo used the following language, that "the reason the farmers were not prosperous was on account of their laziness and triflingness, that the 16 to 1 calamity howlers ought to have 16 stripes to each back." He (Kilgo) used this language in a public lecture at the above named place, which so offended a large number of the best people there that they got up and left the church without waiting to hear more.... July 29, 1898.

... This evidence was excluded on the same technical grounds as the "diamond ring" evidence from Roxboro. Instead of "turning on the light" upon his "record" in North Carolina, the whole effort of the defendant has been to shut it off.

I also offered you the affidavits of A. J. Connor, J. B. Bryan and W. H. Evans, from the county of Northampton, all Methodists and gentlemen of high character.... Mr. Connor who is editor of the "Patron and Gleaner" and Mayor of Rich Square, says:

"That on or about the 2nd day of November, 1896, I heard Dr. J. C. Kilgo deliver a lecture at Pinner's M.E. church in Northampton county, in the course of which he said, in substance, that the men going over the country complaining of the exciting conditions and claiming to have a panacea for the evils of the government were nothing but political demagogues, meaning, as I believe, W. J. Bryan and the advocates of the restoration of the free coinage of silver as set forth in the Chicago platform. In the same connection he said: "There is nothing the matter with the country but laziness." ... His lecture impressed me also as a masterful and ingenious apology and defense of trusts, monopolies and the existing gold standard, and as an indirect covert attack upon the public school system of the State."

They further say the effect of the speech has been unfavorable to the college and will prevent students coming here.

These three are depositions regularly taken and were excluded because your prosecutor (Oglesby) said he did not think they tended to prove Dr. Kilgo's "record in North Carolina," nor his unfitness.... This is a very comfortable arrangement for a man who wants his "record" preserved from publicity.

Can you expect farmers to send their sons to a college whose

President teaches publicly that the laziness of their fathers is the cause of the depression. It is the language used by the taskmasters of Pharaoh of old to the children of the oppression....

Another feature of Dr. Kilgo's record in North Carolina is his manipulation and wire-pulling. If I were to go into his record at the last two or three annual conferences and at many of the District Conferences heretofore, it might make interesting reading, but would raise a nest of hornets about my ears, but Dr. Kilgo has relieved me from any necessity of resorting to so unpleasant a proceeding. Since the meeting was ordered at Dr. Kilgo's instance, for his investigation, and pending that investigation he has visited District Conference after conference. The lamb was not more sure to follow where Mary went than the announcement that the Doctor was attending a district conference was sure to be followed by a notice that Duke and Kilgo were endorsed. This pending a judicial investigation by this Board, which was supposed to be made in good faith, at his instance, whether he ought to be endorsed! The similarity in the language of these resolutions and the singular coincidence as to the care with which his special friends were selected as delegates to the Annual Conference, made the State smile. The hand of the "boss" was recognized, and even the monopoly papers which are always on Dr. Kilgo's side could not refrain any more than other papers from noting that "Dr. Kilgo was running in the primaries." Only one editor that I know of defended him, and that was Mr. Ivey, who is one of the jury which is to pass upon the identical question which those resolutions were determining in advance without evidence—resolutions which were published with remarkable promptness and regularity in the Advocate, though it refused to print a moderately worded resolution signed by Frank C. Robbins and six others ... against the false representations of our agents by which a large sum of money was voted by Congress to our church....

The evidence of the presence of Dr. Kilgo or his special friends at these district conferences where these resolutions were passed, and the fact that many members of this jury voted at them in favor of resolutions endorsing Dr. Kilgo, thus anticipating your verdict, was not denied by any evidence, nor even denied (his usual way) in Dr. Kilgo's speech. The only thing that looked like a defence was the statement in his speech (unsupported by any evidence) that I had written articles in favor of free coinage of silver while on the bench before which such questions might come. If I was wrong (as he intimated) how would that make right this action of the trustees in recording their verdict in favor of Dr. Kilgo at the District Conferences before coming here to vote on it again as impartial jurors. But there is in truth no analogy. The remonetization of silver, the great financial issue, is purely a national question. By no sort of possibility could it come before a State court. But the endorsement of Dr. Kilgo by Trustees voting at District Conferences was a decision by them of the identical question which you are to decide—whether he ought to be endorsed or not.

Then, if further evidence is desired of Dr. Kilgo's capacity for manipulating for his measures, I refer you to the affidavit of T. B. Kingsbury, L.L.D., that Dr. Kilgo sent him a message that he (Kilgo) "had the Methodist preachers at his back; that he had the medicine for him, and he would spread it all about." Here is the deposition. T. B. Kingsbury being sworn, says:

"On or about the 28th of June, 1897, Mr. J. A. Crews reported to me that he had seen and talked with Dr. Kilgo at Morehead City, and that Dr. Kilgo had sent me a message. . . .

" 'Tell Kingsbury I say he is a hypocrite and a fraud.' The threats were: 'I say Kingsbury is a liar and he knows when he lies. I have the medicine for him, and I shall spread it all about. I have a mission, and I mean to destroy him. He must be driven out of North Carolina. I will drive him out. He and I cannot remain in it. He ought to be driven out of the Methodist church. If he is driven from the Messenger he can find nothing to do—no other paper in North Carolina would have him; he cannot get employment out of the State. I can get a place outside. I have the Methodist preachers of the State at my back.' "

WISH TO EVADE EVIDENCE AGAINST HIM

The next thing I am called upon to prove is the statement that Dr. Kilgo wished to evade the evidence I had against him. When it is remembered that I could easily have been given notice, there being a telephone in this building, connected with one where I was, and four daily trains each way, that no notice was given; that if I had attended and produced evidence the Board could not have sustained him, (which he desired so earnestly that he threatened to resign if it was not done) and that my subsequent request for information as to the trial was refused a case has been made on that point for any jury. Now, has it been shown that if opportunity had been given, evidence could have been offered, which should have prevented the finding of the committee that they endorsed Dr. Kilgo and condemned my charges. If it had been in evidence then that Dr. Kilgo had said in Caswell that free silver men ought to have sixteen lashes to the bare back, could you have endorsed that? If it had been shown as now, that he had said in Northampton that the cause of the depression was the laziness of the farmers, and that he made monopoly and gold standard speeches in Sampson and Duplin, could you have endorsed that and denounced my charge, that he favored the gold standard publicly, as unfair? If it had been shown then that he denounced graded schools as dens of vice, and as Christless schools, could you have endorsed him so readily? If it had been shown that he had been a well known wire-puller in South Carolina, and had threatened Dr. Kingsbury with using his wires against him to his hurt among the Methodist preachers, whom he claimed to have at his back, could you have endorsed that? Could you have endorsed his statement that our ladies could be led anywhere by a consideration? Could you have endorsed those and other things that could have been shown against him? If not, then the conclusion is irresistible, he did not want them shown, and that he wished to evade their being shown, for he did not wish to resign, and the Jas. W. Wilson-Jurney card in the Charlotte Observer says he threatened to resign unless you did sustain him.

SPEECH TO DUKE

Now we come to that remarkable speech to Mr. Duke. The reporter who took it down, Zeb Vance Council * has a most excellent character. No attempt was made to attack, though he lives here in Durham, where zealous agents would have gotten such evidence, if to be had. He is a gentleman of intelligence and bears in his name a hereditary approval of the people's truest and greatest friend. He says he is positive as to the language, that he took it down at the time, for he was struck by it that Dr. Kilgo should say that Mr. Duke because of his gift was greater than all these—the primacy at Mecklenburg, the blood shed at Bethel and Cardenas. I did not purport in my letter to give the exact words used by Dr. Kilgo, but I said that in effect he said so and so and Mr. Council's affidavit fully and entirely sustains me. It is this:

"Z. B. Council makes affidavit as follows that on the 7th day of January, he was the local reporter for the Durham Daily Sun, an afternoon paper published in Durham, that he heard the speech

* Now engaged in the printing business in Chapel Hill.

made by Dr. J. C. Kilgo at the residence of W. Duke on the evening of June 7, 1898, when the Richmond Band, the Faculty of Trinity College, some students and others went there for the purpose of serenading Mr. Duke and thanking him for his liberality; that he reported the proceedings for the Durham Sun and the words appearing in quotation marks in the following clipping:

" 'At the conclusion of the address the student body, headed by the Richmond band and faculty, marched down to the residence of Washington Duke, and serenaded him and gave three cheers for Kilgo, Duke and Trinity. Short speeches were made by George Humber, Dr. Robbins and Dr. Kilgo, all expressing their appreciation and thanks to Mr. Duke for his liberality. In the course of his remarks, Dr. Kilgo said, 'The first white child was born in North Carolina, the first Declaration of Independence was signed in North Carolina, the first blood shed of the civil war and present war was shed by a North Carolinian, but greater than these the greatest philanthropist of the South is a North Carolinian" ' [these words] were spoken by Dr. Kilgo on that occasion and were taken down by the affiant in his note book, that he afterwards wrote out the article which appeared in the Durham Daily Sun on the 8th day of June, 1898, and the above language therein attributed to Dr. Kilgo was used by him; that no correction of his report has even been made or requested by any one, and no one has ever suggested to the affiant that it was not accurate.

"And the affiant further says that in the same speech Dr. J. C. Kilgo in speaking of Trinity College, its hopes, benefactors and prospects, said in substance: This (meaning Mr. W. Duke's house) is the president's house. We are just permitting Mr. Duke to use it awhile. Over there on Chapel Hill street (pointing to Mr. B. N. Duke's residence) is the house of a member of the faculty, and there (pointing to Duke's factory) is our industry and we have a bank down town.

"The affiant is not positive of the exact words used by Mr. Duke in this last paragraph as he did not take the words down at the time, yet he is positive most of these words were used by Dr. Kilgo and the language above gives the substance of what was said.

(Signed) "ZEB B. COUNCIL"

"Sworn to and subscribed before me this, the 5th day of June, 1898.

"(Signed) D. C. GUNTER, J. P. (Seal)"

It will be noted that as to the paragraph referred to in my letter, Mr. Council is positive, he took the words down at the time and published them next day. He appeared before you and by oral testimony substantiated what he swore to above. On a strict cross-examination it clearly appeared that he had stated the exact truth as to his speech.

. . . It is true Dr. Kilgo has introduced one or two witnesses who thought that he said "and also" instead of "greater than," but he says he spoke without notes, and all of his witnesses say they took no notes. Mr. Council took notes. He says he knows he was accurate. . . .

The witnesses Dr. Kilgo introduced were members of his Faculty, holding their place at his nod and one or two trustees. . . . Dr. Kilgo has not omitted in this trial to pay his usual tribute to the Dukes. In his speech just made he paid them a grateful and glowing tribute. And even in the depositions he has taken and which have been read in your hearing he has managed to bring out to his credit that one of the Dukes alone pays $800 towards the salary of Mr. Oglesby (your prosecutor) who is pastor both of Mr. Duke and Dr. Kilgo. . . .

The Western North Carolina Conference which is half owner of this College in 1897 passed this resolution:

"In view of the lamentable effects resulting from the use of the cigarette and the rapid growth of this evil; therefore be it

Resolved, That we, the Western North Carolina Conference in session assembled, are opposed to the manufacture, sale and use of cigarettes, and will do all we can to save our people from this terrible evil." . . .

The laws of North Carolina 1889, chapter 374 prohibit Trusts under a penalty of $10,000 fine and ten years imprisonment. . . . A member of this Board has suggested to me that the American Tobacco Company (alias Cigarette Trust) has not been convicted in any court of being a trust. A cause that depends on that defence is already lost. The whole world knows it is a trust. . . .

And well do the tobacco growers of North Carolina know the Cigarette trust which has stifled competition and reduced the prices of the product of their toil one half or three fourths. A few years ago the prosperity of that section was the wonder of the State. But there came a frost, a killing frost, when the Cigarette Trust was formed. It blighted the country worse than a cyclone but palaces are reared in New York and in Durham. . . .

Dr. Kilgo has stated publicly so often as to require no special proof that "After he got a few more Trinity students in the Conference he would make it hot for the preachers educated at other colleges." This is on a par with his speech at Weaversville that "Trinity was coming into its kingdom (he doubtless meant Dukedom) one of these days and the preachers who did not stand by her would be made to feel her power." There you have the "machine" disclosed. Trinity is to run North Carolina. Dr. Kilgo is to run Trinity and the cigarette millions are to run him and to aid him to maintain his supremacy.... The feeling that it is dangerous to oppose Dr. Kilgo has been widely cultivated. It is his chief strength. It has hampered the prosecution in getting the evidence, especially as the attendance of witnesses could not be compelled. From the vast number of letters I have received from laymen, which show that the laity are almost solidly against Kilgoism, I will not quote, but I will read brief extracts from letters received from three ministers (out of many I have received) situated in widely different sections. One writes:

"There were thousands who had not bowed the knee to Baal, so there are many with you that shall be revealed should the matter be carried to the Annual Conference. Ours is not the time in which the spirit of inquisition thrives. I am willing for the Dukes to put their money where they like, but recipients thereof must not try to throttle the right of individual opinion or the expression of it. It argues littleness of mind for one to be putting into publicity man's opinion of himself privately expressed. I do not think you need to fear the outcome of present conditions. Truth triumphs."

Another widely loved minister writes:

"You have my deepest sympathies under the unbrotherly and unjust treatment you have received at the hands of your friends. The outlook for those of us whose honest convictions place us in the minority in the Conference is not all bright or cheering. At what time we shall be "requested" to retire is uncertain. The prospect is indeed gloomy. May the good Lord take care of us."

That brother has evidently felt the edge of the "machine," this new invention which Dr. Kilgo has brought into the Methodist church.

One of the ablest ministers in the church writes: "I believe every charge you make against Dr. Kilgo. The basis (of his support) is the recognition of the American Tobacco Company as a religious institution, and the canonization of the Dukes before they die—an advance step as compared with the papacy."

I have many similar letters from our ministers and large numbers from laymen all over the State.

The Church of God should be the mainstay against the mad tide which now threatens to overwhelm all in a sordid worship of wealth, but they are not all Israel who are of Israel. Church members and ministers are too often in the throng that bow the knee to Baal....

I know it has been told around with effect, members of the Board have told me, "we have a million dollars in sight." If Dr. Kilgo is not sustained, it is possible that it may vanish, and there may be some who shall say what is the harm of plastering up Dr. Kilgo's shortcomings if we keep that beautiful thing in sight. If I am condemned unjustly for having told the truth, there may be some who shall say what is a little injustice like that to losing the sight of so much money.

There was one once who had the whole world in his sight, and he turned his back upon it. It is true it was a long time ago, but we call him Master, and we profess to be his followers.

No duty more unpleasant has ever devolved upon any man than this has been to me. It pains me to be at variance with anybody, especially with any of those whom I have deemed my friends for years. I can not but believe that some influence back of Dr. Kilgo, has planned this as an adroit scheme to create a division between me and some who have been heretofore my friends. But I have been driven, pulled, dragooned into this controversy, which is so opposed to all my feelings. Because I said to a fellow Trustee we had done well to defeat Dr. Kilgo's proposition for a four years term, eleven months later without warning, without notice, I am suddenly censured by my associates, by men whom I esteemed, and am asked to resign. When I asked for information it was denied me. But I kept my wound to myself. I said nothing. Then on information coming from those who voted for my condemnation, it is published in the press. I then gave the facts, Mr. Southgate replied, to which I answered, and from that day in June, two months ago, till now not a word from me or my pen has gone to the press. I let the matter drop in the interest of harmony. Dr. Kilgo afterwards came out in an interview. I made no reply. Unable to keep the fight up in that way, he applied to this Board to investigate him and summon me as a witness, thus choosing his own forum. In his speech here, he boasted that he had re-opened the fight. All this time, pending the investigation, which should be impartial, I observed the propriety of keeping silent. But during this time Dr. Kilgo was going from District Conference to District Conference, and wherever he or his special friends went, resolutions endorsing Dr. Kilgo and Mr. Duke sprang up as flowers at the footsteps of spring. The "Advocate," under the auspices of one of the jury with regularity and dispatch printed these resolutions, and defended Dr. Kilgo, while the "Christian Educator," edited by two of Dr. Kilgo's professors, has in each issue overflowed with volumes of abuse of myself. The papers owned in part or controlled by the Dukes and the entire monopoly press have assailed me. In coming here today to lay these facts before you, I have simply done my duty. I desire no harm to Dr. Kilgo. I have no personal animosity to him, but I am antagonistic to the views he has expressed in the matters I have referred to. I earnestly desire the best good of this college. I think his usefulness here has been fatally impaired for the reasons I have given. I would have preferred not bringing out this evidence against Dr. Kilgo, but he would have it so and the Board ordered it.

I know it is hard to fight this "combination of Blifil and Black George," this union of Kilgo's "machine methods" and the millions of the cigarette trust. I know the forces they can marshal, the papers whose columns they can turn loose on any one, the numerous agents of all kinds they can set in motion. I can not cope with them in use of money. I have never thought the chief end of man was to accumulate wealth. I have tried, in my humble way, to be of some use to my fellow men. I have ever advocated those things which were for the public welfare and not those which served the private interest of great corporations and multi-millionaires. I have thereby made them my enemies. I have little save my good name, and some share in the esteem of my fellow citizens whose interests I have faithfully endeavored to serve, and these things I well know the gigantic power of money will endeavor to take from me. . . .

Your verdict is not unanticipated by me. All the evidence in Dr. Kilgo's behalf has been admitted. More than half that collected against him (with difficulty, in the absence of compulsory process for witnesses) has been rejected. So many members of this Board have recently voted for resolutions endorsing Dr. Kilgo at the District Conferences it would not be easy with the fullest investigation to change your views. But we have not had a full investigation. Dr. Kilgo from the start has insisted on technicalities and the rejection of evidence. Let him be satisfied with a verdict secured by such means. Those windows are open and through them the truth will go out to an honest, an intelligent and an impartial public. They will try the triers. And beyond the silent stars, this gracious, beautiful night sits one from whom no technicalities will exclude the truth, and whose clear vision will be unclouded by any earthly considerations.

TO CLARK FROM JAMES B. LLOYD

Tarboro, N.C.
Sept. 5, 1898

I have just read your able speech, and I can not find language to express my deep indignation and supreme contempt for the methods that were employed to throttle and stifle the truth as to the conduct of Dr. Kilgo. I am not a Methodist, and, therefore, have nothing to do with the management of Trinity College, but, as a citizen of North Carolina, I have the right to express myself when great injustice is done to a person occupying such a high official position as you do.

Candor compels me to say that the methods adopted in the trial of yourself would have been very becoming in the Judge who condemned Socrates to drink the hemlock. But they deserve the severest condemnation at the hands of all fairminded men who love justice and fairplay.

Give your speech wide circulation so the people may judge for themselves.

TO CLARK FROM F. C. HARDING AND FIVE OTHER GREENSBORO LAWYERS *

Greenville, N. C.
September 5th, 1898

We, the undersigned members of the Greenville bar have read with interest the Clark-Kilgo controversy, and feeling that however well armed you may be, on account of the justness of your cause, you will appreciate an expression of approval from us, and we deem it both a pleasure and a privilege to say, that our sympathy has been and is still with you, that we approve of your course, that we wish to compliment you on the splendid courage you have shown and the manly fight you have made, and that we

* W. D. Grimes, I. H. Sugg, W. F. Harding, B. F. Tyson, and W. H. Long.

commend you for the timely rebuke it has given to the growing ecclesiastical power which has already become a menace to intellectual and civil liberty and to many state institutions.

TO CLARK FROM J. A. LEE *

Kinston, N.C.
Sept. 6, 1898

I have just finished reading your able speech for the board of Trustees of Trinity College, printed in Sunday's News and Observer. It is a masterly speech and has a wonderful array of facts and evidence, if I am any judge. I have until recently been defending the President of Trinity and the cause of the College, against some of my leading men. But I can no longer defend them.

My people as well as myself are with you. I admire your course, and firmly believe that you have been unjustly treated. If matters shall reach a crisis in the next Annual Conference, in my judgment some people will be surprised how the conference will vote. This is the first time in my life that I have written such a letter, and taken such a course. I thank you for that speech.

TO CLARK FROM W. B. FLEMING

Ridgeway, N.C.
Sept. 6, 1898

I am a farmer and member of the Methodist Church. If my church sustains Dr. Kilgo and his methods, I will know that it is an enemy to mankind. Up to 1895 I raised tobacco largely, since then I have not raised any, for four years prior to this time I could feel the greed of the Tobacco trust each year more plainly until I was forced to leave off raising the weed or lose the little means that I had accumulated. This loss and inconvenience was as nothing; the use of cigarettes blighted my hopes in an only boy, young man, who was put under the sod last December. May God forbid the church to endorse any evil especially that of the changers. I believe the laity are with you against the almost combined influence of the clergy. You need not go outside of the recent trial to prove "wire pulling." May God Bless you and yours in your work for down trodden humanity.

Personally, I do not know you. My love for justice and bravery have prompted these lines and may God guide you to do and say just the right thing until this controversy is ended.

* Methodist minister.

TO CLARK FROM GEORGE W. GRAHAM

Charlotte, N.C.
Sept. 6, 1898

Your letter received this A.M. also the paper. The News and Observer reached here Sunday and there was a great demand for it. After the people read it they were so indignant at the way you had been treated and scoundrelism of Kilgo that public opinion forced Joe Caldwell * to acknowledge the defeat of Kilgo and to write a very complimentary editorial of you, although it was intermixed with dirt. Charlotte is with you and the general impression here is that had Kilgo put his trust in the Lord instead of tobacco, he would not be smoking so much just now.

TO CLARK FROM CHARLES F. WARREN †

Washington, N.C.
Sept. 7, 1898

...I have followed with interest, your controversy with Dr. Kilgo and the trustees of Trinity College. A private conversation between two trustees of a college is made the basis of official action by the board. It would be but slightly more inquisitorial to hold a trustee accountable for his belief or his unexpressed thought. The methods pursued towards you were those of the Star Chamber. They shock every sense of propriety and fair play. The ecclesiastical and semi-ecclesiastical tribunals sometimes work out curious results. They are not trammeled by law or consistency. I would quickly sever my connection with great prosecution if the solicitor, at every stage of the trial, was admitting away the case of the State. I would regard him as an enemy in my camp and would require him to get out or would get out myself. A verdict reached as this was, from a tribunal constituted as this was, carries no weight. It does not even whitewash. The expected has simply come to pass.

I do not know Dr. Kilgo and never saw him. I was educated outside the State and may be considered impartial between the higher institutions of learning in the State. In my opinion the course of Dr. Kilgo has been very objectionable since he has been in North Carolina.

It is a pity to see the head, professor or trustees of colleges and universities toadying to wealth. It sets up false ideals for young

* Editor of *Charlotte Daily Observer*.
† Lawyer and former member of the General Assembly.

men and defies the dollar. It pollutes the stream at the fountain. The man who can control and shape the higher education of a people can both draft their laws and write their song. The indications are not few and they all point to the attempt to shape in this country the course of instruction in Colleges and Universities that square with the views of benefactors whose wealth and donations are derived from methods denounced by law. These gift bearing Greeks should be feared.

To the ungodly mind it would seem to be a glaring inconsistency to accept an endowment in the stock of a trust against whose manufacturers it is necessary to protect by law students in college under the age of seventeen, but to the faithful, I presume, all these things can be reconciled.

For a college, struggling for years with debt and poverty, the temptation of a generous endowment is almost irresistible. It may come in "questionable shape," as the ghost in Hamlet, but there will be found on the part of trustees little disposition to interrogate it, either as to the motive of the donor or the character of the gift. Those are not likely to dissolve the laws between Duke and Trinity. It would be the truer policy of the college to rely for its support upon a powerful religious denomination and excellence of the course of instruction furnished. It would then build upon the bedrock of public confidence. The temptation of a large endowment is too glittering to put aside. You might console yourself with the homely wisdom of the local poet, commenting upon the refusal of the minister receiving a salary of four thousand dollars to obey an urgent call of duty and to accept a charge where the salary was only two thousand dollars:

> He might have called till He was blue
> Before he'd move from four to two.

You must feel like a man who has been trampled by a herd of wild cattle—bruised, but resolute.

TO CLARK FROM J. H. PEARSON *

Morganton, N.C.
Sept. 5, 1898

I have read with pleasure the justly deserved scoring you have given Kilgo, and beg to extend my congratulations to you for the very able and effectual manner in which it has been done. The

* Editor of the Morganton *Herald*.

people of North Carolina who are freed from corporation and trust influence are with you in this fight, and it is to be regretted that we have not a representative press that would ring clear in a true expression of their opinions.

TO CLARK FROM W. E. EDMONSON

Philadelphia, Pa.
Sept. 7, 1898

I am with you heart, soul and body. Am disgusted with their gag-law "manipulation." Don't let up till the "ring" is broken. I wish I were there to cast my say on the right side. I expect to attend conference.

TO CLARK FROM THE REVEREND CHARLES W. BYRD *

Asheville, N.C.
Sept. 7, 1898

I write to assure you that you have the sympathy of at least our Methodist Ministers in the conflict through which you have passed. I have read your speech as published in the News and Observer. If you did not make out the case I am unable to judge of evidence. Of course, the verdict was made up before you met at Durham, and you were not disappointed, but the verdict of the Trustees will not be the verdict of North Carolina public.

Don't let all this estrange you from the church, but stand up and fight for truth in the future as you have done in the past.

TO CLARK FROM E. J. HOLT

Smithfield, N.C.
Sept. 9, 1898

I have read all I could get out of the papers in the Clark-Kilgo matter and I feel that as a member of the Methodist Church, and one who loves his church and has been taught to reverence our clergy and to believe that they are devoted to justice, fairness, and as a rule are high-toned fair minded men, that I wish to say to you that the action of the Board of Trustees and the prosecutor, Dr. Oglesby,† has disgusted me (and many others) with them. I am sure I have never heard of anything more unfair in my life and as for Dr. Kilgo, if I had a dozen boys to educate and had a barrel

* Methodist minister and Presiding Elder.

† Pastor of Duke's church in Durham. Oglesby acted as prosecutor in the "trial" of Clark before the Board of Trustees.

of money for each boy I would not send them to Trinity while he is at its head. It seems to me that his slander of the women of N. C. is meaner and worse than that of the negro editor, Manly * of Wilmington, N. C. particularly when we consider the source from which each slander came.

You certainly made out your case and while the "court" decided against you the public must and will say that you are right—and that Dr. Kilgo is all and more than you charged against him, and his endorsement by the "court" "places them in a hole" and lowers them to a position in the opinion of all right minded people which must destroy their influence for good for all time to come.

TO CLARK FROM GEORGE A. SHUFORD †

Asheville, N. C.
9/2/98

I wish to express to you my sympathy in your contest with the trustees of Trinity College. I know nothing about the merits of the controversy except what I have gathered from the publications in the newspapers, but I do believe in fair play, and the investigation which the trustees have pretended to make strikes an outsider not only as being farcical, but as a gross violation of the established rules of judicial procedure. It seems to have been simply a whitewashing affair. Instead of benefitting Dr. Kilgo, I am satisfied it will have the contrary effect. It gives the public the impression that there are facts which he is afraid to allow to be brought to light. I have never had any confidence in him since he commenced his warfare on our state institutions. I look on any man who is an enemy of the University and our Normal College at Greensboro as an enemy of the state, and the sooner he gets out of the state the better it will be for our people.

This letter is of course personal, but if you need any further evidence to establish Kilgo's reputation in South Carolina I think I can put you on sources of information.

TO CLARK FROM W. W. VANDIVER

Columbus, N. C.
Sept. 9, 1898

I have read in Sunday's News and Observer, your argument in the Kilgo matter and think you made out your case. My father

* A. L. Manley, Editor of Wilmington *Record.*
† Lawyer.

and grandfather were both Methodist preachers and I am sorry to see the church for which they lived and labored and in which they died, endorse such methods and conduct and ideas as characterize ...[the] marplot and upstart Kilgo.

I desire to ask you if Trinity College owns $100,000 of stock in the Tobacco Trust. In your argument the language seems to carry that meaning.

I wish to write something now and then in my paper which will tend to acquaint the Methodists with John Kilgo and his cigarette college, and will live in the hope that every threat he made against that admirable Christian gentleman, Dr. Kingsbury, will be a boomerang and hit him centerably. The church should get rid of him. I would be obliged for any further information that could be published that would open the eyes of the people of N. C. as to this ecclesiastic demagogue.

TO CLARK FROM A. L. BROOKS *

Mt. Vernon Springs, N.C.
Sept. 9/98

Your speech "published in last Sunday's News & Observer" has added many friends to your list. Surely the board made a mistake when it refused to let you offer that speech in your own defense. Much better for the College and Church had they kept nothing hid. Thousands of good people "and Methodists too" are in full sympathy with you and endorse your course. It has never been my pleasure to meet you, but I have a brother who served with you in the war and I used to think it was his delight to speak in praise of Maj. Walter Clark. I have not seen him in several years.

TO CLARK FROM A. M. AIKENS †

Danville, Virginia
Sept. 11, 1898

I have just finished reading from my friend Webster's paper your complete exposure of that scoundrel Kilgo....

The cowhide well laid on is the punishment for him, and I hope he will have it before he leaves the State.

I believe that most of the preachers who have the easy places in the cities and colleges serve the money power with the same willingness that Kilgo does.

* Greensboro attorney and author of *Walter Clark, Fighting Judge.*
† Prominent business man.

TO CLARK FROM HOWARD F. JONES

Wilson, N. C.
Sept. 28, 1898

I have been "itching" for several weeks to write you and assure you that you have the great body of Methodist laymen at your back and supporting you in your controversy with Dr. Kilgo. The trial was a perfect farce, so far as justice and impartiality was concerned. I wish with all my heart that our hard working Methodist Layman (the man who toils all the day long and receives a mere pittance for his labor, and of that pittance gives liberally to support of the Gospel) could get a chance to vote upon the questions brought out in the trial. I am quite sure the decision of the *lower Court* would be reversed.

I wish, my dear Sir, that you had a faint idea even, of the warm place you hold in our hearts. We feel that we have in you a friend and bulwark of safety against the tools of the great money power. May you live long to serve us in the highest offices within our gift. I wish we could place your name with that of the great Bryan and elect you to preside over the Senate.

I know that my good old Father—who even now attends all quarterly meetings—is with you in your controversy with Dr. Kilgo and so you will find the great Body of Toilers.

TO CLARK FROM E. F. AYDLETT *

Elizabeth City, N. C.
October 6, 1898

Upon my return from Raleigh I find a pamphlet stating it is "A report of the procedings of the investigation of the charges brought by Justice Walter Clark vs Dr. Jno. C. Kilgo". Doubtless you are aware that these pamphlets are being sent all over the state. I write simply to express to you that your many friends in this section feel that you have not been treated fairly in the matter, and they do not hesitate to express themselves. The proceedings by the Trustees are extraordinary and it seems that they had already decided what they would do before hearing the evidence. I have not heard the expression from a single one who does not believe the charges you made were sustained by you from the evidence introduced, and which you had ready to introduce. I write this to give you some idea what a great many people in this

* Lawyer.

section think about the matter, as I thought it would be of some satisfaction to you.

TO CLARK FROM J. M. BANDY *

Greensboro, N. C.
Dec. 3, 1900

Allow me to congratulate you in at last having your controversy with old Kilgo, the *Saint,* placed where the light could shine in on the unfair, unjust methods used against you.

He could not now appeal to Oglesby, Jurney & Co. to sustain him. He could not repress evidence against him and admit evidence in his favor.

Like old Simion, I have waited a long time to see this man Kilgo reap his reward. It has come. The time is indeed refreshing.

I was once a Professor in Trinity College. I saw the pure rot on which it was being moved and founded. I was not mistaken. Every one of us is asked to give up his convictions, and fall down and worship Kilgoism. Thanks! There are few of us who do not propose to do so.

TO CLARK FROM ARTHUR T. ABERNATHY

Philadelphia, Penn.
Dec. 11, 1900

I have noticed with more than Christian gratification the outcome of the Kilgo-Gattis Trial, and am very glad to notice that the people of the state have so generally vindicated your early conceptions of this man Kilgo. Some of us, who as teachers, were not treated with Christian generosity that ought to be characteristic of North Carolina, have watched with considerable interest these actions of imported instructors who have taken our place and attempted to traduce the educational system of our state and of course we feel the deepest gratitude to you for your stand in the entire matter....

* Civil engineer.

VIII

Selected Speeches and Articles

1864–1900

THE CIVIL LAW

WALTER CLARK'S SENIOR SPEECH, CHAPEL HILL, APRIL, 1864

ROME HAS CEASED TO RULE THE WORLD. The slow and silent decays of time, the irruption of barbarians and the effeminacy and rapacity [of] her own citizens have rendered the "Eternal City" little more than a majestic ruin. The magnificent columns of Hadrian and Antonine now serve only as curious relics of the past. The lights are extinguished in the palace of the Cesars. The swallow builds its nest in the Capitol. And the once proud mistress of the world is a needy dependent on the favor of a monarch beyond the Alps. But there is that in the Roman Supremacy, which like the immortal part of man, survives when all the rest has decayed. The legions of Gaul and Illyricum no longer exist. Scipio sleeps with his veterans of Africa and Spain. The Roman *Arms* no longer hold the world in subjection but today the Roman Law rules where the Roman eagles never flew. In the noble words of D'Aguessean "The grand destinies of Rome are not yet accomplished. She rules throughout the world by her reason after having ceased to reign by her authority."

Deriving its origin, far back in the cycles of antiquity, from the laws of Solon and Lycurgus; incorporated into the "Twelve Tables"; enlarged by the Senatus-consulta of the Roman Senate; refined and explained by the fiery eloquence of Tully and the legal learning of Sulpicius; disseminated and rendered supreme throughout the world by the legions of Scipio, Cesar and Pompey; commended to the obedience of mankind by the imperial decrees of the Cesars, enriched by the writings of Papinian, Panlus, Gaius, Ulpian and Modestinus and *finally* abridged, classified, digested and handed down to posterity by the wisdom of Justinian the *Corpus Juris Civilis*—The Roman Civil Law—claims the attention, the admiration, and the wonder of mankind.

Cradled in Arms, nourished in Victory and matured in Luxury the *Civil Law* has kept pace with the advance of civilization, decayed with its decay and revived with its revival. Carried by the Arms of Rome from the pillars of Hercules to the Wall of Severus and the banks of the Euphrates and having ruled for so many centuries alike over barbarians and civilization it has revived at the present day "to be taught and obeyed not only in France, Spain, Germany, Holland and Scotland but in the islands of the

Indian Ocean, and on the banks of the Mississippi and the St. Lawrence."

The conquests of the Roman Law have been more durable and even more extensive than those of her Arms. When the "Northern Hive" poured forth its hordes to the destruction of that power, whose legions had hitherto advanced but to conquest, the Roman eagles drooped the conquered wing and the Roman Empire established by the genius and courage of thirteen centuries disappeared in a few short years from the gaze of History and "like the baseless fabric of a vision, left not a wreck behind". But not so with the Roman Law. Emerging like the Phoenix from annihilation as it were, it spread its sway over the conquering and the conquered with a rapidity which threatened to absorb all codes of civil conduct.

It was on the shores of Britain that the Laws, like the Arms, of Rome received their first repulse. But though opposed by the masculine vigor and free spirit of the Common Law and though the proud barons of Plantagenet arose in their might and exclaimed "Nolumus leges angliae mutari" yet even *there* has the Civil Law formed the basis of the English Law of Personal Property, become the foundation of all decisions in the High Courts of Admiralty and exerted no small influence on the private relations of social life.

While we feel a just pride in the Common Law which our forefathers solemnly declared to be the birthright of every American, we can not but behold with admiration mingled perhaps with some portion of awe that stupendous Code of Laws which ruled for so many centuries the whole of the then known world, which has furnished so much of the Common and the Canon Law, which has become the acknowledged basis of the Law of Nations and which to-day rules without a rival the entire water and so large a portion of the land surface of the globe.

The principles of Justice are eternal. What though the degenerate Roman Senate raised statues inscribed to "Cesar, the Demigod". What though fierce Marius exclaimed that "Laws spake too softly to be heard amid the din of arms". The statues of the one have long since lain in the dust. The name of the other is a "byword and a reproach among nations". While they from the Capitol were giving their imperious commands to the world, hardly from the Curule chair were unobservedly proceeding those early principles of Justice and the Civil Law which will survive when the names of the haughty Dictators are unknown and Rome itself will be no more. The principles of Justice embodied in the Code of Justinian have floated over the wreck of empires, the fall of dynasties and the crash of the political world "calmly as the course of a meteor on dark rolling clouds".

The Civil Law is so intimately connected with the History of the Past, the politics of the Present and the destinies of the Future that it will not fail to attract the study and attention of the scholar, the soldier and the statesman in every age. In the words of the venerable Chancellor Kent "The whole body of the Civil Law will excite never failing curiosity, and receive the homage of scholars as a singular monument of wisdom. It fills such a large space in the eye of human reason; it regulates so many interests of man as a social and civilized being; it embodies so much of thought, reflection, experience and labor; it leads so far into the recesses of antiquity, and it has stood so long against the "waves and weathers of time", that it is impossible, while engaged in the contemplation of the system not to be struck with some portion of the awe and veneration, which are felt in the midst of the solitude of a majestic ruin.

ADDRESS BEFORE THE HESPERIAN AND COLUMBIAN SOCIETIES AT TRINITY COLLEGE

(June 9, 1880)

Fifteen years have passed since last I stood beneath the shadow of these walls. Then these woods and hills were filled with the squadrons, regiments and batteries of a surrendered and disbanding army. Men who had marched from Belmont to Chickamauga, and from Bethel to Bentonville here fused together into the last grand army of the Confederacy yielding to an inexorable fate, and the command of their gallant leader laid down their arms. Here rang out our latest bugles, here rolled our last drum beat, here bronzed brave hearted men wept like tender women, and here, in sight of this spot the glorious starry cross which we had seen so often plunge into the fight and sweep victorious across the ridge of battle was furled and folded *forever*. Here it floated last over an organized army but on the deathless and inalterable page of the past, it has taken its proud stand "By the lilies of France and the Cross of St. George".

Fifteen years ago—it calls up many memories. The expiring agonies of a great and an historic cause can be felt but can not be described. Excepting the "Adieux of Fontainebleau" when Napoleon bade farewell to his eagles history contains no scene as touching as the noble resignation of the disbanding armies at Appomattox and at Trinity.

Fifteen years have passed—and once more I stand upon this spot. Those fifteen years have brought much of trial, but much of comfort too to the land that army loved so well and for which it fought so bravely. I have returned to find the revived and invigorated growth of an institution which as a Methodist new with pride, and as a citizen of North Carolina I sincerely admire. I have returned to look upon the noble faces of a new generation, who know nothing of the din and turmoil of those eventful years, and to whom its glories are a tradition, and as I gaze upon the countenances of the young men, into whose hands must ere long pass the helm of state and the guidance of the affairs of our great Republic, I feel that the men and the scenes of that time belong to the Past, the great, the irreversible and historic past. Our faces are turned towards the setting sun while in the bright countenances before me I see eyes which are turned on the sun which is careering towards a splendid and a brilliant zenith. Such is life.

Time pauses not for man. Labitur et labetur. While the dreamer dreams the hair grows gray.

Peace hath her victories no less than war, and in the noble institution which has arisen here, and in the labors of its distinguished President and his efficient assistants we have that which will redound as much to the advancement of Progress, and the preservation of the principles of liberty, as the deeds of those bloody days when the clash of opinion and antagonistic ideas was marked by the rush of opposing squadrons. In some way the conflict of principle and the advance of civilization is ever, ceaselessly, steadily, going on. When the drum ceases to roll the charge, when the roar of artillery and the patter of musketry have hushed, in the silent labors of the midnight lamp and the whirr of industrial machinery we have the noiseless work of the general planning the campaign, the steady thud of the sapper and miner in the gallery under the enemy's works. Progress is ever onwards. It may change its mode but while the world stands it must go *forward.* Now a principle may be advanced by the charge up the hill at Hastings, now by the repulse before the breastworks of Bunker Hill, and now again by the cogitations of Newton or the inventions of Morse and Stevenson. There is an active principle at work fermenting in the bosoms of mankind which will not let them rest—whose motion is Progress, whose advance is Civilization, whose form is Republicanism, and whose ultimate achievement is universal Christianity.

As my subject to-day, I shall ask to call your attention, necessarily in a perfunctory manner, to the nature of this grain of leaven which is working so great a ferment in the masses of mankind.

No man in this intelligent audience needs to be told that the history of our present civilization is that of the ideas which were incarnated at Bethlehem and which were lifted up to the gaze of all succeeding centuries at Calvary. How profoundly those ideas have penetrated every domain of life—social, educational, religious, legal—it is not necessary for me to say civilization is a reflex of, and a constant approximation to, Christianity. The civilization of any age since the Advent is its degree of Christianity. To trace out this fact and show the deep modifications which the teachings of Christ have wrought in the thoughts and lives of mankind would take more time than this occasion permits. I shall address myself to the bearing those teachings have had upon a subject with which many seem to think that they have little in common, I mean Politics and political affairs. Upon nothing has however their influence been more profound. It is impossible that ideas which assume to control the individual conduct of men should not sway their collective action. Because Christ said that his kingdom was not of this world, it does not follow that it was intended that the management of political affairs was to be entirely turned over to His Satanic Majesty, an idea on which many politicians, at this day, seem to act. The declaration meant no more than that His kingdom was not based on *force* as were the kingdoms of the world, and he immediately adds "for if it was then would my servants fight." In treating this subject of the influence of Christ on Politics, it is naturally divided into the effect on the *form* of government and on the *mode* of administration. In speaking of the influence of the teachings of the Great Master in this connection I shall view him simply as a man. I would have no one misunderstand me. I would not for a moment intimate the slightest doubt upon that mysterious revelation which I so little comprehend but most reverently and devoutly believe of his being God in the flesh. Of his divinity here and elsewhere from the eloquent lips of men who have made His their calling. It is of him as a man and the political effect of his teachings that a layman could now speak.

Mr. Stevens in his great work on the "War between the States" well says that "There is a political force in ideas and that before it constitutions, and compacts and agreements are but as barriers of sand before the resistless march of the ocean." The central idea in the teachings of Christ is that between the supremest of supreme powers and the humblest individual the dignity of manhood needs no human intermediate. In that idea is the germ of the political equality of men and before its irresistible force the forms of government established by kings and oligarchies with their artificial & burdensome inequalities become vain barriers against the might & majesty of popular rights. Christ taught that the poor should possess the kingdom of heaven and that the meek should inherit the earth, that God watches over the humblest of his children with more than parental care, that he is no respecter of persons, that in his eyes all men are equal, and that not many mighty nor many rich are called. The unavoidable, the necessary political effect of such teachings is democracy. He taught neither agrarianism nor sedition but so far as the influence and spirit of such a religion could leaven human society, it was impossible for it not to promote liberty and brotherhood and equality among men.

From such teachings comes the freedom of thought, freedom of speech, freedom of conscience, freedom of action. The highest type of a Christian State is a government of the people, by the people and for the people. Well might the old Roman Emperors recoil from a religion whose teachings would strike off the fetters from subject races as well as from subject men.

The world could not at once receive the great idea. It must permeate trickle, work its way. For ages the rulers of this world used priest craft for their purposes and through the agency of its teachers shackled the freedom of its teaching. But the leaven was always at work. In time it fell into and enlightened the minds of Savonarola, of Luther, of Knox, of Wesley. Its advance has been gradual but steadily accelerated. Christianity first conquered heathendom and gained possession of temporal power, then it conquered its own teachers and Protestantism was its fuller development, and hand in hand with its political work marched social and material progress. Then the seed fell into the minds of Wesley, and Whitefield and the divorce of Church & State followed. At each successive step as men have pondered its teachings human liberty has advanced. The right to think, to speak, to act, has been more and more asserted as men came to feel that in the eye of the ultimate tribunal rich and poor, king and peasant, master and slave stood on the same level. If the thoughts and the acts of this life were to be judged from the same throne and by the same standard whence came the right of a fellow criminal, of men who were to abide the same judgment, to restrict and control our deeds and our thoughts. To the same master we all stood or fell. As I have before said the political result of such teachings was democracy and will become more and more the result as these teachings are thoroughly understood among the masses until we have in the coming ages the Universal Republic.

From Marathon to Morgarten, from Bannockburn to Bunker Hill, fields have grown red in the struggle for the freedom of man but the force of such teachings has crashed through the ranks of tyranny with more fatal effect than the dripping spears of the phalanx at Marathon or the closed and serried charge of the sons of liberty at Morgarten. The leaven of these ideas worked its way in the political measures of meal. The fire which went out from the lowly teacher of Nazareth devoured the cedars of Lebanon—the lofty thrones which dominated and overshadowed the earth. The small stone hewn without hands has grown to a mountain and filled the whole earth. Born in a stable and cradled in a manger Christ came not to enhance the tyranny of earthly rank, without a foot of land to call his own on the soil he trod he was not the supporter of Herod's system but its anti-type, without a roof to cover his head, with poor fishermen for his companions, he came not to bind the chains of Tiberius upon the people but to vindicate the truth that where the spirit of the Lord is, there is liberty. We may speak of Tell, of Bruce of Bannockburn, of Washington, but viewed as a man simply the great Apostle and High Priest of Human Liberty is the carpenter of Nazareth. Lose sight for the moment of his divinity, consider him as a man, as a philosopher and yet we find that these teachings of his have stirred up and moved this "tempest's breath and battle's rage" on which ride the hopes of freedom.

Let the humanitarian deny his divinity, strip him of all except that which made him a man like as one of us, seal up the violated portals of the grave and yet from his last resting place in the rock hewn tomb of Joseph of Arimathea the "pale Galilean" rules the world. Well might the apostate Emperor of a yet unfallen empire exclaim in his last moments "Vicisti, O Galileae!", "You have conquered O Galilean". All the resources, all the might and majesty and power of a great empire wielded by an autocratic energy and an unconquerable will were put in motion to arrest the progress of these ideas but the successor of Constantine admitted in his dying moments the futility of the struggle.

I hardly think this point of view has heretofore been made sufficiently prominent. The freedom with which Christ made us free is certainly a moral freedom, a freedom from sin, but it is also a freedom of thought and action from tyrannical restraint, a freedom from wicked thrones and all human tyranny. It has spoken by the mouth of Peter and Paul, of Luther and Calvin, of Knox and Wesley, but it has spoken too in the cannon of Gustavus Adolphus, of Protestant England against Catholic Spain, in the broadsides of Lepanto, in the cannonade of Valmy, and on whatever field freedom has faced her foes. It has spoken in the still small voice of meditation, of prayer, of exhortation but it has spoken too in the thunders and lightnings of Sinai, in the hoarse throated music of artillery and amid the fiery crash of musketry.

The progress of Christianity ethically means morality, but politically it means republicanism. Other forms of government can not abide the doctrines it teaches. We have but to glance at the history & geography of christendom to find that whenever and wherever civil liberty has been established there Christianity has its noblest and purest realization. It is a most significant fact that since the christian era civil liberty has existed nowhere outside the limits of christendom.

The necessary ultimate political effect of the teachings of Christ being a republican form of government, a government of freedom to think, to say, to act, there remains for your consideration the effect of those teachings on the *mode* of administering the government. And here again there is not that divorce between christian teachings and principles and the administration of public affairs which corrupt men have always insisted upon and desired.

The great danger to our institutions is no longer from without, it is from within. The corruption and degradation which even in the highest places taints so largely the administration of public affairs is at variance with the pure and noble teachings to which we owe our free form of government. Corruption is utterly incompatible with the preservation of our liberty and our institutions. It is a growing cancer on the body politic whose roots have sunk deep and must be eradicated by heroic treatment, by the free and speedy use of the knife, ere those roots strike into a vital part.

Packing Party Conventions is but the preliminary step to a fraudulent count of the popular vote. In either case there is a fraudulent suppression of the popular will upon which our government is based and the men who procure either the one or the other, or connive at it, or knowingly accept the benefit of such conduct deserve more surely the convicts' garb than the honors which a free people should bestow only on the worthy and the good. Such conduct is treason, treason to the people, treason to religion. Conduct which would ruin a man in a private transaction with a fellow man is ten fold more injurious and more infamous when committed against the rights of the body of the people.

The perpetuity of our free institutions depends on our public morals and an enlightened public sentiment. The degradation and pollution which taints so much of the management of our public affairs is a cause of gloomy foreboding to every one who sincerely loves his country and is attached to our noble form of government. It is not too much to say that if we would serve that country and preserve these blood bought institutions, the best ever vouchsafed to man, we must thoroughly and entirely cleanse and purify the political management of our affairs. Nineveh did not repent, the cities of the plain did not repent, Bethsaida and Chorazin and Capernaum did not repent and unless our noble heritage of liberty and our glorious institutions are to share the fate of the massive structures of those ancient cities and struck to earth are to lie shattered in the dust a perpetual reminder of our folly and our sin to remotest ages and all future times there must be a thorough, a searching, and an utter regeneration and purification in the Politics and public affairs of this country.

The first reform in this matter is for the people once and for all to refuse to endorse by their votes and put in high places men with tainted lives and with a reputation for political trickery. Christian men who for temporary expediency sacrifice principle in such matters are pointing the dagger at the body of liberty and belying their christian professions. The distinguished Dr. Haygood well says "The philistines are wise in their generation when they say 'Religion and politics don't mix' for, at first hearing, it sounds like a compliment to religion'. What such men mean—and they are the wire-pulling, convention-packing and sometimes ballot box stuffing set—is, don't spoil our politics with your religion. And well may such be afraid of it for when politics is purified by religion their occupation will like Othello's be *gone* indeed.

Church and Politics should be kept separate—always. But religion is necessary in politics. The devil has already run our politics longer than is safe—for us. A man should carry his religion into his politics just as he carries it into his shop, his store, his law office. The good men of this country must take charge of it and rule it, and put good and true men to rule over us else we are lost indeed. Unless Christianity can save the Republic it will sink by its own corruption as did the heathen republics of Greece and Rome. Think not I despair of our Republic, for ours unlike those of old is founded upon and brought about by the pure and noble teachings of Christ and I believe, and I have an abiding faith, that those teachings will be strong enough to purify, to regenerate and to save it.

Young Gentlemen— You belong to a great and a mignty race, the greatest and mightiest that has arisen and overshadowed the earth with its fame. You belong to the great anglo-saxon race on whose possessions the sun never sets, a race to whose stout keeping the ark of human liberty and human progress has been confided almost as exclusively as the ark of the covenant and the oracles of God, were to the Israelites of old. To you and your comrades of your generation will soon pass the custody of this noble heritage which has been achieved by the high thinking and wrought out by the hard fighting of your race—a race which from Hastings and

Chevy Chase to Appomattox and Isandula has seldom met with defeat and never with dishonor. Upon you will repose the sacred duty of preserving and handing down this great trust to future ages. To the descendants of such sires as yours there can be no fear of any force tyranny can bring. In America at least there is now no open force arrayed against us. In the glance of liberty they have vanished from our front as "The sun's bright lances rout the mists of morning." But there is that other enemy—political corrup[tion] and decay of public and official honesty. To you will fall the duty of routing out and destroying this last enemy of the people and our institutions. You should do it as thoroughly as the Israelites were commanded to do with the philistines and canaanites of their day. The Israelites left their work half done and suffered the penalty. I deeply fear the day is too far spent for our generation to thoroughly perform this great work of political purification. You can and should do it thoroughly. You can see that honest and pure men and none other rule the affairs of a great, a brave and a true people. Do this and the Republic will burst the bonds that surround it, its emblem will float in the majesty of its purity and humanity will stand forth "redeemed, regenerated and disenthralled" in the irresistible might of Political Emancipation.

THE LEGAL ASPECT OF THE TELEGRAPH AND TELEPHONE—ESSENTIAL PARTS OF AN EFFICIENT POSTAL SERVICE

(*Ameri an Law Review,* 1895; rep. Sen. Doc. 205, 54 Cong. 1st sess.)

Many who admit the great advantages, nay, the necessity, of the telegraph and telephone being operated as a part of the postal system are deterred by the inquiry, Is it constitutional? In truth, it is unconstitutional for this essential branch of the postal system to be operated by a private monopoly or in any other manner than by the Government.

When the Constitution placed the post-office in the hands of the Government it conferred its exclusive operation, and with it all means of operating it to the best advantage, upon the Government. The same clause of the Constitution of the United States (Art. I, sec. 8) which empowers Congress to declare war, raise and support armies and a navy, to coin money, regulate commerce, and borrow money on the credit of the United States includes the provision to "establish post-offices and post-roads."

If the power of the Government is exclusive as to the other provisions, it is so also as to the post-offices, for all these powers are conferred by the same clause and by the same words—in the same breath, as it were. The numerous decisions of the United States Supreme Court holding the power of Congress over the post-office and the carrying of mails to be exclusive render unnecessary any discussion of an undisputed point. It is interesting to note, however, that in 1836 Hon. John C. Calhoun, the leader of the strict constructionists, who denied to the General Government all powers not clearly granted, in a report made by him as chairman of a committee of the United States Senate, said: "It must be borne in mind that the power of Congress over the post-office and the mail is an exclusive power." These words have been cited and approved by the Supreme Court of the United States in the case of ex part Jackson so recently as the Ninety-sixth United States Reports, on page 734.

The bestowal of the exclusive right and duty to operate the post-office carried with it the exclusive right and duty to use all the agencies that would make the post office most highly efficient, as such agencies from time to time should be improved or invented. On this principle the first telegraph line was built by a Congressional appropriation under a "strict construction" Administration (Polk's), and the telegraph belonged to the Government from 1844 to 1847, and when, under mistaken notions of economy, it was then turned over to private ownership. Henry Clay, the great Whig leader, and Cave Johnson, the Democratic Postmaster-General, were among the public men who went on record as earnestly protesting against such a step. Indeed, the Supreme Court of the United States, in an unanimous opinion, has held that the telegraph came within the grant of power to establish the post-office. That opinion, delivered by Chief Justice Waite, says:

> The powers thus granted are not confined to the instrumentalities of the postal service known or in use when the Constitution was adopted, but they keep pace with the progress of the country and adapt themselves to the new developments of time and circumstances. They extend from the horse with its rider to the stage coach; from the sailing vessel to the steamboat; from the coach and steamboat to the railroad, and from the railroad to the telegraph, as these new agencies are successively brought into use to meet the demands of an increasing population and wealth.

And Justice H.B. Brown, who is recognized as one of the ablest members of the United States Supreme Court, in the leading article in the August Forum, says:

> If the Government may be safely intrusted with the transmission of our letters and papers, I see no reason why it may not also be intrusted with the transmission of our telegrams and parcels, as is almost universally the case in Europe.

Congress placed the same construction on its powers by chapter 230, acts 1866, which provides that all telegraph lines thereafter built shall be constructed under the notice, and only after the company signing a contract that the Government may at any time take over such telegraph lines upon paying the value of its material.

It will be noted, just here, that so far as railroads are used for the transmission of mail they were promptly, and from the beginning, adopted and used exclusively by the post-office. Whether, in so far as railroads are used for the entirely different purpose of carrying passengers and freight, they shall be taken over by the Government is an entirely different question, standing on its own basis, which has never affected the undeniable right and duty of the Government to use them exclusively, so far as they are used for the carriage of mails. But the telegraph and telephone (so far as used by the public for hire) are, and can be, only used for the transmission of mail, and unquestionably come within the exclusive grant to the Government of operating the post-office. The telegraph and telephone are simply the electric mail, or mail sent by electricity, just as the railway mail is sent by steam agency in preference to the horsepower formerly used in the days of the stage-coaches and horseback riders and canal boats.

When the Government shall assume its duty of sending the mail by electricity railroad companies can still operate their own telegraph lines on their own business, and private telephone exchanges will still exist, just as railroads and others may now send their own letters by their own agents (Rev. Stat., sec. 3984), but not carry them for others for hire. (Rev. State., sec. 3982). Then, as now, the Government would only have the exclusive privilege of carrying mail for hire. (Rev. Stat., sec. 3990.)

This privilege of carrying mail for hire, whether sent by electricity or steam or stagecoach, or on horseback, is an exclusive governmental function, and no corporation or monopoly can legally exercise any part of it. It is the duty of the Government to do it, and to do it in the quickest and most efficient manner, and at the lowest possible rate consistent with the cost.

The Army and Navy and the Departments of Justice are Departments of exclusive governmental functions, in the same manner and to exactly the same extent as the post-office. But suppose that some branch of the Department of Justice (as by turning in fines, penalties, and tax fees), or of the War or Navy, could be made a source of revenue, would it not be singular to turn that revenue paying part of those Departments to a private monopoly, leaving the people to support the nonprofitable part? Yet that is exactly what is done with the Post-Office Department. Though the Post-Office is as exclusively a governmental function as the Army or Navy or the Department of Justice, the Government operates only the slow, antiquated, nonpaying part of the Post-Office, leaving the taxpayers to make up an annual deficit of six or eight million dollars; while the rapid, improved, up-to-date part of the Post-Office, the rapid or electric mail, is operated by a private monopoly and pays a heavy dividend on its watered stock of one hundred and fifty millions—ten times the actual value of its plant. Besides, this system is unjust, for the private monopoly naturally selects the best-paying districts, and a large part of the people are denied the advantages of a modern post-office.

In every country save ours alone the power of the monopoly has failed to maintain a system so unconstitutional and so opposed to the best interests of the public. Hence, in every country except ours the telegraph and telephone are constituent parts of the post-office, with the double result that the post-office facilities of the telegraph and telephone are extended to the country post-offices and the postal revenues show a profit instead of a loss. Notably Great Britain, which has most widely extended the use of the telegraph and telephone as a part of its post-office, shows a large annual profit from its post-office, instead of a deficit, which was usual before the telegraph and telephone were added to that department by Mr. Gladstone in 1870.

But there are those who say that the telegraph and telephone would centralize the Government. Yet it would be hard to see why an efficient postal service is more centralizing than an inefficient one, or why mail sent by electricity or pneumatic tubes (which should be adopted in the large cities) is more centralizing than mail sent by horseback or by steam. It is a puzzle to understand why ownership of telegraph or telephone wires costing less than $10 per mile should imperil the Government, more than the ownership of gunboats, or post-office buildings, or postal cars. If it were the question of adding new functions to the Government, as the ownership of railroads and the carrying of freight and passengers, this argument would be legitimate for debate. But when the Constitution has already turned over the exclusive duty of transmission of mail to the Government, there can be no argument of this kind properly used against the introduction of the most improved methods for the transmission of the mail, whether by electricity or pneumatic tubes.

Telegraphic dispatches would be as sacred in the hands of the Government employees as other mail now is, or as the telegrams are in the hands of the employees of a private corporation. Besides, Government employees, especially under civil service rules and subject to the supervision of public opinion, would be less capable of using the telegraph for partisan purposes, as has been done under corporation ownership, and as was flagrantly attempted to be done in the first Cleveland election, as everyone remembers.

With telephones at all country post-offices, and all villages and the smaller towns, few additional employees would be required, and those few would be added at centers which require the telegraph and where civil service rules obtain. The telephones and telegraph would be put in the post-office buildings already owned or rented by the Government, thus saving the rent of all the buildings now used by the private companies. This, and the saving of the salaries of the officials of the present corporations and the dividends on their largely watered stock, would enable the Government to reduce its tolls to the uniform rate of 10 cents per message independently of the large increase in business.

In Great Britain (by the official report made to this Government in the United States Consular Reports for April, 1895) the increase since the Government has taken over the telegraph and telephone has been tenfold in private messages, and thirtyfold in press messages; and the improvement in promptness of delivery has been from an average of two to three hours under private ownership to an average of nine minutes under Government. This wonderful increase in business has been due to the threefold cause of cheap rates, extension of the lines to all post-offices, and greater promptness in delivery. With wire costing less than $10 per mile there is no reason why the Government should not own a line to every post-office in the Union.

There should be no dicker with private companies about leasing or purchasing. In 1866 they only asked for five years to close up, but when the five years were out they had formed the present great trust and have ever since defied the public.

They have had thirty years' notice to abandon their use of a branch of the governmental functions. In that time they have received hundreds of millions of profits illegally extorted from the toiling masses. They have no claim to extract another dollar by lease or sale of their antiquated or worn-out instruments. Let the Government give the actual value of such wire and material as it may wish to use, and take complete and exclusive possession of the duties of a post-office. Certainly these corporations are entitled to no compensation for franchises or loss of expected profits, since under the act of 1866 every telegraph line has been built under a contract that it should be turned over to the Government upon payment of the assessed value of the material. The franchise has always been the property of the Government, and was only temporarily permitted to be used by the private corporations.

Every postmaster who can talk can use the telephone, and where a telegraph office is required the Government can employ an assistant as operator as easily as any other clerk. Other countries, without exception, are doing this good work of furnishing electric mail facilities at cheap rates to all its people, in the country as well as in the town. Why should this Government, alone of all the world, which claims, par excellence, to be a government of the people and for the people, fail in this constitutional duty of furnishing proper postal facilities and to all its people? The only proper postal facilities for the American people are those which shall extend to every nook and corner of the Republic, which shall be the best that the latest advances in science can offer, and which are furnished as near the exact cost of the service as is possible without profit. Such postal facilities the American people are entitled to demand as a right. They should rest contented with nothing short of this.

THE TELEGRAPH IN ENGLAND

(*The Arena,* December 1895)

As taxes upon the diffusion of intelligence among men and deficiencies in the postal service affect everyone, I condense the following from the official report on the workings of the Government telegraph in England made to our Government by the United States consul at Southampton, England, and printed in the last number of the Consular Reports. He says:

On January 29, 1870, all the telegraphs in the United Kingdom were acquired by the Government from the corporations which had previously operated them, and thenceforward became an integral part of the post-office. The English people owed this great measure in their interest, like so many others, to Mr. Gladstone, who bore down all opposition from the companies, who were making big profits. Till then the districts paying best had ample service, though at high rates (as is still the case with us), while whole sections off the lines of railway were destitute of telegraphic facilities. The Government at once extended the telegraph to all sections and reduced the rate to one cent a word. The following is the result: In 1870, under private ownership, 7,000,000 individual messages and 22,000,000 words of press dispatches were annually sent. Now that the telegraph is operated by the post-office the annual number of individual messages sent is 70,000,000 (ten times as many), and over 600,000,000 words of press dispatches (thirty times as many) are used. This at a glance demonstrates the overwhelming benefit to the public of the change and their appreciation of it.

The press rates have been reduced so low that every weekly country paper can afford to print the latest telegraphic dispatches as it goes to press, and a telegraph or telephone is at every country post-office. In London the telegraph has largely superseded the mail for all the small and necessary details of life—to announce that you are going to dine at a certain house, or to inform your wife that you are detained on business and not to keep dinner waiting, and the like—over 30,000 telegrams being sent daily in that city alone.

The following is quoted from the consul, verbatim:

The service is performed with the most perfect punctuality. It is calculated that the average time employed to-day in the transmission of a telegram between two commercial cities in England varies from seven to nine minutes, while in 1870 (under private ownership) two to three hours were necessary.

The rate of 1 cent a word includes delivery within the postal limits of any town or within 1 mile of the post-office in the country. Beyond that limit the charge is 12 cents per mile for delivery of a message. The telegraph being operated as a constituent part of the postal service it is not possible to state how much profit the Government receives from it, but the English Government does not consider that it should be treated as a source of revenue. It regards it as a means of information and education for the masses and gives facilities of all kinds for its extension in all directions.

This unbiased and impartial report, officially made to our Government, is worthy of thought and consideration. It may be added that in every civilized country except this the telegraph has long since been adopted as one of the indispensable agencies of an up-to-date post-office department. Even in half-civilized Paraguay (as we deem it) they have better postal facilities than we, for the post-office there transmits telegrams at 1 cent a word and rents out telephones at $1 per month.

At present, owing to high rates, 46 per cent of all telegrams in this country are sent by speculators (who thus get an advantage over producers) and only 8 per cent are social or ordinary business messages. In Belgium, where the Government rate is less than 1 cent per message, the social and ordinary business messages between man and man are 63 per cent of the whole. Figures could not be more eloquent as to the vast benefit this confers upon the great mass of people, who bear the bulk of the burdens of any government and receive so few of its benefits. With the telegraphs and telephones operated by our Post-Office Department at moderate rates, say, 5 or even 10 cents per message, a similar change would take place here. Individual and news messages would increase tenfold to thirtyfold, as elsewhere—probably more—and the monopoly now held by speculators would cease.

The average telegraph rate now charged in this country, by the reports to Congress, is 31 cents per message—three times the average rate in all other countries under post-office telegraph service; and experts say that our Government could probably afford, with the vast increase of business, a uniform rate of 5 cents, as the average cost of a message is about 3 cents. According to experts the telegraph plants now in use could be superseded by the Government with a superior plant at $15,000,000, while the present corporations are strangling commerce to earn heavy dividends on a watered stock of over $150,000,000.

According to English experience the transfer of the telegraph to the Post-Office Department would result in (1) a uniform rate of 10 cents for 10 words between all points, or possibly less; (2) an increase in individual messages of at least ten for every one now sent; (3) an increase in press dispatches of thirty words or more for every one now sent; (4) a popularization of the telegraph for all uses, social and business; (5) an increase in the promptness of delivery, the average there being now seven to nine minutes as against two to three hours formerly; (6) no section would be destitute, but at each one of our 70,000 post-offices there would be a telephone or telegraph. By adopting the telephone at most post-offices, instead of the telegraph, the increase in the number of post-offices would be inconsiderable.

The vast influence of the great telegraph monopoly can be used for political purposes by coloring news and in other more direct ways. When the telegraph service is made a part of the post-office and placed under civil-service rules and subject to the direct force of public opinion, the experience in other countries has been that it exerts no more power on party politics than the army or judiciary. Originally the telegraph (in 1846) belonged to the post-office. When it was abandoned to private corporations on account of its supposed expense, Henry Clay, Cave Johnson, and other leaders of both parties had the foresight to foretell the mischief done in abandoning an essential governmental function to private monopoly.

To prevent this great benefit being given to the masses and to preserve the consolidated capital the control of the most efficient avenues of intelligence with the great advantages thus given that element in addition to the enormous tolls it can thus levy on the rest of the nation, there is practically only the inexorable will of one powerful and exacting corporation which has fastened itself on the body politic. It is the oldest trust in this country. It is the pioneer on which so many others have been patterned. It is the most burdensome because its oppressive tolls restrict communication between men and levy a tax on knowledge. It is illegal, since the Constitution requires Congress to establish the Post-Office, to leave this most essential function of a modern, up-to-date postal service in the hands of private corporations.

The telegraph is a source of gigantic emoluments to these corporations, while the Government restricts its postal service to antiquated and more dilatory processes. It is no wonder that such a postal service is not self-sustaining and shows an annual deficit while the telegraph companies pay enormous dividends. In other countries, where the telegraph is a part of the post-office, that department shows annual profits; but the monopoly fastened on us is intrenched in the sympathy of all other trusts. It has the support of the large city dailies (all owned by large capitalists) who fear the competition of dailies in small towns and of the weeklies if news should become free, and its transmission cheaper, over a Government postal telegraph. It is backed by the powerful lobby which it constantly maintains at Washington, paid out of the excessive telegraphic rates still exacted in this country alone out of a long-suffering and too patient people. And not least, it is said that it distributes franks to every Senator and every Member of Congress. How many accept these favors and how many are influenced by them no one knows except the corporation officials, but that they do know may be seen from the fact that tenders of such favors have not ceased.

WHERE SHALL THE GOVERNING POWER RESIDE?

Address before the University College of Medicine, Richmond, Va. April 29, 1897

. . . I must say to you, my young friends, that not in 1861, when the steady tread of the old Confederate regiments first echoed along these streets, and the artillery wagons came rumbling by, and the bugles of marching cavalry rolled along your valleys, was there greater unrest in the minds of the masses of your fellow-citizens North and South, East and West, than there is at this moment of deep, dreamless, apparent peace. The hearts of men are strangely moved within them, for the masses are not satisfied with existing conditions. No one contemplates that the present unrest will culminate, like that of 1861, in armed strife, but all the signs that history has ever given of great impending changes are with us. None are lacking. Conditions, will not, cannot remain as they are. Be assured of that. If you are men worthy of the Revolutionary race of heroes who won our liberties, and equal to the generation which faced the perils of the great civil war without shrinking, you should read and understand the signals of the coming storm.

There are men to whom the present status is very comfortable. They denounce any statement that all others are not as contented as themselves. It was your own great orator who, quoting the inspired seer of Israel, cried out in prophetic language: "They say peace, peace, but there is no peace."

THE CONFLICT OF IDEAS, the conflict of interests is more real at every point of contact than that which Mr. Seward proclaimed an "irrepressible conflict" in 1860. At Cooper Institute, Mr. Lincoln truly declared to a startled generation that the Union could not remain half bond and half free. It is equally true now that this Government cannot be governed partly by freemen and partly by an oligarchy of wealth. One or the other must be sole master of the Republic. The generation of 1860 had not, like this, the benefit of the lessons taught by four terrible years of war, and hence the issue of this day can be settled by ballots—not by bullets.

But it is well for us to comprehend the intensity of the question now to be settled and to understand, once for all, that it will not and cannot be settled till there is a complete triumph for one side and a crushing, hopeless defeat for the other, a catastrophe so full and utter that whatever way it fall out, the victory will be engraved in profound modifications upon our organic law.

Be it understood that I come not before you to express or to advocate any views of my own, or of any party, or of any section. It would be an insult to you and unworthy of myself to use this occasion for such a purpose, but I accept the great thought of Terence, the Latin poet, which St. Augustine tells us was received with thunders of applause by a Roman audience: *"Homo sum, humani nihil a me alienum puto."* "I am a man, and whatever concerns the welfare of my fellowmen can never be without interest to me." Called upon to address educated, talented young men who are to go out and become captains of thought and leaders in the hosts of our Israel, I shall be unmindful of the duties and opportunities of the occasion if I were to waste it in rhetorical platitudes or well rounded sentences signifying nothing—the situation is too grave.

THE ISSUES TOO IMPORTANT, the impending conflict too certain, and the results too great and lasting. If I can say ought to impress upon your ingenuous minds that a great struggle, more important than that of 1861, and as inevitable (though we trust to be settled in a different forum), is before you, and that you will be factors of consequence in that contest, then perhaps not altogether in vain I shall have stood before you. . . .

What are these contending forces, and what is the true issue? Is it the tariff? That is a party issue over which either side predicts beneficial results if it wins, and disastrous consequences if it fails—and alternately one or the other wins, and with better or worse conditions the country goes on. Is it the silver issue, the financial question? That is nearer the mark, yet that question is rather an incident, a symptom, a phase with suggested remedies and not the diseases itself. Nor yet is it the conflict between labor and capital, nor the old, old struggle between State Rights and the centralizing tendencies of the Federal government.

THE VITAL QUESTION LIES DEEPER than any of these. It is that which the Roman republic had to face, which every republican government has had to determine, and upon the answer to which, its continued existence as a republic depends. That question was very dimly and indistinctly discerned in the beginning of this great republic. It took on increased importance after the late civil war. To-day it has become the great underlying question upon which men, instinctively, often unconsciously, perhaps, are taking sides. It is a question which in a Republic must be settled, and there can be no peace until it is, and the result must be safeguarded by profound constitutional changes.

The vital question which this country is called upon to determine and towards the determination of which we are, intelligently it may be, or blindly it may be, groping our way is "Where shall the governing power reside." "Shall it be men or money?" It is not a new question, but in a Republic it is the inevitable question whose determination settles all others. What matters it if the Constitution says that all political power resides in or is derived from the people if it has ceased to be true in fact? The Roman legions bore to the latest days of the empire upon their standards the words, "The Senate and the Roman People," centuries after Augustus and Tiberius and Nero had stamped out the last vestiges of the popular will. There were still Tribunes of the People, and Consuls and a Senate and the forms of a Republic in official documents and proceedings long centuries after the real power had passed from the curia and the comitia to the barracks of the Pretorian Guards, and when there was no will in Rome save their master.

YEARS AFTER THE VICTOR OF MARENGO had been crowned emperor, and the sword of Austerlitz had become the supreme power of France, the French coins and official documents still bore the superscriptions of the republic. The nature of a government is not determined by its forms and titles. These usually remain unchanged long after the governing power has become vested elsewhere. What boots it if on parchment we shall continue to read, "All political power is vested in and derived from the people; all government of right originates from the people, is founded upon their will only, and is instituted solely for the good of the whole," if it is not a living, potential, actual truth?

IF, AS A MATTER OF FACT, great corporations through their agents, whether lobbyists or paid members of the legislature itself, can control a majority of that body, so that the choice of the corporations, and not the genuine choice of the people, is sent to the Federal Hall of Ambassadors to sit as a Senator in Congress, then the parchment declaration is a flaunting lie. If gigantic combinations of wealth can elect or control majorities in State Legislatures or in Congress, so as to shape legislation, if they can be potent in the nomination of Federal or State officials, then the real governing power vests in money, not in men, and your boasted republic is but a once beauteous form from which the spirit has already departed.

This is the question of the hour, which should be pondered and understood with a full grasp of its meaning, and all the consequences which must flow from the displacement of the centre of gravity in government. If this displacement has already measurably taken place, or if there is grave danger of it, the struggle to restore it will bring on the crisis which must determine the real nature of our government. For mark you well this fact: that if multi-millionaires or vast combinations of capital, have succeeded, or shall succeed, to the real control of legislation, they have only won its possession because it can be immensely profitable to them; and if profitable, they cannot afford to run the risk, from time to time, of losing so profitable a domination by popular agitation. They will seek, if they have not already done so, to strengthen themselves by securing THE MAJORITY OF THE FEDERAL SENATE, and an influence in the executive councils, and even more important than that, the majority of appointments to the Federal bench, whose life tenure and uncontrolled power of construing constitutions and statutes will be of invaluable aid. . . . Nor, as time goes by, will the matter stop even with the selection of judicial augurs. Agitation, public agitation, affects values—that horrible *bete noire* of capitalism. Profound constitutional changes, either secured by express enactment or read into the Constitution by servile judges, must lessen the opportunity for agitation by rendering it powerless, and the gradual increase and the maintenance of a large standing army must prevent all thought of resistance. If the money power, as has been charged, and as is believed by many, is already largely in control of government, State and national, then the steps just described will be natural and necessary to protect and preserve that profitable power in their hands, leaving the empty forms of a republic to stand in silent but impotent protest.

On the other hand, if the control of legislation is so highly profitable and important to the money power, it will be an irreparable calamity to the toiling masses to lose it. The founders of the republic fondly believed they had secured it not only for themselves, but for their posterity for all time. If the advocates of popular government win, they in turn, still less than the money power, can rest easy in the victory with the organic law remaining as it is. Experience has shown its weakness and insufficiency. There are many points requiring amendments. It would be tedious, perhaps beyond my power, to point out any except the most obvious. The election of United States Senators by State Legislatures has been so often a perversion of the popular choice and a concession to corporation influences that the public sentiment to confer upon the people of each State, instead of the Legislature, the election of its federal Senators is confined to no party and to no section. The bill to amend the Constitution in that respect has passed the lower House of Congress more than once, and once, at least, by a unanimous vote. The corporations have so far been able to prevent its passage by the Senate itself. The Federal judiciary, by its mode of appointment especially lays itself open to the grasp of great monopolies and combinations, whose influence in such matters is asserted to have become almost irresistible in recent years. The life tenure of office, placing the occupants of the Federal bench beyond reach of public complaint, if their trust is abused, and the finality of their powers as interpreters of the Constitution and statutes, combine to make it essential to the great monopolies to control the appointments in this branch of the government. There are unquestionably MANY ABLE AND SPOTLESS MEN on the Federal bench today, but it has been asserted, and it must be confessed, not without much foundation in fact, that it is rapidly becoming the rule to fill such positions with men whose life work has been that of counsel for great corporations and whose entire training is calculated to bias them upon all questions upon which corporation interests and popular rights must clash. One of the incidents of the coming struggle will be the determined effort to make the Federal judges elective by the people of their respective districts and circuits and for a term of years. This change has already been deemed necessary and been decreed by nearly every State as to its own judiciary, and there are still stronger and more urgent reasons why the people should have more weight and the corporations less in naming Federal judges.

Remember that it was the sage of Monticello who pointed out the "sapping and mining" which would overthrow the Constitution if the ultimate construction of statutes and Constitution was left to so unrepublican an institution as a body of men who were selected for life and without the public having any voice in their selection. Time has proven his wisdom and aggravated the evil he denounced.

There are TWO CLASSES OF MEN ONLY who are likely to oppose the election of United States Senators and United States Judges by the people: First, there are those who accept the phrase of a government of and by the people as a formula merely. They at heart do not believe the people are capable of self-government.

They would never have trusted them with the election of Governors, members of Congress, or the President, and they sincerely fear to trust to the voice of the people the selection of any other officer whatsoever. The other class is that whose self-interest, personal aspirations or orders from those above them bind to oppose popular enfranchisement in the selection of Federal Senators and Judges.

Then there is the great Transportation question. From its economic side it is of vast importance. By secret rebates they can build up and destroy at will cities and individual fortunes. It is too great a power to be entrusted to the hands of a few irresponsible men, the control of whom is generally found to be centered in that modern Babylon by the Thames. Of vast importance from the economic side, the danger is deadly from the governmental standpoint. By the vast number of their employees, the great numbers of the press and the bar whom they retain, and their ready power of concentration of influences upon pivotal points, they have a preponderating weight which can endanger the maintenance of popular government. The suggested remedy of government ownership of railroads is untried here and is fraught with prophesied evils. The remedy sought to be applied in many States of control by means of Railroad Commissions has too often resulted in the railroads selecting the Commissioners and simply adding the Commissions to their assets. The question must needs be solved, but its solution has not yet been found.

IT IS THE OLD RIDDLE OF THE SPHYNX. To fail to answer it is death. There are still other matters which need not be discussed now. Who shall win the victory remains to be seen. But that the inevitable conflict is at hand and that its results will be lasting and will leave its mark in constitutional changes is beyond question.

It should not be lost sight of that in this struggle for the possession of the governing power there is no taint of an agrarian spirit. There is no appreciable element of the American people who are opposed to property rights. It is not opposition to property, but to its combination in vast masses for political purposes, that it may control legislation and the machinery of government in the interest of the combination and against the property rights of others. It was Senator McDuffie who said that legislation could be made the most powerful and exacting of plunderers. There is no hatred of corporations as such. They are essential in the service of civilized life, nay indispensable. Nor even against railroad corporations so far as they keep within the legitimate duties of their creation, but it is when they seek to use their enormous power of wealth and organization for the undue emolument of their owners and by entering the political arena seek to control legislation and public policy that the collision becomes inevitable. The opposition is not to them as servants of the public, but as would be masters of the people. That we have already passed the danger line as to the aggregation of wealth will be seen from this summary from reliable sources: Egypt, Persia and other great empires fell when less than ten per cent. of the people had secured nine-tenths of the accumulated wealth of those empires. The glories of imperial Rome crumbled into dust before the brawny arms of the half-naked barbarians of the northern forests when 1,800 families had garnered the bulk of its wealth. Already to-day, one-half of one per cent. of the people of this country own over one-half of its entire wealth, and nine per cent. of its people seventy-five per cent. of its property. This condition tends rapidly to aggravate itself. To-day in Europe, forty per cent. of the householders are tenants. In this grand young Republic already seventy per cent. of the householders, nearly double the European ratio, do not own but rent their homes. This condition of things has not accidentally happened. It has been brought about by the great corporations and combinations of capital. Already many warning voices have been raised.

. . . In his message to Congress, December 3, 1888, President Cleveland used these striking words: "The communism of combined wealth and capital, the outgrowth of over-weening cupidity and selfishness, which insiduously undermines the justice and integrity of free institutions, is not less dangerous than the communism of oppressed poverty and toil, which exasperated by injustice and discontent, attacks with wild disorder the citadel of rule." He might have said it was a thousand fold more so.

THE REAL MENACE TO MEN OF MODERATE PROPERTY and those seeking to earn a modest competence is not in the poor and weak, but in the colossal and mighty combinations which lay their hands upon States and recoil not on the threshold of the National Judiciary. "Words," said Mirabeau, "Words are things." Aware of this fact, those who serve the money power by speech and pen, are wont to dub those who entertain sentiments adverse to government by money as anarchists, socialists and communists. But be not daunted in this contest by epithets. The very combination of epithets will show that they are words, nothing more. An anarchist is one who is opposed to all government. He is the *ne plus ultra* of individualism. Society has nothing to fear from the few hundred throughout the Union professing that faith. At the very opposite pole are the communists who believe in government for everything, in the community of goods. This system failed under the Apostles themselves who gave it a trial, and is not likely to be tried again with success while poor human nature remains what it is. Between these two opposite poles, anarchism or no government, and communism or government in everything at the other, lies socialism. Every civilized government is to a large extent, and almost in proportion to its degree of civilization, socialistic. The original conception of government was a policeman with a big stick to prevent or punish murder and violence, theft and other crimes, so that person and property might be secure. But we have become far more socialistic than that crude beginning. When taxes were laid on the property and persons of all, whether having children or not, and not in proportion to the number of children, in order to educate other people's children, a most unmistakable stride towards socialism was taken, yet our public schools are now our pride, and justly so. Socialistic, too, is the levy of public taxes to maintain hospitals for the sick, the poor, the insane, the blind and the deaf and dumb. So is the postoffice itself, for what connection is there between government in its original function of preserving the peace and order and the distribution of intelligence? In like manner municipal ownership of lights, water works and street cars—admirable as it is, and admirably as it has operated for the public good—is essentially socialistic. I would not be misunderstood as opposing any of these measures because they are socialistic, nor as advocating further steps in that direction. That is not my purpose, but to call to your minds that whether a measure is to be adopted or not, should depend upon whether it will serve the public welfare, and that it is not to be rejected if the only objection that can be urged is that some one thinks it is socialistic, seeing that so large a part of the better portion of government is already of like nature. We need to be often reminded, indeed we should never forget, that government exists for the people and not the people for the government. It was your own great statesman, Thomas Jefferson, who, for maintaining this sentiment in the opening of the century, brought down upon his head the wrath of those who believed in government by the few.

. . . I have told you of the great and just unrest in the public mind and the dissatisfaction at present conditions. I have called your attention to the fact that the vital and inevitable issue overshadowing all others is whether the governing power shall reside in manhood or in money. I have endeavored to call your attention briefly to the consequences of victory for either side and to some of the remedies suggested. I now again repeat that the disposal of the victory is with your generation, for you shall bear in your hands the issues of life and death for the last great experiment of free government. With you it shall rest whether the silent centuries are all ready to close over the tomb in which shall rest the last hope of humanity.

On your Capitol grounds stands the colossal statue of the world's greatest leader, who won the battle of the free. On eternal guard around him stand the bronzed figures of those who preserved that liberty in civic halls and high debate for many a weary year. Out yonder overlooking "Fame's eternal camping-ground"—in Hollywood cemetery—and the dreamless sleep of many a chieftain and many a soldier, is the peerless form of another of the world's greatest leaders, he who said that "Duty is the noblest word in the English language." Where these immortals have led the way, we, the children of men, can afford to follow.

THE RIGHT TO REGULATE RAILROAD FARES AND FREIGHT RATES

Address before the Law Class of Wake Forest College, May 24, 1897

... SUCCESSFUL AS THIS COLLEGE HAS BEEN, the success of its Law Department has been phenomenal. It began with two students in the sumer of 1894, not quite three years ago. I learn from Prof. Gulley that in the session of 1894-5 it had fourteen students; the catalogue of 1895-6 shows sixty-seven law students, and that of 1896-7 has eighty-six—a number which is not only greater than that of any other law school in the State, but which, I am told, is greater than that of all the other law schools put together. Twenty-eight of its students have already received license to practice and are scattered over this State, Georgia, South Carolina and Virginia, and twenty-five more will apply for license at the September term of the Supreme Court. I learn, too, that your law course requires two years. This is eminently right. Young men lose nothing by taking time to lay broad and deep the foundations of their legal knowledge. There is nowadays too great a disposition to rush out into all the professions with too little preparation.

In nothing is the old maxim, *Festina lente* ("make haste slowly"), wiser than in this matter of procuring a thorough training for the arena on which one is to fight the battle of life. In many of the States three years' legal study is required before admittance to the bar, and in others four years. There are several which require only two years' study. North Carolina is one of the very few States in which only one years' study is required before the law student is permitted to stand his examination before license to practice. This is entirely too little. It is unjust to the bar, and more than all unjust to the young student who should begin his career well grounded in the principles of the law. Your college officials have done well by you and acted wisely for the reputation of the college in exacting a two years' course of study, for your success or failure in after life will reflect upon the college which sends you forth.

... Speaking to young lawyers, the address should properly be upon some legal subject, yet it might not be easy to find one upon which you are not already well posted by your excellent instructor. It occurs to me, however, that there is one upon which many practicing lawyers even are not as well informed as they should be, because its vast importance is of comparatively recent development, and cases involving it have been rarely tried as yet at the bar of the courts of this State—though the subject is on trial at the great bar of public opinion. It is a matter, too, upon which every citizen, be he lawyer or layman, should be thoroughly informed as to his rights and the rights of the public.

I shall, therefore, speak to you tonight upon "The Right of the Public to regulate the charges of Common Carriers, and of all others discharging Public, or quasi-Public Duties." The decisions on the subject by THE SUPREME COURT OF THE UNION have been quite uniform, and have so thoroughly illuminated and settled the whole matter that I can discuss it with small reference to the decisions of other tribunals. . . .

The right of the public to regulate the charges of common carriers, even in times when the public granted no franchise, and conferred no right of eminent domain, is far older than the common law, older even than the civil law, and was recognized by both as a necessary and unquestioned rule. TWENTY-ONE YEARS AGO, IN 1876, the Supreme Court of the United States was first called upon, pointedly, to review and re-affirm the recognized law of the ages, that the sovereign possessed the right to regulate the charges for services rendered in a public employment, or for the use of property affected with a public interest. The particular instance was the constitutionality of an act of the General Assembly of Illinois regulating the charges of warehouses for the storage of grain. It was contended that, unlike railroads and telegraph companies, the public had conferred no franchise by an act of incorporation, nor used the right of eminent domain to take private property for their use, and hence that the right to regulate warehouse rates was not to be placed on the same footing as the unquestioned public right to regulate the charges of common carriers. The underlying principle, however, was held to be broad enough to embrace the public right to fix and control the charges of grain warehouses. Though the pressure of immense interests was brought to bear to swerve the court from the well-beaten track by the aid of the ablest and most skilful members of the bar, it firmly held to the principles which have always been law among Anglo-Saxon people. The court laid down the following principle to which, with one slight deviation, it has ever since adhered:

"1. Under the powers inherent in every sovereignty, a government may regulate the conduct of its citizens towards each other, and when necessary for the public good, the manner in which each shall use his property.

"2. It has, in the exercise of these powers, been customary in England from time immemorial, and in this country from the first colonization, to regulate ferries, common carriers, hackmen, bakers, millers, wharfingers, auctioneers, inn-keepers and many other matters of like nature, and in so doing to fix a maximum charge to be made for services rendered, accomodations furnished and articles sold.

"3. The Fourteenth Amendment to the United States Constitution does not in any wise amend the law in this particular.

"4. When the owner of property devotes it to a use in which the public has an interest, he, in effect, grants to the public an interest in such use, and must, to the extent of that interest, submit to be controlled by the public.

"5. The limitation by legislative enactment of the rate of charges for services rendered in an employment of a public nature, or for the use of property in which the public has an interest establishes no new principle in the law, but only gives a new effect to an old one."

The opinion was rendered by CHIEF JUSTICE WAITE, and is a very able and elaborate one.... It is doubtful if a more important one has been delivered by that court in recent years than this negative which it then and there put upon this attempt, by one of the great monied combinations of the country, to reverse the immemorial law that the public has the right to regulate charges in all matters affected with a public use. The court pointed out that the very learned and just Lord Chief Justice Sir Matthew Hale, centuries ago, had laid it down in his Treatise *De Jure Maris,* that the sovereign could regulate the conduct and tolls of public ferries, and in his Treatise *De Portibus Maris* had laid down the same as the rule of common law as to wharves and wharfingers, and as to all property and avocations "affected by a public interest," and cited many English and American decisions, recognizing this to be a true statement of the well-settled "law of the land." The court in that case well says that in all such matters, "The controlling fact is the power to regulate at all. If that exists, the right to establish a maximum of charge, as one of the means of regulation, is implied. In fact the common law rule, which requires that the charge be reasonable, is itself a regulation as to price. Without it the owner could make his rates at will, and compel the public to yield to his terms, or forego the use. To limit the rate of charges for services rendered in a public employment or for the use of property in which the public has an interest, is only changing a regulation which existed before," and, therefore, the court declared that it is not "a taking of property without due process of law." The court further said, "We know that this is a power which may be abused, but that is no argument against its existence. For protection against abuses by legislatures, the people must resort to the polls, not to the courts." This is a VERY PLAIN AND STRAIGHTFORWARD DECLARATION of the immemorial law, and if that court, under tremendous pressure, has since intimated that the courts might supervise legislative action if the rates should ever be such as to destroy the value of property, it has never infringed upon its declaration, that the people, through its representatives in the law-making body, could prescribe rates and the court, in fact, has never ventured to set aside the legislative rates in a single case ever brought before it as unreasonable, nor has it fixed the precise line at which it would assume to intervene.

By all the decisions the right to fix rates being not a judicial but a legislative power, to be exercised by the legislature itself or through a commission created by it, it logically follows that as the court said in this case, and reaffirmed in Budd vs. New York, 143 U.S., 516, the remedy for a harsh exercise of power (if it should ever happen) is a recourse to the people at the ballot-box, not to the courts. For an unwise or oppressive use of its powers, the Legislature is not subject to the supervision of the judiciary, which is merely a co-ordinate branch of the government. It is only when the Legislature passes an act—whether wisely or unwisely—which is not within the scope of its powers, that the courts can declare it unconstitutional. . . .

Some time has been given to the consideration of MUNN VS ILLINOIS as it is the leading one, in which the force of great combinations of capital was brought to bear to remove the ancient landmarks which protected the people from excessive and unreasonable charges. No case has been more cited since and approved. If at common law the public had a right to regulate the charges of stage lines, grist mills, bakers, chimney-sweeps, inn-keepers and the like, as to whom the public conferred no franchises, for an overwhelming reason it must possess that right as to the modern carriers by rail, whose companies receive their existence from the public will and have the breath of life breathed into them by legislative act. Beyond that, railroad corporations are vested with the power of eminent domain, since power is given to them to take possession of the lands of others, against their will, in order to build their tracks. This could only be done if these corporations are created for the public benefit, since the Constitution forbids private property to be taken "except for public uses."

... THE LEGISLATURE IN ITS LIBERALITY expressly provides in the Act of 1891, creating the Railroad Commission, that if any common carrier shall deem the rates prescribed too low, the company may appeal to the Superior Court. In that court a jury of twelve men can pass upon and settle the fact in dispute whether the rate is reasonable or not. Nothing can be fairer than to submit the question to the same tribunal which settles all disputed issues of fact when the lives, liberty, rights and property of any citizen are at stake.

The right of the public to regulate rates is not restricted to those avocations which are essentially monopolies, as railroads and the like, but it applies to all matters which are affected with a public use. This was carefully considered by the Court of Appeals of New York in People vs. Budd, 117 N.Y., 1, in which it was declared that the right of regulation by the public is not restricted to cases in which the owner has a legal monopoly or some special government privilege or protection, but extends to all public employments and property....

The right of regulation applies also to *water companies,* Spring Valley vs. Schottler, 110 U.S., 347, and in a recent Texas case, the right to regulate the charges of *cotton compresses* is recognized, and there are also cases recognizing the right to regulate charges of *tobacco warehouses* and of warehouses for storing and weighing cotton, and to regulate services and charges of *general warehousemen,* Delaware vs. Stock Yard, 45 N.J. Eq., 50.

The same right of public regulation of rates applies to *street railways,* Buffalo R. Co., vs. Buffalo, 111 N.Y., 132.... And to *canals,* Perrine vs. Canal Co., 9 Howard, U.S., 172, and to *ferries,* Stephens vs. Powell, 1 Ore., 283 ... to *toll roads and bridges,* Covington vs. Sanford, 94 Ky, 689....

And *wharf charges,* Ouachita vs. Aikem 121 U.S., 444; and to *telegraph rates,* Mayo vs. Tel. Co., 112 N.C., 343, ... and to *telephone charges,* although the telephone is covered by a United States patent, Hockett vs. State, 105 Ind., 250....

AS TO GAS COMPANIES, the right of the State to regulate rates either itself or through power conferred upon municipal corporations is beyond controversy.... The power to regulate *water rates* has already been cited . . . and the right to authorize municipal bodies to regulate the *price, weight and quality of bread* is declared upon the precedents to be settled law. . . .

The power to regulate the tolls of *public mills* is declared . . . also the power to fix the rates for the *salvage of logs*. . . . The above are but a few of the cases recognizing the inherent public right to regulate those matters, and there are still many others recognized as subject to public regulation.

It must not be forgotten that there is a BROAD DISTINCTION IN THE LAW, running through all the ages, between the above and similar avocations "affected with a public interest," as to which the sovereign or the public has the right to regulate and fix rates and purely private matters, as farming, selling merchandise, manufacturing and similar matters, which are purely private in their nature, and as to which the public has never claimed or exercised the right of regulation. It is by ignorance, or an affected ignorance, of this broad distinction in the law and which is based on the essential difference in the nature of things, that denial has been sometimes attempted (by those not lawyers) of the right of public regulation in matters as to which the public has always possessed that right.

From the beginning of this State as a Colony, our statute books have borne provisions regulating the tolls of public mills, and until very recent years the county courts fixed the charges of innkeepers, hotels and bar-rooms. The latter regulations have been abandoned of late years, not because the power does not still exist, but because its exercise was no longer required to protect the public, the multiplication of inns and hotels furnishing sufficient protection by reason of competition. The regulation of the tools of grist mills, ferries and the like is still exercised.

AS TO RAILROADS AND PUBLIC CARRIERS, the complete list of decisions uniformly sustaining the public right to fix their charges, both in State and Federal courts, would fill many pages. . . .

The authority of the Legislature to empower a railroad commission to prescribe reasonable rates for common carriers is held constitutional in numerous cases. . . .

The rights of the courts to interfere with the rates fixed by the law-making powers was denied in Munn vs. Ill. and several other cases. . . .

When the question arises whether the Legislature has exceeded its constitutional power in prescribing the rates to be charged by a corporation controlling a public highway, STOCKHOLDERS ARE

NOT THE ONLY PERSONS whose rights and interests are to be considered. The rights of the public are not to be ignored. The court further says that the inquiry as to whether rates are reasonable and just includes whether they are reasonable and just to the public, and adds: "The public cannot properly be subjected to unreasonable rates in order simply that stockholders may earn dividends. If a corporation cannot maintain such a highway and earn dividends for stockholders, it is a misfortune for it and them which the Constitution does not require to be remedied by imposing unjust burdens upon the public."

... The statutory regulation of the rate to be paid for the use of money is another striking instance of legislative authority to regulate rate. And who would contend that the courts have power to intervene and say the legislative rate is too low?

The Supreme Court of the United States has tersely put THE TRUE STATUS OF RAILROADS thus: "They are chartered and built for public benefit. The pecuniary profit of their owners is purely incidental." Many railroad owners and managers would reverse this if they could, and as far as they are permitted they act upon the maxim "Railroads are operated for the benefit of their controllers and managers. The public benefit is purely incidental."

The great hindrance to achieving the public benefit which is the legal object for which these corporations are created is THE RELUCTANCE OF THEIR MANAGERS to concede reasonable and just rates. Some of them act as if they believed that common carriers were a private business and that they have the right to lay upon the public any rate they think fit to raise money enough to pay whatever salaries they see proper to allow themselves, and whatever expenditures they care to make and interest on three or four times the stock and bonds the property really cost. Yet nothing is farther from the law.

Railroad, telegraph, telephone and express companies are *quasi* public corporations, the charges are IN THE NATURE OF PUBLIC TAXATION, and the public have the right to look into the nature of their expenditures and to fix the rates as a reasonable net profit above economical and necessary disbursements. The public right in this regard is fully shown by the uniform and numerous decisions of the courts I have cited to you. With the enhanced value of money and the corresponding fall in the prices of farm produce and of labor, there should be a corresponding fall in passenger and freight rates. This would conduce to the public benefit and convenience, and would at the same time redound to the benefit of the corporations, which instead of carrying a few cars half full of passengers or freight, would find it to their benefit as well as that of the public, to reduce their rates and carry two or three times the number of cars with full loads. The present charges are an embargo on travel and traffic alike.

This has been amply shown by experience in those States in which the public has succeeded in reducing the rates, and by the experience of a line in our own State whose receipts nearly doubled during its reduction of rates. Another striking instance of the reduction of postage rates, which has always been followed by enormously increased receipts. Indeed the two cents per mile passenger rates already prescribed in so many States, and which THE PEOPLE OF THIS STATE ARE DEMANDING, is admitted by the corporations here to be just, since their reports show that their receipts average 2⅕ cents only per mile to each passenger—the enormous addition which makes the charge 3¼ cents to the public is caused by the immense number of free passes issued to office-holders, large shippers, and other influential people or favorites—the very people who need them least—but the corporations need their influence to keep the public quiet under exorbitant exactions. Thus, in effect, roughly speaking, every three passengers who pay 3¼ cents per mile for their own travelling are paying also for the free riding of another, for the railroads carry the dead heads at the expense of the public.

...In 1874, when the Legislature of Wisconsin opened the fight for two cent fares and lower freight rates, their action was sustained by the Supreme Court of the State, Chief Justice Ryan delivering a remarkably able opinion, in the course of which he said, "It may well be that the high rates charged by the railroads have lessened their own receipts by crippling the public interests. The affidavits of experts have been read to the contrary, but they are only opinions, founded indeed on past statistics. Such opinions, founded on such statistics, would have defeated cheap postage, and are helping today to defeat a moderate tariff. Experience often contradicts such theories. The interest of the public in this regard seems to be identical with that of the railroad. We think there must be a point where the public interest in railroads, and the private interest of the corporations meet, where the service of the public at the lowest practicable rate will produce the largest legitimate income to the railroad. It seems to us an utter delusion that the highest toll will produce the largest income. The companies have hitherto absolutely controlled their own rates. The

Legislature now limits them. The companies say the limit is too low. But there is no occasion for heat or passion on either side. The people and the Legislature understand well the necessity of railroads to the State and the necessity of dealing fairly and justly, and even liberally with the companies."

And the same can be said of the people of North Carolina. They are A JUST AND SENSIBLE PEOPLE. They understand the necessity and the benefit of railroads. There is no hostility to the railroads as such. We want more of them. There is no disposition among any of our people to deal other than liberally with these corporations. There is no desire to fix rates unreasonably low. But we know that rates are *unreasonably high*. We know that when one great line voluntarily reduced its rates one-third, it nearly doubled its receipts, and that these lower rates were stopped by an injunction illegally granted at the instance of a rival corporation. Our people know that the railroads were built nearly entirely with our money, and largely with money from the public treasury. We know that by shrewd manipulation the owners of the original stock were forced to sell at a small per cent. of the original cost, and that the controlling management is now chiefly dictated by non-resident multi-millionaires, living in London and New York, and that these railroads, which in the eye of the law "were chartered and built for the public benefit, the pecuniary profit of the owners being incidental only," are now run at "the highest the traffic will bear," for the enrichment of non-residents and with precious little regard to our advantage. We know THE ENORMOUS SALARIES paid its highest officials, who are also provided with sumptuous private palace cars and staffs of servants, private secretaries, lawyers and newspapers at our expense. We know that all of these expenses come out of the toiling masses, from whom they are collected by the station agents as surely and more rigidly than the taxes are collected by the sheriffs and collectors for your State and Federal Governments. And we know too that we have full power through our representatives to fix every charge made by every railroad in the State.

The Supreme Court of the United States has decided in the cases I have quoted to you that the public in fixing rates have the right to know the amount of the salaries of railroad officials and the nature of their disbursements, that it may be seen how high it is necessary to fix rates. If the expenditures are extravagant, as for high salaries, or illegal, as for lobby expenses or running newspapers, those items may be disregarded. The public have the same right to be informed as to all these matters as in regard to the salaries and expenses of its State Government, for it pays them both equally. The railroad managers need to learn that THIS IS NO IMPERTINENT CURIOSITY, but that these are matters of legal right, and that their management and rates are of vital interest to the public who pay every expenditure they make. Yet last winter, when a resolution asking information as to the salaries of the higher railroad officials was introduced, some of them affected to treat it as inquiry into private matters, and secured the defeat of the resolution in the House, though it passed the Senate. They knew the investigation would be damaging, and they dared not let the people know how much they were taxed for railroad salaries and illegal expenses. We know from their own showing that the *pro rata* part of the salaries on one tolerably short railroad was double that paid by the entire State to the Governor and all the other Executive officers of the State Government, and that the salaries and emoluments of more than one official of corporations operating in this State amount to more than a dozen times what the State pays its Governor, and yet both are paid by the people, and come out of their earnings before they can use a dollar for themselves.

In coming to these conclusions, you will see that I have advanced no idea that is not based upon the reiterated decisions of the highest courts in the land. In saying these things I have no desire, nor has anyone, to excite any prejudice against any corporation, except that opposition which should always be aroused in the breasts of freemen by seeing their fellows illegally oppressed, and their meager subsistence taken from them to support the luxury and idleness, and too often the vices of others. We should be men who *"know their rights, and knowing, dare maintain them."*

I know that in all history whenever any man has dared to tell the people their rights, and to tell them that they are oppressed, and that they have the legal right to stop the oppression, it makes him a mark for every hired arrow, and every mercenary bowman. But in the language of Martin Luther, at the Diet of Worms, *"Here I stand—God help me—I can do no other."* When the immortal Vance was asked to say nothing about the abuses of the conscription, that it would all be arranged, he replied: "God forbid that the rights and the honor of North Carolina, and the welfare of her people, should depend upon the grace and mercy of a conscript bureau." And so I say now in your hearing, that

"God forbid that the freedom of North Carolina from unjust exactions, and the welfare of her people, should depend upon the grace and mercy of Pierpont Morgan and such as he." We are entitled to regulate these charges of common carriers among us, as an immemorial right of a free people in all times, and we will accept no petty abatement as a favor from them. The decisions I have quoted conclusively show that the public not only have a right to fix rates, but in doing so they justly should allow nothing for exorbitant salaries, extravagant expenses, illegal disbursements, nor, after discarding these, anything above the expenses of economical management and a moderate interest on the real value of the property, for the law is just, and does not tolerate dividends on watered stocks and bonds.

I could easily show you that the sum illegally wrung from the people of North Carolina above the legal requirements above stated is annually more than DOUBLE THE ENTIRE AMOUNT OF TAXES levied for your State Government. If the men of 1776 are to be commemorated for all time for their resistance to a little illegal tax upon tea, the men who shall hereafter step forward and shall succeed in rescuing North Carolina from the enormous pillage exacted from her and from which her people are staggering without always knowing the reason, will deserve to be remembered

"Far, far on, in summers that we shall not see."

All corporations in North Carolina have not been willing plunderers of her people. Some would reduce rates if others would permit them. Two conventions of the manufacturers and other great industries in the middle and western part of our State, which have been unduly depressed by discriminations against us, and unjust rates, have met and have taken steps looking to some relief. In the eastern part of the State the truckers attempted action last year, but received slight attention. The great railroads, by demanding a pooling bill at the hands of Congress, have admitted that competition is at an end. As that safeguard no longer remains for the public, it is more than ever essential that we should assert and maintain the protection given the public by its right to regulate rates. Yet the body of our people consider the great sums they are unjustly paying as ILLEGAL TRIBUTE MONEY TO THE STRANGER, and they will send to the next Legislature a body of men who will right these wrongs. They can as a right secure a relief for seeking which they will be laughed at when it is asked as a favor. I have shown you that they have full power to secure their own relief, and I could say these things nowhere more appropriately than to the more than four score young men in the largest law school in the State, and in a college maintained by a body of people whose love of civil liberty and human rights is surpassed by none.

When the wicked son of Omri reigned as King over Israel, he was vexed by the free speech of Elijah, and on meeting him he cried out in fierce tones and with flashing eyes, *"Art thou he that troubleth Israel?"* The prophet of Carmel answered him back, *"It is not I that troubleth Israel, but thou and thy house."* And we know that when the supreme test came, and the power was revealed which drove those oppressions and abominations out of the land, the servants of Baal stood in the presence of the mocking servant of God and answered him not a word.

POLITICAL TEACHINGS OF THE GOSPEL

(Address before Raleigh District Sunday School Conference, Franklinton, N.C., June 15, 1897.)

. . . The Sunday school is an agency in developing the highest type of character in the membership of the church. It not only creates zeal in the teacher and brings home to teacher and scholar alike the influence of the sublime precepts of the gospel, to an extent not otherwise obtainable, but it educates Christian people in liberality by teaching children the duty and blessing of giving. It shows them the beauty of Christian lives devoted to the instruction of others. It brightens the lives of little waifs who are brought into contact with children in a happier condition of life, and they are thus reclaimed to the services of humanity and God by seeing that they are not outcasts, but that Christian people care for them and have regard for their welfare. When the children of the poor have the truth impressed upon them, it opens wide the door of opportunity and advancement in life. Countless numbers are thus brought to become useful and prosperous members of society who otherwise would have been the enemies of social government, and of an authority which would mean to them only repression and continued degradation.

These and many other reasons can be given for the vast benefit Sunday Schools have been, not only to the church, but to civilized government as well, for the history of our civilization in every age has been its degree of Christianity. In fact our civilization began with the incarnation at Bethlehem. The seed of mustard has grown till it has become a great tree, and all nations may repose under its branches.

The morality, the virtues, the faith, the benevolence, the resignation under trials, the good will among men taught the children, and their teachers too, by the thorough knowledge of the Scriptures acquired in the Sunday schools have not only a wide and lasting effect upon the tone of society and the conduct of life of those receiving this instruction, but there is another distinct benefit which has probably not been called to your attention.

The highest ideal of government which the ages have evolved, is that a government of the people, by the people, and for the people. Have you ever thought where it came from? The central idea in the teachings of Christ is that between the supremest of supreme power and the humblest individual the dignity of manhood requires and permits no human intermediate. There you have the great thought of the equality of mankind. No one ever conceived, or announced, that idea before. No heathen philosopher ever dreamed it. In every pronouncement He ever made, He taught the nothingness of human rank, the worthlessness of distinctions of wealth. He first taught the brotherhood of man, He taught that men should live not for themselves but for the race, for their fellowmen. He told the rich young man to sell all that he had, to give it to the poor and follow Him. He himself taught, by the sublimity of his example, for he went about doing good. Freedom and liberality were barely conceived of before His day. They were not so much as names even, save in the short-lived republics of Greece and Rome. And in them, having no true basis, they soon withered and perished. In Christ alone the basis of real and lasting freedom was first laid in the equality and brotherhood of the human race. . . .

The world was slow to perceive the full force of the new ideas taught by the Sermon on the Mount, and by every act and speech of the Master. Indeed the world does not yet, after nearly nineteen centuries, fully grasp and comprehend the true intent and meaning of his words. Having eyes to see and ears to hear, we do not understand. The words are yet too strong for us, but we are growing into the light. We are beginning to discern in dim outline the pathway upon which shines the Star of Bethelehem. There are a few who begin to understand fully whither it leads, to the vast masses of men the words are yet too strong for a poor human nature. But all who know that the teachings of Christ are the real source of all democratic forms of government. I do not use the word in a party sense, but in the broader meaning of a government which is in the interest of the people and not in behalf of the privileged few—privileged as in some countries because of inherited wealth, or as in this country, by acquired wealth. In the eyes, and in the plain words of the Master, wealth confers no privileges, but imposes fearful responsibilities and duties. . . .

Our liberty, based upon the gospel of equality and brotherhood, gives us freedom of thought, freedom of speech, freedom of conscience, freedom of action.

The world cannot at once receive these great ideas. They needed time, centuries, to permeate the social fabric, to leaven political institutions, to work their way. When emperors and kings essayed to patronize the church, they but corrupted it by choking the free operation of its cardinal principles. When popes and cardinals took charge, they obstructed the development of the church, for to them equally with the king and emperor, the equality, the brotherhood, the liberty of men were incomprehensible and antagonistic. The master has said, he who would be greatest among you, let him be your servant, and in a true republic the highest official is not a ruler but a servant.

But in spite of king and cardinal, pope and emperor, the political force of the Christian ideas has won its way. The right to think, to speak, to act freely has been more and more asserted as men came to feel that in the eye of the ultimate tribunal, rich and poor, king and peasant, master and slave, stood on the same level. The political effect of such teachings is democracy. The true source of political self government is the religion of Christ, and there is no force more potent for the maintenance of that form of government than these schools, which sow the thoughts of equality, brotherhood and liberty in the minds of children. Here is the seed bed of civil and religious freedom.

Born in a stable and cradled in a manger, the Christ came not to enforce the tyranny of hereditary rank, without a foot of land to call his own he did not exalt the claims of wealth, without a roof to cover his head, and with poor fishermen for his companions, he came not as the champion of power, but to assert the truth that "where the Spirit of the Lord is, there is liberty." . . .

If Christ came to-day who would receive, and who would crucify him? The pure minded little children would receive Him. They did so when he came nineteen centuries ago. . . . And then among the men He would recruit his followers, just as of old, for the "common people heard Him gladly." Those whose faces are darkened by the searching glances of the sun and their hands hardened by toil, would figure largely among His followers. And so would the honest men of whatever profession and whatever calling, who are striving for modest competence, and in whose hearts the greed of gold has not burnt out all traces of humanity and fair dealing and to "that divinity which should be within us." But not many mighty nor many rich shall be called. It was so of old. They who form great syndicates and trusts to rob the people, and those who gather where others have sown would be foremost among those who would crucify Him. . . .

The great evil of this day is the worship of wealth, and it makes no matter to its worshippers that we know thât every vast estate is necessarily accumulated by robbery of the people—for there is a modest limit in the nature of things to the accumulations which can be made by diligence, and thrift and economy and honest industry. The free opportunity for honest accumulations is the glory of our institutions, but these vast estates are not made in that way. They are made by processes which should consign their holders rather to your penitentiaries. Their very size proves they are not honest accumulations. . . .

Our people are being robbed by wholesale. They do not receive the just rewards of their labors. They are being pauperized and kept in want while a few men, by trick and combinations, are gathering to themselves the earnings of a continent. Yet how many leading church members, how many church papers are denouncing the robbers and the wrongs as the Master did, and as it is still written in His word? How many indeed are pursuing an opposite course? I condemn no man. Let each man's conscience answer him.

Search all history, and you will find no age when the robbery of the just earnings of the masses was more systematic, more shameless and less resisted than today. There was never a time when the worship of great riches, however badly acquired, was more open than now. . . .

The Talmud of the Hebrews has a true saying that if "the world shall ever be reformed and saved it will be by the breath of the school-children." And if this world is to be redeemed from this subservience to wealth which subjects our people to robbery and our children to poverty, it will be because of the saving words of the Master which are being impressed upon the tender hearts of the children in the Sunday Schools of the land. There is a saving strength in His words, which if received in simple faith, can redeem the world, both for the time that now is as well as for that which shall be hereafter.

TWELVE REASONS WHY THE TELEGRAPH SHOULD BE RESTORED TO THE POSTOFFICE

(*New Time* Magazine, July, 1897)

Among the many reasons why the telegraph and telephones should be owned and operated exclusively by the postoffice department, there are no less than twelve of such weight that any one of them should be sufficient to cause the adoption of that measure by Congress.

1. The Constitution requires it. That instrument (Art. 1., Sec. 8), places the establishment of postal facilities exclusively in the government. Under that provision, originally the mail was carried on horseback; then by stage coach; then with the advent of steam it was carried by railroad and steamboat. When messages began to be sent by electricity, the government (1844-47), therefore logically adopted and operated the telegraph. When, in a fit of economy, it was turned over to private corporations, Henry Clay, the great Whig leader, and Cave Johnson the Democratic Postmaster-general, earnestly opposed this unconstitutional action. Leading men in all parties since, including five Postmasters-generals, have endeavored to restore the electric mail to the postoffice, but the powerful telegraph lobby has been too powerful in Congress to permit a vote upon the question. Yet, out of eighteen committees to whom successive bills for government ownership have been referred, sixteen have reported favorably, one was noncommittal, and only one was adverse.

2. If the government owned the electric mail, a telegraph or telephone would be established at each of the 75,000 post-offices, and, indeed, the number of post-offices would be greatly increased, whereas now the telegraph goes to only 21,000 selected points, for the private companies, operating purely for profit, naturally seek only points that pay well, while the object of the government would be to serve the greatest number of people, the whole people, if possible, and at bare cost, no profits being desired. The high rates and restricted number of offices now make this great discovery of no benefit to the great mass of the people.

3. The government desiring only to earn expenses could give a uniform low rate of five cents between any two points in the Union. This is the opinion of experts.

4. The government could operate it more cheaply. There would be no enormous salaries to the higher officials, nor would great sums be paid out, as now, to maintain a lobby at Washing-

ton, and at each State capital, and to retain lawyers and editors to influence public opinion. Then the government could save the rent now paid by the companies, as it could use for the telegraph and telephones the same buildings it now owns or rents for post-office purposes at each point.

5. The government, while not paying, as the private companies do, enormous sums—from $100,000 down—as salaries to the higher officials, would, on the other hand, not follow their example in giving starvation wages to the vast army of employees who do the real work. The object of the government not being to earn big salaries and dividends on a six-fold watered stock, it could and would pay a living wage to the operators. Besides, the increased business would largely increase the pay of postmasters at country postoffices.

6. The operators would have some fixity of tenure, being postmasters, and hence not liable to be turned out for voting their choice. In the last campaign every pressure was brought to bear upon the employees of the great corporations, but public sentiment would not have permited the postoffice officials to apply the same pressure to the postmasters.

7. Messages would be, like the mails, more secret. Now the business of every man is at the mercy of the heads of private corporations, which are in no wise subject to public opinion.

8. It would emancipate the press, who are now in the power of the private companies, and must take such news as they send, and dare not be free in discussing certain questions.

9. The cheap rate would enable every weekly paper to take telegraphic dispatches. This would benefit printer and the public starting new papers, and extending the circulation of old ones. In England, when the government took over the telegraphs and adopted cheap rates, the number of press dispatches instantly increased thirty fold—not thirty per cent. merely, but thirty times the former number.

10. All other countries, practically, except Canada, have the telegraph and telephone operated by the government, and at low rates, and in all it has been a success for the government, and a vast benefit to the public. We claim to be a business people, but we are guilty of turning over the best paying part of the post-office—the quick, rapid electric mail—to private corporations, and operate the slow, non-paying part, by the public at a loss, of course.

11. The government placing a telephone at every country post-office, and increasing the number, of course, would, to a large extent, amount to rural delivery, without the expense that an extension of the present city delivery to country districts would be. This would also destroy the isolation which is now the drawback to country life, by putting the country districts in speaking distance of the town. It would enable those in the country to summon a doctor, inquire for freight, ascertain the daily state of the markets, and to communicate with the courthouse when needed as witnesses, or on other business.

12. No millionaires would be created, as now, out of the surplus earnings, but the money, beyond the bare cost of operation would remain in the pockets of the people, while at the same time these facilities would be extended to every nook and corner of the Republic, and become a convenience to the whole people, instead of being, as now, a mere advantage to a few, which is very often to the detriment of the many.

ADDRESS BEFORE THE ELEVENTH ANNUAL CONVENTION OF RAILROAD COMMISSIONERS AT DENVER, COLORADO

(August 10, 1899)

I appreciate the compliment of being requested to address this Eleventh Annual convention of your honorable body, composed of the inter-State Commission and the Railroad Commissioners of thirty-four States. There are few men to whom more important interests are confided than you, upon whom rests a people's hope for the regulation of the great transportation business of this country. Upon your success in the discharge of that duty awaits the public decision whether we shall rest content with this form of regulation, or whether, slowly it may be, or suddenly it may be, but in either event reluctantly, the people shall be forced to take over the ownership of railroads as the sole solution of one of the greatest problems which now vex the public mind.

Your conventions have, I believe, with one exception, been held in the city of Washington. Appropriate, as for many reasons that city is for your gathering and pleasant as it is for any assemblage, you are to be congratulated that for this occasion you have selected the capital of the Centennial State, the centre of the wild and breezy west. Here the air is purer. You are at a higher elevation and can take a broader and more comprehensive view of men and affairs. It would look as if you were at the very centre and hub of the universe, for as Proctor Knott said of the "zenith city of the unsalted seas," the sky fits down at the same distance all around us. At any rate you are at the centre of the great country which stretches from the Mississippi to the Pacific—a section which embraces two-thirds of this Union, though many men east of the Mississippi have never suspected it. Political parties are so little alive to it that all our Presidents save one have come from the one-third of the Union that lies east of the Mississippi, and that one lived on the very bank of the river at Baton Rouge. Two of the three great parties in 1896 combined in the nomination of a candidate from west of the great river, and the probabilities are that he will be nominated again next year.

The mountain barriers which once divided this immediate section from the Golden Slope of the Pacific are like Louis XIV said of the Pyrenees—they exist no longer—for we

> Have ridden our iron stallions down to drink,
> Through the canyons to the waters of the West.

The steel rails of commerce have riveted State to State by bands that can never be burst asunder. Beneath the tread of the iron horse mountains have vanished and rivers ceased to exist.

From the golden mile stone in the Roman Forum radiated those magnificent roads which to this day tell how Rome built for the ages. Along them poured the tide of the Republic's and the Empire's commerce; over them tramped her legions, and as the God Terminus successively removed further and further the limits of her domains, those magnificent viaducts carried to the remotest verges the arts, the literature, the laws, the civilization that was Roman. Indeed her roads made possible the vast extent of her dominion and bound together for so many centuries so many countries in that Roman Peace which created and maintained the civilization and the learning without which humanity would not occupy the advanced stage that it does today.

Suppose for a moment that those Roman roads, the arteries of the empire, had been owned by private companies of millionaires; that not a wheel could roll nor a man move along them, nor even the legions except on terms dictated by the corporations; would not those corporations have had the empire by the throat? Would they not have appointed the consuls and pro-consuls, every Senator, every general and every judge? They would have been the government.

A greater than Rome is before you. In these United States the 190,000 miles of iron way are no less the life arteries of the Republic. Along them pours a tide of travel, of freight, of wealth far beyond what the Roman ways, even those nearest the capital, ever witnessed. Indeed, though our railway system dates back only seventy years, over any one of our many great through lines, the volume of freight and travel exceeds that of the entire world a century ago. It is needless to say that the control of this immense power must be in the government, that is in the people, for with us the government is still in theory at least, the people.

The Supreme Court of the United States held in the Granger cases (Munn v. Illinois, 94 U.S.) and has reiterated in many a case since that time out of mind the control of common carriers and their regulation as to rates and in all other matters, rested in the government. "Though in this country transportation by railroad is carried on by private corporations," said the Inter-State Commerce Commission in their last report (1899) to Congress, "it is essentially a government function. This appears from the necessary conditions of railroad construction. It is a universal maxim that private property can not be taken for private uses, but only for the public use. Yet no railroad can be built without the appropriation of private property. It equally appears from the relation of a carrier's business to the community. A merchant may sell to one customer for one price and to another customer for another price, as best subserves his interest, without violating any sense of right and wrong, but it is universally felt that the rates of public transportation should be uniform to all. The railway is, from its very nature in respect to the greater part of its business, a virtual monopoly. If the business of transportation is essentially a government function, then the government must see that it is properly . . . charged. If it is in essence a monopoly, then it must be regulated. The two things, of necessity, go hand in hand."

This is a very clear statement of the proposition. Railroads can only be constructed by reason of having rights of way condemned for them as a public use, and being a public use, they are necessarily subject to public regulation. Indeed, the fact that you sit here, that we have an Inter-State Commission and thirty-four States or more have their Railroad Commissions, is conclusive that the sovereign, of whom the Supreme Court of the Union and of every State is merely an agency—the sovereign people—have decided once for all that these iron horses shall be bitted and bridled. The sun will not, cannot, go back a single degree on the dial at Ahaz. Mr. Ingalls, President of two great systems, in his address to you last year, frankly said: "Regulation by the people has come to stay and a railroad manager who does not recognize that fact is a back number." He further said that the mass of railway managers fully recognized the permanence of public control and regulation and were earnestly seeking a solution of the difficulties attendant upon it.

No one can doubt that if all railway managers loyally accepted the yoke of the law, all questions of differences between railways and people would be fairly settled by these boards provided by the law for that purpose. It is because many managers do not accept it but resort to injunctions (often issued by their former attorneys, promoted to the bench) to set aside rates, regulations and tax assessments made by your commissions that the present unsatisfactory condition of affairs exists.

It results that the real question—and we are face to face with it—is whether it is practicable to control these great forces, these immense aggregations of capital, by Commissions and by statutes, or shall it be necessary to take the absolute ownership of them over in the government.

In all the countries of the world save Great Britain and the United States, the answer has been that government ownership is indispensable to a safe and just control. Accordingly in almost all other countries, including even the Australian and other British colonies, the railroads, or at least the controlling lines are owned by their respective governments. In the United States and the contracted territory embraced in the British Isles, the experiment of government control, without government ownership, is on trial.

There are evils in government ownership. There are difficulties in government control, unless it has ownership. It is those difficulties which you have had to face since the creation of your respective Commissions. You know their magnitude. The history of your various bodies, and the published proceedings of your meetings in these joint sessions for ten years past, show how fully you have grasped the situation and with what ability you have discussed the problems it presents.

There are many aspects in which the railroad problem presents itself:

1. The relation of common carriers to their stockholders.
2. To one another.
3. To their employees.
4. To the government.
5. Their relation to the humble individuals who are often treated as if they had no right to express their opinions on such serious and intricate matters as railroad management, yet without whom not a car wheel would roll, not a magnate would draw his salary—in short the men upon whose broad shoulders rest the entire support of this immense system—the patrons of the roads.

In looking over your proceedings last session, I see that the invitation was extended to me upon the ground that the investors, the great railroad presidents and their attorneys, the employees, the representatives of the government had been heard by you, and it was suggested that it would not be amiss of the people, "the Joneses who paid the freight," they who supported the railroads instead of being supported by them, should be heard from also, and a friend of mine proposed that I should be selected to represent this "Forgotten Man." Your convention did me the very high honor to ask me to present him and I am before you. This forgotten man elects no president, superintendent or board of directors but he has to bear whatever burdens they see fit to place upon him. He has no voice in fixing the salaries, many of them as high or higher than that of the President of the United States, but he pays them to the last cent. He rarely rides in a palace car or upon a free pass but he pays the fares of those who do. He has no hearing as to the tax which shall be levied for the movement of himself, his produce or his purchases, but he pays it more surely than he does the taxes for the support of his city, State or Federal Government, for the Station Agent, like that other tax collector, the Custom House officer, extends no credit but requires cash in hand.

Speaking for this client you have assigned me, I shall not say that he desires government ownership. On the contrary I think he does not—as yet. He is patient. He is conservative. He is watching it closely; I may even say, doubtfully, but he will give it a fair trial. If it succeeds so much the better. If it shall fail, he will be heard from further.

Let it not be thought that there are limitations upon his power, for from ocean to ocean and from earth to sky, this land and all that in it is, are his. He conquered it with his blood. He created it with His labor and has defended it with His life. As to Constitutions, He made them and He can make others when He deems that justice to Himself and to those dependent upon Him, shall require it. Justice has ever been the attribute of the race to which He belongs, and conservatism His companion, but He can move. He moved at Bunker Hill and an historic flag, the flag of his fathers for long centuries, disappeared from his shores forever. He moved at Philadelphia and a new form of government, alien to the traditions of the race, took its place among the nations to abide forevermore.

I shall therefore, as far as I am able, point out to you a few of the views of this client, some of the causes of complaint which he has told me he has under the present system of government control and which possibly may be remedied without calling in government ownership; and I take it this is what you wish to hear.

The masses of our fellow citizens are intelligent and just. They have no hostility to railroads as such, but only to their abuses. They recognise the immense value of railroads, their indispensable assistance in the development of this country. By individual, city, county, State and National subscriptions they have aided the construction of the railroad system of this country. They have seen individual stockholders "frozen out;" they have seen the more than $500,000,000 of National aid given in lands and bonds, disappear "like the baseless fabric of a vision" and leave scarce a wreck behind. These things they have endured and would even forgive if the present management of these systems was fair and just.

It was a Frenchman who maliciously defined a lawyer as a "gentleman who rescues your property from the enemy and appropriates it himself." It will be small advantage to the public if the railroads develop the country merely to own its profits themselves, for the value of the land depends upon the amount of profits taken out of its produce for transportation.

The returns of the Inter-State Commerce Commission for the year ending 30 of June, 1899, are not yet in but taking the returns for 30 of June, 1898, and making an allowance for increase at the same ratio which they showed over the previous year, it may be roughly estimated that there were 190,000 miles of railway in the United States on June 30, 1899, and that the railroad receipts for the year ending on that day were 1,400 millions dollars of which 500 millions were net profit. It may also be said that two sevenths of the receipts were from passengers of whom more than 600 millions were carried) and that the total of bonds and stocks upon which these corporations were paying dividends and interest is (according to Poor's Manual and other good authorities) something more than double what it would cost to replace all the railroads with their equipment and property of every description. The 100 per cent. or more of bonds and stocks above actual value is due largely, but not altogether to watering, for to some extent it represents extravagance in construction and shrinkage in values.

The immense volume of this business, whose receipts aggregate nearly three times, and whose net revenues about equal, the total receipts of the National Government, shows that it must be regulated by public control in some form. It touches the public welfare at too many points to be left uncontrolled by no considerations superior to the profits of the corporations or the caprices of their managers. At the same time the immense bulk shows also the difficulty of wise or effective supervision and the incalculable harm alike to the carriers and the public if that supervision were done by unskilful or hostile hands.

One of the greatest evils of the present system is the proneness of these corporations to intervene in politics. Realizing that government by the people is only possible when the government is kept untouched by the power of great moneyed combinations, there is nothing which arouses public indignation more than the unconcealed interference of these corporations in the nomination and election of legislators, congressmen, Governors and United States Senators. Their contributions to Presidential campaign funds is a National scandal. Worse than all is their influence in the appointment of the life judiciary of the Federal Government and recent evidence given before the Industrial Commission shows that they are not above tampering with the nomination and election of State judges chosen by the people.

It is not for such purposes as these that corporations are chartered. Their interference in such matters is not to advance but to thwart the public interest. Such expenditures of effort and money are not made without expectation of most adequate returns. They are not necessarily made in behalf of either political party, for the late Jay Gould cynically expressed the truth when he said that in a Democratic district he was a Democrat and in a Republican district a Republican, but in every one a railroad man. This interference in the nomination and election of public officials fatigues popular indignation even more than the lobbies maintained in Congress and State legislatures, to affect legislation and is a great lever towards forcing a demand for government ownership of the railroads.

The greatest evils attendant upon the present system, viewed from a financial standpoint, greater than excessive rates, and more difficult to repress, because secret, is discrimination in rates. By this means individuals and even cities can be destroyed and others built up by their destruction. The Standard Oil Co. which forced the railways to carry its products at 30 cents per barrel while compelling them not only to charge all others 80 cents per barrel, but even to pay the extra 50 cents paid by its rivals into the Standard Oil Treasury, is a sample of the methods of these modern highwaymen, the trusts. The Standard Oil Company is shown to have received from the railroads $10,000,000 bonus by this means in 18 months. Other corporations have followed the same methods until small manufacturers have been crushed out and equality of opportunity which was the boast of our institutions has become non-existent.

The crucial question for solution is whether the interference of great corporations in politics and their secret discrimination in rates, whereby trusts are created and sustained, can be suppressed without resort to government ownership. These evils must be eliminated. The hope of America lies in the very fact that our people will not submit to such abuses much longer.

How shall you suppress these discriminations? Mr. Depew recently stated that certain large establishments could ship goods from Chicago to New York at 35 cents per 100 pounds while others had to pay 75 cents—a difference of $80 per car load, or on a shipment of ten car loads per day a discrimination of a quarter of a million dollars per year; and W. H. Vanderbilt testified before the Hepburn Commission that all large shippers got rebates if they asked for them. How can any individual or any town stand up against the destructive power of such discriminations?

Can they be stopped by voluntary agreements, however solemn between railroad managers? Hear what President Ingalls told you at your last convention. He said: "Men managing large corporations, who would trust their opponents with their pocket books with untold thousands in it, will hardly trust his agreement for the maintenance of tariffs while they are in the room together. Good faith seems to have departed from the railroad world so far as traffic agreements are concerned." If these managers will not trust one another how can the public be expected to have much faith in them?

The Inter-State Commerce Commission seems to agree entirely with President Ingalls-for they say in their 1899 report, "The situation has become intolerable, both from the standpoint of the public and of the carriers. Tariffs are disregarded, discriminations constantly occur, the price at which transportation can be obtained is fluctuating and uncertain. Railroad managers are distrustful of each other and shippers all the while in doubt as to the rates secured by their competitors. The volume of traffic is so unusual as to frequently exceed the capacity of equipment, yet the contest for tonnage seems never relaxed. Enormous sums are spent in purchasing business and secret rates accorded far below the standard of public charges." This is unanswerable proof that those charges are too high and that the general public is victimized. The report goes on, "The general public gets little benefit from these reductions, for concessions are mainly confined to the heavier shippers. All this augments the advantage of large capital and tends to the injury and often to the ruin of small dealers. These are not only matters of grave consequence to the business welfare of the country, but they concern in no less degree the higher interests of public morality." Further on the report says: "The discriminations are always in favor of the strong and against the weak." This condition the present law is powerless to control. If it is asked why the criminal remedies are not applied the answer is they have been without success. The business of railroad transportation is carried on to a very large extent in conceded violations of the law. Men who in every other respect are reputable citizens are guilty of acts which if the statute law of the land were enforced, would subject them to fine or imprisonment."

It would seem that the remedy is easy and simple. It is to give the Inter-State Commission power to reduce rates. When a discrimination of this kind has proven the current rate too high, it should be made the duty of the Commission to reduce the rate to the general public permanently at that figure. A ratchet and pawl arrangement of that kind can alone give the general public justice and stop discriminations.

The bulk of the receipts of railroads, five-sevenths on an average of say one thousand millions dollars in round numbers for the year ending 30 June, 1899, came from the carriage of freights. I have not the time or the knowledge to point out, if indeed any one can, as yet, the most serious defects in the freight rates. So close is the calculation on these points that it is said that ⅛ of a cent per bushel on wheat between Chicago and Liverpool, will determine its rate and we know that 1/10 of a cent per ton per mile added on freight would tax over 100 millions more annually out of the people. There should be no power to add it except by the people's consent, given through the Railroad Commissions.

Our commissions have done a great work in securing improvements in the classification of freights and the publicity of rates, and towards the accuracy of returns—though the reliability of the returns made by railroads is, as yet an unknown quantity. On some systems they can doubtless be relied upon and on others not at all. Until a uniform and reliable system of returns can be compelled, we shall be more or less groping in the dark in our search for that elusive but much desired "reasonable rate," which the law allows.

When there is no suppression or intentional misstatement in the returns, there are sometimes such errors as charging the rental of leased lines to operating expenses—which is in effect making the public pay the rentals for them—and sums spent for lobbying, subsidizing newspapers and such purposes are always covered up in a lump sum, usually under the head of terminal expenses. The traveller and the shipper has to pay for debauching his own public servants.

It is true that compared with foreign countries, there has been a decided reduction in freight rates, and if there were no discriminations, we might think we had approached, in some sections of the country, a fair rate. The introduction of larger engines, labor-saving devices and other economies, however enable the railroads to haul very much cheaper than formerly. By the introduction of larger engines alone, the Union Pacific Railroad saved $1,040,000, in 1894 over the cost of doing the same volume of work in 1890.

That we have not yet reached a reasonable and fair freight rate is shown not only by the frequent reduction to favored parties, but by the large quantities of freight carried from our eastern and indeed our Lake States, over the Canadian Pacific Railroad and thence down to California points, instead of by the natural and shorter routes through our own States. Then while freight rates in the greater part of the Northern and Western States are more reasonable than formerly, those South of the Potomac and Ohio were adjudged excessive by the Inter-State Commerce Commission in the case of "Freight Bureau of Cincinnati v. Cincinnati, New Orleans and Texas Railroad," 167 U.S. 479, which was begun by the Freight Bureau of Chicago and Cincinnati for the purpose of reducing rates from those two cities to eight important cities in the Southern States. No tribunal has ever reversed this finding that these rates were excessive. The United States Supreme Court merely held that the Interstate Commerce Commission had no power to reduce rates—the more is the pity—but it held that Congress could confer that power upon the commission. The statement of Mr. Campbell, general freight agent, proven recently before the Industrial Commission was to the effect that freight rates in the Southern States are exorbitant. Indeed it is a matter of common knowledge and can be shown at any time by a comparison of freight charges on the south side of the Ohio with those on the North.

CRIPPLING THE SOUTH

In fact the embargo laid on the Southern States by the extortionate charges for transportation is the chief factor in retarding its growth. If the members of Congress from those States would unite in support of a bill conferring upon the Inter-State Commerce Commission the right to reduce rates whenever in the opinion of that able and conservative commission rates are excessive, they would do more for the progress and prosperity of that beautiful section than can be done by any other single measure in the ordinary range of legislation. In some sections of the South, the charges are so high, especially in the trucking business, that the real owners of the soil are the London and New York bankers who own the principal railways of the South. Their transportation charges take all the profits, leaving the nominal owners of the soil a mere pittance. Their situation is exactly like that of the people of Ireland, a fine country which is in the same manner impoverished by the Bailiffs carrying all the profits of agriculture to be spent by non-resident landlords in London, whence it never returns. The railroad system of the South is a duplicate of that which impoverishes Ireland, there by the actual ownership of the soil, with us by the ownership of the railroad systems whose exorbitant charges (as adjudged by the Inter-State Commerce Commission) is in the practical perception of all the profits of ownership of the soil, without its inconveniences. One large railroad system in North Carolina last year paid its stockholders (by sundry devices) 156 per cent dividends, which is over 400 per cent. on the price at which the syndicate bought out the State's stock in the road. Though they got back in one year's profits more than four times their investment, they obtained from a Federal judge an injunction against the Railroad Commission reducing their fares to 2½ cents per mile or assessing their property for taxation at one-third of the market value of their stocks and bonds.

You gentlemen can say whether there are instances approaching this injustice or unfairness in your respective States.

While freight rates in the Northern States will compare favorably with those in other countries, in passenger rates the charges in this country are, as a rule, excessive and unjustifiable and of course double so in the Southern States.

HIGH PASSENGER TOLLS

In no particular have the railroad charges been more extortionate nor more unwise than in passenger rates. Upon the liberal estimate of 125 (1/16 of a ton) as the average weight of passengers paying full fare (above 12 years of age) the average charge for passengers per mile is over 30 times, not infrequently 50 times, that charged per pound for freight, notwithstanding passengers load and unload themselves—a consideration which far more than compensates for the carriage of baggage for part of the passengers. This is peculiarly unfortunate for it not only diminishes the revenues of the roads, which could fill their cars, or carry additional cars, without any perceptible addition of expense, but it prevents that free circulation of the population which is so highly educational and which induces new enterprises whereby freight traffic is increased. Wherever reasonable passenger rates have been tried, the result has been not only accommodation to the public, but increased profits to the railways. In thinly settled Russia, as far back as 1894, passenger rates were reduced to 3/4 cent per mile for distances under 106 miles, and lower for longer distances—the fare for 100 miles being 75 cents and for two thousand miles $6.00. This paid so well that since then a further reduction has been made which our Consular agents report profitable. In Belgium workmen living 42 miles from their working places buy weekly tickets good to go and return six times a week for 57 cents a week, and shorter distances in proportion—a good solution of the evils of crowded tenement houses and high rents. In India the rates were 1/2 cent per mile which proved so profitable that recently there has been a reduction to 1/3 cent per mile. In Great Britain, France, Germany, and Austria, travel, equal in accommodation to our second class, averages 3/4 cent per mile.

Among many examples of what lower rates will do in this country, in one of the rate wars, passenger rates from San Francisco to Chicago were reduced from $120 to $15, with the result that the passenger coaches were full, carrying 60 passengers, and bringing $900 per car, when the haul of a load of cattle would have been at usual rates only $220 per car.

There are two reasons possibly why railroad managers prefer higher rates—for it cannot be on account of the profit. One is they prefer a small volume of business at approximately the same profit—the convenience to the public being counted nil. The other is that with high rates, the free passes have a greater purchasing power in influence and in votes, and the same is true of the reduced rates they give the drummers, preachers and others who can influence public opinion, thus making the passenger business a leverage of special privileges to some and not equal rights to all.

ADVANTAGES OF LOW RATES

Judge Cooley, that eminent statesman and jurist, as long ago as 1892, in his address before your convention, pointed out that the railroads in most unmistakable ways, daily admitted their passenger rates to be too high. First, he said, by the large number of persons they carry free; then by the number of those they carry at reduced rates on mileage tickets, the still further reduction to ministers, and the yet further reduction on all conceivable occasions, summer tours, college commencements, political speakings, excursions, and in the occasional rate wars. As that eminent man pointed out, it will be fairer for the public if the corporations, instead of making so many special rates, and crowding the people on excursions and other occasions, would make permanent, all the year round low rates, with exceptional rates to no one and on no occasion. A permanent rate of this kind of one cent a mile first-class, and less for second-class, would pay the roads better than the present system and would give them a popularity they do not now possess, not only by reason of the moderateness of the charge, but from the absence of that air of favor and condescension which attends the granting of lower rates for special occasions and the favoritism or worse, which marks the free pass and reduced rates given to individuals. The greater opportunity given by the reduced rates to laborers to live out of congested cities where their theatre of work lies, and to raise their families amid better surroundings would alone justify the reduction, to say nothing of the greater opportunity to seek at points where labor is needed—against which present railroad rates are a Chinese wall. Owing to our higher passenger fare, only about one-third as many people in proportion to population ride on railroads in this country as in England.

I note in your proceedings that in your meeting four years ago Mr. Cole, of New York, stated that in his State even then the statute required all railroads charging over 2 cents per mile to sell 500 miles tickets for $10, good on any train, in hands of the owner, any member of his family or firm or employee, with the result that the roads were selling ordinary tickets generally at that rate or under.

RATES NORTH AND SOUTH

Instead of passenger rates being moderate and alike to all, they range from 3¼ cents per mile in the Southern States (and were only reduced to that point by the Railroad Commissions) down to one cent on some of the Northern railroads, the average being about two cents. The charges for passengers are thus distributed:

1. To the influential, as newspaper editors, politicians, public officials, relatives of railroad managers and the wealthy, free passes —which means that their fare is being paid by adding the cost of the rate charged the poor and uninfluential.

2. To those with secondary influence, like commercial tourists, employed by wealthy firms reduced rates are given, upon the

1,000 mile ticket system—which is simply a device for the interest on the fare paid in advance, is no consideration to the corporation but the required lump sum can not conveniently be raised by the average man.

3. To ministers of the gospel who will come under obligation to the railroads by special applications therefor, permits to buy tickets at reduced rates are granted as a favor. Thus a padlock is sought to be put on their influence.

4. As an outlet to public disaffection at high rates, lower rates are granted as a special favor to conventions, commencements and the like, and wealthy hotel owners are conciliated by low summer rates.

5. Lastly, the great masses (except on special occasions) are taxed the highest rate possible. Of those least able to bear it, the utmost is exacted. For all this system of favors and special privileges, a very low permanent rate, without exceptions for any occasion or to any person (except railroad employes in the discharge of their duties) should be substituted, with no difference in rate except that justified by difference in accommodation.

A change so just, so much to the benefit of the public and the railroads alike, can not be too soon adopted.

THE FREE PASS EVIL

The evils of the free pass system, and the immoral purposes to which it has been put has met wide public condemnation. Eight great States have put in their Constitutions provisions against it, making it forfeiture of office for any office holder to take a free pass. The Inter-State Commerce Commission has repeatedly decided that free passes are forbidden in all Inter-State Commerce and among States forbidding it by Statute. . . . In that State the railroads absolutely ignored the statute, so much so that I find that the Chairman of the North Carolina Railroad Commission stated to your convention a year ago, that 100,000 free passes were issued annually in that State, and this was seven years after the Act was passed. All during those years, in spite of the law, the railroads had carried that 100,000 of the rich and influential free, by adding the cost of their riding to the tickets of the poor and uninfluential. Since then, the law has been enforced by a fine of $1,000 being laid in two cases (out of, it would seem, 700,000 violations). I see that Van Ost in his work states that one-fifth of the passengers in the West ride free—that is to say that the other four-fifths pay for their riding.

HAS IT BECOME SECRET?

I do not know how far the corrective force of public opinion and the enforcement of the law have abated the free pass injustice, but Judge Cooley, in his address before you, to which I have already referred, intimated that it had merely become secret (like freight discriminations) and that it was carried on by the device of issuing mileage books—for which nothing is paid—instead of free passes. Aside from the injustice of making one portion of the community (and those least able to pay for themselves) pay for the free riding of others, there is the leprosy of the free pass system being the most shameless and most widely spread system of bribery of public officials and others having or supposed to have influence with the public. Beginning as a distribution of transportation to servants of the State, at a time when often the State owned, or had largely aided in the construction of the railroads, its evil tendency was not at first generally understood. If abolished utterly as it should be, railroads could by that fact alone be enabled to reduce passenger fares to accord more with the enhanced value of money—an enhancement which the railroads alone have not reduced charges to meet.

Both as to freight and passenger rates, the courts hold that the States can reduce to a reasonable rate. What is a reasonable rate is a matter of fact, upon evidence adduced, not a question of law. It should be settled by an appeal to a jury, unless the railroad commissions should be held special juries provided for that purpose, and whose conclusions are final, as the Supreme Court held in regard to their valuation of railroad property for taxation. Kentucky Railroad Tax Cases, 115 U.S. 321, a view which is sustained by Judge Cooley in his address before you.

JUDICIAL USURPATION

When a judge issues his injunction against rates prescribed by a State Legislature or a board created by it for that purpose, the Judge simply assumes to substitute his opinion of the reasonableness of a rate for that of the law, and is guilty of usurpation of power, as was recently shown by that eminent judge of the United States Circuit Court, Judge Caldwell, in an address before the Missouri Bar Association.

The fixing of rates of common carriers and the assessment of their property for taxation are essentially governmental functions and the judiciary are not a supervisory, or higher department of government. If there arises any difference as to rates or valuation, it is a question of fact to be determined by the board created by law; or if there is any appeal, under our system of laws it should be settled like all other issues of fact, by a jury—not by a judge.

RAILROAD CASUALTIES

To the Massachusetts Commission belongs the credit of beginning back in 1867 the agitation for safety appliances. To the Inter-State Commerce Commission belong the credit of procuring the act of Congress which requires the use of self couplers, after a date fixed, which the Commmission has extended to January 1st, next, as authorized by the statute. In their last report they say "There were 1,034 fewer employes killed, and 14,062 fewer injured during the year ending June 30, 1897, than during the same reported in 1893. In the Spanish American War 298 were killed and 1,645 wounded. In car coupling alone 219 less were killed and 4,994 less were injured in 1897 than in 1893, when the law was enacted." In 1893 when the statute was passed the casualties from coupling and uncoupling cars were 433 killed and 11,919 injured. In 1897 when the law as to self couplers was only partially complied with the casualties were only 214 killed and 6,283 injured. When the law shall come into full force on January 1st next the casualties from this source should cease entirely. It should not have required a statute to compel the railways to put on this cheap and simple contrivance costing less than $18 per car, the absence of which, at the passage of the statute, was causing the death annually of 433 men and the maiming of near 12,000 others. Indeed the courts in North Carolina and possibly in some other States have held that independent of the statute the railway company was liable for damages for the killing or wounding of any employe when the accident could have been prevented by the use of self couplers.

THE DEADLY CROSSING

More than 4,500 people were killed and 6,300 wounded other than their employes and passengers by railways last year. A very large part of these casualties were at crossings. In England and perhaps all other countries of Europe the railways are required to cross either above or below public roads and streets. This is required in New York as to all new railroads and to some extent as to those already built. But as this change is impracticable as to existing railways in many States owing to the expense, your

Commissions could at least require (if you are authorized by law to regulate crossings, and if you cannot get the authority) that at every crossing on the same grade of a public road or street, the railway company should place an electric gong which shall be automatically rung by the driving wheel of each approaching locomotive by means of a simple contrivance placed at a specified number of feet from each crossing. It would save many hundreds of lives each year. I have seen this device used in the stations in Germany to notify passengers automatically of the approach of the train.

SAFETY APPLIANCES

Electric headlights operated by the engines would be useful in saving many hundreds of lives and injuries annually. According to Railroad Reports to the Inter-State Commerce Commission between 40,000 and 50,000 persons are killed or wounded each year by the railways of the United States—even since the vast saving of life and limb accomplished by the forced adoption of self couplers. This is an annual loss of 25 times as great as that sustained by this country in the Spanish war last year. Any regulation that will procure a reduction of this blood tax should be welcomed by the railways as well as by the public.

The question of the relation of the employes to the railroads does not belong to the province you have assigned me, further than as that relation affects the general public. There is no doubt that a very large part of the collisions and derailments are caused by the over-service required of engineers and others. An accident not long since in our section entailing the loss of many lives was caused by the engineer having been on duty 20 hours out of 24. He was nearly drunk for sleep. The strain upon nerves of a man charged with the responsibility of many lives, who stands at the throttle valve of a 90 ton engine as it is driven across the country on its narrow ribbon of steel, is such that it is doubtful if the law should not prohibit him or other railroad employes on the trains from being engaged more than eight hours out of 24. I believe that is now the law in New York.

TELEGRAPH AND TELEPHONE

Some of your Commissions are charged with the regulation of rates and assessment for taxation of telephones, telegraph and express companies. In all the countries of the world I believe except this and Canada, the telegraph and telephone are part of the post-office system, legally as well as logically, for they are simply methods of communicating intelligence. I have always believed as a lawyer that under the provisions of the Federal Constitution which requires Congress to establish postoffices and postroads, it is its duty to transmit intelligence by wire as well as by rail, by electricity as well as by steam or pneumatic tubes, and as this power vested in Congress is held by the United States Supreme Court to be an exclusive power, that the operation of telegraph and telephones for hire by others than the government is as illegal as their running the postoffice would be. Great Britain which alone has stood with us against government ownership of railroads, has had to leave us on this matter for there the telegraphs are a part of the postoffice department. The rates under government ownership abroad justify the belief that under government ownership here we can have a uniform telegraph rate of ten cents and probably 5 cents for 10 words between any two points in the country and $1 a month or less for rental of a telephone. Back in 1891 Postmaster General Wannamaker said to Congress that if telegrams and telephones were turned over to his office, as in other countries, a uniform rate of ten cents for telegrams and 2 cents for telephonic messages would pay handsomely. If so cheaper rates would be practicable today. Immense public benefit would result from this change. As you are charged with fixing their rates, there is certainly room for large reduction not only from comparison with foreign rates, but from the fact that the Western Union which now has a capitalization, bonds and stocks of $120,000,000 has acquired its plants and its capitalization entirely out of its earnings over and above the steady payment of dividends, for only $440,000 cash—less than half a million—has ever been paid in by its stockholders. This was shown in several Congressional investigations. Though 17 out of 18 Committees of Congress, to whom postoffice ownership of the telegraph has been referred have reported in favor of that measure, as well as four postmaster generals have recommended it, the measure has never yet gotten to a vote owing to the immense lobby maintained by the Western Union monopoly.

THE EXPRESS ANOMALY

It is an anomaly that express companies (which are also in your jurisdiction) should be permitted, thus placing a double tax upon a patient and oppressed people. In other countries the postoffice has a parcels delivery branch, which collects and delivers by wagon parcels at residences like other mail matter, up to 1 and in some countries 16 pounds, and at ½ cent to 1 cent per pound, a small fraction of express charges in this country. In Austria and Germany more than $100,000,000 of goods are annually sent by the Parcels Post. In these matters the United States is a back number. The corporations dwarf us. As long as the express business remains for private emolument, not for public convenience it should be noted that the rates charged by the Postoffice Department abroad show that there is a large margin for reduction of rates under public control here.

MAIL CHARGES

In no particular are railroad rates more exorbitant than those charged for the carriage of the United States mails, 8 cents per pound for an average distance of 440 miles, with a further charge of 200 per cent per year on their cost for rental of postal cars, while the charges to express companies is one half cent per pound or less. This is of interest to the public, as it is the sole cause of a deficit in the postal revenue, and thereby defeats a reduction of letter postage to one cent and a further reduction on other matter. In fact railway rates to the postoffice are often 50 per cent higher than the charge for freight by wagon. This, however, should be remedied by Congress which has full knowledge of the facts and hardly comes within your jurisdiction. The corrective power of public opinion may effect something.

THE MATTER OF VALUATION

Most of your boards, if not all are charged with the valuation of railroad, express and Telegraph and Telephone property for taxation. This is a government function and it has been decided by the United States Supreme Court in Kentucky Railroad Tax Cases, 115 U.S. already cited that the action of such boards is due process of law and final. But there are Federal judges who have issued their injunctions notwithstanding; esteeming their own opinion of the value of such property, superior to that of the boards authorized by law. In North Carolina the railroad companies are taxing the public rates high enough to pay four per cent net, above taxes and all expenditures, upon $120,000,000, but when the Board appointed by law for the purpose assessed their property and franchise at $42,000,000 (about one third the value) those corporations which were owned by non-residents, promptly secured an injunction from a Federal judge. I do not know

ZEBULON BAIRD VANCE
United States Senator from North Carolina.

whether such flagrant cases occur elsewhere, but the result in that State has been universal indignation, except among the newspapers and other agencies in corporation pay. Such action gives an impetus to the growing demand for the election of Federal Judges by the people and for a term of years instead of the present unrepublican life tenure under which they are neither responsible to public opinion nor anything else, and hold their will superior to that of the law. The Acts of a State Legislature are apparently held in sovereign contempt.

"THE BIAS OF TRAINING"

In saying this I wish to be understood as casting no reflection upon my brethren of the Federal bench as a body. Among them are some of the ablest and purest men and best lawyers in the Republic. But unlimited power without responsibility such as is conferred by life tenure with a certainty of no liability to impeachment by a busy Congress is too great a temptation for most men—and when as now, the Federal bench is largely recruited from those whose lives at the bar have been spent as railroad attorneys, and who know that they owe their promotion to the influence of the great corporations who have formerly employed them, it is not strange that some of these judges should yield to the bias of their training.

THE CARDINAL MISTAKE

The cardinal mistake is in assuming that railroads are chartered for a private purpose—the emolument of their managers. They are chartered for public purposes, the convenience and service of the public, the profit of the managers being only incidental to procure the service. When railroads were owned by the original subscribers to the capital stock living along their lines, and the counties and cities which were large stockholders, public opinion exercised through the annual election of the officers was sufficient public control. But now that the railroads have mostly passed into the hands of non-resident syndicates, who care little for public needs and wishes or for aught except profits, the officers are simply local overseers of the non-resident owners. Consequently there is no control except through public opinion formulated in legislative enactment and executed by your commissions created for that purpose. The new doctrine that the judiciary is the Supreme power in the State, to set aside legislative enactments and restrain executive action is promulgated and pushed in the interest of the great moneyed combinations so that when their lobbyists can not defeat legislative action, they may fall back upon the small body of judges in whose selection they can have a hand. But this attempt to suppress the popular will by a judicial oligarchy (which is without warrant in our Constitutions) will prove as futile, as the attempt to suppress the popular will by executive power in England. The result there was that one King lost his head, another his throne and for two hundred years no sovereign has dared to veto an act of Parliament and no judge has ever imagined he had power to declare unconstitutional an act of the legislative body. The corporations which are urging the claims of Judicial Supremacy in this government may bring the bench to ruin, but they cannot destroy the inherent sovereignty of the people, who must speak their will through legislative bodies and have that will executed by such agencies as they shall select. Those who can not trust to the wisdom and justice of the people have no business in a free country.

DETERMINING TAX VALUES

Returning to the matter of taxation there should be no difficulty on that subject, for as the Supreme Court of the United States held in Taylor vs Secor, 92 U.S. 575, the actual value of a railroad and its franchise is exactly that of the market value of all its bonds and stocks. In that case Justice Miller said: "It is therefore obvious that when you have ascertained the current cash value of the whole funded debt, and the current cash value of the entire number of shares, you have, by the action of those who above all others can best estimate it, ascertained the true value of the road, all its property, its capital stock and its franchises; for these are all represented by the value of its bonded debt and of the shares of its capital stock."

"This is a simple and unerring plan," says Senator Ford in the North American Review, "sanctioned by long usage in many States and approved by the Supreme Court of the United States."

There are some States which levy a tax on gross earnings, which is perhaps as fair as any that could be devised. These Commissions were created precisely because the public were dissatisfied with the conduct of the railway, telegraph and express companies and decided to regulate them otherwise than by individual actions in ordinary courts, which few individuals had the financial ability to sustain with such powerful adversaries. It is a defect in all these Acts that no officer is appointed to represent the State, for the amount of an overcharge demanded by the complainant is usually too small to justify him to retain counsel. While the relief, if granted by you being usually a reduction of rates or other general regulation, is of general benefit to the public and of great interest to the corporation which last is therefore usually represented by numerous and able counsel. Their ex parte statements and arguments, the plaintiff being unrepresented put you at a disadvantage. As Judge Cooley said to your convention in 1892, "The people's cause is lost by default." This is a grave defect and should be remedied.

THE CASE SUMMED UP

To sum up for the client you have assigned me: He is just and moderate. He asks no unjust reduction in rates, nor that any undue share of taxation be placed upon the railroads. He knows that he gave these corporations the breath of life and that by the aid of his right of eminent domain they have laid their tracks. He knows that private and public subscriptions to their construction have been often submerged by reconstructions and other methods and that these great corporations are nearly all owned by non-resident bankers—usually in London and New York. My client demands that discriminations be stopped whether secret rebates of freight or free passes or donated mileage books. He demands a just modification of freight rates and especially of those South of the Ohio, which the Inter-State Commerce Commission has adjudged excessive, and that passenger rates should be reduced to something like the rates in other countries, without special privileges to any. He demands that these corporations shall take their hands off our politics and leave the people free to select their own public servants, and that the process of federal judges, whether appointed by corporation influences or not, shall not be prostituted to defeat public control or the assessment of their property for taxation.

He would be glad to see the telegraph, telephone and express (or Parcels Post) made a part of the Postoffice as in other countries, or failing in that, secure a just reduction of their rates by your Commissions. He asks that safety appliances and moderate hours of labor for employees be required in order that the present annual casualty list of 40 to 50,000 killed and wounded may be diminished.

In these demands there is nothing unjust. Railway managers should gladly and frankly concede them. If so, the utmost harmony will prevail. But be assured, nothing less than these things will satisfy the great American people.

It was a railroad king in this country who, when the dissatisfaction of the people, with his rates and his management, was reported to him, replied with brutal frankness. "The people be d——d." Let us hope that there be few like unto him for there is nothing stronger than a wrong unredressed when a great people is the sufferer.

Gentlemen, I thank you for the honor of your invitation and for the patience and attention with which you have heard me.

PREFACE TO THE STATE RECORDS OF NORTH CAROLINA

(1895)

At a period somewhat prior to the death of the late Col. William L. Saunders, the compilation and publication of the COLONIAL RECORDS which, under his efficient superintendence, had reached from the beginnings of the Province down to and inclusive of the year 1776, and filled ten large folio volumes, were suspended. This work was not resumed for some years, till in 1893 the undersigned, at the invitation of the Trustees of the State Library, assumed the continuation of the work of collecting and publishing. It was soon ascertained that the difficulties of the work and the scarcity of material were much greater than had attended the preparation of the ten volumes already issued, and that this scarcity of material, even more perhaps than the failing health of Col. Saunders, had caused him to suspend at the end of the year 1776, instead of bringing the work down to the year 1781, as authorized by The Code, section 3609.

Down to the outbreak of hostilities in 1775, and the flight of Gov. Josiah Martin from the State, copies of all important papers were "sent home" to England, and there preserved in the PUBLIC RECORDS Office. When the State determined upon the publication of her COLONIAL RECORDS a tolerably complete set of these official records were to be found in London. Under the instructions of Col. Saunders, these were copied for the State by W. Noel Sainsbury, Esq., who was admirably fitted for the work by more than forty years acquaintance with these records. After passing through his hands and those of Col Saunders, these copies formed the chief material for the ten volumes which have been issued, the additions from other sources being comparatively insignificant.

But with the year 1776, this source of supply ceased. Copies of official records were no longer sent to England to be filed, and consequently the State is thenceforward thrown upon her home resources for historical records. These are very meagre indeed. For many years after 1776 the Governor and other Executive officers resided at their homes, often at remote points, meeting only when the Legislature was in session. There was no permanent seat of government for nearly a score of years, and no fixed and safe depositories for the public archives. Papers thus scattered and little cared for soon became much disordered and a large portion of them were lost or destroyed. As for those which remained to be transferred to the capital when it became settled at Raleigh, a large part were burned in the fire which destroyed the Capital building in 1832, others were destroyed when Raleigh was taken possession of by the Federal Troops in 1865, and some valuable documents disappeared during the regime of 1868-70, when many new men of doubtful character filled unaccustomed seats in the Legislature and other official positions. Valuable papers from time to time have been loaned to historians and lost, or at least have not been returned, and besides this there has been the natural waste of material kept in ill-ventilated and damp recesses without attention to care.

It may be imagined, therefore, that our early archives are conspicuous from their poverty. Little was to be found therein save such portions of the Executive correspondence as many years after its date had been copied into the Executive letter books and a part of the Journals of the Legislature, some of these last being lost and others mutilated. An attempt was made to supplement our stores from the archives at Washington, but the same waste of material consequent upon a peripatetic capital had lessened the quantity of material to be found there, which had been still further diminished by the burning of the War Department early in the century, and again, a few years later in 1814, when the British captured Washington and destroyed the Public Buildings.

The writer visited and inspected the "Draper" collection preserved in the Capitol of Wisconsin, the Astor and Lennox Libraries in New York, and the State and War, and other Departments in Washington City, and has gathered fragments, as they could be found, from various other sources. After all the collection is very unsatisfactory, but probably represents very nearly the sum total of historical material (not heretofore printed), which at this late day can be gathered together. It must always be a source of lasting regret that the Legislature of 1829 did not accept the offer of Judge Murphey, to collect and publish such of the early archives of the State, as at that date still remained. We possess a bare fragment of the stores accessible to him. The correspondence of Genl. Gates in 1780, so far as it relates to this State, has been copied from the originals on file in the Astor Library in New York, and there is a possibility of securing copies of Genl. Greene's correspondence, 1781-3 relative to North Carolina and North Carolina Troops while commanding the Southern Department. Permission to copy these was given, but the owner having died before it could be done, the letters have now passed into other hands.

Application was made to W. Noel Sainsbury, Esq., to make a more exhaustive search in the PUBLIC RECORDS office in London. The result has been the discovery of a few papers which were overlooked in copying the records for Colonel Saunders and many other papers were found in the South Carolina files in the English records office, the papers of the two Provinces often pertaining to subjects of interest, common to both, not being filed in duplicate. These omitted papers have now all been copied, and appear in the *Supplement* 1730-1776, which occupies the first part of the present volume. Mr. Sainsbury passed away, at a ripe old age in March last, and his death is a distinct loss to this State, whom he has served so well and faithfully.

Governor Elias Carr, the present executive, has been a warm and earnest friend of this labor of gathering and publishing the remnants of our early archives and he has given every possible aid and encouragement to the prosecution of the enterprise. Hon. John C. Scarborough, the head of our educational system, has appreciated the value of the work and has always been its earnest friend. Major Graham Daves, of Newbern, an accomplished scholar, with fine historical attainments and tastes, has made laborious researches in the departments at Washington and has procured copies of all matter to be found there which is fitted for this work. The writer also wishes to express his acknowledgment for advice and assistance to Capt. Sam'l Ashe, of Raleigh, whose scholarship and patriotism are an inheritance from ancestors who have been conspicuous in our State's annals from the earliest dawn of its history.

The General Assembly of 1895, (Chapter 464), extended the period which these archives are to embrace down to January 1790 and authorized the *Index* of the entire work to be prepared. For the lack of an index the volumes already published have so far been of slight service. The literary board have selected for this important task Dr. Stephen B. Weeks, Ph.D., whose experience, application and scholarly attainments are a guarantee of the efficiency of his work. The index will cover the entire series, including both the *"Colonial"* and *"State"* Records, from the beginning to 1790, in one volume.

The title of the volumes now being prepared is necessarily changed to STATE RECORDS, but for convenience, especially in indexing the first volume of the new series will be entitled STATE RECORDS, Vol. XI., the ten preceding volumes being entitled, COLONIAL RECORDS, 1-10.

PREFACE TO
HISTORIES OF THE SEVERAL REGIMENTS AND BATTALIONS FROM NORTH CAROLINA IN THE GREAT WAR 1861-'63 *

More than two thousand years ago Pericles, speaking of his countrymen who had fallen in a great war, said: "In all time to come, whenever there shall be speech of great deeds they shall be had in remembrance." More truly than to the Athenian soldiery can these memorable words be applied to those North Carolinians who for four long years carried the fortunes of the Confederacy upon the points of their bayonets.

With a voting population at the outbreak of the war less than 115,000, North Carolina furnished to the Confederate cause, as appears from Major Gordon's article herein, 127,000 troops, or more than one-fifth of the men who marched beneath the Southern Cross, in addition to the Militia and Home Guards who rendered useful, though short, tours of duty, under State authority. In the first battle of the war, at Bethel, North Carolina was at the front and the first man killed in battle was Wyatt from Edgecombe. When the great tragedy was closing at Appomattox it was the men of Cox's North Carolina Brigade, of Grimes' Division, who fired the last volley at the foe. The two great pivotal battles of the war were Gettysburg in the East and Chickamauga in the West. Upon them turned the issue of the great struggle, and in both the men who fell farthest to the front, nearest to the muzzles of the enemy's guns, were from North Carolina regiments. This is demonstrated not only by the narratives of eye-witnesses in these volumes but by the monuments which the Federal Government has erected on those great battlefields to indicate the "high-water mark" to which the tide of Southern success rose, and from which, after those days of historic struggle, it painfully and slowly but surely ebbed away.

Not, therefore, in boast, but in sober historic truth, on the cover of these volumes, has been inscribed the lines which tell the story of North Carolina's fidelity to duty:

"FIRST AT BETHEL.
FARTHEST TO THE FRONT AT GETTYSBURG AND CHICKAMAUGA.
LAST AT APPOMATTOX."

* The complete title-page is "Histories/of the/Several Regiments and Battalions/from/North Carolina/ in the/Great War 1861-'65/written by members of the respective commands/edited by/Walter Clark/ (Lieut.-Colonel Seventeenth Regiment N. C. T.)./ 1901.

It is to tell the plain, unvarnished story of the men at the front that these sketches have been written by those who participated therein, and by the authority and at the expense of the State they are now printed in order to hand down to posterity an authentic account of what the soldiery of this State suffered and died in the discharge of their duty. It was inscribed upon the stones piled above the Spartan dead who died at Thermopylae: "Stranger, go tell it in Lacedemon that we lie here in obedience to her command." North Carolina can never forget that in obedience to her command more than 40,000 of her bravest, best and brightest young men fill soldiers' graves from "the farthest north" at Gettysburg to that far Southern shore.

"Where the mightiest river runs, mingling with their fame forever."

These dead have not died in vain. The cause of Southern Independence for which they fell has passed forever from among men. Not an advocate remains. But as long as valor shall move the hearts of men, as long as the patient endurance of hardship, and fatigue, and danger in the discharge of duty shall touch us, as long as the sacrifice of life for the good of one's country shall seem noble and grand, so long shall the memory of the deeds recorded in the plain, sober narratives in these volumes, written by men whose gallantry is surpassed only by their modesty, and who were more eager to handle the sword than to use the pen, be preserved and cherished by their countrymen.

The story of these volumes is briefly told. At the meeting of the State Confederate Veterans Association at Raleigh, N. C., in October, 1894, on motion of Judge A. C. Avery, seconded by F. H. Busbee, Esq., it was

"*Resolved,* That a history of each regiment and organization from North Carolina which served in the Confederate Army shall be prepared by a member thereof, and that Judge Walter Clark be requested to select the historians from each command and to supervise and edit the work; and further, that the General Assembly be memorialized to have these sketches printed at the expense of the State."

On motion of Captain W. H. Day, Judge A. C. Avery, General Robert F. Hoke and Lieutenant-Colonel Wharton J. Green were appointed a committee to present this memorial and procure the passage of the legislation desired.

Already at that date (1894) nearly thirty years had passed since the close of hostilities and the steady advance of the years had driven gaps in our ranks wider than those made by the leaden hail of battle. Suitable men for the work were difficult to find for many of the regiments, and when found they often pleaded the press of business, loss of memory and increasing infirmities. But by persistent effort competent historians were secured for each regiment, except the 73d, 74th, 76th, 77th and 78th (which being Senior Reserves, the only resource was to utilize some sketches heretofore written.

But here another difficulty arose. Among those who promised to write the story of their regiments some died and others procrastinated. The latter class was large by reason of the failure of the General Assemblies of 1895 and 1897 to assume the publication by the State. This, however, was done by the General Assembly of 1899, the bill being introduced and eloquently championed by Hon. H. Clay Wall, member from Richmond county and historian of the Twenty-third Regiment. Upon the passage of the act the vacancies caused by death or declination were filled up and the remaining sketches (with a few exceptions) being in hand by the spring of 1900, and the others promised, publication was begun. The printing was, for certain causes, however, so much delayed that the General Assembly of 1901 passed an act to expedite the completion of the work, which is now guaranteed to be finished during the current year.

The work of the several historians and of the Editor has of course been one of love and without pecuniary compensation. We would that our labors could have been worthier of the subject and of our noble comrades living and dead. The State assumed the cost of publication and the work is its property, as the deeds it commemorates are the noblest inheritance of its people and their sure gage of fame.

It was thought that it would add vividness to these pen-and-ink sketches of their deeds to give engravings of as many of the actors in those stirring times as could be readily obtainable. The selection of these was left, of course, to the several regimental historians. No line was drawn at rank. The only restriction has been that each picture shall have been taken "during the war or soon thereafter"—the object being to present the men as they *then* looked—and that the subject made an honorable record in the Great War. Major C. L. Patton, a Southerner residing in New York City and the head of a great publishing house, kindly and without remuneration undertook the supervision of the engravings and their proper grouping to go with the histories of their respective commands. In this way it is believed that the interest of the work has been greatly enhanced and that this will grow as the years diminish the number of survivors. Many of their descendants, perchance, will look back as a patent of nobility to the men whose names or whose features are preserved in these volumes. The cost of the engravings has been defrayed by the relatives or friends of the parties. A few maps have been also added to illustrate the text.

The requirement that the history of each command should be written by a member thereof was to insure authenticity. But as by reason of wounds or other temporary absence few men were every day of the four years present with their commands, and the lapse of time might cause errors of memory, the several historians were requested to refresh their memories by conversation and correspondence with their surviving comrades, and they also had access to the publication by the Government of the invaluable series of "Official Records of the Union and Confederate Armies." In addition, the sketch of each regiment as sent in was published in the newspaper of largest circulation in the section in which the regiment was principally raised, and survivors were requested to note errors and omissions and to communicate them to the writer of the regimental history.

This was a heavy tax upon the columns of the press, but with the patriotism which has always characterized the editors of North Carolina this service was cheerfully and freely rendered without charge or compensation. The Confederate Veterans of North Carolina are greatly indebted for this great service in rendering our histories more full and accurate to the Raleigh *News and Observer* and *Morning Post,* the Wilmington *Messenger* and *Star,* the Charlotte *Observer,* the Fayetteville *Observer,* the New Bern *Journal,* the Asheville *Citizen,* the Waynesville *Courier,* and perhaps others.

During the compilation of these sketches we have up to this date, lost no less than nine of the writers of these sketches by death, Captain John Cowan, Third North Carolina; Captain Neill W. Ray, Sixth North Carolina; Professor H. T. J. Ludwig, Eighth North Carolina; General Rufus Barringer, Ninth North Carolina; Colonel Stephen D. Pool, Tenth North Carolina; Colonel W. J. Martin, Eleventh North Carolina; Sergeant H. C. Wall, Twenty-third North Carolina; General Robert B. Vance, Twenty-ninth North Carolina; Captain M. V. Moore, Sixty-fifth North Carolina, and there were others who died before completing their sketches and for whom substitutes were had.

If errors or omissions of importance are discovered by any of our comrades as these volumes successively issue from the press, they are requested to promptly communicate the needed correction to the historian of the regiment concerned, that proper amendment may be made among the *Errata* in the last volume. The most scrupulous and exact accuracy is earnestly desired in these volumes.

North Carolina has grandly known how to make history. She has till now always left it to others to write it. Hence she has never had full justice done the memory of her sons. With these volumes the reproach is taken away. Herein the historian will find authentic, reliable material, compiled by the gallant men who saw the deeds they narrate. From these volumes some yet unborn Thucydides or Macaulay of the future may draw some of his material for that history which shall transmit to all time the story of this most memorable struggle, and the historians in these pages shall have thus contributed their share in perpetuating the fame of their State and of their comrades to the most distant times.

GENERALS FROM NORTH CAROLINA [1]

By Walter Clark, Lieut.-Col. Seventieth N. C. T.

From General Ainsworth, Chief of the Record and Pension Office at Washington, in whose custody are the "Archives of the War Department of the Confederate States," I have procured the following *certified list* of the Generals appointed from North Carolina, with the date of commission of the highest rank attained by each, and graded accordingly to seniority of commission:

LIEUTENANT-GENERALS.

	Name.	Date of Rank.
1.	THEOPHILUS H. HOLMES	10 October, 1862
2.	* DANIEL H. HILL (not sent to Senate)	11 July, 1863

[1] From *Histories of the Several Regiments....*

* For some unexplained reason, President Davis did not send in General Hill's appointment as Lieutenant-General to the Senate and he was never confirmed as such by that body, though at the President's request and by virtue of the President's appointment he served in that capacity. As Lieutenant-General he commanded a corps in the Army of the West at Chickamauga in 1863. Later he resumed his rank of Major-General.

MAJOR-GENERALS.

	Name.	Date of Rank.
1.	W. H. C. WHITING (killed in battle)	28 February, 1863
2.	ROBERT RANSOM, JR.	26 May, 1863
3.	WILLIAM D. PENDER (killed in battle)	27 May, 1863
4.	ROBERT F. HOKE	20 April, 1864
5.	*STEPHEN D. RAMSEUR (killed in battle)	1 June, 1864
6.	BRYAN GRIMES	15 February, 1865

BRIGADIER-GENERALS.

1.	RICHARD C. GATLIN	8 July, 1861
2.	L. O'B. BRANCH (killed in battle)	16 November, 1861
3.	J. JOHNSTON PETTIGREW (killed in battle)	26 February, 1862
4.	JAMES G. MARTIN	15 May, 1862
5.	THOMAS L. CLINGMAN	17 May, 1862
6.	GEORGE B. ANDERSON (killed in battle)	9 June, 1862
7.	JUNIUS DANIEL (killed in battle)	1 September, 1862
8.	JAMES H. LANE	1 November, 1862
9.	JOHN R. COOKE	1 November, 1862
10.	ROBERT B. VANCE	1 March, 1863
11.	ALFRED M. SCALES	13 June, 1863
12.	MATTHEW W. RANSOM	13 June, 1863
13.	LAWRENCE S. BAKER	23 July, 1863
14.	WILLIAM W. KIRKLAND	29 August, 1863
15.	ROBERT D. JOHNSTON	1 September, 1863
16.	JAMES B. GORDON (killed in battle)	28 September, 1863
17.	*WILLIAM R. COX (temporary)	31 May, 1864
18.	*THOMAS F. TOON (temporary)	31 May, 1864
19.	*W. GASTON LEWIS (temporary)	31 May, 1864
20.	RUFUS BARRINGER	1 June, 1864
21.	*JOHN D. BARRY (temporary)	3 August, 1864

* Major-General Ramseur was a temporary Major-General, and Brigadier-Generals Cox, Toon, Lewis and Barry were temporary Brigadier-Generals. These temporary appointments were peculiar to the Confederate army. They were made to a command whose head was absent in prison or wounded, upon whose return it was contemplated that the temporary appointee would go back to his previous rank, though while occupying his temporary grade he had the same rank and authority as if permanently appointed. In point of fact, each of such appointees held his rank to the close save General Barry, who went back to the colonelcy of the Eighteenth Regiment, being disabled by wounds very soon after his appointment, whereupon General Conner was temporarily placed in command of the brigade until the return of General Lane, the permanent Brigadier, who had been absent wounded.

	Name.	Date of Rank.
22.	ARCHIBALD C. GODWIN (killed in battle)	5 August, 1864
23.	WILLIAM MAC RAE	4 November, 1864
24.	COLLETT LEVENTHORPE	3 February, 1865
25.	WILLIAM P. ROBERTS	21 February, 1865

This is a full list of the Generals appointed from North Carolina. There were several other Generals who were born in North Carolina but who went into the service from other States of which they had become citizens and which justly claim them, as Generals Braxton Bragg, Cadmus M. Wilcox, Jeremy F. Gilmer, Gabriel J. Rains, Felix Zollicoffer, Ben. McCullough, and possibly others. On the other hand, General D. H. Hill, born in South Carolina, had long been a citizen of this State, and General W. H. C. Whiting, born in Mississippi, and General John R. Cooke, of Missouri, threw in their lot with us and were appointed from this State and commanded North Carolina troops the whole war.

General James Conner, of South Carolina, and General Alfred Iverson for a while commanded North Carolina brigades, but they were appointed from their respective states and do not figure properly in a list of Generals from North Carolina.

It is worthy of note that one-half of the Major-Generals and one in four of the Brigadier-Generals from this State were killed in battle or died of wounds during the war.

The parole lists at Appomattox were signed by Bryan Grimes, Major General, and by James H. Lane, John R. Cooke, Matt. W. Ransom, William R. Cox, William MacRae and William P. Roberts as Brigadier Generals. *"Official Records of Union and Confederate Armies, Vol. 95, pp. 1277-1279."* The parole lists at surrender of Johnston's army were signed by Daniel H. Hill and Robert F. Hoke as Major-Generals, and Thomas L. Clingman, W. W. Kirkland and Lawrence S. Baker, Brigadier-Generals. *"Official Records of Union and Confederate Armies, Vol. 98, pp. 1601-1666."* The other general officers from North Carolina above named were at the time of the above surrenders either dead, or wounded, prisoners or on detached service.

REGIMENTS AND BRIGADES.

North Carolina furnished seventy-eight full regiments and some twenty battalions to the Confederacy, besides a few scattering companies and a large number of individuals who served in commands from other States, of both which latter we have no data recorded in these volumes. The composition of brigades was so often changed that it was found useless to record it here. Of the regiments the Tenth, Thirty-sixth and Fortieth were artillery, and the Ninth, Nineteenth, Forty-first, Fifty-ninth, Sixty-third, Sixty-fifth and Seventy-fifth were cavalry regiments. Most of the battalions were artillery or cavalry.

The Seventieth, Seventy-first and Seventy-second Regiments and three battalions were Junior Reserves—boys seventeen years of age, who, however, did good service at the battles of Southwest Creek and Bentonville, and a portion of them at the bombardments of Wilmington and of Fort Branch on the Roanoke, and in other minor actions. They were brigaded and were commanded first by Colonel F. S. Armistead, then by Colonel Nethercutt and later by General L. S. Baker, and composed one of the brigades of Hoke's Division. They also aided at Belfield, Va., to repulse the enemy's advance southward.

The Seventy-third, Seventy-fourth, Seventy-sixth, Seventy-seventh and Seventy-eighth were Senior Reserves, between the ages of forty-five and fifty, and rendered good service, a portion of them being under fire.

All the above, being regularly in the Confederate service, have a part in these volumes.

Besides these there were regiments and battalions of Home Guards, composed of those exempt from Confederate service by reason of being State officers (as justices of the peace, county officials, etc.), or for other causes, who rendered service from time to time, for short tours of duty, under the orders of the Governor. Also, in the early part of 1862 there was service rendered by Militia ordered out for short periods, in emergency, notably those under Brigadier-Generals David Clark, Collett Leventhorpe and Jesse R. Stubbs for the defense of the Roanoke after the fall of Roanoke Island, and a regiment of Militia shared in the battle of New Bern. There was also doubtless valuable service rendered by the Militia in other parts of the State. But from the scope of this work, and the dearth of material at this late date, no adequate account is herein given of the services of our Militia and Home Guards, though at the time their aid was valuable.

NAVAL OFFICERS.

The following appear, in the Confederate Archives, as the highest officers in the Navy, appointed from North Carolina, though there were many others of lesser rank:

Name.		Date of Rank.
James W. Cooke	Captain	10 June, 1864.
John N. Maffitt	Commander	13 May, 1863.
James Iredell Waddell	First Lieutenant	6 January, 1864.

Captain Cooke commanded the ram "Albemarle" at the capture of Plymouth, 20 April, 1864, by General R. F. Hoke, for which victory General Hoke and himself, with the officers and men under their command, were voted thanks by the Confederate Congress. General Hoke's commission as Major-General bears that date in recognition of his service.

Lieutenant James Iredell Waddell, as commander of the "Shenandoah," was the last to bear the Confederate flag, not having heard of the fall of the Confederacy till August, 1865, when he was in mid Pacific.

Commander J. N. Maffitt's services were also conspicuous and are well known.

IX

The Supreme Court of North Carolina*

* Printed in *The Green Bag*, October, 1892, pp. 457-474; November, 1892, pp. 521-540; December, 1892, pp. 569-591.

I

THE TITLE "SUPREME COURT OF NORTH Carolina" dates from the Act of 1805; but the court thus styled consisted of a conference of the circuit judges, and was in fact a mere continuation, with some modifications, of the previous Court of Conference. In the year 1818 the Supreme Court, consisting of judges having appellate duties only, was first established. From 1818 to 1868 it was composed of three judges. The number was increased by the Constitution of 1868, to consist of a Chief-Justice and four Associate Justices. By constitutional amendment the number of Associate Justices was reduced to two, Jan. 1, 1879; but by another amendment it was again increased to four, Jan. 1, 1889.

Since the establishment of the Supreme Court in 1818 the bench has been occupied by twenty-nine judges, of whom seven were Chief-Justices. In this enumeration are included the present occupants of the bench. This article is intended to be a sketch of the twenty-four incumbents of the Supreme Court of North Carolina from its organization in 1818, exclusive of those now on the bench.

The history of our judiciary prior to the Act of 1818, creating a separate and distinct body of Appellate Judges, will justify a cursory notice.

In 1670, under the cumbersome "Fundamental Constitutions of Carolina," which had been drafted by the celebrated philosopher John Locke, we first hear of a Chief-Justice of North Carolina. He was no less a man than Anthony Ashley Cooper, better known to fame as Lord Shaftesbury. He was one of the eight Lords Proprietors to whom the province of Carolina had been granted by the Crown. Lord Shaftesbury had no intention of exercising the duties of the post in person, and appointed one Captain John Willoughby as his deputy. In 1713 we find that Christopher Gale was Chief-Justice. He was born in Yorkshire, England, where his father was rector of a church. He resided and died in Edenton. He left a name that is never mentioned but with respect. The late Col. George Little of Raleigh was a lineal descendant. Gale, owing to difficulties with the Governor, visited England, and was succeeded by Tobias Knight, who was accused (but acquitted) of complicity with the pirate "Blackbeard." He was succeeded by Frederick Jones, of indifferent fame. Gale, having returned from

England, again filled the post. In 1724 Governor Burrington endeavored to eject him, and appointed Thomas Pollock; but the Lords Proprietors retroceded their sovereignty to the Crown in 1729; and in 1731 Gale was superseded by William Smith, who had been educated at an English University, and had been admitted as a barrister at law in England. Governor Burrington appointed John Palin first to succeed him, and then William Little, son-in-law of Gale, who, soon dying, was succeeded by Daniel Hamner. He in his turn yielded to Smith, who had returned from England. In 1740 John Montgomery became Chief-Justice, and was succeeded in 1744 by Edward Moseley, a man of real ability. He died in 1749, and was succeeded in turn by Enoch Hall, Eleazar Allen, James Hassell, and Peter Henly respectively.

In 1746 an important change was made in the Court Law. Up to this time the Chief-Justice sat with from two to ten assistants, who were simple justices of the peace. Indeed it is not certain that all the Chief-Justices even were lawyers. By that act all writs were issued from the court at Newbern, and all pleadings were filed there; but trial of the issues could be had at the *nisi prius* terms held by the Chief-Justice and associates at Edenton, Enfield, and Wilmington. Three Associates were appointed under this act, who were required to be lawyers. Charles Berry became Chief-Justice in 1760, and committed suicide in 1766. In 1767 the Province was divided into five judicial districts,—Edenton, Newbern, Wilmington, Halifax, and Hillsboro,—in each of which towns a court was held twice each year by the Chief-Justice and his Associates. The Chief-Justice was Martin Howard, and the Associates were Richard Henderson and Maurice Moore. Judge Henderson was the father of Chief-Justice Leonard Henderson, and Judge Moore was the father of Justice Alfred Moore, of the U. S. Supreme Court. This Act of 1767 expired at the end of five years; and in consequence of disagreement between the Governor and the Legislature, there were no courts in the Province between 1773 and 1777. After August, 1775, till the Judiciary Act adopted Nov. 15, 1777, by the new State government, the judicial functions were perforce discharged by the Committees of Safety.

Under the Provincial government the Chief-Justice was a member of the Council of Upper House of the General Assembly, which also shared largely in the executive functions. The Constitution of 1776, on the contrary, made both the Executive and Judiciary dependent upon the General Assembly, which was elected annually. Though the judges were to hold office during good behavior, their offices could be abolished at the will of the legislature, and there was no inhibition against a decrease of their salaries. The Constitution of 1835 prohibited a decrease of a judge's salary during his continuance in office. The Constitution of 1868 made the Supreme Court a part of the Constitution and beyond repeal by legislative action, and fixed the term of office at eight years, and made it an independent part of the Government, free from control by the legislative or executive departments. The judiciary inferior to the Supreme Court is still, however, left subject to legislative action, except that the term of office of the Superior Court judges is fixed at eight years, and the salary of no judge can be diminished during his continuance in office.

By the Judiciary Act of 1777 the State was divided into six districts,—Wilmington, Newbern, Edenton, Hillsboro, Halifax, and Salisbury. In 1782 Morganton was added, and in 1787 Fayetteville, making eight in all. At each of these a court was held twice each year by three judges. The first judges elected were Samuel Spencer of Anson, Samuel Ashe of New Hanover, and James Iredell of Chowan. After riding one circuit Iredell resigned, and was succeeded by John Williams of Granville. Iredell was a very able man, and was subsequently appointed by Washington a Justice of the Supreme Court of the United States. Judge Ashe held office till he was elected Governor in 1795, Spencer till his death in 1794, and Williams till his death in 1799. The death of Judge Spencer was singular. In old age he was asleep on a warm day in a chair under the shade of a tree. A turkey cock, enraged by a red cap or handkerchief which the Judge wore to keep off the flies, assaulted him. Either by the blow of the gobbler, or by the fall from his chair caused by the assault, the old Judge died.

To this court belongs the distinction of being the first to assert the power and duty of the bench to declare an act of the legislature void for unconstitutionality. This it did in the case of Bayard *v.* Singleton, at May Term, 1786, shortly before similar action by the Supreme Court of Rhode Island. New York followed with a similar decision in 1791, South Carolina in 1792, and Maryland in 1802. This was novel and strong action then. There were no precedents for it. In England, there being no written Constitution, any action of the Parliament had always been conclusive on the courts, at least since arbitrary government by the Crown had ceased.

In 1790 Halifax, Edenton, Newbern, and Wilmington were constituted the Eastern Riding; and Morganton, Salisbury, Fayetteville, and Hillsboro the Western Riding. Two judges were to hold each term of court, the number being increased for that purpose to four by the election of Judge Spruce McKay. In 1799 James Glasgow, Secretary of State, and others having been charged with fraudulent issue of land warrants, the legislature passed an act for the court to meet twice a year in Raleigh for the trial of these causes, and incidentally to hear appeals in causes accumulated in the district courts, the act to expire in 1802. This act, however, so far as hearing appeals was concerned, was in 1801 extended for three years, and the court was styled the "Court of Conference." In 1804 this was made a court of record, and the judges required to file written opinions. In 1805 the title was changed to the "Supreme Court,"—surely a tardy recognition of the constitutional provision of 1776,—and the Sheriff of Wake was made marshal of the court. In 1806 the districts were increased to six ridings, two additional judges being elected, and a superior court was for the first time to be held twice a year at the courthouse in each county, and by one judge. The judges were to ride each circuit in rotation, as is still the law, and as it has been continuously since 1806, with the exception of the years 1868-1876. The provision requiring this is now in the Constitution. In 1810 the judges hearing appeals in the "Court of Conference" were required to write out their opinions "at full length," and to elect a Chief-Justice. John Louis Taylor was the first and only judge who filled the post. By the same act a seal and motto were directed to be established for the court, and any party to an action in the Superior Court, civil or criminal, was given the right of appeal. Any two of the six judges sitting in conference at Raleigh as a supreme court constituted a quorum.

In the year 1818 the Supreme Court, as contemplated by the Constitution of 1776, and substantially as it has ever since existed (barring an increase in the number of judges, and the constitutional provisions as to tenure of office, and independence of the other departments of the government, as above noted), was established. The bill was introduced by Hon. William Gaston, who many years after became one of the most illustrious members of the court he had contributed to create.

The salary was fixed at that date at $2,500,—a figure at which it still stands, though owing to the changes in values the present salary is not much more in fact than one third of the sum allowed by our forefathers seventy-four years ago. The salary of the Superior Court judges, previously $1,600, was then fixed at $1,800. This has since been raised to $2,500. The legislature elected John Louis Taylor, Leonard Henderson, and John Hall the first judges.

Taylor and Hall were elected from the Superior Court bench, and Henderson had recently resigned from it. Till the Constitution of 1868 the tenure was for life or good behavior, and the judges were elected by the legislature, the Chief-Justice being chosen by his associates. Since 1868 the term of office has been fixed by the Constitution at eight years, as has been stated, and the office of Chief-Justice is a distinct one from that of Associate Justice, though there is no difference in point of emolument or functions, save that the Chief-Justice presides. The mode of election, too, since 1868 is by the people. In event of a vacancy the Governor appoints till after the next general election for members of the General Assembly. The new court began work Jan. 1, 1819, and its first decisions appear in the 7 N. C. Reports (3 Murph.).

Among the decisions prior to the establishment of the new court we note that the court in those days made numerous adjudications upon bets on horse-races, from which they have been relieved by the Act of 1810 making all betting illegal. In Williams *v.* Cabarrus, 1 N. C. 19, decided in 1793, will be found the ethics which should govern in horse-racing laid down with a fulness and accuracy which indicate thought and a thorough knowledge of the race-track; and there are many similar cases: McKensie *v.* Ashe, 2 N. C. 578; Hunter *v.* Parker, 3 N. C. 373, and others. In State *v.* Knight, 1 N. C. (Taylor, 44), Judge Taylor lays down a principle which has just been reaffirmed after the lapse of nearly a century, in State *v.* Cutshall, 110 N. C. 538, that the legislature cannot make an extraterritorial act punishable in this State. In the same volume, in State *v.* Carter, occurs one of those unaccountable decisions which made the old criminal law so often a trespass upon the common-sense of mankind. In that case the defendant had been convicted of a deliberate and malicious homicide, yet the judgment against the murderer was arrested because in the indictment in the word "breast" the vowel *a* (which is unpronounced) was omitted by clerical error. Such fantastic mental phenomena have long since become impossible, as the legislature, by repeated and very plain enactments, have provided that errors and omissions of form, and not of substance, shall be disregarded, and the courts have now very long since abandoned such trifling with justice. In this very case it is refreshing to see that Judge Taylor dissented from the decision of the court. It is also to be noted that in those days an appeal lay for the State in criminal cases from a verdict of not guilty. State *v.* McLelland, 1 N. C. (Conf. 523), and State *v.* Hadcock, 3 N. C. 348. This was not reversed till as late as the year 1809 by the decision in State *v.* Jones, 5 N. C. 257, and then upon the wording of the new statute regulating appeals.

On p. 469 of the 3 N. C., the conscientious reporter saves himself from all possible responsibility by this remark at the end of the report of the case of Clark *v.* Arnold: "The reporter is bound by his duty to the public to question at least one part of this decision." Then, after giving his reasons why the court was in error, he courteously adds: "But let it be remembered, once for all, that I impute this, as well as every other mistake of Judge Hall, to the hurry of business. I believe the government at this time has no officer who more deserves its confidence. Yet I cannot agree to disseminate wrong legal opinions out of respect to the opinion of any one." State *v.* Smith, 5 N. C. (1 Murph.) 218, is an indictment for fraudulently procuring a certificate of survey to be issued from the public-land office, etc. Its singularity lies in the fact that the defendant then, and for many years after, was State Senator continuously till elected Governor in 1810; the prosecutor was Alfred Moore, then an Associate Justice of the United States Supreme Court. The Surveyor, who was alleged *particeps criminis,* frequently thereafter served as a member of both branches of the General Assembly. The case is evidently a historical puzzle for some Dryasdust to investigate and elucidate. The new court, as we have said, began its labors Jan. 1, 1819; and its decisions begin with the 7th N. C. Reports (3 Murph.).

John Louis Taylor, chosen by his associates the first Chief-Justice, was when elected to the Supreme Court the oldest judge in commission on the Superior Court bench, to which he had been elected in 1798. He was born in London, but of Irish parentage, March 1, 1769. At the age of twelve years he was removed from his widowed mother, and brought to this country by his elder brother, James Taylor. By the assistance of his brother, he obtained, though in an imperfect degree, the benefits of a classical education at William and Mary College in Virginia, an eminent institution in those days, from which went out four Presidents,—Jefferson, Madison, Monroe, and Tyler—Chief-Justice Marshall, Gen. Winfield Scott, and many other distinguished men. He was compelled to leave college before graduation; and after reading law without preceptor or guide, he was admitted to the bar in 1788, before he was twenty, and located in Fayetteville. In 1792, 1793, 1794, and 1795, he was elected to the legislature from Fayetteville, then a borough town. In 1794 he was a candidate before the General Assembly for the office of Attorney-General, but was defeated by Blake Baker. He removed to Newbern in 1796, and in 1798 he was elected a Judge of the Superior Court. In 1818 he had held that office consecutively twenty years, during ten of which he had been Chief-Justice of the court held by the judges of the Superior Court in Conference. He died Jan. 29, 1829, and is buried in the cemetery at Raleigh. In 1802 he published Taylor's Reports, which now form a part of 1 N. C. Reports. In 1814 he published the first volume of the North Carolina Law Repository, and in 1816 the second volume of the same, and in 1818 Taylor's Term Reports. These three volumes are now united in one, known as the 4 N. C. Reports. As originally printed, the Repository contained much interesting matter (other than decisions of the court) which has now been omitted in the reprint. In 1817 he was appointed by the General Assembly jointly with Judge Henry Potter of the United States District Court for North Carolina to publish a revision of the statute law of the State. This revisal, known as Potter's Revisal, came out in 1821. In 1825 Judge Taylor published a continuation of this work, including the Acts of 1825. This is known as Taylor's Revisal. He also published a treatise on executors and administrators. He possessed a singular aptitude for literature, and would have excelled in composition if his "jealous mistress," the law, had given him opportunity. His elocution was the admiration of all who heard him. His style of writing is preserved to us in his opinions, and in beauty of diction they are not surpassed, if equalled, by any of his successors. Chief-Justice Taylor came to that post at forty-nine years of age, and during the ten years he presided in the new court his opinions, which are to be found in Murphey's last volume and Hawk's four volumes (now known as 7th to 11th N. C. Reports inclusive) and in part of 16 N. C., form at once his judicial record and his lasting eulogy. His opinions before his elevation are to be found in the prior volumes, 1st to 6th N. C. His charge to the grand jury of Edgecombe in 1817 is a model in style and subject matter. It was published by request of the grand jury. Of his character as a man his associates place their estimate on record in a tribute to be found in the 16 N. C. (1 Dev. Eq.) 309, as follows: "Of the Chief-Justice as a man, we are unwilling to trust ourselves to speak as we feel. We loved him too well and too long to make the public the depository of our cherished affections. If there ever heaved a kinder heart in human bosom, it has not fallen to our lot to meet with it. If ever man was more faithful to friendship, more disinterested, humane, and charitable, we have not been so fortunate as to know him. When we think of these excellencies,—when we call to mind the instances in which we have seen them illustrated in practice, and felt their kindly influence,—and when we look around into the wide world to search for those who may supply his place in our affections, the exclamation involuntarily arises,—

> "Vale! Vale!
> Heu quanto minus est, cum reliquis versari
> Quam tui meminisse."

Judge Taylor was twice married. By his wife Julia Rowan he had one child, a daughter, who married Major Junius Sneed, of Salisbury. A son of theirs, John Louis Taylor Sneed, became Attorney-General of Tennessee. His second wife was Jane Gaston, sister of Judge Gaston, by whom he had a daughter who married David E. Sumner, of Gates County, and left descendants in Tennessee. Judge Taylor also had a son who died without issue. His name, therefore, can be transmitted to posterity only in his good works which "do follow him." Judge Taylor was succeeded as judge by John D. Toomer, and as Chief-Justice by Leonard Henderson.

Chief-Justice Leonard Henderson was the son of Judge Richard Henderson of colonial times, and was born, Oct. 6, 1772, on Nutbush Creek, in that part of Granville County which is now in Vance. As an evidence of the frugality and industry of the times, it is said his mother taught her sons as well as her daughters to card and spin. A county and two prosperous towns preserve this illustrious family name to posterity. His brother Archibald was equally distinguished as a lawyer. Archibald married the sister of Governor Alexander, and represented the Salisbury district two terms in Congress,—the same district for which his grandson, Hon. John S. Henderson, is now the worthy representative in Congress for the sixth term. Two other brothers of Judge Henderson were distinguished lawyers, while another was Comptroller of the State, and long Clerk of the Supreme Court; and his uncle, Major Pleasant Henderson, a Revolutionary soldier of distinction, succeeded Judge Haywood as clerk of the House of Commons in 1796, and retained the office through all the mutations of parties and men for forty years, and by annual elections. A sister of Judge Henderson was the wife of Judge McKay, already mentioned, and a niece was the wife of Judge Boyden of the Supreme Court in more recent years.

Judge Henderson's early education was limited. He studied law under Judge Williams, and located at Williamsburg. Soon after he came to the bar he married his cousin, Frances Farrar, who was a niece of Judge Williams. The young couple being poor, Judge Williams, who was wealthy, generously gave them a fair settlement in life to begin the world. For several years Leonard Henderson was clerk of the District Court at Hillsboro. In 1808 he was elected to fill the vacancy on the Superior Court bench caused by the death of his brother-in-law, Judge McKay. His election was the higher compliment because a majority of the legislature belonged to the opposite political party. The duties of the office he discharged with ability and fidelity for eight years, resigning in 1816. In 1818, as already stated, he was elected to the Supreme Court bench. The election took place Dec. 12, 1818. The candidates were John Louis Taylor and John Hall, who had been in continuous service on the Superior Court bench twenty and eighteen years respectively; Henderson, who after service of eight years had recently resigned; Henry Seawell, who was still on the bench after five years' service; Archibald D. Murphey, who, with a high reputation as an able lawyer and an elegant scholar, had greatly distinguished himself in a seven years' service in the State Senate, where he had been foremost in advocacy of a system of Internal Improvements and Public Schools; and Bartlett Yancey, a distinguished lawyer, who had served four years as a member of Congress, and who was then and for many years after Speaker of the State Senate. There was no scarcity of material. The majority in the legislature was of the opposite political party to Henderson, as had been the case in 1808; yet on the first ballot Henderson and Hall were elected. On the second ballot Taylor was by a narrow majority elected, and was chosen by his associates Chief-Justice, being their senior in judicial service, though junior in years to Judge Hall. Judge Battle, who had studied law with him and was his personal friend, in his excellent sketch of him deplores that Judge Henderson, "in common with too many of our distinguished lawyers and public of that day, had become imbued with the French infidelity which was rife in their youth," and that in consequence he had not "that purity of manners and morals which the genuine spirit of Christianity alone can produce." He says, however, that his integrity was beyond question, and that he was charitable in act and in speech, temperate, candid, and truthful. His religious views are said to have been much modified in his latter days. He was kind, sociable, and courteous, a fine conversationalist, and very popular. Among his law students were his successors, Chief-Justice Pearson and Judge Battle. He was elected to the Supreme Bench on the first ballot, together with a personal friend but political opponent, over four other gentlemen of the highest reputation and influence. He was a good lawyer, and stands in the front rank as a judge. He was restive of precedent when he considered it in conflict with principle. He did not have the same degree of regard for the maxim, *Stare decisis,* which was so prominent a feature with Judge Taylor; but he had an honest, strong mind, and his arguments show an earnest grasping after the truth. Later in life he could not endure the fatigue of reading many books, and he relied on his recollection of principles and his powers of argumentation. Hence with his later opinions, as with Pearson's, and for the same cause, there is small citation of authority. A fair specimen of his knowledge and powers can be found in Taylor *v.* Shuford, 11 N. C. (4 Hawks) 126, on the difficult subject of estoppel and warranty, which he discusses with clearness and force, without citation of any decided case or elementary work. On the death of Judge Taylor, in 1829, Judge Henderson was elected by his associates Chief-Justice, and served till his death, which took place at his residence near Williamsboro, August 13, 1833. He had four sons and two daughters, and through them has many descendants, who look back with pride to the record of his honored and useful life. Among his descendants are A. E. Henderson, a prominent lawyer of Caswell County, and the wife of the late Governor Scales. He was succeeded as Judge by William Gaston, and as Chief-Justice by Ruffin.

Judge John Hall, who was elected to the Supreme Court at its organization together with Taylor and Henderson, was the senior of them both, having been born in Augusta County, Va., May 31, 1767, near Waynesboro, a small village now on the railroad from Staunton to Richmond. He was the youngest of the children of Edward Hall and Elizabeth Stuart, his wife. Edward Hall was a native of Ireland, who first settled in Pennsylvania, but afterward removed to Virginia in 1736. Judge Hall received an excellent education, and was a graduate of William and Mary College, where he was a fellow-student of Bishop Ravenscroft, and possibly of Chief-Justice John Louis Taylor. He studied law in Staunton, Va., under his kinsman, Judge Stuart, who was the father of Hon. A. H. H. Stuart, Secretary of the Interior under President Fillmore. In 1792 Judge Hall removed to Warrenton, N. C., where he continued to reside till his death. His manners were diffident and reserved, and his talents, though considerable, were not striking; but such was the favorable impression made by his character and industry that, though he came to Warrenton a total stranger, and possessed no influential connections, eight years thereafter he was elected, at thirty-three years of age, a judge of the Superior Court, then the highest judicial office in the State. On the adoption of the present Superior Court system in 1806, he rode the circuits of the State in rotation. As there were then six circuits, he had held court in succession in every county of the State four times, when in December, 1818, he was elected to the Supreme Court, being chosen on the first ballot. He discharged the duties of the office with credit and fidelity. On the death of Chief-Justice Taylor, though the senior in years and judicial service, he did not insist upon succeeding to the office, and concurred in the selection of Judge Henderson as Chief-Justice. Owing to a painful and distressing malady, he resigned, December, 1832, and died soon thereafter, at his residence in Warrenton, Jan. 29 ,1833. Although not a brilliant or showy man, he possessed a sound judgment and extensive legal attainments. He was eminently a safe judge, thoroughly impartial and unbiassed. Throughout life his character was unblemished. In 1804 he was elected Grand Master of Masons, and though taking no part in politics, he was in 1829, while still retaining his position on the bench, elected as one of the Presidential Electors on the Jackson ticket. His judicial opinions were brief, plain, and to the point. In person he was considerably above middle size, with handsome features and a florid complexion. He left eight children, one of whom—Hon. Edward Hall—was appointed Judge of the Superior Court in 1840, and served a short term on the bench with much reputation. Judge John Hall was succeeded on the Supreme bench by Judge Daniel.

Archibald DeBow Murphey, though never elected a member of the Supreme Court, is entitled to a place in this list of the occupants of the bench, as by special commission he discharged its duties for part of three terms. Under a clause in the act creating the court, the Governor was authorized to detail a Judge of the Superior Court by special commission to sit instead of a judge of the Supreme Court in causes where one of its members had been counsel or had an interest in the result. Judge Henderson had been elected from the bar, where he had been in full practice, and there were many of these causes. Judge Murphey was specially commissioned by Governor Branch, and sat in several cases at May term 1819, 7 N. C. 428; at November term 1819, 7 N. C. 566;

at June term 1820, 8 N. C. 77, 82, 86, 92, 126. Indeed his concurrence with Chief-Justice Taylor (8 N. C. 96) against Judge Hall's dissent sustained the validity of the Moses Griffin will, under which Newbern has ever since possessed the "Griffin" school. Judge Daniel (afterward for many years a judge of the Supreme Court) was also commissioned and sat at May term 1819, in several causes (7 N. C. 54, 503). The act was repealed in 1821, being considered of doubtful constitutionality.

The fame of Judge Murphey is very dear to the State, and he was worthy of any honors she could bestow upon him.

His father, Col. Archibald Murphey, was a prominent citizen of Caswell County, and bore a part in the military service of the Revolution, for which the citizens of that patriotic county were specially distinguished. At his father's residence near Red House, and seven miles from Milton, Judge Murphey was born in 1777, a member of a family of seven children. He entered the State University in 1796, and graduated with the highest distinction in 1799. Such was the reputation he had acquired that he was immediately appointed Professor of Ancient Languages in the University, which position he held for three years, maturing that taste for liberal studies which always distinguished him.

He was admitted to the bar in 1802 after a meagre course of legal study, but advanced rapidly to the front rank in the profession. The bar is not a place where a false reputation for talents can be maintained. His practice for years was not exceeded by any lawyer in the State, and he had most able competitors and contemporaries at the bar,—the two Hendersons, Cameron, Norwood, Nash, Seawell, Yancey, Ruffin, Badger, Hawks, Mangum, Morehead, Graham, and many others. Governor Graham says of him: "He had a Quaker-like plainness of aspect, a scrupulous neatness in an equally plain attire, an habitual politeness, and a subdued simplicity of manner which at once won his way to the hearts of juries, while no Greek dialectician had a more ready and refined ingenuity, or was more fertile in every resource of forensic gladiatorship." Though a charming and successful advocate, he more especially delighted in the equity practice, which he deemed "the application of the rules of Moral Philosophy to the practical affairs of men." He was a skilful pleader; and his chirography, neat and peculiar, was almost as legible as print,—an unusual thing with lawyers.

From 1812 to 1818, he was continuously, by annual election, a Senator from Orange, and on this new theatre shone even more conspicuously than in his profession. He inaugurated a new era in the public policy of the State, and exerted for years probably a greater influence than any other citizen of the State. He was the foremost and ablest advocate, indeed the originator, of a system of internal improvements and of common schools in North Carolina. His papers and addresses on these subjects would do credit to DeWitt Clinton or John C. Calhoun. One of these memoirs was published in 1822, with high commendation in the "North American Review," then edited by Hon. Edward Everett. He was a firm friend to the State University. In 1822, by appointment of North Carolina, he was heard before the Tennessee legislature, and adjusted the disputed claims of the University to lands in that State. He also was the first who aroused an interest in our State history. He proposed, indeed, to write a history of North Carolina (though never able to accomplish it), and procured from the Revolutionary survivors, then rapidly passing away, much valuable material and information, which but for him would have been irretrievably lost. In one of his letters he says: "We know nothing of our State, and care nothing about it. We want some great stimulus to put us all in motion, and to induce us to waive little jealousies and combine in one general march to one great purpose."

In 1818 he came near being elected to the bench of the new Supreme Court, though he had never presided—as the successful candidates all had—on the Superior Court bench. He was elected to fill one of the vacancies on the Superior Court bench, and held the office for two years, during which time he sat, as we have seen, by special commission, part of three terms upon the Supreme Court. He resigned in the fall of 1820. In 1819 he published three volumes of reports, the 5, 6, and 7 N. C. (formerly 1, 2, and 3 Murphey). Of these, the first two covered the decisions of the old Supreme Court (from 1804 to 1818), and the last contained the decisions of the new Supreme Court for 1819,—the first year of its existence. We are so accustomed now to official reporters and a prompt publication of the decisions of the court of last resort, that we cannot understand the full extent of the benefit conferred on the profession then by the editing and publishing of the decisions, the larger part of which had remained in manuscript for so many years.

As a literary character, Judge Murphey should be classed as one of the first men in the nation. His style had all the charm of Goldsmith or Irving. In Latin, Greek, and French his proficiency was such that he read the standard authors with pleasure and for amusement. He was thoroughly familiar with the English classics; and, though in this self-taught, he had no small attainments in the sciences. His oration before the two literary societies of the University in 1827 was the first of a long series of like addresses by distinguished men at the annual Commencements, but has never been surpassed by any. It has been a model of its kind. Its commendation by Chief-Justice Marshall in a letter to its author adds to its interest, and renders it historical.

In the latter years of his life he struggled with disease and financial embarrassment, the latter the result of over-sanguine investments. But to the last his gifted mind, when his chronic rheumatism permitted him to appear in the court-room, shone out in its noonday splendor, and at all times his hours of pain and misfortune were solaced

> "With silent worship of the great of old,
> The dead but sceptred sovereigns,
> Who rule our spirits from their urns."

He died at Hillsboro, his place of residence, Feb. 3, 1832, and is buried in the Presbyterian churchyard, where repose so many of our illustrious dead. He left two sons, Dr. Murphey of Mississippi, and Lieutenant Murphey of the United States Navy. A beautiful and growing town in the western-most county of the State preserves his name, and our State itself the recollection of his fame.

John DeRossett Toomer was born at Wilmington, March 13, 1784. He was educated in part at the University of North Carolina, but did not graduate. He was elected Judge of the Superior Court in 1818, but resigned the next year. On the death of Chief-Justice Taylor in 1829, Judge Toomer was appointed by Governor Owen in June to the Supreme Court till the legislature should meet in December, 1829, when Judge Thomas Ruffin was elected by that body. Thus Judge Toomer's stay upon the Supreme bench was brief, and he did not have opportunity to develop his powers; but the opinions he filed afford proof that if time had been given, he would have achieved a reputation equal to that of almost any judge who has occupied the seat. A judge who has capacity is like a tree in good soil,—he *grows*. Time is necessary to him. It is only an inferior man who does not improve by experience and study. Judge Toomer's opinions are thirteen in law cases to be found in 13 N. C. (2 Dev.), and two in equity cases in 16 N. C. (1 Dev. Eq.). For many years he was president of the branch bank of the Cape Fear at Fayetteville. He represented Cumberland in the State senate in 1831 and 1832, and was a member of the convention to revise the Constitution in 1835. In 1836 he was again elected a judge of the Superior Court, to succeed Judge Strange, who had been elected to the United States Senate. In 1840, on account of ill-health, he resigned, and was succeeded on the Superior bench by W. H. Battle. Judge Toomer was welcomed back to the bar, and located at Pittsboro, in Chatham County, where he lived till his death, Oct. 27, 1856, in the seventy-third year of his age. He was an eloquent speaker, an agreeable writer, of fine literary attainments, and an amiable and urbane gentleman.

> "None knew him but to love him,
> None named him but to praise."

He was succeeded on the Supreme Court bench, as already stated, by Judge Ruffin.

The hunter in the Indian jungle discovers by unmistakable signs when the king of the forest has passed by. So the lawyer who turns over the leaves of the North Carolina Reports, when he comes upon the opinions of Thomas Ruffin, instantly perceives that a lion has been there.

Thomas Ruffin, the eldest child of his parents, was born in King and Queen County, Virginia, Nov. 17, 1787. His father, Sterling Ruffin, was a very zealous and a very pious minister of the Methodist church. His mother was cousin-german to Chief-Justice Spencer Roane of the Supreme Court of Virginia. His father sent his son at a suitable age to a classical academy in Warrenton, N. C., taught by Marcus George, an Irishman, and a teacher of high reputation. Among his schoolmates there were Cadwalader Jones and Weldon N. Edwards. From this academy he was transfered to Nassau Hall, Princeton, N. J. His father, who was a deeply pious man, was controlled, it is said, in the selection of this college in preference to William and Mary and other colleges then popular, by a desire to secure him as much as possible from the usual temptations of college life by placing him in an institution whose reputation for the maintenance of authority and discipline stood high, as it did at Princeton. Young Ruffin graduated there in 1805, being sixteenth in a class of forty-two members. Gov. James Iredell was his roommate; and among his college friends and contemporaries who afterwards achieved prominence were Samuel L. Southard and Theodore Frelinghuysen, of New Jersey; Joseph R. Ingersoll, of Philadelphia; Stevenson Archer, of Maryland; and many others. On his return home he entered the law office of Daniel Robertson, Esq., in Petersburg, and remained with him during 1806 and 1807. Here he had as fellow-students Gen. Winfield Scott and Judge John F. May. Mr. Robertson was a Scotchman by birth, a learned scholar and advocate, who gained high distinction as a lawyer. He reported the debates in the Virginia Convention which adopted the Federal Constitution and the trial of Aaron Burr for high treason. In his autobiography General Scott refers to subsequent occasions when he had met Judge Ruffin, especially in Washington, in the spring of 1861, when the latter was serving as a member of the Peace Congress; and he expresses the opinion that "if the sentiment of this good man, always highly conservative (the same as Crittenden's) had prevailed, the country would have escaped the sad infliction of the war."

Rev. Sterling Ruffin, his father, having suffered financial reverses, removed to Rockingham County, N. C., in 1807, and his son soon followed. He continued his studies in the law office of Judge Murphey, and was admitted to the bar in 1808. He located in Hillsboro, and on Dec. 7, 1809, married Miss Anne Kirkland of that town, the daughter of William Kirkland, a leading citizen. In 1813, 1815, and 1816, he was a member of the House of Commons from the borough of Hillsboro, and in the last-named year was Speaker of the House. In 1815 and 1816 the town of Hillsboro was represented by Judge Ruffin, and the county by Judge Murphey in the Senate, and Judge Nash in the House. It is said that on first coming to the bar Judge Ruffin's efforts at argument were diffident, and his speech hesitating and embarrassed. His friends candidly advised him to abandon the profession, but he felt that he had the "root of the matter" in him, and held on. He was well grounded by his studies in a knowledge of the law, and experience soon cured his defects of speech. At a strong bar he soon became a leader, and in 1816, while Speaker of the House, he was chosen a judge of the Superior Court to fill the vacancy caused by the resignation of Duncan Cameron. This position he resigned after two years on the circuit, and returned to a lucrative practice at the bar. He was an indefatigable student, and a frame of iron permitted him any amount of application. For forty-three weeks of the year he had engagements in court which he kept regardless of weather and bad roads. He also was for one or two terms reporter of the Supreme Court, but was compelled to relinquish the position by the demands of his practice. His work as reporter will be found in the first part of the 8th N. C. (1 Hawks). In the summer of 1825, upon the resignation of Judge Badger, he again accepted the position of judge of the Superior Court, and during the next three years he administered its duties in such a manner that he was generally designated by public opinion for the succession to the Supreme Court upon the occurrence of the first vacancy.

In the fall of 1828 the stockholders of the State Bank of North Carolina, at Raleigh, at whose head were William Polk, Peter Browne, and Duncan Cameron, in view of its embarrassments and threatened litigation, prevailed on him to take the presidency of the bank with an increased salary and with the privilege of practising his profession. He again resigned his judgeship, and, accepting the offer, by his diligence and practical business knowledge and the faith imparted by his acceptance of its headship, he effectually reinstated the bank in public confidence, and relieved it of its embarrassments. About this time there being a vacancy in the United States Senatorship by the appointment of Governor Branch to the head of the Navy Department, he was solicited to become a candidate for the vacancy, with strong prospects of success. This he declined, saying, as he often did, that "after the labor and attention he had bestowed upon his profession he desired to go down to posterity as a lawyer." While employed on the affairs of the bank, he still remained in full practice at the bar, and his reputation as a lawyer suffered no eclipse. On the death of Chief-Justice Taylor, in 1829, Governor Owen appointed to the Supreme Court Judge Toomer, a lawyer of deserved eminence in the profession, and of a singularly pure and elevated character; but public opinion and the sentiment of the bar had so decidedly marked out Judge Ruffin for the succession that when the legislature met in the fall of that year he was elected to the position.

Upon the death of Chief-Justice Henderson in 1833, Judge Ruffin was elected Chief-Justice by his associates, and served as such nineteen years. In the autumn of 1852, while at the height of his fame and not yet oppressed by the weight of years, he resigned his office, intending to retire forever from the profession and the studies in which he had won renown. But in 1858, on the death of his friend and successor Chief-Justice Nash, he was called by the almost unanimous voice of the legislature, though in his seventy-second year, to resume his place upon the Supreme Court bench. This he did, but did not insist upon resuming the Chief-Justiceship, which went to Judge Pearson. After something over a year's service, his failing health made his duties irksome, and he resigned a second time, and retired finally from judicial life. It is his singular fortune to have resigned twice from both the Superior Court and Supreme Court bench. It is worthy of note, too, that in 1848 all three of the Supreme Court judges (Ruffin, Nash, and Battle), the Governor (Graham), and one of the United States Senators (Mangum) were from the single county of Orange. Already, from 1845 to 1848, two of the Supreme Court (Ruffin and Nash), the Governor (Graham), and one United States Senator (Mangum) had been from that county; while at the legislature of 1841 both United States Senators (Graham and Mangum) were elected from the same county of Orange, in which the Chief-Justice also then resided. From 1852 to 1858 two of the three Supreme Court judges were again from Orange, as two out of the three (Smith and Merrimon) were from Wake from 1883 to 1889. In the latter year the number of judges was increased to five. Thus, in our State, geographical considerations have had small weight in the selection for non-political offices in which fitness alone is of importance.[1]

During the six years between Chief-Justice Ruffin's resignation in 1852 and his re-election in 1858, and again after his second resignation in 1859, he accepted the office of justice of the peace in Alamance County, to which he had then removed, and held the county court with the lay justices as their presiding justice. Another most eminent lawyer, Thomas P. Devereux, the author of Devereux's Reports, having retired from the bar upon falling heir to a princely fortune, discharged the same duty for years as presiding justice of the peace in the county court of Halifax; and George E. Badger, ex-U. S. Senator and ex-judge, presided in the same manner as a justice of the peace in Wake County. The law is well said to be a jealous mistress; but Judge Ruffin took an intelligent and practical part in agriculture and horticulture. During the recess of his courts, for thirty-five years, while at the bar and on the bench, as well as after his retirement from both, he found recreation in these pursuits, and in the rearing of live-

1 It may also be noted that in 1815 the Governor (Miller), both United States Senators (Macon and Turner), and Judge Hall were from the same county,—Warren. It is a singular coincidence that before serving together in the United States Senate, Macon and Turner had served together in the Revolutionary War as privates in the same company in Colonel Hogun's Seventh North Carolina Regiment. There is probably no parallel case in the history of the Senate.

stock and in the improvement of breeds. It was no mere compliment to a distinguished citizen when the Agriculture Society of North Carolina in 1854 elected him to its Presidency, but a tribute to his eminence in that calling to promote the interests of which the Society had been founded. He was also one of the soundest and ablest financiers in the State. We have already seen the demand for his services as President of the leading bank in the State, and his success in restoring its prestige and credit.

By his industry, frugality, and capacity for the management of property, he accumulated a large estate. He owed little of it to his profession; for soon after he had achieved a lucrative practice he was called to the bench, on which, notwithstanding four successive resignations, he spent the greater part of his active life, receiving the moderate salary attached to the judicial office in North Carolina.

Until superseded by the changes in 1868, he had been for many years the oldest Trustee of the State University, and took an active interest in promoting its welfare.

After the failure of the "Peace Conference" of 1861, as to which President Buchanan adds his testimony to that of General Scott, that the voice of Judge Ruffin was for peace, he accepted a seat in the Convention of 1861. When war began, his influence was for its earnest and zealous prosecution. When defeat at last came, he yielded an honest submission, and in good faith renewed his allegiance to the government of the United States. After the war he sold his farm and returned to Hillsboro, where he died, Jan. 15, 1870, after an illness of but four days, in the eighty-third year of his age. He raised a family of thirteen children. One of his sons, Thomas Ruffin, Jr., became a judge of the Superior and Supreme Courts, and as such will have notice further on in this article.

As an advocate Chief-Justice Ruffin was vehement but logical. He placed small reliance on rhetoric, and appeals to the imagination. His mind was broad, analytic, and grasping. He was physically and mentally capable of vast application, and he did not spare himself any amount of labor. Indeed of him it was true, "Labor ipse est voluptas." He was in the habit of exercising his mental faculties by daily going over the demonstration of some theorem in mathematics. He reached greatness like most great men (especially lawyers), not by the sudden sweep of an eagle's wing, but

"While others slept
He toiled upward in the night."

His capacity as a business man was shown in the executive talent displayed by him on the Superior Court bench, where there is full scope for it, and in which particular the occupants of that bench are more often lacking than in a knowledge of law. In administering the criminal law upon the circuit, the extent of punishment depends very largely on the discretion of the judge. Judge Ruffin's sentences, while not cruel, were such as to be a terror to evil-doers. His practical mind saw that punishment was not vengeance visited upon the criminal, nor was it intended to be reformatory, but rather an example to deter others from the commission of offences, and that the protection to law-abiding men was to prevent violations of law by fear of punishment. He was no sentimentalist. He knew that the investigation and the punishment of crime was expensive to the good men of the community, and by the nature of his sentences he left no doubt of his intention to fulfil the purpose of the court by visiting offences against law with unpleasant consequences to the evil-doer. Consequently, wherever he rode the circuit crime decreased. He sat upon the Supreme Court bench twenty-three years consecutively, from 1829 to 1852, during nineteen years of which he was Chief-Justice, besides one year and a half after his return to the bench. His opinions thus covered nearly a quarter of a century, and will be found in 35 volumes, from 13 N. C. (2 Dev.) to 45 N. C. (Bus.) inclusive, and also in the 51 & 57 N. C. He wrote while on the bench more opinions than any other judge. His opinions embrace almost every topic of the civil and criminal law. They are usually long, full, and show the concentration of a powerful mind upon the subject in hand. His opinions are well beaten out. The print of the hammer is there. His opinions have been cited with approbation by the Federal and State supreme courts, by eminent text-writers, and have been quoted as authority in Westminster Hall. He reached the rare distinction of being equally great both in the common law and as an equity lawyer. Pearson probably equalled him as a common-law lawyer, but fell far short of him in the grasp and application of the great principles of equity.

While conservative, as judges and lawyers necessarily are, he was not a Chinese copyist "of things long outworn." Where the condition of things in this country as compared with England, or improved modes of thought, or "the better reason" called for a modification of precedent, he did not hesitate to declare it. In the criminal law he was above the pettiness of "word-splitting," and obeyed the will of the legislature,—so often expressed in enactments previously slighted by the courts,—that technicalities should be disregarded by the judges when not of the substance of the issues involved. In State *v.* Moses, 13 N. C. (2 Dev.) 452, he construed the statute to mean that all defects and omissions in indictments are cured, except the omission of an averment of matter essential to constitute the crime charged. This certainly was the clear intent of the law-making power. He says: "This law was certainly designed to uphold the execution of public justice, by freeing the courts from those fetters of *form, technicality,* and *refinement* which do not concern the substance of the charge and the proof to support it. Many sages of the law had before called nice objections of this sort a disease of the law and a reproach to the bench, and lamented that they were bound down to strict and precise precedents, neither more brief, plain, nor perspicuous than that which they were constrained to accept. In all indictments, especially those for felonies, exceptions extremely refined, and often going to form only, have been, though reluctantly, entertained. We think the legislature meant to *disallow the whole of them,* and only require the *substance;* that is, a direct averment of those facts and circumstances which constitute the crime to be set forth." In 1796 the North Carolina legislature amended the common-law rule by prohibiting judges from expressing an opinion on the facts. The example has been followed in only a very few States, and the common-law rule still prevails in the United States and most of the State courts, as well as in all other English-speaking countries. In this same case (State *v.* Moses) Judge Ruffin takes his stand against an extension of the purport of this statute by judicial construction, and intimates that "the administration of the law would be more certain, its tribunals more revered, and the suitors better satisfied, if the judge were required (as formerly) to submit his views on *the whole case,* and after the able and ingenious but interested and partial arguments of counsel, to follow with his own calm, discreet, sensible, and impartial summary of the case, including both law and fact. Such an elucidation from an upright, learned, and discreet magistrate, habituated to the investigation of complicated masses of testimony, often contradictory, and often apparently so, but really reconcilable, would be of infinite utility to a conscientious jury in arriving at a just conclusion, not by force of the Judge's opinion, but of the reasons on which it was founded, and on which the jury would still have to pass. If this duty were imposed on the Judge, it is not to be questioned that success would, oftener than it does, depend on the justice of the cause, rather than the ability or the adroitness of the advocate."

During his service on the bench two notable departures were made from the English precedents in equity, simplifying our system and freeing it from embarrassments: (1) Adhering to the Statute of Frauds, and refusing to decree specific performance of a verbal contract of sale of land upon part performance; (2) Discarding the doctrine of vendor's lien upon land sold on credit. Womble *v.* Battle, 38 N. C. 193. There were also other salutary reforms, since recognized and acted on by many able courts, in support of which Chief-Justice Ruffin delivered strong and convincing arguments. His familiar knowledge of affairs, especially with banking and accounts, and his practical knowledge of our many-sided, every-day life was of great advantage to him on the bench. He was, as Tennyson says of Wellington, "rich in saving common-sense."

In State *v.* Morrison, 14 N. C. 299, he laid down the doctrine, since followed in every State but one (Black Int. Liquors, § 507) that on an indictment for retailing liquors without license, the burden is on the defendant to show the existence of a license. His opinion in "Hoke *v.* Henderson," 15 N. C. (4 Dev.) 1, holding that an officer has an estate in his office, and though the legislature may destroy the office (when not prohibited by the Constitution), yet it cannot continue the office, and transfer the estate in it to another, is a most able argument, which received the notice and high encomium of Kent and other constitutional writers. It was the main authority relied on by Mr. Reverdy Johnson in the second argument of *Ex parte* Garland before the United States Supreme Court,—a case involving the power of Congress by a test oath to exclude lawyers from practice in that court for participation (on the Southern side) in the late war between the States, and upon which Mr. Johnson won his case. In State *v.* Benton, 19 N. C. 196, he established clearly the practice as to trials for homicide and challenges to jurors. In Railroad *v.* Davis, 19 N. C. 452, he established the doctrine (then a new one) of the right of the legislature to provide for condemnation of a right of way for railroad purposes, and that in such cases the land-owner did not have a constitutional right to a trial by jury to assess the damages, but was remitted to whatever mode of assessment might be provided by the legislature, and that payment of compensation did not necessarily precede the taking possession of the right of way. In Irby *v.* Wilson, 21 N. C. 568, in a very able opinion, he maintains that while the domicile of the husband is that of the wife for some purposes, yet where they have adverse interests, as in a suit between them, her domicile is where she actually resides; and that hence in an action for divorce, where a wife had left the State for many years, a decree of divorce obtained by the husband in the State where he continued to reside, without actual service upon the wife, is a nullity. In Webb *v.* Fulchire, 25 N. C. 485, is laid down the proposition that where a man is cheated out of his money, though it is in playing at a game forbidden by law, he may recover back what he has paid from the person who practised the fraud upon him. The game in this case was "three-card monte," and the learned Judge seems as much puzzled as to how the trick was worked as the simple-minded plaintiff himself. State *v.* Rives, 27 N. C. 297, is a very interesting decision, which holds that while the interest of a railroad company in its right of way can be sold under execution, the corporate franchise is not liable to such sale. In Attorney-General *v.* Guilford, Ib. 315, is discussed a subject which is still sometimes a *vexata questio* in this State, and the Chief-Justice holds therein that the county authorities are not bound to grant license to retail spirituous liquors to every one who proves a good moral character, nor have they, on the other hand, the arbitrary power to refuse at their will all applicants for license, if properly qualified; and further, that the county authorities, having a discretion to a certain extent in granting such licenses, a mandamus will not lie to compel them to grant a license to any particular individual, though he may have been improperly refused a license, the only remedy, if the license is perversely and obstinately denied, being by indictment. *Apropos* of this, counsel for the applicant to retail, in one of the recent cases in this State, observed with much *naïveté* that he did not understand the object of this requirement, and that he did not see why a man needed a good moral character to qualify him to sell intoxicating liquors. Fleming *v.* Burgin, 37 N. C. 584, maintains the proposition that actual notice of an unregistered incumbrance does not affect a subsequent incumbrance or purchase for value. In State *v.* Boyce, 32 N. C. 536, is a very interesting discussion of the right of the owner of slaves to permit them to meet and dance on his premises on Christmas eve and other holidays without being responsible for keeping a disorderly house. He says: "We may let them make the most of their idle hours, and may well make allowances for the noisy outpourings of glad hearts, which Providence bestows as a blessing on corporeal vigor united to a vacant mind . . . There was nothing contrary to morals or law in all that, adding as it did to human enjoyment, without hurt to any one, unless it be that one feels aggrieved that these poor people should for a short space be happy at finding the authority of the master give place to his benignity, and at being freed from care and filled with gladness."

Take him all in all, we have not seen "his like again." By the consensus of the profession he is the greatest judge who has ever sat upon the bench in North Carolina, and those few who may deny him this honor will admit that he has had no superior. In political opinions he was a follower of Jefferson; but this did not prevent his reverence for Chief-Justice Marshall, who was his personal friend, as was also Chancellor Kent. He was succeeded as Judge by Battle (on Battle's second call to the Supreme bench), and as Chief-Justice by Nash, both from his own county of Orange. When he left the Supreme Court bench in 1859, after having been recalled to it, he was succeeded by Judge Manly.

II

Joseph John Daniel was a resident of Halifax County, in which he was born Nov. 13, 1784. He entered the University in 1804, but left after a brief stay, and studied law under Gen. William R. Davie at Halifax. He represented that borough town in the legislature in the years 1807 and 1815, and the county in the same body 1811 and 1812. He was elected a judge of the Superior Court in 1816, to fill the vacancy caused by the resignation of Judge Leonard Henderson. This position he filled with fidelity sixteen years, and at June Term, 1820, of the Supreme Court, sat in a few cases in that court by special commission, as already mentioned in the sketch of Judge Murphey. In 1832, upon the resignation of Judge Hall, he was elected to succeed him upon the Supreme Court bench. He discharged the duties of that post till his death, which took place at Raleigh, Feb. 10, 1848. While in service on the bench he was a member from Halifax of the Constitutional Convention of 1835, in which his colleague, Judge Gaston, was also a member.

Judge Daniel's opinions have always been great favorites with the profession. They are the shortest to be found in our reports, yet they are clear, to the point, and dispose of the whole subject in hand. Wheeler in his History says of him: "He was remarkable for his patience, profound legal knowledge, and general learning, especially in history. His character was one of innocent eccentricity, and if he possessed the 'wisdom of the serpent,' truly, it might well be said, the 'harmlessness of the dove' also belonged to him. The elevation of office and the dignity of position never changed the native simplicity of his character and the unadulterated purity of his republican principles." Upon Judge Daniel's death in 1848, Chief-Justice Ruffin, who had been so intimately associated with him for sixteen years, said of him, "He had a love of learning, an inquiring mind, and a memory uncommonly tenacious; and he had acquired and retained a stock of varied and extensive knowledge, and especially became well versed in the History and Principles of the Law. He was without arrogance or ostentation, even of his learning; he had the most unaffected and charming simplicity and mildness of manners, and no other purpose in office than to 'execute justice and maintain truth.' " But he needs no tongue or pen to praise him. His eulogy was written by his own hand in the judicial opinions which still remain to instruct us. It is not uncommon to be fulsome in speaking of the dead, seeking the favor of the living rather than the cool impartial award of history, and presenting a fancy sketch for which the delineator is "indebted to his imagination for his facts, and to his memory for his wit." Nothing was more foreign to the character of Judge Daniel. He knew himself how to speak truly and to the point, and to stop when he had made himself understood. Like Cromwell, he would have said, "Paint me as I am." He made no pretensions to greatness. He was a strong man and a just judge. He was a good lawyer, and deservedly ranks high up in the legal pantheon.

Unlike Ruffin, he had no spheres of activity off the bench; though possessed of a great memory and an accurate knowledge of history, unlike Murphey, he has left us nothing from his pen except his decisions, and, unlike Gaston, he did not achieve eminence either in politics or literature. He was a lawyer, pure and simple, and among lawyers his fame "must live or bear no life." He is said to have possessed no eloquence as an advocate, but to have made his way at the bar by learning and diligence.

An anecdote often told of him may be pardoned here. At church on one occasion with the Chief-Justice, when the collection plate was approaching, he could find nothing but a five-dollar gold piece in his pocket. "Ruffin," said he, "lend me a quarter." The Chief-Justice did not have it. "Lend me a half or a dollar." A shake of the head was the reply. He slammed the gold piece in the plate, saying in desperation "D—n you, go!"

Judge Daniel's opinions will be found in twenty-one volumes of the Reports, to wit, 14 and 15 N. C., 17 to 30 N. C. inclusive, and 36 to 40 N. C. inclusive, embracing the Law and Equity reports for sixteen years, beginning December Term, 1832. His opinions are of Spartan brevity, usually half a page or less, and very rarely indeed exceeding one page. The following may be turned as fair specimens of his style of thought and expression: State *v.* Stalcup, 23 N. C. 30 and State *v.* Wilson, Ib. 32, as to the requisite averments and proof in indictments for riot, and Hardin *v.* Borders, as to the same in actions for malicious prosecution. In Mitchell *v.* Mitchell, Ib. 257, he construes a will in a fourth of a page; and in Gaither *v.* Teague, 26 N. C. 65, he decides a question as to the admissibility of evidence in less than five lines. Fleming *v.* Straley, 23 N. C. 305, discusses evidence on a question of domicile. State *v.* Fore, Ib. 378, holds that as to indictments, if the sense be clear and the charge sufficiently explicit, nice objections should be disregarded. Ballew *v.* Clark, 24 N. C. 23, is a ruling that a party signing an instrument can plead that he was insane when he did it, and that the old doctrine that a man cannot stultify himself had long been exploded. Rowland *v.* Rowland, Ib. 61, decides that in a civil action against several who have a joint interest, the declaration of one as to a fact within his own knowledge is evidence against all the other defendants also. Copeland *v.* Copeland, 25 N. C. 513, is a decision in half a page that an overseer from whom a slave is retreating had no right to shoot at him to stop him, and that the owner of a slave which is unjustifiably injured while hired out, can recover damages for the injury. Locke *v.* Gibbs, 26 N. C. 42, is a ruling that one may recover damages for a malicious prosecution of his slave. Smith *v.* Low, 27 N. C. 197, holds that the return of a ministerial officer of his acts out of court, unlike the records of the court, is only *prima facie* correct, and not conclusive. Needham *v.* Branson, Ib. 426, decides that where a conveyance of land is made to husband and wife, they do not take as joint tenants or as tenants in common, but by entireties, and on the death of one the entire estate devolves upon the other. Wright *v.* Mooney, 28 N. C. 22, holds that a judgment in one court is a set-off in an action in assumpsit in another court. State *v.* Gherkin, 29 N. C. 206, rules that falsely putting a witness's name to a bond which does not require a subscribing witness does not vitiate the bond, and is not a forgery. Coon *v.* Rice, Ib. 217, construes a case coming under the rule in Shelley's Case. State *v.* Thomas, Ib. 381, holds it to be error in the judge to tell the jury that they must find for one of the parties unless they believe his witness had committed perjury.

Judge Daniel's will is in eight lines. In it "he disposed of a large estate, gave his blessing to his children and his soul to his God." He was ten years at the bar, and thirty-two years consecutively a judge,—sixteen years on the Superior Court and sixteen on the Supreme Court. For eleven years (1833-1844) Ruffin, Daniel, and Gaston sat together on the Supreme Court bench of North Carolina. No State has surpassed that bench in ability and learning. To our own judicial annals that time is what—

"The golden prime of good Haroun al Raschid"

is to Eastern story.

On Jan. 1, 1822, Judge Daniel married Miss Maria B. Stith. He left surviving him one son, William A. Daniel, Esq., of Weldon, and two daughters, through whom he has many descendants; among them Jacob Battle, Esq., of Rocky Mount, one of the ablest young lawyers of eastern North Carolina; the wife of Dr. R. H. Lewis, of Raleigh; and Armistead C. Gordon, of Staunton, Va., author of the beautiful idyl "My boy Kree."

Judge Daniel was succeeded on the bench by Hon. W. H. Battle.

The name of Gaston is one upon which North Carolinians love to linger. A county and two towns, Gastonia and Gaston, bear his name. Chief-Justice Henderson is the only other judge whose popularity has received a like testimony. William Gaston was born in Newbern, N. C., Sept. 19, 1778. His father, Dr. Alexander Gaston, was a native of the North of Ireland, but of Huguenot descent, and a graduate of Edinburgh Medical College. He had been a surgeon in the English army, but resigned and settled in Newbern. During the Revolution he was an ardent patriot, serving both as captain of volunteers, and as surgeon in the army. In August, 1781, when Major Craig advanced towards Newbern, the emboldened tories captured the town. Dr. Gaston, in attempting to escape, pushed hurriedly off in a boat with a companion, the river being close by his house. The tories fired over the heads of his wife and children, who were on the wharf; and he fell mortally wounded. He left a young widow almost without means, and two children,—a son then three years old, the subject of this sketch, and a daughter who in after years became the wife of Chief-Justice John Louis Taylor.

An early anecdote will illustrate the training he received at the hands of his mother. "William," said one of his playmates, "what is the reason *you* are always head, and *I* am always foot of my class?" "If I tell you the reason," replied the seven-year-old boy, "you must keep it a secret, and promise to do as I do. When I take my book to study, I always say a prayer my mother has taught me, that I may be able to learn my lessons." His companion could not remember the words of the prayer; and that evening William was found by his mother behind the door, writing out the prayer for his friend to commit to memory. His mother was a devoted Catholic, and such her distinguished son remained through life.

At thirteen years of age he was sent to Georgetown Catholic College, D. C. whence the Rev. Mr. Plunkett wrote his mother that he was "the best scholar and the most exemplary youth we have in the college." His health suffering from too close application, he was wisely called home for some months of rest. After some months' study under the Rev. Mr. Irving, he was sent to Princeton, where he entered the junior class, and graduated there in 1796 with the highest honor. He said the proudest moment of his life was when he announced this fact to his mother.

On his return to Newbern he studied law with Francis Xavier Martin, a native of France, a leading lawyer, author of Martin's N. C. Reports, and of a history of North Carolina, afterwards appointed by Mr. Jefferson judge in Mississippi Territory, and who was a judge of the Supreme Court of Louisiana thirty-one years, 1815-1846, out-living his distinguished pupil. In 1798 Judge Gaston was admitted to the bar, being then twenty years of age. In 1800 he was elected to the State Senate, and in 1808 Presidential Elector for that district, the electors being then chosen by districts in this State. In 1808, 1809, 1824, 1827, 1828, and 1831 he represented the town of Newbern in the House of Commons, being chosen Speaker of that body in 1808, and afterwards; and in 1800 (as already stated), 1812, 1818, and 1819 he was in the State Senate. He was defeated for Congress in 1810 by William Blackledge, but was elected in 1812, taking his seat in 1813 and again in 1815. He at once took a leading part. Mr. Webster, in reply to an inquiry from a member of Congress from Ohio, "who was the greatest of the great men in the War Congress," said, "The *greatest* man was William Gaston;" adding, with a smile, "I myself came in along after him." With equal magnanimity, Henry Clay, in conversation at Raleigh, said: "I once differed with Gaston, but afterwards found that Gaston was right." Several of his speeches, especially those on the "Loan Bill" and the "Previous Question," are models of parliamentary debate. He was the leader of the

Federal party, and opposed to the Administration. After two terms in Congress he voluntarily returned to his practice. In the State Senate, in 1818, he drafted and introduced the bill which established the Supreme Court of this State. The statute book of North Carolina is full of proofs of his wisdom. His speech on the State Currency in 1828, and in defence of the Constitution in 1831, and in 1827, in opposition to a bill introduced by Frederick Nash (himself afterwards Chief-Justice) to reorganize the Supreme Court, are among his most notable efforts. His most brilliant legislative action was in the State Convention of 1835 (while still on the Supreme Court bench), when he secured the repeal of the constitutional restrictions upon Catholics. He was a superb orator and a most persuasive advocate. His address before the Literary Societies at the University of North Carolina in 1832, and at Princeton in 1834, are models of their kind.

Upon the death of Chief-Justice Henderson, in 1833, Gaston was elected without solicitation or suggestion from himself to the Supreme Court bench, as Associate Justice, Judge Ruffin becoming Chief-Justice. He was then fifty-five years of age, and the senior in years of both his associates,—Ruffin and Daniel. His election was indeed a marked compliment to his personal eminence; for in the fifty years which elapsed between the creation of the Supreme Court in 1818, and its *bouleversement* in the cataclysm of 1868, this was the only instance of the election to that bench of any one who had not previously served upon the Superior Court bench. Indeed, all others were taken directly from that bench except Judge Henderson, and he, after having served many years as a Superior Court judge, had only recently resigned when elected to the Supreme Court on its organization. Gaston had been thirty-five years in full practice at the bar before he was called to the bench; but his opinions are singularly free from that disposition to choose sides which is so often observed in judges who come late to the bench, and who generally are swayed by strong preconceived views on some subjects. In 1835, as already stated, he was a leading member of the Convention of 1835 to amend the Constitution. When called to the bench in 1833, the Constitution contained a provision, the famous thirty-second article, rendering ineligible to office any one who "denied the truth of the Protestant religion." Judge Gaston was a devout and consistent member of the Roman Catholic church. He accepted his election to the bench, and maintained, in a very strong and remarkable letter, that there was no organization, form of faith, or creed which could be called *the* Protestant religion, that no Catholic as such denied any truth held by Protestants, and that, considering the general tenor of the Constitution, it was clear that this provision was not *intended* to disqualify Catholics from office. All possible question on the subject was laid to rest by the amendments to the Constitution made by the Convention of 1835.

In 1840 Judge Gaston was solicited by the then dominant party to accept the post of United States Senator. This was no mere compliment. He could have been elected without a contest. But like Chief-Justice Ruffin, under similar circumstances, he declined the proffered honor. In a letter to Gen. John G. Bynum, October, 1840, he expressed his refusal, and that upon the ground that the duties of the post he then filled were "as important to the public welfare as any services which I would render in the political station to which you invite me."

Judge Gaston's opinions are well rounded, and betray scholarship as well as legal learning. Among those most deserving of notice are State *v.* Will, 18 N. C. 121, which holds that if a slave in self-defence, under circumstances strongly calculated to excite his passions of terror and resentment, kills his overseer or his master, the homicide under such circumstances is not murder, but manslaughter. The opinion is a clear, intelligent discussion of the rights of the slave in such circumstances. The case is further remarkable for the very full and able briefs of counsel (printed in the report of the case) by B. F. Moore, George W. Mordecai, and Attorney-General J. R. J. Daniel. Indeed the brief of Mr. Moore, in this case, first gave him that established reputation which ripened in a few years into the admitted leadership of the North Carolina bar.

In State *v.* Haney, 19 N. C. 390, Judge Gaston lays down the rule, since settled law, that the unsupported testimony of an accomplice, if it produces entire belief in the prisoner's guilt, is sufficient to warrant a conviction, and that the propriety of cautioning the jury against placing too much confidence in testimony of that nature must be left to the discretion of the trial judge. In Thomas *v.* Alexander, 19 N. C. 385, he lays down, what is now also settled law, that on appeal the presumption is in favor of the correctness of the proceedings and judgment below, and that such judgment will be affirmed unless the appellant shows that there was error. In State *v.* Manuel, 20 N. C. 122, he affirms the constitutionality of the act requiring defendants convicted of crime to work out the fine and court costs, and that this is not prohibited by the clause forbidding imprisonment for debt, that while the fine and costs may be collected as a debt by execution, they are also a punishment, and therefore the defendant can be imprisoned if he fails to pay. He also discussed citizenship, naturalization, and alienage. The opinion is a very able and thoughtful one, and presents a fair specimen of his literary style and method of reasoning. Parrott *v.* Hartsfield, 20 N. C. 203, is a short opinion in which he discusses the right of the owner of sheep to kill a sheep-killing dog, though not taken in the act.

In McRae *v.* Lilly, 23 N. C. 118, he settled the practice already once before laid down, and ever since followed in this State, that setting aside a verdict for excessive damages is a matter of discretion in the presiding judge, and not a question of law, and hence the granting or refusal of such motion is not reviewable by the Supreme Court. Clary *v.* Clary, 24 N. C. 78, is a very interesting opinion, holding that a witness who has had opportunities of knowing and observing a person whose sanity is impeached, may not only depose to the facts he knows, but may also give his opinion or belief as to his sanity or insanity.

Judge Gaston died in harness, and like a soldier in the discharge of his duty. Death is impartial. It is Horace who says,—

> "Pallida mors equo pulsat pede
> Pauperum tabernas, regumque turres."

On Jan. 23, 1844, while in attendance upon the court and in his usual health, he was suddenly stricken with apoplexy. By use of suitable remedies he revived, and entered into cheerful conversation with his friends, for he was an engaging conversationalist. He was relating the particulars of a social party at Washington some years before, and was speaking of one who on that occasion avowed himself a free-thinker in religion; "from that day," said Judge Gaston, "I always looked on that man with distrust. I do not say that a free-thinker *may* not scorn to do a mean action, but I dare not trust him. A belief in an all-ruling Providence, who shapes our ends and will reward us according to our deeds, is necessary. We must believe and feel that there is a God *all wise and almighty.*" As he pronounced this last word, he raised himself up to give it emphasis, there was a rush of blood to the brain, his body fell back lifeless, and his spirit stood in the presence of the Master. He thus passed away in the sixty-sixth year of his age.

In the beautiful cemetery at Newbern, a plain, massive monument of white marble stands, with no inscription save the single word "Gaston." There is need of no other. The rest is already known when the living stand in the presence of the ashes of so illustrious a man. Yet his contemporaries in their own behalf, not his, might not inappropriately have handed down to posterity their estimate of his life-work by adding at the base those grand but simple words in which, on the presentation of the resolutions of the bar upon the occasion of his death, Chief-Justice Ruffin in his reply summed up the opinion of the court, of the bar, and of the public: "*We* knew that he was a good man and a great judge." Both houses of the General Assembly passed unanimously resolutions expressing a deep sense of the public loss,—an unusual circumstance. His death was incidentally the occasion of a singular proceeding. The Supreme Court continued in session, though the vacancy was not immediately filled. Upon the receipt below of the certificate of opinion from the Supreme Court, affirming the judgment in a capital case, Judge Pearson, then upon the Superior Court, took judicial cognizance that there were but two judges upon the upper bench when the decision was rendered, and ruled that the action of that court was extra-judicial and invalid except when composed of three judges, and refused to execute the mandate. This action, coming up for review (State *v.* Lane, 26 N. C. 434), it was reversed, the opinion by Chief-Justice Ruffin holding that upon the death of one of the judges of the Supreme Court the two surviving judges have full power and authority to hold the court and exercise all its functions. An exactly similar case happened in South Carolina last year, after the death of Chief-Justice Simpson; and that court came to the same conclusion as ours.

Judge Gaston was in his day one of the most popular men the State has ever known. His popularity, too, was of that solid character eloquently described by Lord Mansfield as that "which follows a man, not that which is run after, but which, sooner or later, never fails to do justice to the pursuit of noble ends by noble means."

One great element of his abiding popularity, in addition to his high integrity and great talents, was his unswerving devotion to his native State. When solicited to accept emolument and fame elsewhere, he always replied: "Providence has placed me here, and 't is my duty, as well as pleasure, to do what I can for my native State." We have seen why he declined a seat in the United States

Senate. In a letter to one of his daughters he said: "The resources of our State lie buried and unknown; when developed, as they must be erelong, she will be raised to a consequence not generally anticipated."

His talents, his character, and his attainments were such that Chief-Justice Marshall was heard more than once to say that he would cheerfully resign if, by so doing, he could secure the appointment of Judge Gaston in his stead. He was so well-rounded a man, so uniformly great, that he did not show his full stature; just as a tall but well-proportioned man does not seem as high as a less symmetrical one of the same height. The sharp contrast of his excellence with that in which he is deficient is needed.

Gaston's goodness, benevolence, and mildness of manner were so attractive that his mental superiority was less noted than it would have been in a man with less to recommend him. Of him it might truly be said,—

> "His life was gentle, and the elements
> So mixed in him, that Nature
> Might stand up and say to all the world,
> 'This was a man.' "

His love of his State found expression in the following poem, which has been adopted by universal consent as our State hymn. It is too well known in North Carolina to be repeated; but as your magazine has a national circulation, a poem from so eminent a Judge may be worthy of being given at length.

The Old North State

Carolina, Carolina, Heaven's blessings attend her;
While we live we will cherish, protect, and defend her.
Though the scorner may sneer at, and witlings defame her,
Our hearts swell with gladness whenever we name her.
  Hurrah! hurrah! the old North State forever.
  Hurrah! hurrah! the good old North State.

Though she envies not others their merited glory,
Say, whose name stands the foremost in liberty's story?
Though too true to herself e'er to crouch to oppression,
Who can yield to just rule a more loyal submission?
  Hurrah, etc.

Plain and artless her sons, but whose doors open faster
At the knock of the stranger, or the tale of disaster?
How like to the rudeness of their dear native mountains
With rich ore in their bosoms, and life in their fountains!
  Hurrah, etc.

And her daughters, the queen of the forest resembling;
So graceful, so constant, yet to gentlest breath trembling;
And true lightwood at heart: let the match be applied them,
How they kindle and flame! Oh, none know but
    who've tried them.
  Hurrah, etc.

Then let all those who love us love the land we live in,
(As happy a region as on this side of Heaven,)
Where Plenty and Freedom, Love and Peace smile before us,
Raise aloud, raise together the heart-thrilling chorus,
  Hurrah! hurrah! the old North State forever.
  Hurrah! hurrah! the good old North State.

The tune, it need hardly be added, is that of Heber's well-known hymn, beginning,—

"When through the torn sail the wild tempest is streaming,
And o'er the dark wave the red lightning is gleaming."

Some one has said, "The style is the man." The following extract from Gaston's address at the University presents the style and the man:—

"Honestly seek to serve your country, for it is glorious to advance the good of your fellow-men, and thus, as far as feeble mortals may, act up to the great example of Him in whose image and likeness you are made. Seek, also, by all honest arts, to win their confidence, but beware how you ever prefer their favor to their service. The highroad of service is indeed laborious, exposed to the rain and sun, the heat and dust; while the by-path of favor has apparently at first much the same direction, and is bordered with flowers and sheltered by trees, 'cooled with fountains and murmuring with waterfalls.' No wonder then that, like the son of Abensina, in Johnson's beautiful Apologue, the young adventurer is tempted to try the happy experiment of uniting pleasure with business, and gaining the rewards of diligence without suffering its fatigues. But once entered upon, the path of favor, though found to decline more and more from its first direction, is pursued through all its deviations, till at length even the thought of return to the road of service is utterly abandoned. To court the fondness of the people is found, or supposed to be, easier than to merit their approbation. Meanly ambitious of public trust without the virtues to deserve it; intent on personal distinction, and having forgotten the ends for which alone it is worth possessing, the miserable being, concentrated all in self, learns to pander to every vulgar prejudice, to advocate every popular error, to chime in with every dominant party, to fawn, flatter, and deceive, and becomes a demagogue. How wretched is that poor being who hangs on the people's favor! All manliness of principle has been lost in this long course of meanness; he dare not use his temporary popularity for any purposes of public good in which there may be a hazard of forfeiting it; and the very eminence to which he is exalted renders but more conspicuous his servility and degradation. However clear the convictions of his judgment, however strong the admonitions of his as yet not thoroughly stifled conscience, not these, not the law of God, nor the rule of right, nor the public good, but the caprice of his constituents, must be his only guide. Having risen by artifice, and conscious of no worth to support him, he is in hourly dread of being supplanted in the favor of the multitude by some more cunning deceiver. And such, sooner or later, is sure to be his fate. At some unlucky moment, when he bears his blushing honors thick upon him (and well may such honors blush), he is jerked from his elevation by some more dexterous demagogue, and falls unpitied, never to rise again."

Surely these are noble words.

Judge Gaston was thrice married: (1) in 1803 to Miss Susan Hay, daughter of John Hay, the eminent lawyer, of Fayetteville; (2) in 1805 to Hannah, daughter of General McClure,—she died in 1813; (3) in 1816 to Miss Worthington, of Georgetown. Through his last two wives he has numerous descendants. A daughter by his second wife was the first wife of Judge Matthias E. Manly, of the Supreme Court of North Carolina. The only child of that union married a son of Rev. Dr. Francis L. Hawks, of New York, and died a few years since, leaving several children. Judge Gaston was thus the brother-in-law of Chief-Justice Taylor, and the father-in-law of Judge Manly. He was succeeded on the bench by Frederick Nash of Orange.

Frederick Nash was born, Feb. 9, 1781, in the old Colonial Palace at Newbern, his father, Abner Nash, being then Governor of the State. He had been elected in December 1779, to succeed

Richard Caswell, who was the first Governor under the republican form of government. Governor Nash was a member of the Continental Congress from 1782 to 1786, and died in the latter year at Philadelphia, while attending Congress. His wife was the widow of the Royal Governor, Arthur Dobbs. His brother, Francis Nash, was mortally wounded at Germantown, Oct. 4, 1777, and is buried at Kulpsville, not far from Philadelphia. The Nash family was prominent among the early colonists of North Carolina.

When Washington visited Newbern on his Southern tour in 1791, Frederick Nash was presented to him as the nephew of General Nash. He took the boy on his knee, and placing his hand on his head, reminded him of his brave and patriotic uncle as a bright exemplar to follow. This the boy never forgot.

Frederick Nash was sent, when quite young, to Williamsboro, to the school of the Rev. Mr. Patillo, a Presbyterian clergyman, under whom Chief-Justice Henderson had also studied. He was prepared for college by Rev. Mr. Irving, of Newbern, who had likewise prepared Judge Gaston; and like him he entered Princeton College, whence he graduated with the second distinction in 1799. In this class were John Forsythe, afterwards Governor of Georgia, Secretary of State under Jackson, etc.; and James C. Johnston of Edenton. Nash studied law, and was admitted to the bar. In 1804, and again in 1805, he represented the town of Newbern in the House of Commons. In 1808 he removed to Hillsboro, and represented the county of Orange in the House 1814 and 1815, and the town of Hillsboro in the same body 1827 and 1828. Down to the Convention of 1835 the elections to the legislature were annual, and six towns were each entitled to a member in the Commons: Halifax, Newbern, Wilmington, Fayetteville, Hillsboro, and Salisbury. In 1807 he was elected a Trustee of the University, then a life position, and was always its warm friend.

In 1815 he introduced a bill in the legislature for the suppression of duelling, and supported it in an able and eloquent speech. On his removal to Hillsboro he purchased the dwelling of his friend and kinsman, Judge Cameron, and resided there till his death.

In 1818 he was elected judge of the Superior Court, and filled the duties of that responsible position till his resignation in 1826. He possessed those qualities which Lord Campbell (himself an eminent judge) has designated as essential to a good judge: "Patience in hearing, evenness of temper, and kindness of heart." He was again elected to the Superior Court bench in 1836, upon the resignation of Judge Norwood. Upon the death of Judge Gaston of the Supreme Court bench, in 1844, he was elected to succeed him, being then in his sixty-fourth year. Upon the resignation of Chief-Justice Ruffin in 1852 he was elected by his associates Chief-Justice. He died at his home in Hillsboro, Dec. 5, 1858, in the 78th year of his age. His opinions show a familiarity with the precedents and a singular chasteness and felicity of expression.

Among his opinions the following may be noted as giving a fair specimen of his style and reasoning: (State *v.* Perry, 44 N. C. 330), as to challenges to jurors, special venire, conduct of the jury, and conduct of a trial in a capital case. In Rives *v.* Guthrie, 46 N. C. 84, it is held in a learned opinion that the word "months" in the Statute of Limitations means *lunar,* not *calendar* months. This, however, has since been changed by statute. In State *v.* Moore, 46 N. C. 276, it is ruled that where, by special Act, the county authorities were forbidden to issue license to retail liquor in the limits of an incorporated town, without the written consent of the town authorities, a license issued without such written consent is void, and will not protect the retailer from an indictment. The same point came up again this year (1892), and was ruled the same way (Hillsboro *v.* Smith, 110 N. C. 417). Clements *v.* Hunt, 46 N. C. 400, holds that declarations of deceased members of a family are competent to prove the date of birth of a member of the family, though it may also be recorded in the family record, the one kind of evidence being of no higher dignity than the other. Miller *v.* Black, 47 N. C. 341, since thrice affirmed, decides that an action may be maintained in the courts of this State, though both plaintiff and defendant are citizens of other States. State *v.* Samuel, 48 N. C. 76, holds that where a husband slays, on the spot, one taken in the act of adultery with his wife, it is manslaughter, not murder. The Georgia Statute makes homicide under such circumstances excusable. It would add to the respect for the law if this were the statute everywhere; for juries will invariably acquit on the ground of emotional insanity or some other pretext. In a recent case in this State where *jury* law and *book* law came in conflict, the jury returned without a verdict, and told the court there was a conflict between the *law* and the *evidence,* and that a verdict was impossible.

In 1856 the legislature laid a general tax on *all salaries.* The question arose whether this tax could apply to judicial salaries in purview of the provision of the Constitution forbidding that they be diminished during the term of office. Chief-Justice Nash at the instance of the court addressed a letter to Hon. Joseph B. Batchelor, the then Attorney-General, stating that the court felt a delicacy in expressing an opinion upon a subject in which the members of the court were interested, and asked his opinion as the highest law officer of the State. The very able reply of the learned Attorney-General is published in the appendix to the 48 N. C. (3 Jon.), and is to the effect that the power to tax salaries is the power to diminish them, and is therefore prohibited by the Constitution. This has ever since been deemed the law in this State.

Judge Nash married in 1803 Miss Mary Kollock at Elizabethtown, N. J. He and his wife were devoted members of the Presbyterian Church. They left several children; among them Henry K. Nash, long a prominent lawyer in Hillsboro, and Misses Sarah and Maria Nash, principals of the famous female school in Hillsboro, to whose excellent training and care so many men are indebted for most excellent wives, whom their husbands deem the best in the State.

Judge Nash spent a long life of honor and usefulness, and dying "left no blot on his name." Truly,

> "The remembrance of the just
> Smells sweet, and blossoms in the dust."

He was succeeded on the bench by Hon. Matthias E. Manly of Craven.

William Horn Battle was born in Edgecombe County, Oct. 1, 1802. Elisha Battle, the founder of the family and a prominent member of the Baptist Church, removed to Edgecombe County, in this State, from Virginia in 1743. He served for many years in the legislature for that county, and was a member of the provincial congress at Halifax in 1776, which framed the State Constitution. Joel Battle, the father of Judge Battle, was an influential and enterprising citizen of the same county, and established the Rocky Mount Mills, which remained till recently in the Battle family. Judge Battle graduated at the State University in 1820, delivering the valedictory, then deemed the prize of the second-best scholar. Among his classmates were the distinguished lawyer B. F. Moore and Bishop Otey; and among his college mates his future associate, Chief-Justice Pearson. He was the eldest of six brothers, all of whom were educated at the University. He read law with Judge Henderson, and was licensed to practice in 1824. In January, 1827, he removed to Louisburg. He had not the qualities to push him early to the front in his profession. He won his way by industry and fidelity. The voters of the county in which he resided were almost unanimous in support of Jackson's administration, while Judge Battle belonged to the opposition. He was little calculated for political life, but he had the courage of his opinions. He was twice defeated for the legislature, but on a third venture he was elected, in 1833, to the House of Commons, and in 1834 he was again elected by an increased majority. After his election three fourths of the voters of the county signed a petition to him to vote for Hon. Bedford Brown for U. S. Senator, who was of the opposite political party, and in deference to the will of the people, upon whose consent our form of government is based, he so voted. He was not misled by these successes, so complimentary to him, and which were due to public confidence in his character, from his true vocation, and after this never again attempted the thorny path of politics.

As early as 1832 Judge Battle published a second edition of 1 Haywood's Reports (now 2 N. C.), annotated with references to subsequent decisions and statutes. This work, manifesting his learning, ability, and patience, gave him at once an established reputation. It was followed by similar annotated reprints of several other volumes of the earlier reports. From 1834 to 1839, in conjunction with T. P. Devereux, he was Reporter to the Supreme Court, and published 4 volumes of Law and 2 of Equity Reports, which are now known as 18 to 22 N. C. Reports. These were the halcyon days of the court; Ruffin, Daniel, and Gaston being then the judges constituting the court. In 1835 he was appointed, in conjunction with Governor Iredell and Judge Nash (afterward Chief-Justice), to revise the statute law of the State. In 1836-1837 the legislature adopted their work, the "Revised Statutes," with small alteration. This work owes much of its excellence to Judge Battle's indefatigable labor and thorough knowledge of the statute law and the decisions.

In 1839, Mr. Devereux having resigned, Judge Battle became sole Reporter; but before he had issued a volume, Judge Toomer having resigned, he was appointed by Governor Dudley to succeed him on the Superior Court bench, and was elected by the legislature when it met later in the same year. His work as sole Reporter is in the first part of 23 and 36 N. C. Reports (1 Ire. and 1 Ire. Eq.). To add to his modest salary as judge, like many of our judges, he found it best to open a law school. For that purpose and to educate his sons he removed in 1843 to Chapel Hill. In 1845 he was elected by the trustees of the university professor of law, but without salary, and opened the law school, which lasted until 1866. A large percentage of the lawyers of the State owe much of their professional attainments to his faithful and careful instruction. All his students remember him with respect and affection. Among his students were three of his successors on the Supreme Court bench,—Davis, Shepherd, and Clark.

Learned, firm, patient, courteous, incorruptible, and impartial, his administration of justice on the Superior Court bench met with an approval which marked him out for promotion. In May, 1848, upon the death of Judge Daniel, he was appointed by Gov. Wm. A. Graham to fill the vacancy upon the Supreme Court bench until the meeting of the ensuing legislature. That body failed to confirm the appointment, and Judge Pearson was elected. The reason given was that there was already a governor, a U. S. Senator, and three judges in the county of Orange where Judge Battle resided. There being, however, a vacancy upon the Superior Court bench, he was immediately elected thereto without opposition, being the choice of both political parties. Members of the legislature without distinction of party united in a letter requesting him to accept the office. Urged thus and by many friends outside of the legislature, he accepted the position, and again entered upon the discharge of the duties of Superior Court judge. In 1852, upon the resignation of Chief-Justice Ruffin, Judge Nash became Chief-Justice, and Judge Battle was elected to the Supreme Court bench by an almost unanimous vote and without distinction of party. He filled the position till 1865, when all the State offices were declared vacant. He was then again elected to the Supreme Court bench, and occupied the post until the new Constitution was adopted in 1868, under which the judges were elected by the people. The State being in the control of the opposite political party, he then returned to the practice at the bar in connection with his sons Kemp P. and Richard H. Battle. In 1876 he was chosen President of the Raleigh National Bank. In 1877 his son, Hon. Kemp P. Battle, having been elected President of the university, Judge Battle returned to Chapel Hill, and was again professor of law.

In 1866 Judge Battle published a Digest of the North Carolina Reports, in three volumes. In the preface to the third volume he says that he "has read over every case ever reported in North

Carolina from the beginning to the end." To these he afterwards added a fourth, bringing the work down to the year 1874, and including the seventieth volume of Reports. In 1872 he was again appointed by the legislature to revise our statutes. Though alone on the commission, and not even given the aid of a clerk, he produced at the end of a year's time the volume known as "Battle's Revisal."

Judge Battle was probably more thoroughly familiar with the case law of North Carolina than any other judge who ever sat on the bench. His opinions were expressed in clear, simple language, without effort at show or effect. He knew the precedents. He eschewed judicial legislation. He had no pet system or ideas to promote. He was eminently a safe judge. In the consultation-room he was invaluable. In more than one instance his dissenting opinions have since been held to be the correct declaration of the law, as notably in his dissenting opinion in State *v.* Barfield, 30 N. C. 344 (at his first term), in which he held, against Ruffin, C. J., and Nash, J., that in a trial for murder, evidence of the character of the deceased as a violent and dangerous man is admissible if there is evidence tending to show that the killing was in self-defence, or where the evidence is wholly circumstantial, and the character of the transaction is in doubt. The view of Judge Battle is now held to be the law in this State (State *v.* Turpin, 77 N. C. 473, and subsequent cases).

His opinions at his first term will be found in 30 N. C., and after his return to the bench in 44 N. C. to 63 N. C. inclusive. Among those that it may be interesting to note are Melvin *v.* Easley, 46 N. C. 387, holding that medical and other scientific books are not admissible in evidence, though *experts* may be asked their opinion and the grounds for it, which may be found in part on such books. In Commissioners of Raleigh *v.* Kane, 47 N. C. 288, it is held that the granting or refusing license to sell liquor, being to a certain extent discretionary with the county authorities (when within their power), their action cannot be reviewed, either by appeal or certiorari. State *v.* Peter Johnson, 48 N. C. 266, enunciates the well-established doctrine, that in trials for murder, if the killing by a deadly weapon is proved, the burden shifts, and is upon the prisoner to show all matters of excuse or mitigation. This was affirmed again by Judge Battle in State *v.* Willis, 63 N. C. 26. In Lane *v.* Railroad, 50 N. C. 25, it is held that where a corporation has been brought into court under a wrong name, the court has power to amend the process by striking out that name and inserting the right one, the defendant being already in court by service upon its officer. State *v.* Glen, 52 N. C. 321, is a leading case, discussing the rights of the public and of riparian owners over unnavigable streams. In State *v.* Williams, 52 N. C. 446, it is held that in trials for murder, where the identity of the body is destroyed by fire or other means, the *corpus delicti* may be proved by presumptive or circumstantial evidence.

In person, Judge Battle was rather below medium size. He was simple in his manners, cordial, and without affectation. Though gentle and quiet in his demeanor, he was firm and fearless in the discharge of duty.

In June, 1825, he married Miss Lucy Martin Plummer, the daughter of Kemp Plummer, a prominent lawyer of Warrenton. He was exceedingly fortunate in his choice of a wife. With her he enjoyed near half a century of a domestic happiness rarely granted to man. They lived to rear eight children to years of maturity. There were two noble sons, whose souls went up to God amid the smoke of battle, fighting for the Confederacy. Among the others are, (1) Hon. Kemp P. Battle, Treasurer of the State, 1866-1868; and from 1877 until his recent resignation President of the University, and now Professor of the newly established Chair of history in that institution. (2) Richard H. Battle, of Raleigh, one of the leading lawyers of North Carolina and President of the State Agricultural Society. He was State Auditor 1864-1865. (3) Dr. W. H. Battle, a prominent physician of Anson County.

For forty years Judge Battle was a communicant of the Protestant Episcopal Church, and for a quarter of a century a member of its diocesan and general conventions. His walk in life and conversation were without reproach.

"The good gray head which all men knew"

was indeed, as it should aways be, a mark for honor. His old age was accompanied by

"Honor, love, obedience, troops of friends."

He died at Chapel Hill, March 14, 1879, in the seventy-seventh year of his age. When the inevitable hour came, he had no preparation to make; but

"Soothed and sustained
By an unfaltering trust, approached his grave
Like one who wraps the drapery of his couch
Around him, and lies down to pleasant slumbers."

When the new Supreme Court was established under the Constitution of 1868, the number of judges was increased to five. Chief-Justice Pearson and Judge Reade of the old Court were retained, and Judge Battle, owing to the change in the political complexion of the State, was succeeded by Judge W. B. Rodman, the two additional judgeships going to Judge Dick and Judge Settle.

The name of Richmond Mumford Pearson, fifth Chief-Justice of North Carolina, is written in legible characters,

"High on the dusty roll the ages keep."

Ascending the bench at thirty-one years of age, his judicial career covered nearly forty-two years of unbroken service—twelve years on the Superior Court bench, and nearly thirty on the Supreme Court, of his native State, and of these last over nineteen years as Chief-Justice. He had ability, industry, and time. The net result was a great judge, of which his State and his profession have cause to be proud. He was the equal of Ruffin, if not his superior, as a common law lawyer. He had probably more originality, and, as far as he went, was as accurate. He only fell behind Ruffin in his thorough grasp of the great principles which are applied in the administration of Equity. To the casual reader Ruffin seemed a very remarkable thinker. Those who will read the cases cited in his opinions will increase their admiration for his learning at the expense of his originality. In this he was the greater judge. Ruffin was made by his labor, and labored to the last, as the sunflower

"Turns on her god when he sets
The same look she turned when he rose."

But with Pearson, towards the last, as with Chief-Justice Henderson, reading became irksome. So long accustomed to pronounce the law, his later opinions are often rather his conclusions than a statement of the reasons by which they were reached. Few will deny Ruffin's rank as our greatest judge. None will deny Pearson's claim to the second place, except those who claim for him the first.

Judge Pearson was born June 28, 1805, in Rowan County, N. C. His grandfather, Richmond Pearson, was a native of Dinwiddie County, Va., who removed to this State, and settled in the forks of the Yadkin. He was an officer of the Revolutionary War, and was captain of a company at Cowan's Ford when Gen. Wm. Lee Davidson was killed. Among his children by his first wife were Gen. Jesse A. Pearson, who commanded a regiment in Gen. Joseph Graham's N. C. Brigade sent against the Creeks in 1814; Hon. Joseph Pearson, Member of Congress 1809-15; and a daughter who married Judge John Stokes, United States District Judge for North Carolina; and among his children by his second wife was the subject of this sketch. His mother, Miss Mumford, was the daughter of an ex-officer of the British navy. She was married twice before she was nineteen years of age. Colonel Pearson was her second husband.

Judge Pearson's early education was under John Mushat at Statesville and at Washington City, where the expenses of his education were defrayed by his half-brother, Hon. Joseph Pearson; his father, an enterprising merchant and planter, having failed in business in 1812. He graduated at the University of North Carolina in 1823, at the age of eighteen, with the highest honors in his class. Among his classmates were Daniel W. Courts, and Judge Robert B. Gilliam; and among his college mates, Gov. Wm. A. Graham, Judge John Bragg of Alabama, Thomas Dews, Judge Augustus Moore, John W. Norwood, David Outlaw, Wm. J. Bingham, Ralph Gorrell, Gov. Henry T. Clark, Dan'l M. Barringer, Abraham Rencher, Judge Anderson Mitchell, Attorney-General J. R. J. Daniel, A. O. P. Nicholson and Bishop Otey of Tennessee, B. F. Moore, and his own future associates on the Supreme Court, Judges W. H. Battle and M. E. Manly. He studied law under Chief-Justice Henderson, and received his license in 1826. He began practice at Salisbury, and his rise was at once rapid and marked. For four years (1829-32) he represented Rowan in the House of Commons, the Senator from the county at that time being Judge David F. Caldwell. In 1835 he was a candidate for Congress against Hon. Abraham Rencher and Hon. Burton Craige, but was defeated by Mr. Rencher. In 1836 he was elected Judge of the Superior Courts, T. P. Devereux being his competitor, and rode the circuits of the State till December, 1848, when he was elected to the Supreme Court, as heretofore stated, over Judge Battle, who had been appointed by the Governor to fill the vacancy caused by the death of Judge Daniel. On the death of Chief-Justice Nash, in 1858, he was elected by his associates, Judges Battle and Ruffin (who were both on the bench for a second time), Chief-Justice. During the war he took a very bold stand in maintaining the writ of Habeas Corpus. He was a candidate for the Constitutional Convention of 1865, but was beaten by Mr. Haynes. When all civil offices were declared vacant that year, he was re-elected to the Supreme Court by the legislature, and served till the Constitution of 1868, when, all offices being again vacated, he was elected Chief-Justice by the people. He was nominated by both political parties, and of course elected without opposition.

In 1870, Governor Holden having declared martial law in certain counties, many leading men were imprisoned by military authority,—the State militia under Kirk. Application for a writ of Habeas Corpus was made to Judge Pearson. Obedience to the writ issued by him was refused by the military. Owing to his attitude as to this matter during the war, high hopes were entertained that he would enforce the efficacy of the great writ of right. After hearing argument (Ex parte Moore, 64 N. C. 802), however, he decided that he could not direct its execution in opposition to the will of the Governor, without danger of civil war, and declared the "judiciary exhausted." This is not the place to discuss a question on which so much has been said, and which is as yet still viewed as much from the political standpoint as the legal one. It is enough to say that upon his decision being announced, a wave of disappointment swept over the State, like that which a nation feels, when one who

> "Might have lighted up and led his age
> Falls back in night."

The prisoners were afterwards released upon a Habeas Corpus issued by Judge Brooks of the United States Court, whose process the officer did not dare to disregard. Judge Pearson has placed his defence, and the concurrence in and approval of his course by his brethren of the bench, on record (65 N. C. 349). Governor Holden was afterwards impeached and removed from office. Chief-Justice Pearson under the Constitution presided at the Impeachment trial. Whatever feeling there was against the Chief-Justice at the time was largely kept under by the influence of those who had studied law under him. They were numerous and influential, and to a man devoted to him. And the public at large, however much they differed as to the propriety of his course at this juncture, are disposed, as a magnanimous people, to forget it, and remember only his excellence. With them

> "Fresh stands the glory of his prime;
> The later trace is dim."

These sketches are not intended as eulogies, but as history. Though not assuming to sit in judgment upon a matter which is yet debated, still it is proper to notice the event, and to say that on this occasion of his life, whether his action was right or wrong, he did not receive the popular approval which so signally and generally marked his judicial career. In January, 1878, on his way to Raleigh to open the spring term of the court, while crossing the Yadkin River in a buggy, he was stricken with paralysis, and died at Winston, Jan. 5, 1878, in the seventy-third year of his age.

His career on the Supreme Court is the longest in our annals, nearly thirty years; and his opinions are so numerous we can only refer briefly to a few of them. They are usually as clear as a bell, and evince a strong personality in the writer. Wiswall *v.* Brinson, 32 N. C. 554, is an interesting opinion which holds (Ruffin, C. J., dissenting) that where one is injured by the negligence of a contractor who undertakes to remove a building across the street, the owner of the building is answerable in damages. Mills *v.* Williams, 33 N. C. 558, decides that the legislature has the same power to repeal an act establishing a county as it has to create or divide a county. Leggett *v.* Bullock, 44 N. C. 283, rules that as between the parties a mortgage is valid without resignation. Capehart *v.* Mahoon, 45 N. C. 30, discusses the difference between common and special injunctions. State *v.* McIntire, 46 N. C. 1, holds that if it appears from the record and the face of the pardon that the Governor was misinformed, the courts will hold the pardon void. The ruling in Thompson *v.* Thompson, 46 N. C. 430, is that the widow is entitled to dower in land covenanted to be conveyed to her husband. State *v.* Haywood, 48 N. C. 399, is authority that the omission to discharge any duty imposed by law, which concerns the public, is indictable. In Shaw *v.* Moore, 49 N. C. 25, it is held that one who believes in a Supreme Being who will punish sin in this world, though not in a world to come, is a competent witness. Ashe *v.* DeRossett, 50 N. C. 299, is upon the difference between remote and proximate cause in an action for damages. State *v.* Smith, 53 N. C. 132, explodes the old maxim, "Falsum in uno, falsum in omnibus." Morse *v.* Nixon, 51 N. C. 293, learnedly discusses the right to kill a "chicken-eating hog." Melvin *v.* Easley, 52 N. C. 356, is an interesting discussion, each of the judges filing opinions, as to the validity of sales made on Sunday. Cotton *v.* Ellis, 52 N. C. 545, holds that a *mandamus* will issue to the Governor to require him to do an act merely ministerial. After war became flagrant there were many cases of parties seeking to be discharged from alleged illegal detention in the army by Habeas Corpus. In all these cases Judge Pearson was a strenuous supporter of the right of the courts to examine into the legality of such detention. He held that the writ was not suspended by the emergency of the times. The cases can be examined by those who will turn to them. In re Graham, 53 N. C. 416; In re Bryan, 60 N. C. 1; Gatlin *v.* Walton, Ib. 325; In re Roseman, Ib. 368. Davidson College *v.* Chambers, 56 N. C. 253, is the counterpart of the recent great suit in which Cornell University was a party; and the court here also decided that the college could only take so much of a legacy as added to the property it already held would not be in excess of the limit specified in its charter.

In re Martin, 60 N. C. 153, is an opinion given at the request of the Governor as to his right to declare an office vacant and fill it by appointment. In re Hughes, 61 N. C. 57, and Cooke *v.* Cooke, Ib. 582, are discussions of the legal status of the State as it was left by the results of the war.

State *v.* Farrow, 61 N. C. 161, is short, but entirely in Pearson's peculiar style. It says enough and in very few words. State *v.* Haywood, 61 N. C. 376, establishes the test upon the trial of an issue of insanity. After the Convention and legislature of 1868, there were large issues of State bonds which were assailed as fraudulent and illegal. The matter was often before the courts. It is discussed by Pearson in Galloway *v.* R. R., 63 N. C. 147, and other cases. Numerous cases also arose as to the validity of acts of State and county authorities during the war, especially as to the validity of bonds issued by a county to provide its citizens with salt, etc. These were held void on the ground that they were issued to provide means to avoid the results of the federal blockade, and therefore in aid of the Confederacy. Leak *v.* Comm'rs, 64 N. C. 132.

In R. R. *v.* Reid, 64 N. C. 155 and 226, the court held invalid an alleged exemption of certain R. R. corporations from taxes. On appeal to the United States Supreme Court this was overruled; but the present year a similar question has been raised, and the exemption, so far as drawn in question, again ruled invalid, but upon a different ground entirely (Alsbrook *v.* R. R., 110 N. C. 137), and an appeal to the United States Supreme Court has again been taken.

On page 785, et seq., of the 64 N. C. are the opinions of C. J.

Pearson and the other judges as to the legislative term of office, which opinion was rendered in consequence of a resolution of the General Assembly requesting it. Kane *v.* Haywood, 66 N. C. 1, is a discussion of the power of the court to disbar an attorney who has embezzled the money of his client.

The Constitution of 1868 introduced the Homestead provision in this State and the reformed Code of Civil Procedure. Both have given rise to numerous decisions; but they cannot be noticed here, except the ruling that the homestead was valid against action for *torts* in Dellinger v. Tweed, 66 N. C. 206 (Pearson and Rodman dissenting). The consequence has been the passage of many statutes making indictable acts which were previously punishable only on the civil side of the docket by actions for damages. State *v.* Jefferson, 66 N. C. 309, holds that the judge cannot discharge a jury by telegraphing the clerk to do so; and in State *v.* Branch, 68 N. C. 186, it is held that the judge cannot bring the Grand Jury into open court and examine witnesses before it there. Crummen *v.* Bennet, 68 N. C. 494, holds that the fraudulent conveyance of a homestead does not forfeit the owner's right to claim it against creditors. In Green *v.* Green, 69 N. C. 294, Pearson, C. J., says: "We take this notice of the brief of Mr. B——, out of respect for the learned counsel, and with the hope that it will be an admonition to counsel not to overlook the facts of the case in order to present 'a nice point of law.' " Cloud *v.* Wilson, 72 N. C. 155, is a construction of the Constitution as to the judicial tenure of office. State *v.* Neely, 74 N. C. 425, is an indictment for an assault with intent to commit rape, and is known as the "chicken-cock" case, from the learned discussion between the Chief-Justice and Judge Rodman as to that fowl. The dissenting opinion, however, has since been held correct in State *v.* Massey, 86 N. C. 658.

The opinions of Chief-Justice Pearson will be found in forty-seven volumes, from 31 N. C. to 77 N. C. inclusive. They represent a vast amount of labor and thought, much of which is of permanent value.

Many characteristic anecdotes are related of him. One only is here given. Some one when he was a young man asked him why he allowed the Bishop to confirm him, intimating that he thought the future Chief-Justice was not exactly prepared. "Well," said Pearson, "when I was baptized, my sponsors stood surety for me. I thought I ought to surrender myself in discharge of my bail." He was not an idolator of other men's thought, and did not hesitate to overrule a precedent if he thought it wrong or in the progress of events had become an anachronism. He would say, "You can't make an omelet without smashing an egg, nor clear a road through a forest without cutting down a tree." He was idolized by his students and reverenced by the bar. He had his foibles, but "not one that came near his heart." Before the war he was a Whig in politics, and after 1868 a Republican. He used many original expressions. Among them, for instance, in a burglary case, speaking of a chimney which was low and easy of entrance, he said "a traveling dog or an enterprising old sow" might have easily entered the house, and therefore no one ought to be held guilty of burglary for entering (State *v.* Willis, 52 N. C. 192). He spoke of the repartee and rejoinder of counsel between themselves as "crossfiring with small shot." His familiar and often quoted expression that a case was "on all fours" with another means that it is *in consimili casu.* Then there is his ruling (since overruled), that a fraudulent debt embraced in a deed of assignment to secure creditors renders the whole void, "as one rotten egg spoils an omelet" (Palmer *v.* Giles, 58 N. C. 75.) Numerous others of his homely and vigorous expressions might be collected, and would be entertaining reading if there was space for them. He was not eloquent in words or imagery, but the clearness and precision with which he expressed himself, backed frequently by homely but forcible turns of expression, gave his opinions a vigor and a charm which are often lacking in more carefully prepared productions. He discharged his duty conscientiously, and every term he went through the entire docket and gave every litigant a hearing. He was a patient, attentive, and *understanding* listener. He saw through a case quickly on the argument, and as it were by intuition.

In 1868 a number of leading members of the bar signed a "Protest" which resulted in several of the signers being attached for contempt. The proceedings will be found in Ex parte Moore, 63 N. C. 397. It is only referred to here as a part of the history of the times, and as the sole occasion in the history of the State when there has been antagonism between the bench and the bar. Happily the feeling then aroused was of very short duration. Five of the "protestants" have since sat on the Supreme Court bench themselves: two were ex-Governors, three have since been Governors of the State, and two United States Senators.

In 1831 he located in Mocksville, and in 1832 married the daughter of United States Senator John Williams of Tennessee, and niece of Hugh L. White, also a Senator from that State, and

Whig candidate for the Presidency in 1836. By her he had ten children, three of whom survived him.

One of them is Richmond Pearson, Esq., of Asheville, one of the most prominent and wealthiest men of western North Carolina; and one of his daughters was the first wife of the late Governor Fowle. In 1847 he removed to Richmond Hill in Surry County, where he lived till his death, and maintained the famous law school at which so many of the lawyers of North Carolina were educated; among them three of his future associates, Settle, Bynum, and Faircloth, besides Avery and Ruffin, who afterwards came on the court. He stated that he had taught over a thousand law students in his life. His first wife having been several years dead, in 1859 he married Mrs. Mary Bynum, the widow of Gen. Jno. Gray Bynum, and daughter of Charles McDowell of Morganton. There was no issue of this marriage; but Mrs. Pearson's son by her first marriage, Hon. Jno. Gray Bynum, is one of the present Judges of the Superior Court.

Chief-Justice Pearson was succeeded by Hon. W. N. H. Smith, who was appointed Chief-Justice by Governor Vance.

Matthias E. Manly is the last of the judges who ascended the bench in *ante bellum* days. He was born in Chatham County, N. C., 13 April, 1800, and was a younger brother of Gov. Charles Manly and of the Rev. Dr. Basil Manly. He graduated at the University in 1824, in the same class with Gov. Wm. A. Graham, Judge Augustus Moore, David Outlaw, and Thomas Dews. He was for a while tutor of mathematics in the University. He studied law under Governor Manly, and located in Newbern. He was elected in 1834 and 1835 to the House of Commons from that town, being its last member, as borough representation was abolished by the Convention of 1835. He was elected in 1840 Judge of the Superior Court, in the place of Judge Edward Hall, who had been appointed by the Governor to fill the vacancy by the resignation of Judge R. M. Saunders. The duties of this post he discharged with fidelity for nineteen years, until December, 1859, when he was elected to the Supreme Court to fill the vacancy caused by the second retirement of Judge Ruffin. He served upon that bench till the offices of the State were declared vacant in 1865, when Judge E. G. Reade was elected to succeed him. Judge Manly was Speaker of the State Senate in 1866, and was elected by that legislature to the United States Senate jointly with Governor Graham, but they were not allowed to take their seats. He then resumed practice at Newbern. where he remained till his death.

For a quarter of a century—nineteen years on the Superior Court bench and six years on the Supreme Court—he rendered his State faithful judicial service. His stay on the Supreme Court was mostly during the war, when there was not much litigation. His opinions will be found in five volumes; *i. e.* 52, 53, 58, 59, & 60 N. C. Among them may be noted State *v.* Bandon, 53 N. C. 463, in which he discusses insanity as a defence for crime. He also filed an opinion in Melvin *v.* Easley, 52 N. C. 356, in which the judges differed among themselves as to the validity of a sale upon Sunday. The Habeas Corpus cases during the war have already been cited in the sketch of Chief-Justice Pearson. As a proof of Judge Manly's impartiality, it may be noted that his first four opinions were in appeals in cases tried by himself while on the Superior Court bench. In these he reversed himself in two cases and affirmed two. (52 N. C. 12, 14, 16, 19.)

After his retirement from the bench, like Ruffin, Badger, and Devereux, he presided as one of the magistrates over the county court until that court was abolished in 1868.

He died at Newbern, 9 July, 1881, in the eighty-second year of his age. His first wife was the daughter of Judge Gaston. After her death he married Miss Simpson. He left one child by his first wife, and several children by his second. Among the latter are Capt. Matt Manly, for years Mayor and Postmaster of Newbern, and Clement Manly, the popular and rising lawyer of Winston, who bids fair to add to the hereditary honors of a family which has already given Gaston and the two Manlys to the State.

Judge Manly was a sound and well-read lawyer. He possessed the sincere regard and the entire confidence of the people of North Carolina, and

"Bore without abuse the grand old name of gentleman."

Like Judge Gaston, he was a member of the Roman Catholic Church. He was succeeded, as has been stated, by Judge Edwin G. Reade.

III.

Edwin Godwin Reade was born at Mt. Tirzah, Person Co., N. C., Nov. 13, 1812. His father, Robert R. Reade, died when the subject of this sketch was very young, leaving a widow and three young sons with small means. In early life he aided to support the family by work on the farm, in the carriage and blacksmith shop, and in the tanyard. At eighteen years of age he started out to procure an education. As soon as he had made sufficient progress he entered the Academy of Rev. Alex. Wilson, and paid for his own preparation for college by teaching the younger boys the rudiments he had himself so recently learned; but instead of entering college he read law in 1833 under himself at home by studying the law books which a retired lawyer kindly loaned him. He received license to practise in 1835. Previous to that, at the June term of the court, when, according to the custom of the times, the candidates announced themselves, he astonished every one by declaring himself a Whig candidate for the legislature, and in a well-prepared speech arraigned the administration of President Jackson. This was certainly bold, as at the last election there had been but eleven anti-Jackson votes cast in the county. He made such an effective canvass that he was beaten by only one hundred votes. He at once attained prominence, and his rise at the bar was rapid. In 1855 he was nominated without solicitation Whig candidate for Congress against Hon. John Kerr, one of the finest orators in the State, and after a brilliant canvass was elected. He declined to be a candidate for re-election. In 1863 he was appointed by Governor Vance Confederate States Senator, and at the expiration of the appointment he was in the same year (1863) elected Judge of the Superior Court. When all offices were declared vacant in 1865, he was re-appointed by the Governor provisionally, and served as such till elected by the legislature Judge of the Supreme Court, to succeed Judge Manly. In 1866 and again in 1867 he was elected Grand Master of Masons. In 1868, when, by the terms of the new Constitution, the judges were to be chosen by the people, Judge Reade, like Chief-Justice Pearson, was nominated by both the Democratic and Republican parties, and was elected without opposition. He filled the duties of that office till the expiration of his term, Jan. 1, 1879. He was then elected President of the Raleigh National Bank, which was somewhat embarrassed. Like Chief-Justice Ruffin under similar circumstances, he speedily redeemed the credit of the bank. He remains to-day its efficient head. He was chosen almost unanimously a delegate to the State Convention of 1865, and was elected its President by acclamation. This was the Convention called to readjust our relations with the Federal Government. On taking the chair Judge Reade made a memorable address beginning:

"We are going home," which attracted wide attention. With the exception of one term in Congress, Judge Reade has never taken an active part in politics. On Mr. Lincoln's election Hon. Jno. A. Gilmer, then in Congress from North Carolina, wrote to Judge Reade at the instance of Mr. Seward, to know whether he would accept a seat in the Cabinet. This he declined, but strongly urged Mr. Gilmer to accept.

It is said of him when in his prime that in the history of the State he never had his superior as an advocate before a jury. He speaks with such logic and simplicity as to give eloquence and fervor to his speeches, which persuade and convince. His methods at the bar are fitly described in the following extract from his address before the State Bar Association since his retirement from the bench, in which, after speaking of his frequently sitting up all night to prepare a case for trial, and his contempt for counsel who pleaded lack of preparation, and his indulgence to the opposite side before trial whenever not to the prejudice of his own client, he says: "My practice was to allow a brother to supply defects, correct errors, and do almost anything he desired to do *in fixing up his case before trial;* but when the trial commenced and swords were drawn, I threw away the scabbard and *fought for a funeral.*" He was a caustic and trenchant writer. Many of his articles and addresses have been published in pamphlet form, and merit preservation by being collected and published as a volume.

He sat on the Supreme bench thirteen years. His opinions are usually short, always terse and clear. They are to be found in the nineteen volumes from 61 N. C. to 79 N. C. inclusive. Among his opinions may be noted: Wood *v.* Sawyer, 61 N. C. 251, the famous Johnston Will case in which the ablest counsel summoned from all parts of the State appeared, and in which was involved the validity of the will of James C. Johnston, disposing of the largest estate in North Carolina. The case was tried below by Chief-Justice Merrimon, then upon the Superior Court bench, and the opinion affirming the judgment on appeal is by Judge Reade. The issue was the sanity of the testator. Graham, Bragg, Vance, and Eaton appeared for the caveators; and Moore, Smith, Heath, Gilliam, Conigland, Phillips, and Battle *contra.* Such an array of legal talents was never before or since, in the history of this State, assembled in one case. In the well-known cases of Jacobs *v.* Smallwood, 63 N. C. 112, Hill *v.* Kesler, 63 N. C. 437, and others, he held that the Homestead exemption was valid against debts created prior to the adoption of the Homestead law. In one of these cases (Jacobs *v.* Smallwood), he says that the homestead is secure to the owner against all comers, "from turret to foundation stone." This ruling was afterwards reversed, however, by the United States Supreme Court in Edwards *v.* Kearsey, 96 U. S. 595. In Sutton *v.* Askew, 66 N. C. 172, it is held that the act restoring the common law right of dower does not apply to land acquired prior to the passage of the act. People *v.* McKee, 68 N. C. 429, decides that the Governor, and not the legislature, has the power of appointment to office. State *v.* Jones, 69 N. C. 16, rules that the court has no power to grant a rehearing in a criminal case. Green *v.* Castlebury, 70 N. C. 20, settled the practice as to trials by referees. State *v.* Parrott, 71 N. C. 311, held that any one has a right to tear down an obstruction (here a railroad bridge) to the free navigation of a river. State *v.* Elwood, 73 N. C. 189, holds that in trials for murder when the killing is proven or admitted, malice being implied, if the defendant fails to show any matter of excuse or mitigation, it is not error to tell the jury that if they believe the evidence it is their duty to find the defendant guilty of murder. People *v.* Staton, 73 N. C. 546, decides that the clerk of a court appointed by a *de facto* judge, who is himself afterwards ousted by the courts, has a superior title to one appointed by the *de jure* judge after judgment in his favor and entrance into office under it. In Lee *v.* Dunn, 73 N. C. 595, it is held that a requirement that a sheriff shall produce a receipt for taxes before induction into office for a second term is constitutional, and imposes no additional qualification for office. Grady *v.* Comm'rs, 74 N. C. 101, held that the creation and alteration of townships was left with the legislature. State *v.* Miller, 75 N. C. 70, discusses the statute of this State forbidding the judges of the trial courts from limiting counsel as to the length of their speeches.[1] In State *v.*

[1] From the remotest time and in all countries one of the recognized duties of the judge has been to economize the time of the courts in all proper respects including a due supervision of the length of argument by counsel. Iowa and North Carolina are the only States which have departed from this rule by statutes which forbid the trial judge from limiting either the number or length of speeches. In Iowa a legal journal says (possibly jocularly) that when counsel begin the argument, the judge goes off to a game of billiards. It may be doubted if the innovation has been of any good effect in North Carolina; for judges have never been prone to restrict argument unduly, while the existence of the power and duty, in proper cases, to do so prevented abuse. The statute has been thought by some to lengthen materially the terms and expense of our courts without corresponding benefit. It is certain that there is now greater opportunity for abuse, as the lawyer is not responsible to the public for the conduct of the court as the judge was. The statute, however, does not extend to the Supreme Court, which is protected by the Constitution from legislative interference.

Overton, 77 N. C. 485, it is held that a defendant in a criminal action has no constitutional right to be present in the Supreme Court on the argument of his appeal. State *v.* Hoskins, 77 N. C. 530, decides that a revenue officer indicted for an offence committed under color of his office has a right to remove the action into the Federal court. Perry *v.* Shepherd, 78 N. C. 83, discusses the writ of Prohibition. State *v.* Driver, 78 N. C. 423, discusses "excessive punishment," and is a case that once attracted considerable attention. Holiday *v.* McMillan, 79 N. C. 315, considers the separate estates of married women. In a "Note to the Profession," 68 N. C. 133, Judge Reade recommends sending up on appeal only so much of the record as is really necessary, and Pearson, C. J., does the same in a note on page 166 of the same volume.

Judge Reade's first wife was Miss Emily Moore, of the family of General Moore (of Revolutionary fame) and of Bishop Moore. She died in 1871, and he subsequently married Mrs. Mary E. Parmelee, widow of Benjamin J. Parmelee, of Washington, N. C. Judge Reade has no children by either marriage. He is a consistent member of the Presbyterian church, which he joined early in life, and of which he has been a ruling elder more than thirty-five years. He is charitable and unostentatious. He has risen by his own exertions, and by dint of talent and a determination to succeed.

The bench elected to go into office at the end of Judge Reade's term was Democratic, and reduced by constitutional amendment to three in number. He was succeeded by Judge Thomas S. Ashe.

William Blount Rodman was born at Washington, N. C., June 29, 1817. The founder of the Rodman family was John Rodman, a Quaker, who went from Ireland to Barbadoes in 1686. His sons emigrated to Rhode Island. Judge Rodman's father was a native of New York. He removed about 1800 to this State, and married a daughter of John Gray Blount, to whose care Judge Rodman was left by the early death of both his parents. He graduated at the University with the first honors in 1836. He read law with Judge Gaston, and was licensed to practise in 1838. He soon acquired a large practice. Among numerous important cases in which he was of counsel, he appeared for the defendant in the famous trial of Geo. W. Carrowan for murder. He entered the war as captain of a company, and was in the battle of Newbern, 14 March, 1862, and went with Branch's Brigade to Virginia as quartermaster. He was soon appointed, by President Davis, presiding officer of a military court, with the rank of colonel. He served in this capacity till the close of the war. His considerable estate was almost entirely destroyed by the results of the great civil conflict, and he began life anew.

He was elected to the Convention of 1868. Many of the most important provisions of the Constitution adopted by it are due to his pen or his active support. To him is especially due the credit of the provision that the tax on $300 of property shall never exceed the tax on the polls. The object of this clause, known as the "equation of taxation" clause, is apparent, and originated with him. It was not in any other State Constitution. Messrs. Rodman, Tourgee, and Victor Barringer were the Commissioners who prepared and reported to the legislature our present Code of Civil Procedure. Judge Rodman also prepared a Code of Criminal Law and Procedure. Unfortunately this latter was not adopted. He also drafted the Landlord and Tenant Act, the Act concerning Marriages, and the Drainage of Swamplands Act, and many others. In 1868 he was elected by the people a Justice of the new Supreme Court. His opinions will be found in seventeen volumes, 63 N. C. to 79 N. C. inclusive. The judicial term of office is eight years, but it was held (Loftin *v.* Sowers, 65 N. C. 251, and opinion 64 N. C. 785) that the term of the judges first elected ran for eight years after the next general election, which was two years after the adoption of the Constitution. The effect was to make the term of the judges first elected ten years. Judge Rodman served the full term of ten years, which expired Jan. 1, 1879. He and Judge Reade were the only two of the five judges elected in 1868 who served till the end of their terms.

Judge Rodman was one of the best read men who have sat upon our Supreme Court. He wrote a large number of most important opinions while on the bench. These are too numerous to be all referred to. As specimens of his style and modes of thought, the following may be noted: Robbins ex parte, 63 N. C. 309, as to the law of contempt. It is there held that the court can tax the costs of a case against counsel who has been guilty of gross negligence. Hyman *v.* Devereux, 63 N. C. 624, decides that if a bond secured by mortgage be renewed, the new bond retains the same security. Norfleet *v.* Cromwell, 64 N. C. 1, is an instructive opinion upon covenants running with the land. McConnell *v.* McConnell, 64 N. C. 342, gives the history of the doctrine of color of title in North Carolina. Simmons *v.* Wilson, 66 N. C. 336, denies the right of county commissioners to levy a tax exceeding double the State tax, except for a special purpose and when authorized by the legislature. Pullen *v.* Comm'rs, 66 N. C. 361, holds the right of taxation is unlimited, except as prescribed by the Constitution. In Turner *v.* R. R., 70 N. C. 1, the decision is that when a free pass for life is given to one by vote of the stockholders, the pass is a mere license which the company may revoke at their pleasure. Pippen *v.* Wesson, 74 N. C. 437, holds that a married woman has no power to contract a debt, or enter into an executory contract, even with the written consent of her husband, unless her separate estate is charged with it, either expressly or impliedly, by its being for her benefit. London *v.* Headen, 76 N. C. 72, is an unusual case, not likely to occur often, since it enforces the collection of a penalty against a party for refusing an office. Warlick *v.* White, 76 N. C. 172, is as to the legitimacy of children born in wedlock, and the right to exhibit the child to the jury. Branch *v.* R. R., 77 N. C. 347, is an instructive opinion upon the exercise of the police power of the State over common carriers, and the mode of computing time in penal statutes. In Miller *v.* Miller, 78 N. C. 102, an action for divorce, his opinion received at the time some adverse criticism, caused probably even more by the tone of the opinion than by the conclusion he reached. In London *v.* Wilmington, 78 N. C. 109, and Gatlin *v.* Tarboro, Ib. 119, is discussed the matter of town taxation. In Oldham *v.* Kerchner, 79 N. C. 106, and Lewis *v.* Rountree, Ib. 122, very full consideration is given the rules as to the measure of damages. State *v.* Swepson, 79 N. C. 632, holds that a verdict of not guilty procured by the fraud or trick of the defendant is a nullity, and the defendant can again be put on trial for the same offence.

Judge Rodman has always been a student. His opinions are valuable and instructive. He spent the greater part of a long life—

> "Mastering the lawless science of our law,
> That codeless myriad of precedent,
> That wilderness of single instances."

The profession and the public are indebted to him for his valuable aid in introducing the reformed system of practice and for many useful statutes. He still lives at Washington, N. C., and practises law in partnership with his son.

In 1858 he married Camilla, daughter of Wiley Croom of Alabama. She died in 1887, leaving six children, one of whom, Capt. W. B. Rodman, Jr., is a prominent lawyer of Washington, N. C.

The Democratic party in 1878 having elected its nominees for the bench, Judge Rodman retired at the end of his term, Jan. 1, 1879, and was succeeded by John H. Dillard.

Robert Paine Dick was born at Greensboro, N. C., Oct. 5, 1823. His father, Hon. John M. Dick, was Judge of the Superior Court nearly thirty years, from 1832 till his death, in October, 1861.

Judge Robert P. Dick graduated at the University of North Carolina in 1843 with distinction. He read law with his father, and was admitted to the bar in 1845. He was United States District Attorney for North Carolina from 1853 till the acceptance of his resignation in April, 1861. He was a candidate for elector on the Douglas ticket in 1860. He was a member of the State Convention of 1861, and signed the Ordinance of Secession. He was State Senator from Guilford, 1864-65. In May, 1865, he was appointed by President Johnson United States District Judge for North Carolina, but resigned in two months and before qualifying, being unable to take the "iron-clad" oath. In March, 1867, he was a member of the Convention that organized the Republican party in this State, and in April, 1868, he was elected Justice of the Supreme Court. In June, 1872, he resigned, after a service of four years, upon his appointment by President Grant as United States District Judge for the newly created Western District of North Carolina, which position he still fills.

His opinions will be found in four volumes, from 63 N. C. to 67 N. C. inclusive. They are well written, as have also been his opinions upon the United States District Court. He is fond of literature, and is probably the best biblical scholar in the State. He has delivered several admirable addresses on literary occasions which have been published in pamphlet form. He married, in 1848, Miss Mary Adams of Virginia. A daughter of his married the eldest son of Hon. Stephen A. Douglas.

Judge Dick is a pleasing speaker and writer. He has for years been a ruling elder in the Presbyterian church and a Sunday-school superintendent. He is very courteous and agreeable in his manners. He has a large circle of friends and no enemies.

Upon his resignation from the Supreme Court, his colleague, Judge Settle, who was elected with him in 1868 but who had resigned in 1871, was appointed to succeed him.

Thomas Settle was born in Rockingham County, Jan. 23, 1831. His father, Thomas Settle, was Member of Congress 1817-21, Speaker of the House of Commons in the State Legislature

1827-28, and Judge of the Superior Court for nearly a quarter of a century, from 1832 till his resignation in 1854.

The subject of this sketch graduated at the State University in 1850 in the same class with John Manning and Prof. W. C. Kerr. Among his college mates were United States Senators Ransom and Pool, Governor Scales, Generals Pettigrew and Bryan Grimes, Dr. E. Burke Haywood, President Battle of the University, Rev. Dr. Thomas E. Skinner, Major Rufus S. Tucker, Oliver H. Dockery, Seaton Gales, Peter M. Hale, David M. Carter, Francis E. Shober, and many others who have since achieved prominence. He read law with Judge Pearson, with whom he afterwards sat on the Supreme Court, and was licensed to practise in 1854. He was a member of the legislature from 1854 to 1859, and was elected Speaker of the House in 1858. He was chosen elector in 1856 on the Buchanan ticket. In 1860 he was a supporter of Stephen A. Douglas, who had married his kinswoman. He entered the war in 1861 as captain of a company in the Third N. C. Regiment. At the end of twelve months' service he resigned, was elected Solicitor of his district, and served almost continuously till 1868. He was a member of the Convention of 1865; also a member of the State Senate of 1865-66, and was elected its President. In April, 1868, he was elected a Justice of the Supreme Court. He resigned after his appointment as minister to Peru, Feb. 18, 1871, and was succeeded by Hon. Nathaniel Boyden.

Judge Settle returned from Peru in 1872, was President of the National Convention of that year, which nominated Grant for a second term, and a candidate for Congress against Gen. J. M. Leach, by whom he was defeated by a narrow majority. Judge Dick having resigned, Judge Settle was, Dec. 5, 1872, reappointed to the Supreme Court by Governor Caldwell, and served till 1876. Upon his nomination that year as Republican candidate for Governor against Vance, he resigned and entered the canvass, which was one of the most notable ever known in the State. It was conceded that each party had named its strongest man. Vance was elected by 13,000 majority. Jan. 30, 1877, Judge Settle was appointed United States District Judge for the District of Florida. He held that office till his death, which occurred Dec. 1, 1888, in the fifty-eighth year of his age.

He married the daughter of Tyre Glenn. His son, Thomas Settle, has been for six years the very efficient Solicitor of the Ninth Judicial District, and was the Republican candidate for

Congress in his district at the recent election. One sister of Judge Settle married the Democratic Governor and United States Senator, David S. Reid; and another was the wife of Hon. O. H. Dockery, the Republican candidate for Governor in 1888. His brother, Col. David Settle, is a leading Democrat.

Judge Settle's opinions, when first upon the bench, will be found in 63, 64, and 65 N. C., and, during his second occupancy of the bench, in 68 N. C. to 75 N. C. inclusive. His opinions are generally short. His bias was for political, not judicial life. He merely "bivouacked in the Supreme Court in his march from one political position to another;" but he was a man of unquestioned ability, and had he turned his attention to law exclusively, he would have ranked higher as a judge. Among his opinions may be noted State *v.* House, N. C. 315, upon the larceny of animals *ferae naturae.* State *v.* Linkhaw, 69 N. C. 214, is a singular case. The defendant had a peculiar manner of singing which convulsed the congregation with laughter; but as it was found as a fact that he sang *bona fide,* and the best he could, the court held that he was not indictable under the act for disturbing a religious congregation. The opinion is serious and short. It is a dictinct loss to the world that it could not have been written by Irving Browne or Seymour D. Thompson. State *v.* Oliver, 70 N. C. 60, overrules the old doctrine that a man had a right to whip his wife (if he could) provided he used a switch no larger than his thumb, and gallantly holds that he has no right to chastise her at all.

State *v.* Collins, 70 N. C. 241, holds that the judge, being responsible for the conduct of the court over which he presides, has had, from immemorial time, the power (though rarely exercised) to guard against a waste of time by speeches of counsel of inordinate length. This decision, however, gave rise to the act of assembly depriving judges of control over the time of the courts in that respect. In Wilmington *v.* Yopp, 71 N. C., it is held that the commissioners of a town have the right to assess the cost of paving the sidewalks of a street upon the owners of the abutting property. State *v.* R. D. R. R., holds that the legislature had no power to prohibit a change of gauge by a railroad corporation. Since the subsequent decisions of the United States Supreme Court in the "Granger" and other cases, that the legislature has supervisory and police powers over all corporations, this decision would now hardly be considered authority. But the subject at that time was *terra incognita.* As it was, Judge Rodman did not sit, Judge Bynum dissented, and it was always understood that

Chief-Justice Pearson was *dubitante*. Skinner *v.* Hettrick, 73 N. C. 53, is an interesting discussion of the right of fishery in navigable waters. Upon his second resignation Judge Settle was succeeded by William T. Faircloth.

Nathaniel Boyden was born in Conway, Mass., Aug. 16, 1796. He was a soldier in the War of 1812. He entered Williams College in 1817. He went thence to Union College, New York, where he graduated in July, 1821. His father was a Revolutionary soldier, who died in 1857, aged ninety-four. Judge Boyden came to Guilford County, N. C., in 1822. He was admitted to the bar in December, 1823, and settled in Stokes County, near Germantown. In 1832 he removed to Surry, which county he represented in the House of Commons in 1838 and again in 1840. In 1842 he removed to Salisbury, where he resided till his death. He represented Rowan County in the State Senate in 1844, and in 1847 he was elected a member of the Thirtieth Congress. He declined a re-election, and continued in practice at the bar till raised to the bench. He attended forty-eight courts each year, and practised regularly in twelve counties. He was a member of the State Convention of 1865, and in 1868 was elected as a Republican to the Fortieth Congress. Upon Judge Settle's first resignation, he was appointed by Governor Caldwell, in May, 1871, to the Supreme Court. He was then in his seventy-fifth year. He died at Salisbury, Nov. 5, 1873, having served on the bench two years and a half. His opinions will be found in five volumes, 65 to 69 N. C. inclusive. He was a very successful practitioner. While on the bench he was said to have been especially useful on questions of practice. He was a good lawyer, possessed a strong and cultivated mind, and was endowed with an extraordinary memory. Many of his opinions might be cited with profit. A fair specimen of his style, and his practical turn of mind will be found in Horton *v.* Green, 66 N. C. 596, which was an action for deceit and false warranty in the sale of a mule.

He married in 1825, in Stokes County, Miss Ruth Martin, by whom he had several children, but left surviving him only two, N. A. Boyden of Yadkin and Jno. A. Boyden of Salisbury. After her death he married in December, 1845, Mrs. Jane Mitchell, widow of Dr. Lueco Mitchell, daughter of Hon. Archibald Henderson and niece of Chief-Justice Leonard Henderson. By her he left one son, A. H. Boyden, one of the most prominent and popular citizens of Salisbury. In 1873 Judge Boyden attended the Commencement at Union College, being the fifty-second anniversary of his graduation, and found only one person who had been at college with him.

Judge Boyden was succeeded by William P. Bynum.

William Preston Bynum was born June 20, 1820, in Stokes County, N. C. He graduated at Davidson College, with the highest honors, in 1843. He read law with Judge Pearson, with whom he afterwards sat on the Supreme Court, and was admitted to the bar in 1844. His license was the last one signed by the lamented Gaston, who died so suddenly. He located in Rutherfordton, but after his marriage removed to Lincolnton. In 1861 he was appointed by Governor Ellis Lieutenant-Colonel of the second N. C. Regiment. His future associate on the Supreme Court, Judge Faircloth, was Quartermaster of this regiment; and the Major was the future General and Judge W. R. Cox. Judge Bynum was in the battles around Richmond and at the first battle of Fredericksburg. After the death of Colonel Tew, he became Colonel. Early in 1863 he was elected Solicitor and returned home. He continued in this position for eleven years, and until promoted to the Supreme Court. He was a member of the State Convention of 1865, and State Senator 1865-66, by which body he was elected Solicitor. He was appointed by Governor Caldwell, Nov. 20, 1873, to the Supreme Court bench to fill the vacancy caused by the death of Judge Boyden, and occupied the post till the expiration of his term, Jan. 6, 1879. He then settled in Charlotte to practice law; but being a man of means, has paid no great attention to business. His opinions are to be found in 70 N. C. to 79 N. C. inclusive,—nine volumes. They are clear, strong, and able. He has a vigorous mind, was a capital judge, and thoroughly impartial. He wrote many excellent opinions. The following may be quoted as specimens: Armfield *v.* Brown, 70 N. C. 27, which holds that if a reference is compulsory the objecting party is entitled notwithstanding to a jury trial of the issues arising on the pleadings, —*aliter* if the reference is by consent. In re Schenck, 74 N. C. 607, holds that the writ of Habeas Corpus does not lie for one imprisoned by the final judgment of a court of competent jurisdiction, even where the judgment is erroneous. The remedy is by *certiorari*. If such plain provisions of law were not overlooked, we should not have the scandal of subordinate Federal judges using the writ of Habeas Corpus to bring before themselves cases which should regularly go up to the United States Supreme Court by writ of error to the highest State court. Huffman *v.* Click, 77 N. C. 55, holds that medical books are not admissible in evidence, and that counsel cannot read extracts from them as part of his speech,—*aliter* as to books upon the "exact sciences." State *v.* Turpin holds that in a trial for murder the character of the deceased for violence is competent if there is evidence tending to proved self-defence, or if the evidence is circumstantial and the nature of the transaction is in doubt. This sustained the dissenting opinion of Battle, J., in State *v.* Barfield, and is now held settled law. State *v.* Morris, 77 N. C. 512, discusses the right of the legislature to repeal or modify charters and to revoke licenses. Citizen's National Bank *v.* Green, 78 N. C. 247, holds that the income from the homestead and personal property exemption and the natural increase of the latter are not exempt from execution. Doggett *v.* R. R., 78 N. C. 305, is an interesting discussion of negligence and damages therefor, when proximate and when remote. Mizell *v.* Simmons, 97 N. C. 182, is an instructive case upon boundary, course, distances, and description of land. Manning *v.* Manning, 79 N. C. 293 and 300, is an action of ejectment brought by the wife against her husband. The questions involved are novel, and the opinion shows careful consideration of the subject.

Judge Bynum married the sister of Judge W. M. Shipp, and is uncle to Judge Jno. Gray Bynum, both of the Superior Court bench. He is a near relative of Senator Wade Hampton. His elder brother was John Gray Bynum, whose widow married Chief-Justice Pearson. He has one son, Rev. W. S. Bynum, of the Episcopal church. Judge Bynum had no successor to the seat he filled, as at the expiration of his term the constitutional amendment went into effect reducing the Supreme Court judges to three in number.

William Turner Faircloth was born in Edgecombe County, N. C., Jan. 8, 1829. He graduated at Wake Forest College, 1854, with distinction. His means being limited, he taught school in vacation, and thus earned a large part of the means to pay his expenses at college. He studied law with Judge Pearson, and was admitted to practice Jan. 1, 1856, and was almost immediately elected County Solicitor. In May, 1856, he removed to Goldsboro, where he has ever since resided. During the war he was Quartermaster of the Second North Carolina Regiment; Louis Hilliard, afterwards a judge of the Superior Court, being Commissary. His future associate on the Supreme Court, Judge Bynum, and Judge W. R. Cox of the Superior Court, were field officers in the same regiment. He served the whole war, and was at the surrender at Appomattox. He was a member of the Convention of 1865, and also of the legislature of 1865-66. By this legislature he was elected Solicitor, and filled the position till all offices were declared vacant in 1868. He was a member of the State Convention of 1875, together with Justices Avery and Shepherd, who are now on the court. He was appointed by Governor Brogden, Nov. 18, 1876, to fill the vacancy on the Supreme Court, caused by the second resignation of Judge Settle. He served till the expiration of his term, Jan. 1, 1879. He then returned to the practice of his profession at Goldsboro, where he still resides. He canvassed the State in 1884, as candidate for Lieutenant-Governor on the Republican ticket, and in 1888 was the candidate of the same party for Justice of the Supreme Court, but was defeated with his party on both occasions. He is a member of the Baptist church, and a man of pure character and upright walk in life. Beginning with himself, as his principal stock in trade, he has accumulated a handsome estate. He has been a successful lawyer.

His opinions will be found in five volumes, from 76 N. C. to 79 N. C. inclusive. There may be noted State *v.* Brooks, 76 N. C. 1, which holds that carnal knowledge of a married woman obtained by fraud in personating her husband does not amount to rape. State *v.* Smith, 77 N. C. 488, decides that the burden being on the defendant, on a trial for murder, to show mitigating circumstances, if the jury are left in doubt as to the matters alleged in extenuation, the verdict should find him guilty of murder. Hymans *v.* Dancy, 79 N. C. 511, discusses excusable neglect upon a motion to set aside a judgment upon that ground. State *v.* Barham, 79 N. C. 646, is upon the requirements in an indictment for profane swearing.

Judge Faircloth has been a director in the Wil. & Weldon and A. & N. C. R. Roads. He is also a trustee of Wake Forest College and of several other institutions.

He married, in 1867, the daughter of the late Council Wooten, of Lenoir County, but has no children.

At the end of his term of office the number of Supreme Court Judges was reduced to three; hence, like Judge Bynum, he had no successor. The two senior Associate Justices were Reade and Rodman, who were succeeded by Justices Ashe and Dillard, and Chief-Justice Smith was elected his own successor.

William Nathan Harrell Smith, sixth Chief-Justice, was born in Murfreesboro, N. C., Sept. 24, 1812. His father was a native of Connecticut, a graduate of Yale, and a physician. He removed to this State in 1802 and died in 1813.

Judge Smith graduated at Yale in 1834, and studied law at its law school. Among his college mates were Morrison R. Waite, the future Chief-Justice of the United States, Wm. M. Ewarts, since Secretary of State, Samuel J. Tilden, and Edwards Pierrepont, minister to England. He obtained license to practise law in North Carolina, but soon removed to Texas. After a stay of six months he returned to this State. In 1840 he was elected to the lower house of the legislature from Hertford, and in 1848 to the State Senate. By the legislature of that year he was elected Solicitor for his district, and was re-elected four years later, serving two full terms. In 1857 he was the Whig candidate for Congress against Henry M. Shaw, but was beaten by a few votes. In 1858 he was a candidate against the same competitor and was elected. Though this was his first term in Congress, he came within one vote of being elected Speaker, and would have been chosen, it is said, had he agreed to appoint E. Joy Morris, Chairman of the Committee on Ways and Means, in the interest of Protection. His competitors for the Speakership were Hon. John Sherman, Republican, and Thomas S. Bocock, of Virginia, Democrat. Mr. Sherman having withdrawn, Mr. Pennington, of New Jersey, was elected Speaker. Mr. Smith served out his term in Congress, and was present at the inauguration of President Lincoln. He was elected to the Confederate States Congress, and served in it the entire period of the war (1861-65). In 1865-66 he was again a member of the State legislature; and the passage of the act to permit colored people to testify was due to him, as was also the enactment of Lord Denman's act permitting parties in civil cases to be witnesses. In 1870 he removed to Norfolk, Va., to practise law. Though all his life a political opponent of Governor Holden, when the latter was by that legislature impeached and tried, Judge Smith was retained as one of his counsel. In 1872 he removed to Raleigh, and entered into partnership with Hon. George V. Strong. The law firm of Smith & Strong continued for several years. Upon the death of Chief-Justice Pearson, Mr. Smith was appointed, Jan. 14, 1878, by Governor Vance as Chief-Justice. This is the only instance in this State of a Chief-Justice being appointed who was not already one of the justices of the court. When Judge Smith was promoted directly from the bar to the chief place on the court, the four associate justices, though gentlemen of experience and learning, were all of the opposite political party to the appointing power. He was elected by the people that fall for a term of eight years. In 1886 the bench, then consisting of Smith, Ashe, and Merrimon, were re-nominated and re-elected. Chief-Justice Smith and Judge Ashe were each at the time of their re-election in their seventy-fifth year. There is probably no other case of two out of three judges of the highest court of a State being re-elected at such age. No higher compliment could have been paid their efficiency, or been more expressive of the unwillingness of the people to make changes on that court. The term of office on the Supreme Court, which was previously for life, was changed by the Constitution of 1868 to a term of eight years. But since the change there has been no instance of a judge of that court being defeated for a renomination, and none has been defeated for re-election, except in 1878, when the bench passed from the Republican to the Democratic party.

Judge Smith was an excellent advocate, a fluent speaker, a strong judge. Labor was a pleasure to him. Though for ten years of his service there were but three judges on the bench, the business of the court, representing the ultimate litigation of a million and three quarters of people, never got for a day in arrears. The work, however, was too heavy; and by constitutional amendment the number of judges was again increased to five, Jan. 1, 1889. He did not long enjoy the relief afforded by this addition, but died Nov. 14, 1889. Owing to the vast increase of business with the growth of the State in population and wealth, the work done by Chief-Justice Smith and his two associates in these ten years of service equals that done by the court during its first thirty years. The pages of the reports during these ten years exceed in number of pages, and contain far more cases in number, than the reports for the first thirty years from the organization of the court in 1818 down to 1848. His opinions are to be found in 78 N. C. to 104 N. C. inclusive, twenty-seven volumes.

Among them may be noted the following: Overby *v.* Build. and Loan Asso., 80 N. C. 56, which settled the law governing building and loan associations. Ruffin *v.* Harrison, Ib. 208, which holds that when one is both administrator and guardian, upon closing one trust the law transfers the liability to the other; but that until the first trust is closed the sureties on the bond for the discharge of that trust are still liable. Scarborough *v.* Robinson, Ib. 409, decides that an act of the legislature is invalid until signed by the speakers; and though the journals may show that the bill passed each house the requisite number of times, the courts cannot by mandamus compel the speakers to sign it. In Washington Toll Bridge *v.* Commissioners of Beaufort, Ib. 491, it is held (page 498) that though a contract made by a State with a corporation is protected by the United States Constitution, when the attempted contract is for an alienation of any of the "essential powers of government" it is inoperative and void. This same doctrine has been recently reaffirmed by the court in Alsbrook *v.* Railroad, 110 N. C. 137. Mowery *v.* Salisbury, 82 N. C. 175, holds that a town tax on dogs is valid. Lord *v.* Hardin, Ib. 241, rules that church property cannot be subjected to payment of a pastor's salary. N. C. Railroad Co. *v.* Alamance, Ib. 259, decides that a statute to collect taxes for past years is constitutional. Cain *v.* Commissioners, 86 N. C. 8, upholds the validity of the "no fence law" and of local assessments as distinct from taxation. This is affirmed in many cases since, notably Commissioners *v.* Commissioners, 92 N. C. 180. Hannon *v.* Grizzard, 89 N. C. 115, discusses "residence" and "domicile" in connection with eligibility to office, and the same is considered in Lee *v.* Mosely, 101 N. C. 311, in reference to the right of homestead.

Ellison *v.* Raleigh, Ib. 125, and Doyle *v.* Raleigh, Ib. 132, discuss the right of a city council to deprive one of its members of his seat upon the ground of ineligibility, and the proper remedy. Stanly *v.* Railroad, Ib. 331, decides that in a suit against a corporation it need not be averred that it has been incorporated, and if that is disputed it should be done by answer. This is affirmed in Ramsay *v.* Railroad, 91 N. C. 418. University *v.* Harrison, 90 N. C. 385, discusses escheats, and the presumption of death from long absence. State *v.* McNinch, Ib. 695, rules that an officer making an arrest is not liable for excessive force if used in good faith and without malice. Churchill *v.* Ins. Co., 92 N. C. 485, holds that where a lawyer is to discharge a duty, not purely professional, he is merely an agent, and his neglect is the neglect of his client. This is followed in many cases, especially in Abrams *v.* Ins. Co., 93 N. C. 60, and Finlayson *v.* Accident Association, 109 N. C. 196, and is involved in a more recent case which has been much discussed by the profession,—Williams *v.* Railroad, 110 N. C. 466. Asheville *v.* Aston, 92 N. C. 578, holds that the second story of a house, when held separately, may be recovered in an action of ejectment. Williams *v.* Railroad, 93 N. C. 42, decides that a common carrier is not bound by a bill of lading issued by its agent, unless the goods are actually received for shipment, even though the bill has been transferred to a *bona fide* holder for value. Halstead *v.* Mullen, Ib. 252, draws the distinction between a defective statement of a cause of action and a statement of a defective cause of action. Barksdale *v.* Commissioners, Ib. 472, holds that though the Constitution requires the common schools to be kept open for four months, this will not authorize the exceeding of the limit imposed in another section of the Constitution upon the rate of taxation. Puitt *v.* Commissioners, 94 N. C. 709, decided an act unconstitutional which applied the poll tax collected on white people to the white schools and the poll tax from the colored race to the education of colored children. State *v.* Miller, 94 N. C., held that a fine of $2,000 and thirty days in jail was not excessive punishment for keeping a gambling-house under the circumstances of that case. After sundry attempts to evade this decision, the fine was eventually paid in full. Duke *v.* Brown, 96 N. C. 127, is one of many cases holding that a majority of the qualified voters and not merely of those voting, is necessary to enable a municipal corporation to loan its credit. In Hannon *v.* Grizzard, 96 N. C. 293, and s. c. 99 N. C. 161, it is held that when the Commissioners refuse to induct into office a person elected thereto upon the bona fide belief that he is ineligible, an action against them for damages will not lie, although on a *quo warranto* it is adjudged that such person was entitled to the office. In re Griffin, 98 N. C. 225, holds that where an act punishable as a contempt is also a violation of the criminal law, an indictment will lie, notwithstanding the punishment imposed for the contempt. State *v.* Thomas, Ib. 599, rules that where a defendant in a criminal action voluntarily becomes a witness in his own behalf, he waives his privilege of refusing to answer questions which may tend to criminate him. Threadgill *v.* Commissioners, 99 N. C. 352, is a decision that counties are not liable for torts unless liability is imposed by statute. Hammond *v.* Schiff, 100 N. C., is a discussion of the right of lateral support to a party wall. State *v.* Lyle, Ib. 497, discusses the rights of a town or city in condemning land for streets. State *v.* Cross and White, 101 N. C. 770, is the well-known case against the Cashier and President of the State National Bank for forgery. DeBerry *v.* Nicholson, 102 N. C. 465, discusses the rights of the parties and the powers of the canvassing board in a contested election case. Edwards *v.* Dickson, Ib. 519, considers the status of an unregistered deed.

Judge Smith married, Jan. 14, 1839, Miss Mary Olivia Wise,

of Murfreesboro. He left two sons, William W., a general insurance agent and E. Chambers Smith, a prominent lawyer and late Chairman of the Democratic State Executive Committee, both of Raleigh. Judge Smith was a consistent member of the Presbyterian church. His character was spotless, his patriotism beyond question. Having exceeded the bounds of man's appointed years,—

"Life's labors done,
Serenely to his final rest he passed,
While the soft memories of his virtues yet
Linger like twilight hues, when the bright sun is set."

With the exception of Chief-Justices Ruffin and Pearson, he is deemed second to no judge who has sat upon the bench in North Carolina. Had he come to the post as early in life as they, and spent his career in developing his judicial qualifications, it may be doubted if he had not fully equalled them. No ability however striking, can make up for the lack of time and opportunity. He was in his sixty-sixth year when he first went upon the bench.

For long years in varying positions he labored for the public weal. Never for an hour of that time did public confidence waver in his integrity or his entire capacity for the work assigned. And now "his memory like a slow fading twilight long shall dwell in the hearts of a people he served so faithfully and well."

He was succeeded as Chief-Justice by Hon. A. S. Merrimon.

Thomas Samuel Ashe was born, July 21, 1812, in that part of Orange County, N. C., which is now Alamance. He was a great-grandson of Judge Samuel Ashe, who has already been mentioned in these sketches as one of the three judges who constituted the entire judiciary of North Carolina from 1777 till 1795, when he became Governor of this State.

The subject of this sketch graduated at the State University in 1832, in the same class with James C. Dobbin, Secretary of the Navy under Pierce, and United States Senator Thomas L. Clingman. He studied law under Chief-Justice Ruffin, and located at Wadesboro in 1836. In 1842 he was elected as a Whig to the lower house of the legislature, and in 1854 to the State Senate. He was Solicitor of his judicial district from 1848 to 1852, and left an abiding recollection of his faithfulness and ability among the people of that section. He was nominated for Congress in 1858, but declined the nomination. During the war he was a member of the Confederate Congress from his district, and was then elected to the Confederate State Senate. In 1868, in "Reconstruction days," he was Democratic candidate for Governor, but was defeated by Governor Holden. In 1872 and 1874 he was elected to the United States Congress, and served upon the Judiciary Committee. He was one of the committee of three which was examining James G. Blaine as to the Credit Mobilier when further examination was stopped by Mr. Blaine's illness. In 1876 he was elected a justice of the Supreme Court of North Carolina, to succeed Judge Reade, and in 1886 was nominated by acclamation and re-elected, being then in his seventy-fifth year.

He was second to few men on the bench. He possessed excellent qualifications for a judge. But both ability and experience are necessary in creating a great judge. He was in his sixty-seventh year when he first went upon the bench. Judge Ashe's opinions are good specimens of strong nervous English. His opinions are to be found in sixteen volumes, 80 N. C. to 95 inclusive. Among these may especially be read State *v.* Bowman, 80 N. C. 432, as to the construction of the constitutional provision in regard to the ridings of the judges; Whitaker *v.* Smith, 81 N. C. 340, which holds that an overseer is not entitled to file a laborer's lien for his services; Taylor *v.* Harris, 82 N. C. 25, which construed the computation of time as to the services of a summons ten days before court. Tabor *v.* Ward, 83 N. C. 291, rules that retroactive laws involving no criminal element are not unconstitutional. Hester *v.* Roach, 84 N. C. 251, is a construction of the Mill-dam Act. Wharton *v.* Moore, 84 N. C. 479, is a discussion of the doctrine of betterments. Katzenstein *v.* R. R., Ib. 688, sustains the validity of the statute imposing a penalty upon railroads for failure to forward freight. State *v.* Knight, Ib. 789, holds that indictments for the higher offences should not ordinarily be quashed, and has been recently cited with approval in State *v.* Skidmore, 109 N. C. 795, and State *v.* Flowers, Ib. 841. Wilmington *v.* Macks, 86 N. C. 88, sustains the validity of a town tax upon lawyers. Keeter *v.* R. R., 86 N. C. 346, rules that it is the duty of a railroad company to provide a sufficient number of cars for the prompt forwarding of all freight. The same doctrine has since been applied by the court to the furnishing of cars for passengers in Purcell *v.* R. R., 108 N. C. 414. The right to an order of restitution when a judgment is reversed is laid down in Boyett *v.* Vaughan, 86 N. C. 725. Cumming *v.* Bloodworth, 87 N. C. 83, holds that there can be no lien upon the homestead for materials furnished. Muller *v.* Commissioners, 89 N. C. 171, defines the duties and powers of county commissioners in granting license to retail liquor. Knight *v.* Houghtalling, 94 N. C. 408, is a case in which the unusual "Writ of Assistance" was granted. Hodges *v.* Williams, 95 N. C. 331, is an interesting case as to the rights of riparian owners.

Judge Ashe was a fine specimen of manhood. His days were, in the general opinion of the public, shortened by the excessive labor exacted of the Supreme Court, which during his entire occupancy of the office consisted of only three judges.

He died at his home in Wadesboro, Feb. 4, 1887, in the seventy-fifth year of his age. He married early in life Miss Burgwyn. He left one son, Samuel T. Ashe, a popular member of the bar, who lives at Durham; and several daughters, one of whom married James A. Lockhart, a lawyer of Wadesboro, who is one of the most prominent men in that section of the State; and another married Hon. Richard H. Battle, of Raleigh, who has been already mentioned.

Judge Ashe was a model judge and a model man. In many particulars he very nearly resembles Gaston, his illustrious predecessor. Like him, he went late to the bench; like him, he developed great judicial capacity; and like him, he left a character above reproach, and obtained a great and lasting popularity. The examples of both will live for good.

> "Were a star quenched on high,
>   For ages would its light
> Still travelling downward from the sky
>   Shine on our mortal sight;
>
> "So when a good man dies,
>   For years beyond our ken
> The light he leaves behind him lies
>   Upon the paths of men."

Judge Ashe was succeeded by Joseph J. Davis.

John H. Dillard was born in Rockingham County, N. C., Nov. 29, 1819. He entered the University of North Carolina, but after a year and a half left on account of ill health. He afterwards entered William and Mary College, and graduated at its law school in 1840. He began the practice of law at Richmond, Va., then removed to Patrick Court House, Va., and became commonwealth's attorney. In 1846 he returned to Rockingham County, N. C., and from 1848 to 1861 he was a law partner of Judge Ruffin, who succeeded him, on the Supreme Court bench. In 1862 he entered the army, and served one year as captain of a company in the Forty-fifth North Carolina Regiment. In 1868 he removed to Greensboro, where he has ever since resided. For many years he was county attorney and clerk and master for Rockingham County. In 1878 he was elected to the Supreme Court, and began his labors Jan. 1, 1879, succeeding Judge Rodman. There being, as stated, only three judges then upon the bench, his health gave way under a conscientious effort to keep up with the mass of work devolved upon the court, and to the regret of every one he resigned, Feb. 11, 1881, after a service of a little more than two years.

His opinions sustain his standing as one of the foremost lawyers in the State. They are to be found in four volumes, 80 N. C. to 83 N. C. inclusive. Among them should be noted Riggan *v.* Green, 80 N. C. 236, that a deed of a lunatic is voidable, not void; since affirmed in Odom *v.* Riddick, 104 N. C. 515. Wright *v.* Hemphill, 81 N. C. 33, as to the right to reassemble the jury to complete their verdict. Cobb *v.* O'Hagan, Ib. 293, lays down the duty of a client to give proper attention to his case, and not to leave the matter absolutely to his counsel, without further attention on his part. Jones *v.* Mial, 82 N. C. 252, that where the plaintiff sues on a special contract, if he fails on that he may recover upon a quantum meruit without amendment of his complaint. This has since been followed in several cases, especially in Stokes *v.* Taylor, 104 N. C. 394.

Judge Dillard married, in 1846, Miss Ann I. Martin, of Henry County, Va. He has several children.

Judge Dillard is very much loved. A large fine-looking man, with a large brain and kindly heart, he looks more like a bishop than a layman. He is unostentatious,

> "And as the greatest only are,
> In his simplicity sublime."

He is the only lawyer in North Carolina who does not appreciate how great a lawyer Judge Dillard is. For many years, he and Judge Dick (of the United States District Court, and formerly of the North Carolina Supreme Court) have maintained an excellent law school at Greensboro. He was succeeded by Thomas Ruffin.

Thomas Ruffin, the fourth son of Chief-Justice Thomas Ruffin, was born Sept. 21, 1824, at Hillsboro. He was prepared for college by Samuel Smith, and one of his schoolmates was Judge Jno. H.

Dillard, his lifelong friend. He graduated at the University of North Carolina, in 1844, with honors. Among his classmates were L. C. Edwards and Walter L. Steele, and among his college mates Gen. Rufus Barringer, Judges R. P. Dick, and Samuel J. Person. He read law under his father, and began practice at Yanceyville in 1846. In 1848 he removed to Wentworth, and formed a law partnership with Judge John H. Dillard. In 1850 he represented Rockingham County in the House of Commons. In 1856 he was elected Solicitor, and served till his resignation in March, 1860. He was an unusually strong prosecuting officer. He entered the army in 1861 as a captain in the Thirteenth North Carolina Regiment. In October, 1861, he was appointed by Governor Clark a Judge of the Superior Court, to fill the vacancy caused by the death of Judge John M. Dick. He rode the fall circuit. He then resigned, and returning to the army was, in March, 1862, promoted to be Lieutenant-Colonel of his regiment. He was wounded at the desperate battle of South Mountain, Md., Sept. 14, 1862, and resigned March 13, 1863. He displayed great courage, coolness, and capacity on the battlefield. In the latter part of the war he served as member of an Army Court in the Western Army. After the war he resumed practice at Graham, but in 1868 removed to Greensboro, and formed a law partnership with Judge Dillard and Jno. A. Gilmer, who afterwards became a Superior Court Judge. In December 1870, his health becoming seriously impaired, he abandoned the practice, and removed to Hillsboro, where he ever after resided. For a while he was an insurance agent. His health being somewhat restored in 1875, he returned to the bar and formed a partnership with John W. Graham. Upon the resignation of Judge Dillard, Feb. 11, 1881, he was appointed by Governor Jarvis to succeed him upon the Supreme Court. In 1882 he was nominated by the Democratic party to the same post, and elected. The labor of the court was too heavy for three judges, and, like Judge Dillard, he soon found that he could not remain on the bench and *live*. He resigned, Sept. 23, 1883, after a service of two years and a half, and resumed the practice of law with Hon. John W. Graham at Hillsboro. His opinions will be found in five volumes, 84 N. C. to 89 N. C. inclusive. They are a lasting monument to his industry and ability. Attention may well be called to the following: Muse *v.* Muse, 84 N. C. 35, which holds that a husband in a divorce suit may be ordered to pay alimony out of the proceeds of his labor when he owns no property. Wilson *v.* Seagle, Ib. 110, discusses the duty of an appellant in perfecting his appeal. Wallace *v.* Trustees, Ib. 164, hold that the corporate powers of a municipal corporation may be revoked, leaving the creditors to seek relief by an appeal to the legislature. Murrill *v.* Murrill, Ib. 182, is one of many decisions holding that a new action will not lie when the same end can be attained by a motion in the original cause. Long *v.* McLean, 88 N. C. 3, decides that the constitutional provision abolishing imprisonment for debt has no application to actions in tort. Bevers *v.* Park, Ib. 456, holds that the heir may plead the statute of limitation to a debt of his ancestor in a proceeding by the administrator to sell land for assets to pay the debts. Syme *v.* Riddle, Ib. 463, rules that the husband is still entitled *jure mariti* to the services and earnings of the wife, and that this has not been altered by the constitution nor the "marriage act." Dougherty *v.* Sprinkle, Ib. 300, holds that a married woman cannot be sued before a justice of the peace upon any liability incurred during coverture. He was strong in his convictions, and clear and forcible in his expression of his views.

He had no superior as an advocate at the bar of North Carolina. In the legal traditions of the State, he and Judge Reade—heretofore mentioned—stand as advocates *facile principes.* He was exceedingly courteous and winning in his manner; but when his duty or his interest required it, he could be a very thunderbolt. For some reason, he never once sat for his portrait or photograph. Hence he is the only one of the judges an engraving of whom is not presented in these sketches. He married, early in life, Miss Mary Cain, of Hillsboro, and left her surviving him with three sons and a daughter.

He died at Hillsboro, May 23, 1889.

> "He gave his honors to the world again,
> His blessed part to Heaven, and slept in peace."

He was succeeded by A. S. Merrimon.

Joseph John Davis was born, April 13, 1828, in that part of Franklin County which is now in Vance. His grandfather, William Davis, was a soldier of the Revolution. He attended Wake Forest College one year, and subsequently went to the University of North Carolina, but did not graduate. He read law under Judge Battle, and was admitted to the bar in 1850, and located at Oxford, but three years later removed to Louisburg. In 1862 he entered the army as Captain in the Forty-Seventh North Carolina

Regiment. He was not one of those who, moved by ambition, went to "seek for glory in the smoky purlieus of the cannon's mouth." With him then, as always, the controlling motive was a high sense of duty to the people among whom Providence had cast his lot. He was captured in Pettigrew's charge at Gettysburg, July 3, 1863, and was a prisoner at Fort Delaware and Johnson's Island till paroled just before the close of the war. After the war he began the practice of his profession at Louisburg, where he resided henceforth till his death. He was elected to the legislature of 1866 from Franklin County. In 1874 he was elected a member of Congress from the Raleigh district, and served for six years. He then resumed the practice of his profession till 1887, when upon the death of Judge Ashe, he was appointed by Governor Scales, February, 1887, to the vacancy upon the Supreme Court bench. In 1888 he was nominated by the Democratic party and elected to the same post. The promotions to the Supreme bench in North Carolina, as elsewhere, have usually been from those who have seen service on the Superior Court bench. In the fifty years from the organization of the court till 1868 Judge Gaston was the only exception. In 1868, when the State passed into the control of a new political party, Judges Pearson and Reade only, out of the five elected to the Supreme Court, had served on the lower bench. When the State again passed back to the Democratic party in 1878, two of the three Supreme Court judges were taken from the bar. But since then all the judges of the Supreme Court have seen service on the Superior Court bench, excepting only Judges Davis and Burwell.

His opinions will be found in fifteen volumes, 96 N. C. to 110 N. C. inclusive. During the last three years of his life his health was impaired, but he strove with fidelity to discharge the important trust confided to him. Among his opinions should be noted Hodge *v.* Powell, 96 N. C. 64, which holds that while a married woman cannot be estopped by a contract she will not be allowed to repudiate her acts, when to do so would permit her to perpetrate a fraud. Efland *v.* Efland, Ib. 488, which recognizes that when an equitable element is involved the Superior Court at term has jurisdiction of a proceeding to assign dower. Cagle *v.* Parker, 97 N. C. 271, discusses the question of easements and how they may be created. Hussey *v.* R. R., 98 N. C. 34, maintains that an action will lie against a corporation for torts such as slander, libel, and malicious prosecution. McCanless *v.* Flinchum, Ib. 358, is a very full discussion of the homestead. State *v.* Emery,

Ib. 668, is one of many cases sustaining the widely recognized doctrine that on the trial of an indictment for retailing liquor without license, the burden is on the defendant to show a license. Smith *v.* R. R., 99 N. C. 241, is one of many cases in this State holding that if the facts be admitted or proved, what is negligence or contributory negligence is a question of law. Troy *v.* R. R., Ib. 298, lays down what is now the settled rule as to contributory negligence. Foundry Co. *v.* Killian, Ib. 501, decides that unpaid balances on subscription to the capital stock of a company may be subjected to the payment of its debts. Michael *v.* Foil, 100 N. C. 178, considers the doctrine of privileged communication as applicable to lawyer and client. Goodman *v.* Sapp, 102 N. C. 477, holds that in civil cases the failure of a party to go upon the stand as a witness is the proper subject of comment whenever the circumstances are such as would make the non-introduction of any other witness the subject of comment. This has since been considered and reaffirmed in Hudson *v.* Jordan, 108 N. C. 10, and s. c. 110 N. C. 250.

Judge Davis married, in October, 1852, Miss Catherine Shaw, of Louisburg, by whom he left several children. She died in 1881; and in 1883 he married Miss Louisa Kittrell, who survives him.

Judge Davis died at his home in Louisburg, Aug. 7, 1892. No man ever more completely had the entire confidence of the people. His name was the synonym of candor, honesty, and singleness of purpose.

For the last few months his life was perceptibly ebbing away, and when the end came,

> "Night dews fall not more gently to the ground,
> Nor weary worn-out winds expire more soft."

His funeral was one of the most largely attended ever seen in his section, and everything betokened the love, esteem, and profound respect of the people among whom he had so long lived. He was succeeded by Judge James C. MacRae.

THE PRESENT COURT.

These sketches were not intended to embrace the present occupants of the bench. A sense of propriety forbids.

The following bare data are taken from publications heretofore made.

Augustus Summerfield Merrimon, the seventh Chief-Justice, was born in Transylvania County N. C., Sept. 15, 1830. In 1860 he was elected to the House of Commons, and in 1861 he entered the army as Quartermaster, with the rank of Captain, but was soon elected Solicitor of his district, and served till the close of the war. He was elected a Judge of the Superior Court in 1866, but resigned in August, 1867, rather than obey orders issued by military authority. He was nominated by the Democratic party for Supreme Court judge in 1868, but was defeated with his ticket. He was the Democratic candidate for Governor in 1872, and was again defeated; but the legislature that winter elected him to the United States Senate, and he served 1873-79. Upon the resignation of Judge Ruffin he was appointed by Governor Jarvis, Sept. 29, 1883, to succeed him as Associate Justice of the Supreme Court, and at the next general election he was elected by the people. Upon the death of Chief-Justice Smith he was appointed by Governor Fowle, Nov. 16, 1889, to succeed him, and was elected by the people in 1890. His opinions begin in the 89 N. C.[1]

James Edward Shepherd was born in Nansemond County, Va., July 26, 1846. During the war he was a telegraph operator in Western Virginia. He studied law under Judge Battle; admitted to the bar in 1869. He was a member of the Constitutional Convention of 1875. He was appointed by Governor Jarvis Judge of the Superior Court, August, 1882, and elected by the people the same year. Upon the increase of the Supreme Court to five members, he was elected one of the additional judges, and took his seat Jan. 1, 1879. He resides in Washington, N. C. His opinions begin in the 102 N. C. Upon the death of Judge Merrimon he was appointed by Governor Holt, Nov. 16, 1892, Chief-Justice. He was succeeded as Associate-Justice by Armistead Burwell.

Alphonso Calhoun Avery was born, Sept. 11, 1835, in Burke County; graduated at the University in 1857; studied law under Chief-Justice Pearson; admitted to the bar in 1860; saw service in the army in 1861-64; elected State Senator in 1866 and again in 1868, but the last time not allowed by military authority to take his seat. He was a member of the Constitutional Convention in 1875. He was elected Judge of the Superior Court in 1878, and re-elected in 1886. Upon the adoption of the amendment to the Constitution increasing the Supreme Court to five in number, he and Judge Shepherd were elected the two additional judges; and he took his seat, Jan. 1, 1889, for a term of eight years. His opinions begin in the 102 N. C. He resides in Morganton.

[1] Chief-Justice Merrimon died since the above was put in type, at his home in Raleigh, N. C., Nov. 14, 1892. He was succeeded by Hon. J. E. Shepherd.—ED.

Walter Clark was born in Halifax County, Aug. 19, 1846; graduated at the University in 1864; saw service in the war (1861-65) except one year while at the University. When the number of Superior Court judges was increased from nine to twelve in 1885, he was appointed by Governor Scales, April 15, 1885, one of the additional Superior Court judges, and was elected in 1886 by the people. Upon the appointment of Judge Merrimon as Chief-Justice, he was appointed by Governor Fowle to succeed him as Associate Justice Nov. 16, 1889, and was elected by the people in 1890. His opinions begin in the 104 N. C. He resides in Raleigh.

James Cameron MacRae was born in Fayetteville, Oct. 6, 1838. He obtained license to practise law in 1859. He saw service in the war (1861-65). He was a member of the legislature of 1874-75. He was appointed by Governor Jarvis, in July, 1882, Judge of the Superior Court, to succeed Judge Bennett, and was elected by the people the same year. His term expiring in 1890, he returned to the bar. Upon the death of Judge Davis he was appointed by Governor Holt, Aug. 24, 1892, to succeed him, and was elected by the people at the general election this fall. He resides in Fayetteville, N. C. His opinions will begin in the 111 N. C.

Armistead Burwell was born in Hillsboro, Orange County, N. C., Oct. 22, 1839, and is a son of Rev. Robert Burwell, then pastor of the Presbyterian Church at that place. He graduated at Davidson College, 1859, with the first honors. He then engaged in teaching, and was in Arkansas when the war broke out. He served through the war with troops from that State, and was severely wounded in 1864 before Atlanta. He resumed teaching in Charlotte after the war; studied law, and was licensed to practise in 1869. He located in Charlotte, where he has resided ever since. Since 1877 he has been continuously a State Director of the North Carolina Railroad, being reappointed by each successive Governor. He was State Senator in 1880. Upon the death of Chief-Justice Merrimon, Justice Shepherd being promoted, Judge Burwell was appointed by Governor Holt to be Associate-Justice, Nov. 16, 1892.

The work of all courts is in a large measure temporary; but there is a still larger part which abides and shapes the future. Our civilization is like the coral islands, built by individual and forgotten workers, on whose labors each successive generation climbs to higher things. The work of the courts is a potent factor in our civilization. It bears the impress of the present, but remains to instruct the future, as imprints of a passing shower of ages ago are preserved in strata of sandstone. In like manner, much of the work shaped out by the conjoined labor of bench and bar will have its effect long ages after the men of this generation and all memory of them

> "Like thin streaks of morning cloud shall have
> melted into the infinite azure of the past."

To fix for a few fleeting moments longer the memory of a few of the laborers ere their names shall already sound strange in the courts and the land where they labored, is the object of sketches such as these.

Chief-Justice Taylor was born in England; Chief-Justice Ruffin, Judges Hall and Shepherd were born in Virginia; Judge Boyden in Massachusetts. The other twenty-five were native North Carolinians.

Judge Settle was the youngest judge, having ascended the bench at thirty-seven. Next came the elder Ruffin, Pearson, Murphey, Shepherd, and Clark, who all went on at forty-two or forty-three. Judge Nash went on at sixty-three, and was in his seventy-second year when made Chief-Justice. Judge Smith went on the bench at sixty-five, Ashe at sixty-six, Boyden at seventy-four, and yet served two and a half years. Smith and Ashe were each in their seventy-fifth year when elected the second time. The longest service was by Pearson, twenty-nine years on the court, and the elder Ruffin, near twenty-five years. Each of these was nineteen years Chief-Justice.

As to religious persuasion, six were Presbyterians,—Nash, Reade, Dick, Smith, Avery, and Burwell; two Roman Catholics,—Gaston and Manly; two Methodists,—Merrimon and Clark; one Baptist,—Faircloth; one or possibly two were members of no church; and the remaining eighteen, being nearly two thirds of the whole number, have been Episcopalians.[1]

[1] The death of Chief-Justice Merrimon occurring after this article was in type, a more lengthy sketch of him which was sent us could not be inserted. A notice of him, however, will be found in our obituary columns. In the first column of Part I. (October number) of this article the total number of judges there given as twenty-nine should be changed to thirty.—ED.

SUMMARY.

Judges in Order of Appointment.	County or Place of Birth.	Residence when Elected.	Years on Supreme Court.	When term began.	Age when elected to Supreme Court.	Years on Superior Court.	Age at Death.	Remarks.
1. Taylor, C. J.	England	Craven	10	1818	49	20	59	10 years C. J.
2. Henderson, C. J.	Vance	Granville	15	1818	46	8	61	4½ years C. J.
3. Hall	Virginia	Warren	14	1818	51	18	65	
4. Murphey	Caswell	Orange	—	1820	43	2	54	Special service three terms.
5. Toomer	New Hanover	Cumberland	½	1829	45	5	72	Twice on Superior Court.
6. Ruffin, C. J.	Virginia	Orange	24	1829	42	5	82	Twice on each b. 19 years C. J.
7. Daniel	Halifax	Halifax	15	1832	47	16	63	
8. Gaston	Craven	Craven	11	1833	55	—	66	
9. Nash, C. J.	Craven	Orange	14	1844	63	16	77	6 years C. J.
10. Battle	Edgecombe	Orange	16	1848	45	12	76	Twice on each bench.
11. Pearson, C. J.	Rowan	Rowan	29	1848	43	12	72	19 yrs. C. J. 2d and 3d elections fr. Yadkin.
12. Manly	Chatham	Craven	6	1859	59	19	91	
13. Reade	Person	Person	13	1865	53	2	Living.	

14. Rodman	Beaufort	Beaufort	10	1868	51	—	Living.	
15. Dick	Guilford	Guilford	4	1868	44	—	Living.	U. S. Dist. Judge.
16. Settle	Rockingham	Rockingham	7	1868	37	—	57	Twice on bench.
17. Boyden	Massachusetts	Rowan	2½	1871	74	—	77	
18. Bynum	Stokes	Lincoln	5	1873	53	—	Living.	
19. Faircloth	Edgecombe	Wayne	2	1876	47	—	Living.	
20. Smith, C. J.	Hertford	Wake	12	1878	65	—	77	12 years C. J.
21. Ashe	Alamance	Anson	8	1879	66	—	74	
22. Dillard	Rockingham	Guilford	2	1879	59	—	Living.	
23. Ruffin	Orange	Orange	2½	1881	57	½	65	
24. Merrimon, C. J.	Transylvania	Wake	9	1883	53	1½	62	3 years C. J.
25. Davis	Vance	Franklin	5½	1887	58	—	64	
26. Avery	Burke	Burke	Since Jan., '89	1889	53	10	Now on bench.	
27. Shepherd, C. J.	Virginia	Beaufort	Since Jan., '89	1889	42	6½	" "	C. J. Nov., '92
28. Clark	Halifax	Wake	Since Nov., '89	1889	43	4½	" "	
29. MacRae	Cumberland	Cumberland	Since Aug., '92	1892	54	8½	" "	
30. Burwell	Orange	Mecklen-burg	Since Nov., '92	1892	53	—	" "	

INDEX

www.ingramcontent.com/pod-product-compliance
Lightning Source LLC
LaVergne TN
LVHW090254210926
848480LV00001B/13
9780807868522